MASS MEDIA

Fourth Edition

Editor
Joan Gorham
West Virginia University

Joan Gorham completed her undergraduate work at the University of Wisconsin and received masters and doctoral degrees from Northern Illinois University. She currently teaches courses in mass media effects as well as nonverbal, intercultural, and instructional communication at West Virginia University. Dr. Gorham is the author of *Commercial Media and Classroom Teaching,* she has published numerous articles on communication in instruction, and she was the recipient of one of her institution's 1995 teaching excellence awards. She regularly teaches graduate classes dealing with media literacy for teachers throughout the state of West Virginia.

Annual Editions
A Library of Information from the Public Press
Dushkin/McGraw-Hill
Sluice Dock, Guilford, Connecticut 06437

Visit us on the Internet—http://www.dushkin.com

The Annual Editions Series

ANNUAL EDITIONS is a series of over 65 volumes designed to provide the reader with convenient, low-cost access to a wide range of current, carefully selected articles from some of the most important magazines, newspapers, and journals published today. ANNUAL EDITIONS are updated on an annual basis through a continuous monitoring of over 300 periodical sources. All ANNUAL EDITIONS have a number of features that are designed to make them particularly useful, including topic guides, annotated tables of contents, unit overviews, and indexes. For the teacher using ANNUAL EDITIONS in the classroom, an Instructor's Resource Guide with test questions is available for each volume.

VOLUMES AVAILABLE

- Abnormal Psychology
- Adolescent Psychology
- Africa
- Aging
- American Foreign Policy
- American Government
- American History, Pre-Civil War
- American History, Post-Civil War
- American Public Policy
- Anthropology
- Archaeology
- Biopsychology
- Business Ethics
- Child Growth and Development
- China
- Comparative Politics
- Computers in Education
- Computers in Society
- Criminal Justice
- Criminology
- Developing World
- Deviant Behavior
- Drugs, Society, and Behavior
- Dying, Death, and Bereavement
- Early Childhood Education
- Economics
- Educating Exceptional Children
- Education
- Educational Psychology
- Environment
- Geography
- Global Issues
- Health
- Human Development
- Human Resources
- Human Sexuality
- India and South Asia
- International Business
- Japan and the Pacific Rim
- Latin America
- Life Management
- Macroeconomics
- Management
- Marketing
- Marriage and Family
- Mass Media
- Microeconomics
- Middle East and the Islamic World
- Multicultural Education
- Nutrition
- Personal Growth and Behavior
- Physical Anthropology
- Psychology
- Public Administration
- Race and Ethnic Relations
- Russia, the Eurasian Republics, and Central/Eastern Europe
- Social Problems
- Social Psychology
- Sociology
- State and Local Government
- Urban Society
- Western Civilization, Pre-Reformation
- Western Civilization, Post-Reformation
- Western Europe
- World History, Pre-Modern
- World History, Modern
- World Politics

Cataloging in Publication Data
Main entry under title: Annual Editions: Mass media. 1997/98.
   1. Mass media—Periodicals. I. Gorham, Joan, *comp.* II. Title: Mass media.
ISBN 0–697–37321–5   301.16′05   ISSN 1092–0439

© 1997 by Dushkin/McGraw-Hill, Guilford, CT 06437, A Division of The McGraw-Hill Companies.

Copyright law prohibits the reproduction, storage, or transmission in any form by any means of any portion of this publication without the express written permission of Dushkin/McGraw-Hill, and of the copyright holder (if different) of the part of the publication to be reproduced. The Guidelines for Classroom Copying endorsed by Congress explicitly state that unauthorized copying may not be used to create, to replace, or to substitute for anthologies, compilations, or collective works.

Annual Editions® is a Registered Trademark of Dushkin/McGraw-Hill,
A Division of The McGraw-Hill Companies.

Fourth Edition

Cover image © 1996 PhotoDisc, Inc.

Printed in the United States of America

Printed on Recycled Paper

Editors/Advisory Board

Members of the Advisory Board are instrumental in the final selection of articles for each edition of ANNUAL EDITIONS. Their review of articles for content, level, currentness, and appropriateness provides critical direction to the editor and staff. We think that you will find their careful consideration well reflected in this volume.

EDITOR

Joan Gorham
West Virginia University

ADVISORY BOARD

Alison Alexander
University of Georgia

Robert Bellamy
Duquesne University

Brenda K. Cooper
Utah State University

Stanley B. Cunningham
University of Windsor

William Dorman
California State University
Sacramento

Arthur M. Fried
Plymouth State College

Jarice Hanson
University of Massachusetts
Amherst

Phyllis Lang
University of North Carolina

Kathleen Lowney
Valdosta State University

Janette Kenner Muir
George Mason University

Elizabeth M. Perse
University of Delaware

Deborah Peterson-Perlman
University of Minnesota
Duluth

Michael J. Porter
University of Missouri
Columbia

Paula C. Renfro
Southwest Texas State University

Reed W. Smith
Georgia Southern University

Debra Olson Tolar
Antelope Valley College

William H. Young
Lynchburg College

Staff

Ian A. Nielsen, Publisher

EDITORIAL STAFF

Roberta Monaco, Developmental Editor
Addie Raucci, Administrative Editor
Cheryl Greenleaf, Permissions Editor
Deanna Herrschaft, Permissions Assistant
Diane Barker, Proofreader
Lisa Holmes-Doebrick, Program Coordinator
Joseph Offredi, Photo Coordinator

PRODUCTION STAFF

Brenda S. Filley, Production Manager
Charles Vitelli, Designer
Shawn Callahan, Graphics
Lara M. Johnson, Graphics
Laura Levine, Graphics
Mike Campbell, Graphics
Juliana Arbo, Typesetting Supervisor
Jane Jaegersen, Typesetter
Marie Lazauskas, Word Processor
Larry Killian, Copier Coordinator

# To the Reader

In publishing ANNUAL EDITIONS we recognize the enormous role played by the magazines, newspapers, and journals of the *public press* in providing current, first-rate educational information in a broad spectrum of interest areas. Many of these articles are appropriate for students, researchers, and professionals seeking accurate, current material to help bridge the gap between principles and theories and the real world. These articles, however, become more useful for study when those of lasting value are carefully *collected, organized, indexed,* and *reproduced* in a *low-cost format,* which provides easy and permanent access when the material is needed. That is the role played by ANNUAL EDITIONS. Under the direction of each volume's *academic editor,* who is an expert in the subject area, and with the guidance of an *Advisory Board,* each year we seek to provide in each ANNUAL EDITION a current, well-balanced, carefully selected collection of the best of the public press for your study and enjoyment. We think that you will find this volume useful, and we hope that you will take a moment to let us know what you think.

According to the results of a 1994 survey by Veronis, Suhler, and Associates, the average American spends 3,295 hours each year—the equivalent of 137 days or 82 40-hour work weeks—consuming mass media messages. Of these hours, 1,539 are spent watching television, 1,061 listening to the radio, 261 listening to recorded music, 168 reading newspapers, 99 reading books, 84 reading magazines, 51 watching videos at home, 11 watching movies in theaters, and 21 playing video games. Along with schools, the church, and the family, mass media have great potential for shaping American society. And, just as schools and families have been blamed for a variety of society's ills, these media have taken their fair share of heat.

The mass media are a part of the fabric of American society. Learning how to critically evaluate media messages—asking, Who created this message? What is its intent? How objective is it? How does what I am seeing or hearing reflect and/or shape real-world realities?—is a part of being literate in today's society. The organization of these readings reflects this media literacy perspective. Unit 1 provides an introduction to concerns that have been raised about the impact of mass media on children, on daily living, and on society. Unit 2 explores media as sources of news and information as well as their influence on social agendas and attitudes. Units 3 and 4 introduce questions of media ethics and examine the power of media's visual images. Unit 5 addresses the relationships among advertising, media content, and popular culture. Unit 6 examines media influences on American politics. Finally, unit 7 takes a look ahead at the shape of tomorrow's media.

You will find that the writers included in this collection frequently use television as a reference point in describing how mass media messages are shaped and interpreted. This is a reflection of the media focus of the public press and of television's rapid acceptance and continuing presence as the "massest" of mass media. Most of the articles, even those that are primarily descriptive, include an editorial viewpoint and draw conclusions or make recommendations with which you may disagree. These editorial viewpoints are more frequently critical than they are complimentary. They are not necessarily my opinions and should not necessarily become yours. I encourage you to debate these issues, drawing from the information and insights provided in the readings as well as your own experiences as a media consumer. If you are an "average" American, you have spent a great deal of time with mass media. Your own observations have as much value as those of the writers whose work is included in these pages.

The articles selected for inclusion in this fourth edition of *Annual Editions: Mass Media* reflect three issues of particular concern in the mid-1990s. The first is the ongoing debate over whether and how to regulate media content, particularly inclusion of themes of sex and violence. The second is a renewed debate over ethics in news coverage, an outgrowth of analyses of media and the O. J. Simpson criminal trial. The third is a heightened awareness of the changing media landscape that has followed in the wake of shifts in regulatory policy affecting electronic media and a flurry of business mergers resulting in newly integrated media-communications-entertainment enterprises.

As always, those involved in producing this anthology are sincerely committed to including articles that are timely, informative, and interesting reading. We value your feedback and encourage you to complete and return the postage-paid *article rating form* on the last page of the book to share your suggestions and let us know your opinions.

B. Gorham

Joan Gorham
Editor

Contents

UNIT 1

Living with Media

Seven selections discuss the impact of mass media on daily living and on society.

To the Reader	iv
Topic Guide	2
Overview	4

1. **TV without Guilt: Group Portrait with Television,** David Finkel, *The Washington Post Magazine,* January 16, 1994.
   David Finkel presents a portrait of life in one American family—the Delmars—and *the impact of television* on the rhythms of its *daily routines.* — 6

2. **Can TV Save the Planet?** Chip Walker, *American Demographics,* May 1996.
   Chip Walker looks at *television use and preferences* among teenage viewers worldwide and the impact of television on global *consumer values.* — 12

3. **Sexuality and the Mass Media: An Overview,** Jane D. Brown and Jeanne R. Steele, *SIECUS Report,* April/May 1996.
   Jane Brown and Jeanne Steele argue that television, magazines, radio, advertising, and news media are all preoccupied with *sexuality.* They explore potential *mainstreaming, social learning, and agenda-setting effects* of media's sexual themes. — 16

4. **Gendered Media: The Influence of Media on Views of Gender,** Julia T. Wood, from *Gendered Lives: Communication, Gender, and Culture,* Wadsworth Publishing Company, 1994.
   Julia Wood contends that media exert a powerful influence on how we view men and women, minorities, and the elderly. The *effects of media's images* on male/female roles and interactions, perceptions of our bodies, and abuse of and violence against women are explored. — 23

5. **Cause and Violent Effect: Media and Our Youth,** Barbara Hattemer, *The World & I,* July 1994.
   Barbara Hattemer presents a *cause-effect argument linking violent and sexually explicit media content to changes in social attitudes and behavior.* Following a review of supportive evidence from media effects research, she concludes with a call for increased media self-regulation reminiscent of the Motion Picture Production Code that served as an industry standard from 1930 to 1966. — 33

6. **Battle for Your Brain,** John Leland, *Newsweek,* October 11, 1993.
   Beavis and Butt-Head represent a new kind of rude, loser-hero popular in the media that is produced to attract teenage and young adult audiences. John Leland explores the extent to which their portrayals shape versus reflect social realities and attitudes. — 41

7. **Chips Ahoy,** Richard Zoglin, *Time,* February 19, 1996.
   The *V chip* offers what appears to be an easy solution to concerns about making television viewing a safe-for-children activity. Richard Zoglin explains driving forces behind V chip legislation and new dilemmas posed by its presence. — 45

The concepts in bold italics are developed in the article. For further expansion please refer to the Topic Guide and the Index.

UNIT 2

Information and Influence

Eight articles provide critical perspectives on mass media as a source of news and information.

Overview — 48

8. **Tuning Out the News,** Howard Kurtz, *Washington Post National Weekly Edition,* May 29–June 4, 1995. — 50
   In recent years, more media outlets have been providing news and information than ever before; however, according to Howard Kurtz, little of it is getting through to a sizable segment of the population. Kurtz discusses reasons *why much of the American public has little interest in news media.*

9. **Should the Coverage Fit the Crime?** Joe Holley, *Columbia Journalism Review,* May/June 1996. — 54
   Joe Holley goes inside KVUE-TV in Austin, Texas, following reporters and editors who are operating under a new policy that redefines traditional "if it bleeds, it leads" philosophies of airing *news of crime and violence.*

10. **All in the Family,** Marc Gunther, *American Journalism Review,* October 1995. — 60
    Media megadeals such as Disney's acquisition of Capital Cities/ABC and periodic additions to Rupert Murdoch's News Corp. holdings pose major challenges for news media. Marc Gunther explores the questions of both *corporate seeding* and *corporate censorship* of news topics.

11. **VNRs: News or Advertising?** Robert B. Charles, *The World & I,* September 1994. — 65
    A *video news release (VNR)* is a film clip, usually a minute or two in length, produced by a public relations firm and made available to television stations and networks by satellite feed. Robert Charles discusses how and why VNRs find their way into news broadcasts and the pros and cons of their being there.

12. **The Gospel of Public Journalism,** Alicia C. Shepard, *American Journalism Review,* September 1994. — 71
    The goal of public journalism is to reconnect citizens with their newspapers, their communities, and the political process. Attentive to *public feedback,* public journalism also takes a *"feedforward"* stance in its advocacy for community change.

13. **A Medical Breakthrough,** Jerome Aumente, *American Journalism Review,* December 1995. — 77
    Network *coverage of health and medical issues* fits well in the current climate of public interest in news with personal relevance. Jerome Aumente examines the challenges of medical reporting.

14. **Under Siege,** Linda Fibich, *American Journalism Review,* September 1995. — 82
    Recently, the public has shown an ever-increasing level of *contempt for mainstream media.* Linda Fibich reviews some of the reasons for this hostility and offers a few responses from media people.

15. **CBS, *60 Minutes,* and the Unseen Interview,** Lawrence K. Grossman, *Columbia Journalism Review,* January/February 1996. — 88
    In late 1995 the CBS show *60 Minutes* elected to kill an interview with the highest-ranking executive ever to blow the whistle on the tobacco industry. How this impacts on *the power of the media* is examined by Lawrence Grossman.

The concepts in bold italics are developed in the article. For further expansion please refer to the Topic Guide and the Index.

UNIT 3

Defining the Rules

Six selections explore how presenting newsworthy information can be complicated by considerations of what is ethically right and wrong.

Overview

16. **The Media and Truth: Is There a Moral Duty?** Paul Johnson, *Current*, December 1992.
    Based on 40 years of experience working with media organizations, Paul Johnson explains "seven deadly sins of the media": distortion, worshiping false images, theft of privacy, murder of character, exploitation of sex, poisoning the minds of children, and abuse of power. He then proposes "ten commandments" for *moral conduct* by all those who exercise media power and influence.

17. **"How Do You Feel?"** Fawn Germer, *American Journalism Review*, June 1995.
    When tragedies are covered, journalists must often make difficult decisions that *balance getting the story against sensitivity to its subjects.* Fawn Germer presents the techniques and the ethical dilemmas of chasing interviews.

18. **Gotcha!** Robert Lissit, *American Journalism Review*, March 1995.
    The *use of hidden cameras* by news reporters is not new; however, the recent development of relatively inexpensive cameras that are extremely small and silent has reopened the debate over when or if their use is ethical. Robert Lissit presents examples and repercussions of undercover photography.

19. **Anonymous Sources,** Alicia C. Shepard, *American Journalism Review*, December 1994.
    Defenders of *confidential sources* argue that they bring to light important stories that would otherwise never surface; opponents contend that their use undermines journalism's credibility. Alicia Shepard describes past and present cases and attitudes toward reporting information from unnamed informants.

20. **When Checkbook Journalism Does God's Work,** Louise Mengelkoch, *Columbia Journalism Review*, November/December 1994.
    Louise Mengelkoch describes a case that has convinced her that *sensationalism, checkbook journalism, and the tabloid press have virtue* in their willingness to empower the powerless.

21. **Are Quotes Sacred?** Fawn Germer, *American Journalism Review*, September 1995.
    Fawn Germer discusses perspectives on the degree to which it is and is not ethical to *clean up, condense, or otherwise alter quotations.*

100

102

106

111

116

123

126

The concepts in bold italics are developed in the article. For further expansion please refer to the Topic Guide and the Index.

UNIT 4

The Power of Images

Six articles explore the power of visual images and raise questions of their effects—from engendering emotional responses to reinventing reality.

Overview — 130

22. **Missing on the Home Front,** George H. Roeder Jr., *National Forum,* Fall 1995. — 132
    Photographs in *Life* magazine and other illustrated publications, newsreels, and films played a major role in educating Americans as to the nature of World War II. Thousands of photographs deemed likely to undermine home front morale were censored. George Roeder discusses these *images the public did not see,* and why they were withheld.

23. **Where Have All the Heroes Gone?** Christopher Hanson, *Columbia Journalism Review,* March/April 1996. — 137
    Christopher Hanson chronicles changes in the way journalists have been portrayed in popular films, tapping into the preconceptions of the audience and feeding back a cynical image that undercuts *perceptions of news professionals.*

24. **The Final Frontier,** Richard Corliss, *Time,* March 11, 1996. — 141
    Richard Corliss presents a brief history of *Hollywood's image of what it is like to be homosexual.* Homosexual characters have been shown as a joke, as figures of suave decadence, as fearful monsters, and as victims or martyrs. "Growing up, we all find ourselves, in part, by finding aspects of ourselves onscreen. Gays didn't."

25. **TV's Black Flight,** Christopher John Farley, *Time,* June 3, 1996. — 143
    Christopher John Farley describes a shift in television entertainment programming that has largely separated "white programming" from *"minority programming,"* segregating audiences who seek images of themselves.

26. **What the Jury Saw: Does the Videotape Lie?** Michael B. Rosen, *Bostonia,* Winter 1992–1993. — 145
    This analysis of the Rodney King and Marion Barry trials, in which videotaped records were important components, includes a brief history of photography and commentary on *the value of film as propaganda.*

27. **Photographs That Lie: The Ethical Dilemma of Digital Retouching,** J. D. Lasica, *Washington Journalism Review,* June 1989. — 151
    Digital technology has made it possible to retouch photographs in almost any manner without any evidence of tampering. Retouching photographs is not new, but the sophistication and ease of digital technology make it ever more prevalent. Where do you draw the line?

The concepts in bold italics are developed in the article. For further expansion please refer to the Topic Guide and the Index.

UNIT 5

A Word from Our Sponsor

Five selections explore relationships among advertising, media content, and popular culture.

Overview 154

28. **Sex, Lies, and Advertising,** Gloria Steinem, *Ms.,* July/August 1990. 156
    Writing in the first advertisement-free issue of *Ms.,* Gloria Steinem discusses experiences with advertisers that led to the magazine's decision to increase subscription rates and sever its *dependence on advertiser revenue. Dictated conditions* by various manufacturers on the placement of company advertisements within articles are described.

29. **Hollywood the Ad,** Mark Crispin Miller, from *Seeing through Movies,* Pantheon Books, 1990. 165
    While movies have not traditionally incorporated advertisements or depended on advertisers as a source of revenue, there is a current trend to cut deals for financial backing in exchange for *placing product plugs within films.* Mark Miller gives several examples of this trend and concludes that the art of film is becoming indistinguishable from the techniques of advertising.

30. **Your Show of Shills,** Leslie Savan, *Time,* April 1, 1996. 174
    Leslie Savan explains *the increasingly blurred line between programming and advertising on network television,* where "advertising's osmotic bleed into entertainment has turned into an arterial gush."

31. **Why Won't Television Grow Up?** Vicki Thomas and David B. Wolfe, *American Demographics,* May 1995. 176
    Vicki Thomas and David Wolfe explain how the absence of television programming that appeals to older consumers is influenced by *advertisers' interest in reaching a youthful target audience.* The authors contend that few media or advertising executives understand demographic trends or consumer habits and that dividing a market by age is a dated and narrow perspective.

32. **Children in the Digital Age,** Kathryn C. Montgomery, *The American Prospect,* July/August 1996. 180
    Almost one million children in the United States are now using the *World Wide Web,* and 3.8 million have Web access. Kathryn Montgomery argues that new on-line services for children are being developed in a highly commercialized media culture and sees troubling consequences of *advertisers' moving into children's cyberspace.*

UNIT 6

The State of the Nation

Five articles examine how mass media have influenced the way American political leaders are elected and how they govern.

Overview 186

33. **Reshaping the World of Politics,** Lee Edwards, *The World & I,* November 1994. 188
    Lee Edwards discusses *the impact of both traditional media and newer information technologies* on political parties, campaign strategies, political rhetoric, and the way that public officials communicate.

34. **Hoodwinked!** James McCartney, *American Journalism Review,* March 1996. 193
    Political candidates recognize the power of the media in *shaping agendas that influence voter decisions.* Politicians are often portrayed as victims of the press; however, they can also be sophisticated manipulators of news coverage. James McCartney traces campaign myths fed to and embraced by media in presidential contests from 1960 through 1992.

The concepts in bold italics are developed in the article. For further expansion please refer to the Topic Guide and the Index.

35. **Over the Line?** Sherry Ricchiardi, *American Journalism Review,* September 1996.   201
   Sherry Ricchiardi profiles Christiane Amanpour's coverage of Bosnia as an example of ***advocacy reporting*** that hits hard in covering national policy and presidential decisions.

36. **The Power of Talk,** Howard Fineman, *Newsweek,* February 8, 1993.   206
   The 1992 presidential campaign brought with it a new twist: ***talk-show politics.*** Larry King, Rush Limbaugh, and call-in talk show hosts around the country are finding an increasing market for political commentary. Howard Fineman notes the power of such programs in initiating grassroots activism, and he wonders whether they misdirect government priorities by forcing responses to the angry minority who use this forum.

37. **The Boys on the 'Net,** Wendall Cochran, *American Journalism Review,* April 1996.   209
   Politicians have discovered that they cannot ignore ***new technology*** as a means of getting their messages out to voters as well as to journalists. Wendall Cochran marks 1996 as the year politics discovered the World Wide Web, the Internet, and e-mail as resources of choice.

UNIT 7

The Shape of Things to Come

Six selections explore new media technologies and the changing landscape of mass media forms, consumption, and regulation.

Overview   212

38. **The Age of Convergence,** Philip Moeller, *American Journalism Review,* January/February 1994.   214
   The convergence of ***computers, fiber optics, and cable*** has led to high-profile research and development efforts to determine what consumers want and how they will use new media technology. Philip Moeller examines the future of ***news media*** organizations in an interactive media environment.

39. **Cyberspace Journalism,** Carol Pogash, *American Journalism Review,* June 1996.   220
   Electronic newspapers and magazines are reinventing the look and feel of news reporting and presentation. Carol Pogash describes life at HotWired, the migration of news mavericks to cyberspace, the potential for profit, and the future of online publishing.

40. **The Amazing Video Game Boom,** Philip Elmer-Dewitt, *Time,* September 27, 1993.   225
   For 20 years leaders in the entertainment industry have dismissed ***video gaming*** as removed from the mainstream of American media. Recently, however, telemedia giants have spent millions of dollars developing partnerships that are aimed at redefining ***the future of television and movie entertainment media*** through video game technology.

The concepts in bold italics are developed in the article. For further expansion please refer to the Topic Guide and the Index.

41. **Immaculate Reception,** Marshall Jon Fisher, *The Sciences,* 230
March/April 1996.
Digital televisions can send and receive electronic mail, gain access to the Internet, transmit startlingly lifelike images, and enable viewers to select the camera angles with which they view them. Marshall Jon Fisher describes the development and promises of ***digital television technology,*** along with its limitations and problems.

42. **Who Owns Digital Works?** Ann Okerson, *Scientific American,* 234
July 1996.
Ann Okerson examines questions about ***how to apply current copyright law to new media formats.*** To what extent are works "published" in cyberspace protected by law? How can we track who owns what, assuming that ownership makes sense at all? What are the liabilities of Internet providers? What does "fair use" mean in the electronic environment?

43. **The Biggest Thing Since Color?** Michael Krantz, *Time,* 239
August 12, 1996.
Some half-a-dozen companies have jumped into manufacturing ***TV-PC hybrids,*** a means of bringing the 85 to 90 percent of American homes that are not connected to the Internet into its Web. Michael Krantz wonders whether surfing the Net is something couch potatoes will really care to do.

Index 241
Article Review Form 244
Article Rating Form 245

The concepts in bold italics are developed in the article. For further expansion please refer to the Topic Guide and the Index.

Topic Guide

This topic guide suggests how the selections in this book relate to topics of traditional concern to students and professionals involved with the study of mass media. It is useful for locating articles that relate to each other for reading and research. The guide is arranged alphabetically according to topic. Articles may, of course, treat topics that do not appear in the topic guide. In turn, entries in the topic guide do not necessarily constitute a comprehensive listing of all the contents of each selection.

TOPIC AREA	TREATED IN	TOPIC AREA	TREATED IN
Advertising	2. Can TV Save the Planet? 3. Sexuality and the Mass Media 4. Gendered Media 7. Chips Ahoy 11. VNRs: News or Advertising? 28. Sex, Lies, and Advertising 29. Hollywood the Ad 30. Your Show of Shills 31. Why Won't Television Grow Up? 32. Children in the Digital Age 39. Cyberspace Journalism	Government Influence	7. Chips Ahoy 11. VNRs: News or Advertising? 22. Missing on the Home Front 34. Hoodwinked! 41. Immaculate Reception 42. Who Owns Digital Works?
		Industry Self-Regulation	5. Cause and Violent Effect 7. Chips Ahoy 9. Should the Coverage Fit the Crime? 16. Media and Truth 18. Gotcha! 19. Anonymous Sources
Children and Media	1. TV without Guilt 2. Can TV Save the Planet? 3. Sexuality and the Mass Media 5. Cause and Violent Effect 6. Battle for Your Brain 7. Chips Ahoy 32. Children in the Digital Age 40. Amazing Video Game Boom	Libel	18. Gotcha! 19. Anonymous Sources 21. Are Quotes Sacred?
		Magazines	3. Sexuality and the Mass Media 4. Gendered Media 10. All in the Family 22. Missing on the Home Front 27. Photographs That Lie 28. Sex, Lies, and Advertising 39. Cyberspace Journalism
Cultivation Theory	3. Sexuality and the Mass Media 4. Gendered Media 5. Cause and Violent Effect 23. Where Have All the Heroes Gone? 24. Final Frontier		
Ethics	9. Should the Coverage Fit the Crime? 11. VNRs: News or Advertising? 12. Gospel of Public Journalism 13. Medical Breakthrough 15. CBS, 60 Minutes, and the Unseen Interview 16. Media and Truth 17. "How Do You Feel?" 18. Gotcha! 19. Anonymous Sources 20. When Checkbook Journalism Does God's Work 21. Are Quotes Sacred? 22. Missing on the Home Front 27. Photographs That Lie 35. Over the Line?	Media Effects Research	3. Sexuality and the Mass Media 4. Gendered Media 5. Cause and Violent Effect 7. Chips Ahoy 32. Children in the Digital Age
		Media Ownership	10. All in the Family 29. Hollywood the Ad 38. Age of Convergence 40. Amazing Video Game Boom 41. Immaculate Reception
		Media Sex	3. Sexuality and the Mass Media 4. Gendered Media 5. Cause and Violent Effect
Family Values	1. TV without Guilt 3. Sexuality and the Mass Media 5. Cause and Violent Effect	Media Use	1. TV without Guilt 2. Can TV Save the Planet? 3. Sexuality and the Mass Media 8. Tuning Out the News 25. TV's Black Flight 31. Why Won't Television Grow Up? 32. Children in the Digital Age 38. Age of Convergence 40. Amazing Video Game Boom 43. Biggest Thing Since Color?
Federal Communications Commission (FCC)	5. Cause and Violent Effect 7. Chips Ahoy 41. Immaculate Reception		
Gatekeeping	10. All in the Family 15. CBS, 60 Minutes, and the Unseen Interview 22. Missing on the Home Front		
Gender Stereotypes	4. Gendered Media		

TOPIC AREA	TREATED IN	TOPIC AREA	TREATED IN
Media Violence	3. Sexuality and the Mass Media 4. Gendered Media 5. Cause and Violent Effect 6. Battle for Your Brain 7. Chips Ahoy 9. Should the Coverage Fit the Crime? 29. Hollywood the Ad 40. Amazing Video Game Boom	Photography	18. Gotcha! 22. Missing on the Home Front 26. What the Jury Saw 27. Photographs That Lie
		Political Coverage	8. Tuning Out the News 12. Gospel of Public Journalism 19. Anonymous Sources 33. Reshaping the World of Politics 34. Hoodwinked! 35. Over the Line? 36. Power of Talk 37. Boys on the 'Net
Minority Images	4. Gendered Media 24. Final Frontier 25. TV's Black Flight		
Movies	4. Gendered Media 5. Cause and Violent Effect 22. Missing on the Home Front 23. Where Have All the Heroes Gone? 24. Final Frontier 29. Hollywood the Ad 40. Amazing Video Game Boom	Radio	3. Sexuality and the Mass Media 36. Power of Talk
		Ratings	7. Chips Ahoy 31. Why Won't Television Grow Up?
Music/MTV	2. Can TV Save the Planet? 4. Gendered Media 5. Cause and Violent Effect 29. Hollywood the Ad	Right to Privacy	16. Media and Truth 18. Gotcha!
		Social Learning Theory	3. Sexuality and the Mass Media 5. Cause and Violent Effect 6. Battle for Your Brain
New Technologies	7. Chips Ahoy 27. Photographs That Lie 32. Children in the Digital Age 33. Reshaping the World of Politics 37. Boys on the 'Net 38. Age of Convergence 39. Cyberspace Journalism 40. Amazing Video Game Boom 41. Immaculate Reception 42. Who Owns Digital Works? 43. Biggest Thing Since Color?	Tabloid News	18. Gotcha! 20. When Checkbook Journalism Does God's Work
		Talk Shows	1. TV without Guilt 3. Sexuality and the Mass Media 36. Power of Talk
		Televison	1. TV without Guilt 2. Can TV Save the Planet? 3. Sexuality and the Mass Media 4. Gendered Media 5. Cause and Violent Effect 6. Battle for Your Brain 7. Chips Ahoy 8. Tuning Out the News 9. Should the Coverage Fit the Crime? 11. VNRs: News or Advertising? 13. Medical Breakthrough 15. CBS, 60 Minutes, and the Unseen Interview 25. TV's Black Flight 30. Your Show of Shills 31. Why Won't Television Grow Up? 40. Amazing Video Game Boom 41. Immaculate Reception 43. Biggest Thing Since Color?
News Reporting	3. Sexuality and the Mass Media 8. Tuning Out the News 9. Should the Coverage Fit the Crime? 10. All in the Family 11. VNRs: News or Advertising? 12. Gospel of Public Journalism 13. Medical Breakthrough 14. Under Siege 15. CBS, 60 Minutes, and the Unseen Interview 17. "How Do You Feel?" 18. Gotcha! 19. Anonymous Sources 20. When Checkbook Journalism Does God's Work 21. Are Quotes Sacred? 22. Missing on the Home Front 26. What the Jury Saw 27. Photographs That Lie 34. Hoodwinked! 35. Over the Line? 37. Boys on the 'Net 38. Age of Convergence 39. Cyberspace Journalism		
		V Chip	7. Chips Ahoy
		Video News Release (VNR)	11. VNRs: News or Advertising? 13. Medical Breakthrough
		World Wide Web	32. Children in the Digital Age 37. Boys on the 'Net 39. Cyberspace Journalism 42. Who Owns Digital Works?
Newspapers	8. Tuning Out the News 10. All in the Family 12. Gospel of Pubic Journalism 19. Anonymous Sources 21. Are Quotes Sacred? 22. Missing on the Home Front 27. Photographs That Lie 34. Hoodwinked! 38. Age of Convergence		

Living with Media

We live in a mediated society, one in which the forms and formats of mass media continue to evolve as audiences shift and technologies change. The five largest U.S. newspapers have a combined daily circulation of over 6 million. The average American reads 11.6 different magazine issues per month. On a typical day, 95 percent of Americans report listening to the radio at some point in their routines. In 1994 major motion picture studios produced 168 films, and movie theaters sold 1.29 million admission tickets.

In the United States, 98 percent of households have television. Of those television households, 99 percent have color television, 81 percent have one or more VCRs, 64 percent have basic cable, 38 percent have two or more television sets, and 28 percent have three or more sets. The average household receives 27 television stations and has television on about 47 hours per week; 1995 figures from the Nielsen Media Research Organization indicate that adult women log an average of 5 hours and 1 minute of television viewing each day, while adult men watch 4 hours and 17 minutes per day. It has been estimated that the average child will have watched 5,000 hours of television by the time he or she enters first grade and 25,000 hours by the end of high school—nearly twice as much time as will be spent in a classroom from first grade through graduation from college.

The media have been blamed for just about everything from a decrease in attention span to an increase in street crime, to undoing our capacity to think. In *Amusing Ourselves to Death* (Penguin, 1986), social critic Neil Postman suggests that the cocktail party, the quiz show, and popular trivia games are reflections of society's trying to find a use for the abundance of superficial information given us by the media—and useful for little else than attempts to impress one another with small talk. Peggy Noonan, a former network writer who worked as a speechwriter during the Reagan administration, has observed that experiences are no longer "real" unless they are ratified by television (which is why, she says, half the people in a stadium watch the game on monitors rather than watching the field). Marie Winn's memorable description of a child transfixed by television, slack-jawed, tongue resting on the front teeth, eyes glazed and vacant (*The Plug-In Drug*, Penguin, 1985) has become an often-quoted symbol of the passivity encouraged by television viewing.

Questions of whether or not and to what extent media influence our behaviors, values, expectations, and ways of thinking are difficult to answer. While one bibliographer has compiled a list of approximately 3,000 citations of English-language articles focusing just on children and television (and all written within the last 35 years), the conclusions drawn in these articles vary. Isolating media as a causal agent in examining human behavior is a difficult task, complicated by the challenge of understanding the complexities of the mind; differences in the context in which media are consumed (e.g., the personal, nonmedia experiences of the consumer and the extent to which media content is actively versus passively processed); the difficulty of finding representative control

UNIT 1

groups who have not been exposed to media; and the challenge of determining long-range effects. Thus, while researchers have found it difficult to prove that mass media *are* responsible for significant changes in individual consumers and in society as a whole, they have also found it difficult to prove that they *are not* linked to such changes.

Media messages serve a variety of purposes: They inform, they influence public opinion, they sell, and they entertain. They frequently do all of these things, sometimes below the level of consumers' conscious awareness. Children watch *Sesame Street* to be entertained, but they also learn to count, to share, to accept physical differences among individuals, and (perhaps) to desire a Sesame Street lunch box. Adults watch crime dramas to be entertained, but they also learn that they have the right to remain silent when arrested, how (accurately or inaccurately) the criminal justice system works, and that the world is an unsafe place.

Nicholas Johnson, a former chairman of the Federal Communications Commission, has noted, "Every moment of television programming—commercials, entertainment, news—teaches us something." While we may enter the media world to be entertained, the values and behaviors that we experience there have the potential of affecting social reality. The articles in this section were chosen to give readers a feel for concerns that have been raised regarding these implicit lessons of mass media content.

"TV without Guilt: Group Portrait with Television" provides a candid look at how television has become ingrained in the rituals of one family's daily life. As evidenced by readers' responses to this article, it strikes a controversial chord in its reflection of both how we use television and what we learn from it. "Can TV Save the Planet?" extends commentary on television use beyond the borders of the United States, claiming that the only thing adults around the world are more likely to do on a given day than watch television is to brush their teeth.

While some media consumers, such as Bonnie Delmar, a subject of the first article, express their love of television without guilt, Jane Brown and Jeanne Steele (see "Sexuality and the Mass Media: An Overview") are more critical of the effects of media use and content. All forms of mass media are, they charge, preoccupied with sexuality, contributing to "the patterns of sexual behavior we see in society today: early and unprotected sexual intercourse with multiple sexual partners, and high rates of unintended pregnancies." Similarly, Julia Wood, in "Gendered Media: The Influence of Media on Views of Gender," contends that media are harmfully perpetuating stereotypical expectations and attitudes about male/female roles and interactions. In "Cause and Violent Effect: Media and Our Youth," Barbara Hattemer links violent and sexually explicit media to changes in social attitudes and behavior, and John Leland questions whether or not television characters Beavis and Butt-Head have reinforced new cultural values of cynicism, stupidity, and crudity in his essay, "Battle for Your Brains."

In contrast to these cautionary views, Richard Zoglin, in his essay "Chips Ahoy," suggests that critics are too quick to blame media, particularly television, for society's evils. Countercritics such as Zoglin argue that the U.S. culture is more likely to drive the media than be driven by them; the popularity of mass media depends on their reflecting and preserving the status quo. The writer raises questions about the methodologies of studies cited as "proof" of media's harmful effects, and he notes that people who consume a lot of media often do so for a reason. They may be of lower socioeconomic status, more passive in nature, less intelligent than others, or socially alienated—all factors that are likely to be actual causes of effects that were attributed to their heavy media use.

Each of the writers whose views are included in this section agrees that media have the potential of influencing behavior and values. Each agrees that media content has changed over the years. However, they differ in the degree to which they believe that individual media consumers, particularly children, are shaped by what they encounter through media. Some argue that changes in media content simply reflect changes in social norms and attitudes; others claim that media provide role models and cultivate attitudes that drive social change.

Looking Ahead: Challenge Questions

After reading the unit's first article, compare your family's use of television with the way television was used in the Delmar household. Beyond the question of quantity of television watching, how accurately do you feel this portrait reflects the typical family's relationship with television?

What is your response to television characters Beavis and Butt-Head? Do you find them humorous? Why or why not? Why do you agree or disagree with John Leland's explanation for their appeal?

How solid is the evidence of a cause-effect relationship between exposure to violent content in mass media and actual aggressive or violent behavior? To what degree can scientific research resolve questions of such media effects? Do you find the arguments of media critics or countercritics more compelling? Why?

To what degree do media portrayals of women, men, families, religion, patriotism, ethnic minorities, sexuality, and violence reflect changing social norms? To what degree do they shape social norms? Why has each been criticized? With which criticisms do you agree and disagree?

… Article 1

TV Without Guilt

Group Portrait With Television

One family's love affair with the tube

David Finkel

The first TV to come on is the one in the master bedroom, a 13-inch Hitachi. The time is 8:20 a.m. The alarm clock goes off, and Bonnie Delmar opens her eyes and immediately reaches over to the night stand for the remote. Her husband, Steve, has already left for work. The children are still asleep. The house is quiet. On comes CBS because Bonnie was watching the David Letterman show when she drifted off the night before. She watches "This Morning" for a few minutes, catching up on what has happened in the last seven hours in the world beyond her Gaithersburg home, and then she switches to NBC in time for the weather and Willard Scott. Later in the day, she will tell about a dream she once had. "I dreamt I was married to Willard Scott," she will say. "I was going to my 10th high school reunion, and I was excited that everyone was going to see that I was married to a celebrity, but then I wasn't excited because it was Willard Scott. You know?"

The second TV to come on is the 19-inch Zenith in the bedroom of Bonnie's daughter, Ashley, age 7 years and 10 months. The time is now 8:45, 40 minutes before school begins, and Ashley and her younger brother, Steven, get dressed while watching "The Bozo Show." The Zenith is the newest TV in the house, purchased a few weeks before to replace the 26-inch Sony console that had been in Ashley's room until the color picture tube went bad. "She threw a fit when the console broke," Bonnie says of Ashley's initial reaction. "She was, like, 'I won't watch TV in my room anymore,' so Steve and Steven went out and got her a new TV, and she wasn't at all happy about it. I mean, she went in her room and cried about it. She actually cried. She wanted a big screen. I actually laughed at her. I said, 'You've got to be kidding,' and that made her more furious. She was saying, 'How can you give me such a small TV?' But, anyway, that's over. She's fine now." On the screen this morning, Bozo is standing next to a child who is attempting to throw a ping-pong ball into a succession of six buckets. She does this and wins several prizes, and Ashley and Steven jump around the bedroom cheering while Bonnie, who has been watching with them, claps her hands. "Wow!" she says. "What a great day."

The third TV to come on is the 27-inch Hitachi by the kitchen table. It's now a few minutes after 9, time for "Live—Regis & Kathie Lee." This Hitachi has an especially complex remote, but Steven has mastered it, despite being only 6. He picks it up and changes the channel to "Barney and Friends." "I love you, you love me," the Barney theme song begins, but Steven sings his own variation, learned from Ashley, who learned it at school. "I hate you, you hate me, he sings, "let's kill Barney one two three, with a great big knife, stab him in his head, pull it out and then he's dead." "Steven!" Bonnie says, laughing. "How's it really go?" "I don't know," Steven says. He picks up the remote again and switches to cartoons, while Bonnie, who wants to watch "Regis & Kathie Lee," goes over to the counter by the sink and turns on the five-inch, black-and-white, battery powered Panasonic.

It is now 9:10 a.m. in the Delmar house. Fifty minutes have gone by since the alarm. Four TVs have been turned on. It will be another 16 hours before all the TVs are off and the house is once again quiet.

By the sink, Bonnie continues to watch "Regis & Kathie Lee."

At the table, Ashley and Steven watch Speedy Gonzales in "Here Today, Gone Tamale."

Looking at them, it's hard to imagine three happier people.

"Mom," Ashley says later, after she has gone to school and come home and resumed watching TV, "I'm going to watch TV in Heaven."

"You're going to watch TV in Heaven?" Bonnie says.

"Yeah," Ashley says.

"Well," Bonnie says, "let's hope they have it on up there."

Of all the relationships of modern civilization, none is more hypocritical than the relationship between an American family and its television set.

We say we don't watch TV except occasionally, and yet, according to Nielsen figures, we have it on an average of 7½ hours a day. We worry that TV causes violent behavior, and yet we keep watching violent shows. We complain that TV is getting too graphic, and yet we are buying sets with sharper pictures and larger screens. We insist we have better things to do than watch TV, and yet every night, on every street, shooting through the gaps in closed blinds or around the edges of drawn curtains is the electric blue glow that is the true color of our lives.

TV is our angst. TV is our guilt. We watch it. We worry about it. We blame it. We watch it some more. We feel bad about how much we really watch it. We lie.

Except for the Delmars.

"I just don't buy it that too much TV is bad for you," says Steve, 37, the chief financial officer of a company that makes

From *The Washington Post Magazine,* January 16, 1994, pp. 9-15, 24-27. © 1994 by The Washington Post. Reprinted by permission.

1. TV without Guilt

automated telephone answering systems, who gets home from work around 7, eats dinner while watching Dan Rather and Connie Chung, settles down in the den by the 19-inch Sony, watches a few hours of sports, goes back to the bedroom, turns on the Hitachi and falls asleep with it on because Bonnie can't fall asleep if it's off. "Nobody wants to admit they watch television—it's got the connotation: 'the boob tube'—but all these people, what are they doing? I'm not sure if they have any more intellect. It's not like they're all going to the Smithsonian or anything."

"Let's see," says Bonnie, 35, a housewife and former restaurant hostess with a bachelor's degree in elementary education, totaling up how much TV she watches a day. "It just depends on if I'm home or not. Almost always, the TV is on from 4 o'clock to the end of 'David Letterman.' It depends, though. If I'm home, I'm watching. Probably nine hours a day is average. There are some days I might actually watch 16, 17 hours, but there are some days I'm out and about, and I don't get to watch as much."

At the Delmars', there are six TVs, counting the old Sony console that is now in the guest room, and plans are to refinish the basement and add two more. At the Delmars', not only is the TV always on, it is virtually a member of the family, part of nearly every significant moment in their lives.

Bonnie remembers her honeymoon. "The cable went out," she says. "It wasn't out for long, six hours maybe, but I was pretty mad."

She remembers Steven's birth. "Steven was born during the halftime of a Redskins game," she says. "It was a Monday night, 'Monday Night Football,' a big game. I was actually pushing, and Steve and the doctor were watching the game right down to the last second."

She remembers Ashley's birth. "I cut out the TV guide the day she was born," she says. "I thought that would be interesting." She gets Ashley's baby book. "Look—'Webster' was on, in first run. 'Mr. Belvedere.' 'Diff'rent Strokes.' 'Falcon Crest.' 'Fall Guy.' 'Miami Vice.' 'Dallas.' 'Dynasty.' 'Knight Rider.' God, can you believe it? Wow."

She remembers when Ashley and Steven were conceived. "I don't watch TV during sex, if you want to know," she says, laughing. "I'm capable of turning it off for five minutes."

But not much longer than that. Certainly not for an entire day, Bonnie says. In fact, she says, she can't remember the last time a day passed without her watching something. "It would be very hard for me to make it through a day," she says. "It's almost an automatic reflex at this point."

The same goes for the kids, who, until recently, were allowed to watch as much TV as they wanted. Then came the night when Steve awakened well after midnight—Bonnie says it was toward 4 a.m.—and found Ashley sitting up in bed watching the Cartoon Network. Now the rule for the kids is no TV after 11 p.m. on school nights, but other than that, anything goes. "The kids watch everything from 'Barney' to 'Beavis and Butt-head,'" Bonnie says. There is no embarrassment in the way she says this, not even the slightest hint of discomfort. There is nothing other than brightness and happiness, for that is what she feels about TV.

"I love it. I love it. I can't help it. I love it," she says. "Why should I be ashamed of saying that?"

3 p.m. The 27-inch Hitachi is on. Time for "Maury Povich." So far this day, Bonnie has watched parts of "Regis & Kathie Lee," "Jerry Springer," "Broadcast House Live," "Geraldo," "American Journal," "Loving," "All My Children," "One Life to Live" and "John & Leeza," and now she is watching Povich talk from his New York studio to a woman named Happy Leuken who weighs more than 600 pounds and is in a Boston hospital weight-loss program. "God, it's so sad," Bonnie says, looking at Happy, who is spread over her hospital bed like raw dough, chatting away. Now she and the rest of the viewing audience see what Happy can't, that Happy's hero, exercise guru Richard Simmons, is standing outside the door to Happy's room, poised to dash in and surprise her with a bouquet of flowers. "Watch," Bonnie says. "He loves to cry. He'll come in. He'll cry. She'll cry. The audience will cry. I might cry too." In he runs. Happy looks surprised. The studio audience applauds. He embraces her. The studio audience cheers. He kisses her big neck. The cheers get louder. She kisses him on the lips. "There he goes," Bonnie says. "He's working up to it. He's starting to blink."

She keeps watching. "Did you know he was on 'General Hospital?'" she says. "It was years and years ago. He was running an exercise class. There was one character, a heavyset character, who was in the class, and I thought they were going to transform her into something beautiful, but I guess she wouldn't lose any weight because they dropped the story line."

Bonnie not only knows this about Richard Simmons, she knows everything about everybody. To her, TV is more than entertainment, it's a family of actors who share histories and links.

Earlier in the day, when she was showing off some school lunch boxes she has collected over the years, she got to the "Get Smart" lunch box and found herself thinking about Dick Gautier, who played Hymie the Robot, and Julie Newmar, who she thinks played opposite Gautier in one or two episodes and definitely played Catwoman in "Batman," as did Eartha Kitt and Lee Meriwether, who was also in "The Time Tunnel" and whose daughter was a model on "The Price Is Right." "Kyle. Kyle Meriwether," she said. "She used to substitute when one of the other girls, like Janice, couldn't make it." A little later, when the soap opera "Loving" came on, Bonnie said of an actress: "That woman is married to Michael Knight, who plays Tad in 'All My Children,' and she was married to David Hasselhoff, who played a character named Michael Knight in that show 'Knight Rider.' Isn't that weird?" Now, looking at Maury Povich, she says, "Can you believe Maury Povich is married to Connie Chung?"

So of course she knows about Richard Simmons, who is now sitting on Happy's bed, congratulating her on the 50 or so pounds she has lost, absently rubbing his thumb up and down her exposed lower leg. Over the years, there's been all kinds of research done on the effects of television on viewers, including, fairly recently, a study on the effects of the TV set itself, which showed that the bigger the screen is, the more involved a viewer

1. LIVING WITH MEDIA

feels. It also noted that people are buying bigger TVs all the time, something that Steve, who has looked at a 35-inch Mitsubishi, is considering for the basement. For now, though, the 27-inch Hitachi is the biggest screen in the house, which, as Simmons keeps rubbing Happy's leg, rubbing it, rubbing it, rubbing it, seems plenty big enough. "That kind of grosses me out," Bonnie says, and she leaves the house to pick up the kids from school.

The school is just down the street. In fact lots of things in Bonnie's life are just down the street: the toy store where she buys Ninja Turtle dolls for Steven and "Beverly Hills, 90210" dolls for Ashley; the pizza place that is always advertising two pizzas with up to five toppings each for $7.99; the grocery store where she buys Cap'n Crunch, and Flintstone Push Ups in Yabba Dabba Doo Orange, and all the other things the kids want after seeing them on TV. The school is closest of all, so close that when Bonnie has the windows open and the TV volume down she can hear the kids squealing and laughing on the playground.

She is back in a few minutes. The TV is still on, and as the car doors open and close, Happy Leuken is still chatting away, talking now about how the hospital allows conjugal visits. Now Happy's husband is talking about their own conjugal visit, about how exciting it was that, for the first time in years, his wife was able to lift her legs onto the bed by herself, and how much he's liking her body, really *really* liking it—and that's what Ashley and Steven come home to.

They run into the house, stop by the TV, listen. Some parents might worry about this, but not Bonnie. She simply goes into the kitchen and begins getting out snacks. If the kids have a question, she figures, they'll ask it, and if they don't they'll probably get bored and change the channel. Sure enough, Steven picks up the remote and changes to cartoons. He and Ashley sit at the kitchen table. Bonnie pours them sodas. She gets them Rice Krispies treats. She defrosts some Ball Park Fun Franks—"Michael Jordan endorses these," she says—and serves them with potato chips, which Ashley dips in ketchup. The kids keep watching. Eating. Watching. Then they run back to Ashley's room to watch cartoons on her TV, and Bonnie changes the channel to Sally Jessy Raphael, where the topic is "moms who share their daughters' boyfriends."

"Don't you love watching this?" she asks during a commercial. "Can you tell me you're not enjoying this? I love seeing how people live." Even the worst shows, she says, have value if for no other reason than she gets to see what other lives are like. "Lesbians. Homosexuals. Transvestites," she says, listing people she has met through TV. "Spiritualists. Occultists. Teenage runaways. Teenage drug addicts. Teenage alcoholics. Child stars who are in trouble. Politicians. Bald men. People with physical problems. Cancer survivors. Siamese twins." Now she will learn about moms and daughters who share the same boyfriends, and tomorrow, according to a commercial, she will meet "a man who had his private parts enlarged—on the next Maury."

She agrees it's a strange group of people. Nonetheless, she keeps watching as one of the moms on the show says she and her daughter run a phone sex line and pretend to have orgasms while actually eating donuts and painting their nails.

"You know, TV really does open up your eyes about how many people in the world there are, and how different they are," Bonnie says. "I mean without TV, who would exist? Just these middle-class people I see every day. I wouldn't know anything else was going on."

She watches to the end.

Then, with the kids, she watches "Full House."

Then they watch "Saved by the Bell."

Then she watches the local news.

Then Steve comes home and the entire family eats dinner and watches Dan Rather and Connie Chung.

Then, sometimes with Steve, sometimes with the kids, sometimes by herself, Bonnie watches "Jeopardy," "Mad About You," "Wings," "Seinfeld," "Frasier," "The Mary Tyler Moore Show," "The Dick Van Dyke Show," "The Tonight Show" and "The Late Show With David Letterman. Toward the end of "Letterman" she falls asleep, awakens long enough to turn off the TV and falls back asleep until 8:20 a.m., when she reaches woozily for the remote and starts all over again.

Not that TV is the only thing Bonnie does. "I don't just sit and watch TV," she says. "I'll clean while I watch. I'll read the paper. I'll work on crafts. I like making doll-house furniture with Ashley. I'll fold laundry." She also reads books, volunteers at the school several times a week and works on the yard.

But almost all of this involves TV, at least peripherally. The crafts are done in front of the Hitachi, and whenever she cleans the house she takes the portable Panasonic along to the rooms that don't have a TV. The book she is reading at the moment is by Howard Stern, and the book she's reading with Ashley, which came from a school book club, is about Stephanie, one of the characters on "Full House."

From time to time, her friends poke fun at her about all of this, but she doesn't mind. Sometimes Steve does too—"the walking TV Guide," he calls her—but she doesn't mind that either. They've been married nearly 10 years now, and even though she once turned down a free weekend in Jamaica with Steve in part because the hotel room didn't have a TV, he says of her, "If everybody was like Bonnie, the world would be a helluva lot better place."

"I'd definitely like to have a perfect family," she is saying one evening.

"She'd like to have the Beaver Cleaver family," says Steve.

"I would. You know I've had people tell me that Steven looks like Beaver," she says, adding that she always tells them, "Thank you."

"You do?" says Steve.

"Yeah," says Bonnie. "It's a compliment."

"Bonnie's life tends to be dictated by what she sees on television," Steve says, rolling his eyes.

"You think a lot of stuff on television is ridiculous," Bonnie says to him.

"Yeah, I do. For instance, talk shows. Why would anyone want to watch these shows all the time?"

"You learn a lot," Bonnie says.

"Like what?"

8

1. TV without Guilt

"About everything."

"Like enlarged sex organs?"

"Yeah," Bonnie says.

"It's like the National Enquirer," Steve says. "Pretty soon there'll be a show on two-headed cabbages."

"But you know what?" Bonnie says. "I always have something to talk about at parties."

"That's true," Steve says.

"For instance," Bonnie says, "do you know how many women the average man sleeps with in his lifetime?"

"What's your source for this?"

"Geraldo."

"The man who put skin from his butt on his head?"

"Seven. The answer is seven," Bonnie says. "Don't you find that interesting?"

So there is conversation in the Delmar house too, as well as family time, when everyone watches a show together. "We all watch 'Home Improvement,'" Bonnie says. "We all watch 'Seinfeld.'" They also watch "Married . . . With Children," a show that has been called sexist, misogynous, soft pornography and worse. But it also has about 20 million regular viewers, including the Delmars, who try to watch it every week.

This week, however, Bonnie announces she wants to watch a special on CBS, "a show that was on when I was little, and I want to watch it very much."

"What is it?" Steve asks.

"'The Waltons Reunion,'" Bonnie says.

"Oh, God. I thought they died," Steve says.

"I *loved* that show," Bonnie says.

"But Mom . . ." Ashley says.

"Mom . . ." Steven says.

"If you want to sit quietly, you can sit here and watch," Bonnie says. "But be quiet. Mommy wants to watch this."

And so Ashley and Steven go off to watch "Married . . . With Children" by themselves.

"Channel Two Five," Bonnie calls to them as they run down the hallway, so they'll know what to press on the remote.

They go to Ashley's room, a room in which they spend a couple of hours every day, just them and whatever they want to watch. Steven has his own bedroom a few steps away, but because he doesn't yet have a TV he is in Ashley's room more than his own, usually falling asleep and spending the night in her queen-sized bed. The bed has a heart-shaped pillow on it with a picture of Zack, from "Saved by the Bell," along with the inscription "Sweet Dreams." "Ashley loves Zack," Steven says about that. "He's her love muffin." There is also a dresser drawer filled with videotapes of children's movies—"We probably have a hundred," Steven says—as well as a Super Nintendo game, a VCR, a videotape rewinder, a cable outlet and of course, the new 19-inch Zenith, on which Al Bundy, one of the "Married . . . With Children" characters, is saying to his wife, Peg, as their neighbor Marcy listens, "I'm telling you, Peg, I'm so hot, if Marcy wasn't here I'd take you on the floor right now."

To which Peg says, "Get out, Marcy."

To which Ashley and Steven, hearing every word of this exchange, say nothing. They just keep listening as Al and Peg get in an argument about sex, and Peg says to Al that TV is the "only thing you've turned on in 20 years," and Al says to a Peg, "Well, if you came with a remote and a mute button, I might turn you on too."

Wordlessly, Ashley and Steven watch the show until it ends and then run back out to Bonnie. "How was it?" she asks, and that's all she asks—not so much because she doesn't care what her children watch but because she and Steve don't see any reason to worry about it.

"You know why?" Bonnie says the next day, when the kids are in school and she is making them a surprise for when they get home, a concoction of cereal, pretzel sticks, butter and brown sugar. "Because I really trust my kids. If there's anything bad, they'll tell me about it."

She puts the pan in the oven. On the Hitachi, Maury Povich is about to show a videotape of a convenience store clerk being shot during a robbery. "It's so as graphic, you might not want to watch," he warns.

If TV's so bad, Bonnie says, why are her kids doing so well? If it's so bad, why is Steven so happy, and why is Ashley excelling in school? Just the other day, at a parent-teacher conference, Ashley's teacher called her a terrific student and concluded by saying to Bonnie, "You will be seeing great things from Ashley"—and to Bonnie's way of thinking TV is one of the reasons why. As she said after the conference, "I have friends who think it's terrible that I let my kids eat candy, that I let my kids watch TV, that I don't have a lot of rules, but I'll tell you what: Set my kids and their kids in the same room and see who's better behaved. They're really, really sweet kids. And a lot of these parents who try to do everything right—no TV, lots of reading, lots of rules, trying to do everything perfectly—let's face it. Their kids can be real pains in the neck."

The smell of melting butter and brown sugar fills the kitchen. On the Hitachi, the convenience store clerk is on the ground, bleeding, yelling for help.

"I think they're doing good," she says of her kids. "I don't think TV has corrupted them at all. Who knows, you know? We won't know for 15, 20 years. But right now, they seem okay."

3:20. Time to go pick them up.

Once, last year, when Ashley was in first grade and Steven was still at home, Bonnie decided to let Ashley walk to school, just as she had done when she was child growing up. That's when she lived in Wheaton, in a split-level, in a time when she and everyone else felt absolutely, unquestionably safe. Year after year she would walk to school, walk home at lunch time to eat a peanut butter sandwich and watch "The Donna Reed Show," walk back to school, walk back home. The first day Ashley did this, though, the very first day, she came home with a note alerting parents that a man in a van had been seen loitering near certain bus stops, taking photographs of little children. So that was the end of that. For some reason the world has changed, Bonnie says, although she doesn't think the reason is TV.

The kids run in and plop down at the kitchen table. At this time of day, the decision about what to watch on the Hitachi is

1. LIVING WITH MEDIA

theirs, and they switch to Daffy Duck as they dig into the cereal-and-pretzel mix.

Another day, they decide to stick with "Maury Povich." "That lady is so skinny you can see her bones," Ashley says as the camera focuses on a woman who is almost skeletal.

"That lady has an eating disorder," Bonnie says.

"What's an eating disorder?" Ashley asks.

And so, because of TV, Ashley and Steven learn about eating disorders.

Later, they watch "Beverly Hills, 90210," in which the plot revolves around a boy who forces himself on a girl.

And so Ashley and Steven learn about date rape.

Eleven o'clock comes. Time to turn off the Zenith, according to the new rule of house. The night before, Ashley cried when Bonnie did this—"It's not *fair*," she yelled—but this night, in the darkened room, Bonnie sits on the edge of the bed and traces her fingers over her children's faces in light, lazy circles, and soon their eyes are shut.

And so Ashley and Steven learn to go sleep without TV.

Thirty years ago: Bonnie is small. The TV is black and white. There is one TV in the entire house, no cable, no remote, no VCR, just a TV in the corner of the living room with an antenna on top and Red Skelton on the screen, and Bonnie is laughing so hard she is rolling around on the carpet. She is allowed to stay up as late as she wants, and watch as much TV as she wants, and there has never been a happier child.

Thirty years later: Ninety-eight percent of American households have TV, according to Nielsen Media Research; 66 percent have at least two TVs; 77 percent have at least one VCR; 62 percent get cable; and TV is under scrutiny by everyone from politicians who are proposing ratings for TV shows and video games, to academicians and sociologists who produce study after study about its dulling effects on developing brains, to a group of 20 worried women who come together one evening at an elementary school in Silver Spring, not far at all from the neighborhood where Bonnie grew up.

Bonnie isn't among them. Bonnie, in fact, would never go to such a meeting, and neither would Steve, who says of such things, "These people who get so rabid, they should be taking it easy." The women, though, feel exactly the opposite. Members of a loosely organized group called the Mothers Information Exchange, they have come to hear about the effects of TV from Amy Blank, who is with the Maryland Campaign for Kids' TV, an organization that monitors children's programming on area TV stations. All of the women have children. All see TV as something to be concerned about. Several of the women go so far as to say they feel truly afraid of what TV might be doing to their children, and what they hear over the next 90 minutes doesn't make them feel any less anxious.

"As we'll learn this evening, we have an incredible relationship with that box over there," says Blank, an edge of direness in her voice, motioning toward a TV that is hooked up to a VCR. "We can't remember when we didn't have it in our lives. That's really profound. We don't have people in our lives this long, some of us. We've had this thing in our lives all our lives. It's incredible."

She asks the women how many TV sets they own.

"We have five."

"We have four."

She asks how many hours a day the TVs are on.

"Six."

"Three-and-a-half."

"Oh God, this is embarrassing."

"Are you including Barney videos?"

"Do you have to include your husband?"

She turns on the TV and shows a videotape, in which the announcer says that "in a typical television season, the average adolescent views 14,000 instances of sexual contact or sexual innuendo in TV ads and programs."

She turns on an opaque projector and shows a chart that says: "Most children will see 8,000 murders and 10,000 acts of violence before they finish elementary school."

"They won't do any other thing, other than eat or sleep, that many times," she says. "That's what we're teaching them. It's okay to kill 8,000 people. It's okay to hurt or maim 10,000 people. It's okay. TV does it, so it's okay."

She shows another chart of what parents should do, a list that includes limiting the amount of time children watch TV.

"I think we're seeing tremendous effects on our kids and on our society," she says. "I mean, we're a broken society. We really are. We're struggling. There's so much incredible pain out there. And many of us just don't know where to hide, and don't know what to do.

"I want to show you one last thing," she says, and on the TV comes a clip from "The Simpsons," a show she detests so much that, earlier in the evening, when one of the mothers said she thought "The Simpsons" could be funny at times, she said, "Bart should be shot."

This clip, though, she likes. It is of Marge Simpson, the mother, writing a letter to a TV station.

"Dear Purveyors of Senseless Violence," she begins.

"I know this may sound silly at first, but I believe that the cartoons you show to our children are influencing their behavior in a negative way. Please try to tone down the psychotic violence in your otherwise fine programming.

"Yours truly, Marge Simpson."

"Dear Valued Viewer," the station manager writes back. "In regards to your specific comments about the show, our research indicates that one person cannot make a difference, no matter how big a screwball she is."

"I'll show them what one screwball can do!" Marge says to that.

Blank snaps off the TV.

"Well," she says, "I don't think any of us are screwballs," and with those words and the vision of 8,000 murders in their minds, the women head off into the darkness of prime time.

Meanwhile, back in Gaithersburg, where the Delmars are watching TV, life is as untroubled as usual.

Thursday, 8 p.m. Time for "The Simpsons." But it's also time for "Mad About You," which Bonnie, Steve and Steven want to watch, so Ashley goes back to her room by herself.

She turns on her TV. She sits at her desk, takes out some paper and pastels and starts to draw. Five minutes go by. Ten minutes.

1. TV without Guilt

On the screen, a character named Krusty the Klown is reciting a limerick: "There once was a man from Enis . . ."

Now Bart is sticking the leg of a chair in the garbage disposal, turning it on and riding it like a bronco.

Now he is talking about how something "sucks."

But Ashley doesn't notice. She is completely involved in getting what she sees at the moment in her mind down on paper. She draws some white clouds in a blue sky. Now she draws a flower with blue petals and a pink center, and now she writes under the flower, "This is Steven."

She puts down her pastels, looks at what she has done, holds it up, explains the title:

"I think he looks like a flower."

She runs out to the kitchen table and climbs onto the lap of Bonnie, who is, of course, busy watching TV, but not so busy that she can't give her daughter a hug, and in this way another evening passes by. Around 9, Ashley lies on the floor in front of the TV and does her spelling homework. At 10, she is back on Bonnie's lap. "I love you," she says to Bonnie as 10:30 comes and goes. "Kiss me."

Sometimes, Bonnie says, she thinks her life could be a TV show, although she isn't quite sure what kind of show it would be.

She knows it wouldn't be a drama, she says, not yet anyway, because not enough dramatic things have happened, at least not directly to her. There have been friends with cancer, friends with bad marriages, friends who have suffered all kinds of traumas, but the only drama in her own life came a few years ago, when she found herself engaged in an escalating internal dialogue about mortality. For reasons she is still unsure of, she would make a dentist's appointment and wonder if she would live long enough to go, or she would buy milk and wonder if she would make it through the expiration date. Finally, in tears one day, she told her mother about this, and gradually the thoughts went away, bringing an end to a time that was certainly interesting, Bonnie says, and even momentarily disturbing, but hardly the stuff of TV.

So it wouldn't be a drama, she says, and neither would it be a talk show. There is, of course, plenty of talking in the Delmar house, but it's the talk of any family rather than of TV. The phone rings. It's Steve. "Hi," Bonnie says. "What time will you be home?" At the table, Steven takes a big bite out of a sandwich. "Chew carefully," Bonnie says. "Peanut butter can make you choke." There are, on occasion, longer, deeper, more philosophical discussions, but those too are internal dialogues that usually come into her mind late at night, when everyone is asleep except Bonnie, who's trying one more time to go to sleep without being lulled there by TV. "I think that's the reason I have to have the TV on," she says. "If it's not on, I think. I think, I think, I think." About: "Everything. I know this sounds weird, but I think about ways the economy could be solved. Really. I think about NAFTA. I think about how my life could be better. I think about TV. It's an intense thing. I won't think about one solution, I'll think about 20. I get into all these ideas, and then I think I'll write a letter to Bill Clinton, or to Dear Abby, or someone else. And then . . . then I'll think no one wants to hear what I'm thinking, so I'll just turn the TV on, and eventually I'll drift off.

"That's the thing about TV," she says. "You don't have to think."

So: not a drama, not a talk show.

Obviously, then, it would have to be a situation comedy, which Bonnie says is fine with her because, after all, "isn't everybody's life a sitcom kind of life?"

True enough, a lot of what goes on at the Delmars' seems exactly that. Days almost always begin brightly and end with hugs, and in between there's no telling what exactly will happen.

Like the time Bonnie went out to mow the lawn, got on the rider mower, started picturing Eddie Albert "bouncing on that tractor" and began singing the theme song to "Green Acres." Not once did she sing it, not twice, but over and over, for more than an hour, until she realized the kid across the street was looking at her like she was from another planet. Which is why whenever she has mowed the lawn since, she has hummed.

Or how about the time she was actually on TV? It was right after Ashley was born, and she had to make a fast trip to the grocery store. She grabbed a sweat shirt out of the dryer, hurried through the store with her baby and was in line to pay, thinking how big and unattractive she must look, when she noticed the checkout guy kind of smiling at her. How nice, she thought, suddenly feeling better about herself. "And then I came home and realized I had a pair of underwear and a sock stuck to my back," she says. "Static cling. I had walked through the whole store that way. Well, okay, I can handle that. But the next week one of the local TV stations had some cameras in the store, and they asked if they could talk to me and film me walking with my baby, and I said sure, and I'll bet all the Giant people were watching that night, and the checkout guy said, 'Hey! That's the lady who had the underwear stuck to her back!' "

So: a situation comedy.

" 'Life With the Delmars,' " Bonnie says it could be called, and it would have four characters:

The dad.

"He'd be hard-working," she says. "He'd be a character who's in and out, one of those characters where you don't see too much of him, but funny. And fun."

The son.

"Kindergarten student. Enthusiastic. Mischievous. Rambunctious."

The daughter.

"Definitely precocious. She'd act like a teenager, a teenager wannabe. Stubborn. Funny."

And the mom.

"Let's see," she says. "Who am I?"

She thinks. Thinks some more. Can't come up with a description, so she thinks instead about who might watch such a show.

"*I'd* watch it," she says.

Can TV SAVE THE PLANET?

SUMMARY

Television isn't creating a global village, but a global mall. In a world united by satellite technology, teenagers the world over share many consumer attitudes because they watch many of the same TV shows and commercials. Global teens already have some strong brand preferences, but there's still plenty of room to develop global brands by paying attention to youth.

Chip Walker

Chip Walker is global trends director of The BrainWaves Group, a division of DMB&B in New York City.

As focus groups go, this one is fairly typical. On one side of a two-way mirror, a group of teenagers sits around a table talking with a moderator about clothing preferences. On the other side, observers from an advertising agency eat M&Ms and occasionally take notes. A relatively small group of brand names keeps coming up: Levi's and Calvin Klein jeans, Timberland boots, and Adidas and Nike footwear. What is the most important source of fashion information? No surprise: it's TV ads. To an American observer, the unusual thing about this group is the fact that the only English words being spoken are the brand names. This is Bangkok.

Worldwide access to commercial television is creating a global consumer culture. But it isn't the homogeneous "global village" that pundits have been predicting. Regional differences in attitudes, values, and beliefs still abound. In many areas, they are stronger than ever. Yet TV is creating a common culture of consumption. More than ever, people around the world know about and want the same types of branded goods and services. Rather than a global village, mass exposure to TV is creating a global mall.

The global consumer culture is most clearly seen among young people who have grown up on a steady diet of television. While these young people still clearly belong to indigenous cultures based on religion and national identities, they have all learned to understand marketing in much the same way.

"In some markets, there has been a concern that western media will cause national identity and values to suffer," says Janet Scardino, vice president of international marketing at MTV Networks. "What we've seen is that the media don't change values or ethics. They are much more likely to impact kids' behavior as consumers. We're seeing a growing commonality among global youth as it relates to media habits and spending habits."

"Young people are certainly more global in outlook and behavior," says Tom Miller, senior vice president of Roper Starch Worldwide in New York City. "The primary reason for this is the influence of popular culture emanating from the U.S. and the U.K."

TV is becoming the great unifying force in the world. Thus, the course of the future may not lie so much in the hands of governments, or political or religious movements, but rather in the hands of those who shape commercial TV. This in turn provokes the question: If TV really does unite the world and marketers control TV, what kind of world is in store?

A GLOBAL MALL

TV isn't just an activity. It's become one of the most popular ways to spend leisure time since the invention of the nap. Virtually all households in North America have a television, according to a 1995 Roper study. The only thing people in these countries are more likely to do on a given day than watch TV is brush their teeth; 95 percent brush and 91 percent watch the tube. Related items such as "shampooed hair" and "read a magazine" rate considerably lower, at 52 percent and 35 percent, respectively. In fact, just 32 percent took a nap.

While Americans appear to be the number-one couch potatoes, our fellow viewers around the world are not far behind. Middle Easterners watch the most (3.6 hours per day), followed by North

2. Can TV Save the Planet?

The Most Common Denominator

Watching TV surpasses other forms of media consumption and even personal hygiene in much of the world.

(percent of adults participating in selected activities in the past day, by region of the world, 1995)

	all	North America	Latin America	Western Europe	Central Europe	Ex-USSR	Asia
Brushed teeth	95%	96%	97%	94%	95%	80%	98%
Watched any TV	91	93	86	90	91	90	92
Read a newspaper	63	65	46	68	74	41	72
Listened to the radio	57	59	69	71	71	49	46
Took a shower	55	78	93	64	58	30	36
Shampooed hair	52	65	72	52	41	24	46
Read a magazine	35	32	27	42	50	10	42
Took a bath	32	24	5	20	39	16	50

Source: Roper Starch Worldwide, New York, NY

Americans, including Mexicans (2.9). Western Europeans watch the least, at 2.5 hours a day. Only work and sleep take up more of our time than TV does.

Here in the U.S., our adjustment to the TV life has been gradual. During the 1960s and 1970s, most households had access to only a handful of channels. With the advent of cable, we gradually got more. But elsewhere in the world, communities have gone from no TV to dozens of channels overnight, thanks to satellite-dish technology. The average planetary citizen can choose from 12 channels, finds Roper. North Americans get the largest channel selection, averaging 27. Western Europeans are a distant second, with 14. Latin Americans and Central Europeans average 12 choices, Middle Easterners 11, and Asians 9. Residents of the former Soviet Union have the most limited channel choice, with 4.

As media markets have grown more sophisticated and consumer demand has surged, local programming has proliferated. Gone are the days when a dubbed rerun of "Dynasty" or "Dallas" suffices for viewers worldwide. What remains unchanged is the popularity of western genres—soaps, sitcoms, talk shows, movies—and most pervasive of all, the ads.

American advertising agencies dominate the global marketplace by huge margins. Seven of the top-ten global shops are U.S.-based.

Nearly everyone agrees that the impact of mass TV watching is seen most clearly among today's youth. Think of it this way: During a time of crisis, people in more than 200 countries can tune in to news on CNN or BBC World Service Television and watch the same news reports at the same time. But imagine a group that tunes in to the same type of

> **Americans are the world's greatest couch potatoes, but other countries are not far behind.**

programming, complete with ads, every day. MTV now reaches over 239 million viewers in 68 countries, most of them teens and young adults.

What is the nature of this emerging global consumer generation? Most multinational studies understandably focus on those with the most money—adults. But what about teenagers? The New World Teen Study was designed as the first global syndicated quantitative study to focus on this target. Conducted in schools among 6,500 15-to-18-year-olds, the study provides a read on the attitudes, lifestyles, values, and consumer behavior of teens in 26 countries.

A WORLD UNITED

The New World Teen study reveals that global teens are a generation with startling commonalities as consumers. Despite differing cultures, middle-class youth all over the world seem to live their lives as if in a parallel universe. They get up in the morning, put on their Levi's and Nikes, grab their caps, backpacks, and Sony personal CD players, and head for school.

Spending time with friends and watching television tie as teens' most enjoyable way to spend free time. In fact, eight of teens' top-ten activities are media-related. For TV programming, teens prefer movies above and beyond all else. Music videos, stand-up comedy, and sports are also hugely popular. The hottest international sport in the mid-1990s is basketball, rather than soccer or football. The Chicago Bulls are enormously popular among teens in many countries.

Teens watch both locally produced and foreign programming. A look at the top TV programs in a dozen countries, put together by DMB&B International Media Group in London, shows that the movie

1. LIVING WITH MEDIA

Home Alone was a huge hit among teen TV viewers in Indonesia. In Russia, the now defunct American soap "Santa Barbara" is a top-ten rated show among kids aged 11 to 17, and Brazilian teens' hearts beat for the dramatic series "ER." On Godzilla's home turf, Japanese teens tune in to American science fiction with "The X-Files."

MTV is probably the most impressive global youth TV phenomenon, however. With separate indigenous music video networks including MTV Latino, MTV Brazil, MTV Europe, MTV Mandarin, MTV Asia, MTV Japan, and MTV India, the network has the ability to reach a large proportion of the world's youth literally overnight. "Kids are tuned in to music and music videos more than ever, but it's not necessarily the same music," says MTV's Scardino.

Because music tastes are highly localized, over 90 percent of MTV's airtime is locally programmed and produced. Still, a look at the top-five music videos shows that teens around the world share some of the same musical tastes. During the week of January 8, 1996, Madonna, Queen, and the Rolling Stones topped the charts for MTV Latino. Silverchair was hot in Brazil, and Michael Jackson and Tina Turner were in the top five on MTV Europe.

DEVELOPING GLOBAL BRANDS

The good news for marketers is that teens who watch commercial TV also tend to consume more. For example, teens who watch MTV music videos are much more likely than other teens to wear the teen "uniform" of jeans, running shoes, and denim jacket, finds the New World Teen Study. They are also much more likely to own electronics and consume "teen" items such as candy, sodas, cookies, and fast food. They are much more likely to use a wide range of personal-care products, too.

The ability to reach the world's teens virtually overnight via the medium of TV is particularly crucial to marketers when you consider that in the high-growth regions of Latin America and the Far East, people under age 18 represent a majority of the population. Not only does global youth represent the adult of tomorrow, it is a sizable market in and of its own right today. It's important to keep in mind, however, that you can't necessarily address teens with an adult-oriented message. TV's homogenizing power means that, as consumers, teens frequently have much more in common with each other than they do with their parents. They can also have significant influence over the brands their parents buy.

Governments around the world, particularly more oppressive regimes, are wary of television's power. "TV changes people," says Jon Vanden Heuvel of Columbia University's Freedom Forum Media Studies Center. "The impact of having TV everywhere is that it is a great leveler. It raises expectations. The 'have nots' start to want to have. It makes them impatient with things like government or run-away inflation that get in the way of having what they want."

For years, the Chinese government tried to keep out the influence of what it viewed as western decadence. But with the advent of satellite dishes, it has virtually given up. Some observers have even credited the removal of the Berlin Wall to the power of TV. "As East Germany began to get western TV and the media prohibition there declined, it became less OK for them not to have the things they saw others had," says Vanden Heuvel.

World consumers may never be a completely homogenous group. Still, the availability of mass TV via channels like ESPN, CNN, BBC, Discovery, and MTV is creating an opportunity to communicate to world consumers en masse, much the way network TV did in the U.S. during the 1950s and 1960s. Some saw this era as the "golden age" of American advertising. It's possible that we are headed for another, even larger golden age of growth and prosperity in global advertising.

What can marketers expect in the future? The first and foremost effect is continued growth in global branding. Continued growth of the global middle class* will lead to greater disposable income, and the growth of global TV will provide consumers with solid ideas about how to spend the money. Recent efforts by the likes of IBM are only the tip of the iceberg.

* See "The Global Middle Class," September 1995.

The TV Teens Love

Maybe it's because they've had so much exposure, but teens in the U.S. are more likely than teens elsewhere to like everything they see on TV.

(percent of 15-to-18-year-olds who like selected types of TV programs, by region of the world, 1995)

	U.S.	Europe	Latin America	Far East
Movies	93%	91%	86%	90%
MTV/music videos	85	77	82	80
Stand-up comedy	72	49	63	59
Olympic games	69	64	70	56
Sports	69	53	65	56
Talk shows	66	37	45	46
News	65	44	44	40
Cartoons	65	54	55	69
Academy awards	62	39	52	47

Source: New World Teen Study, The BrainWaves Group

Teens' Top Nine

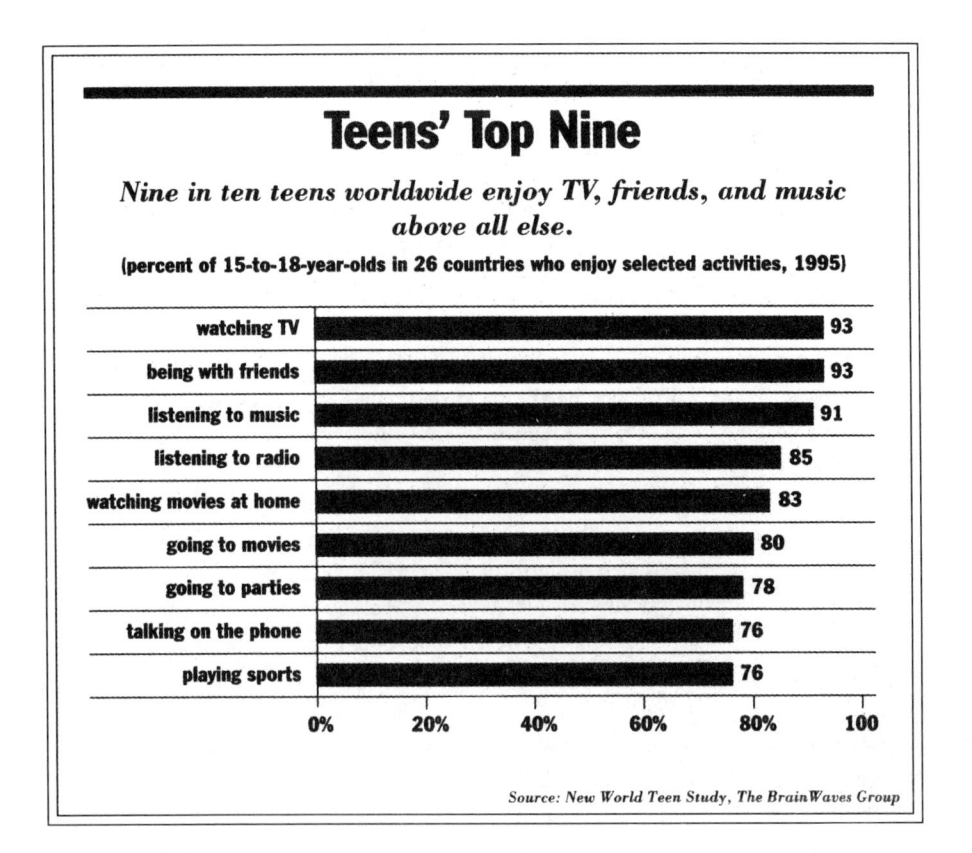

Nine in ten teens worldwide enjoy TV, friends, and music above all else.

(percent of 15-to-18-year-olds in 26 countries who enjoy selected activities, 1995)

Activity	Percent
watching TV	93
being with friends	93
listening to music	91
listening to radio	85
watching movies at home	83
going to movies	80
going to parties	78
talking on the phone	76
playing sports	76

Source: New World Teen Study, The BrainWaves Group

The opportunity for global advertising directed at younger consumers is enormous. One of the most important findings of the New World Teen study is that, in many product categories, there are no perceived brand leaders. And in some categories where there is a perceived leader, it's not teens' favorite brand. This indicates an opportunity for new youth brand leaders to emerge. Both facts signal opportunities to become teens' favorite, today and tomorrow.

Advertisers interested in targeting the planet's future adult consumers must remember to "stay real." No matter where they live, teenagers struggle with the opposing forces of worry and optimism. The prevailing result in light of these conflicting forces is a down-to-earth mindset. From a lengthy battery of attitudinal items, the one that teens most agree with worldwide is: "It's up to me to get what I want out of life." Half agree that "most advertising can't be believed," and nearly as many, 44 percent, say that most people can't be believed.

2. Can TV Save the Planet?

To communicate with such a cynical yet hopeful target, it is important to think first of the solid realism that unites the world's young people. With this in mind, marketers can stand back and examine the differences that are truly relevant to each situation. When do cultural distinctions need to be addressed? When should advertising be cast differently by market? Only by offering sensitivity and respect to teens can marketers expect to leverage the power of the newly emerging youth-driven consumer culture.

Behind the Numbers Wave I of the New World Teens Study is the first syndicated quantitative international study of teens' attitudes, lifestyles, values, and consumer behavior. Wave I interviewed more than 6,500 teenagers in 26 countries around the world in late 1994. The study's second wave, available this spring, covers more than 20,000 respondents in 40 countries. For more information, contact Chip Walker at (212) 468-4246 or Elissa Moses at (212) 599-0700. Roper Starch Worldwide surveyed nearly 38,000 adults in 40 countries in March and April 1995. For more information, contact Tom Miller or Toni Shields of Roper Starch at (212) 599-0700. Information on global teens' favorite TV shows was compiled by the DMB&B International Media Centre in London. For more information, contact Judy Thomas at 44-11-630-0000. MTV: Music Television provides information on global teens' favorite music videos. For more information, contact Janet Scardino at (212) 258-8000. For additional information about international media habits, see two Freedom Forum publications: "The Unfolding Lotus: East Asia's Changing Media" and "Changing Patterns: Latin America's Vital Media." Both are available from the Freedom Forum Media Studies Center, Columbia University, 2950 Broadway, New York, NY 10027; telephone (212) 678-6600.

Article 3

SEXUALITY AND THE MASS MEDIA: AN OVERVIEW

By Jane D. Brown, Ph.D. and Jeanne R. Steele, M.S.
School of Journalism and Mass Communication
University of North Carolina
Chapel Hill, NC

Regardless of age or gender, all but the rarest of Americans are exposed to sexual images, allusions, and talk in the media on an almost daily basis. Sexually attractive models beckon from billboards, and talk shows showcase sexual anomalies. Television soap operas, prime-time series, movies, music lyrics and men's, women's, and teen magazines draw heavily on sexual themes.

TELEVISION

More Americans have television sets than phones, and the television is on about seven hours per day in the average home.[1] In addition, about a third of Americans' free time is spent watching television, more than the next ten most popular leisure activities combined.[2] African-Americans watch 50 percent more television than other groups[3], and children and teenagers from low-income households watch more television than other children.[4] Current content analyses suggest a remarkable consistency across programming—with sexuality far more explicit today than it was in the days of Ozzie and Harriet's twin beds.[5]

On prime-time television. The most recent comparative study of specific sexual behaviors during prime time on the major broadcast networks found an average of 10 instances of sexual behavior per hour[6], a slight decrease in the overall rate since a similar study was conducted four years earlier.[7] The drop, however, occurred primarily in the least explicit sexual category—physical suggestiveness—and was offset by a 50 percent increase in the rate of heterosexual intercourse, defined as talk about, implied, or actual physical portrayals of sexual intercourse.

When sexual behavior in promotions for upcoming shows was added, the rate per hour increased from about 10 to more than 15, painting a picture more in line with public perceptions and supporting the idea that networks frequently use "sex as bait" to increase their ratings.[8]

More alarming, given current rates of sexually transmitted diseases (STDs) and unplanned pregnancy, analysis showed that few programs ever mentioned the negative consequences that may result from having sexual relations. In fact, references to pregnancy prevention and STD prevention both showed declines from the already low rates in the earlier study. Thus, a typical viewer would see about 25 instances of sexual behavior for every one instance of preventive behavior or comment. And, even then, the message may not be the most desirable—all the coded references to STDs or pregnancy prevention were in a joking context.

On the soaps. Traditionally steamier than prime-time programming, daytime soap operas have received substantial research attention because of their strong appeal for women and adolescents. A recent analysis of sexuality on the soaps found that top-rated soap operas averaged 6.6 sexual incidents per hour compared to about half that number 10 years earlier. Talk about safe sexual relations and contraception was still relatively rare—six references in 50 episodes, against a backdrop of 15 different story lines about pregnancy over a two-month period.

In addition, sexual intercourse between unmarried individuals remained the staple on the five shows studied.[9] Nearly one in 10 of the characters involved in any sexual activity was involved in extramarital relationships. Although there was lots of talk about pregnancy, there were not many babies—only 22 appearances by toddlers aged four and under.[10]

On the daytime talk shows. Sexuality on the soaps looks almost tame compared to topics discussed on daytime talk shows. The new breed—including Ricki Lake, Sally Jessy Raphael, Jenny Jones, Montel Williams, and Geraldo Rivera—compete for guests willing to make public confessions about intimate sexual relations and feelings. "Catfights and rowdy showdowns" keep viewers tuned in, so producers shop for controversy and on-air confrontations.[11] Sometimes they get out of hand: Jonathan Schmitz was charged with murder in the death of Scott Amadure, a young man who declared his attraction to Schmitz during a taping of a *Jenny Jones* show on secret admirers.[12]

On cable and video. Adult programming that portrays explicit sexual behavior is cable television's fastest growing segment.[13] With the advent of a fiber optic infrastructure, a projected 500 channels are expected to include even more such content. The video cassette player (VCR) also provides greater access to sexually explicit materials.

According to recent content analyses, sexual relations are more frequent and more explicit in movies than in any other medium. Virtually every R-rated film contains at least one nude scene, and some of those most popular with adolescents contain as many as 15 instances of sexual intercourse in less than two hours.[14] Despite the R rating that supposedly restricts viewing to people over 18 years of age unless accompanied by an adult, two-thirds of a sample of high school students in Michigan reported that they were allowed to rent or watch any movie they wanted, and the movies they most frequently viewed were R-rated.[15]

On music videos. Even before Elvis was prohibited from shaking his hips on *The Ed Sullivan Show*, popular music was synonymous with sexuality. Especially appealing to youth,[16] popular music and now music videos contain frequent references to relationships, romance and sexual behavior—the very stuff young people are most interested in as they work on constructing a sense of who they are and what they value.[17] Music videos, now available on at least five major cable networks, may be especially influential sources of sexual information for adolescents because they combine visuals of adolescents' favorite musicians with the music. Many of the visual elements are sexual.[18] Rap music is particularly explicit about both sexuality and violence.[19] Perry argues that the explicit "sexual speak" of African-American women rappers follows in the liberating tradition of the "blues," which gave voice to African-American women's sexual and cultural politics during the years of migration to northern states. This striving for empowerment may explain why some rap musicians have responded to concerns about unsafe sexual relations and have included alternative messages. Some rap music includes talk of "jimmy hats" or condoms. An album by the female rap group Salt 'n' Pepa is about the pleasures and responsibilities of sexual relationships.

RADIO

Frank discussions about sexuality—ranging from Dr. Ruth's on-air psychological counseling to the sexual banter of disc jockeys hired to capture the teen/youth adult audience as they drive to school or work—are common on radio. Content analyses are rare, however, given the diversity of local radio programming and the speed with which local radio personalities rise and fall in popularity.

MAGAZINES

Magazines are another important source of relationship and sexual information, especially for women and adolescent girls. In a recent survey, more than a quarter (26 percent) of women aged 30 to 49 reported that magazines are the source they most typically rely on (second only to health care professionals) for information about birth control.[20]

In 1994, the 12 largest women's magazines (including *Better Homes and Gardens, Family Circle, Woman's Day, Good Housekeeping,* and *Ladies' Home Journal*) had a combined circulation of more than 40 million, according to the Audit Bureau of Circulations. Other magazines such as *Parents* (circulation 1.84 million) and *Soap Opera Digest* (1.46 million) also are read by a largely female audience.

Although publishers' statements reveal subtle differences in the market niche each is trying to attract, women's magazines until recently have focused on two broad topics: what a woman should do to get a man *(Cosmopolitan)* and what a woman should do once she has the man and his children *(Redbook)*. Specifically, *Cosmopolitan* claims to deal with the emotional side of women's lives while *Redbook* is edited for "young working mothers with children…women who face the challenge of balancing family, home, and career."

Other magazines have attempted to include other aspects of women's lives: *Working Woman* and *Savvy* are targeted toward women who work outside the home. *Health* is for "active women who have made the pursuit of good health an integral part of their daily lives."[21] But even in these magazines, the emphasis remains primarily on women's lives as they revolve around making themselves attractive enough to catch and keep a man.

Reproductive issues are infrequently covered. Despite their focus on women's lives, these magazines rarely cover reproductive issues such as abortion that might alienate some readers, and, thus, indirectly, advertisers who are looking for large or tightly segmented circulations. As the controversy surrounding abortion has escalated, the largest women's magazines have published only a few articles.[22] *Glamour* and *Mademoiselle* have carried more articles (although still only about one a year) than the others. *Family Circle, Ladies Home Journal,* and *Woman's Day* carried five or fewer articles during the two decades from 1972–1991.

Advertisers exert a great deal of control over magazines—both over editorial content and whether they should/could exist at all—because advertising revenue accounts for at least half of the income of most magazines. According to its editor-in-chief, *Glamour* was able to include more articles about abortion than the other magazines because reader surveys showed that readers were pro-choice and, thus, advertisers were less concerned that such content would alienate readers.[23]

Ms. magazine, the only women's magazine explicitly dedicated to feminism and the facts about women's sexuality, struggled for 20 years to attract enough advertising. Traditional advertisers, such as cosmetics companies, made such heavy demands on editorial content (e.g., no cover photos of women without makeup) that the magazine has given up advertising and today relies solely on a hefty subscription price ($35 for six issues) for revenue.[24] Although now editorially freer, *Ms.* has dropped from a circulation of 500,000 to about 170,000 due to the price increase.[25]

1. LIVING WITH MEDIA

Sexuality in Teen Magazines. The teen magazine, *Sassy*, initially suffered from an advertiser boycott organized by the far right after early issues included such articles as "Losing Your Virginity and "Getting Turned On." Despite the editors' dedication to providing "responsible, direct information about [sexuality]" and the appreciative response of readers and parents, the magazine was forced to remove the "controversial" content to stay in business.[26]

Today, advertisers appear less concerned about adult scruples as they compete to capture their piece of the growing (both in terms of size and spending power) youth market.[27] *YM*—originally titled *Calling All Girls* before metamorphizing to *Polly Pigtails, Young Miss*, and, finally, to *YM* (Young and Modern)—recently beckoned readers with a "special sealed section," a play on the brown paper wrapper typically associated with pornography. Titled "Getting Intimate," the section featured eight straight-talking pages about sexuality issues. One page was devoted to STDs—who gets them, how they are spread, what the symptoms are, and how they are treated. Another page relied on a mix of first-person accounts, professional advice, and "surprising sex stats" to help readers answer the question: "Sex: Ready or Not?" This combination of peer-talk and solid data about sexual issues in a girls' magazine signals a positive trend.

ADVERTISING

Paradoxically, many of the same advertisers who have exerted pressure to keep responsible sexuality information out of the media often use sexual appeals to sell their products. A study of 4,294 network television commercials found that one of every 3.8 commercials includes some type of attractiveness-based message.[28]

Although most advertisements do not directly model sexual intercourse, they help set the stage for sexual behavior by promoting the importance of beautiful bodies and products that enhance attractiveness to the opposite sex. Advertisers like Calvin Klein, Guess jeans, and Benetton have pushed the limits of sexual suggestiveness with their use of bared flesh, childlike models, and intertwined limbs.

The frequent portrayal of women as interested only in attracting men or as prizes to be won, may lead to the disempowerment of women in sexual relationships. If a woman does all she can to attract a man, can she say no when he wants the sexual relationship she supposedly has been offering? And if she does say no, should a man believe her?

NEWS MEDIA

Although rarely thought of as sexuality educators, the news media at the least help keep sexual behavior salient. The American public and policymakers frequently are faced with news stories about abandoned babies, abortion clinic violence, and controversies over condom availability programs. Sometimes referred to as agenda setters, the media are in a unique position to get people thinking about specific issues.

The media sometimes are reluctant to cover issues that do not meet traditional criteria for news worthiness, including being relevant to middle-class Americans.[29] Because newspapers and news magazines compete for the same kinds of readers, they publish stories that have remained remarkably consistent in subject matter and point of view across the last three or four decades, despite more women in the newsroom.[30] According to another study, the same has been true for women's magazines which, despite more women (although still few) in high editorial positions, continue to treat their women audiences in the same "stereotypical ways that men editors had in the 1960s."[31]

HIV/AIDS provides an excellent example of the power of media to keep a sexually related topic off the agendas of both the public and policymakers. Because the disease initially was thought to affect only homosexuals and intravenous drug users, groups deemed to be outside the "mainstream" by many editors and reporters, very few stories on HIV/AIDS appeared until mid-1985, four years after the Centers for Disease Control had reported more than 350 deaths. *The New York Times,* an influential agenda setter for both other media and policymakers, was especially slow in covering the topic.[32]

PREOCCUPATION WITH SEXUALITY

In sum, all forms of mass media, from prime-time television, to music, music videos, magazines, advertising and the news media include information about sexual behavior. The media provide a window on a world preoccupied with sexuality. In this media world, heterosexual activity is frequent, recreational, and, most often, engaged in by unmarried partners. These partners usually do not discuss their sexual relationship or use contraceptives, yet they rarely get pregnant. If a woman does get pregnant, she rarely considers abortion as an alternative, and even more rarely has one.[33]

The financial and emotional problems associated with parentless or single-parent families sometimes are portrayed, but generally are resolved harmoniously and quickly. Thus, we might expect that exposure to such content at least contributes to the patterns of sexual behavior we see in society today: early and unprotected sexual intercourse with multiple partners, and high rates of unintended pregnancies.

RESEARCH ON THE ISSUE

Sensitivity to sexuality as a topic has restricted research. Only a handful of studies have attempted to link exposure with beliefs, attitudes, or subsequent behavior.

The few studies that do exist consistently point to a relationship between exposure and beliefs, attitudes, and behaviors. Ultimately, which comes first may not be the most important question. Of greater significance is the cumulative effect of media saturated with the sounds, images, and politics of sexuality.

Traditional communication research and a growing body of interdisciplinary work by psychologists, anthropologists, sociologists, and cultural theorists point to a process of cultivation, agenda-setting, and social learning that affects every aspect of our lives.

"MAINSTREAMING" OF AMERICA

According to one perspective, television is the most powerful storyteller in American culture, one that continually repeats the myths and ideologies, the "facts" and patterns of relationships that define our world and "legitimize the social order."[34]

Television tells its stories through prime-time sitcoms and series, daytime soap operas and talk shows, news and sports, and a steady stream of commercials that fuel the entire television industry. And it does so throughout the lifespans of its viewers. According to the "cultivation hypothesis," a steady dose of television, over time, acts like the pull of gravity toward an imagined center.

Called "mainstreaming," this pull results in a shared set of conceptions and expectations about reality among diverse viewers. Tests of the hypothesis have found, for example, that "heavy" television viewers are more likely to believe the world is "mean and dangerous," apparently because of frequent exposure to violence on television.[35]

Researchers have found that college students who watch soaps are more likely than their nonviewing counterparts to overestimate the occurrence of divorce and single parenthood. Interestingly, given the paucity of such portrayals on the soaps, viewers also overestimated the number of abortions[36] and the incidence of STDs[37] in the real world.

Other studies have looked at the cultivation of gender-role stereotypes and have found evidence that television nurtures their continuing presence in American society.[38] Studies of adolescents also have found that heavy television viewing is predictive of negative attitudes toward remaining a virgin.[39] A variety of other factors also enter the picture—ethnicity, class, and gender affect both program preferences and the meanings that are drawn from media content. But, in general, our media culture sells sexuality without consequences.

SETTING AMERICA'S AGENDA

Other researchers see the mass media as agenda-setters that not only tell people what is important in the world around them, but also how to think about the events and people who inhabit that world.[40]

Using words and images as their palette, news anchors, reporters, and photographers paint pictures of a world peopled by villains and victims, good guys and bad guys. Over time, the many little dramas that make up the day's news events take on a life of their own—the news media's pictures of the world actually become the world in the minds of thousands of viewers and readers.

As professional storytellers, the news media not only control which stories get told, they also decide how they get told. Called "framing," this aspect of newsmaking helps shape an individual's understanding of events and may affect behavior.[41] Highly charged issues such as abortion or teen pregnancy require careful treatment by newsmakers. Rather than framing them as juicy controversies—the stuff on which ratings are built—editors and reporters would do well to examine their motives and methods before fueling the deep rifts that divide society on these issues.

In a detailed account of how the abortion debate developed in Fargo, ND, in the 1980s, anthropologist Faye Ginsberg describes what happens when the media sacrifice socially responsible coverage for "good television": "By picking up violent or near-violent action as 'newsworthy,' to the neglect of the less dramatic but more representative work, most coverage of the abortion issue unwittingly colludes with the radical behavior of a vocal minority—for whom visibility is a preeminent goal—even when condemning it."[42]

By framing issues in particular ways, the media contribute to the creation of moral panics[43] over perceived threats (for example, the teen pregnancy "epidemic"). As Blumer put it, a "social problem exists primarily in terms of how it is defined and conceived in society."[44] By applying the "epidemic" label to teenage pregnancy, the media helped create an environment that justifies the use of stringent, authoritarian measures to fight a social disease somehow brought on by its "victims." When coupled with the people's "common knowledge" about epidemics and disease, the media framing of the issue makes it relatively easy to blame teenage mothers for failing to take reasonable precautions rather than looking for ways to improve the material conditions of teenage mothers or the effectiveness of health education programs.[45] Either way, the media can be, and often are, central to the process.

SOCIAL LEARNING

Few studies have directly considered the question of most fundamental concern: Does exposure to sexuality issues in the media cause those who see it to engage in sexual behavior earlier and in riskier ways? Two studies have found correlations between watching higher doses of "sexy" television and early initiation of sexual intercourse.[46] Although neither study was designed to sort out effectively which came first—the exposure to sexual content or the sexual behavior—both suggested that exposure to sexual content is related to early sexual intercourse among teens.

This is not much to go on, but both studies support the

1. LIVING WITH MEDIA

ideas of social learning theory that guide a great deal of research on how media affect behavior. Basically, the theory predicts that people will imitate behaviors of others when those models are rewarded or not punished for their behavior. Modeling will occur more regularly when the model is perceived as attractive and is similar to the imitator and the modeled behavior is salient, simple, prevalent, has functional value, and is possible.[47] Thus, the theory would predict that teens who spend more time watching television will imitate behavior that includes depictions of attractive characters having sexual intercourse who rarely suffer any negative consequences.

MEDIA VIOLENCE

More than 1,000 studies, using a variety of research techniques—including laboratory and field experiments, cross-sectional and longitudinal surveys, and meta-analyses—consistently have found small positive relationships between exposure to violent content in the visual media (primarily television and movies) and subsequent aggressive and antisocial behavior.[48] As some theorists have pointed out, although such an effect may seem small, media are one of the many factors that contribute to human behavior that could be modified most readily.[49]

One of the most compelling of the naturalistic studies of television violence found that the homicide rates in three countries (the United States, Canada, and South Africa) increased dramatically 10 to 15 years after the introduction of television.[50] Although early television is not remembered as particularly violent, the earliest content analyses conducted in the mid-1960s in the United States reported the number of violent acts per hour at rates similar to current fare. (Remember all those cowboy shoot-'em-ups?)

Would analyses of the incidence of unplanned pregnancies and the introduction of television draw similar conclusions? It is not an unreasonable expectation. Further studies very likely will find patterns of effects similar to those established for violent content.

USING THE MEDIA

Health advocates have developed three basic strategies for using the mass media in the interest of healthy sexual behavior:

- **Public information campaigns** where media are used to generate specific effects in a large number of people within a specified period of time.[51] Such campaigns are usually more successful when advertising space is purchased and heavy reliance is not placed on public service announcements (PSAs).

- **Media advocacy** where health advocates generate their own news. This calls for knowledge of how the media work as well as using that knowledge to get issues on the media agenda. Public policies that affect access to and affordability of sexuality education, contraception, and abortion are logical targets of such advocacy.

- **"Edutainment"** where socially responsible messages are incorporated into entertainment media such as music, television dramas, soap operas, and magazine articles. The longer formats allow more time for developing complex messages such as how to negotiate condom use or how to choose an appropriate birth control method.[52] The primary drawback to the education-entertainment strategy in the United States is that the media are unlikely to include portrayals they consider potentially controversial.[53]

SUGGESTIONS FOR THE FUTURE

In sum, existing research supports a qualified yes to the question: Do media affect sexual attitudes, beliefs, and behaviors? At this point, researchers know more about what kinds of media portrayals of sexuality are available than about their effect on audiences.

Key communication theories (cultivation, agenda setting, and social learning) and years of research on other kinds of communication effects suggest, however, the increasingly frequent, unprotected, and consequence-free sexual behavior depicted in all forms of mass media do affect American's sexual beliefs and behaviors.

Here are some conclusions to guide future investigations and research:

- **Television is not the only medium of concern.** Teenagers, especially, turn to other forms of media—particularly music, movies, and magazines—as they seek clues about who they want to be or should be in the larger culture. Women rely on women's magazines. These are important sources of sexual information for further research. New forms of communication, including the Internet, which is becoming an important source of sexuality information, also should be included in future inquiry.

- **There is no such thing as "the" media audience.** As media grow increasingly fragmented and specialized, so do their audiences. Previous research shows that audiences often select different media based on ethnicity, gender, age, and class. African-Americans are more likely to watch television shows, listen to music, and read magazines featuring African-Americans. Men will seldom read women's magazines. People with a college education are more likely to watch news and public affairs programs. People who do not work during the day are more likely to watch soap operas. Future research should focus on who is watching what, and why.

- **Media effects will not be uniform across audiences.** Researchers need to pay closer attention to developmental, lifestyle, and cultural issues. It is reasonable to expect that teens involved in sexual relationships will seek out sexual media content because it is relevant. Possible cultural differences in interpretation of sexual content were clear in a study of rock star Madonna's early controversial video "Papa Don't Preach."[54] White college students, particularly women, thought it was about a pregnant girl telling her father she is pregnant and wants to keep her unborn child. African-American males, in contrast, frequently retold the story as a girl asking her father's permission to be with her boyfriend. For them, the "baby" was a boyfriend. Learning about differences in interpretation will add to an understanding of the media's effects on sexuality.

- **Interdisciplinary research will be most valuable.** Increasingly, researchers are recognizing that media effects are best understood when studies are conducted from multiple perspectives. New breakthroughs might be forged by bringing multidisciplinary teams together to study how the media affect everyday life.

- **Media producers should be held accountable.** The economics of the media industry cannot be ignored. Advertisers, publishers, producers, and investors in the huge media conglomerates all have one thing in common. They do what they do to make money. Industry officials and academicians need to ask what can reasonably be expected of media owners and producers. What are the ethical implications of programming and business decisions? What form should social responsibility take?

The sexual health and happiness of future generations will be affected by whether we consider the media only as a backdrop or as an important piece of the cultural fabric.

This article is based on a paper originally commissioned by the Henry J. Kaiser Family Foundation and was presented last fall by Dr. Brown and Ms. Steele during a session on "Sex and Hollywood: Should There Be a Government Role?" The session was part of a series on "Sexuality and American Social Policy" sponsored by the Kaiser Family Foundation and the American Enterprise Institute. It was adapted for the SIECUS Report by the authors.) — **Editor**

REFERENCES

1. G. Gerbner, L. Gross, M. Morgan and N. Signorielli, "Growing Up with Television: The Cultivation Perspective," in J. Bryant and D. Zillman, eds., *Media Effects: Advances in Theory and Research* (Hillsdale, NJ: Lawrence Erlbaum, 1994), 17-41.

2. G. Gerbner, "Women and Minorities, A Study in Casting and Fate" (A report to the Screen Actors Guild and the American Federation of Radio and Television Artists, June 1993), 3.

3. U.S. Congress, Office of Technology Assessment, *Adolescent Health, Vol. II: Background and the Effectiveness of Selected Prevention and Treatment Services* (Washington, DC: U.S. Government Printing Office, 1991).

4. "Violence and Youth: Psychology's Response" (Summary report of the Commission on Violence and Youth of the American Psychological Association, 1993).

5. K. Childers and J. D. Brown, "No Blank Slate: Teen Media Awareness Mirrors Upbringing," *Media and Values*, 46 (1989): 8-10.

6. D. T. Lowry and J. A. Shidler, "Prime Time TV Portrayals of Sex, 'Safe Sex' and AIDS: A Longitudinal Analysis," *Journalism Quarterly*, 70, no. 3 (1993): 628-37.

7. D. T. Lowry and D. E. Towles "Prime Time TV Portrayals of Sex, Contraception, and Venereal Diseases," *Journalism Quarterly*, (1989): 66.

8. D. T. Lowry and J. A. Shidler, "Prime Time TV," 635.

9. B. S. Greenberg and R. W. Busselle, "Soap Operas and Sexual Activity" (A report submitted to the Kaiser Family Foundation, October 1994).

10. Ibid.

11. C. Champagne, "When Push Comes to Shove," *All Talk: The Talk Show Magazine* (a special issue of *Soap Opera Digest*), 1995, p. 57.

12. C. Small, "Jenny's Shameful Pandering," *The Raleigh* (NC) *News & Observer*, March 28, 1995.

13. M. Kaplan, "You Get What You Pay For: Everything You Ever Wanted to Know about Cable Sex," *Us*, August 1992, p. 79.

14. B. S. Greenberg, M. Siemicki, S. Dorfman, et al., "Sex Content in R-Rated Films Viewed by Adolescents," in B. S. Greenberg, J. D. Brown and N. L. Buerkel-Rothfuss, eds., *Media, Sex and the Adolescent* (Creskill, NJ: Hampton Press, 1993), 29-44.

15. N. L. Buerkel-Rothfuss, J. S. Strouse, G. Pettey and M. Shatzer, "Adolescents' and Young Adults' Exposure to Sexually Oriented and Sexually Explicit Media," in B. S. Greenberg, J. D. Brown and N. L. Buerkel-Rothfuss, eds., *Media, Sex and the Adolescent* (Creskill, NJ: Hampton Press, 1993), 99-114.

16. J. D. Brown, K. W. Childers, K. E. Bauman, and G.G. Koch, "The Influence of New Media and Family Structure on Young Adolescents' Television and Radio Use," *Communication Research*, 17, no. 1(1990): 65-82.

17. J. R. Steele and J. D. Brown, "Adolescent Room Culture: Studying Media in the Context of Everyday Life," *Journal of Youth and Adolescence*, in press.

18. C. D. Hansen and R. D. Hansen, "The Content of MTV's Daily Countdown: 'Dial MTV' for Sex, Violence, and Antisocial Behavior" (Unpublished paper, Oakland University, Rochester, MI).

19. I. Perry, "It's My Thang and i'll Swing It the Way That i Feel!," in J. G. Dines and J. M. Humen, eds., *Gender, Race and Class in Media: A Test-Reader* (Thousand Oaks, CA, Sage, 1995), 524-30.

1. LIVING WITH MEDIA

20. *Unplanned Pregnancy: Table 142* (New York: Louis Harris and Associates, Inc., 1994).

21. *Consumer Magazines and Agri-Media Source*, 17, no. 4 (1995).

22. J. Ballenger, "Uncovering Abortion: Sisterhood Is Cautious," *Columbia Journalism Review* (March, April 1992): 16.

23. Ibid.

24. G. Steinem, "Sex, Lies & Advertising," *Ms.*, July/August 1990, pp. 18-28.

25. M. Braden, "Ms. Doesn't Miss the Ads," *The Quill*, January/February 1992, pp. 22-5.

26. E. Larson, "Censoring Sex Information: The Story of *Sassy*." *Utne Reader*, July/August 1990, pp. 96-7.

27. M. Cox, "New Magazines for New Cliques of Teens," *The Wall Street Journal*, March 14, 1994, p. B1.

28. A. C. Downs and S. K. Harrison, "Embarrassing Age Spots or Just Plain Ugly? Physical Attractiveness Stereotyping As An Instrument of Sexism on American Television Commercials," *Sex Roles*, 13, nos. 1 and 2 (1985): 9-19.

29. S. Klaidman, "Roles and Responsibilities of Journalists," in C. Atkin and L. Wallack, eds., *Mass Communication and Public Health: Complexities and Conflicts* (Newbury Park, CA: Sage, 1990), 60-70.

30. G. L. Bleske, "Ms. Gates Takes Over: An Updated Version of a 1949 Case Study," *Newspaper Research Journal*, (fall 1995): 88-97.

31. L. Jolliffe and T. Catlett, "Women Editors at the 'Seven Sisters' Magazines, 1965-1985: Did They Make a Difference?," *Journalism Quarterly*, 71, no. 4 (1994): 800-08.

32. J. W. Dearing and E. M. Rogers, "AIDS and the Media Agenda," in T. Edgar, M.A. Fitzpatrick, and V. S. Freimuth, eds., *AIDS: A Communication Perspective* (Hillsdale, NJ: Lawrence Erlbaum, 1992), 173-94.

33. B. T. Roessner, "Why Doesn't TV Ever 'Choose' Abortion?," *The Raleigh (NC) News & Observer*, April 21, 1994, p. 7E.

34. G. Gerbner, L. Gross, M. Morgan and N. Signorielli, "Growing Up with Television: The Cultivation Perspective," in J. Bryant and D. Zillman, eds., *Media Effects: Advances in Theory and Research* (Hillsdale, NJ: Lawrence Erlbaum, 1994), p. 18.

35. Ibid.

36. N. L. Buerkel-Rothfuss and S. Mayes, "Soap Opera Viewing: The Cultivation Effect," *Journal of Communication*, 31, no. 3 (1981): 108-15.

37. N. L. Buerkel-Rothfuss and J. S. Strouse, "Media Exposure and Perceptions of Sexual Behaviors: The Cultivation Hypothesis Moves to the Bedroom," in B. S. Greenberg, J. D. Brown and N. L. Buerkel-Rothfuss, eds., *Media, Sex and the Adolescent* (Creskill, NJ: Hampton Press, 1993), 225-47.

38. M. Morgan, "Television and Adolescents' Sex-Role Stereotypes: A Longitudinal Study," *Journal of Personality and Social Psychology*, 43, no. 5 (1982): 947-55; N. Rothschild, "Small Group Affiliation As a Mediating Factor in the Cultivation Process," in G. Melischek, K.E. Rosengren, and J. Stappers, eds., *Cultural Indicators: An International Symposium* (Vienna: Verlag der Osterreichischen Akademie der Wissenschaften, 1984), 377-87.

39. J. A. Courthright and S. J. Baran, "The Acquisition of Sexual Information by Young People," *Journalism Quarterly*, 57, no. 1 (1980): 107-14.

40. M. McCombs and D. Shaw, "The Evolution of Agenda-Setting Research: Twenty-five Years in the Marketplace of Ideas," *Journal of Communication*, 43, no. 2 (1993): 58-67; G. M. Kosicki, "Problems and Opportunities in Agenda-Setting Research," *Journal of Communication*, 43, no. 2 (1993): 100-27.

41. S. Iyengar, *Is Anyone Responsible? How Television Frames Political Issues* (Chicago, IL: University of Chicago Press, 1991).

42. F. D. Ginsburg, *Contested Lives* (Berkeley, CA: University of California Press, 1989), 117.

43. S. Hall, C. Critcher, T. Jefferson, J. Clarke and B. Roberts, *Policing the Crisis: Mugging, the State, and Law and Order* (New York: Holmes & Meier Publishers, Inc., 1978).

44. H. Blumer, *Symbolic Interactionism* (Englewood Cliffs, NJ: Prentice-Hall, 1969), 300.

45. W. R. Neuman, M. R. Just and A. N. Crigler, *Common Knowledge: News and the Construction of Political Meaning* (Chicago, IL: University of Chicago Press, 1992).

46. J. D. Brown and S. F. Newcomer, "Television Viewing and Adolescents' Sexual Behavior," *Journal of Homosexuality*, 21, nos.1 and 2 (1991): 77-91.

47. A. Bandura, "Social Cognitive Theory of Mass Communication," in J. Bryant and D. Zillmann, eds., *Media Effects: Advances in Theory and Research* (Hillsdale, NJ: Lawrence Erlbaum, 1994).

48. G. Comstock and V. Strasburger, "Deceptive Appearances: Television Violence and Aggressive Behavior: An Introduction," *Journal of Adolescent Health Care*, 11 (1990): 31-44.

49. Ibid.

50. B. S. Centerwall, "Television and Violence: The Scale of the Problem and Where to Go from Here," *Journal of American Medical Association*, 267 (1992): 3059-63.

51. E. M. Rogers and D. Storey, "Communication Campaigns," in C. Berger and S. Chaffee, eds., *Handbook of Communication Science* (Newbury Park, CA: Sage, 1987), 817-846.

52. V. Freimuth, "Theoretical Foundations of AIDS Media Campaigns," in T. Edgar, M. A. Fitzpatrick, and V. S. Freimuth, eds., *AIDS: A Communication Perspective* (Hillsdale, NJ: Lawrence Erlbaum, 1992), 91-110.

53. J. D. Brown and K. Walsh-Childers, "Effects of Media on Personal and Public Health," in J. Bryant and D. Zillman, eds., *Media Effects: Advances in Theory and Research* (Hillsdale, NJ: Lawrence Erlbaum, 1994), 389-415.

54. L. Wallach, "Improving Health Promotion: A Critical Perspective," in R. E. Rice and C. K. Atkin, eds., *Public Communication Campaigns* (Newbury Park, CA: Sage), 353-36.

Gendered Media: The Influence of Media on Views of Gender

Julia T. Wood

Department of Communication, University of North Carolina at Chapel Hill.

THEMES IN MEDIA

Of the many influences on how we view men and women, media are the most pervasive and one of the most powerful. Woven throughout our daily lives, media insinuate their messages into our consciousness at every turn. All forms of media communicate images of the sexes, many of which perpetuate unrealistic, stereotypical, and limiting perceptions. Three themes describe how media represent gender. First, women are underrepresented, which falsely implies that men are the cultural standard and women are unimportant or invisible. Second, men and women are portrayed in stereotypical ways that reflect and sustain socially endorsed views of gender. Third, depictions of relationships between men and women emphasize traditional roles and normalize violence against women. We will consider each of these themes in this section.

Underrepresentation of Women

A primary way in which media distort reality is in underrepresenting women. Whether it is prime-time television, in which there are three times as many white men as women (Basow, 1992 p. 159), or children's programming, in which males outnumber females by two to one, or newscasts, in which women make up 16% of newscasters and in which stories about men are included 10 times more often than ones about women ("Study Reports Sex Bias," 1989), media misrepresent actual proportions of men and women in the population. This constant distortion tempts us to believe that there really are more men than women and, further, that men are the cultural standard.

Other myths about what is standard are similarly fortified by communication in media. Minorities are even less visible than women, with African-Americans appearing only rarely (Gray, 1986; Stroman, 1989) and other ethnic minorities being virtually nonexistent. In children's programming when African-Americans do appear, almost invariably they appear in supporting roles rather than as main characters (O'Connor, 1989). While more African-Americans are appearing in

---

MEDIA'S MISREPRESENTATION OF AMERICAN LIFE

The media present a distorted version of cultural life in our country. According to media portrayals:

White males make up two-thirds of the population. The women are less in number, perhaps because fewer than 10% live beyond 35. Those who do, like their younger and male counterparts, are nearly all white and heterosexual. In addition to being young, the majority of women are beautiful, very thin, passive, and primarily concerned with relationships and getting rings out of collars and commodes. There are a few bad, bitchy women, and they are not so pretty, not so subordinate, and not so caring as the good women. Most of the bad ones work outside of the home, which is probably why they are hardened and undesirable. The more powerful, ambitious men occupy themselves with important business deals, exciting adventures, and rescuing dependent females, whom they often then assault sexually.

From *Gendered Lives: Communication, Gender, and Culture* by Julia T. Wood, Chapter 9, pp. 231-244. © 1994 by Wadsworth Publishing Company, Inc. Reprinted by permission.

1. LIVING WITH MEDIA

prime-time television, they are too often cast in stereotypical roles. In the 1992 season, for instance, 12 of the 74 series on commercial networks included large African-American casts, yet most featured them in stereotypical roles. Black men are presented as lazy and unable to handle authority, as lecherous, and/or as unlawful, while females are portrayed as domineering or as sex objects ("Sights, Sounds, and Stereotypes," 1992). Writing in 1993, David Evans (1993, p. 10) criticized television for stereotyping black males as athletes and entertainers. These roles, wrote Evans, mislead young black male viewers into thinking success "is only a dribble or dance step away," and blind them to other, more realistic ambitions. Hispanics and Asians are nearly absent, and when they are presented it is usually as villains or criminals (Lichter, Lichter, Rothman, & Amundson, 1987).

Also underrepresented is the single fastest growing group of Americans—older people. As a country, we are aging so that people over 60 make up a major part of our population; within this group, women significantly outnumber men (Wood, 1993c). Older people not only are underrepresented in media but also are represented inaccurately. In contrast to demographic realities, media consistently show fewer older women than men, presumably because our culture worships youth and beauty in women. Further, elderly individuals are frequently portrayed as sick, dependent, fumbling, and passive, images not borne out in real life. Distorted depictions of older people and especially older women in media, however, can delude us into thinking they are a small, sickly, and unimportant part of our population.

The lack of women in the media is paralleled by the scarcity of women in charge of media. Only about 5% of television writers, executives, and producers are women (Lichter, Lichter, & Rothman, 1986). Ironically, while two-thirds of journalism graduates are women, they make up less than 2% of those in corporate management of newspapers and only about 5% of newspaper publishers ("Women in Media," 1988). Female film directors are even more scarce, as are executives in charge of MTV. It is probably not coincidental that so few women are behind the scenes of an industry that so consistently portrays women negatively. Some media analysts (Mills, 1988) believe that if more women had positions of authority at executive levels, media would offer more positive portrayals of women.

Stereotypical Portrayals of Women and Men

In general, media continue to present both women and men in stereotyped ways that limit our perceptions of human possibilities. Typically men are portrayed as active, adventurous, powerful, sexually aggressive, and largely uninvolved in human relationships. Just as consistent with cultural views of gender are depictions of women as sex objects who are usually young, thin, beautiful, passive, dependent, and often incompetent and dumb. Female characters devote their primary energies to improving their appearances and taking care of homes and people. Because media pervade our lives, the ways they misrepresent genders may distort how we see ourselves and what we perceive as normal and desirable for men and women.

Stereotypical portrayals of men. According to J. A. Doyle (1989, p. 111), whose research focuses on masculinity, children's television typically shows males as "aggressive, dominant, and engaged in exciting activities from which they receive rewards from others for their 'masculine' accomplishments." Relatedly, recent studies reveal that the majority of men on prime-time television are independent, aggressive, and in charge (McCauley, Thangavelu, & Rozin, 1988). Television programming for all ages disproportionately depicts men as serious, confident, competent, powerful, and in high-status positions. Gentleness in men, which was briefly evident in the 1970s, has receded as established male characters are redrawn to be more tough and distanced from others (Boyer, 1986). Highly popular films such as *Lethal Weapon, Predator, Days of Thunder, Total Recall, Robocop, Die Hard,* and *Die Harder* star men who embody the stereotype of extreme masculinity. Media, then, reinforce long-standing cultural ideals of masculinity: Men are presented as hard, tough, independent, sexually aggressive, unafraid, violent, totally in control of all emotions, and—above all—in no way feminine.

Equally interesting is how males are *not* presented. J. D. Brown and K. Campbell (1986) report that men are seldom shown doing housework. Doyle (1989) notes that boys and men are rarely presented caring for others. B. Horovitz (1989) points out they are typically represented as uninterested in and incompetent at homemaking, cooking, and child care. Each season's new ads for cooking and cleaning supplies include several that caricature men as incompetent buffoons, who are klutzes in the kitchen and no better at taking care of children. While children's books have made a limited attempt to depict women engaged in activities outside of the home, there has been little parallel effort to show men involved in family and home life. When someone is shown taking care of a child, it is usually the mother, not the father. This perpetuates a negative stereotype of men as uncaring and uninvolved in family life.

Stereotypical portrayals of women. Media's images of women also reflect cultural stereotypes that depart markedly from reality. As we have already seen, girls and women are dramatically underrepresented. In prime-time television in 1987, fully two-thirds of the speaking parts were for men. Women are portrayed as significantly younger and thinner than women in the population as a whole, and most are

> **JILL**
>
> I remember when I was little I used to read books from the boys' section of the library because they were more interesting. Boys did the fun stuff and the exciting things. My mother kept trying to get me to read girls' books, but I just couldn't get into them. Why can't stories about girls be full of adventure and bravery? I know when I'm a mother, I want any daughters of mine to understand that excitement isn't just for boys.

depicted as passive, dependent on men, and enmeshed in relationships or housework (Davis, 1990). The requirements of youth and beauty in women even influence news shows, where female newscasters are expected to be younger, more physically attractive, and less outspoken than males (Craft, 1988; Sanders & Rock, 1988). Despite educators' criticism of self-fulfilling prophesies that discourage girls from success in math and science, that stereotype was dramatically reiterated in 1992 when Mattel offered a new talking Barbie doll. What did she say? "Math class is tough," a message that reinforces the stereotype that women cannot do math ("Mattel Offers Trade-In," 1992). From children's programming, in which the few existing female characters typically spend their time watching males do things (Feldman & Brown, 1984; Woodman, 1991), to MTV, which routinely pictures women satisfying men's sexual fantasies (Pareles, 1990; Texier, 1990), media reiterate the cultural image of women as dependent, ornamental objects whose primary functions are to look good, please men, and stay quietly on the periphery of life.

Media have created two images of women: good women and bad ones. These polar opposites are often juxtaposed against each other to dramatize differences in the consequences that befall good and bad women. Good women are pretty, deferential, and focused on home, family, and caring for others. Subordinate to men, they are usually cast as victims, angels, martyrs, and loyal wives and helpmates. Occasionally, women who depart from traditional roles are portrayed positively, but this is done either by making their career lives invisible, as with Claire Huxtable, or by softening and feminizing working women to make them more consistent with traditional views of femininity. For instance, in the original script, Cagney and Lacey were conceived as strong, mature, independent women who took their work seriously and did it well. It took 6 years for writers Barbara Corday and Barbara Avedon to sell the script to CBS, and even then they had to agree to subdue Cagney's and Lacey's abilities to placate producer Barney Rosenzweig, who complained, "These women aren't soft enough. These women aren't feminine enough" (Faludi, 1991, p. 150). While female viewers wrote thousands of letters praising the show, male executives at CBS continued to force writers to make the characters softer, more tender, and less sure of themselves (Faludi, 1991, p. 152). The remaking of Cagney and Lacey illustrates the media's bias in favor of women who are traditionally feminine and who are not too able, too powerful, or too confident. The rule seems to be that a woman may be strong and successful if and only if she also exemplifies traditional stereotypes of femininity—subservience, passivity, beauty, and an identity linked to one or more men.

The other image of women the media offer us is the evil sister of the good homebody. Versions of this image are the witch, bitch, whore, or nonwoman, who is represented as hard, cold, aggressive—all of the things a good woman is not supposed to be. Exemplifying the evil woman is Alex in *Fatal Attraction,* which grossed more than $100 million in its first four months (Faludi, 1991, p. 113). Yet Alex was only an extreme version of how bad women are generally portrayed. In children's literature, we encounter witches and mean stepmothers as villains, with beautiful and passive females like Snow White and Sleeping Beauty as their good counterparts.

Prime-time television favorably portrays pretty, nurturing, other-focused women, such as Claire Huxtable on "The Cosby Show," whose career as an attorney never entered storylines as much as her engagement in family matters. Hope in "Thirtysomething" is an angel, committed to husband Michael and daughter Janey. In the biographies written for each of the characters when the show was in development, all male characters were defined in terms of their career goals, beliefs, and activities. Hope's biography consisted of one line: "Hope is married to Michael" (Faludi, 1991, p. 162). Hope epitomizes the traditional woman, so much so in fact that in one episode she refers to herself as June Cleaver and calls Michael "Ward," thus reprising the traditional family of the 1950s as personified in "Leave It to Beaver" (Faludi, 1991, p. 161). Meanwhile, prime-time typically represents ambitious, independent women as lonely, embittered spinsters who are counterpoints to "good" women.

Stereotypical Images of Relationships Between Men and Women

Given media's stereotypical portrayals of women and men, we shouldn't be surprised to find that relationships between women and men are similarly depicted in ways that reinforce stereotypes. Four themes demonstrate how media reflect and promote traditional arrangements between the sexes.

Women's dependence/men's independence. Walt Disney's award-winning animated film *The Little Mermaid* vividly embodies females' dependence on males for identity. In this feature film, the mermaid quite literally gives up her identity as a mermaid in order to

1. LIVING WITH MEDIA

become acceptable to her human lover. In this children's story, we see a particularly obvious illustration of the asymmetrical relationship between women and men that is more subtly conveyed in other media productions. Even the Smurfs, formless little beings who have no obvious sex, reflect the male-female, dominant-submissive roles. The female smurf, unlike her male companions, who have names, is called only Smurfette, making her sole identity a diminutive relation to male smurfs. The male dominance/female subservience pattern that permeates mediated representations of relationships is no accident. Beginning in 1991, television executives deliberately and consciously adopted a policy of having dominant male characters in all Saturday morning children's programming (Carter, 1991).

Women, as well as minorities, are cast in support roles rather than leading ones in both children's shows and the commercials interspersed within them (O'Connor, 1989). Analyses of MTV revealed that it portrays females as passive and waiting for men's attention, while males are shown ignoring, exploiting, or directing women (Brown, Campbell, & Fisher, 1986). In rap music videos, where African-American men and women star, men dominate women, whose primary role is as objects of male desires (Pareles, 1990; Texier, 1990). News programs that have male and female hosts routinely cast the female as deferential to her male colleague (Craft, 1988; Sanders & Rock, 1988). Commercials, too, manifest power cues that echo the male dominance/female subservience pattern. For instance, men are usually shown positioned above women, and women are more frequently pictured in varying degrees of undress (Masse & Rosenblum, 1988; Nigro, Hill, Gelbein, & Clark, 1988). Such nonverbal cues represent women as vulnerable and more submissive while men stay in control.

In a brief departure from this pattern, films and television beginning in the 1970s responded to the second wave of feminism by showing women who were independent without being hard, embittered, or without close relationships. Films such as *Alice Doesn't Live Here Anymore, Up the Sandbox, The Turning Point, Diary of a Mad Housewife,* and *An Unmarried Woman* offered realistic portraits of women who sought and found their own voices independent of men. Judy Davis's film, *My Brilliant Career,* particularly embodied this focus by telling the story of a woman who chooses work over marriage. During this period, television followed suit, offering viewers prime-time fare such as "Maude" and "The Mary Tyler Moore Show," which starred women who were able and achieving in their own rights. "One Day at a Time," which premiered in 1974, was the first prime-time program about a divorced woman.

By the 1980s, however, traditionally gendered arrangements resurged as the backlash movement against feminism was embraced by media (Haskell, 1988; Maslin, 1990). Thus, film fare in the 1980s included *Pretty Woman,* the story of a prostitute who becomes a good woman when she is saved from her evil ways by a rigidly stereotypical man, complete with millions to prove his success. Meanwhile, *Tie Me Up, Tie Me Down* trivialized abuse of women and underlined women's dependence on men with a story of a woman who is bound by a man and colludes in sustaining her bondage. *Crossing Delancey* showed successful careerist Amy Irving talked into believing she needs a man to be complete, a theme reprised by Cher in *Moonstruck.*

Television, too, cooperated in returning women to their traditional roles with characters like Hope in "Thirtysomething," who minded house and baby as an ultratraditional wife, and even Murphy Brown found her career wasn't enough and had a baby. Against her protests, Cybill Shepherd, who played Maddie in "Moonlighting," was forced to marry briefly on screen, which Susan Faludi (1991, p. 157) refers to as part of a "campaign to cow this independent female figure." Popular music added its voice with hit songs like "Having My Baby," which glorified a woman who defined herself by motherhood and her relationship to a man. The point is not that having babies or committing to relationships is wrong; rather, it is that media virtually require this of women in order to present them positively. Media define a very narrow range for womanhood.

Joining the campaign to restore traditional dominant-subordinate patterns of male-female relationships were magazines, which reinvigorated their focus on women's role as the helpmate and supporter of husbands and families (Peirce, 1990). In 1988, that staple of Americana, *Good Housekeeping,* did its part to revive women's traditional roles with a full-page ad ("The Best in the House," 1988) for its new demographic edition marketed to "the new traditionalist woman." A month later, the magazine followed this up with a second full-page ad in national newspapers that saluted the "new traditionalist woman," with this copy ("The New Traditionalist," 1988): "She has made her commitment. Her mission: create a more meaningful life for herself and her family. She is the New Traditionalist— a contemporary woman who finds her fulfillment in traditional values." The long-standing dominant-submissive model for male-female relationships was largely restored in the 1980s. With only rare exceptions, women are still portrayed as dependent on men and subservient to them. As B. Lott (1989, p. 64) points out, it is women who "do the laundry and are secretaries to men who own companies."

Men's authority/women's incompetence. A second recurrent theme in media representations of relationships is that men are the competent authorities who save women from their incompetence. Children's litera-

> **PAUL**
>
> I wouldn't say this around anyone, but personally I'd be glad if the media let up a little on us guys. I watch those guys in films and on TV, and I just feel inadequate. I mean, I'm healthy and I look okay, and I'll probably make a decent salary when I graduate. But I am no stud; I can't beat up three guys at once, women don't fall dead at my feet; I doubt I'll make a million bucks; and I don't have muscles that ripple. Every time I go to a film, I leave feeling like a wimp. How can any of us guys measure up to what's on the screen?

ture vividly implements this motif by casting females as helpless and males as coming to their rescue. Sleeping Beauty's resurrection depends on Prince Charming's kiss, a theme that appears in the increasingly popular gothic romance novels for adults (Modleski, 1982).

One of the most pervasive ways in which media define males as authorities is in commercials. Women are routinely shown anguishing over dirty floors and bathroom fixtures only to be relieved of their distress when Mr. Clean shows up to tell them how to keep their homes spotless. Even when commercials are aimed at women, selling products intended for them, up to 90% of the time a man's voice is used to explain the value of what is being sold (Basow, 1992, p. 161; Bretl & Cantor, 1988). Using male voice-overs reinforces the cultural view that men are authorities and women depend on men to tell them what to do.

Television further communicates the message that men are authorities and women are not. One means of doing this is sheer numbers. As we have seen, men vastly outnumber women in television programming. In addition, the dominance of men as news anchors who inform us of happenings in the world underlines their authority ("Study Reports Sex Bias," 1989). Prime-time television contributes to this image by showing women who need to be rescued by men and by presenting women as incompetent more than twice as often as men (Boyer, 1986; Lichter et al., 1986).

Consider the characters in "The Jetsons," an animated television series set in the future. Daughter Judy Jetson is constantly complaining and waiting for others to help her, using ploys of helplessness and flattery to win men's attention. *The Rescuers,* a popular animated video of the 1990s, features Miss Bianca (whose voice is that of Zsa Zsa Gabor, fittingly enough), who splits her time evenly between being in trouble and being grateful to male characters for rescuing her. These stereotypical representations of males and females reinforce a number of harmful beliefs. They suggest, first, that men are more competent than women. Compounding this is the message that a woman's power lies in her looks and conventional femininity, since that is how females from Sleeping Beauty to Judy Jetson get males to assist them with their dilemmas (McCauley, Thangavelu, & Rozin, 1988). Third, these stereotypes underline the requirement that men must perform, succeed, and conquer in order to be worthy.

Women as primary caregivers/men as breadwinners. A third perennial theme in media is that women are caregivers and men are providers. Since the backlash of the 1980s, in fact, this gendered arrangement has been promulgated with renewed vigor. Once again, as in the 1950s, we see women devoting themselves to getting rings off of collars, gray out of their hair, and meals on the table. Corresponding to this is the restatement of men's inability in domestic and nurturing roles. Horovitz (1989), for instance, reports that in commercials men are regularly the butt of jokes for their ignorance about nutrition, child care, and housework.

When media portray women who work outside of the home, their career lives typically receive little or no attention. Although these characters have titles such as lawyer or doctor, they are shown predominantly in their roles as homemakers, mothers, and wives. We see them involved in caring conversations with family and friends and doing things for others, all of which never seem to conflict with their professional responsibilities. This has the potential to cultivate unrealistic expectations of being "superwoman," who does it all without her getting a hair out of place or being late to a conference.

Magazines play a key role in promoting pleasing others as a primary focus of women's lives. K. Peirce's (1990) study found that magazines aimed at women stress looking good and doing things to please others. Thus, advertising tells women how to be "me, only better" by dyeing their hair to look younger; how to lose weight so "you'll still be attractive to him"; and how to prepare gourmet meals so "he's always glad to come home." Constantly, these advertisements empha-

> **JOANNE**
>
> I'd like to know who dreams up those commercials that show men as unable to boil water or run a vacuum. I'd like to tell them they're creating monsters. My boyfriend and I agreed to split all chores equally when we moved in together. Ha! Fat chance of that. He does zilch. When I get on his case, he reminds me of what happened when the father on some show had to take over housework and practically demolished the kitchen. Then he grins and says, "Now, you wouldn't want that, would you?" Or worse yet, he throws up Hope or one of the other women on TV, and asks me why I can't be as sweet and supportive as she is. It's like the junk on television gives him blanket license for doing nothing.

1. LIVING WITH MEDIA

size pleasing others, especially men, as central to being a woman, and the message is fortified with the thinly veiled warning that if a woman fails to look good and please, her man might leave (Rakow, 1992).

There is a second, less known way in which advertisements contribute to stereotypes of women as focused on others and men as focused on work. Writing in 1990, Gloria Steinem, editor of *Ms.*, revealed that advertisers control some to most of the *content* in magazines. In exchange for placing an ad, a company receives "complimentary copy," which is one or more articles that increase the market appeal of its product. So a soup company that takes out an ad might be given a three-page story on how to prepare meals using that brand of soup; likewise, an ad for hair coloring products might be accompanied by interviews with famous women who choose to dye their hair. Thus, the message of advertisers is multiplied by magazine content, which readers often mistakenly assume is independent of advertising.

Advertisers support media, and they exert a powerful influence on what is presented. To understand the prevalence of traditional gender roles in programming, magazine copy, and other media, we need only ask what is in the best interests of advertisers. They want to sponsor shows that create or expand markets for their products. Media images of women as sex objects, devoted homemakers, and mothers buttress the very roles in which the majority of consuming takes place. To live up to these images, women have to buy cosmetics and other personal care products, diet aids, food, household cleaners, utensils and appliances, clothes and toys for children, and so on. In short, it is in advertisers' interests to support programming and copy that feature women in traditional roles. In a recent analysis, Lana Rakow (1992) demonstrated that much advertising is oppressive to women and is very difficult to resist, even when one is a committed feminist.

Women's role in the home and men's role outside of it are reinforced by newspapers and news programming. Both emphasize men's independent activities and, in fact, define news almost entirely as stories about and by men ("Study Reports Sex Bias," 1989). Stories about men focus on work and/or their achievements (Luebke, 1989), reiterating the cultural message that men are supposed to do, perform. Meanwhile the few stories about women almost invariably focus on their roles as wives, mothers, and homemakers ("Study Reports Sex Bias," 1989). Even stories about women who are in the news because of achievements and professional activities typically dwell on marriage, family life, and other aspects of women's traditional role (Foreit et al., 1980).

Women as victims and sex objects/men as aggressors. A final theme in mediated representations of relationships between women and men is representation of women as subject to men's sexual desires. The irony of this representation is that the very qualities women are encouraged to develop (beauty, sexiness, passivity, and powerlessness) in order to meet cultural ideals of femininity contribute to their victimization. Also, the qualities that men are urged to exemplify (aggressiveness, dominance, sexuality, and strength) are identical to those linked to abuse of women. It is no coincidence that all but one of the women nominated for Best Actress in the 1988 Academy Awards played a victim (Faludi, 1991, p. 138). Women are portrayed alternatively either as decorative objects, who must attract a man to be valuable, or as victims of men's sexual impulses. Either way, women are defined by their bodies and how men treat them. Their independent identities and endeavors are irrelevant to how they are represented in media, and their abilities to resist exploitation by others are obscured.

This theme, which was somewhat toned down during the 1970s, returned with vigor in the 1980s as the backlash permeated media. According to S. A. Basow (1992, p. 160), since 1987 there has been a "resurgence of male prominence, pretty female sidekicks, female homemakers." Advertising in magazines also communicates the message that women are sexual objects. While men are seldom pictured nude or even partially unclothed, women habitually are. Advertisements for makeup, colognes, hair products, and clothes often show women attracting men because they got the right products and made themselves irresistible. Stars on prime-time and films, who are beautiful and dangerously thin, perpetuate the idea that women must literally starve themselves to death to win men's interest (Silverstein et al., 1986).

Perhaps the most glaring examples of portrayals of women as sex objects and men as sexual aggressors occur in music videos as shown on MTV and many other stations. Typically, females are shown dancing provocatively in scant and/or revealing clothing as they try to gain men's attention (Texier, 1990). Frequently, men are seen coercing women into sexual activities and/or physically abusing them. Violence against women is also condoned in many recent films. R. Warshaw (1991) reported that cinematic presentations of rapes, especially acquaintance rapes, are not presented as power-motivated violations of women but rather as strictly sexual encounters. Similarly, others (Cowan, Lee, Levy, & Snyder, 1988; Cowan & O'Brien, 1990) have found that male dominance and sexual exploitation of women are themes in virtually all R- and X-rated films, which almost anyone may now rent for home viewing. These media images carry to extremes long-standing cultural views of masculinity as aggressive and femininity as passive. They also make violence seem sexy (D. Russell, 1993). In so doing, they recreate these limited and limiting perceptions in the thinking of another generation of women and men.

In sum, we have identified basic stereotypes and

themes in media's representations of women, men, and relationships between the two. Individually and in combination these images sustain and reinforce socially constructed views of the genders, views that have restricted both men and women and that appear to legitimize destructive behaviors ranging from anorexia to battering. Later in this chapter, we will probe more closely how media versions of gender are linked to problems such as these....

Pathologizing the Human Body

One of the most damaging consequences of media's images of women and men is that these images encourage us to perceive normal bodies and normal physical functions as problems. It's understandable to wish we weighed a little more or less, had better developed muscles, and never had pimples or cramps. What is neither reasonable nor healthy, however, is to regard healthy, functional bodies as abnormal and unacceptable. Yet this is precisely the negative self-image cultivated by media portrayals of women and men. Because sex sells products (Muro, 1989), sexual and erotic images are the single most prominent characteristic of advertising (Courtney & Whipple, 1983). Further, advertising is increasingly objectifying men, which probably accounts for the rise in men's weight training and cosmetic surgery. Media, and especially advertising, are equal opportunity dehumanizers of both sexes.

Not only do media induce us to think we should measure up to artificial standards, but they encourage us to see normal bodies and bodily functions as pathologies. A good example is the media's construction of premenstrual syndrome (PMS). Historically, PMS has not been a problem, but recently it has been declared a disease (Richmond-Abbott, 1992). In fact, a good deal of research (Parlee, 1973, 1987) indicates that PMS affected very few women in earlier eras. After the war, when women were no longer needed in the work force, opinion changed and the term *premenstrual tension* was coined (Greene & Dalton, 1953) and used to define women as inferior employees. In 1964, only one article on PMS appeared; in 1988–1989, a total of 425 were published (Tavris, 1992, p. 140). Drug companies funded research and publicity, since selling PMS meant selling their remedies for the newly created problem. Behind the hoopla, however, there was and is little evidence to support the currently widespread belief that PMS is a serious problem for a significant portion of the female population. Facts aside, the myth has caught on, carrying in its wake many women and men who now perceive normal monthly changes as abnormal and as making women unfit for positions of leadership and authority. Another consequence of defining PMS as a serious problem most women suffer is that it leads to labeling women in general as deviant and unreliable (Unger & Crawford, 1992), an image that fortifies long-held biases against women.

Menopause is similarly pathologized. Carol Tavris (1992, p. 159) notes that books describe menopause "in terms of deprivation, deficiency, loss, shedding, and sloughing," language that defines a normal process as negative. Like menstruation, menopause is represented as abnormalcy and disease, an image that probably contributes to the negative attitudes toward it in America. The cover of the May 25, 1992, *Newsweek* featured an abstract drawing of a tree in the shape of a woman's head. The tree was stripped of all leaves, making it drab and barren. Across the picture was the cover-story headline "Menopause." From first glance, menopause was represented negatively—as desolate and unfruitful. The article focused primarily on the problems and losses of menopause. Only toward the end did readers find reports from anthropologists, whose cross-cultural research revealed that in many cultures menopause is not an issue or is viewed positively. Women in Mayan villages and the Greek island of Evia do not understand questions about hot flashes and depression, which are symptoms often associated with menopause in Western societies ("Menopause," 1992, p. 77). These are not part of their experience in cultures that do not define a normal change in women as a pathology. Because Western countries, especially America, stigmatize menopause and define it as "the end of womanhood," Western women are likely to feel distressed and unproductive about the cessation of menstruation (Greer, 1992).

Advertising is very effective in convincing us that we need products to solve problems we are unaware of until some clever public relations campaign persuades us that something natural about us is really unnatural and unacceptable. Media have convinced millions of American women that what every medical source considers "normal body weight" is really abnormal and cause for severe dieting (Wolf, 1991). Similarly, gray hair, which naturally develops with age, is now something all of us, especially women, are supposed to cover up. Facial lines, which indicate a person has lived a life and accumulated experiences, can be removed so that we look younger—a prime goal in a culture that glorifies youth (Greer, 1992).

Body hair is another interesting case of media's convincing us that something normal is really abnormal. Beginning in 1915, a sustained marketing campaign informed women that underarm hair was unsightly and socially incorrect. (The campaign against leg hair came later.) *Harper's Bazaar,* an upscale magazine, launched the crusade against underarm hair with a photograph of a woman whose raised arms revealed clean-shaven armpits. Underneath the photograph was this caption: "Summer dress and modern dancing combine to make necessary the removal of objectionable hair" (Adams, 1991). Within a few years, ads promoting removal of underarm hair appeared in most women's magazines, and by 1922, razors and depilatories were

1. LIVING WITH MEDIA

firmly ensconced in middle America as evidenced by their inclusion in the women's section of the Sears Roebuck catalog.

Media efforts to pathologize natural physiology can be very serious. As we have seen in prior chapters, the emphasis on excessive thinness contributes to severe and potentially lethal dieting, especially in Caucasian women (Spitzack, 1993). Nonetheless, the top female models in 1993 are skeletal, more so than in recent years (Leland & Leonard, 1993). Many women's natural breast size exceeded the cultural ideal in the 1960s when thin, angular bodies were represented as ideal. Thus, breast reduction surgeries rose. By the 1980s, cultural standards changed to define large breasts as the feminine ideal. Consequently, breast augmentation surgeries accelerated, and fully 80% of implants were for cosmetic reasons ("The Implant Circus," 1992). In an effort to meet the cultural standards of beautiful bodies, many women suffered unnecessary surgery, which led to disfigurement, loss of feeling, and sometimes death for women when silicone implants were later linked to fatal conditions. Implicitly, media argue that our natural state is abnormal and objectionable, a premise that is essential to sell products and advice for improving ourselves. Accepting media messages about our bodies and ourselves, however, is not inevitable: We can reflect on the messages and resist those that are inappropriate and/or harmful. We would probably all be considerably happier and healthier if we became more critical in analyzing media's communication about how we should look, be, and act.

Normalizing Violence Against Women

Since we have seen that media positively portray aggression in males and passivity in females, it's important to ask whether media messages contribute to abuse of and violence against women. There is by now fairly convincing evidence (Hansen & Hansen, 1988) that exposure to sexual violence through media is linked to greater tolerance, or even approval, of violence. For instance, P. Dieter (1989) found a strong relationship between females' viewing of sexually violent MTV and their acceptance of sexual violence as part of "normal" relationships. He reasoned that the more they observe positive portrayals of sexual violence, the more likely women are to perceive this as natural in relationships with men and the less likely they are to object to violence or to defend themselves from it. In short, Dieter suggests that heavy exposure to media violence within relationships tends to normalize it, so that abuse and violence are considered natural parts of love and sex.

Dieter's study demonstrates a direct link between sexual aggression and one popular form of media, MTV. Research on pornography further corroborates connections between exposure to portrayals of violence against women and willingness to engage in or accept it in one's own relationships (Russell, 1993). Before we discuss this research, however, we need to clarify what we will mean by the term pornography, since defining it is a matter of some controversy. Pornography is not simply sexually explicit material. To distinguish pornography from erotica, we might focus on mutual agreement and mutual benefit. If we use these criteria, pornography may be defined as materials that favorably show subordination and degradation of a person such as presenting sadistic behaviors as pleasurable, brutalizing and pain as enjoyable, and forced sex or abuse as positive. Erotica, on the other hand, depicts consensual sexual activities that are sought by and pleasurable to all parties involved (MacKinnon, 1987). These distinctions are important, since it has been well established that graphic sexual material itself is not harmful, while sexually violent materials appear to be (Donnerstein, Linz, & Penrod, 1987).

Pornographic films are a big business, outnumbering other films by 3 to 1 and grossing over $365 million a year in the United States alone (Wolf, 1991). The primary themes characteristic of pornography as a genre are extremes of those in media generally: sex, violence, and domination of one person by another, usually women by men (Basow, 1992, p. 317). More than 80% of X-rated films in one study included scenes in which one or more men dominate and exploit one or more women; within these films, three-fourths portray physical aggression against women, and fully half explicitly depict rape (Cowan et al., 1988). That these are linked to viewers' own tendencies to engage in sexual violence is no longer disputable. According to recent research (Demare, Briere, & Lips, 1988; Donnerstein et al., 1987; Malamuth & Briere, 1986), viewing sexually violent material tends to increase men's beliefs in rape myths, raises the likelihood that men will admit they might themselves commit rape, and desensitizes men to rape, thereby making forced sex more acceptable to them. This research suggests that repeated exposure to pornography influences how men think about rape by transforming it from an unacceptable behavior with which they do not identify into one they find acceptable and enticing. Not surprisingly, the single best predictor of rape is the circulation of pornographic materials that glorify sexual force and exploitation (Baron & Straus, 1989). This is alarming when we realize that 18 million men buy a total of 165 different pornographic magazines every month in the United States (Wolf, 1991, p. 79).

It is well documented that the incidence of reported rape is rising and that an increasing number of men regard forced sex as acceptable (Brownmiller, 1993; Soeken & Damrosch, 1986). Studies of men (Allgeier, 1987; Koss & Dinero, 1988; Koss, Dinero, Seibel, & Cox, 1988; Koss, Gidycz, & Wisniewski, 1987; Lisak & Roth, 1988) have produced shocking findings: While the majority of college men report not having raped anyone, a stunning 50% admit they have coerced, manipulated, or pressured a woman to have sex or have had sex with her after getting her drunk; 1 in 12 men at some colleges has engaged in behaviors meeting the legal definition of rape or attempted rape; over 80% of men who admitted to acts that meet the definition of rape did not believe they had committed rape; and fully one-third of college men said they would commit rape if they believed nobody would find out.

Contrary to popular belief, we also know that men who do commit rape are not psychologically abnormal. They are indistinguishable from other men in terms of psychological adjustment and health, emotional wellbeing, heterosexual relationships, and frequency of sexual experiences (Segel-Evans, 1987). The only established difference between men who are sexually violent and men who are not is that the former have "hypermasculine" attitudes and self-concepts—their approval of male dominance and sexual rights is even stronger than that of nonrapists (Allgeier, 1987; Koss & Dinero, 1988; Lisak & Roth, 1988; Wood, 1993a). The difference between sexually violent men and others appears to be only a matter of degree.

We also know something about women who are victims of rape and other forms of sexual violence. Between 33% and 66% of all women have been sexually abused before reaching age 18 (Clutter, 1990; Koss, 1990). The majority of college women—up to 75%—say they have been coerced into some type of unwanted sex at least once (Koss, Gidycz, & Wisniewski, 1987; Poppen & Segal, 1988; Warshaw, 1988). A third of women who survive rape contemplate suicide (Koss et al., 1988). It is also clear that the trauma of rape is not confined to the time of its actual occurrence. The feelings that accompany rape and sexual assault—fear, a sense of degradation and shame, anger, powerlessness, and depression—endure far beyond the act itself (Brownmiller, 1975; Wood, 1992b, 1993f). Most victims of rape continue to deal with the emotional aftermath of rape for the rest of their lives (Marhoefer-Dvorak, Resick, Hutter, & Girelli, 1988).

What causes rape, now the fastest growing violent crime in the United States (Doyle, 1989; Soeken & Damrosch, 1986)? According to experts (Costin & Schwartz, 1987; Koss & Dinero, 1988; Koss, Gidycz, & Wisniewski, 1987; Scott & Tetreault, 1987; Scully, 1990), rape is not the result of psychological deviance or uncontrollable lust. Although rape involves sex, it is not motivated by sexual desire. Authorities agree that rape is an aggressive act used to dominate and show power over another person, be it a man over a woman or one man over another, as in prison settings where rape is one way inmates brutalize one another and establish a power hierarchy (Rideau & Sinclair, 1982). Instead, mounting evidence suggests that rape is a predictable outcome of views of men, women, and relationships between the sexes that our society inculcates in members (Brownmiller, 1975; Costin & Schwartz, 1987; Scott & Tetreault, 1987; South & Felson, 1990).

Particularly compelling support for the cultural basis of rape comes from cross-cultural studies (Griffin, 1981; Sanday, 1986), which reveal that rape is extremely rare in cultures that value women and feminine qualities and that have ideologies that promote harmonious interdependence among humans and between them and the natural world. Rape is most common in countries, like the United States, that have ideologies of male supremacy and dominance and a disrespect of women and nature. Cultural values communicated to us by family, schools, media, and other sources constantly encourage us to believe men are superior, men should dominate women, male aggression is acceptable as a means of attaining what is wanted, women are passive and should defer to men, and women are sex objects. In concert, these beliefs legitimize violence and aggression against women.

While the majority of media communication may not be pornographic, it does echo in somewhat muted forms the predominant themes of pornography: sex, violence, and male domination of women. As we have seen, these same motifs permeate media that are part of our daily

---

MYTHS AND FACTS ABOUT RAPE

Myth	Fact
Rape is a sexual act that results from sexual urges.	Rape is an aggressive act used to dominate another.
Rapists are abnormal.	Rapists have not been shown to differ from nonrapists in personality, psychology, adjustment, or involvement in interpersonal relationships.
Most rapes occur between strangers.	Eighty percent to 90% of rapes are committed by a person known to the victim (Allgeier, 1987).
Most rapists are African-American men, and most victims are Caucasian women.	More than three-fourths of all rapes occur within races, not between races. This myth reflects racism.
The way a woman dresses affects the likelihood she will be raped.	The majority—up to 90%—of rapes are planned in advance and without knowledge of how the victim will dress (Scully, 1990).
False reports of rapes are frequent.	The majority of rapes are never reported (Koss, Gidycz, & Wisniewski, 1987). Less than 10% of rape reports are judged false, the same as for other violent crimes.
Rape is a universal problem.	The incidence of rape varies across cultures. It is highest in societies with ideologies of male dominance and a disregard for nature; it is lowest in cultures that respect women and feminine values (Griffin, 1981).

1. LIVING WITH MEDIA

lives, which generally portray males as dominating in number, status, authority, and will. Substantial violence toward women punctuates movies, television—including children's programming—rock music, and music videos, desensitizing men and women alike to the *unnaturalness* and unacceptability of force and brutality between human beings. Thus, the research that demonstrates connections between sex-stereotypical media and acceptance of sexual violence is consistent with that showing relationships between more extreme, pornographic media and acceptance of and use of violence....

REFERENCES

Adams, C. (1991, April). The straight dope. *Triangle Comic Review*, p. 26.
Allgeier, E. R. (1987). Coercive versus consensual sexual interactions. In V. P. Makosky (Ed.), *The G. Stanley Hall Lecture Series* (Vol. 7, pp. 7–63). Washington, DC: American Psychological Association.
Baron, L., & Straus, M. A. (1989). *Four theories of rape in American society*. New Haven, CT: Yale University Press.
Basow, S. A. (1992). *Gender: Stereotypes and roles* (3rd ed.). Pacific Grove, CA: Brooks/Cole.
The best in the house. (1988, October 19). *New York Times*, p. 52Y.
Boyer, P. J. (1986, February 16). TV turns to the hard-boiled male. *New York Times*, pp. H1, H29.
Bretl, D., & Cantor, J. (1988). The portrayal of men and women in U.S. commercials: A recent content analysis and trend over 15 years. *Sex Roles*, 18, 595–609.
Brown, J. D., & Campbell, K. (1986). Race and gender in music videos: The same beat but a different drummer. *Journal of Communication*, 36, 94–106.
Brown, J. D., Campbell, K., & Fisher, L. (1986). American adolescents and music videos: Why do they watch? *Gazette*, 37, 9–32.
Brownmiller, S. (1975). *Against our wills: Men, women, and rape*. New York: Simon and Schuster.
Brownmiller, S. (1993, January 4). Making female bodies the battlefield. *Newsweek*, p. 37.
Carter, B. (1991, May 1). Children's TV, where boys are king. *New York Times*, pp. A1, C18.
Clutter, S. (1990, May 3). Gender may affect response and outrage to sex abuse. *Morning Call*, p. D14.
Costin, F., & Schwartz, N. (1987). Beliefs about rape and women's social roles: A four-nation study. *Journal of Interpersonal Violence*, 2, 46–56.
Courtney, A. E., & Whipple T. W. (1983). *Sex stereotyping in advertising*. Lexington, MA: D. C. Heath.
Cowan, G., Lee, C., Levy, D., & Snyder, D. (1988). Dominance and inequality in X-rated videocassettes. *Psychology of Women Quarterly*, 12, 299–311.
Cowan, G., & O'Brien, M. (1990). Gender and survival vs. death in slasher films: A content analysis. *Sex Roles*, 23, 187–196.
Craft, C. (1988). *Too old, too ugly, and not deferential to men: An anchorwoman's courageous battle against sex discrimination*. Rockland, CA: Prima.
Davis, D. M. (1990). Portrayals of women in prime-time network television: Some demographic characteristics. *Sex Roles*, 23, 325–332.
Demare, D., Briere, J., & Lips, H. M. (1988). Violent pornography and self-reported likelihood of sexual aggression. *Journal of Research in Personality*, 22, 140–153.
Dieter, P. (1989, March). *Shooting her with video, drugs, bullets, and promises*. Paper presented at the meeting of the Association of Women in Psychology, Newport, RI.
Donnerstein, E., Linz, D., & Penrod, S. (1987). *The question of pornography: Research findings and policy implications*. New York: Free Press.
Doyle, J. A. (1989). *The male experience* (2nd ed.). Dubuque, IA: William C. Brown.
Evans, D. (1993, March 1). The wrong examples. *Newsweek*, p. 10.
Faludi, S. (1991). *Backlash: The undeclared war against American women*. New York: Crown.
Feldman, N. S., & Brown, E. (1984, April). *Male vs. female differences in control strategies: What children learn from Saturday morning television*. Paper presented at the meeting of the Eastern Psychological Association, Baltimore, MD. (Cited in Basow, 1992.)
Foreit, K. G., Agor, T., Byers, J., Larue, J., Lokey, H., Palazzini, M., Patterson, M., & Smith, L. (1980). Sex bias in the newspaper treatment of male-centered and female-centered news articles. *Sex Roles*, 6, 475–480.
Gray, H. (1986). Television and the new black man: Black male images in prime-time situation comedies. *Media, Culture, and Society*, 8, 223–242.
Greene, R., & Dalton, K. (1953). The premenstrual syndrome. *British Medical Journal*, 1, 1007–1014.
Greer, G. (1992). *The change: Women, aging, and menopause*. New York: Alfred Knopf.
Griffin, S. (1981). *Pornography and silence: Culture's revenge against nature*. New York: Harper and Row.
Hansen, C. H., & Hansen, R. D. (1988). How rock music videos can change what is seen when boy meets girl: Priming stereotypic appraisal of social interactions. *Sex Roles*, 19, 287–316.
Haskell, M. (1988, May). Hollywood Madonnas. *Ms.*, pp. 84, 86, 88.
Horovitz, B. (1989, August 10). In TV commercials, men are often the butt of the jokes. *Philadelphia Inquirer*, pp. 5b, 6b.
The implant circus. (1992, February 18). *Wall Street Journal*, p. A20.
Koss, M. P. (1990). The women's mental health research agenda: Violence against women. *American Psychologist*, 45, 374–380.
Koss, M. P., & Dinero, T. E. (1988). Predictors of sexual aggression among a national sample of male college students. In V. I. Quinsey & R. Orentky (Eds.), *Human sexual aggression* (pp. 133–147). New York: Academy of Sciences.
Koss, M. P., Dinero, T. E., Seibel, C. A., & Cox, S. L. (1988). Stranger and acquaintance rape: Are there differences in the victim's experience? *Psychology of Women Quarterly*, 12, 1–24.
Koss, M. P., Gidycz, C. J., Wisniewski, N. (1987). The scope of rape: Incidence and prevalence of sexual aggression and victimization in a national sample of higher education students. *Journal of Consulting and Clinical Psychology*, 55, 162–170.
Leland, J., & Leonard, E. (1993, February 1). Back to Twiggy. *Newsweek*, pp. 64–65.
Lichter, S. R., Lichter, L. S., & Rothman, S. (1986, September/October). From Lucy to Lacey: TV's dream girls. *Public Opinion*, pp. 16–19.
Lichter, S. R., Lichter, L. S., Rothman, S., & Amundson, D. (1987, July/August). Prime-time prejudice: TV's images of blacks and Hispanics. *Public Opinion*, pp. 13–16.
Lisak, D., & Roth, S. (1988). Motivational factors in nonincarcerated sexually aggressive men. *Journal of Personality and Social Psychology*, 55, 795–802.
Lott, B. (1989). Sexist discrimination as distancing behavior: II. Prime-time television. *Psychology of Women Quarterly*, 13, 341–355.
MacKinnon, C. A. (1987). *Feminism unmodified: Discourses on life and law*. Cambridge, MA: Harvard University Press.
Malamuth, N. M., & Briere, J. (1986). Sexual violence in the media: Indirect effects on aggression against women. *Journal of Social Issues*, 42, 75–92.
Marhoefer-Dvorak, S., Resick, P., Hutter, C., & Girelli, S. (1988). Single-versus multiple-incident rape victims: A comparison of psychological reactions to rape. *Journal of Interpersonal Violence*, 3, 145–160.
Maslin, J. (1990, June 17). Bimbos embody retro rage. *New York Times*, pp. H13, H14.
Masse, M. A., & Rosenblum, K. (1988). Male and female created they them: The depiction of gender in the advertising of traditional women's and men's magazine's. *Women's Studies International Forum*, 11, 127–144.
Mattell offers trade-in for "Teen Talk" Barbie. (1992, October 13). *Raleigh News and Observer*, p. A3.
McCauley, C., Thangavelu, K., & Rozin, P. (1988). Sex stereotyping of occupations in relation to television representations and census facts. *Basic and Applied Social Psychology*, 9, 197–212.
Menopause. (1992, May 25). *Newsweek*, pp. 71–80.
Mills, K. (1988). *A place in the news: From the women's pages to the front page*. New York: Dodd, Mead.
Modleski, T. (1982). *Loving with a vengeance: Mass-produced fantasies for women*. New York: Methuen.
Muro, M. (1989, April 23). Comment: New era of eros in advertising. *Morning Call*, pp. D1, D16.
The new traditionalist. (1988, November 17). *New York Times*, p. Y46.
Nigro, G. N., Hill, D. E., Gelbein, M. E., & Clark, C. L. (1988). Changes in the facial prominence of women and men over the last decade. *Psychology of Women Quarterly*, 12, 225–235.
O'Connor, J. J. (1989, June 6). What are commercials selling to children? *New York Times*, p. 28.
Pareles, J. (1990, October 21). The women who talk back in rap. *New York Times*, pp. H33, H36.
Parlee, M. B. (1973). The premenstrual syndrome. *Psychological Bulletin*, 80, 454–465.
Parlee, M. B. (1979, May). Conversational politics. *Psychology Today*, pp. 48–56.
Peirce, K. (1990). A feminist theoretical perspective on the socialization of teenage girls through *Seventeen* magazine. *Sex Roles*, 23, 491–500.
Rakow, L. F. (1986). Rethinking gender research in communication. *Journal of Communication*, 36, 11–26.
Richmond-Abbott, M. (1992). *Masculine and feminine: Gender roles over the life cycle*. New York: McGraw-Hill.
Rideau, W., & Sinclair, B. (1982). Prison: The sexual jungle. In A. Scacco, Jr. (Ed.), *Male Rape* (pp. 3–29). New York: AMS Press.
Russell, D. E. H. (Ed.). (1993). *Feminist views on pornography*. Colchester, VT: Teachers College Press.
Sanday, P. R. (1986). Rape and the silencing of the feminine. In S. Tomaselli & R. Porter (Eds.), *Rape* (pp. 84–101). Oxford, UK: Basil Blackwell.
Sanders, M., & Rock, M. (1988). *Waiting for prime time: The women of television news*. Urbana, IL: University of Illinois Press.
Scott, R., & Tetreault, L. (1987). Attitudes of rapists and other violent offenders toward women. *Journal of Social Psychology*, 124, 375–380.
Scully, D. (1990). *Understanding sexual violence: A study of convicted rapists*. Boston, MA: Unwin Hyman.
Segel-Evans, K. (1987). Rape prevention and masculinity. In F. Abbott (Ed.), *New men, new minds: Breaking male tradition* (pp. 117–121). Freedom, CA: Crossing Press.
Sights, sounds and stereotypes. (1992, October 11). *Raleigh News and Observer*, pp. G1, G10.
Silverstein, B., Perdue, L., Peterson, B., & Kelly, E. (1986). The role of the mass media in promoting a thin standard of bodily attractiveness for women. *Sex Roles*, 14, 519–532.
Soeken, K., & Damrosch, S. (1986). Randomized response technique: Application to research on rape. *Psychology of Women Quarterly*, 10, 119–126.
South, S. J., & Felson, R. B. (1990). The racial patterning of rape. *Social Forces*, 69, 71–93.
Spitzack, C. (1993). The spectacle of anorexia nervosa. *Text and Performance Quarterly*, 13, 1–21.
Stroman, C. A. (1989). To be young, male and black on prime-time television. *Urban Research Review*, 12, 9–10.
Study reports sex bias in news organizations. (1989, April 11). *New York Times*, p. C22.
Tavris, C. (1992). *The mismeasure of woman*. New York: Simon and Schuster.
Texier, C. (1990, April 22). Have women surrendered in MTV's battle of the sexes? *New York Times*, pp. H29, H31.
Unger, R., & Crawford, M. (1992). *Women and gender: A feminist psychology*. New York: McGraw-Hill.
Warshaw, R. (1988). *I never called it rape*. New York: Harper and Row.
Wolf, N. (1991). *The beauty myth*. New York: William Morrow.
Women in media say careers hit "glass ceiling." (1988, March 2). *Easton Express*, p. A9.
Wood, J. T. (1992b). Telling our stories: Narratives as a basis for theorizing sexual harassment. *Journal of Applied Communication Research*, 4, 349–363.
Wood, J. T. (1993a). Engendered relationships: Interaction, caring, power, and responsibility in close relationships. In S. Duck (Ed.), *Processes in close relationships: Contexts of close relationships* (Vol. 3). Beverly Hills, CA: Sage.
Wood, J. T. (1993c). *Who cares: Women, care, and culture*. Carbondale, IL: Southern Illinois University Press.
Wood, J. T. (1993f). Defining and studying sexual harassment as situated experience. In G. Kreps (Ed.), *Communication and sexual harassment in the workplace*. Cresskill, NJ: Hampton Press.
Woodman, S. (1991, May). How super are heros? *Health*, pp. 40, 49, 82.

Cause and Violent Effect

Media and Our Youth

Barbara Hattemer

Barbara Hattemer is president of the National Family Foundation. For many years, she has educated the public about the effects of violent and sexually explicit media, most recently through promoting her book Don't Touch That Dial: Impact of the Media on Children and the Family.

Recent headlines proclaim increasing youth violence: "4 Teenagers Charged in Murder of Tourist," "Pupils Told To Run for Their Lives—Teacher Describes Terror in Classroom," "FSU Student Murdered, Sister Raped—18-year-old Beaten to Death, Sister Tied to Tree in Ocala National Forest."

Youth crime is on everyone's mind. It is the focus of virtually every political campaign of 1994. There is talk of boot camps, stricter laws, trying children as adults for committing serious crimes, larger prisons, harsher sentences, gun control, curfews. Take the kids off the streets so we can feel safe again! Keep them home! Why? So they can watch more murder and rape on television and video?

How weary we have grown of the statistics on how many murders every high school graduate has seen. According to the American Psychological Association, even before leaving elementary school, the average child has seen eight thousand murders and one hundred thousand acts of violence on television.

Social science, clinical concepts, and common sense all agree that what children watch affects who they become, what they believe, what they value, and how they behave.[1]

EARLY INFLUENCE OF TV

Television's influence on our children starts earlier than most of us realize. Andrew Meltzoff found that fourteen-month-old infants can watch an unfamiliar toy being dismantled and reassembled on television and repeat the actions twenty-four hours later. Even at this early age, television acts as a guide to real-life behavior. Throughout childhood, children learn by imitating what they see others doing.

Two-to six-year-old children cannot evaluate the messages they receive from the media they watch. They simply accept what they see as normal behavior. Children cannot tell the difference between reality and fantasy until the fifth or sixth grade. Six-to twelve-year-olds imitate what they see and hear without fully understanding the consequences of what they are doing. Most adoles-

---

[1]. Unless otherwise noted, the material in this paper is thoroughly referenced in *Don't Touch That Dial: The Impact of the Media on Children and the Family,* by Barbara Hattemer and H. Robert Showers, Huntington House, 1993.

1. LIVING WITH MEDIA

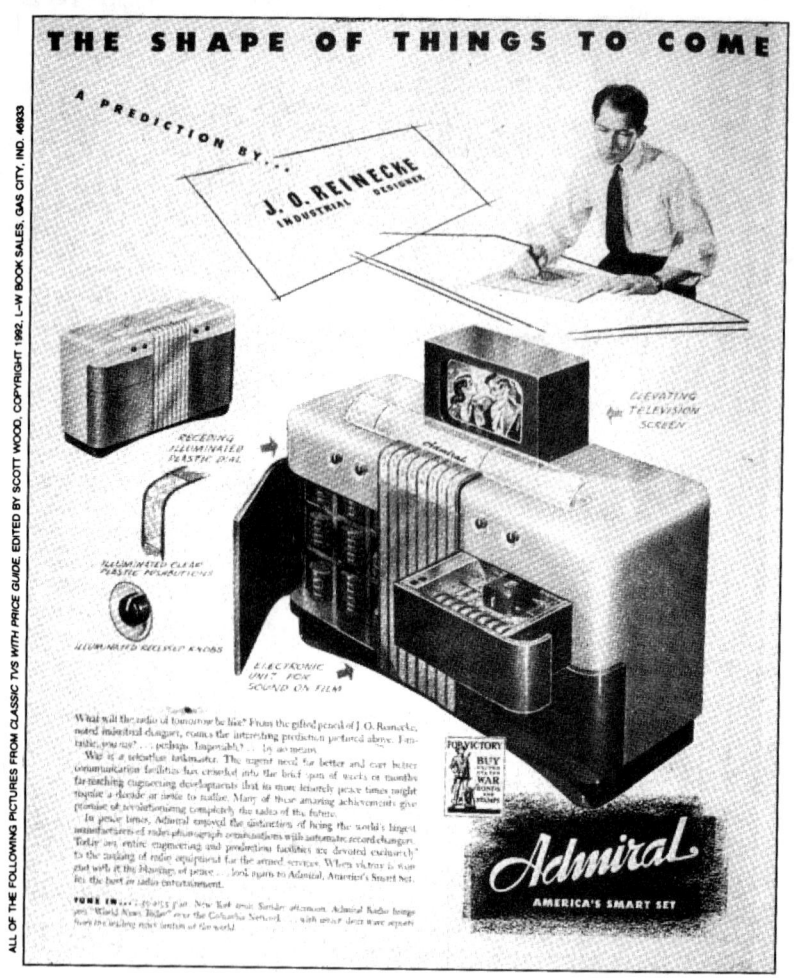

■ Early models of TV sets suggest the cultural place of television; here an advertisement from *Collier's* in November 1942 shows an Admiral "vision."

cents do not have a fully developed, internal set of morals and values. They accept the conduct they see in the media as the social norm and integrate it into their own behavior patterns.

What are the predominant messages of television, movies, and other media that our children are accepting and imitating? That violence is an everyday occurrence and an acceptable way of solving problems and that promiscuous sex is normal and expected of everyone, including younger and younger children. These two messages merge as the philosophy of pornography, once thought to be limited to sleazy adult bookstores and out-of-the-way art cinemas, has been mainstreamed. The rape myth—that women secretly want to be raped and that they enjoy forced sex—has so permeated our children's minds that 65 percent of boys and 47 percent of girls agreed with a survey question that "it was acceptable for a man to force sex with a woman if he had been dating her for more than 6 months."

While television has unlimited potential for good, at the present time its influence on children's lives is largely negative. Television programming, according to Dr. Paul Howard, prominent Boston psychiatrist, is so hostile and aggressive it produces tremendous anxiety in young watchers. "One weekend of children watching television," he declared, "undoes a whole week of psychotherapy for my young patients."

Television and violence have been almost synonymous since television became a part of nearly every home. As far back as 1977, nine of every ten TV programs contained violence. Today, while there is more variety, there are more sources of violence than ever before. In addition to violent action-adventure movies and television dramas, violence pervades music videos, rap songs, documentaries, commercials, and news broadcasts. The networks provide up to 10 violent acts per hour; cable, up to 18 violent acts per hour; and children's cartoons, 32 violent acts per hour. Movies like *Teenage Mutant Ninja Turtles* raise the count to 133 violent acts per hour. The body count is rising, too: *Total Recall*, 74 dead; *Robocop 2*, 81 dead; *Rambo III*, 106 dead; and *Die Hard 2*, 264 dead.

Mass-produced, cheap industrial violence is something quite new in our culture. The new heroes glamorize violence for its own sake. The violence is the story, not an element necessary to the telling of a story. Add to this the influence of violent video games and fantasy games that encourage children to spend hours planning how to kill or maim more successfully. Mix in violent comic books and serial-killer trading cards, and you have a culture that gives its children a steady diet of violent role models but very little old-fashioned nurture and direction from parents.

VIOLENT YOUTH

For nearly a decade, judges and police officers have been exclaiming that they have never before seen rapists and murderers who

5. Cause and Violent Effect

are so young. The news, in its promotion of the sensational, keeps the tragic headlines ever before us. What some feared might one day happen is indeed happening. The subculture that has long been singing about beating up women, killing parents, and murdering for fun has surfaced.

One-half of the sex offenders in this country are now under the age of eighteen! A 1988 Michigan crime report stated that 681 juveniles who averaged fourteen years of age were convicted of sexually assaulting children who averaged seven years of age. These are not always violent or deeply troubled children; they are children who have been exposed too early to material they cannot process without imitating. They see it on cable in their own homes, they hear it on the telephone. Dial-a-porn companies have admitted that 75–85 percent of their customers are children. Overstimulated by what they see and hear, they act it out on younger siblings or playmates.

Violent crime is up 560 percent since 1960 and is rising. There are three million incidents of school crime every year. In 1993 alone, the rate of violent encounters in schools rose 34 percent in the state of Florida. Rape, assault, and murder have replaced chewing gum, talking in class, and throwing wads of paper, the greatest school problems in the forties. From 1987 to 1991, teenagers arrested for murder increased 85 percent. In 1990, forty-two hundred teenagers were killed by guns. In New York City, one in five teenagers carries a weapon to school; and one in twenty, a gun. On any one day, 135,000 children carry guns to school across the nation.

It is said that we have always been a violent society, but there is a new callousness among our young people. Many studies have found that using pornography increases men's callousness toward and distrust of women, as well as their inclination to rape. Research also has revealed that 100 percent of our high schoolers have seen soft-core pornography, and 90 percent of high school boys and 80 percent of girls have seen hardcore pornography. The younger they are when they see it, the more likely they are to want to imitate it.

Horror movies aimed at young teens desensitize them to violence and create an ever-increasing appetite for it. If the camera angle allows the child to see the

■ **The television as center of the family, as seen by Magnavox in 1950.**

action through the eyes of the madman, a subtle shift takes place. He identifies not with the passive victim but with the active perpetrator. In his imagination, it is the child himself who wields the knife, the ax, or the deadly weapon. Identifying with the aggressor, he senses the thrill of momentary power over another and learns to enjoy committing a crime.

Park Dietz declares that exposing boys to films showing women being mutilated in the midst of sex scenes is the best way to raise a generation of sexual sadists. One study found that Freddy of *Nightmare on Elm Street* and Jason of *Friday the 13th* are better known to ten-to thirteen-year-olds than Abraham Lincoln and George Washington. Seven- to twelve-year-olds name horror movies as their favorites and say they like seeing people killed and enjoy watching pain and torture. Freddy is the star of not only a series of movies, but a televi-

1. LIVING WITH MEDIA

sion series, a comic book, 900 number, toys, and trading cards. The mayor of Los Angeles named a holiday for him. We are teaching our children to look to mass murderers as their role models.

Film critic Roger Ebert sees a basic change taking place in society regarding women in danger. The sympathy of the audience has moved from the woman to the killer. As the camera takes the killer's point of view, the lust to kill is placed, not in the character of the killer, but in the audience.

Too often, that audience is full of impressionable children. They can buy a ticket to any G or PG film and often slip into R-rated films in a mall complex. (They laugh when asked if they have trouble getting in to see R-rated movies, and producers boast that if they make the movies, children will find a way to see them.) At video stores and libraries, even the pretense of restricting children from R-rated movies is gone. With the notable exception of Blockbuster video stores, there is no age restriction for obtaining violent movies.

REAL-LIFE AGGRESSION

No one today doubts that our children are seeing massive amounts of violence in a wide variety of media presentations. Moreover, a vast amount of scientific research proves that watching violence on the screen is causally related to real-life aggression. Since the 1968 National Commission on the Causes and Prevention of Violence, a series of government commissions and reports and a consensus of medical associations have all found a link between screen violence and violent behavior.

The television and motion picture industries have been successful in casting doubt on such findings by saying that some studies show an effect and others do not, but the studies that show the fewest effects have been sponsored by the industry. We now have over three thousand studies telling us that watching violent films increases violent behavior. Research has found that preschool children who frequently watch violent cartoons behave aggressively. First graders who watch aggressive cartoons exhibit more hostile behavior in school than first graders who watch neutral programming or even a football game. Because the impact is greater the more realistic the violent scenes are, researchers fear the more realistic human characters in today's cartoons may have an even greater influence on children.

Leonard Eron and Rowell Huesman conducted an important longitudinal study, following eight year olds for twenty-two years. They found that children who watched large amounts of violent television at age eight were more likely to be engaged in criminal behavior at age thirty. Not only did they commit serious crimes, they also punished their children more harshly and were much more aggressive when drinking.

Studies before and after the introduction of television in an area reveal an increase in aggressive behavior after the arrival of television. Two years after television was introduced into Notel, Canada, physical aggression among children increased 160 percent.

A study by Brandon Centerwall focused on the effects of childhood exposure to television violence on adult criminal behavior in larger populations, comparing the effect of television on the roughly comparable white populations of the United States, Canada, and South Africa. Fifteen years after television was introduced into the United States and Canada, white homicide deaths had risen 93 percent and 92 percent, respectively. At the same time, in South Africa, where there was no TV, the white homicide rate had dropped 7 percent. Yet, eight years after South Africa received TV, the rate had already increased 56 percent, indicating that, in fifteen years, it would be close to that of the United States and Canada. In fact, by 1987, twelve years after television had been introduced into South Africa, the white homicide rate had risen by 130 percent.

Centerwall looked for every possible alternative explanation, completing another eleven studies on factors such as the baby boom, urbanization, economic trends, alcohol consumption, capital punishment, civil unrest, and the availability of firearms, but he could find none. He ruled out such factors as the U.S. civil

5. Cause and Violent Effect

While television has unlimited potential for good, at the present time, its influence on children's lives is largely negative.

rights movement and the Vietnam War because these did not affect Canada. He concluded that exposure to violent programming on television is causally related to roughly one-half the twenty thousand yearly homicides in the United States and one-half the rapes and assaults as well.

His conclusions held up when he looked at populations within the United States that acquired television at different times. When television appeared in the early 1950s, it was an expensive luxury. Since blacks tended to lag behind whites by about five years in acquiring television sets, he predicted that the white homicide rate would rise before the black homicide rate in the United States. In fact, the white homicide rate began to rise in 1958, while the black homicide rate dropped consistently throughout the next four years. Similarly, those regions of the United States like New York and New Jersey that acquired television before other sections of the country were also found to have an earlier increase in the homicide rate.

Centerwall believes that the lag of ten to fifteen years between the introduction of television and the rise in the homicide rate indicates that the greatest effect is on children under the age of twelve. In the past, it took these children ten to fifteen years to grow up before they were old enough to commit homicide. Today, however, children are not waiting to become adults to begin committing adult crimes. Youth crime is growing at a much faster rate than adult crime. The past ten years have seen an increase of 55 percent in the number of children arrested for murder. Centerwall explains this as the snowballing effect. The first generation raised on television learned values from the adults in their lives as well as from the TV set. With the increasing dominance of the media in society, the passing on of values from the older generation has diminished, while the second and third generations raised on TV have increasingly taken their values from the media culture.[2]

LETHAL VIOLENCE

The increase in the seriousness of juvenile crime may be explained further by the fact that violence has become increasingly graphic and gory. According to journalist David Barry, the juvenile delinquency portrayed in 1950s' movies "consisted almost entirely of assaults with fists and weapons which left victims injured, but alive. It was non-lethal violence. The notion of American teenagers as killers was beyond the threshold of credibility."[3]

Since then, he says, the level of criminal violence reported in everyday news stories has become almost unrecognizable. He offers the following statistics as evidence of the effect of the first twenty-nine years of television on crime in the United States. In 1951, there were 6,820 murders, 16,800 rapes, and 52,090 robberies. By 1980, these had increased to 23,000 murders, 78,920 rapes, and 548,220 robberies—vastly more than the 47 percent population increase from 150 million to 220 million. The murder rate is increasing six times faster than the rate of population growth. It is now the leading cause of death for black youths and the second leading cause of death of all fifteen-to twenty-four-year-olds. Violence is the leading cause of injury to fifteen-to forty-four-year-old women. The U.S. Centers for Disease Control calls it both a leading public health issue and an epidemic.

Researchers offer numerous explanations of how and why media violence translates into real-life violence. They theorize that when a child observes vio-

---

2. An interview with Brandon Centerwall, M.D., "A Tale of Three Countries: Homicide Rates Rise after Television's Arrival," *Media and Values*, no. 62.
3. David Barry, "Growing Up Violent," *Media and Values*, no. 62.

lence used as a means of solving conflicts, the event is recorded in his brain and stored in his memory bank. This scene can be reinforced by subsequent violent scenes, which eventually blend into a general script of how to react to conflict. The more graphic the violence, the more likely it will catch the child's attention and become part of a script stored in his memory, waiting to be retrieved when he faces a similar conflict situation in real life.

Older children are particularly responsive to violence that is realistic or close to their personal experience and thus seems likely to happen in real life. Younger children are more likely to identify with and imitate violent behavior if the character is attractively portrayed. The more that children of all ages identify with a violent character, the more likely they are to be aggressive themselves.

Watching violence primes the pump and starts a network of associations. As media violence is absorbed into a person's thoughts, it activates related aggressive ideas and emotions that eventually lead to aggressive behavior. What a child observes as the associative networks in his brain are developing is of paramount importance.

Violence that is rewarded or left unpunished appears to be sanctioned in a child's mind. It is, therefore, much more likely to be imitated. Violence that appears to be justified or portrayed as necessary for a good cause is even more likely to be imitated. One reason the large amount of violence in Japanese films does not produce as much real-life violence as in the United States is the way that Japanese

---

Excerpts from the *Motion Picture Production Code*, in force from 1930 to 1966

GENERAL PRINCIPLE:

The sympathy of the audience shall never be thrown to the side of crime, wrong-doing, evil or sin.

PARTICULAR APPLICATIONS:

The technique of murder must be presented in a way that will not inspire imitation.

Brutal killings are not to be presented in detail.

Methods of crime should not be explicitly presented.

The use of firearms should be restricted to essentials.

SPECIAL REGULATIONS ON CRIME:

Action suggestive of wholesale slaughter of human beings, either by criminals, in conflict with police, or as between warring factions of criminals, or in public disorder of any kind, will not be allowed.

There must be no suggestion, at any time, of excessive brutality.

Action showing the taking of human life, even in the mystery stories, is to be cut to the minimum. These frequent presentations of murder tend to lessen regard for the sacredness of life.

There must be no display, at any time, of machine guns, sub-machine guns or other weapons generally classified as illegal weapons in the hands of gangsters, or other criminals . . .

REASONS UNDERLYING
PRINCIPLES AND APPLICATIONS:

If motion pictures consistently hold up for admiration high types of characters and present stories that will affect lives for the better, they can become the most powerful natural force for the improvement of mankind.

Hence the important objective must be to avoid the hardening of the audience, especially of those who are young and impressionable, to the thought and fact of crime. People can become accustomed even to murder, cruelty, brutality, and repellent crimes, if these are too frequently repeated.

5. Cause and Violent Effect

■ A 1971 RCA record cover reproduces the myth that TV watching is a family affair.

films portray violence, highlighting the pain, suffering, and tragic consequences that follow. They teach an altogether different lesson than America's glamorized violence.

Not everyone reacts the same way to violence. Poorly nurtured children with few inner strengths and without internalized boundaries are more susceptible to its influence than well-nurtured children who have received a strong value system from their parents. Children who are undersupplied with parental love are often angry and chaotic inside. They are drawn to violent films, heavy metal music, and gangster rap because it reflects their inner turmoil. It both reinforces and offers approval for their negative attitudes. The combination of being undersupplied with parental nurture and overstimulated by violent media can be deadly.

VIOLENCE IN MUSIC

In 1989, the American Medical Association concluded that music is an even greater influence on teens than television. This is because they have more exposure to heavy metal music than to either pornography or horror films. MTV has introduced a whole generation of children to songs that glorify pleasure seeking and irresponsibility. Its videos contain thirteen violent acts per hour, and four out of five of them mix violence with sex.

Rock stars are always available to young people starving for attention and understanding. They offer children unqualified acceptance. They appear to meet their needs and understand their chaotic emotions better than their parents. Prolonged listening to hard-rock music correlates with many negatives, from the mildly troubling to the very serious: increasing discomfort in family situations, a preference for friends over family, poor academic performance, increased chemical dependency, violence, stealing, and sexual activity. It makes disturbed adolescents feel powerful and in charge.

There is a strong relationship between antisocial or destructive behavior and listening to rock music with destructive themes. The preference for heavy metal music among juvenile delinquents is almost three times as high as among the general population of high schoolers. This music is filling our children's heads with rebellion, raw sex, violence, and a hatred and abuse of women of a degree never seen before. For example:

> Tie her down, she knows what's waiting for her.
> Nothing too cruel, so beat her 'til she's red and raw,
> Crack the whip, it hardly stings the bitch.
> "She Like It Rough," Thrasher

Much of heavy metal music reflects a fascination with the occult:

> I am possessed by all that is evil, the death of your God I demand, I spit at the virgin you worship, and sit at Lord Satan's right hand . . .
> "Welcome to Hell," Venom

> We are instruments of evil, we come straight out of hell.
> We're the legions, haunting for the kill.
> "Demons," Rigor Mortis

1. LIVING WITH MEDIA

Newsweek speaks of the ability of rap music to alienate, of its imagery and lyrics as "pure confrontation." It educates our children on the crime and rage of inner-city life and fills their heads with rebellion, hate, and more raw sex. While the courts rule in favor of hateful speech, our culture struggles with how to deal with entertainment that spews hatred into children's minds.

THE FAMILY ANTIDOTE

Research has found that the best defense against the media is a strong family that makes an effort to impart values and gives children clear boundaries. Youths from families with well-defined value systems use them to interpret what they observe. Teenagers from homes in which family members communicate openly and engage in an active viewing style, discussing programs with their children, are less influenced by what they see.

Violent programming has a greater impact on boys than on girls, a greater impact on young men who are already callous than on those who are sensitive, and a greater impact on those from the inner city who experience violence in their daily lives. The latter, by their own admission, are more aroused by filmed violence, give it higher approval ratings, and watch more of it. With thousands of violent models stored in their memories and more aggressive associations implanted in their minds, why are we surprised when they react violently to real-life situations?

The entertainment industry could help our troubled children by cutting back on the number of violent portrayals, by making them less graphic and attention getting, and by emphasizing the sorrowful consequences of violence rather than glamorizing and making heroes of violent men.

A possible solution is granting the Federal Communications Commission the power to include excessive violence in the broadcasting standard that limits indecency and obscenity on radio and television. Government censorship cannot raise the moral tone of the nation. A better answer is the return to standards and voluntary limits. Nothing shows so clearly how far we have fallen as a nation from the values we once agreed upon than a look at the old Motion Picture Production Code, in force from 1930 to 1966, which stated

> Motion picture producers recognize the high trust and confidence which have been placed in them by the people of the world. . . . They recognize their responsibility to the public because of this trust and because entertainment and art are important influences in the life of the nation.

But a code should apply to television, cable, and satellite as well. Government hearings and citizen complaints could serve to pressure the industry to consider an updated and revised code for all its products.

For this to become a reality, citizens must demand a better balance between creative freedom and social responsibility, between anything for a profit and serving the public interest. The industry must stop the "Can you top this!" mentality, which makes each sequel more graphic and gory than the one before. We must become more discriminating viewers and stop watching violent programs. We must enter into dialogue with the industry, thanking studios and networks for every good offering and supporting them at the box office and in the ratings races. We must support the sponsors of good programs and protest irresponsible companies at stockholders' meetings.

A return to standards is a better solution than labels. Parental advisories give permission to label and then go ahead and produce even more violent material. We need to recapture the essence of the old motion picture code, which declared that "there is no real substitute for successful self-government in industry" and that "self-regulation is wholly consonant with freedom of expression."

Battle for Your Brain

Stupidity, served with knowing intelligence, is now TV's answer to real smarts. And no one serves it like the crude and rude Beavis and Butt-head.

John Leland

It is television at its most redeeming. A whale swims gracefully across the screen as the narrator mourns its imminent destruction. Watching in their living room two boys, about 14, are visibly moved. Their eyes widen, their nostrils twitch uncomfortably. One boy's lips stiffen around his wire braces. The only hope, the narrator says, "is that perhaps the young people of today will grow up more caring, more understanding, more sensitive to the very special needs of the creatures of the earth." It is a rich moment, ripe with television's power to make remote events movingly immediate. The boys can watch idly no longer. Finally one turns to the other and asks, "Uh, did you fart?"

The boys are Beavis and Butt-head, two animated miscreants whose adventures at the low end of the food chain are currently the most popular program on MTV. Caught in the ungainly nadir of adolescence, they are not nice boys. They torture animals, they harass girls and sniff paint thinner. They like to burn things. They have a really insidious laugh: *huh-huh huh-huh*. They are the spiritual descendants of the semi-sentient teens from "Wayne's World" and "Bill and Ted's Excellent Adventure," only dumber and meaner. The downward spiral of the living white male surely ends here: in a little pimple named Butt-head whose idea of an idea is, "Hey, Beavis, let's go over to Stuart's house and light one in his cat's butt."

For a generation reminded hourly of its diminished prospects, these losers have proven remarkably embraceable. "Why do I like 'Beavis and Butt-head'?" asks Warren Lutz, 26, a journalism major at San Francisco State. "You're asking me to think, dude." Created by beginner animator Mike Judge, 30, for a festival of "sick and twisted" cartoons last year, Beavis and Butt-head have become a trash phenomenon. T shirts, hats, key rings, masks, buttons, calendars, dolls are all working their way to malls; a book, a comic book, a movie, a CD and a Christmas special are in the works. David Letterman drops a Beavis and Butt-head joke almost nightly; later this fall the pair will become a semiregular feature on his program. As their notoriety reached Fort Lewis College in Durango, Colo., archeology students have started calling Jim Judge, Mike's father, Dr. Butt-head. "Whenever any . . . 8- to 12-year-olds find out I'm related to Beavis and Butt-head," he says, "I become a god to them." Beavis and Butt-head, whose world divides into "things that suck" and "things that are cool," are clearly the new morons in town.

They are also part of a much wider TV phenomenon, one that drives not just stupid laughs but the front-page battle now being waged for control of Paramount Pictures. It is the battle to play road hog on the Information Highway. As cable technology continues to expand our range of viewing options, the old boundaries of propriety and decency no longer apply. Beavis and Butt-head join a growing crowd of characters who have found a magic formula: nothing cuts through the clutter like a slap of bracing crudity. Nothing stops a channel surfer like the word "sucks."

Stupidity, served with a knowing intelligence, has become the next best thing to smarts. Letterman's signature "Stupid Pet Tricks" bit, now 11 years running, introduced a new voice to television: ironic, self-aware, profoundly interested in the ingrained dumbness of the tube. Instead of dumbing down, it made smart comedy out of the process of dumbing down—and it clicked. Barry Diller successfully built Fox into the fourth network on a shockingly *lumpen* cartoon family, the Simpsons, and an even more *lumpen* real one, the Bundys of "Married . . . With Children." Nickelodeon's cartoon "The Ren & Stimpy Show," the highest-rated original series on cable, follows the scatological adventures of a Chichuahua and a cat, sometimes not getting much farther than the litter box. The network's new contender, "Rocko's Modern World," wallows down a similarly inspired low road. Its first episode, in which a home-shopping channel called "Lobot-o-shop" pitched items like tapeworm farms for kids, beat "Ren & Stimpy" in the ratings. And the widely loved and hated radio host Howard Stern has taken his act to E! Entertainment Television. "There's a purity to [this] kind of ignorance," says "Beavis and Butt-head" writer David Felton, at 53 MTV's oldest staff member.

1. LIVING WITH MEDIA

This Is Your Reel Life

Channel surf's up in Chicago. In a week, Windy City-zens can expand their minds with plenty of retro TV.

'BEWITCHED': Bothered and bewildered by the news? You'll be even more confused if, in channel-flopping, you spot two different Darrens. — 5 times

'BONANZA': Can't find "Battlestar Galactica" on the dial but need a Lorne Green fix? Catch him on the Ponderosa in all his pre-Alpo splendor. — 8 times

'CHARLIE'S ANGELS': Aaron Spelling's TV jiggle-magic made Farrah Fawcett a '70s star, featuring hot-pants-style karate and lots of teeth. — 10 times

'DRAGNET,: Duhn-duhn-duh, duhn-duh-dah-daaaaaah. Dunh-duh-dah, dun-duh-dah dah dah. Dunh-duh-duh, duhn-duh-dah dun. — 11 times

'F TROOP': How the West was really won by "Gilligan's Island" types in army uniforms. And check out those very un-P.C. Indians. — 7 times

'THE FLINTSTONES': Pre-Jurassic park rock! Watch Fred's weight unaccountably fluctuate from episode to Stone Age episode. — 11 times

'GILLIGAN'S ISLAND': Bob Denver's panicky ensign makes Beavis look well adjusted. The real question: who is the Professor sleeping with? — 5 times

'I DREAM OF JEANNIE': Monitor Hagman's hair: eraserhead to Sonny Bono and back again. Eden's harem pants would be cool with Doc Martens. — 5 times

'LEAVE IT TO BEAVER': Good parenting? Ward and June try to shepherd the Beave through an idyllic '50s childhood. Result: the '60s. — 10 times

'THREE'S COMPANY': This Carter-era ménage à trois hit No. 1 in the Nielsens. Was this the gay '70s, or what? — 5 times

---

"Going back to the basic point where thinking begins. And staying there."

But they are not just any losers, this lineage of losers. They are specifically *our* losers, totems of an age of decline and nonachievement. One in five people who graduated from college between 1984 and 1990 holds a job that doesn't require a college education. If this is not hard economic reality for a whole generation, it is psychological reality. Loser television has the sense to play along; it taps the anxiety in the culture and plays it back for laughs. Homer Simpson works in a nuclear power plant. Al Bundy sells shoes. Beavis and Butt-head work at Burger World and can't even visualize the good life. In one episode, as an act of community service, they get jobs in a hospital. Sucking on IV bags, planning to steal a cardiac patient's motorized cart, they agree: "It doesn't get any better than this, dude."

The shows also all share a common language. When "Beavis and Butt-head" producer John Andrews, 39, needed to put together a writing staff, he first called Letterman head writer Rob Burnett for suggestions. "Most of this stuff is done by overeducated guys who grew up reading Mad Magazine, National Lampoon, and watching 'Animal House' and 'Saturday Night Live'," says Matt Groening, creator of the Simpsons. "Scripts are based on what comes out of the collective memory of the writers, which is mostly memories of sitting in front of a TV set growing up." More than just throwbacks to the intelligently dumb television of the Three Stooges and Ernie Kovacs, the current shows are broad immersions in pop culture, satirical and multitiered. They address an audience that can view reruns of "Gilligan's Island" and "I Dream of Jeannie" half as camp, half as the fabric of shared experience. "The smarter you are, the more you see single events on different levels simultaneously," says Fernanda Moore, 25, who likes "The Simpsons," "Ren & Stimpy" and "Beavis and Butt-head." A doctoral candidate at Stanford, Moore is the daughter we all crave and perhaps fear. "Dumb people I know," she says, "aren't self-referential."

Of course, this is only one way to watch the shows. Lars Ulrich, drummer in the band Metallica, was delighted one day to spot Beavis wearing a Metallica T shirt. Yet he was also alarmed. "I would have to say—as little as I want to say it—that I think there are people like that. I'm not sure dumb is the right word. I would go more in the direction of the word ignorant." Either way, as the channels open up, the ship of fools is now sailing at full capacity.

At MTV's offices in New York last week, the ship was running through some rough waters. MTV from the inside is a Marshall McLuhan rec room, a place where precociously creative young people invent cool ways to frame ugly heavy-metal videos. In the production area of "Beavis and Butt-head," these young people had a problem. "I don't know," said the show's creator, Mike Judge, in a voice hauntingly close to Butt-head's (Judge does the voices for most of the characters). The staff was watching an unfinished episode in which Bill Clinton visits Beavis and Butt-head's high school, and something just didn't feel real. As MTV political reporter Tabitha Soren introduced the president to the assembly on screen, Judge's face just lost its air. "Do you really think she could hear [Butt-head] fart from across the gym?" he asked. It was a pressing question; the show was set to air in less than a week. The staff was hushed. Finally someone offered, "If it was a big one she could." Judge considered. "No way."

The fast success of the show, along with the rapid production pace, has been a shock to Judge. Since he moved to New York from Dallas in February, he says, he hasn't met anyone except the people he works with. His office at MTV is spare, the walls empty except for a few

6. Battle for Your Brain

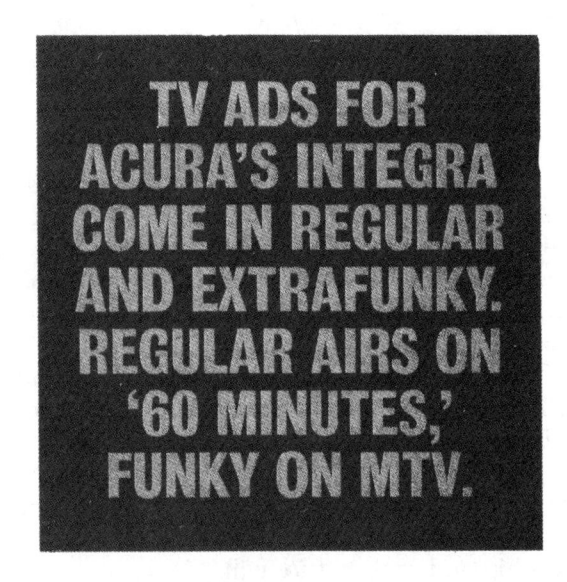

> **TV ADS FOR ACURA'S INTEGRA COME IN REGULAR AND EXTRAFUNKY. REGULAR AIRS ON '60 MINUTES,' FUNKY ON MTV.**

pictures of Beavis and Butt-head and a snapshot of his daughter, Julia, almost 2. In his locker is a stuffed Barney dinosaur, a bottle of Jack Daniel's and a Gap jacket. "You know what's weird?" he says, with a gentle Southwestern accent. "Every now and then I'll say, 'Well, that's pretty cool,' and I can't tell if that's something I would have said before or if I'm doing Butt-head." In a file on his desk, he keeps a drawing of a black Beavis and Butt-head, renamed Rufus and Tyrone. At the moment he has no plans for them. For all their anti-P.C. offensiveness, Beavis and Butt-head have yet to cross the line into race humor. "Actually," says Kimson Albert, 22, one of four African-American artists on the show's staff, "the creator and producer are the most P.C. people."

Judge grew up in Albuquerque, N.M., by his own description "just the most awkward, miserable kid around." He played trumpet in the area youth symphony and competed on the swim team and made honor roll at St. Pius X High School. For kicks, he and his friends used to set fires, just to see how many they could keep going at once and still be able to stomp them out. Three years ago, after working at a couple of unhappy engineering jobs, Judge bought himself a $200 animation kit. His first short, "Office Space," aired on last month's season première of "Saturday Night Live." His third, completed in January 1992, introduced the characters Beavis and Butt-head. It was about torturing animals. He called it "Frog Baseball."

"I was a total animal lover," he says. "When I did the storyboard, I didn't want people to see what I was working on. I thought, 'I don't want to show this to anybody; why am I doing this?'" Even now Judge looks back on "Frog Baseball" with mixed feelings: "I never thought that's what I'd be known for."

Gwen Lipsky, 34, is MTV's vice president of research and planning. When she tested "Beavis and Butt-head" before a target audience last October, she noticed something peculiar. "The focus group was both riveted and hysterical from the moment they saw it. After the tape was over, they kept asking to see again. Then, after they had seen it again, several people offered to buy it from me." Almost without exception, she says, the group members said Beavis and Butt-head reminded them of people they knew. "Interestingly, the people in the focus group who seem the most like Beavis and Butt-head themselves never acknowledge that the characters are them."

Susan Smith-Pinelo, 24, knows them well. A graduate of Oberlin, she is an artist working at what "Generation X" writer Douglas Coupland calls a McJob, as a receptionist at the Sierra Legal Defense Fund. "People laugh at Beavis and Butt-head, Wayne and Garth," she says. "Our generation can relate to this lunatic fringe of teenagers who have fallen out of society, live in a world of TV . . . It's kind of sick, but we like to laugh at them and say, 'I'm not a loser'."

Dick Zimmermann is not a twentysomething and is not amused. A retired broadcasting executive from Larkspur, Calif., Zimmermann, 44, won a state lottery worth nearly $10 million in 1988. Early last summer, while channel surfing, he caught Beavis and Butt-head in the infamous cat episode—touchy ground for anyone involved with the show. Even today it makes Judge uneasy. "They never did this thing with the cat," he says, defensively. "They just made a joke about it: what if you put a firecracker in Stuart's cat's butt." Five days after the show ran, when a cat was found killed by a firecracker in nearby Santa Cruz, Zimmermann put up a $5,000 reward and went to the press. The cause of death, he told Larkspur's Inde-

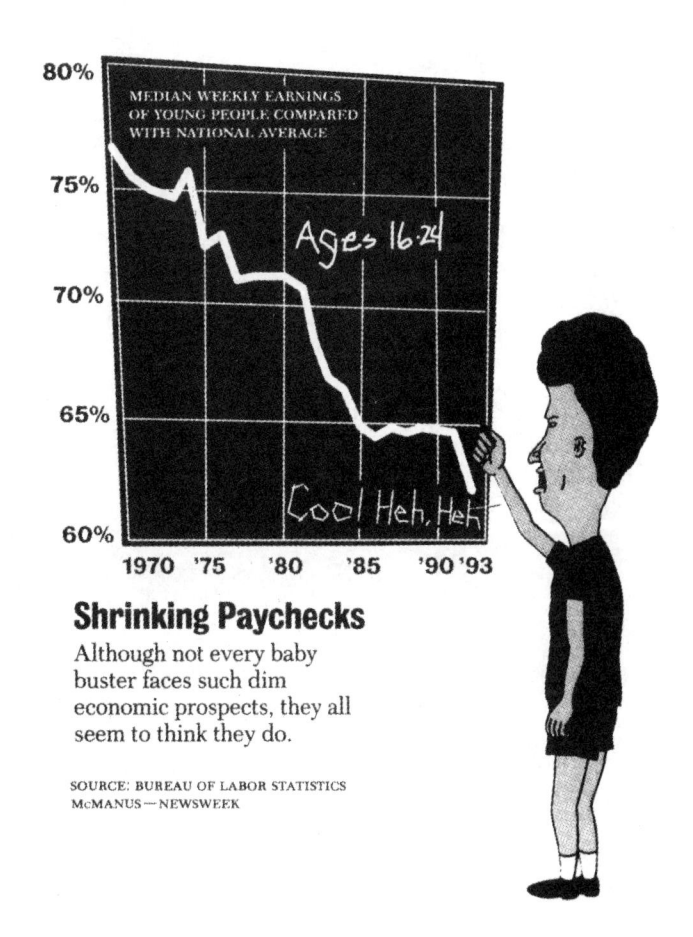

Shrinking Paychecks
Although not every baby buster faces such dim economic prospects, they all seem to think they do.

SOURCE: BUREAU OF LABOR STATISTICS
McMANUS—NEWSWEEK

1. LIVING WITH MEDIA

pendent Journal in a front-page story, was "Beavis and Butt-head." Opening a hot line, he mounted a one-man campaign against the program. "I admit that shows like 'Cops' are obviously very violent," he told NEWSWEEK, "but at least there is the element of good triumphing over evil. The thing about 'Beavis and Butt-head' that caught my eye was the total lack of redeemability. [They] engage in arson, petty theft, shoplifting, auto theft, credit-card fraud, cruelty to animals and insects—not to mention their attitude toward women."

The infamous cat episode will never air again. Three other episodes are also out of circulation, and the show has softened considerably this season. All involved are particularly sensitive because the show runs in family hours: at 7 and 11 p.m. weekdays, and in the afternoon on Saturdays. "The sniffing-paint-thinner we probably shouldn't have done," Judge concedes. "But I'm new to this. I thought of this show as going on at 11, no one's ever going to see it. I think it should run once at 11. We have toned it down."

Gwen Lipsky contends that young kids don't watch the show, that 90 percent of the audience is over 12. But part of the show's appeal is that, yes, these are dangerous, irresponsible messages. "They'll do stuff that we want to do but don't have the guts to do," says, Alex Chriss, 14, who dropped his karate classes to watch Beavis and Butt-head. "On one episode they stole a monster truck and ran over a hippie guy singing save-the-earth songs. We go around mimicking them—not what they say, but how they say it."

Of course, such mimicry is not always harmless, and it is here that we probably need some parental caution. Beavis and Butt-head don't have it; confronted with an image of a nuclear family at the table, Butt-head asks, "Why's that guy eating dinner with those old people?" But other children do. Bill Clinton likes to watch "American Gladiators" with Chelsea; they enjoy the camp value together. And there are lessons to be learned, even from television that prides itself on not doling out lessons. "The whole point of [Beavis and Butt-head] is that they don't grow up," says Lisa Bourgeault, an eighth grader at Marblehead Middle School in Marblehead, Mass. "That's what's hip and cool. But *we* will."

Let's hope so. As our former vice president once put it, with an eloquence few scripted TV characters could match, "What a waste it is to lose one's mind, or not to have a mind." To which, like Beavis and Butt-head, we can only reply, "Huh-huh. Huh-huh. Cool."

With CAREY MONSERRATE *and* DANZY SENNA *in New York,* CARL HOLCOMBE *in San Francisco,* TIM PRYOR *and* MARK MILLER *in Los Angeles and bureau reports*

CHIPS AHOY

As a new study warns that violence saturates the airwaves, a technological quick fix promises to help. But will the V chip really protect our children?

Richard Zoglin

On NBC's *Law & Order* last week, a white racist set off a bomb that killed 20 people on a New York City subway train. Tori Spelling, in the CBS movie *Co-Ed Call Girl,* grabbed a gun and shot a sleazy pimp. Batman (the cartoon character) was almost thrown into a vat of flames by the Penguin. Lemuel Gulliver (the Ted Danson character) battled gigantic bees in the land of Brobdingnag. And Nick Nolte and Eddie Murphy slapped around bad guys in the umpteenth cable showing of *48 HRS.*

It was, in other words, a pretty typical week of TV in the mid-'90s America. Another week, in the view of troubled parents and concerned politicians, in which TV continued to assault youngsters with violent images, encouraging aggressive behavior in a culture where handguns and street violence are rampant. But it was also a landmark week that brought new hope to many parents worried that scenes like the above are doing untold damage to their kids.

As President Clinton signed into law the sweeping telecommunications bill passed by Congress, he officially launched the era of the V chip. A little device that will be required equipment in most new TV sets within two years, the V chip allows parents to automatically block out programs that have been labeled (by whom remains to be seen) as high in violence, sex or other objectionable material. Last week also saw the release of a weighty academic study that said, in effect, it's about time. Financed by the cable industry and conducted by four universities, the study concluded that violence on TV is more prevalent and more pernicious than most people had imagined. Of nearly 2,700 shows analyzed in a 20-week survey of 23 channels, more than half—57%—were said to contain at least some violence. And much of it was the kind that, according to the study, can desensitize kids and encourage imitation: violence divorced from the bad consequences it has in real life.

The study drew an outcry from network executives, who argued, with some justification, that they have reduced the amount of violence they air and have added warning labels for the little that remains. Indeed, a UCLA study (financed by the networks) last year found "promising signs" that levels of network violence are declining. And upon closer scrutiny, the new study's methodology does seem to overstate the case a bit. Nevertheless, it pins some hard numbers on a problem that is popping up increasingly in the public forum: What effect is TV violence having on kids? And what should we do about it?

Politicians of all stripes have jumped in. Democratic Senator Paul Simon has held well-publicized hearings on TV violence and first proposed that networks sponsor independent audits like last week's report. Bob Dole last year called for action against violence on TV as well as in movies and rock music. Democratic Senator Joseph Lieberman of Connecticut last week joined the conservative Media Research Center in urging the networks to clean up the so-called family hour, the first hour of prime time each evening. President Clinton and Vice President Gore have both embraced the V Chip and called for a summit meeting on TV violence with top network and cable executives at the end of February. The antinetwork rhetoric from many reformers sounds strikingly like that directed against another industry charged with making a harmful product. "The TV industry has to be socially responsible," says Harvard child psychiatrist Dr. Robert Coles. "We're now going after the tobacco companies and saying, 'Don't poison people.' It seems to me, the minds of children are being poisoned all the time by the networks. I don't think it's a false analogy."

The analogy depends, of course, on accepting the proposition that TV has a harmful effect on young viewers. Researchers have been sparring over that question for years, but the debate seems to have swung in favor of the antiviolence forces. The study released last week did no original research on the effect TV violence has on children's behavior. But it summarized a growing body of research and concluded that the link between TV violence and aggressive behavior is no longer in doubt.

Even if true, the exact nature and extent of that link is unclear. Is the effect of watching TV violence brief or lasting? Is TV as important a factor in fostering societal violence as economic poverty, bad schools and broken homes? And in any event, is it really possible—or desirable—to manage kids' exposure to a cultural environment that can never be entirely beneficial or benign? From gangster movies in the '30s to horror comics and rock 'n' roll in the '50s, pop culture has always been strewn with pitfalls for youngsters. Sheltering kids from such things is largely futile; most seem to survive in spite of it.

The current wave of concern about TV violence seems oddly timed. The violent action shows that flourished on TV a decade or so ago—*The A-Team; Magnum, P.I.; Miami Vice*—have largely disappeared. The few crime shows left are cerebral dramas like *Law & Order* and *NYPD Blue,* which, though grittier than the older shows, have little overt violence. The sniggering sex talk on network sitcoms is a far more alarming trend. But even if there are some shows that young kids should be shielded from, the question is whether all TV should be held to the standard of safe-for-children. If TV were to be scrubbed clean for kids, it would be a pretty barren place for adults.

The V chip offers what appears to be an easy solution to this problem. Rather than removing or trying to tone down objectionable shows, it enables parents simply to keep them out of kids' reach. The current V-chip technology, developed by a Canadian engineer named Tim Collings, is essentially a computer chip that, when installed

1. LIVING WITH MEDIA

in TV sets (added cost: as little as $1), can receive encoded information about each show. Parents can then program the TV set to block out shows that have been coded to indicate, say, high levels of violence. If, after the kids have gone to bed, parents want to watch Tori Spelling on a shooting spree, they can reverse the blocking by pushing one or more buttons.

The V chip will be welcomed by many parents who despair of monitoring the multitude of TV programs available to their kids. The device has already been a godsend for politicians—a way of seeming to take action on TV violence while avoiding sticky issues of censorship or government control. Most children's activists welcome the device, yet recognize it is not a panacea. "The V chip doesn't do anything to decrease violence," says Arnold Fege of the National Parent-Teacher Association. "There are parents who are not going to use it at all. But it does give parents some control."

Widespread use of the V chip is probably years off. New TV sets are not required to have them for at least two years (legal challenges from the networks are expected to extend that further), and there are still all those chipless RCAs and Sonys currently in people's living rooms. Every set in the house would have to have the V chip, or else kids could just go into the bedroom to watch forbidden shows. Some critics warn, moreover, that it's only a matter of time before kids learn how to break the code and counteract the blocking mechanism.

The trickiest problem of all is, Who will rate the shows, and how they will be rated? The telecommunications bill encourages the networks to devise their own rating system; if they haven't done so in a year, the FCC is empowered to set up a panel for creating one. One possible system is currently being tested in Canada. Programs are given a rating of from 0 to 5 in each of three categories: violence, sex and profanity. By setting their V-chip dial to numbers of their choice, parents can block out all shows with higher than that level of offensive material.

Some V-chip critics see the centralized rating concept as too rigid. They support instead one of several devices currently in development that enable parents to make their own choices of which shows to block out. FCC chairman Reed Hundt, a V-chip booster, contends that it will be only "the first of a slew of products. I predict remote-control devices with selection programs. There will be a variety of ways to receive TV."

Broadcasters, for their part, object that a ratings system mandated by the government threatens their free-speech rights. "A centralized rating system that is subject to review and approval by the government is totally inconsistent with the traditions of this country," says NBC general counsel Richard Cotton. "This legislation turns the FCC into Big Brother." Former CBS Broadcast Group president Howard Stringer argues, "The V chip is the thin end of a wedge. If you start putting chips in the television set to exclude things, it becomes an all-purpose hidden censor."

The rhetoric may invoke the First Amendment, but the networks' more pressing concern is the bottom line. The V chip will, inevitably, reduce the potential audience for shows marked with the scarlet letter. That means advertising revenue will go down. What's more, a violence label may scare off many advertisers and thus cause programmers to steer clear of provocative shows. "The thing nobody is taking into account," says *Law & Order* creator Dick Wolf, "is that there's going to be a V-chip warning on *Homicide, NYPD Blue, Law & Order, ER, Chicago Hope*—any of the adult dramas that deal with real-life substantive issues. Once that happens, you are going to have a television landscape that's far, far different from what you have today."

There is another possible scenario. If the networks and advertisers learn to live with a V rating, producers might find themselves liberated—able to produce even more adult fare, secure in the knowl-

---

So What's On in Tokyo?

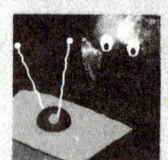

IS THE REST OF THE WORLD AS CONCERNED about sex and violence on TV as America? Channel surf elsewhere and U.S. television begins to seem as though it were run by so many Roman Catholic schoolgirls. In Japan—where TV programming is virtually unregulated and concerns about media amorality are scant—prime-time TV is a mixed menu of soft-core porn, bloodletting drama and violent animation. Log some viewing time in Brazil, and you will find erotic soaps and specials featuring naked women dancing the samba in heels and sparkling body paint. This kind of spectacle could just as easily turn up on European TV, where nudity, sex and tastelessness are also unavoidable. Consider *The Word*, a lewd late-night variety show that aired on Britain's Channel 4 for five years and once depicted a viewer eating other peoples' scabs. (Don't tell Ricki Lake.)

So where do foreign broadcasters draw the line? In Britain, where programming is regulated by the TV industry and the government, shows considered unfriendly to families are prohibited from airing before 10 p.m. Similar rules apply throughout Europe. Definitions of unsuitable fare are so vague, however, that networks often run what turns out to be objectionable programming and pay the penalties later. The Independent Television Commission, one of various monitoring groups in Britain, recently fined MTV Europe $90,000, in part for running explicit sex-themed talk shows in the morning and early evening. In France a government-operated FCC equivalent known as the CSA fined two French networks a total of $2 million in 1989 for airing violent movies during prime-time hours.

Efforts to curtail indecency have been far more efficient in Germany. Starting in 1993 the country's leading TV manufacturer voluntarily included V chips in new sets. The chip can automatically block out movies that the German film-industry board has deemed unacceptable for young audiences. The chip also filters out all TV shows—including soft-core porn—that individual stations decide are potentially inappropriate. The FSF, a TV industry watchdog group, frequently guides networks in scheduling. In December 1994 it convinced the RTL network to run the *Mighty Morphin Power Rangers* on a weekly rather than daily basis, following public outcries that the show preached combativeness.

In Canada, where concerns about violence on TV have been mounting as clamorously as they have in the U.S., broadcasters air expurgated versions of the *Power Rangers*. Canada is also experimenting with V-chip technology in several cities. This week a third round of tests will begin in about 400 homes where encoded programming will allow parents to selectively block out material rated on a scale of 0 to 5 for offensiveness. So far the V chip has sparked few objections in Canada. By mid-March the government is expected to decide whether or not to enact it as law.
—*By Ginia Bellafante, with bureau reports*

edge that children will be shielded from it. Which could, of course, lead either to more sophisticated adult fare or sleazier entertainment. Says Wolf: "If all these shows have warnings on them, you could have a situation where producers are saying to standards people at the networks, 'I've got a warning. I can say whatever I want. I can kill as many people as I want.'"

THEY'RE ALREADY KILLING A LOT, if the National Television Violence Study is to be believed. Billed as the "most thorough scientific survey of violence on television ever undertaken," the study not only found a surprisingly high percentage of violent shows; it also made some damning observations about the way violence is presented. According to the survey, 47% of the violent acts shown resulted in no observable harm to the victim; only 16% of violent shows contained a message about the long-term negative repercussions of violence; and in a whopping 73% of all violent scenes, the perpetrator went unpunished. These figures, however, were based on some overly strict guidelines: perpetrators of violence, for example, must be punished in *the same scene* as the violent act. By that measure, most of Shakespeare's tragedies would be frowned on; Macbeth, after all, doesn't get his comeuppance until the end of the play.

The study found significant variations in the amount of violence across the dial. On network stations, 44% of the shows contained at least some violence, vs. 59% on basic cable and 85% on premium channels like HBO and Showtime. Yet it was the broadcast networks that squawked the loudest. "Someone would have to have a lobotomy to believe that 44% of the programs on network television are violent," exclaims Don Ohlmeyer, NBC West Coast president. (Actually, the study referred to network stations, meaning that syndicated shows like *Hard Copy* were also included.) "Since I've been here, I can't think of a program we've had that's glorified violence, that hasn't shown the pain of violence and attempted to show there are other ways to resolve conflicts."

The researchers' definition of violence did, at least, avoid some of the absurdities of previous studies, in which every comic pratfall was counted. Violent acts were defined as those physical acts intended to cause harm to another; also included were verbal threats of physical harm as well as scenes showing the aftermath of violence. Thus, finding a body in a pool of blood on *NYPD Blue* counts as a violent act; Kramer bumping into a door on *Seinfeld* does not. A cartoon character whacking another with a mallet counts; but the accidental buffoonery of *America's Funniest Home Videos* doesn't.

Yet just one of these acts was enough to classify a program as violent. In addition, the survey covered a number of cable channels—among them USA, AMC, TNT, HBO and Showtime—whose schedules are filled with network reruns (including many action shows like *Starsky and Hutch* and *Kung Fu)* or theatrical films. This served to boost the overall totals of violent shows while masking the fact that violence in the most watched time periods—network prime time—has declined.

"We didn't want to get into a show-by-show debate," says Ed Donnerstein, communications and psychology professor at the University of California at Santa Barbara, where most of the monitoring was done. "We didn't want to point fingers." George Gerbner, former dean of the University of Pennsylvania's Annenberg School for Communication and a longtime chronicler of TV violence, agrees with the study's big-picture approach. "Anytime you give a name of a program, it lends itself to endless quibbling," he says. "The question is not what any one program does or doesn't do. The question is, What is it that large communities absorb over long periods of time?"

Whatever its defects, the study could have a major impact as development of the V chip begins. "This is the foundation of any rating system that will be developed," says Representative Edward Markey of Massachusetts, the V chip's original champion in Congress. The irony is that some of the most objectionable shows, in the survey's view, are cartoons and other children's shows: they are the ones that portray violence "unrealistically," without consequences or punishment. "When you show a young kid somebody being run over and they pop back up without harm, that's a problem," says Donnerstein. Maybe so, but a kid who grows up without Batman or Bugs Bunny misses something else: a chance to engage in playful fantasy. And the V chip can't make up for that.

—*Reported by Hannah Bloch/Washington, Georgia Harbison and William Tynan/New York and Jeffrey Ressner/Los Angeles*

Information and Influence

With the advent of television, media scholar Marshall McLuhan predicted the coming of a "global village" in which communication media would transcend the boundaries of nations: "Ours is a world of allatoneness. 'Time' has ceased, 'space' has vanished. We now live in . . . a simultaneous happening." In naming CNN founder Ted Turner its 1991 Man of the Year, *Time* noted that, a generation later, CNN had begun to make McLuhan's prophecy come to pass. The availability of a worldwide, 24-hour news network has changed news from something that *has happened* to something that *is happening*. As president, George Bush was quoted as having said to other world leaders, "I learn more from CNN than I do from the CIA."

The reporting of news and information was not, in the beginning, considered an important function within media organizations. The first "newspapers" focused more on political advocacy and editorializing than on attempting to provide a comprehensive or objective overview of newsworthy events. Television news was originally limited to 15-minute commercial-free broadcasts presented as a public service. Over the years, however, the news business has become big business. Television news operations are intensely competitive, locked in head-to-head popularity races in which the loss of one ratings point can translate into a loss of $10 million in advertising revenue.

Perceptions of news sources vary among consumer groups. According to a recent Harris Poll, college graduates overwhelmingly rate newspapers as being more accurate and providing more complete news coverage than television. However, 47 percent of adult Americans pick television news as providing greater variety and completeness of coverage, and the share of consumers who rely on television for news has grown steadily for three decades.

The first article in this section addresses the issue of public response to news media. In "Tuning Out the News," Howard Kurtz notes that, despite the growing number of news sources and the around-the-clock availability of news information, many adults report that they are too busy to follow the news, or are suspicious of the media, or find the news too depressing. Kurtz's commentary reflects Arthur Hailey's observation in his novel *The Evening News*: "People watch the news to find out the answers to three questions, Is the world safe? Are my home and family safe? and, Did anything happen today that was interesting?" Given cursory answers to those questions, viewers are satisfied that they are "keeping up," although the total amount of news delivered in a half-hour newscast would, if set in type, hardly fill the front page of a daily newspaper.

The second and third articles in this section address the issues of news selection and spin. Media expert Wilbur Schramm has noted that "hardly anything about communication is so impressive as the enormous number of choices and discards and interpretations that have to be made between [an] actual news event and the symbols that later appear in the mind of a reporter, an editor, a reader, a listener, or a viewer. Therefore, even if everyone does his job perfectly, it is hard enough to get the report of an event straight and clear and true." Schramm's comments point to the tremendous impact of selectivity in crafting news messages. What gets into the media and what does not are influenced by choices made by individuals with personal opinions, causes, and biases. The process of making these decisions is called gatekeeping.

Gatekeeping is necessary. News operations cannot logistically cover or report every event that happens in the world from one edition or broadcast to the next. The concerns associated with the reality of gatekeeping relate to whether or not the gatekeepers abuse the privilege of deciding what information or viewpoints the mass audience receives. Simply being selected for media coverage lends an issue, an event, or an individual a certain degree of celebrity—the "masser" the medium, the greater the effect. Thus, the privilege of choice grants considerable power. Some contend that there is a sensationalist bias in news coverage, a criticism to which some news organizations are responding (see "Should the Coverage Fit the Crime?"). Others worry that media ownership megadeals pose a major challenge to providing objective coverage of parent companies and their pet issues. The reports "All in the Family" and "CBS, *60 Minutes*, and the Unseen Interview" address this issue.

The remaining articles in this section explore the changing landscape of contemporary news and information coverage. News, by definition, is timely: It is "news," not "olds." Decisions regarding what stories to play and how to play them are made under tight deadlines. Satellite broadcasting, lightweight electronic field equipment, computer-generated graphics, and sophisticated access to archive information have dramatically decreased the time required to access, package, and disseminate news. Reporters and editors have less time to investigate, reflect, and evaluate. News media are under enormous pressure to fill time and space with quality visuals under tightened budgets. The competitive nature of news media values gatekeeping choices that attract audiences.

Within this climate, the use of news pieces produced by public relations firms and made available to television stations and networks by satellite feed becomes increasingly attractive. Video news releases (VNRs) are fully pack-

UNIT 2

aged audiovisual story clips; B-rolls are voiceless video clips that can be played behind a voiceover from the local news reporters. These prepackaged stories are frequently well made and may have clear news value; however, they generally include an editorial slant, an element often lost on the average viewer. In "VNRs: News or Advertising?" Robert Charles discusses the pros and cons of VNR use and recommends that news consumers must learn the difference between editorial and straight news copy to maintain a "healthy skepticism" that separates information from influence.

The issue of VNRs is raised again in "A Medical Breakthrough," along with other challenges of covering health and medical issues. With intense efforts of medical associations and research groups to maintain a competitive edge, it can be difficult for medical reporters to evaluate the objectivity of newsworthy information. Further, the attraction of playing up the human interest element of health and medical stories frequently stretches the boundaries of objective reporting. Another example of the blurring of traditional canons of news objectivity is the fast-growing movement toward public journalism, also known as public service journalism, civic journalism, or community-assisted reporting. Alicia Shepard discusses this trend in "The Gospel of Public Journalism," explaining the positions of both its advocates and its critics.

Linda Fibich, in "Under Siege," addresses perceptions of public contempt for mainstream media and offers responses from news media insiders (such as "It is the hot issues of our times that stir most of the criticism. The messenger covering those issues draws the attention and the apparent hostility" and "The public is skeptical of all big institutions, the media included. And I think that's healthy").

Looking Ahead: Challenge Questions

To what extent does Howard Kurtz's profile of people "tuning out the news" reflect your experiences? Discuss whether or not disinterest in news is the media's fault. To what extent should making news more interesting/appealing be a priority of news media?

What are some implications of the tendency for news organizations to blur the line between information and influence? What is your opinion of the use of VNRs? Of public journalism?

Try to watch newscasts on two different networks on the same evening (perhaps one in the early evening and one in the late evening). Record the stories covered, in the order in which they are reported, and the time devoted to each. Did you notice any patterns in the reporting? Were there any differences in the way stories on the same topic were presented? Did you note any instances in which editorial or entertainment values were reflected in story selection or coverage? What conclusions do you draw from your findings?

Tuning Out the News

The media deluge is simply washing over much of the public

Howard Kurtz

Howard Kurtz, Washington Post Staff Writer

LUTHERVILLE, MD. Elizabeth Yarbrough, a school cafeteria worker here, hadn't heard that Republicans in Congress wanted to end the federal school lunch program and turn it over to the state. She doesn't know the name of her congressman. And she's "not real familiar" with the "Contract With America," which Republicans made the centerpiece of the first 100 days they controlled the House. She watches some television news and listens to Howard Stern, but buys the Baltimore Sun only on Sundays, for the want ads.

"I unfortunately don't pay much attention," says Yarbrough, 35. "I haven't seen any improvement of anything in this country for so long. It doesn't really matter who's in power. The little guy is just squashed like a bug."

It seems, on the surface, like a paradox. At a time when there are more media outlets providing more news and information that ever before, why is so little of it getting through to a sizable segment of the population?

The plain fact is that much of the American public has simply tuned out the news—that is, the kind of traditional news, heavily laden with politicians and official proceedings, routinely covered by the mainstream press. These people see journalists as messengers from a world that doesn't much interest them.

Some of the reasons for this disconnect emerged in a recent series of conversations here in the Baltimore suburbs. Some people say they are simply too busy with work and family to follow the news. Others are rather suspicious of the media. Still others see a depressing sameness to the drumbeat of headlines.

"If they'd put more happy stories in the news, I'd read it more," says Rhonda Burris, 28, a clerk for the Baltimore welfare department who cleans offices at night. "It's usually someone got killed, someone's baby feel out the window. I don't want to hear it."

Jean Langston, 44, an insurance claims examiner who often works a second job until midnight, is too busy to bother with newspapers. "I've bought papers and carried them around for three or four days and never gotten to it," she says.

Len Pross, 48, a letter carrier who likes talk radio, finds most news organizations slanted. "Too many news people want to be Rush Limbaughs," he says. "The news is chopped up into bits and pieces. You don't get a whole story."

Norman Brown, 51, a furniture salesman, says he is too busy for daily news reports—but he makes time for such programs as "The Oprah Winfrey Show" and "Geraldo!" "They have interesting topics, daughters running around with their mother's boyfriend. "It's entertaining," he says.

Some of this lack of interest may stem from the way that media organizations define and package the news, news that many people find irrelevant to their daily lives. Some of it may involve a new generation of well-educated, well-compensated journalists who identify more with society's elite than with working-class Americans.

But much of it has to do with a growing sense of alienation from the political system, and the belief that the major media are an integral part of that system. Some of those interviewed say they are not angry at the press, but disgusted with what the press, in their eyes, represents.

"A vicious circle may be at work: cynical coverage tailored to a cynical public, which makes the public more cynical and begets more cynical coverage," Paul Starobin of the National Journal wrote in Columbia Journalism Review.

All this has contributed to a striking degree of ignorance about national affairs. According to recent polls for various new organizations:

- Only half of those surveyed could name Newt Gingrich as the speaker of the House, although 64 percent knew that Judge Lance Ito is presiding over the O. J. Simpson trial.
- Just four in 10 are familiar with the Republicans' "Contract With America," despite an avalanche of publicity since the 1994 campaign.
- Only half know that Congress approved the North American Free Trade Agreement, one of the biggest political battles of the Clinton presidency.

8. Tuning Out the News

- Only 24 percent said Congress has cut the federal budget deficit by billions of dollars; nearly half said it had not. Since Clinton took office the deficit has declined by nearly $100 billion.
- Just one in three said Congress had raised taxes on the very rich; half said it had not. The Clinton economic package raised income taxes on the wealthiest 1 percent of taxpayers.

Political strategists, whose job is to break through the media static, say news reports are competing for attention with the likes of "Roseanne," "Hard Copy" and "Cops," which apparently resonate more with some viewers than Dan Rather, Tom Brokaw and Peter Jennings, the main networks' nightly news anchors.

"The problem with the 'Contract With America' is there's no visual," says Frank Luntz, the Republican pollster who helped shape the contract. "There's no blood, no guns going off, no policemen knocking down people's doors. There's nothing to make people look up and stamp it on their brain."

Many analysts say the media, with their emphasis on conflict, convey more heat than light about public issues. They say too many journalists cover public affairs as an insider's game in which all politicians are assumed to be scheming and devious.

Others see the press as a willing conveyor belt for propaganda. "There's a lot of misinformation in political campaigns that gets quoted in the press without the press providing a refereeing function," says Kathleen Hall Jamieson, dean of the Annenberg School of Communications at the University of Pennsylvania. "The he-said-she-said style of journalism minimizes the likelihood the public will know whether he or she is telling the truth."

On issue after issue, news stories—such as those reporting that Clinton raised income taxes on the wealthy—seem to have little impact. A Wall Street Journal poll last year found that 43 percent expected to pay more in income taxes. Even among those making less than $20,000—a group whose taxes were cut—26 percent expected to pay more.

"There was a largely knee-jerk response that whenever government does something, I'm going to end up paying the bill," says Stanley Greenberg, Clinton's pollster.

When it comes to news, the country is split along demographic lines. Those who are vitally interested in the sort of news carried by the Baltimore Sun or other papers are older, more affluent and better educated.

According to a survey by the University of Chicago's National Opinion Research Center, only a third of those under 30 read a newspaper every day, compared to three-quarters of those over 65. Less than half of those without a high school diploma read a paper every day, compared to more than two-thirds of those who have attended graduate school. Regular readers include fewer than four in 10 of those earning $15,000 to $20,000 a year, but seven in 10 of those earning more than $60,000.

Newer forms of media are filling the vacuum. Many people who don't bother with newspapers listen to talk radio or watch daytime talk shows or tabloid television. These programs deal in a more emotionally charged way than the mainstream press with such issues as sex, race, welfare and affirmative action.

The Washington Post recently asked a research firm to select a dozen Baltimore-area residents who do not read a newspaper every day and are interested in talk radio or daytime talk shows. These people, none of whom has a college degree, seemed distinctly uninterested in the Republican revolution on Capitol Hill. Although the Contract With America has received an avalanche of news coverage, most knew nothing about it.

Clarence Lowery, 65, a retired asbestos worker, cannot name any provision in the contract but nonetheless dismisses it as "politician lies. They always say they're gonna do something and they can't."

Rhonda Burris, the city clerk, knows only that the Republicans are "trying to cut this and cut that. . . . It doesn't seem like they can do anything for me. They just talk."

Melissa Sharrow, 32, a sales representative, thinks the contract involves trading with other countries. "I don't pay much attention [to politics] because it upsets me," she says.

Clearly, the daily clamor of charges and countercharges between the White House and Congress is but a faint echo by the time it penetrates the lives of many Americans.

Over dinner one recent evening, four Baltimore County residents said they were unaware of the recent congressional battle over term limits, or that the House had voted on it the previous month. "That's one of the things Newt won't bring up now because he wants to keep his job," says Len Pross, the letter carrier.

Still, some news manages to permeate pop culture. All those at the dinner know that Gingrich's mother had told CBS's Connie Chung that her son had called Hillary Rodham Clinton "a bitch." And all know that Clinton had said on television that he wears briefs, not boxers.

Elizabeth Yarbrough recalls Gingrich saying on television that "women could not possibly go into battle because they'd get infections in the trenches," as she puts it. But she cannot identify any policy Gingrich advocates.

Many people trust news reports far less than their own experience, or what they have heard from acquaintances and relatives. "I have a friend who works for the government and he says he hardly does anything and he gets a raise every year," says Norman Brown, a furniture salesman.

Yarbrough has two children, and her husband is unemployed after working 15 years for a bakery equipment company that moved to Florida. About stories she reads on an improving economy, Yarbrough says, "I don't believe that. I go to the grocery store and see the price of everything going up. My husband calls these places, there's no contracts, no jobs."

Several people suggest that journalists and policians do not understand the welfare issue. Jean Langston, the claims examiner, says her sister, a school secretary with four children, had to go on welfare temporarily after losing her job. "They don't know about these situations," Langston says.

Many people tend to remember colorful news reports that confirm what they already believe. Pross, a Christian activist who is educating his 11-year-old at home, said he heard on the conservative radio show "Focus on the Family" that Hillary

2. INFORMATION AND INFLUENCE

A Great Divide Between the Media and the Public

More than half the public agrees with House Speaker Newt Gingrich of Georgia that the press has been too cynical and negative in covering the new Congress, but eight in 10 national journalists disagree.

Two-thirds of the public believes that President Clinton's character problems have been overplayed by the media, but two-thirds of national journalists reject such criticism.

More than half the public says homosexuality should be discouraged, but eight in 10 journalists believe it should be accepted.

These are among the findings of a survey of 515 journalists and 2,000 others made public by the Times Mirror Center for the People and the Press. The study depicts a yawning gap between the way journalists and their customers view politics, social issues and the news business.

"There appears to be a cultural divide that the press itself acknowledges," says Andrew Kohut, the center's director. "The public is saying the national media is part of the problem. They identify more of the 'gotcha' journalism and out-of-control journalism with national news organizations."

Many reporters and news executives are sharply critical of their profession. Half the journalists surveyed say the media haven't adequately covered the potential consequences of the "Contract With America," the GOP blueprint for the first 100 days of Congress. Three-quarters admit they give too little attention to complex issues.

Two-thirds of national journalists—and more than half of those from local media outlets—say they give short shrift to positive news. More than two-thirds say they are too focused on misdeeds and personal failings of public figures. More than half agree that journalists are too cynical.

Yet they may be less cynical than the people they serve. More than half the national journalists surveyed gave officials in Washington high marks for honesty and integrity, about three times the proportion of non-journalists who say they feel that way. Local journalists were twice as likely as ordinary citizens to have high regard for federal officials.

Times Mirror found a generation gap on this question, with journalists in their thirties—dubbed "the Vietnam-Watergate generation"—the most cynical, followed by those 40 to 55. Journalists over 56 were described as the least cynical.

On other questions, the public delivered a significantly harsher verdict on the media. Only one journalist in 10 sees media sensationalism as a serious matter, but more than two in 10 non-journalists do. "We want to be recognized as serious, high-minded, sophisticated professionals who do important work for the country, but also we want the freedom to peer into rape victims' bedroom windows," one Washington journalist is quoted as saying.

Asked if news coverage has improved, 37 percent of the public said no, 15 percent volunteered negative views and 15 percent did not answer. All told, two out of three members of the public had nothing or nothing good to say about the media.

THESE DIVERGING VIEWS WERE PARTICULARLY APPARENT IN assessing political coverage. Even two-thirds of the Republicans surveyed said the press had made too much of Clinton's character problems. But this coverage is no accident. More than eight in 10 national journalists say they view Clinton's character as weak. And a majority feel that coverage of the administration has been shaped by this perception. Still, nearly half the national journalists concede that they may have undercovered Clinton's achievements.

Though large majorities of the public have said the press is making too much of the Whitewater affair, most of the national journalists surveyed say the scandal has been covered about right. One-third say it has been overcovered, and only 5 percent believe it has been undercovered. By contrast, more than four in 10 talk radio hosts say they want more reporting on Whitewater.

THE GAP BETWEEN JOURNALISTS AND THE PUBLIC MAY BE greatest on cultural issues. Only one in five of the national journalists attend church or synagogue regularly, half the rate of the public. Two-thirds of the public say the personal values of journalists make it difficult for them to understand religion and family values.

Politically, only 5 percent of national journalists describe themselves as conservative, compared to 39 percent of the public. Nearly two-thirds of national journalists called themselves moderates, and 22 percent said they were liberal, slightly more than the general population. The Times Mirror center said liberals were more likely to work at national newspapers, and conservatives in local television.

There were sharply divergent views on which parts of the media do the best job. Members of the public like local television news the best, with more than two-thirds giving it high marks. But national journalists turned up their noses at local TV, which drew good reviews from only 15 percent.

Similarly, more than 90 percent of journalists give high marks to such national newspapers as The New York Times, The Washington Post and the Los Angeles Times, but just over a third of the public does so. Nearly half said they did not know enough to offer an opinion.

Members of Congress, who often receive upbeat coverage from hometown stations, rate local television four times higher than they do network news, according to the survey. However, though two-thirds of the lawmakers praise national newspapers, only one-third like their local papers.

Most journalists pointed the finger of blame elsewhere, with more than eight in 10 giving their own news organizations high marks. Some journalists attribute the media's problems to television news, especially local television, while local TV staff blamed local papers.

"They acknowledge the problem, but it's someone else's problem," Kohut says. "I guess you could interpret that as defensiveness."

—*Howard Kurtz*

8. Tuning Out the News

Clinton is working on a U.N. treaty under which "children's rights could supersede the rights of parents."

Burris says she recalls reading that members of Congress receive free private school scholarships for their children. Yarbrough still talks about a pair of "PrimeTime Live" reports on government waste that are more than two years old.

"They were showing these people who do idiotic things like measure the flow rate of ketchup, making $40,000 to $50,000 a year," she says. "I never realized there were that many unnecessary jobs."

Yarbrough recalls reading in a newspaper that "they were thinking of getting rid of this department where they sit around collecting $80,000-a-year paychecks for doing absolutely nothing." Reminded that as a cafeteria worker she is a government employee, she says: "I'm feeding kids. I'm doing something productive."

Many of these folks grew up reading the Baltimore Sun or Baltimore News American in their parents' homes. But somewhere along the way they lost the habit.

"A newspaper is not something I relish reading," Pross says. "It's much easier to sit in front of the tube and have someone tell you something." Langston says it "just drives me crazy" when front-page stories jump to an inside page.

When she was growing up, Langston says, her father would chew over the news with the egg man and the bread man as they made deliveries to the house. Today, she and others say, they almost never discuss politics with friends or relatives.

Their lives revolve around work, children and church, not news cycles. Burris drives her children to sporting events and dance recitals. For Langston, who cares for her daughter and niece, it's dance practice and choir rehearsal. Brown is single and self-employed. "My job takes up all my time," he says. "I have a tremendous amount of paperwork. I listen to the news, but it goes in one ear and out the other. You hear the Republicans and the Democrats saying the same things."

They get their media fix on the run. Langston keeps an eye on "Good Morning America" or "Today" while getting ready for work, and reads Good Housekeeping on the supermarket line. Pross listens to Rush Limbaugh while delivering the mail. Burris watches "Entertainment Tonight" and reads People because she likes to keep up with the movie stars. Brown reads Time—"I like the pictures"—and Money, and listens to a Baltimore radio host.

They use words like "repetitive" and "monotonous" to describe the news. And they have pet peeves that seem to encapsulate their doubts about the media. Pross says he finds ABC's Sam Donaldson "arrogant" and doesn't like the way he covers the White House, although Donaldson has been off that beat since 1989. Langston objects to the O. J. Simpson trial coverage. "The reporters give their opinions and it's as if he's already guilty," she says. "Because of the experience of black people and the problems we've had, we don't want to say he's guilty until we've seen all the facts."

Pross says he finds Limbaugh entertaining but that "I don't agree with him about everything. I don't like the way he puts down everyone just because they may be a liberal. Of course, that's what sells him. He's puffed up."

In this highly skeptical environment, few had kind words for the president. Burris said it seems like Hillary Clinton is running the White House. Yarbrough says she was excited by Bill Clinton during the 1992 campaign but that the last time he was on television, "I kind of wandered off and said, 'What else is on?'"

Like several of her neighbors, Yarbrough feels slightly guilty about being poorly informed. But, she says, "It's more trouble than it's worth to listen to the news and get your hopes up."

Should the coverage fit the crime?

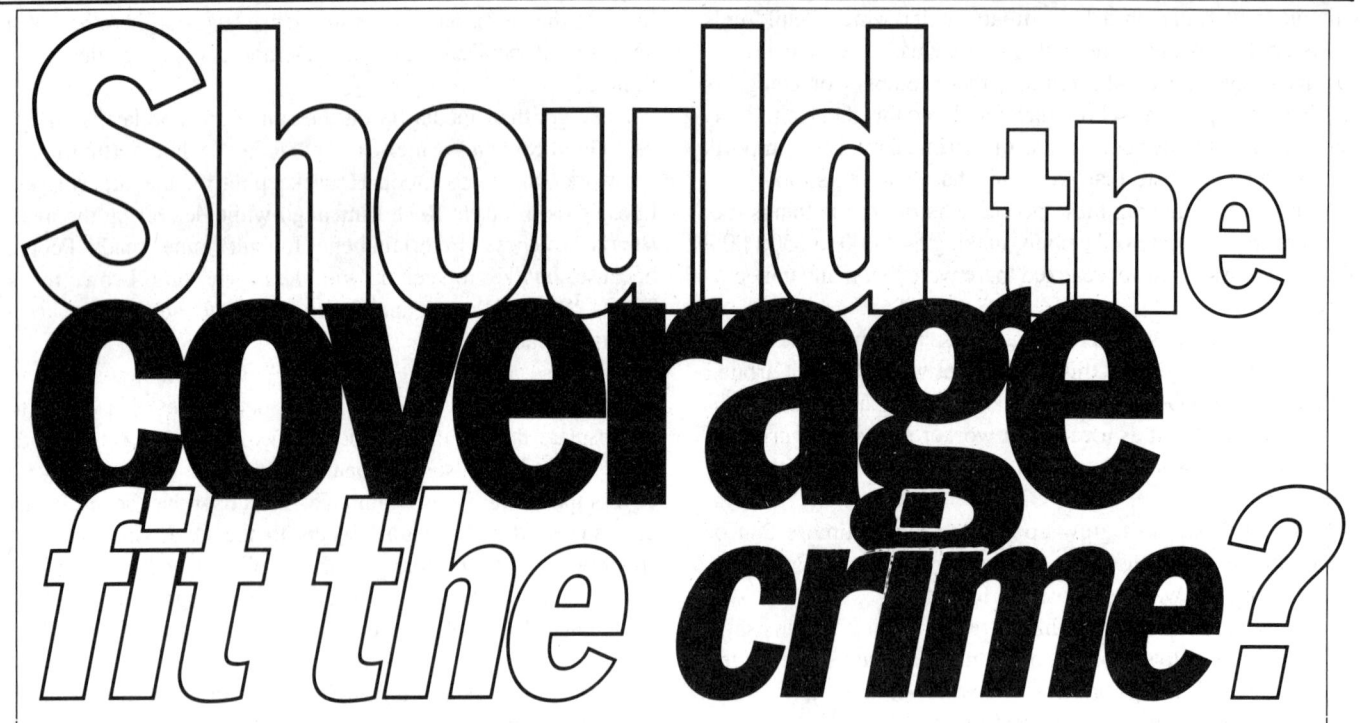

A Texas TV station tries to resist the allure of mayhem

by Joe Holley

It's 10 o'clock and news viewers across the country know where they'll be for the next few minutes: at the scene of the crime.

Crime and violence — what the Denver-based Rocky Mountain Media Watch calls "mayhem" — are as ubiquitous on local news shows as the winsome male-female anchor team and the happy chat between bite-sized bits of coverage. Critics argue that this mayhem not only crowds out more legitimate news but skews reality, that local TV newscasts must share responsibility for the fact that, at a time when crime rates across the country are going down, public anxiety about crime continues to rise.

What if a TV news operation refused to cover crime in the same old way? Would crime still make the same noise in the community? Would the station?

Since the beginning of the year, Austin's ABC affiliate, KVUE-TV, a Gannett station, has been trying to find out. KVUE's experiment not only has given Austin viewers something of a choice, but it has forced the station's staff to reassess long-held assumptions about how to cover crime, or even whether to cover it. It has forced reporters, editors, and news directors to ask that more basic question: What is news?

Partly because violent crime is relatively rare in the city, Austin TV has never been terribly crime-obsessed. But after a complicated network-affiliation swap last year, the local CBS station, re-named K-EYE, hit the market with a bagful of gimmicks, razzle-dazzle graphics, and hyperbole, focusing attention on the way crime gets covered. K-EYE's yen for mayhem may be only slightly more knee-jerk than its competitors', but its approach underscored the public's impression that local TV news thrives on violence and disaster.

Joe Holley is a writer who lives in Austin.

9. Should the Coverage Fit the Crime?

Although K-EYE's ratings remain in single digits nearly a year after the affiliation shuffle, the station has stayed with its format.

It was KVUE, meanwhile, the longtime ratings pacesetter, that decided to try to break its Pavlovian response to the squawking police scanner and the melodramatic visuals.

Now, before a crime story makes it on the air on KVUE, it must meet one or more of five criteria:

1) Does action need to be taken?
2) Is there an immediate threat to safety?
3) Is there a threat to children?
4) Does the crime have significant community impact?
5) Does the story lend itself to a crime-prevention effort?

No sooner were these guidelines installed on January 21 than they were tested by a trio of murder stories. In early February, in the small town of Elgin, thirty miles east of Austin and in the KVUE viewing area, three men shot and killed each other during a Saturday-night brawl. The triple murder failed to make the KVUE newscast.

The station's three competitors aired the story. "When somebody's killed, that's news," says Jeff Godlis, K-EYE's news director. But to Mike George, KVUE's news manager, the incident was unfortunate, but it wasn't news. George points out that a KVUE reporter drove to Elgin twice to investigate. She found that the men, all Mexican nationals, were not permanent Elgin residents, and that the dispute that prompted the shootings was an isolated incident fueled by drugs and alcohol.

"There was no immediate threat to public safety, no threat to children, and there was really no action that you would take, other than to say 'I don't want to go to that part of Elgin,'" says Cathy McFeaters, KVUE's executive producer. "It really wasn't a crime-prevention story, so then the question becomes significant community impact, and the reaction that we got by just asking people about it was that they weren't too concerned." Staff members worried that some might think the reason this story did not air had to do with the nationality of the killers and victims. "We talked about whether it would make a difference if these guys were from Lubbock or New York or wherever," McFeaters says. "It didn't."

The second story, during the third week of the experiment, involved a man who stabbed his wife in the front yard of their home and then barricaded himself inside the house. Some of KVUE's competitors reported live from the scene.

Cathy McFeaters, executive producer

Carole Kneeland, news director

"Being number one revolved around the lowest common denominator, and I got disgusted with it" — Cathy McFeaters

KVUE's reporter on the scene found that the man inside the house was eighty-two years old, could barely walk, and was nearly blind. He had no criminal record and seemed to present no threat to neighbors or to the police. Again, the incident didn't meet the guidelines, and KVUE did not air the story.

The third story took place in a Wal-Mart parking lot, where a twenty-one-year-old man, after an argument inside the store with two teenagers, was shot and killed when he walked outside. Because the perpetrators were at large at the time of the newscast, thus meeting the threat-to-public-safety guideline, and because the shooting happened in a busy Wal-Mart parking lot, the story easily met KVUE's guidelines.

"Austin police need your help today," KVUE anchor Walt Maciborski began. "They are looking for suspects in a murder at a Wal-Mart store. The shooting happened in the parking lot of the store in Northeast Austin last night. . . . Police arrested a sixteen-year-old at his home this morning and charged him with murder. They are looking at store surveillance tape to find other suspects." A seventeen-year-old was later arrested and charged.

McFeaters, KVUE's thirty-one-year-old executive producer, is the catalyst for the crime-coverage experiment. An associate producer at KVUE during and after her college years at the University of Texas at Austin, she then went to the Gannett station in Jacksonville, Florida, and took a job in 1991 as a producer at ABC's WSOC in Charlotte, North Carolina. That ABC affiliate bears the dubious distinction of being the ninth-worst station for excessive "mayhem" out of a hundred that the Rocky Mountain Media Watch group examined last fall. (The top three stations on the "mayhem index" are WLKY-TV, Louisville, Kentucky; KNBC-TV, Los Angeles; and KFOR-TV, Oklahoma City.)

"That was the first time I had worked for a metered market, where you live or die by the daily ratings," McFeaters recalls. "You lead with crime. I always understood the thing about ratings, because I'm a very competitive person, and I love to be first. But being number one revolved around the lowest common denominator, and I got disgusted with it. But how could I argue, because we were doing really well?"

The solution, McFeaters thought, was to leave the business. She reached the nadir, she says, with a story about bestiality;

2. INFORMATION AND INFLUENCE

she'd rather not recall the details. But in plotting her escape from WSOC, she discovered by accident that KVUE had an opening. Her boss there would be Carole Kneeland, a respected broadcast veteran who happened to share McFeaters's concerns about crime coverage.

Kneeland, who is forty-seven, was the capital bureau chief for nearly eleven years for Dallas's WFAA-TV before becoming KVUE's news director in 1989. Like McFeaters, she has long been concerned about what she calls local TV's over-coverage of crime and disaster. For her, a story that KVUE ran last fall seemed to crystallize the issue. A pickup truck swerved off the highway and into the playground of a day care center, killing a child. It was a poignant story, but it happened in California. The story ran in Austin and elsewhere for one reason: the heartbreaking video of the little body lying on the playground.

Not long after that, Kneeland and McFeaters began putting together their crime-coverage concept. The station had been convening monthly community meetings for the previous year, and from those meetings they already knew that the coverage of crime and violence was a persistent viewer complaint.

"We wouldn't even have to ask about it specifically," Kneeland says. "We'd say, 'What do you think about local news coverage?' The first thing they'd always react with was, 'It's too violent. It's too sensational.' Or, 'There's too much crime coverage with no significance.'"

"I remember talking to Carole, and I said, just jokingly, 'I just wonder what would happen if no one covered crime?'" McFeaters recalls. "It wasn't like a mission of mine or anything; it was almost out of spite for Charlotte."

It was also a marketing strategy, she admits. "That is not why we are doing it, but that's certainly a part of it. I felt sure that people would appreciate this and would watch us because of it."

The two women encouraged the news staff to begin analyzing how — and why — the station was covering crime stories. "The reasons [reporters] gave about why something ought to be covered — 'Somebody ought to do something about that!' or 'It affects the community' — gradually became the categories," Kneeland recalls. Informal criteria evolved over a period of three or four months.

The station's general manager, Ardyth Diercks at the time, signed off on the experiment in early December; Kneeland and McFeaters laid the final guidelines out for the staff on January 10. With a promotion barrage and explanatory spots during the newscasts, the station put the plan into practice a week and a half later.

A number of viewers complain that they got tired of *hearing* about the new approach. Indeed, until March, the explanation and promotion of the new guidelines were woven right into the newscast. A crime story typically concluded with a graphic of the new guidelines, with big red check marks on which guidelines the story was deemed to have met. There were oral explanations as well. "Today's marijuana bust is an example of a crime-fighting or crime-prevention effort, one of the guidelines we're using now to change the way we cover crime," anchor Judy Maggio told her viewers in February. "The project is KVUE Listens To You On Crime. We're still going to cover crime, but we're doing it in a less violent and sensational way. We would like to hear your feedback." She went on to say that she and "Bob" — co-anchor Bob Karstens — would host a discussion about the station's new crime-coverage philosophy on America Online that evening.

KVUE Listens to you on Crime
Guidelines
- ☐ Immediate Threat
- ☐ Threat to Children
- ☐ Take Action
- ☐ Significant Impact
- ☐ Crime Prevention Efforts

Mike George, news manager

Judy Maggio and Bob Karstens, co-anchors

"We confirmed that there were three dead on the scene, and the thought process began right then: Is this going to meet the guidelines?" — reporter Greg Groogan

The response to the experiment itself has been overwhelmingly positive. "A big congratulations to KVUE for the efforts to keep unimportant violence off television..." reads a typical fax. "We are not interested in gory details about who got smeared on the interstate, who got murdered, etc." reads another.

Austin Police Chief Elizabeth Watson, an outspoken advocate of community policing in this rapidly growing city of more than half a million people, also endorses KVUE's new approach, while she is critical of K-EYE's razzle-dazzle. "I think that it is commendable for a major TV news station to really take a look at responsible reporting, commendable from a community service standpoint," she says. "Sensationalized reporting fuels fear. It makes people feel powerless."

9. Should the Coverage Fit the Crime?

But when does "responsible reporting," to use Chief Watson's term, become a kind of cheerleading for local law enforcement or a device for self-censorship? In the first few weeks of the experiment, the station seemed to be blurring the distinction between straight reporting and being "a responsible member of the community." Its incessant efforts to tease out crime-prevention tips in every story often sounded more like police public-service announcements than news stories.

"We've got these neat little guidelines," reporter Kim Barnes says, "which means we've got to give a solution, so let's give some tips. My concern is that so much of our focus

Wendy Erikson, reporter and weekend anchor

story is worth putting on the air. And if it's worth putting on the air, is it worth "packaging," giving it the full story-and-pictures approach? "This policy makes us think about the way we cover crime," George says. "It's just like any other story: we ask the question 'Why is this important?' "

"What we're trying to get away from is an automatic response to the way we cover crime," McFeaters says. "We're not trying to deny the ugliness in the world; that's not what this is about. However, we have a responsibility not to give that ugliness more play than it deserves."

McFeaters draws a sharp distinction between what KVUE is doing and the "family-sensitive" approach, pioneered by WCCO-TV in Minneapolis, one of a handful of stations around the country that are spurning violent, manipulative, and emotion-laden newscasts. The Minneapolis station pledges that its 5 P.M. newscast will never contain material that a family with children watching would find offensive. To McFeaters, such a pledge is a gimmick, in effect a kind of self-censorship. The Minneapolis station, she says, allowed the perception to develop that it had, in effect, "gone soft" on crime. She doesn't want that to happen to KVUE, and the station's promotional efforts are aimed at heading off that notion.

"The world is violent. Your ignorance of it doesn't make it less violent" — a KVUE viewer

and concern is on getting the sidebar [the crime-prevention tips] that we're not getting the who, what, when, and where — which is our primary job."

Some viewers consider the KVUE experiment an effort to avoid reality. "Grow up," one viewer urged in another fax. "The world is violent. Your ignorance of it doesn't make it less violent. It only makes it more palatable to you when you stick your heads in the sand."

A similar objection came from Joe Phelps, pastor of an American Baptist church in an Austin suburb. "Frankly," the minister wrote in an op-ed piece that ran in the *Austin American-Statesman*, "hearing about violence is the least we can do to remain connected with our fellow citizens, our kin, who experience such tragedy. The reporting should not be sensationalized. Pictures may not always be appropriate. But the reality that people kill and are killed on a regular basis is newsworthy. We need to hear it."

Competitor K-EYE, meanwhile, is trying to make a little ratings hay with that no-crime perception of KVUE. "Is your newscast giving you all the news?" K-EYE's latest promo asks, a not-so-subtle dig at KVUE's highly publicized crime diet.

For Kneeland, McFeaters, and others at KVUE, the perception that the station no longer covers crime has been frustrating. When critics call, Mike George takes pains to explain the distinction the station makes between covering a crime story and airing it. His reporters listen to the police scanner just as they always have, he explains, and they still investigate crime and violence. But after they've asked the questions and nosed around the crime scene, they now have to decide whether the

It is a Monday night toward the end of February, and McFeaters and Kneeland have called a meeting of the newsroom staff to assess their experiment. Minutes after anchors Bob Karstens and Judy Maggio wrap up the 6 P.M. newscast with a bit of happy chat with weatherman Mark Murray, the staff gathers around a white oval table in the corner of the large, airy newsroom. Behind them, floor-to-ceiling inverted-V windows in a stark white wall offer views of suburban Austin at dusk.

Maggio and Karstens sit side-by-side at one end of the table, just as they do on the set. Reporters, editors, producers, directors, news managers, engineers, and photographers, a couple of dozen in all, slouch in chairs and on desks or lean against the wall around the table. Several of their colleagues scurry about the newsroom getting ready for the 10 P.M. newscast. It's a youthful-looking group; the average age is probably under thirty.

Three video cameras record the gathering as McFeaters opens the meeting with a videotape of another gathering — a viewer focus group that had met several times over a two-month period. The seven members of this group — young and old; black, white, and brown; male and female — are thoughtful and articulate and uniformly supportive of the station's crime-coverage experiment. "I have to be perfectly honest," says Ora Houston, a grandmotherly African-American woman. "I have not missed the crime or the mayhem or the stabbings. It's like my life is much more settled, it's calmer. We know crime's going on. In our neighborhood, we're trying to be proactive about it, but we don't need to see it every day."

The tape ends. Standing in the shadows away from the table, McFeaters says, "Let's start with some of your frustrations."

A reporter replies: "Sometimes it's difficult when there's something you're not covering, and you know the other sta-

2. INFORMATION AND INFLUENCE

KVUE-TV reporters Robbie Owens, Kim Barnes, and Greg Groogan

tions are covering it, and you wonder whether you're doing your job." Another says she worries about digging for the deeper angle and slighting the "who, what, when, where, why. Are we fulfilling our core responsibility?" Someone else, expanding on the thought, suggests a billboard-type graphic that would display such information, without pictures.

students at the University of Texas.

"We confirmed that there were three dead on the scene," he recalls, "and the thought process began right then. 'Is this going to meet the guidelines? If this was murder, was the murderer still at large? Was there an issue of public safety?'"

It seemed that a graduate student in engineering had shot his wife and four-year-old daughter and then turned the gun on himself. "We had a hook," Groogan says. "It was the first murder on UT properties since the Charles Whitman shootings from the UT tower in 1966. That wasn't a bad hook, but that wasn't going to cut it under our new guidelines."

"Sensationalized reporting fuels fear. It makes people feel powerless" — Police Chief Elizabeth Watson

Somebody else comments that "People are saying, 'Oh, y'all are the station that doesn't cover crime anymore.'"

"One of the frustrations is that we've made the decision that this particular life is more important than another one," reporter and weekend anchor Wendy Erikson says. "A family is out there saying, 'My family deserved at least a fifteen-second notice.'"

"Of course, we make those decisions all the time," McFeaters replies, "when we don't report the death of someone with AIDS or cancer or a baby that's died of SIDS." She adds that the only strong complaint she's heard about the experiment is about the promotion. "They're saying, 'All right, already! Quit telling us what you're going to do and just do it!'"

The group discusses ratings and how long the experiment might last if ratings slip. "Hypothetically, what if it costs us number one?" asks reporter Greg Groogan, surveying the faces of his colleagues. "Do we stand on principle, or do we backtrack?" Groogan urges taking a stand.

"I think we do have a more intelligent group of people here in Austin than in other cities," Carole Kneeland says, "so if it can work anywhere, I think it will work here."

Everyone around the table on Monday night was keenly aware that the experiment had undergone its most severe test just a day earlier, February 25. Groogan, who usually covers politics and investigative projects, had been doing weekend duty as part of a skeleton staff. He had arrived at work on Sunday thinking that he had made it through more than a month of the experiment without having to make a critical news judgment. A few minutes later he and photographer Chris Davis were rushing to the scene of a shooting at an apartment complex for married

Meanwhile, University of Texas police had found a weapon and told Groogan they had a 911 tape of the woman calling for help. Campus police were slow to provide much more, and the 5:30 newscast was looming. "We still weren't there," Groogan recalls, "at least for the early show."

If not for the guidelines, Groogan would already have been back at the station with a story in the can. Viewers might not have seen body bags, as they did on K-EYE that evening, but they might have heard the 911 tape and gotten the details about three violent deaths. Now, however, Groogan couldn't find a justification for airing the story: there was no immediate threat to the community, the crime itself was solved, and there was really nothing to say about prevention. There seemed to be no significant community impact; the family was new to the apartment complex, and the neighbors barely knew them. The guideline about children? In this case, the child was dead.

Back at the station, Sunday anchor Wendy Erikson had another killing on her hands, and another decision about the guidelines — an apparent drive-by shooting on Austin's predominantly black and Hispanic east side that had taken place late Saturday night. The suspect was in custody, there was no threat to children, no threat to the community.

"We were between a rock and a hard place," Groogan says. "With our limited weekend staff, we could follow both stories and still not get them on the air. We called Carole at home."

Erikson, thirty, is from suburban Chicago, where, she says, "I grew up watching death and destruction" on TV. She would have aired both Sunday stories without a second thought — before the experiment. Now she found herself in something of an ironic situation. Kneeland wanted to run the drive-by shooting story, but Erikson didn't believe it met the criteria Kneeland herself had developed. "Our credibility is on the line," Erikson told her boss.

"Carole told us to start digging on both, looking for larger issues," Groogan recalls. "She said, 'We cannot drop these stories. If we don't go on the air, that's the price we pay, but we cannot use these guidelines as an excuse not to cover them. Our job is to gather facts and then decide whether to air. The guidelines are not an excuse for not doing the nuts-and-bolts job of reporting.'"

Groogan and other reporters dug. Although neither story made the 5:30 newscast (except for a brief mention of the East Austin murder), Erikson fully aired them both at 10.

The story of the apparent murder/suicide at the university apartment complex focused on the immediate community's response to the tragedy. The residents of the apartment complex gathered at sunset on a playground and talked over what had happened, among themselves and with Groogan. Groogan also listened as counselors talked to the residents about signs of domestic abuse, which was an issue in the investigation, and what they could do to help prevent it.

Groogan believes that the guidelines forced him to stay with the story, and that this extra effort paid off in context and perspective. "In this place," Groogan reported at 10 that night, "where small children are constantly at play, there is a new fear — a fear of guns. They're supposed to be illegal on all university property. Residents wonder if other neighbors have ignored the ban." The visuals were subdued — the apartment complex, children playing there, and, from a distance, the residents in discussion.

KVUE also determined that the other shooting, in East Austin, had significant community impact as well, and in ways KVUE might have missed had it covered the incident simply as a drive-by shooting. Groogan and reporter Robbie Owens — who was pulled off another story to explore the community's response — discovered a predominantly black neighborhood eager to let the rest of Austin know that this was not just another stereotypical incident. "Although this is a terrible time for Bobby Reed's family and friends, they want Austin to know that this was not a gang shooting or a crack deal gone bad," Robbie Owens explained on the air. "It was a family gathered — laughing, talking, and eating enchiladas. Then, witnesses say a white man pulled up, exchanged some words — including a racial slur aimed at the black family gathering. They say he then fired a shotgun, hitting two people, one of them Bobby Reed, who died. But tonight some family and friends say their concern right now is not about hatred, but about loss."

"We had a family pleading for peace, and the community impacted was more than just that block where he lived," Cathy McFeaters says. "It was all of East Austin, all of black Austin."

"I believe that Sunday night newscast was a litmus test," Groogan says. "To Wendy's credit and to our producers' credit, they didn't want to be hypocrites. To Carole's credit, she sensed that by digging a little deeper and looking a little wider, we could still cover those stories without breaking our commitment."

Wendy Erikson still feels a little unsettled by that Sunday experience, however. On the earlier newscasts, "all other stations aired both stories," she recalls, "and I was literally anchoring and feeling that we weren't covering crime. We had four people dead on a quiet Sunday, and we weren't covering it. I've been taught to present the facts, and now I'm in this position where I'm having to decide whether this particular story is something I feel viewers should see.

9. Should the Coverage Fit the Crime?

> "I'm in transition. I'm uncomfortable with the guidelines right now, but part of me does feel good thinking I may somehow be contributing to a change in our society" — Wendy Erikson

"I'm in transition," she adds. "I'm uncomfortable with the guidelines right now, but part of me does feel very good thinking I may somehow be contributing to a change in our society."

Is changing society a journalistic concern? Can new journalistic guidelines also be promotional vehicles? And can thoughtful coverage of important local issues, crime included, compete with gripping images of maimed victims and distraught relatives? "Crime is punctuation," anchor Bob Karstens says. "It grips people. It's hard-edged. The challenge for us is to find stories with the same hard edge that aren't crime stories." McFeaters, who takes pride in the flashy Florida TV tricks she picked up in Jacksonville, believes KVUE can offer good journalism *and* good TV.

She acknowledges that ratings will ultimately determine the fate of KVUE's experiment, but she hopes the station doesn't rush to judgment. "They usually give news directors and anchors two or three years, football coaches two or three seasons before they off 'em," she says. "I don't think you draw any conclusions by one book." If ratings slip, McFeaters says she'll blame the presentation, not the concept, and she'll press to keep trying.

"We characterize it as an experiment, because it is," she says, but adds, "It's not an experiment in the sense that there's an end to this; it's not a one-shot deal. There's no way that at the end of the month Carole or I can walk out into the newsroom and announce, 'OK, now we can start covering crime the way we were.' This newsroom is forever changed. Everyone is going to look at how they cover crime differently from now on."

The February ratings came out in mid-March. They were KVUE's best ever. The station increased its already-solid ratings lead for every newscast, reaching its highest numbers in a decade for its 10 P.M. show. The crime-coverage experiment continues.

ALL IN THE FAMILY

The media megadeals pose a major challenge to the networks: Will ABC and CBS be able to provide unfettered coverage of their parent companies and their pet issues?

MARC GUNTHER

Marc Gunther has covered television since 1983 and is the author of "The House That Roone Built: The Inside Story of ABC News."

THE DEBUT OF THE F/X CABLE NETwork on June 1, 1994, was big news in the New York Post. The network, which features a perky breakfast show, a daily pet show and fading reruns of "Fantasy Island," was welcomed with a full-page spread, written by television reporter Steve Bornfeld. Readers who tried to tune to f/X, though, were bound to be frustrated—the network, at the time, was not carried by a single cable system in New York City.

Insiders knew right away what was going on. The Post and f/X are both owned by Rupert Murdoch's News Corp. What was presented as objective journalism in Bornfeld's story was, in fact, puffery, as Bornfeld, a respected writer who was subsequently forced out of the paper, now confirms.

"Not only did we run a splashy story on the day they debuted, but we ran a splashy story on the day after they debuted about a network that no one in the five boroughs of New York could see," Bornfeld says. "My choice was to write the stories or be fired. I didn't like it very much. But there was no shame about it at the Post."

Evidently not. The Post even ran the phone numbers of New York cable systems for readers to call and ask about f/X—without disclosing that the newspaper and the cable network share a common owner.

The Post's coverage is an extreme example of problems that can arise when news organizations become part of much bigger corporations with diverse interests.

But the example points to the kinds of problems that await journalists at Capital Cities/ABC and CBS, which on consecutive days this past summer announced their plans to merge with Disney and Westinghouse. Similar mergers will surely follow, driven by what ABC media analyst Jeff Greenfield has called "the most significant trend in American communication: the growing belief that bigger is better." At press time Time Warner was negotiating to acquire Turner Broadcasting, which owns CNN.

The result, some believe, will be that many more reporters will be forced to engage in a kind of journalistic incest when covering their corporate parents and siblings. If nothing else, that will fuel second-guessing of news judgments, suspicions about the hidden agendas of news outlets and questions about journalists' independence and credibility.

"Any news division is quite rightfully suspect when reporting on the interests of its corporate parent," says ABC's David Marash, a "Nightline" correspondent who covered the Disney-ABC deal. "It's a significant concern."

Jeff Chester, executive director of the Washington-based Center for Media Education, which opposes media concentration, goes further. "You cannot trust news organizations to cover themselves," he says, citing as an example television's meager coverage of the telecommunications debate last summer in Congress.

Consider just a few of the questions raised by the megadeals:

▶ Will film critic Joel Siegel of ABC's "Good Morning America" feel free to deliver a withering critique of Disney's next big animated movie?

▶ When the Capital Cities-owned Kansas City Star does a Florida travel section, will Disney World be featured on the cover?

▶ Will CBS' "60 Minutes" investigate the nuclear industry's efforts to market "safe" plants abroad and at home, a drive led by Westinghouse?

Such hypothetical questions can't be answered yet, of course. Spokespeople for ABC News and CBS News say the networks will do business as usual, without regard for their new corporate parents.

Perhaps. But the experience of past media mergers suggests that it won't always be easy. The best way to get a feel for the thickets that await journalists at the newly merged companies is to look at the performance of news organizations that already face potential conflicts with

10. All in the Family

corporate owners: Murdoch's properties, the magazines that are part of entertainment giant Time Warner, and NBC News and its parent company, General Electric.

NBC NEWS AND GE HAVE MADE PEACE, though it didn't come easily, while Time Warner's magazines have shown their independence, despite merciless second-guessing. But evidence suggests that two of Murdoch's print outlets, the Post and to a lesser degree TV Guide, have displayed some favoritism when reporting on Murdoch's television properties.

The Post's f/X coverage is the most blatant example. After the full-page spread for opening day, the newspaper followed up with a story headlined "Smooth Start for f/X"—the journalistic equivalent of reporting that a house did not catch fire. J. Max Robins, a TV columnist for Variety, was so struck by the puffery that he wrote that the Post went "embarrassingly overboard."

The Post also tried to shield Fox from negative ink, according to Bornfeld, the former reporter. When filmmaker Woody Allen told a gathering of TV writers that he had no plans to watch a Fox movie about Mia Farrow, Bornfeld filed an item but says it never made the paper.

The Post also neglected to report that Steve Powers, an on-air reporter fired by Fox-owned WNYW-TV Channel 5, filed an age discrimination suit against the station. Bornfeld says his editors told him to ignore it.

Adam Buckman, the Post's TV editor, denies any bias. About the f/X coverage, Buckman says, "We were told to cover the launch of f/X, but we also covered the launch of every other cable network, often in the same way. It was kind of a slow news day and there was nothing else going on."

He disputed the charge that he had squelched a story about Powers' suit against Fox, saying, "I have a vague recollection that we missed it." Post critics "feel completely and totally free to pan Fox shows," Buckman says, and in fact Fox shows have been slammed by the paper.

At TV Guide, Managing Editor Jack Curry says the Fox connection does not come into play when assigning or editing stories. "We have been given absolute independence," he says. He's backed up by former staffer Howard Polskin, who wrote a tough cover story on Fox's "Married...With Children" in 1989, the year after Murdoch bought the magazine. "There was absolutely no interference," Polskin says.

But two others familiar with the internal workings of TV Guide, who requested anonymity, say the Fox factor does make a difference. They cite the magazine's less than aggressive coverage of the embarrassing failure of Chevy Chase's late-night show on Fox. TV Guide ran only a single brief story during the show's six-week run, one that sounded an upbeat note, promising "radical surgery" and "a splashy relaunch of the program." Curry says there wasn't enough lead time for a longer piece and that TV Guide skewered Chase in its best-and-worst of TV year-end issue.

When Bernard Weinraub, a New York Times entertainment reporter, did a freelance piece for TV Guide about Don Rickles and his Fox sitcom, "Daddy Dearest," a Rickles wisecrack about Murdoch was edited out, insiders say. Weinraub says his memory of the incident was vague, but he recalled being told that the joke "cut a little close to the bone."

In contrast to the Post, TV Guide editors and writers haven't given any breaks to Murdoch's f/X. But the cable channel was aided in its early days by the 13-million circulation magazine's decision to list f/X programs in some editions when bigger networks, notably NBC-owned CNBC, a business and talk channel, weren't listed at all. Murdoch and NBC executives were engaged in a bitter feud at the time, after NBC complained to the Federal Communications Commission that News Corp. had acquired its Fox stations illegally.

"We were, by far, the largest network not being carried by TV Guide. This was a growing frustration," says Brian Lewis, a CNBC vice president. "F/X launched with 18 million and, bing, they were listed." CNBC was carried into 48 million homes before it was listed.

Only after NBC, one of TV Guide's biggest advertisers, threatened to pull its ads did CNBC shows get listed.

FEW NEWS ORGANIZATIONS HAVE COME under as much scrutiny as Time Warner since Time Inc. and its magazines merged with Warner Bros. in 1990. The company owns movie studios, television, and book and music publishing businesses. The week the merger happened, Time blundered by choosing not to cover it except in an editor's note. Not long after, the magazine drew more criticism by doing a cover story on Warner Books author Scott Turow, just as the movie based on Turow's "Presumed Innocent" was being released by Warner Bros.

Since then the second-guessing has been nonstop. But there's scant evidence, at least in recent years, that Time Warner has gone easy on itself. Last June, for example, Richard Zoglin, a Time senior writer, was handed a sizzling potato: covering Time Warner's response to charges by Sen. Robert Dole and former Secretary of Education William Bennett that the company's music, movies and TV shows were contributing to America's moral decline. He produced an unsparing account that predicted, correctly, that Warner's music division would gradually back away from violent and misogynist rap. Among his observations: "The standards of taste at Warner

61

2. INFORMATION AND INFLUENCE

labels…have at times seemed extraordinarily lax." Other Warner embarrassments, such as the tacky talk show "Jenny Jones" distributed by the company, also took a pasting.

The story was edited by James R. Gaines, Time's managing editor, and Norman Pearlstine, the editor in chief of the Time magazine group. According to Zoglin, they made it tougher. "They wanted to air more of the dirty laundry," he says. "We put in things that made others in the company very uncomfortable, I learned later."

Zoglin was equally biting in his assessment of Warner TV's new WB Network when it premiered in January. He wrote: "The first batch of shows on WB and UPN (the new Paramount network) will convince no one that they are bringing something new to TV…. Is there room for two more networks offering another load of laugh tracks, retreads and raunchy wisecracks?"

One Time Warner insider says such reporting reflects the split in the huge conglomerate between the respectable East Coast magazines and the freewheeling West Coast music, movie and TV operations. Even if true, that only goes to show that, in fact, the magazines are free to take on their corporate brethren.

How else to explain the fact that Entertainment Weekly, another Time Inc. magazine, told its readers that Warner Bros. movie executives Robert Daly and Terry Semel "reportedly can't stand" Michael Fuchs, the HBO chairman who was put in charge of Warner Music last May? Senior writer Dana Kennedy wrote: "Some say the job so consumed him that he has no life."

Entertainment Weekly strives to treat Warner "like any other studio," says Managing Editor James W. Seymore. Sometimes that can be tricky—last fall, feuding Warner music executives Robert Morgado and Doug Morris furiously lobbied the magazine to gain primacy on EW's list of the most powerful people in entertainment. "People were trying to manipulate us, but they do that all the time," Seymore says. "We got caught in a power struggle."

Time's vaunted tradition of separation of church (editorial) and state (business) has helped the magazine group. "In a sense, the arrogance of Time works to its advantage," Zoglin says. "We don't feel we can be pushed around."

WALT DISNEY CO.

DISNEY
Revenues: $10.1 billion
TV: KCAL-TV, Los Angeles, Touchstone Television, Buena Vista Television
Cable: Disney Channel
Feature films: Walt Disney Pictures, Touchstone Pictures, Caravan Pictures, Hollywood Pictures, Miramax Films
Music: Walt Disney Records and Hollywood Records
Publications: Hyperion Press, magazines, comics
Retail: Licensing and retail ventures including 380 Disney Stores
Sports: National Hockey League Mighty Ducks
Theme parks: Walt Disney World, Disneyland, minority holding in Disneyland Paris, licensing, management and consulting fees from Tokyo Disneyland
Other: Disney Interactive, Walt Disney Cruise Lines

CAPITAL CITIES/ABC
Revenues: $6.4 billion
TV: ABC network, 10 TV stations
Radio: 10 FM stations, 11 AM stations, ABC radio networks with 3,400 affiliates
Cable: 80 percent of ESPN, 50 percent of Lifetime, 37.5 percent of Arts & Entertainment, 50 percent of Tele-Munchen (Germany), 33 percent EuroSport, cable interests in Japan, Germany, France and Scandinavia
Publishing: Newspapers including the Kansas City Star and Fort Worth Star-Telegram, Fairchild Publications, Institutional Investor, Los Angeles Magazine, Multichannel News, Chilton Publications, other specialized publications
Multimedia: ABC Online joint ventures for IMAX films, video games, CD-ROMS, etc.

SOURCES: Broadcasting Magazine, Hoover's Handbook Database

THE GE-NBC MARRIAGE BEGAN TESTILY, in part because GE-appointed managers curbed spending and demanded layoffs at NBC News. GE executives showed little appreciation for the news division's independence and, as a result, helped bring about several incidents of self-censorship and meddling.

The tone was set at the top by GE Chairman Jack Welch. In an interview with Electronic Media, former NBC News President Lawrence Grossman said Welch told him, "Don't bend over backwards to go after us just because we own you." Grossman also said Welch urged him to have NBC reporters avoid using the phrase "black Monday" after the 1987 stock market crash, to avoid spooking the markets. Grossman was fired in 1988.

A 1990 "Today" show segment on consumer boycotts excluded any mention of the far-reaching boycott of GE products by the group INFACT, over GE's role as a producer of nuclear weapons. Todd Putnam, editor of National Boycott News and a guest on the segment, says a "Today" producer warned him not to discuss the boycott against GE. NBC said afterwards that the producer was exercising her independent news judgment.

Other incidents also raised doubts about self-censorship. A 1989 "Today" show segment on defective bolts on planes, bridges and nuclear plants was edited to avoid mention of GE, which bought some of the bolts for its nuclear plants. Only after being criticized did "Today" mention GE's involvement in a follow-up segment.

In the last several years, though, GE has become supportive of NBC News, recognizing its profit-making potential. GE spent $15 million on a new studio for "Today," helped NBC News expand distribution into Europe and Asia, and brought in a strong leader in NBC News President Andrew Lack. While GE continues to make news—the company has been touched by several scandals, ranging from charges of fraud and money-laundering in connection with military jet engine sales to gross mismanagement of its former subsidiary Kidder Peabody—NBC has covered these stories without controversy.

Still, all the networks struggle over how to cover themselves and their corporate interests. When Congress debated telecommunications policy last summer, the broadcast networks provided scant coverage. ABC News' "Nightline" was a notable exception: Anchor Ted Koppel and reporter Jeff Greenfield delivered a thorough look at the biggest change in communications law in 60 years, one that would reduce or abolish government regulation of local and long distance phone companies, cable operators, radio and television. As businesses, the networks had plenty to like about the bill, which would increase the license terms for TV stations from five to 10 years and ease local and national limits on how many stations any one company can own.

"The major commercial networks, ABC among them, stand to make a great deal of money," Koppel reported. "You have probably not heard a great deal about that, though, on television, not because anyone has told us not to cover the story—truly, the people we work for wouldn't do that—but neither is any one of us under the impression that they are especially happy that we have chosen to critically examine the hand that feeds us."

ABC, CBS, NBC and Fox all declined to comment for the "Nightline" piece, Koppel reported. Nor had any of the network news organizations paid much attention to the "significant political contributions by the telecommunications industry, some $18 million in this decade, to current members of the House and Senate," according to Greenfield.

Jeff Chester, with the Center for Media Education, says the networks did a terrible job covering the bill, with the exceptions of "Nightline," PBS' "MacNeil/Lehrer NewsHour" and a segment on ABC's "Good Morning America."

"Nowhere did any of the TV nightly newscasts identify, even once, that their companies were lobbying to influence this legislation," says Chester. "It's not censorship, but self-censorship," he adds, predicting that aggressive reporting will become even more scarce as the companies grow bigger. "How will Disney-ABC News treat the phone companies when they are delivering programming over Ameritech's lines?"

The Disney-Capital Cities/ABC combination will pose a special challenge for journalists inside the merged entity because its interests are so vast (see boxes). And potential conflicts abound: "Good Morning America" covers mov-

WESTINGHOUSE/CBS

WESTINGHOUSE ELECTRIC CORPORATION

- **Revenues:** $8.8 billion
- **TV:** 8 TV stations, Group W Productions
- **Radio:** 8 FM stations, 10 AM stations
- **Electronic systems:** Radar, space and military equipment
- **Government and environmental services:** Waste management services
- **Power generation:** Fossil fuel power plants
- **Energy systems:** Nuclear fuel and nuclear power plant services and technology
- **Mobile refrigeration units:** Thermo King
- **Office furniture and equipment:** The Knoll Group

CBS

- **Revenues:** $3.7 billion
- **TV:** CBS Network, 7 TV stations, CBS Entertainment Productions
- **Radio:** 13 FM stations, 8 AM stations, CBS radio network
- **Cable:** Production agreements with A&E and The Travel Channel

SOURCES: Broadcasting Magazine, Hoover's Handbook Database

ies, ESPN reports on Anaheim's Mighty Ducks, "World News Tonight" has examined violence in the movies, "Prime-Time Live" profiled "Pulp Fiction" star Samuel L. Jackson, and the Kansas City Star writes about the sitcom "Home Improvement." Soon those topics will be all in the family.

What's more, entertainment news has become political news. Sen. Dole and President Clinton have both called upon Hollywood to curb movie violence. Dole's wife, Elizabeth, sold $15,000 of Disney stock after she learned that Disney, through its Miramax subsidiary, distributed "Priest," a film about a gay priest and a sexually active straight priest that was originally scheduled for an Easter weekend release.

Disney Chairman Michael Eisner sent out all the right signals when the merger was announced, assuring employees that he wouldn't interfere with ABC News. "I don't see the Walt Disney Co. coming in and doing anything in news," he said.

That seemed to please ABC News President Roone Arledge, who told the Wall Street Journal that Eisner "knows that to be successful, we sometimes do stories that make people unhappy." While Eisner has a reputation as a hands-on, autocratic chief executive, network executives say that he knows his handling of the news division will be seen as a litmus test by many at ABC.

Film critic Joel Siegel told "Good Morning America" viewers that he expects no trouble. "Siskel and Ebert have been syndicated by Disney for 10 years, not a hint of any kind of pressure or impropriety," he said. "And, in fact, I face this problem here. Cap Cities produces Broadway plays which I have panned in this studio. They produced 'Cats' and right here I

2. INFORMATION AND INFLUENCE

said I saw better choreography from people trying to run across Broadway than I saw on the stage. It's part of being a critic. It is integrity."

Jane Amari, managing editor for design and features at the Kansas City Star, says: "I don't really think it's a problem for the journalists." TV Critic Barry Garron agrees, saying he's written about ABC for years without thinking about their common ownership. The paper does have, however, a policy of disclosing to readers when it is covering one of its own companies' products.

At ESPN, John Walsh, senior vice president and executive editor of the network, expects no difficulties. The network's credibility, he says, is vital, and Disney won't squander it to hype a Disney-sponsored event or team. ABC's Marash, who spent a year working for ESPN, agrees, saying, "That is as straight up and honorable a journalistic organization as any of the network news divisions."

The CBS-Westinghouse merger is much smaller than the Disney-ABC deal, but concerns at CBS News have been heightened because of the way it is being handled. Westinghouse, for example, didn't make clear at the merger announcement who would actually run CBS. Then Michael Jordan, Westinghouse's CEO, waited more than a week before visiting CBS News, which set off more alarms among tradition-minded journalists. "He talked about the stations and about radio, about everything but news," says a CBS News producer who requested anonymity. "We feel like an afterthought."

Westinghouse's other businesses include electric-power generating equipment, such as for nuclear power plants, advanced electronic systems and mobile refrigeration. Reciting the Top 10 items on the Westinghouse "to do" list one night, CBS "Late Night" host David Letterman joked, "Lead story on every CBS newscast: Westinghouse appliances still dependable and affordably priced!" Actually, Westinghouse no longer makes refrigerators or toasters.

Westinghouse's nuclear interests are no joke, however, to liberal critics. "Westinghouse and GE are the Coke and Pepsi of nuclear power," says Karl Grossman, a veteran environmental journalist and a professor at the State University of New York at Old Westbury. "Now you have two of the four major networks owned by the nuclear industry."

Potential customers for Westinghouse and GE nuclear plants include China, Indonesia, South Korea and, if safety concerns can be overcome, utilities in the United States.

Will CBS' "60 Minutes" or NBC's "Dateline" investigate nuclear safety? Not likely, says Karl Grossman.

"Censorship in the United States really functions as a sin of omission," he says. "The reporters will know that this is a very, very sensitive issue in the eyes of management. The investigative reporting that is desperately needed, when it comes to nuclear technology, will just not happen."

The networks dismiss such talk. Don Hewitt, the executive producer of CBS' "60 Minutes," says his program has never ducked stories that might offend the company's owners and advertisers. This year, for example, "60 Minutes" did a powerful profile of Victor Crawford, a tobacco industry lobbyist who became an anti-tobacco activist after he was stricken with cancer. CBS Chairman, President and CEO Laurence Tisch owns Lorillard, a tobacco company.

"We've done a lot of things on cigarette smoking and cancer," says Hewitt, "and I never heard a peep. When Ford was our biggest sponsor, we took on the Ford Pinto as an unsafe car." Whether other newsmen without Hewitt's moxie will feel the same way remains to be seen.

> *"Any news division is quite rightfully suspect when reporting on the interests of its corporate parent," says ABC's David Marash.*

VNRs: NEWS OR ADVERTISING?

Robert B. Charles

Robert B. Charles is an attorney in the litigation department of the Washington, D.C., firm of Weil, Gotshal & Manges.

The nightly news is not what it used to be. Today, much of what we see on CNN, ABC, NBC, CBS, and the local news hour is a novel composite, featuring video news releases (VNRs) produced by public relations firms.

If you are surprised, you are not alone. The truth is unsettling. Nightly news is no longer exclusively the product of network or local news crews but is a deft combination of network or station originated stories and corporate or politically sponsored footage. In fact, according to a recent Nielsen Media Research Survey, about 80 percent of U.S. news directors air VNRs several times a month, and 100 percent of American television newsrooms now use VNRs in their newscasts.

So, what are VNRs? Who pays for them? Who is producing and distributing them? Why do television stations and networks use them? Have they eroded the quality and objectivity of news reporting or improved the precision of nightly news? What ethical questions do they raise? And what, after all, should viewers be doing while corporate and political sponsors, PR firms, broadcasters, and others grapple with the changing nature of nightly news?

In this article, the spotlight is turned on these little-asked questions.

WHAT ARE VNRs?

Simply put, a VNR is a film clip, maybe a minute or two in length, usually produced by a public relations firm and made available to television stations and networks by satellite feed. Dozens of PR firms now produce VNRs. Hundreds of commercial companies sponsor them, hoping for favorable coverage of a story relating to their particular business, and upward of 700 local stations now use them in their nightly news broadcasts.

Moreover, Congress and the White House have gotten into the act. Congress creates VNRs in its own fully equipped, taxpayer-funded television station in the belly of the Rayburn Building in Washington. Meanwhile, the Clinton administration hires out, paying companies like Medialink of New York—at taxpayer expense—to transmit VNRs by satellite to stations around the country.

Fully defining a VNR is tougher than one might think. Some network representatives and stations distinguish between audiovisual VNRs and so-called B-rolls, or voiceless film clips, which are presumed to be closer to what their own crews might shoot. Still others broaden the VNR definition to include any film not shot by a news organization itself, counting even space shuttle footage or Defense Department "file" tapes as VNRs.

But concern is generated chiefly by VNRs that are corporate or politically sponsored for the express purpose of garnering favorable television coverage under the guise of independent, third-party reporting.

More than 4,000 VNRs were distributed to news programs last year by satellite distributors such as industry leader Medialink of New York.

Medialink makes VNRs available to television stations and networks by alerting newsroom computers of a VNR "story" and providing the time and satellite feed coordinates. As Medialink explains, "High-priority designations set off 'flash' signals

2. INFORMATION AND INFLUENCE

in newsroom computer systems, bringing the alert to the immediate attention of editors and producers." Multiple transmissions, faxes, and phone calls then supplement the effort.

But long before newsrooms can decide whether to air a VNR, someone has to create and pay for it. Typically, PR firms create VNRs, and corporate or political clients pay. Thus, A.V.S. Post in Washington, a company with 15 years of VNR experience, has clients from Burger King and Xerox to the AFL-CIO.

Examples are legion. VNR producer Hilton/Sucherman Communications in New York does VNR work for Exxon, Allied Signal, Bristol-Myers Squibb, Merrill Lynch, IBM, Goldman Sachs, Lehman Brothers, the Tribune Company, and Pacific Gas & Electric. Aurora-4 Video Arts of New York serves VNR clients as diverse as Avis, Cannon, 800Flowers, Nikon, and the New York Islanders.

Not surprisingly, VNRs are also diverse. Thus, Gourvitz Communications of New York last year produced a VNR for Univision on use of the Spanish language in the United States, a B-roll for Crayola Crayons on its "Celebration of 90 Years of Color," and year-end VNR business reports for Sony, 3M, and Platinum Guild, each with placement on at least 50 stations.

Likewise, Auritt Communications in New York got paid for a B-roll to promote Madonna's book *Sex*, and News/Broadcast Network (NBN) of New York did the VNR for Calgene's "Flav'r Sav'r" bioengineered tomatoes. As John Bailey, director of marketing for NBN, explained, "Everybody in the TV business needed that piece of footage to run as they read the 10-or 20-second story."

Says Bailey, "It was a legitimate business story: the first whole food, genetically engineered, approved by the Food and Drug Administration for human consumption."

Did the VNR work? Coverage, says Bailey, was astonishing, reaching "something like 300 or 400 broadcasts, on every network, every station, making it the single most viewed new-product announcement video release ever."

What do corporate sponsors pay for such VNR news exposure? Interviews reveal a range from $10,000 to $100,000 for production of a single VNR. And, it is clear, sponsors expect something in return.

■ *Frequent customer:* **Cable News Network regularly uses a satellite feed to pick up VNRs.**

WHY DOES TV USE VNRs?

NBN's Bailey was unusually candid. Local news stations "have no budget, fewer [camera] crews than they used to have, and don't travel first class anymore; those days are over.

"Almost every news director you ever ask," Bailey continued, "will respond, 'We rarely use [VNRs], if ever, and if we do, we always identify them.' Well, it's complete bull."

Confirming Nielsen's numbers, a network source who requested anonymity added that local stations are "tempted" to run VNRs in their news hour because they are under enormous financial pressures.

Interestingly, however, disclaimers of VNR use are not limited to local stations. Several calls to CNN headquarters in Atlanta produced firm denials that VNRs are regularly used by CNN, and a call to ABC News brought a similar disclaimer.

Yet, calls to various VNR producers confirmed that CNN does use a satellite feed to pick up VNRs—and not so irregularly. Medialink and other VNR vendors identified specific instances when, by using a new electronic tracking system called Signa, they could tell CNN had often picked up VNRs. Signa, of course, was developed because VNR sponsors want to know whether, when, where, and how often their VNRs are used.

In addition, a number of VNR vendors list CNN as a client, for example, NBN of New York and American Film & Video of Maryland. Others list CNN as a user of their VNRs, among them, Impressive Images of Atlanta and MG Productions of New York.

Nor is CNN the only media giant that appears to be reluctant to admit using VNRs. ABC, NBC, and CBS each profess "rare" or no

---

Congress creates VNRs in its own fully equipped, taxpayer-funded television station in the belly of the Rayburn Building in Washington.

---

recent use of VNRs, yet each network is touted as a client or recipient of VNRs by leading VNR producers. The latter group includes Edit Masters of New Jersey, Hilton/Sucherman Productions, Neal Marshad Productions of New York, the News Group of Florida, Orbis Broadcast Group of Chicago, Impressive Images, and MG Productions.

One explanation for the contradiction and the stout network denials of VNR use is that networks may be defining VNRs narrowly as full-run, voice-over, unedited film clips or promotional material, whereas VNR producers define VNRs more broadly, including any film clip they produced and the network ran, whether for 2 or 30 seconds, edited or not, with or without voice, or for a corporate, trade association, public service, or government sponsor.

Still, it is clear that television stations across the country are using VNRs at an accelerating pace and for fairly obvious financial-crunch and ease-of-retrieval reasons.

POSITIVE ASPECTS

Are VNRs eroding the quality and objectivity of news reporting or improving the precision, scope, and timeliness of the news? What ethical questions are raised by expanding VNR use?

In August 1992, a *New York Times* article noted that "deadline-pressured, budget-crunched news staffs routinely use portions of video news releases slickly produced by vested interests in the health care industry, without telling the audience that part of what they're seeing is from slanted sources." Health care aside, are VNRs one more threat to objective reporting?

To hear VNR sponsors, producers, and satellite distributors talk, these costly film ventures are mere modern-day news releases, little different from an old printed press release. They simply announce something the sponsor believes is newsworthy and distantly hopes will be covered on the evening news.

Indeed, common VNR types include the following: development of a new drug (for example, last year's VNR on the proposed drug Detoxohol, for speedier metabolism of alcohol); the opening of a new foreign market or product line (as with McDonald's in Russia or Calgene's new tomato); new environmental policies (like Dow Chemical's announcement of a nonpolluting chemical plant); industry discoveries (for example, last year's announcement by the Yogurt Association that yogurt may help prevent colds by boosting immunity); or a company press conference to refute a government charge (as when General Motors rebutted charges of a defective truck).

Other incentives operate to create newsworthy VNRs. The vice president for marketing of Pintak Communications International, a Washington-based VNR producer, noted in an inter-

2. INFORMATION AND INFLUENCE

view that "we owe it to ourselves and our clients to say to a client, 'That's a great concept, but it's not news.'" Why? Because, "one bad experience, and there goes your reputation."

Pintak has created some unique VNRs. On location in Armenia last year for a fundraising VNR sponsored by an Armenian-American organization, Pintak caught what the networks needed: film of the cruel Armenian winter of 1993. "We had the first video coming out of Armenia on what life was like during that winter of starvation and energy shortages," says Pintak's spokesman, and it ran on all networks.

Thus, in fairness, although corporate VNRs have even been derided by critics as "fake news," there are two sides to the debate, and both deserve to be heard. Most corporate VNRs are not blunt PR instruments or frame-by-frame product promotions, as critics charge. Instead, they tend to be pinpoint reports on something a broadcaster might legitimately consider newsworthy.

Another good example is the Pepsi VNRs last year that disproved reports of syringes in Pepsi bottles. Nick Peters, vice president of marketing at Medialink, points out the value to both Pepsi and the public from these VNRs. The first Pepsi VNR showed that Pepsi bottles are inverted just before filling, making insertion of a foreign object impossible. The second showed footage caught by a store camera of the actual tampering.

Before looking at the arguments sponsors leave on the cutting room floor, we should also sweep clean some common confusion. VNRs are not "infomercials," the long-play advertisements made memorable by Ross Perot. Unlike infomercials, VNRs seldom run in their entirety and do not eliminate editor discretion. VNRs are offered free to stations, which can chop, dub, or snip prior to airing.

THE 'FAKE NEWS' CHARGE

Ironically, the toughest critic of VNRs has been *TV Guide*, which recently spearheaded an attack on the PR industry and VNR sponsors under the eye-popping headline "Fake News." *TV Guide* and others take issue with use of any film not produced by a network or station.

Of course, the allegation of "fake news" is serious and raises important ethical questions. Nevertheless, erecting straw men in the debate over VNR use is hardly helpful. *TV Guide*'s across-the-board condemnation of VNRs amounts to slaying a straw man. It oversimplifies and disserves the public with sensational overtones. Who, after all, would *not* be outraged at a conspiracy of networks, local stations, PR firms, and corporate sponsors to promote "fake news"?

The VNR debate has grown beyond that allegation and is now evolving toward defining clear guidelines for ethical use of VNRs. One question being raised is, What responsibilities does a news organization have for ensuring continued reliability and accuracy when it imports a B-roll or VNR into the nightly news?

I put that question to David Bartlett, president of the Radio/Television News Directors Association (RTNDA), the primary professional association of electronic journalists. To begin with, he admitted, there is a natural tension between PR firms and news directors: "They [corporate sponsors and PR firms] are trying to peddle a story, and we [electronic broadcasters] are trying not to be used."

But there is more to it than this, isn't there?

"Yes, today's VNRs are not like those phony, packaged stories put out by PR firms in the past," which were deceptive, says

11. VNRs

■ *Caught in the act:* A woman places a syringe in an opened can of Diet Pepsi and then "discovers" it.

Bartlett. Today, news directors have just one obligation: source disclosure. "If you disclose to your audience clearly where the material came from . . . for example, plastering 'NASA VIDEO' on the screen when you show a NASA video, then so be it." The station has done its job, as "there's nothing wrong with VNRs per se," says Bartlett.

But that analysis seems, if essentially true, still somehow incomplete. Even proper source identification does not erase favorable images, shots like a sun rising behind a fast-food chain as it opens in Moscow; staged interviews of well-made-up CEOs, lab technicians, or employees; gorgeous evergreen settings for corporate environmental initiatives; and the simple tricks of lighting, composition, angle, and filter—all used to create the "perfect" VNR.

Yes, source identification is important, but even sourced VNRs can alter the news, conveying a favorable impression of a sponsor's product or business. Although this may not warrant slowing VNR use, it should be reason enough for heightened viewer caution. Being put at ease by source identification is like trusting that you have erased from jurors' minds impressions drawn from inadmissible evidence with a simple jury instruction. Quite often, the impression remains. And the residual impression left by a fully identified VNR is still much of what a VNR sponsor has paid for.

But, returning to location, do news directors have an unequivocal obligation to disclose the source of every VNR used as "news"? RTNDA's Bartlett hedges: You could argue that the VNR source need not be disclosed if the station believes that the credibility of the story is not called into question, he says. It seems, then, that much of the industry is united around a "sometimes yes, sometimes no" standard.

Source disclosure is, today, the nub of the VNR debate. Already, an ethics code for the PR industry on VNRs has surfaced. The Code of Good Practice for Video News Releases emerged in 1992 and continues to be promoted by the Public Relations Society of America (PRSA), a group of 35 PR firms.

MEDIA ETHICS

What about a code of ethics on VNRs for television and electronic journalists? Electronic journalism is divided. At one end, people like Fred Friendly, national dean of journalism and Columbia Journalism School professor, insist that source identification be a minimum ethical requirement.

Interviewed for this article, he sounded a note close to *TV Guide*, saying use, under some circumstances, is unacceptable. He added, "When I talk to students, I tell them, 'Don't touch these things with a ten-foot pole.'"

Friendly's skepticism is balanced by those more trusting of industry ethics. RTNDA's Bartlett says, "I can't speak for every station, and I would be naive to say that every station adheres to the high standard of ethics I wish they would, but I think the vast majority follow sound ethical behavior" when using VNRs.

Other industry sources estimate that source disclosure nears 80 percent. But many VNR producers, who track their VNR use electronically through Signa, are less sanguine. A spokesman for Pintak Communications explained why he believes local stations run VNRs uncredited. "They [local stations] don't want to be seen as

2. INFORMATION AND INFLUENCE

VNR PRO

Most of today's VNRs are targeted reports on subjects that have a legitimate claim to newsworthiness in the eyes of broadcasters.

Because the VNR is a professional video that has been produced at corporate or political expense, it represents a big cost savings for cash-strapped news organizations.

Some VNRs can provide footage of obscure or fast-breaking events that might otherwise be unobtainable.

The occasional VNR can actually enhance the public good, as happened with a news video released by Pepsi that debunked the possibility of syringes in Pepsi bottles.

VNR CON

News organizations can become marketers for a slew of products they might otherwise not choose to advertise.

Politicians can use taxpayer funds to produce videos whose purpose is to enhance their reelection prospects.

Political VNRs can avoid the tough questions, becoming soft-sell advertisements for a particular public policy.

There is no code of ethics in the electronic media industry governing the handling of VNRs.

Bartlett explains why political VNRs are problematic: "Take President Clinton trying to peddle whatever he's trying to peddle this week: The danger is that the audience might think that an interview with President Clinton was generated in a way that it was not. Often, the station did not call the White House and secure a hard-hitting interview."

So? "The White House doesn't want you to know that they are spending taxpayers' money peddling these phony interviews with the president," explains Bartlett. "I mean, that harms his credibility." But, he adds, "that applies to [VNRs by] any politician, since members of Congress do it routinely."

Where does all this leave us? Fully 81 percent of the American public gets most of its news from television, according to a 1992 Roper poll. The average VNR, according to Medialink, will "get 30 to 40 airings and reach 2 to 4 million confirmed viewers," with some reaching "tens of millions of viewers" and rare VNRs reaching the whole viewing nation, (for example, the Pepsi VNRs got 3,170 airings and reached 500 million viewers).

In the end, although VNRs offer certain palpable advantages, including cost savings for news organizations, footage of obscure or fast-breaking events, and even rare opportunities to enhance the public good, they present risks to the public, including potential inaccuracy and deception.

The bottom line? Viewers should not believe everything they see and should maintain a healthy skepticism when viewing the news. There appears to be no grand conspiracy to promote "fake news," but there is growing risk that your news is deftly weighted in favor of an opinion you might not have had when you sat down and picked up the remote.

relying on what, unfortunately, has been categorized as industrial propaganda."

Source identification is plainly not a vendor problem, because most identify their VNR sponsor. Medialink, for example, has named sponsors since its founding in 1987. President Larry Moskowitz spelled out Medialink's policy: "While no one here tells a news director he *must* use the name of the sponsor, it has always been our policy to name the sponsor, since we feel news personnel need to know who paid for the VNR."

Thus, with a code of ethics already in place for the PR industry, the next place to turn for insistence on ethical VNR use is to the electronic media industry. Observers say that what is needed is a VNR-specific code of ethics for the electronic media industry, applicable to both corporate and politically sponsored VNRs.

THE GOSPEL OF PUBLIC JOURNALISM

Adherents of the fast-growing movement say news organizations must listen more closely to their audiences and play more active roles in their communities if they are to flourish. But nonbelievers worry it will hurt credibility by turning the media into a player rather than a chronicler.

Alicia C. Shepard

AJR contributing writer Alicia C. Shepard examined coverage of Paula Corbin Jones' allegations in our July/August issue.

IMAGINE YOU'RE A NEWSPAPER EDITOR FACED with declining circulation, dwindling ad revenues and the feeling that you and your community are like an unhappily married couple barely on speaking terms. You have big problems and no clue how to fix them.

You're not alone. Many newspaper editors and publishers are worried about the state of journalism. And many are gravitating toward the hottest secular religion in the news business, public journalism.

Inside the tent, preachers Davis "Buzz" Merritt Jr. and Jay Rosen are warning that newspapers, communities and democracy itself will die unless journalists and the public team up in a search for solutions to community woes. Dozens of editors like what Merritt and Rosen have to say and are joining the faithful.

But some doubters are uneasy. They fear the movement poses a threat to traditional journalistic values.

The goal of public journalism—a.k.a. civic journalism, public service journalism or community-assisted reporting—is to "reconnect" citizens with their newspapers, their communities and the political process, with newspapers playing a role not unlike that of a community organizer. According to the gospel of public journalism, professional passivity is passé; activism is hot. Detachment is out; participation is in. Experts are no longer the quote-machines of choice; readers' voices must be heard.

Public journalists are tired of not being allowed to care passionately about their communities and act on their convictions; they believe they have to play major roles in solving the problems of their cities, towns and neighborhoods. "We are part of the community, so they're our problems too," says Marty Steffans, news manager for public life of the Dayton Daily News.

The public journalism movement is sweeping through newsrooms from Bremerton, Washington, to Charlotte, North Carolina. Television and radio stations are joining too. The nascent movement—heavily influenced by, but hardly limited to, Knight-Ridder papers—is still defining itself. That makes it hard to pin down precisely what it is and harder to convert those who treasure the traditional approach to journalism.

So far its components include asking readers to help decide what the paper covers and how it covers it; becoming a more active player and less

2. INFORMATION AND INFLUENCE

an observer; lobbying for change on the news pages; finding sources whose voices are often unheard; and, above all, dramatically strengthening the bonds between newspaper and community. At its heart is the assumption that a newspaper should act as a catalyst for change.

Newspapers such as the Wichita Eagle and Charlotte Observer are among those that have refocused their political coverage on the concerns of ordinary people rather than those of politicians, handlers and spinmeisters.

Some papers, including the Dayton Daily News and Minneapolis' Star Tribune, have sponsored neighborhood roundtables in readers' homes. The Huntington Herald-Dispatch in West Virginia, the Boulder Daily Camera in Colorado and the Daily Oklahoman have held town meetings or convened community discussions designed to solve stubborn social problems. The Wisconsin State Journal established a panel of community leaders to give feedback before stories were published.

One obstacle to grasping public journalism is the lack of an easy-to-understand user's manual. It's a movement fond of jargon that newspaper people traditionally scorn: connectivity, capacity building, values clarification. And the phenomenon comes in a wide variety of flavors. What's considered public journalism at the Wichita Eagle may be entirely different than what's happening at the Boston Globe or the Virginian Pilot & Ledger-Star in Norfolk—yet still part of the same movement.

"The most important thing we can say about public journalism is we're still inventing it," says Rosen, a journalism professor at New York University. "There aren't any experts, really. We are making it up as we go along."

To devotees of traditional journalism, the movement causes discomfort—and skepticism. These "agnostics" remain outside of Merritt's and Rosen's tent in protest. Isn't public journalism, they ask, what first-rate newspapers have been doing all along? Is today's version just a market-driven gimmick to boost circulation?

If readers are dictating what a paper should write, aren't journalists abrogating their responsibility? Shouldn't reporters be community chroniclers rather than boosters?

"My problem is that we're running around saying, 'Eureka, we've found it,'" says Eugene L. Roberts Jr., managing editor of the New York Times. "I'm not sure we ever lost it."

Adds Leonard Downie Jr., executive editor of the Washington Post: "No matter how strongly I feel about something that's going on out there, my job is not to try to influence the outcome. I just don't want to cross that line, no matter how well-meaning the reasoning might be for crossing it."

Despite the detractors, public journalism is gaining support among those eager to try unconventional approaches. "I think the movement is one of the most significant in American journalism in a long time," says Marvin Kalb, director of the Joan Shorenstein Center on the Press, Politics and Public Policy at Harvard University. "This is not a flash in the pan phenomenon. It's something that seems to be digging deeper roots into American journalism and ought to be examined very carefully."

THE PUBLIC JOURNALISM MOVEMENT began somewhat earlier in Georgia, but its first prominent manifestation was born out of frustration over the 1988 presidential campaign coverage. Many believed the media had been transfixed by negative campaign tactics, obsessed with horse race coverage and oblivious to issues that mattered to voters. "At the time of the '88 campaign, everyone felt they had been taken to the cleaners," says Kalb. "The people had become disconnected from the political process."

The Post's Downie thinks two other factors also have contributed to public journalism's growth spurt: a desire to boost circulation, and to win popularity for editors uncomfortable with criticism. "It appears that you are doing something good and then people will love you for it," says Downie. "I'm just not going to worry about being loved or not."

But Buzz Merritt, editor for 18 years of Knight-Ridder's Wichita Eagle, says he was most concerned about the disheartening political campaign of 1988. Barely half of the electorate voted; the last time that had happened was in 1924. But Merritt didn't blame the public; he blamed the media, with its preoccupation with charges and countercharges and poll results.

A week after the election, Merritt wrote a column. The gist was that there needed to be a new compact among politicians, journalists and voters. Since the politicians wouldn't change, Merritt concluded, it was up to the journalists. Two years later, Merritt devised a way to force the candidates to discuss issues before the 1990 vote.

"We did a number of things and in effect changed the campaign," Merritt recalls. "We abandoned neutrality in whether people should vote. We actively were getting people to register and urging them to vote"—through the news pages. (Other papers are making similar efforts. Oregonian Editor Sandra Mims Rowe has said, "I'd rather increase voter turnout 10 percent than win a Pulitzer.")

The Voter Project, which the Eagle carried out in partnership with KAKE-TV, the local ABC affiliate, conducted surveys and focus groups to find out what readers thought the crucial issues were. It then tried to keep the candidates focused on them, downplaying charge-countercharge campaign rhetoric.

On six Sundays before election day, the paper gave in-depth treatment to the issues chosen by readers and outlined the candidates' positions on them. The paper produced reader-friendly voter guides and distributed them to subscribers and non-subscribers alike.

> On six Sundays before election day, the Wichita Eagle gave in-depth treatment to the issues chosen by the readers and outlined the candidates' positions on them.

12. Gospel of Public Journalism

"It took a while to re-educate ourselves to become aggressive about issues," wrote then-Managing Editor Steve Smith, who coordinated the project. "We had become transcribers to political campaigns—getting A's statement and B's response and so forth. We had to train ourselves to be a little nasty" in forcing candidates to answer specific questions about real issues.

In the summer of 1992, the concept was expanded to the People Project: Solving It Ourselves, an undertaking which sought solutions to government gridlock, family stress, crime and poor education.

The challenge was also to get beyond mere consciousness-raising. Too often news operations focus attention on one problem, then move onto the next, leaving the follow-up to government officials and editorial writers. Public journalists, say movement mainstays Merritt and Rosen, must be willing to stay in the fray and act as facilitators and referees, although not necessarily as partisans.

In the People Project, the Eagle teamed up with KSNW-TV and KNSS radio. It hired researchers from Wichita State University to conduct in-depth interviews with 192 residents. Others were invited to telephone, fax or write their ideas about what's wrong and how to fix it. "There were hundreds of voices in the People Project (as it ran in the paper) and not a single expert or politician," says Merritt proudly.

The People Project not only focused on community ills but highlighted success stories and gave reams of information on how people could volunteer. "It was good journalism, comprehensive journalism, but it was much more," James K. Batten, chairman and CEO of Knight-Ridder and a champion of public journalism, has said. "In the copy, in the headlines, in the news pages as well as the editorial page, the Eagle pointed out the problems as the community was describing them and then insisted the community itself had to get busy to solve them."

While no one can definitely attribute it to the project, volunteerism in the schools rose by more than a third after the series, Merritt says. And a survey indicated reader satisfaction with the Eagle had jumped by more than 12 percent.

KANSAS EDITOR MERRITT, 57, AND NEW York professor Rosen, 38, are considered the fathers of the public journalism movement. They met in 1991 at a seminar for journalists in New York City sponsored by the Kettering Foundation, which had asked Merritt to speak about the Voter Project. "Jay and I began to talk and we realized that we were all sort of thinking along the same lines about what ought to happen in journalism," recalls Merritt.

Now Merritt, with 42 years in daily journalism, and Rosen, a reporter in Buffalo in the late 1970s, lecture together, appear individually at conferences and hold seminars. They recently conducted the third public journalism conference at the American Press Institute in suburban Washington, D.C., where the converted preached to each other. Merritt is taking a year off to write a book on public journalism. Rosen heads the nonprofit Project on Public Life and the Press at New York University, which he created in September 1993 with a $513,832 grant from the Knight Foundation to monitor experiments.

And many are experimenting. Currently, 171 news organizations are working with the Project on Public Life and 95 initiatives are underway, according to Lisa Austin, the project's research director. They range from splashy "let's fix our cities" projects to requiring staffers to talk to readers. In each case, public journalism experiments are tailored to the town.

At the Des Moines Register in 1993, reporters, photographers, artists and editors were assigned to hold open-ended conversations about community concerns with at least four area residents. The results were used to design an opinion poll about major local issues.

In other public journalism initiatives:

▶ The Wisconsin State Journal in Madison and a local PBS station assembled citizens on "grand juries" and mock legislatures to deliberate a property tax plan, the national budget, gambling and health care reform.

▶ After boxer Mike Tyson's rape conviction in 1992, the Indianapolis Star commissioned a poll on racial attitudes, then used the findings to shape stories for a week-long series. The local ABC affiliate ran stories on the same topics, with each medium promoting the other's stories.

▶ The News Journal in Wilmington, Delaware, teamed up with a Chamber of Commerce-sponsored think tank to hold a summit on the state's economic problems. The paper conducted five town meetings prior to the summit to hear readers' views, promoted the meetings and helped pay for the summit. No one from the paper actually participated in the two-day event.

Although not officially part of Rosen's movement, Gannett newspapers such as the News Journal have been going in the same direction under the company's News 2000 program, launched in June 1991 for Gannett's 82 dailies. That summer each paper conducted surveys and held town meetings and focus groups, hearing from more than 75,000 residents in Gannett communities about what they liked and disliked about the papers.

WHILE PUBLIC JOURNALISM MEANS many things, one of the highest-profile examples was quite similar to the one sponsored by the Wichita Eagle. The Charlotte Observer, another Knight-Ridder paper, built on the Wichita experience and created an election coverage model in 1992 that many papers are copying.

> *Although not officially part of the public journalism movement, Gannett newspapers have been going in the same direction under the company's News 2000 program.*

2. INFORMATION AND INFLUENCE

Like the Eagle, the Observer abandoned horse race election coverage, concentrating instead on the issues that mattered most to voters. Not surprisingly, it found that residents were worried about the economy, crime and drugs, taxes, health care, education, the environment, and the disintegration of family and community life. Half of the 1,000 participants agreed to serve on a citizens' panel to keep the Observer on track.

In January 1992, then-Editor Rich Oppel introduced the project on the front page. A week later, the paper ran an analysis of the agenda set by the voters.

The paper asked candidates to take specific stands on each of the issues selected by readers. When Democratic U.S. Sen. Terry Sanford refused to explain his position on one issue, the paper printed white space under his picture. Sanford didn't let that happen again.

The Observer staff was initially suspicious, says then-City Editor Rick Thames.

Asking readers' questions at press conferences was especially awkward for reporters. "Other reporters would turn around and look at them like 'What are you doing?'...when they would say: 'Mary Smith of Matthews would like to ask you this question,'" Thames recalls.

Observer reporters asked their own questions, too. But Thames, now an assistant managing editor, noted a qualitative difference. His reporter might ask a candidate about strategy. "The voter question would say: 'I work hard. I can't get loans. What are you going to do for people like me?'" says Thames. "A reporter wouldn't have asked that question."

The Charlotte effort attracted the interest of a key player in another medium and had a broader impact as a result. This year National Public Radio teamed member stations with the Seattle Times, San Francisco Chronicle, Boston Globe, Dallas Morning News and Wichita Eagle to try new approaches to election coverage.

NPR Editorial Director John Dinges says the stations are trying to merge traditional narrative with the voices of individual people so listeners can hear citizens thinking issues through.

"I was very influenced by Charlotte," says Dinges, who's heading the effort. "I wanted to do what they were doing: to let people set the agenda for the election rather than let them be led around by candidates and their handlers."

SINCE 1992, DAYTON, OHIO, HAS BEEN shaken by a series of murders by young people. In March, an 11-year-old shot his two sisters, 3 and 5, killing the younger one.

The Cox-owned Dayton Daily News responded with an ambitious project on youth violence. "Kids in Chaos" was designed to solve the problem, with help from residents. The goal, wrote Editor Max Jennings in April, was to strengthen and support community efforts toward curbing the unprecedented violence and saving Dayton's kids.

The project, run in conjunction with WHIO, the local CBS affiliate, began with more than 400 family roundtables where groups of six or more, lured by free pizza, discussed the problem. In May, the paper began showcasing weekly stories about successful community efforts to help kids. It also cosponsored a conference for 120 local experts dealing with youth violence. But the experts won't dominate the series the paper plans to run, says editor Marty Steffans, who intends to use young voices more than those of adults. "We want the effort to be extremely personal,...to really show how juvenile violence affects our lives and our future," Steffans has written.

As an example of aiming for the personal, Steffans cited a piece about a straight-A student who was gang-raped. The 14-year-old girl and her mother each wrote about the rape without seeing what the other had written.

This month, the paper plans to publish an eight-day series on youth violence that will rely heavily on information collected from teenagers and preteens. Included will be a resource guide with advice for worried parents.

The effort might have stopped there. But not this time, Steffans vows. Tucked inside the series will be a 12-page tab designed to guide and provoke further discussion. If all goes according to plan, the tab will become the bible for some 25 town hall forums that the paper will sponsor with community groups. "If we pull it off, it will be the largest public policy discussion in our community since the Great Flood of 1913," she says.

The paper is completely committed to the effort but Steffans says it knows when to drop out. "If you're doing a good public journalism project, you let the other organizations take the lead," she says. "If newspapers become overly involved in a project, chances are good that it will ultimately fail."

Steffans says the paper can cooperate with the community and still maintain its watchdog role. For instance, the Daily News worked with the police on the project, she says. "But if the police do something wrong, we'll come back at them with guns blazing. They know that."

While the Daily News used pizzas to bring people together to discuss youth violence, the Spokesman-Review in Spokane, Washington, bought them last year for groups willing to talk about Spokane's future. "We heard from hippies trapped in the '60s, people from zip codes that we never got mail from, elderly people living in the community for a very long time, 14-year-olds who really just wanted the pizza," says the paper's editor, Chris Peck.

Staffers also padded their Rolodexes with new names and numbers for future stories.

Peck is working on yet another way to practice public journalism: He's reinventing the editorial pages. This year, rather than filling the op-ed page with the George Wills and Ellen Goodmans, he opened it up to the public. Peck eliminated the position of editorial page editor. Now, two "interactive editors" help readers get their opinions in shape for publication.

"It brings a whole different voice into a very stilted part of the paper," says Peck. "What I hope we can do is develop a model for recasting the opinion page as the laboratory of public journalism."

TURNING OVER THE EDITORIAL PAGE TO the community may be new (although columns by non-journalists are increasingly prevalent on the nation's op-ed pages). But are focus groups, surveys and asking community residents what they care about revolutionary techniques?

"I mean, great God, this is radical?" asks Howard Schneider, a Newsday managing editor. "It's the most traditional thing that any newspaper worth anything has always done. Good newspapers go out to the community.... This is not a radical new notion that you also report on what the public cares about."

Adds the Post's Len Downie, "I hope I've been practicing public journalism for the 30 years I've been in the business." While Downie applauds using focus groups and surveys, he is adamantly opposed to any kind of public participation by journalists.

Downie doesn't vote, rarely reads editorial pages and says he tries not to form opinions on matters covered by the Post. Even with his city in deep trouble, he says his job is to do nothing except tell readers what is happening.

"We've got a terrible fiscal problem in the District and we cover the hell out of it," he says. "But we don't want our coverage to tell people how they should deal with it. That's up to the voters and the Congress and the city council and the mayor."

The Times' Gene Roberts, who's also wary of the movement, may in a sense have been a pioneer public journalist. That makes him wonder if the movement isn't using smoke and mirrors to hype what's been going on for decades.

In the mid-1950s, Roberts was a reporter for the Goldsboro News-Argus in North Carolina. The paper recognized that farmers were too dependent on tobacco and needed to find other ways to make a living. Week after week, Roberts found and wrote about farmers who were making it without relying on tobacco.

Such success stories are now cited by public journalists as important ways for newspapers to "connect" with the community. "I thought that was a legitimate role for a newspaper and still think that way," says Roberts, former executive editor of the Philadelphia Inquirer and now on leave from the University of Maryland College of Journalism. "But we were careful not to get in or usurp the political process."

Skeptics worry that public journalists will get too deeply involved in that process to remain balanced in their reporting. Newsday's Schneider believes that once a newspaper begins to lead the parade rather than cover it, its credibility is in danger. In his view, newspapers should spotlight a problem, solicit reader feedback and aggressively follow the story until it's resolved.

Marvin Kalb has similar concerns. "A journalist who becomes an actor, in my view, is overstepping the bounds of his traditional responsibility," he says. "When the journalist literally organizes the change and then covers it, I'm uncertain about such traditional qualities as detachment, objectivity, toughness…. The whole point of American journalism has always been detachment from authority so that critical analysis is possible."

WHAT HAPPENED AT SCRIPPS Howard's Bremerton Sun in Washington would certainly give the critics pause. In October 1991, angry citizens fought off an effort by developers to buy 600 acres of forest. They wanted the county commission to buy the land, but it didn't have the money.

Mike Phillips, editor of the 40,000-circulation paper, did what editors do: He wrote an editorial saying that if preservation were important, the money had to be found. The day it appeared, he received numerous calls from residents asking him to do something. Along with a local Realtor and banker, Phillips persuaded Kitsap County commissioners to sponsor a meeting. Afterward, with the Sun driving the effort, a citizen education organization was formed to figure out how to save the open space.

The Sun called for volunteers and arranged for training so they could host meetings to decide which parcels of land should be preserved. In all, 47 meetings were held and 1,500 people participated. "The Sun provided background and other workshop materials, published the citizen plan in a 24-page special section and conducted two telephone polls," according to a summary by the Project on Public Life and the Press.

County commissioners responded. They put a $70 million bond issue on the ballot in September 1992. It failed, but the citizen's group began a nonprofit advocacy organization that tries to keep open space issues on the public agenda. Phillips is no longer involved.

As the process unfolded, a Sun reporter had to cover a campaign sponsored by her own paper. Phillips says the reporter didn't have trouble writing about her boss and that he encouraged stories about opposition to the plan. (The reporter, Julie McCormick, declines to discuss the campaign.) According to the summary of the project, Phillips concedes that he, the banker and the real estate agent openly used their power to pressure the county commission into taking action.

"I worried that we were going too far," Phillips says. "So did my staff…. But they realize

> "WHEN *the journalist literally organizes the change and then covers it, I'm uncertain about such traditional qualities as detachment, objectivity, toughness," says Marvin Kalb.*

2. INFORMATION AND INFLUENCE

we are trying very hard here to walk the line and stay on the right side of it. But we are willing to walk the line."

To some, such an approach seems perilously close to the bad old days, when powerful figures like William Randolph Hearst used their newspapers to promote pet causes and candidates.

"I know newspapers will tell you they are only going out to develop a civic culture, to get people involved," says Newsday's Schneider. "But inevitably once a newspaper gets identified as a particular advocate for a position, the dangers are self-evident. Once you lose your credibility and your ability to speak with authoritativeness, you're losing everything."

Critics, too, are wary of substituting the judgments of community leaders for those of editors. In making editorial decisions based on referenda, newspapers are merely feeding readers what they want to read and not necessarily what they need to know. John Bare, writing in the Media Studies Journal, noted that courageous editors are often lonely voices on sensitive issues like sexual mores or race.

"Two decades ago, outspoken newspaper editors in the South who denounced Jim Crow and endorsed civil rights were hated in their communities," wrote Bare, a doctoral student in journalism at the University of North Carolina. "Speaking out against racism was a noble but dangerous tactic, yet the progressive writings of these editors eventually helped bring about change. If those editors had established their news agenda by survey research, however, they certainly would have found that citizens wanted something else."

Newsroom resistance can slow down the cause of public journalism, as it did at the St. Paul Pioneer Press. In 1991 the paper hired syndicated columnist Neal Peirce and a team of urban affairs experts to draft a plan for the city's future. "Response was dismal in the newsroom where staffers believed they could have produced a report as good as Peirce's, given similar resources," according to a summary of the project.

Young reporters tend to be the least receptive, says Merritt. Many would rather be saying "gotcha" to a crooked mayor than helping to forge a consensus. "Generally speaking, the more veteran people understand it," says Merritt. "The older people know what we are doing now is not working."

A positive public journalism experience often overcomes resistance and erases doubts, say devotees. That's what happened in Bremerton, according to Phillips; reporters found it was more fun dealing with "real" people than bureaucrats. But the concept can be frightening: "I envisioned having deep, meaningful conversations and nothing available for tomorrow's paper," says Steve Brook, news editor of the State in Columbia, South Carolina.

Whether public journalism will be successful—and radically change journalism—is tough to measure.

"In the short term, we're not going to solve all these problems," Merritt says. "This has to do with the long term. The way we do business can be changed if enough people understand public journalism.

"There must," he adds, "be a purpose in what they do beyond telling the news."

A MEDICAL BREAKTHROUGH

Once the province of correspondents without a clue, network medical reporting now showcases specialists who use their expertise to sort through the confusing welter of reports, studies, developments and "cures."

JEROME AUMENTE

Jerome Aumente is a professor and director of the Journalism Resources Institute at Rutgers University and is writing a book on health and medical coverage.

It's the morning after his "CBS Evening News" report on the frustration many Americans feel about seemingly contradictory health studies. And Dr. Bob Arnot, M.D., the network's medical correspondent, points to it as an example of how things have changed in network coverage of health and medical issues.

His report dissected conflicting research into the benefits of margarine versus butter, and contradictory studies about the benefits of vitamin E in treating heart disease. He told viewers why different doses, varied test groups or misinterpreted statistics could breed contradictory results.

Arnot did the report because he was concerned about the "tremendous retaliatory wave of patients who say 'Forget it—we don't trust you anymore. We are going to have our steaks and we are going to have our french fries.' Red meat consumption is at a 50-year high. It is just through the roof. People are absolutely fed up with phony food news."

There is a new edge to health and medical coverage provided by ABC, CBS, NBC and CNN. It reflects the evolution of the health and medical beat from a haphazard collection of unconnected stories a few decades ago to a prime network assignment now handled by seasoned medical journalists like Arnot, who know as much, if not more, than the researchers and physicians they cover. And they're not afraid to challenge them.

For Dr. Sidney Wolfe, director of the Public Citizen Health Research Group, a Washington, D.C., research and health advocacy group that has spearheaded efforts toward health reforms, the reporting of Arnot and his counterparts at the other networks represents a major turnaround.

When Wolfe left his research post at the National Institutes of Health in 1971 to create Public Citizen he found an "appalling lack" of journalists with expertise covering health. There were exceptions in print, such as Victor Cohn at the Washington Post and Lawrence Altman at the New York Times, he says but "there wasn't very much going on in the networks."

Today, there is CBS' Arnot and Dr. Timothy Johnson, medical editor at [ABC] News who did doctoral studies in immunology; and

2. INFORMATION AND INFLUENCE

In the 1980s a string of major medical stories including the artificial heart experiments and the AIDS pandemic firmly anchored the medical beat as a network necessity.

George Strait, ABC medical correspondent, who did his undergraduate work in biology and his graduate studies in biochemical genetics.

"It is much better. There is no comparison," says Wolfe, who is interviewed frequently on national newscasts as well as programs such as "Nightline." He attributes the improved coverage to hard-edged, critical questioning, and the expertise of the correspondents.

But there is room for improvement, says Julia Moore, who was the executive director of Physicians for Social Responsibility until August. "The good news is networks do try to take complicated issues and make them accessible to the public," she says. "The bad news is that they do it superficially and in itty-bitty pieces here and there and don't give larger, big-picture reporting."

Others are concerned that easy access to medical journals and studies can lead to less skeptical reporting, particularly at smaller news organizations. Says Dan Rutz, managing editor of CNN's health/medical news and senior medical correspondent, "People are more willing to take stuff that is spoon fed them and put it on without question. That's not good."

WOLFE RECALLS A TIME WHEN health reporting was a "circus scene" because reporters lacked the background, time or training to dig out the true story and to distinguish between valid and faulty research. At cancer conferences in the 1970s, he says, "you would get a lot of very uncritical reporting of the new cures for cancer or breakthroughs in causes of cancer, and most of it was just junk.

"Most of it, if you looked at the data that was being presented and asked reasonable questions, you would say, 'Why is somebody writing about this?'"

But today's network health reporters bring more background and experience to the job. ABC's George Strait believes his science education makes it "more difficult for scientists to obfuscate." Researchers, he says, "are no more immune to putting a spin on things than politicians... and it is easier for me to get through the spin and figure out what the data really does mean."

In 1982 when ABC News sought to distinguish itself from its competitors, it introduced "Special Assignment" segments and Strait, then a general assignment correspondent, did several on the medical field. Roone Arledge, head of the news division, named Strait as ABC's full time health/medical specialist.

"It just exploded. There was a great appetite to do these stories, and it was a topic that local news organizations had begun to put a specialist on," Strait recalls. Until then, nobody at the network was tracking the key medical and science journals for the kind of news coverage that has since become a staple.

In the 1980s a string of major medical stories including the artificial heart experiments, the outbreak of the herpes epidemic and then the AIDS pandemic, firmly anchored the medical beat as a network necessity. Strait was the first American network journalist to report on AIDS from Zaire (the crew had to smuggle out the videotape when the Zairians changed their minds about open coverage). A few years later, Strait did special segments on health topics from the Soviet Union when Mikhail Gorbachev's glasnost opened the door. Since that time the international health scene has grown rapidly, and it is not unusual to see CBS' Arnot reporting overseas on the medical angles of the Persian Gulf War, or on refugee famine and disease in the Sudan and Somalia, or to see NBC's Bazell tracking AIDS developments in Europe, Africa, South America and the Caribbean.

Timothy Johnson of ABC was a physician at Massachusetts General Hospital in Boston when a colleague who invested in a local ABC-TV affiliate hired him to do a weekly medical talk show. This led to appearances on "Good Morning America" beginning in 1975, and eventually to a full time spot at ABC News in 1984.

Arnot was medical director of the National Emergency Service, which oversees emergency rooms and emergency response services performed by 2,500 physicians in 116 hospitals nationwide. He later was a physician for the Olympic Winter Games in Lake Placid, New York, where he ran a sports medicine clinic. He did occasional television reports, and in 1982 CBS offered him a full time spot.

Like ABC's Johnson, who encouraged him to try TV reporting, Arnot has given up his medical practice. He has since reported for the CBS morning news and "48 Hours," but now focuses primarily on the "CBS Evening News with Dan Rather."

After doing doctoral studies in immunology, Robert Bazell wrote for Science magazine and then for the New York Post before joining NBC in 1976. The science correspondent for NBC News, he also reports for "Today" and "Dateline NBC."

With their specialists on board, the networks are also devoting more time to health and science issues. CNN, for example, is making a major commitment to health coverage. Rutz, managing editor of the network's health and medical unit, oversees a 24-member team of producers and on-air correspondents based in Atlanta and Washington that also includes units on nutrition and parenting. Rutz is also a correspondent for CNN's "News from Medicine," which airs several times daily, and coanchor of the weekly "Your Health."

"Any time we have had research done on audience interests, health news always figures prominently," says Rutz, who has been with CNN for 14 years. Other networks and health associations report high viewership, which contributes to keeping health coverage a front-burner issue.

At the commercial broadcast networks, breaking health stories often lead the evening news shows. And weekly special segments, such as Bazell's "Health Watch" on NBC, have become a staple of network newscasts. Collectively, the networks help frame the medical agenda for a nation absorbed with the subject.

Interviews with correspondents and health professionals cite a number of reasons for high viewer interest. A population of aging baby boomers increasingly facing life-threatening diseases, such as breast and prostate cancer, environmental health threats and a frayed, potentially bankrupt health care system, have increased the appetite for health news coverage. Add to that the fact that health care involves hundreds of billions of dollars, a gargantuan chunk of annual federal expenditures and high political stakes.

Many point to the explosion of consumer activism during the 1980s as the impetus that drives people to demand more information in order to make health and lifestyle decisions. ABC's Johnson says this development occurred simultaneously with "obvious changes in medicine when physicians became less distant, less God-like, sort of more human, more available, more approachable." The increase in shared decisionmaking between patients and physicians also bolsters interest in health coverage.

ON A TYPICAL DAY AT HIS OFFICE AT Rockefeller Center in New York City, Bazell fielded a sitdown interview while also handling phone calls about a new tick outbreak, the dangers of hormone replacement and yet another new gene discovery. Bazell says it's critical for medical reporters to approach their specialty with a healthy dose of skepticism so they don't become conduits for incorrect information. "There are a lot of times that people make statements that are outright stupid and foolish, and lie, and they need to be exposed for that," says Bazell.

ABC's Johnson is based in Boston but is all over the network doing long-form pieces for "20/20" or "Nightline," as well as evening news spots and "Good Morning America." He believes health reporting has taken on "more production values, less talking heads" and is more investigative and "biting edge in how it looks at things."

He mentions a recent piece he did for "20/20" on "how certain heart drugs were approved in the 1980s before they were really studied," and another report on a breast cancer study in which data were falsified.

Johnson, like his colleagues, struggles to make sense of constantly changing research data. "Science tends to discover ongoing truth. It's never got the final truth." He says it's crucial to remind viewers that factors such as varying doses given to test populations can affect the outcome of research.

At CBS, Arnot says the seemingly endless parade of often conflicting studies leaves viewers "bombarded and confused." As a result, he says, it is better for journalists to avoid giving consumer advice. His approach is to help viewers understand "we are building data" and to encourage them to talk with support groups or a personal physician before making a health decision.

"At The New England Journal of Medicine, the editor once took me through their back archives and he said, 'You know what? Almost every single thing that was published in the year 1959 is now a lie. All we are trying to do is to figure out how to publish the best lies,'" Arnot says, explaining how "truth" can change as scientists retest and revise their theories.

Arnot blames a triad comprised of the medical industry, researchers and journalists making unwarranted claims or reaching premature conclusions about medical research for conditioning the public to expect black-and-white answers, and making them impatient with gray, tentative data.

Arnot cites a highly publicized medical journal study with a huge base of participants that showed possible connections between breast cancer and the use of estrogen in birth control pills or hormone replacement therapy after menopause. A subsequent study from a competing journal used a far smaller sample and seemed to refute the larger study. Result: more confusion for the viewer.

"What we have really been trying to do is to educate the viewers and say, 'Look, there hasn't been that blind, placebo-controlled, enormous study that is really going to give the answers. So until that is done hedge your bets. You really don't know,'" Arnot says.

CNN's Rutz says the news media, both print and broadcast, must resist a tendency to overdramatize stories with exaggerated "breakthrough" reports, especially in cancer and AIDS coverage. He blames slip-ups on journalists with insufficient background "who sometimes are not knowledgeable enough in the field to realize that a story isn't what it appears."

BUT RUTZ INSISTS BLAME MUST ALSO GO to the science newsmakers who "face a great deal of pressure now for research grants...and others who hire public relations representatives to pitch their work. They can package things in a pretty slick way and suck you in if you are not careful." He finds an increase in PR efforts by medical establishments and universities that tout clients whose work will appear in upcoming reports of scholarly research studies.

Some of the pitches can be bizarre. Rutz once received a mailing containing a cassette player that said: "Hi, this is your heart talking" when he lifted the lid. It was sent by a firm pushing a heart remedy. He has received a pig's umbilical cord in formaldehyde from a firm promoting animal fetal tissue for surgical re-

A POPULATION of aging baby boomers, environmental health threats and a frayed, potentially bankrupt health care system have increased the appetite for health news coverage.

2. INFORMATION AND INFLUENCE

> Robert Bazell says "hospitals... and research institutions are being massively threatened with cuts, and there is a lot of pressure from institutions to publicize themselves."

pairs. Once he even received a fake bullet with a message attached to "bite the bullet"—a grab for attention by a hospital touting its outpatient surgery services.

Bazell also sees a situation "where hospitals, in particular, and research institutions are being massively threatened with cuts, and there is a lot of pressure from institutions to publicize themselves." Government institutions facing the congressional budget ax also urgently seek publicity.

Another concern raised by TV medical correspondents is about the best way to handle reports on the results of studies from research journals. The New England Journal of Medicine and the Journal of the American Medical Association (JAMA), for example, provide weekly reports to the news media that often get heavy play.

Such reports are sent out several days in advance and are embargoed with a strict release date timed to favor the evening news broadcasts. JAMA even has its own regular video news releases (VNRs), available free to networks and local television stations via satellite.

Arnot of CBS dislikes the journal publicity blitz: "There is no question that the journals load up so they attract press attention." He said a journal might cluster a series of articles and an editorial for maximum attention. This, in addition to a carefully timed press conference, many times makes the story "inescapable."

Coverage of the dangers of cholesterol, for example, is fueled by a barrage of studies in scholarly journals, and advertising and public relations campaigns from the food industry and other segments of the health industry, Arnot says. There are so many cholesterol stories, he adds, because someone is spending a lot of money promoting the idea.

Arnot says CBS is "shying away from the journals because they trap you...into doing a story that has been around and you sort of build on it." It makes the journal editors the agenda-setters, he says, and "the people are fed up with the journals." While he says he values the fact that the journals are peer-reviewed—their articles are screened by scientists before publication to ensure scientific validity—and report on properly controlled test results, he believes the news media should make less of studies in their early stages and spend more time on enterprise reporting.

Daniel Maier, director of news and information for the Chicago-based American Medical Association and its journal, defends the way his organization, one of the more aggressive publicity seekers, disseminates information. The journals, he says, perform a valuable service by supplying the media with quality-controlled medical research data that are closely scrutinized by research experts, information they might not have otherwise. Maier also cites data the AMA has provided through its publications in the ongoing debate over smoking and the dangers of cancer that counter claims made by the tobacco industry.

Dr. Jerome Kassirer, editor in chief of the New England Journal of Medicine, says his organization doesn't do any self-promotion. "We don't think that's our responsibility. Our journal is written for physicians and our subscribers," he says. "We think it's appropriate for them to interpret data for themselves."

At the Annals of Internal Medicine, editor Frank Davidoff says only on rare occasions does his publication send out press releases or hold press conferences. He says one example is an upcoming series of five articles on how physicians can deal with issues of domestic violence as one in which the magazine had "some material of unique and special importance."

NBC's Bazell says he values the quality of the journals' work, but is troubled by embargoes. He points to the way one embargo was enforced at The New England Journal of Medicine by a former editor who Bazell said "was the most draconian about this—the authors were not allowed to discuss their results until it was published in the journal. I think that is a bad situation."

Bazell attended a conference in the 1980s at the National Institutes of Health "to deal with this because there were real horror stories of things that had public health implications but were kept from the public for months because people wanted their publication in a prestigious medical journal."

In one case, he recalls, results of a steroid injection that relieved spinal cord injuries were the subject of a major trial. "It was held up for several months because the editor of the [journal] did not want people to talk about it and the scientists went along with it." The editors of the science journals would counter that the fragmented release of study results can cause confusion and harm if the news media report the results prematurely. But a truce seems to prevail today between the journals and health correspondents. Now, Bazell says, "if there is a major finding about treatment of some disease, the results are announced immediately and the person can later publish in the journal and it is not withdrawn."

News organizations also receive numerous VNRs, sent by medical associations, pharmaceutical companies and other organizations with an interest in health coverage. But while these VNRs can make a health reporter's job easy, they must also be viewed with a dose of healthy skepticism.

To make coverage more accessible, producers and correspondents are abandoning technical, jargon-laden reports in favor of segments that engage viewers in more human terms. Rutz of CNN sees a greater use of anecdotes, more focus on people, a more conversational style and more

13. Medical Breakthrough

emphasis on editing, graphics and technical values in the future of medical journalism.

"I think it is healthy as long as we don't cross the line and just abandon our principles entirely in favor of production techniques," Rutz says. "We've got to keep our priorities straight, but our goal is to first of all to impart better information."

Rhonda Rowland, a CNN medical correspondent and former senior producer who now covers breaking medical and health news, appears on "Your Health," a weekly show, in addition to producing in-depth features. She, too, cites a growing tendency to humanize stories, to be more consumer oriented and to provide news and information people can use "to live their lives in a healthy way."

As CNN's only female medical correspondent, she believes it's important for her to not only do general coverage but also to examine health from a woman's perspective. She has done a show on breast cancer, as well as special reports on drug abuse, alcoholism, depression, menopause and estrogen replacement therapy.

"Women have different stresses in life—combining work with family, those sorts of things," Rowland says. "With issues like menopause, there are still a lot of social factors associated with that, and men can't always—because they are not there, they are not living it—they are not able to understand it quite as well."

She says that while network TV health coverage has improved over the past several years, it could be better. This feeling is echoed by Julia Moore, former executive director of Physicians for Social Responsibility in Washington, D.C., a group with about 20,000 members that focuses on environmental health threats. Moore praises network coverage but says it tends to overpersonalize stories. "What we generally have are stories that deal with one individual's confrontation of a disease or medical challenge," she says. "We don't have much of an effort to talk about the bigger picture: What are the implications? Why is one person's experience typical or atypical as a whole? Viewers find that confusing and draw their own conclusions, which may or may not be accurate." She also criticizes the networks for lack of follow-up on important stories.

Dr. Michael Jacobson, who directs the Center for Science in the Public Interest in Washington, D.C., says he is grateful for the extensive TV coverage of his organization's studies, such as those on the nutritional pitfalls of Mexican and Chinese food, fast food restaurants and movie popcorn drenched in fats. But when Center reports noted the positive qualities of seafood, or reported on a highly successful campaign to introduce low fat milk into an entire community's diet, they were virtually ignored, Jacobson says. "Television likes to cover controversy and problems. When we have good news or praise one thing or another, there is typically no coverage of that," he says.

Both the national health correspondents who cover the field and the public interest groups concerned with better health news see remarkable changes for the better, but there's still a long way to go in terms of informing viewers about complex issues.

Strait and others believe health care reform remains an issue that merits close attention, despite the perception by some that viewers tuned out past coverage. Strait emphasizes a special need to cover the human side of the story: people with inadequate coverage or no health insurance at all.

Others, like Arnot, believe that new technologies such as the Internet and the whole new panoply of multimedia technology will substantially alter the way health and medical information is delivered. Arnot predicts that computer-based information and satellite delivery will bring health news to the most remote African villages just as it does to the most cosmopolitan cities in North America.

He envisions health information being shared worldwide through broadcasting, cable, computers and the information superhighway. "It will become this magnificent tool because television is going to be everywhere," Arnot says exuberantly. "To slide on the back of that with this tremendous export we have, which is this engineered medical knowledge, I just think it is a magnificent future."

To make coverage more accessible, producers and correspondents are abandoning jargon-laden reports in favor of segments that engage viewers in more human terms.

UNDER SIEGE

The public's contempt for the mainstream media seems more intense than ever before. Can this relationship be saved?

Linda Fibich

Linda Fibich, a former assistant managing editor of the Milwaukee Journal, teaches at the University of Maryland College of Journalism. She wrote about the Newhouse newspapers in our November 1994 issue.

Ask news professionals to describe the mood out there about their craft and many use similar words: "Mistrustful. Cynical. Resentful," says Sandra Mims Rowe, editor of the Oregonian in Portland. "Critical, skeptical, hostile, unhappy," says Los Angeles Times media critic David Shaw.

"Angry," says Jim Gels, publisher of the Duluth News-Tribune in Minnesota. "At times hostile. Almost, in some cases, unwilling to listen."

Explaining our business is often an exercise in self-defense. Michael Marcotte, news director for KPLU-FM, an NPR affiliate at Pacific Lutheran University in Tacoma, Washington, recalls his recent speech to a civic group in Fircrest, population 5,500. He started to tell his audience that "journalism should be as good as it's ever been," when "suddenly I'm the lightning rod for all this contempt."

Hostility toward the media underlies the outrage over Connie Chung's "between you and me" exchange with Newt Gingrich's mother and the bipartisan support for Sen. Robert Byrd's effort to force journalists to disclose their outside income if they want to cover the Senate. Debate on the proposal quickly became a press-bashing exercise; not a single senator rose to defend the beleaguered media.

It's become harder not to take the criticism personally. Gels relates a summer encounter at the golf course, when a business acquaintance demanded to know how he could hire such ignorant, badly prepared reporters. "This was unsolicited, unprompted, after a 'good morning' exchange," says Gels. The incident was "a bit of an anomaly," but Gels says he's heard similar stories from others.

Ed Breen, managing editor of the Chronicle-Tribune in Marion, Indiana, asks, "Is anyone telling you that it isn't as much fun as it used to be?"

The Mood Out There

"Critical, skeptical, hostile, unhappy."
— DAVID SHAW, *Los Angeles Times media critic*

Americans have had a falling out with the Fourth Estate, enough so that reader and viewer attitudes today are the stuff of major news stories, not just academic and trade journals. Their complaint is consistent, and rising in intensity: Journalism is "too negative, too negative, too negative," says Andrew Kohut, director of the Times Mirror Center for the People & the Press. The bad blood is such that a majority of participants in a recent center survey said that the press gets in the way of the country's efforts to solve its problems.

What this means is in dispute among journalists. To many, a bad reception goes with the territory. But to others, the bleak surveys and grim anecdotes lay down a challenge. Behind them is a public sense of betrayal. And behind the betrayal are high expectations of the press, many the same expectations that we have of ourselves. The common ground deserves attention.

WHY SO MUCH ANGER AGAINST THE media? James Warren, the Chicago Tribune's outspoken Washington bureau chief, cited some of the reasons at a forum last May at American University.

"I was just jotting some notes to myself, and realizing the extent to which people do view us as hypocritical, privacy-invading, emotionally and practically remote from them, paternalistic and prone to frequent error," he said. "And there's ample evidence to support each of those beliefs. All of which melds into what I find a very depressing—visceral almost—disdain of us."

Seated to Warren's right was Joann Byrd, then the Washington Post's ombudsman. From some 45,000 telephone calls in her three-year tenure, Byrd told the assembly, she had concluded that "people don't see journalism as public service anymore."

Instead they believe "that journalists are engaged in self-service—getting ratings, selling newspapers or making their careers,...that our ideas about detachment are so much hogwash.... They feel cheated, I think, that the rules changed and nobody told them."

14. Under Siege

A month before the forum, U.S. News & World Report's John Leo noted in a nationally syndicated column that there were three sessions on "Why America Hates the Press" during the American Society of Magazine Editors meeting in New York. "The self-flagellating panel discussion is almost a must at media conventions," he wrote.

Besides the talk were treatises. Leo mentioned two: In a December issue of The New Yorker, Adam Gopnik attacked the media's "weird, free-form nastiness." In March, Paul Starobin of the National Journal took to the pages of the Columbia Journalism Review to castigate the "cynical" Washington press corps as "A Generation of Vipers."

Leo might have put his own magazine on the list. U.S. News in January identified the press' key excess as "edge" or "attitude," closing the piece with a quote from Marvin Kalb, the NBC veteran who is now director of Harvard's Joan Shorenstein Center on the Press, Politics and Public Policy. "Why do Americans hate the press?" Kalb asked. "Because you deserve it."

The public rancor comes against a backdrop of deep concern about the future of traditional news outlets. Newspaper circulation continues to decline. Two more U.S. cities—Houston and Milwaukee—have become one-paper towns, and the highly regarded New York Newsday folded in July. The networks and newsweeklies struggle against marginalization in an ever-fragmenting marketplace. New media are on the rise in forms that much of the public finds more responsive, from talk radio to the Internet.

So if the mainstream media seem feverish with self-examination, they aren't lacking cause. But have Americans really come to hate the press? Or have they just turned up the volume of a not-so-recent message—that they're fed up with the very forms, conventions and behavior that disturb the press itself?

As Leo observed in the April column, "So many people are so mad at reporters and journalists...they fail to notice how many reporters and journalists share their opinions." Put that way, what looks like a ruinous parting could actually present opportunities for reconciliation. They lie where the public mood converges with our own doubts about our performance.

THE AMERICAN PUBLIC HAS ALWAYS HAD a cranky side in its view of the press. Twenty-one years ago, the Gallup organization asked 611 adults how much confidence they had in the mass media when it came "to reporting the news fully, accurately and fairly." Sixty-nine percent reported either "a great deal" or "a fair amount." But between a quarter and a third—29 percent—reported "not very much" or "none at all." And this was in April 1974, just months before Richard M. Nixon resigned his presidency over the Watergate scandal—when journalists,

> "Mistrustful. Cynical. Resentful."
> —SANDRA MIMS ROWE, editor, the Oregonian

> "Angry. At times hostile. Almost, in some cases, unwilling to listen."
> —JIM GELS, publisher, the Duluth News-Tribune

> "Sensitive, slightly suspicious, less trusting."
> —ED BREEN, managing editor, the Chronicle-Tribune in Marion, Indiana

according to the rosy view from the '90s, were the saviors of the republic.

Those numbers are almost reversed today. In January, an NBC/Wall Street Journal poll of 500 adults found that only 26 percent had a "very positive" or "somewhat positive" impression of the news media. Fifty percent had either "somewhat negative" or "very negative" impressions, and 22 percent described themselves as "neutral."

"There's more criticism of the way the press conducts its business, particularly its watchdog role," Kohut says. "And the attitude is more fundamentally negative than in years."

Gallup surveys show that in the dozen years from 1981 to 1993, the share of Americans who felt that journalists had high ethical standards slid by more than a quarter, from 30 percent to 22 percent.

These are disturbing findings, to be sure. However, in the puckish words of Robert Lichter, codirector of the Center for Media and Public Affairs, "it's important not to be too negative in writing about negativity," lest you contribute to the negativism surrounding the media. Lichter says the public may be "surly. Certainly suspicious. But I think somewhere in there you'd have to use ambivalent."

Deep in a 1993 poll, the Los Angeles Times asked 1,703 respondents whether they had more, less or the same amount of confidence in the news media as they had five years before. The largest share—43 percent—reported that their confidence was unchanged. Thirty-two percent had less, with most citing sensationalism, incomplete or selective reporting, bias or unfairness, and inaccuracy. Nearly a quarter, 23 percent, actually reported a rise in confidence. Their top reasons demonstrated a healthy appetite for information: more news coverage, more and new technology, and immediate or live coverage.

That data may be spun in any number of ways, some grim. One reading, however, leaves wiggle room for optimism: People haven't given up. Many recognize and appreciate that changes in the media will deliver even more of what they want and need to know. What they complain about includes the same things a lot of thoughtful journalists dislike about the way the job is being done.

The correlation between the public's attitude and the press' isn't perfect. But even on points where a minority of the press agrees with the charges against it, the minorities are large, in the neighborhood of 40 percent.

Early this year, the Times Mirror Center compared views of the media among the public, the press, and national and local opinion leaders. "What we found is that the public had a favorable attitude toward the press, but objected to some of its practices," Kohut says. While the public gave overall grades of A and B to the print and electronic media, he adds, the press was also judged "too intrusive, too negative, driving controversies rather than just reporting on them."

2. INFORMATION AND INFLUENCE

Meanwhile, Kohut says, "the press owns up to a lot of its own criticism." The spring study, titled "The People, the Press & their Leaders," found that a majority of the newspeople surveyed thought that public anger with the press was justified, either in unqualified terms or in part.

Forty-seven percent of those working for the national media and 56 percent of the local journalists polled answered either yes or a qualified yes when asked if there was validity in the charge that "the personal values of people in the news media often make it difficult for them to understand and cover such things as religion and family values."

An overwhelming 80 percent of the national journalists and 75 percent of the locals agreed that "too little attention is paid to complex issues." And 58 percent of the national sample and 51 percent of the local agreed with the public's complaint that "the press inadequately covers positive developments."

The biggest difference between the press' self-assessment and the views of its audience was over the adversarial nature of the media. But even here, a third of the journalists found validity in charges that "the press is more adversarial than necessary." Meanwhile, 41 percent of the national journalists and 33 percent of the locals said that in covering the personal and ethical behavior of politicians, the press was fueling controversy rather than only reporting the news.

The survey made headlines for its finding that the press is less cynical than the public in its view of politicians. The news value was in the element of surprise, given the hits the press takes for excess cynicism. Some observers, however, were at no loss to explain.

"The press sees leadership up close and personal, and sees the good with the bad," Kohut says. "The public, increasingly, sees only the bad."

WE KNOW WHAT'S WRONG, WELL enough that when we hear it described a lot of us squirm.

In 1989, The New Yorker's Janet Malcolm wrote "The Journalist and the Murderer," an account of how author Joe McGinniss maintained Dr. Jeffrey MacDonald's cooperation during research for the book "Fatal Vision." MacDonald was kept in the belief that the book would cast doubt on his guilt in the celebrated murders of his pregnant wife and two children, even after McGinniss' opinion began to tilt against him.

"Every journalist who is not too stupid or too full of himself to notice what is going on knows that what he does is morally indefensible," Malcolm observed in her opening paragraphs. "He is a kind of confidence man, preying on people's vanity, ignorance or loneliness, gaining their trust and betraying them without remorse."

"I think it's supposed to be my job to take the yelling.... For some reason, people just really enjoy bashing us. And I think it's perfectly fine...," says NBC's Gwen Ifill.

Malcolm soon would face ethical problems of her own, accused of fabricating quotes in a legal battle that ultimately went to the U.S. Supreme Court. Still, the "Fatal Vision" story caused discomfort in America's newsrooms. At the Milwaukee Journal, a veteran editor tacked Malcolm's piece to a bulletin board with a memo recommending it to the brave. Anyone but a journalistic virgin or saint had committed McGinniss' offense.

Eugene Assaf is an attorney with the Washington office of Kirkland & Ellis, a Chicago law firm that represents a number of corporate clients against the media. It handled the 1993 lawsuit against NBC after "Dateline" rigged the explosion of a General Motors truck. Assaf indicts several practices that he feels contribute to journalism's credibility problems, specifying that he does not speak for his firm or its clients:

"Reporters request to talk about subject X, and you sit down for the interview and they start pulling out documents that relate to Y and get hostile," he says. Such behavior is "increasingly common, not the exception."

He finds fault with an unexceptional strategy of investigative reporting: "The [last-minute] call to the subject…. One does not get to participate in the formation of the story. The story is already done." The reporter may refuse to go off the record, when he has likely done so with others as the story progressed. He imposes a deadline. "The story is going to run in a couple of days. Ask how long they've been working on it, and they tell you three months," Assaf says. "That's not fair."

Assaf doesn't see much bias of the ideological variety. The liberal-conservative paradigms "avoid the issue," which to him is bias in favor of negativism.

Assaf's comments could be dismissed as self-interested. But like Malcolm's McGinniss story, the lawyer's observations prick the conscience.

Howard Kurtz, media reporter for the Washington Post and author of the 1993 newspaper critique "Media Circus," pulls no punches: "I think we bear 95 percent of the responsibility for the low repute in which we are held. In no other profession would top executives scratch their heads and wonder why it is that a substantial proportion of the customers think they're scum."

NEWSPAPER OMBUDSMEN DEAL WITH unhappy readers for a living. How do they gauge the public mood about the media? While suggesting that some perspective is in order—"People who like what the paper is doing do not call us," wrote Gina Lubrano of the San Diego Union-Tribune—several of the eight ombudsmen who replied to an AJR questionnaire gave the critics their due.

Ombudsman Pat Riley of the Orange County Register summarized the common themes in his response: "The dread blame-the-messenger factor," inescapable since the media must deliver some bad news; allegations of bias; accuracy problems; the ready availability of live coverage, which has enabled Americans to judge for themselves and to catch errors of fact or opinionated nuance in reporting.

John Sweeney, public editor for the News Journal in Wilmington, Delaware, wrote that the press "makes an easy target. We make too many mistakes. We're hard to read. We avoid real issues and go for scandal or inside politics. We still think we're the only game in town. And we really don't listen to our critics...no matter what we say."

Jean Otto of Denver's Rocky Mountain News wrote that the public seems "willing to draw lines that the media, whose primary concern is news, have been unwilling to accept. Every time an ordinary person, or even a public figure, faces a battery of reporters and photographers out to get a story, people put themselves in that person's shoes and hate the press for going too far."

Otto also teaches journalism, and finds her students "much more restrained about what they think journalists should do. They want respect for people's privacy, public figures and celebrities no less than the family next door.... They often put human values above news values and think the media do too little of that."

The Boston Globe's Mark Jurkowitz wrote that "in many ways, the media seem to have given up all pretense of being objective middlemen, simple purveyors of information. All over the TV and radio dial, journalistic pundits constantly proffer their boisterous opinions on the weighty issues of the day, reinforcing citizens' perceptions that they are not simply delivering the news, they are shaping the news. If that's the case, they are much fairer game for people who are unhappy with the news they read and see."

In the view of many experts, the relationship between the mainstream press and mainstream America can be summed up in a single word: alienated. For a complex variety of reasons, they say, the press is out of touch with the real concerns of real people, especially on two fronts—political and cultural. And the real people, meanwhile, have it in for the press.

"Journalists have made a virtue of alienation," says Jon Katz, a longtime newspaper editor and former media critic for Rolling Stone and New York magazine who now writes for Wired. "If you ask a journalist, 'Do you know people are ticked off at you?' they'll say, 'Yeah, it means I'm doing my job.'"

William Greider, a former Washington Post assistant managing editor, remarked upon alienation in his book, "Who Will Tell the People": "Like the other primary political institutions, the press has lost viable connections to its own readers and grown more distant from them.... As an institution, the media have gravitated toward elite interests and converged with those powerful few who already dominate politics. People sense this about the news, even if they are unable to describe how it happened or why they feel so alienated from the newspapers that purport to speak for them."

The 1992 presidential campaign was instructive. It marked the first time that both major party candidates, not to mention a renegade third, made substantial use of "new media"—talk shows, MTV, other electronic forums with voters. It was an end run around the press corps. Far from objecting, the citizenry was enlivened.

"Ross Perot went to the extreme length of shunning the press and mocking it," Thomas E. Patterson, a Syracuse University political scientist, wrote in his 1993 book, "Out of Order." Perot's "fights with the press helped him: Each time he criticized the press, the switchboard of his Dallas headquarters lit up with calls from people volunteering to join his campaign."

And there is research to support the notion that the public views the press as part of the problem.

Five years ago, the Kettering Foundation sought to assess the health of American democracy. With the Harwood Group, a Maryland public issues research firm, the foundation conducted focus groups in 10 U.S. cities. When the work was done, David Mathews, Kettering's president, wrote that there was nothing less accurate than the popular view that the public is apathetic about public affairs.

"In fact, they are just the opposite," Mathews concluded in "Citizens and Politics: A View from Main Street America." "They feel as though they have been locked out of their own homes—and they react the way people do when they have been evicted from their own property." When people named "exactly who dislodged them from their rightful place in American democracy," they pointed at "politicians...at powerful lobbyists, and—this came as a surprise—at people in the media. They see these three groups as a political class, the rulers of an oligarchy that has replaced democracy."

When the Kettering researchers probed their focus groups on the subject of the media, participants complained that oversimplified sound bites left them bereft of any real substance, that reporting on policy issues was hampered by media negativism. "Scouring the streets for personal scandals, badgering some people on aspects of their personal lives, playing up arguments over small points between campaigners and among officeholders—it is this kind of coverage that troubles the American people," the study concluded.

The public journalism movement, an effort to "reconnect" newspapers to their communities, grew in part out of such frustration with political coverage dominated by charges and countercharges and inside baseball at the expense of substantive issues that affect voters (see "The Gospel of Public Journalism," September 1994).

The Ombudsmen Speak

"It's the hot issues of our times...that stir most of the criticism. The messenger covering those issues draws the attention and the apparent hostility."
—LARRY FIQUETTE, *St. Louis Post-Dispatch*

Readers' anger "has been mined by talk show hosts whose political agendas attract listeners of like mind.... They fan distrust of the written word by telling listeners what they want to hear."
—GINA LUBRANO, *San Diego Union-Tribune*

2. INFORMATION AND INFLUENCE

"IF YOU HAD ONLY ONE LINE," JEAN Gaddy Wilson advises, it should be this: "Demographics is destiny." Wilson, executive director of New Directions for News at the University of Missouri, says the mainstream media have fallen behind the demographic curve and all that it portends.

Newspapers, newsweeklies, conventional television represent old authority to many Americans, she observes. "Old authority doesn't fit current reality. People live very different lives than the events that are put forward every day [as news].... 'Roseanne' and 'The Simpsons' teach us more about ourselves."

Wilson notes that no one thing has caused this disconnect. She names a few contributors: "One in eight of us was born in a foreign country.... Men are becoming single parents.... Well-educated women are choosing to have kids without men. The vast changes in aging. People don't retire, they undertake another career.... Forty-six percent of children 13 to 17 own a computer."

Media content too often fails to fit the dynamic demographics, she says. Moreover, it follows the old formulas with slavish dedication.

And so Americans fail to see themselves in the one form of commerce protected by their Constitution. That their perplexity and disappointment convert to anger doesn't surprise Wilson. "This was once a place you could trust," she says of the press. "It's as if your mother said she loved you and she turned out to be terrible."

Wired's Katz feels that two developments in particular have put the mainstream press in trouble: First is the "tragic alienation of the young, which has come about through a relentless attack [through the media] on youth culture." The message traditional media deliver to youth is that they are stupid slackers, that they can't or won't read, Katz says.

Second is a trend that he thinks history will view "as a terrible mistake—this broadening of the journalistic mandate to include people's privacy. Journalists have actually permitted themselves to become the new moral squads...[and] I think people resent it tremendously."

He says the latter development, which made Donna Rice, Gennifer Flowers and Paula Corbin Jones household names, has made the journalistic agenda completely different from the public agenda.

JIM WARREN SAYS BLAME FOR THE CURRENT mess must be shared. "Yeah, we screw up...," he told the American University audience. "But I also think that somewhere out there is a basic misunderstanding of what we do, how we do it and our role in a democracy."

Max Cacas, NPR's news operations

"Every time an ordinary person, or even a public figure, faces a battery of reporters and photographers... people put themselves in that person's shoes and hate the press for going too far."
—JEAN OTTO, *Rocky Mountain News*

"No, I don't think Americans hate us. They get angry at us, they despair of us, they sometimes feel betrayed by us and...they sometimes pity us in their perception that we have strayed from our mission of presenting the news dispassionately...."
—PAT RILEY, *Orange County Register*

producer, makes similar points. When Americans complain that mainstream media content is irrelevant to their lives, Cacas says, they are failing to uphold their end of an implicit democratic bargain.

"Think about your news junkie.... For the most part, that person is going to be well-educated. And then—I hate to say this—I look at the average American who says he doesn't understand why we should care about the U.S.-Japan trade dispute.... People aren't being told that the way to understand this is to study."

San Diego's Lubrano acknowledges that a core of her paper's readers have valid complaints. But beyond them are people who get "angry when newspaper stories do not reflect their values and opinions.... That anger has been mined by talk show hosts whose political agendas attract listeners of like mind.... They fan distrust of the written word by telling listeners what they want to hear."

Larry Fiquette, readers' advocate for the St. Louis Post-Dispatch, believes much anti-media sentiment amounts to shooting the messenger: "It's the hot issues of our times...that stir most of the criticism," he wrote. "The messenger covering those issues draws the attention and the apparent hostility.... The anger we're hearing stems more likely from Americans' impatience with their leaders' efforts to solve the nation's intensifying problems."

David Bartlett, president of the Radio-Television News Directors Association, says bleak assessments are magnified by the fact that "the press is the most self-examining and self-critical institution in the world" and by the self-interested nature of much criticism from the outside.

Bartlett says the words he'd choose to describe the public's view of the media mood would be "a lot less negative than our critics would have us believe.... The public is skeptical of all big institutions, the media included. And I think that's healthy.... I think it's a gross and self-serving misreading of the various polls and studies to suggest that the public is hostile. As long as I'm doing better than the politicians I write about, I'm content."

NBC reporter Gwen Ifill no doubt spoke for many when she observed at American University, in what seemed like a single breath, "We spend an inordinate amount of time navel-gazing, looking at ourselves and saying, 'Oh-woe-is-me-why-do-they-hate-us, oh no—they're yelling at me!'

"I think it's supposed to be my job to take the yelling.... For some reason, people just really enjoy bashing us. And I think it's perfectly fine.... I don't think that we can expect or demand anyone to feel sorry for us. We are in wonderful perches. I get to sit in the front row and ask the president of the United States questions. I am paid better than most average people for doing what I get to do and what I love to do."

Here she almost paused. "So it doesn't bother me a lot that people hate me."

BUT FOR EVERY BRAVE FRONT, EACH suggestion that the mainstream news media simply go about their business and wait for the pendulum to swing, there is a news professional troubled by the public mood and searching for a way to respond.

Boston's Jurkowitz: "I think we ignore these issues at our grave peril." San Diego's Lubrano: "To be stoic about public opinion is suicide, especially when reader complaints are justified." Duluth's Gels: "No brainer. We all should be worried about it. [It's] the cancer of readership decline."

Advice abounds, from within and without media ranks. At its core is recognition that the mainstream media must communicate more responsively and responsibly, and do both more nimbly. One suggestion recurs: listen. We can't occupy the center of an information universe that no longer has one.

To Jean Gaddy Wilson, "the great yawning opportunity for the media is for them to listen to the people who receive the messages" and change according to the feedback they hear, "just as a number of restaurants are having to develop foods that are low fat—getting rid of the damaging material."

Richard C. Harwood, consultant on the Kettering study, says journalists must ask different sorts of questions and listen differently to the answers elicited—in effect, to share power in shaping coverage. This means, he says, "opening up the conversation rather than looking for the quote for the third graf."

Syracuse University's Patterson tells journalists to "stop making themselves the center of their stories," a problem he says is greater in television but which nonetheless occurs in print. If the messages themselves are given more play, he says, the interpretations journalists love to make will naturally have more credibility.

Lubrano noted that "fewer than 40 newspapers in this country feel they owe their readers a forum by establishing ombudsmen positions. Ombudsmen will not stop readers from being angry at newspapers, but they will give them a voice. Our readers like the idea of having someone around whose job it is to listen to them, especially in these days of voice mail and changing technology."

From Indiana, Ed Breen acknowledges that "if you talk to old codgers like myself, we sat around newsrooms for 30 years and issued decrees about what was good for newspapers. We listen more to readers these days." He mentions Gannett's News 2000 program, which at the Chronicle-Tribune includes a reader advisory group that meets monthly. The paper receives—and runs—more letters to the editor. Asked if the techniques are working, Breen says, "I think it's too soon to tell."

Gels suggests that news executives "get more in touch at the level where things actually happen—reporters, newsmakers, assigning editors—and truly listen…. Empathize with our readers, and figure out how something is going to affect them before we print it."

At the Oregonian, Sandy Rowe keeps a file filled with clippings dating back to the 1980s, "all of which have a lede: Credibility of news media has never been lower." She believes the press has heard the message, but that "we have not acted on it enough. Too many of us have tried to see it as someone else's problem, as a problem of perception." Acting on the message, she acknowledges, "has to be a long process, not an event."

She urges journalists to develop expertise. "Not enough of us know enough about the subjects we report on. And when there weren't as many media outlets and things weren't as complex, that may have been satisfactory." It isn't any longer, she says.

Doesn't the public bear part of the blame for the decay of public discourse? Is there a laziness factor out there? Rowe regards the question as irrelevant. "We can only take responsibility," she says, "for our share."

> "This was once a place you could trust," Jean Gaddy Wilson says of the press. "It's as if your mother said she loved you and she turned out to be terrible."

Article 15

CBS, 60 Minutes, and the Unseen Interview

Lawrence K. Grossman

Lawrence K. Grossman is the author of The Electronic Democracy: Reshaping Democracy in the Information Age *and former president of NBC News and PBS.*

The controversy over the aborted *60 Minutes* tobacco segment has raised enough issues and questions to fill an imposing journalistic tome on news practices, policies, and ethics. On one level it can be argued that for the public, CBS's decision last October to kill its interview with the highest-ranking executive ever to blow the whistle on the tobacco industry produced noteworthy results:

♦ Thanks to CBS's decision, the devastating allegations by the former vice president of research and development at Brown and Williamson Tobacco Corporation (B&W) captured continuing front-page coverage in the nation's press. The leaks about his charges probably got more sustained notice than the broadcast itself would have. They focused public attention on allegations that B&W, the nation's third-largest tobacco company, squelched research on "safer" cigarettes; altered documents to remove damaging references to the "safe cigarette" project; used an additive known to cause cancer in laboratory animals in its pipe tobacco; and in testimony by its chief executive, lied to Congress about the addictive qualities of tobacco.

> The leaks about the charges in the interview probably got more sustained notice than the broadcast itself would have

♦ Government agencies have been encouraged to investigate a conspiracy to cover up evidence on the dangers of smoking, examine the question of perjury before Congress, look into accusations that the industry's scientific research is deceptive, and seek evidence that tobacco companies have deliberately chosen not to make less harmful products even though they have the ability to do so.

♦ Americans have been alerted to the fact that tobacco companies and others, when faced with damaging exposure, are increasingly resorting to expensive, intimidating, take-no-prisoners litigation to circumvent the First Amendment, strong-arm the press, silence witnesses, and keep important facts from coming to the public's attention.

◆ The nation has also learned of the growing vulnerability of mainstream news organizations, which are becoming relatively minor subsidiaries of huge global corporations with multiple financial interests. Top corporate executives are paid to concentrate on their companies' bottom line and stockholders' returns rather than on their news divisions' responsibilities to the public. That vulnerability was exposed last summer when ABC caved in to a $10 billion libel suit by Philip Morris (see "ABC, Philip Morris, and the Infamous Apology," CJR, November/December).

The *60 Minutes* controversy also served to tarnish the reputations of the network, of CBS News and of *60 Minutes*, the longest-running, most successful, and most honored news program in television history. Several of its squabbling big guns were taken down a peg or two. The tough newsmen who demand that others answer their questions didn't do so well with questions aimed at them.

On the personal level, the episode left several major casualties in its wake, among them: Jeffrey Wigand, a former B&W head of research, whose cover was blown as the CBS News source who pinpointed alleged tobacco company malfeasance; Lowell Bergman, a highly respected investigative producer for *60 Minutes*, charged by colleagues in the press with using flawed and unorthodox newsgathering tactics, and exercising questionable journalistic judgment; and Ellen Kaden, the widely admired general counsel of CBS, blamed for "running scared," "caving in," and even possibly "being guilty of a serious conflict of interest" in making the decision to cancel the *60 Minutes* exposé rather than risk a major lawsuit.

But before looking at the lessons for journalism to be learned from the many issues involved in the *60 Minutes* tobacco episode, here is the story of what happened, based on press reports, mostly from *The New York Times*, *The Wall Street Journal*, the New York *Daily News*, *The Washington Post*, and trade publications, and on interviews with principals at CBS who were directly involved. (Most stipulated that our conversations should be off-the-record and on deep background. A very few of the principals did not return phone calls or would not talk about the episode at all.)

THE REPORTING

Lowell Bergman of *60 Minutes* met Jeffrey Wigand in February 1994, while working on an investigative story about another tobacco company. The story alleged that Philip Morris had developed a cigarette that passed lower incendiary level tests and at the same time passed smokers' taste tests. Then, fearing lawsuits stemming from years of making cigarettes that were not "fire-safe," the company decided to kill the project and label its records about the work done on "fire-safe" cigarettes as attorney work product. That way, the records would be safe from discovery procedures by plaintiffs and government officials.

Bergman, a highly respected, independent-minded, and award-winning investigative producer, a twelve-and-a-half-year veteran of *60 Minutes*, had obtained 800 to 1,000 pages of confidential Philip Morris documents. An anti-tobacco activist tipped him off to a former B&W executive who lived in Louisville and who might be able to analyze the papers and help out as an expert consultant. Bergman called the former executive at home several times, but he would not come to the phone. Finally, using an old investigative reporter's trick, Bergman phoned late at night, woke him up, and said he'd be in Louisville at 11 A.M. the following morning, sitting in the lobby of the Seelbach Hotel reading *The New York Times*.

The executive who showed up in the hotel lobby at 11 A.M. was Jeffrey Wigand. A chemist with a doctorate in endocrinology and biochemistry, Wigand went to work for B&W in 1989 as vice president of scientific research, expecting to help develop a less harmful cigarette, his friends say. He was fired in March 1993, according to his lawyer, after B&W decided to kill his research. Once a $300,000-a-year executive, Wigand is now a $30,000-a-year Louisville high school teacher. He has two young daughters, one with spina bifida.

Wigand left B&W with a severance agreement that paid him for two years and continued his family's health insurance. In turn, Wigand had signed a confidentiality pledge. Not long afterward, in September 1993, B&W sued Wigand, suspending his pay and health insurance, after learning that he had complained about the terms of his severance to another executive at the company who also was being fired. In November, a tougher "nondisclosure settlement agreement" was negotiated and Wigand's severance and health insurance were reinstated.

Although Bergman did not know it when they first met in Louisville in February 1994, Wigand had been called more than a year earlier to testify in a Justice Department investigation of the industry's efforts to develop a "fire-safe" cigarette. In keeping with his confidentiality agreement, Wigand notified B&W about the Justice Department's summons. B&W provided him with counsel to protect its interests in preserving the company's confidential information. (This fall, B&W sued Wigand for breach of his nondisclosure pledge. In its complaint B&W charged that despite Wigand's sworn testimony to the Justice Department stating that the company was *not* able to translate its safer-cigarette research into the development of a "fire-safe" cigarette, the former executive had submitted an affidavit saying just the opposite in a Massachusetts case involving Philip Morris.)

At their first meeting in the Louisville hotel lobby, Bergman showed the former tobacco research executive eighteen pages of tobacco company documents, asked Wigand if he understood the scientific language and material in them and, satisfied that he did, offered to hire him as an expert consultant for *60 Minutes* to interpret the material and verify its contents. After the Louisville meeting, an agreement was quickly struck with the CBS News business affairs/legal department that called for Wigand to work as an expert consultant for *60 Minutes* for no more than ten days to provide a confidential report on the Philip Morris documents and be available to testify in court if CBS News were sued for its *60 Minutes* piece. The contract also specified that Wigand would not talk about any matters concerning B&W, and would not appear on the air.

Shortly before the *60 Minutes* story ran, Wigand came to New York to screen the final version of the piece and check its

2. INFORMATION AND INFLUENCE

accuracy. The story on Philip Morris and inflammable cigarettes aired in March 1994. Wigand was reported to have been paid an estimated $12,000 for out-of-pocket expenses and per diem on that assignment. The exact figure has never been revealed. Network news divisions customarily pay between $500 and $1,000 a day for expert consultants. So CBS's payments to Wigand for his time and expenses working on that *60 Minutes* piece were not out of line with general network practice. Not at all clear, though, was whether Wigand's work for CBS violated his confidentiality agreement. CBS's assignment involved Philip Morris, not B&W, but Wigand's knowledge of the tobacco industry's practices came from his work at B&W.

In any event, the trial judge in the Massachusetts case disallowed Wigand's appearance on the ground, among others, that the defense would be unable to adequately cross-examine Wigand without causing him to breach his agreement with B&W.

After the *60 Minutes* story on Philip Morris's incendiary cigarettes ran in March 1994, Bergman kept Wigand on his "tickler list," calling him periodically. Wigand told Bergman he had gotten a subpoena from the antitrust division of the Justice Department, as well as summonses to testify on cigarette health issues from Representative Henry A. Waxman and the Food and Drug Administration. Wigand was becoming known as an antismoking expert. (Under the terms of his contract with B&W, Wigand had to notify the tobacco company before he talked to the government officials, which he did. But apparently he had felt no obligation to tell B&W about his work for CBS News on the Philip Morris story.)

In April, Wigand, greatly disturbed, called Bergman to tell him he had received two anonymous telephone death threats against his family, warning him to lay off the tobacco industry. He and his wife were frightened, but were afraid to call the local police, evidently concerned about the tobacco company's influence in town. Arrangements were made to help get the Wigands in touch with the FBI, which put on a phone cover that recorded several hang-up calls from pay phones, but no death threats.

Sources at CBS say Wigand told Bergman that when his B&W severance pay ran out in March 1995, he'd be prepared to talk to *60 Minutes* about his experiences there. The two kept in occasional touch. Those contacts were reported to the CBS legal department, which raised no objection.

In March, Bergman submitted a "blue sheet" to *60 Minutes* proposing an investigative story on B&W. The "blue sheet" said a former executive of the company would be ready to talk soon. The proposal warned that B&W was a litigious company that had won a $3 million libel suit, a record judgment, against CBS in the 1980s for a commentary by Walter Jacobson, a newsman on a CBS-owned station in Chicago. The commentary had accused B&W of pandering to children to hook them on cigarettes.

A few weeks later, *60 Minutes* staff producers went to Louisville to meet with Wigand. They had a pleasant dinner in a French restaurant and talked in "general terms" but did not get into specifics. Then, in April, a producer returned with an audio recorder to debrief Wigand. On that trip, a source inside CBS says, the producer learned that Wigand's confidentiality agreement would not expire on March 25, the date his severance pay ended, and flew back to New York with copies of the Wigand settlement documents.

Nevertheless, the producers knew in general terms what Wigand might say, even without yet getting him on tape or on camera. During that period, the University of California at San Francisco obtained papers revealing previously undocumented tobacco industry activities, especially activities of B&W and its parent company, the British American Tobacco Company (now B.A.T. Industries). B&W sued the university in an attempt to have its papers removed from the library shelves, claiming they had been taken illegally from the confidential files of its outside law firms.

In July 1995, articles focusing on the tobacco company documents at the University of California were published in a special issue of *The Journal of the American Medical Association (JAMA)*. In its thirty-nine-page section, *JAMA* described the "massive, detailed, and damning evidence of the tactics of the tobacco industry" that the documents revealed. The papers, *JAMA* said, were "from Brown and Williamson Tobacco Corporation (B&W), the British American Tobacco Company (B.A.T.), and other tobacco interests provided by an anonymous source, obtained from Congress, and received from the private papers of a former B.A.T. officer."

B&W eventually lost its suit against the university and the complete indexed document set remains on deposit in the Archives and Special Collections Department of the University of California, San Francisco, Library and Center for Knowledge Management. (They are available on CD-ROM and via the Internet's World Wide Web at http://www.library.ucsf.edu/tobacco.)

Throughout the early summer of 1995, Wigand tried to decide whether or not to go on camera for *60 Minutes*. He was nervous and uncertain. At one point, Wigand and his wife, who worked nights in a Louisville clothing store to supplement Wigand's teaching income, flew to New York, presumably to be interviewed on videotape, but they backed out at the last moment. Wigand's wife, in particular, was deeply anxious, concerned, and worried about the fallout from his anticipated *60 Minutes* appearance. Sources say Wigand wanted to tell the story out of concern for what the tobacco company was doing to the health of its millions of customers and out of guilt for keeping quiet about his own inside knowledge of what he considered to be its criminal activities, even if his speaking out would clearly violate his confidentiality agreement. Wigand thought he might be able to get out from under the tough nondisclosure restrictions on the grounds that, he felt, the agreement was "virtually extorted from him" and that it should not be enforceable, because it required him to hide information about the company's alleged criminal activities.

In June, Wigand's lawyer asked CBS News to provide written indemnification for his client's legal fees and costs if he were to be sued for libel by B&W as a result of his appearance on *60 Minutes*. One of CBS's in-house lawyers who works on *60 Minutes* matters, Jonathan Sternberg, responded that CBS would agree to indemnify Wigand for libel as long as he went on camera and told the truth.

In July, the *60 Minutes* producers learned that the Justice Department had opened a criminal inquiry into possible perjury by top tobacco company executives in their testimony before a congressional committee denying that nicotine is addictive. It looked as if Wigand would be called in that inquiry to testify about his research at B&W. They also learned that Wigand was listed as an expert defense witness for ABC in the Philip Morris-R.J. Reynolds libel suit. The *60 Minutes* staff felt a certain urgency about getting Wigand on videotape so that if in any of his court appearances, he should be ordered not to talk to the press, Wigand would be able to say an interview with *60 Minutes* had already been videotaped without violating a court order. The *60 Minutes* group also wanted "to get his information in the can" so they would have time to corroborate his assertions and check his statements with information that was available in the B&W papers and other sources. (The documents at the University of California covered the years before Wigand started working at B&W.)

On August 3, Wigand and his wife finally agreed to be interviewed by Mike Wallace. Because the Wigands were still so fearful about what they were doing, Bergman gave Wigand a hand-written note assuring him that CBS would not air the interview without first getting his permission, and stating that they would discuss the matter further on September 3, a month after the taping. The show felt the need to have a commitment by a date certain, rather than risk dragging out the issue indefinitely. In a later interview with *The New York Times* Bergman explained that his intent "had not been to give Mr. Wigand any sort of 'veto power' over the report, but instead to be considerate of the difficult position in which Mr. Wigand found himself" in view of the effects a lawsuit was likely to have on his financial situation and the health problems in his family.

Later in August, after the interview had been recorded, CBS received a letter from Wigand's attorney, Richard Scruggs, stating that he wanted CBS's libel indemnity extended to Wigand's wife, who had also been interviewed by Mike Wallace. In addition, the attorney asked, what would happen if his client were hit with a lawsuit for breach of his nondisclosure contract, as was a likely prospect. He proposed that CBS indemnify Wigand in the event of a breach of contract lawsuit as well. CBS rejected that request, while agreeing to indemnify the Wigands for libel as long as they told the truth. Later Scruggs wrote to CBS stating that if CBS broadcast the interview, it would be considered to have agreed to indemnify his client not only against libel claims but also against possible breach of his nondisclosure contract.

TO BLACK ROCK

It was during this period, sources say, that the matter moved outside the circle of the regular *60 Minutes* staff on Manhattan's West Fifty-seventh Street, and traveled over to the thirty-sixth floor of "Black Rock," the elegant CBS corporate headquarters on Sixth Avenue, where the CBS legal department has its offices. According to one account, a copy of the CBS correspondence about indemnification was sent to *60 Minutes* senior producer Phil Scheffler, the internal journalistic ombudsman for the series, keeper of its editorial standards, and an experienced, respected news executive. Scheffler passed the correspondence along to CBS News president Eric Ober, who forwarded it to Ellen Kaden, the general counsel for CBS. A former litigation specialist, she is well regarded in the industry for her intelligent approach to corporate problems. At the time, she was deeply involved in the merger and acquisition agreement between CBS and its about-to-be new owner, Westinghouse. According to other reports, Kaden had already been alerted to the story by two CBS lawyers, Jonathan Sternberg and Richard Altabes, who worked for her and dealt with *60 Minutes* matters. Kaden decided that she had better become directly involved.

On September 5, Bergman, who lives in Berkeley, California, stopped in New York on his way to London, where he was going to try to corroborate the information in the Wigand interview with retired executives of B.A.T. Industries, B&W's parent. Instead, Bergman was told he had to stay in New York and meet at Black Rock the next day with Sternberg and Altabes. In his more than twelve years at CBS Bergman had never set foot in the CBS corporate headquarters. The long session with the two lawyers on September 6 to review all the facts was the first in a series of three intense meetings that culminated in the decision to abandon the Wigand interview.

A rough assembly of the *60 Minutes* piece had already been put together. After the September 6 meeting at Black Rock, the tape assembly was refined and a draft script prepared for discussion at future meetings on the subject. On September 12, all the CBS principals gathered in Eric Ober's conference room to discuss the case: Bergman, CBS general counsel Kaden, *60 Minutes* executive producer Don Hewitt, CBS News president Ober, senior producer Scheffler, the in-house lawyers, and correspondent Mike Wallace. Sources say that Ober had specifically asked Kaden to come to the meeting along with the other lawyers. At the meeting, which went on for hours, Bergman briefed the group on the story's status. He mentioned that Wigand had recently been subpoenaed in the criminal investigation involving allegations of perjury by top tobacco officials. That inquiry was said to be concentrating on the two executives whose statements were the most damaging, Andrew H. Tisch, until recently chairman of Lorillard Tobacco Company, and James W. Johnston, chairman of R.J. Reynolds Tobacco. Tisch is the son of Laurence Tisch; the Tisch family controls Loews Corporation, which also owns Lorillard and, before the Westinghouse deal went through, was CBS's parent company. Lorillard, meanwhile, was negotiating to buy six cigarette brands from B&W. A participant in the meeting in Ober's conference room was reported to have asked sardonically whether anyone there really expected any of them to tell Laurence Tisch that his son might be indicted with the help of a *60 Minutes* source.

At the meeting, they discussed the fact that Wigand had been listed as a witness in the Philip Morris-R.J. Reynolds libel suit against ABC, and that B&W had intervened to block his appearance. The case against ABC, which had just been settled the month before, with ABC paying Philip Morris a reported $15 million for legal costs and apologizing for the story, was much on everyone's mind. They also reviewed Wigand's involvement in the Boston case against Philip Morris, dealing

2. INFORMATION AND INFLUENCE

with deaths from fires caused by cigarettes. That was the case in which B&W alleged that Wigand had contradicted himself.

Much of the meeting, a number of those present said, was spent trying to find ways to present the story while minimizing the risk to *60 Minutes*, CBS News, and CBS itself. Hewitt proposed to block out Wigand's face and not reveal his name. Ober suggested trying to tie the story to Wigand's grand jury testimony. The lawyers doubted that would help the situation. They discussed whether Wigand's nondisclosure contract might be unenforceable in view of the public interest considerations in exposing the truth and the existence of a whistleblower protection law in Kentucky, the likely venue for a B&W lawsuit. They discussed whether Wigand could sue to get out from under the nondisclosure contract, an effort that could drag on for years. Another option was to do the story without Wigand, but the news people, especially Wallace, argued vehemently for keeping the interview in.

Hewitt, someone at CBS said, viewed the tobacco exposé as a potentially big, high-visibility, muckraking opportunity that could help his show during the fall sweeps period. Ratings had been falling that season, mostly because CBS had lost the rights to televise National Football League games, the show's powerful lead-in, and because of the recent defection of key CBS affiliates to other networks.

There was reportedly no discussion of how the story might affect the tobacco interests of Larry Tisch or the impending merger with Westinghouse. The participants engaged in what one source described as a "typical newsroom analysis of the issues facing *60 Minutes*." Several participants reported that general counsel Kaden warned that, like ABC, they could be risking a $10-billion to $15-billion lawsuit over the story. But the CBS lawyers present were careful not to suggest that the information, if true, should be withheld.

The September 12 meeting concluded with the general counsel's decision to retain outside counsel to examine the extent of the risk, and, specifically, give an opinion on CBS's exposure on the breach of contract issue. The next day, Ober, who had said little during the meeting, was asked to clarify the status of the story. He is said to have replied, "The corporation will not risk its assets on the story and that should be clear from yesterday's meeting."

Bergman, a CBS source said, then asked one of the in-house lawyers whether he could go to Louisville to debrief their source and, if possible, get whatever diaries and records he could so they would at least have all the facts at their disposal. The lawyers offered no objection, so a few days later Bergman flew to Louisville and headed to Wigand's house. Not long after he arrived, the phone rang. Bergman was told to leave immediately and do nothing that B&W might be able to construe as evidence of CBS's interference with their contract with Wigand. The general counsel was deeply concerned about a possible tortious interference suit against CBS by the tobacco company regarding that contract. Bergman did as he was told and left Louisville.

THE OUTSIDE COUNSEL

On October 2, more than a month before anything on the tobacco story was to run on *60 Minutes*, the last general meeting on this subject convened in Ober's conference room. This time Kaden, who was too busy to go across town to the CBS news center, participated by speakerphone from her office in Black Rock. She discussed the fact that CBS had retained P. Cameron DeVore as outside counsel to examine the legal issues surrounding the Wigand interview. DeVore, a partner in a Seattle law firm, is a nationally known, highly respected, and well-liked First Amendment defense lawyer. He was counsel for CBS in the 1983 Chicago libel case won by B&W, although nobody blamed DeVore for the loss. Unlike prominent First Amendment defense attorney Floyd Abrams, who had been retained by ABC to help draft its apology to Philip Morris and who represents the tobacco industry on a commercial speech issue, DeVore had no tobacco industry clients.

DeVore's information about the facts and background of the *60 Minutes* piece came from information he received from the CBS in-house lawyers. No one at *60 Minutes* or CBS News ever talked to DeVore before or after he provided his opinion. Over the speakerphone, Kaden reported to the group in Ober's conference room that DeVore had indeed confirmed her view that if *60 Minutes* went forward with the interview, it would face the likelihood of a substantial lawsuit and a risk that CBS might be found guilty of tortious interference. Other issues existed as well, such as whether CBS could even broadcast Wigand's interview without his permission, which had not yet been granted. There was concern that other facts may not yet have surfaced in view of the story's long gestation period. To this day, no one at *60 Minutes* has heard or seen DeVore's report, if, indeed, it was ever written. No one at CBS News knows whether in DeVore's opinion the odds of losing a lawsuit would be big or small, whether it was a close call or a major risk, or whether some of the problems he found could have been resolved with further work on the story.

A major concern expressed was the potential cost of a lawsuit. There was a consensus at CBS that if it were to lose the case in the tobacco-friendly state of Kentucky, the company could face a sizable financial verdict and a long and expensive appeals process. Unlike Virginia, where the Philip Morris case against ABC was brought and where punitive damages are limited by statute to a maximum of $650,000, in Kentucky no statute restricts the amount of a verdict in such cases. Moreover, in order to bring an appeal in Kentucky, CBS would be required to put up a deposit of 10 percent of the judgment against it. If the judgment were in the billions, the deposit obviously would be sizeable. People talked about whether the story was worth "betting the company" for.

THE DECISION

Kaden concluded that, based on all she had heard and what she knew about the nature of the parties involved, the interview posed too many problems and risks to be shown on *60 Minutes*. Too many questions remained, she felt, and any further efforts by CBS to find the answers might only serve to solidify the case against it for tortious interference.

Although CBS Broadcast Group president Peter Lund did not return my phone call asking about his role in the decision, others directly involved in the discussions confirm that Lund was consulted and said the interview should not run. Similarly, CBS News president Eric Ober would not discuss the case other than to refer to his memo to the CBS News organization of November 19, which said, "The decision was made by CBS NEWS management in consultation with CBS attorneys."

Former CBS chairman Laurence Tisch, by contrast, was not reluctant to talk about his role, or rather his total lack of a role. Tisch said not only did he play no part in making the decision, he knew nothing about the matter until after the interview had been scuttled, when he was informed by Kaden of "her decision." The CBS chairman was in the hospital during that period, undergoing surgery for acute appendicitis. And since the *60 Minutes* issue involved tobacco, Tisch said, it would not have been brought to him to resolve in any event. During the years he was chairman of the broadcasting company, Tisch said, *60 Minutes* and other CBS News programs produced many hard-hitting tobacco stories. Don Hewitt, no admirer of Larry Tisch, as both he and Tisch were quick to point out, confirmed that the chairman had never raised any questions about the program's tobacco exposés.

Just how seriously Hewitt regarded the prospect that CBS might risk losing billions of dollars if *60 Minutes* were to run the story was reflected in a speech he gave at the National Press Club in Washington, D.C., on October 17. Hewitt cited an investigative report about the tobacco industry that *60 Minutes* was working on: "We have a story that we think is solid. We don't think anybody could ever sue us for libel. There are some twists and turns, and if you get in front of a jury in some states where the people on that jury are all related to people who work in tobacco companies, look out. That's a $15 billion gun pointed at your head. We may opt to get out of the line of fire. That doesn't make me proud, but it's not my money. I don't have $15 billion. That's Larry Tisch."

ENTER THE PRESS

With the air date for the story approaching, on Thursday, November 9, the tobacco controversy erupted in the press. In a page one story, *The New York Times* broke the news that "CBS's lawyers ordered the news program *60 Minutes* not to broadcast a planned on-the-record interview with a former tobacco company executive who was harshly critical of the industry." The *Times* story revealed that the reason for killing the interview was not a threat of a suit for libel, but the fear that CBS might be held legally responsible for causing the executive to break a nondisclosure agreement with the tobacco company. Both Wallace and Hewitt were quoted as agreeing with what *The Times* called "the lawyers' decision." Wallace commented, "The ABC lawsuit did not chill us as journalists from doing the story. It did chill the lawyers, who with due diligence had to say, 'We don't want to, in effect, risk putting the company out of business.'"

In the same article, CBS News president Ober denied that the interview was shelved solely for legal reasons. "We looked at the story very carefully," Ober said. "A contract is a contract. I felt for a number of reasons, both editorially and legally, that changes had to be made in the piece." Ober's comment is puzzling because when he saw it, the story was still in rough cut form and any editorial changes he required could most likely have been made before the segment was aired. According to one source, Ober objected to the fact that Wigand's death-threat allegations led the story, a problem that could readily have been fixed. On the other hand, Ober's editorial concern may have referred to the question of whether CBS had the right to run the interview at all since Wigand had yet to give his permission. Any further effort to persuade Wigand would have been seen by the lawyers as adding to the risk of a tortious interference lawsuit.

On the heels of the *Times*'s revelations, the CBS News team began to act in public like a dysfunctional family, as one critic described it. Dan Rather lashed out at his network's lawyers for forcing *60 Minutes* to "back down." "I'd rather take my chances in front of a jury than take my chances in front of corporate lawyers," Rather told syndicated radio host Don Imus. *The Washington Post* quoted Mike Wallace, "We argued with the attorneys and we lost." The *Post* quoted anonymous CBS employees who attributed the decision to the fact that "CBS executives did not want to impede the [Westinghouse] takeover which, with the cashing out of stock options, will bring CBS News president Eric Ober $1.46 million and general counsel Ellen Oran Kaden, who led the legal team, $1.19 million." Ober's response labeled those assertions "absurd" and "a self-serving cheap shot."

> Using an old reporter's trick, Bergman phoned late at night and told the source he'd be sitting in the lobby of the Seelbach Hotel the next morning, reading the *Times*

On Sunday morning, November 12, the *Times* published a withering editorial charging CBS with cowardice and worse. That night, *60 Minutes* broadcast its watered-down version of the tobacco story. Narrated by Mike Wallace, it examined how cigarette manufacturers try to prevent important information from reaching the public. Only a small piece of the Wigand interview was included, without showing his face or revealing his name, and with another voice reading his words about the death threats. Wallace said that *60 Minutes* had requested interviews with B&W and the other tobacco companies, but they refused.

In an unprecedented "personal note" at the end of the broadcast, Wallace expressed his dismay "that the management at CBS had seen fit to give in to perceived threats of legal action against us by a tobacco industry giant. . . . We lost out, only to some degree on this one, but we haven't the slightest doubt that we'll be able to continue the *60 Minutes* tradition of reporting such pieces in the future without fear or favor." About this personal note, the *Daily News* reported that "Peter Lund, who as president of the

2. INFORMATION AND INFLUENCE

CBS Broadcast Group approved Wallace's remarks for broadcast, said he initially resisted doing so. 'My visceral reaction,' Lund said, 'was that he [Wallace] was not going to go on our air and say he was dismayed by this management decision.... Although it seemed unusual and precedential and I'm not sure that I'd approve it for some other program at some other time, I said, You know what? Go ahead.'"

GOING PUBLIC

On Monday, November 13, Charlie Rose, the PBS late-night talk show host, invited Wallace, former *Washington Post* editor Ben Bradlee, and First Amendment lawyer Victor Kovner on his show to talk about what had happened. That evening, as Wallace was leaving his CBS News office to tape the show, he ran into fellow *60 Minutes* correspondent Morley Safer and invited him to come along. "Sure, why not?" Safer replied.

On the show, the two flailed away at the CBS lawyers. Safer described the tortious interference question as "not really hav[ing] much case law going for it." "It is out of the question," he assured Rose, that Wallace and the producer "induced this guy [the interviewee]." "[H]e wasn't paid, he wasn't threatened, he wasn't promised anything other than an opportunity to speak, an opportunity to ... exercise his First Amendment rights on our air." Safer added, "To me, it's an open-and-shut case for CBS News, and I am, as Mike is, dismayed by the decision of our lawyers."

On the issue of tortious interference, attorney Kovner, who teaches this aspect of the law, insisted that the cases are rare, "maybe a couple a year, out of the tens of thousands of claims." If, for example, Kovner hypothesized, CBS had paid this interviewee $10,000, that would raise an issue, but, "According to Morley, there was no payment. There was no inducement.... The law could not be more clear.... CBS is not liable, as a matter of law ... for tortious interference with contractual relations."

When, later in the Rose show, Kovner learned from Wallace that Cam DeVore was the outside counsel who raised questions about the story's risk, he quickly changed his view: "If Cam DeVore issued such an opinion, there are facts that we don't know and I think CBS management has a duty to at least set forth some of them because the implications are, quite frankly, ominous."

Three days later, on November 16, the same day that CBS stockholders met to vote on the Westinghouse buyout, *The Wall Street Journal* published a page one story that had some surprising new facts. CBS LEGAL GUARANTEES TO *60 MINUTES* SOURCE MUDDY TOBACCO STORY, read the *Journal*'s headline. It reported that CBS had not revealed the facts that the *60 Minutes* source had been given a $12,000 consulting fee for a previous show, that CBS had granted him indemnity against libel lawsuits and veto power over the CBS News report, and that CBS had not received permission from the interviewee to air the interview. The *Journal* came to the conclusion: "There's more to CBS's recent decision to kill a hard-hitting tobacco story than meets the eye."

The next day, the New York *Daily News* published the name of the *60 Minutes* source (not that lawyers at B&W would have had the slightest trouble figuring out the identity of the anonymous former tobacco company executive) and someone at CBS News leaked the entire transcript of the never-aired *60 Minutes* interview to the paper.

The *News* reported all of Wigand's major allegations: "According to the transcript," the *News* said, "Wigand charged that Brown and Williamson scrapped plans to develop a safer cigarette and knowingly used a pipe tobacco additive that causes cancer in lab animals. He also said he believed a company executive had committed perjury by testifying in Congress that nicotine is not addictive." Former B&W chief executive officer Thomas E. Sandefur, Jr., was quoted as telling Wigand, "If we pursue a safer cigarette, it would put us at extreme exposure with every other product. I don't want to hear about it any more."

The *News* article went on to reveal that Wigand told *60 Minutes* that the tobacco company's lawyers "altered documents in an attempt to delete any references to the company's efforts to make a 'safer cigarette,'" and that Sandefur had perjured himself in his congressional testimony because he knew that cigarettes were "a delivery device for nicotine." Wigand said, according to the story, that "Brown and Williamson knowingly continued to use a pipe tobacco flavoring additive known as Coumarin despite laboratory evidence that it caused tumors in the livers of mice. 'I wanted it out [to the public] immediately, and I was told it would affect sales, and I was to mind my own business,' Wigand said. Questioned by Wallace, Wigand said the company used the additive at 'a hundredfold the safety level.'"

Giving details about the anonymous death threats, the *News* said that "shortly after informing Brown and Williamson of his contact with Justice Department investigators, Wigand told *60 Minutes*, he got two threatening phone calls. In one call he said he was warned: 'Don't mess with tobacco.' In the second call, he said, the same voice warned him to 'leave tobacco alone or else you'll find those kids [his children] hurt. They're pretty girls now.'" Asked by the *News* about the transcript of the unseen interview, Wigand said, "Read it, and do what you like with it. I have no comment."

The following day, Saturday, November 18, newspapers reported that B&W accused CBS of "improperly persuad[ing] Wigand to reveal information about the company" and accused Wigand of breaching his confidentiality agreement. B&W's vice president of corporate communications, Joseph Helewicz, charged CBS with leaking the transcript even though the network was "properly unwilling" to go on the air with the interview. The tobacco company sent a letter to CBS charging that publication of the interview by the *News* "constitutes a further violation of B&W's legal rights, including intentional, knowing and malicious interference with B&W's contractual right and adds significantly to the harm suffered by B&W." Wigand's lawyer was quoted in *The Wall Street Journal* as saying that Wigand was "upset that the story was leaked," and adding that the leak was in violation of Wigand's understanding with CBS when he gave the interview.

At the same time, the press quoted with relish a statement

put out by Morley Safer claiming Wallace had "sandbagged" him on the Charlie Rose show by not leveling about the tobacco story. His CBS News colleagues, Safer said, had "deliberately suppressed" the agreements with Wigand, and Wallace had left him "twisting slowly in the wind." Safer publicly apologized to Charlie Rose and his audience for misleading them the previous Monday night. He also apologized to the CBS lawyers who, Safer wrote, "it seems were exercising more due diligence than the people accusing them of caving in." In an interview with *The New York Times*, Safer lobbed another grenade at his own colleagues: "It gets very, very muddy when money has crossed the palm."

Safer's outburst prompted an exasperated Bergman to defend himself by sending a memo to the staff: "Morley apparently felt no responsibility on his part to check out his facts before making damaging allegations about me. . . . Let me reassure you that nothing was 'suppressed.'" The producer also revealed that the staff was "under instruction from the general counsel not to reveal *anything*."

Andy Rooney, *60 Minutes*'s curmudgeonly commentator, entered the fray. In his syndicated newspaper column, Rooney charged that Hewitt had demanded cuts in his on-air commentary criticizing CBS chairman Tisch and the decision not to run the tobacco interview. "I couldn't decide whether to quit or sigh in relief," Rooney wrote. "Instead of doing either, I cut out some of the objectionable portions of my script and gave them the shortest piece I've ever done at *60 Minutes*." Rooney then chastised Hewitt for taking off for Europe in the midst of the fracas. In his *60 Minutes* script on November 19, Rooney concluded, "What happened here at *60 Minutes* last week is good evidence of how difficult it is to report on business . . . in this case, the tobacco business. See you next week, maybe."

In an interview with *The Washington Post* that ran three weeks later, Hewitt defended his insistence on cutting Rooney's script. "I'm perfectly comfortable with lawyers making decisions for the corporation they represent," he said. "What I'm not comfortable with is anybody trashing an organization and taking a paycheck at the same time. You don't like what they did? Leave!"

News president Eric Ober tried to regain control of the situation. In a two-page memo, Ober did his best to set out news management's position on the issues to the staff. "Many different factors were weighed in determining whether the proposed story carried legal risks and journalistic problems," Ober wrote, but he emphasized, "nothing improper was done during the newsgathering process by anyone involved." Ober was especially critical of the "inappropriate" conduct of some who disagreed with the decision not to air the interview, saying "the free-for-all that ensued resulted in the identification of a confidential source. Allowing the identity of a confidential source to become known is one of the most egregious violations of journalistic ethics and tradition. . . . While we do not know who released the source's name or how a draft transcript of the report was removed from CBS News and delivered to another news organization [the *News*], CBS News greatly regrets this and will provide full indemnification to the source."

Thus, CBS was forced to take the very step it had refused to take two months earlier. It put itself on the hook to indemnify Wigand for breaking his nondisclosure contract. An internal analysis from the *Times*'s legal department was critical of CBS's timidity. It concluded, "Without even putting up a fight, CBS has managed to create an ugly precedent. 'Tortious interference with contract' has now been added to the legal armory of enemies of the press without so much as a single [court] decision endorsing it."

THE LEGAL FINE POINTS

Along with the press feeding frenzy came many lawyers, most of them First Amendment specialists, offering their professional opinions in articles, letters to the editor, and responses to reporters' questions. The *Times* quoted Joseph B. Jamail, the Houston lawyer for Pennzoil, which won a lawsuit against Texaco for tortious contractual interference with Pennzoil's planned merger with Getty Oil. The $10.5 billion judgment for Pennzoil had put Texaco into bankruptcy court in 1987. Still, Jamail was surprised that CBS would pull back from its tobacco exposé. "If you've got as much backbone as a banana, you go with that one," he said. "I just don't see the damages."

In a letter to *The Wall Street Journal*, Floyd Abrams deplored the attacks on CBS general counsel Ellen Kaden for carrying out her obligations to advise CBS of what risks were posed.

> "I'd rather take my chances in front of a jury than take my chances in front of corporate lawyers," said Rather

And in a forum at the Columbia Graduate School of Journalism, Abrams revealed that in about a third of his cases, his media clients are being sued for claims that circumvent the First Amendment and libel law. He cited cases of claims against the press for contract violations, fraud, intrusion into privacy, intentional infliction of emotional injury, federal and state RICO laws, and even the Ku Klux Klan Act prohibiting wearing disguises in certain circumstances. Although plaintiffs' lawyers "have been very creative and often failed," Abrams said, "there's no doubt that I consider a clear and present danger to broadcast journalism . . . the proliferation of these other sorts of claims as to which we simply don't know the answer . . . about whether there is First Amendment protection or not."

The strongest legal attacks against CBS's decision to suppress its tobacco interview appeared in *The National Law Journal* and *New York Law Journal*. In the former, Jane E. Kirtley, executive director of the Reporters' Committee for Freedom of the Press, argued that "It is a sad day for the First Amendment when journalists back off from a truthful story that the public needs to be told because of fears that they might be sued over the way they got the information."

2. INFORMATION AND INFLUENCE

In a *New York Law Journal* column, James C. Goodale, who was general counsel for the *Times* during the Pentagon Papers case, went even further. Assuming the information *60 Minutes* had was "not only true but also in the public interest," Goodale wrote, "it would seem very difficult for *60 Minutes* to lose a suit" for broadcasting the interview. He called it "a slam dunk win. . . . Once the court is required to determine whether the publication of the embargoed facts is in the public interest, the case is over."

THE LESSONS

Assuming the facts are as reported here and there aren't any major pieces to the puzzle missing, what can we learn from the *60 Minutes* experience?

We start by acknowledging the basic reality that no news story is perfect, as anyone who has ever been the subject of a news report and anyone who knows a good deal about the matter being reported on will readily testify. No news story that I've ever been involved with, including this article, has been entirely without flaws, no matter how meticulous the reporter and the editor. That is especially true of an investigative report, which by definition tries to uncover facts that people go to great lengths and often great expense to hide. And the victim of an exposé, especially a rich and powerful victim, will seize on the slightest error to discredit the entire story. In his breezy memoir, *A Good Life,* Ben Bradlee talks about his "eternal horror" at a major mistake *The Washington Post* made during Watergate reporting secret testimony at a grand jury hearing. "The denials exploded all around us all day like incoming artillery shells. No one can imagine how I felt. We had written more than fifty Watergate stories, in the teeth of one of history's great political cover-ups, and we hadn't made a material mistake. Not one. . . . And now this. . . . [It] caused us anguish we had never felt before." Notwithstanding the blunder, the *Post* carried on, of course, and brought down a president.

Many of the First Amendment lawyers who commented publicly on the *60 Minutes* case, talked about the rising threat to journalism from bold, aggressive corporate litigation that seeks to circumvent the press' traditional First Amendment protection. In recent years, the courts have been closing the door on giving protection to news media, especially in newsgathering. There is a growing perception that networks and broadcasters have run amok, poking cameras in keyholes, barging in with the police, intruding on citizens' privacy, showing no consideration for grieving parents and distraught children, and making ordinary people miserable in the glare of its camera's lights. There is a sense that the news media, as a result of their aggressive reporting on subjects of mere prurient interest rather than true public significance, are tearing away the civil rights of their subjects. The press is reaping the rewards of its own excesses, and now faces a tough, uphill argument before the courts; its First Amendment defenses are being limited. It is essential that the press begin to think about these issues in *journalistic* as opposed to *legal* terms.

Still, while corporations like B&W and others seek to erode First Amendment standards through tough, relentless litigation that applies new areas of law to media cases, there is no evidence yet that they are winning significant battles or shockingly large judgments. A recent analysis by the Libel Defense Resource Center concludes, "As a general proposition, these claims have not fared well for plaintiffs." James Goodale said, "As far as I know, no news organization has ever been sued for what it published solely on a claim of inducing breach of contract."

Media companies, especially big, rich ones, have an obligation to fight fire with fire, and take on belligerent and litigious plaintiffs rather than be bullied by them. During my term at NBC News, Lyndon LaRouche, a sometime presidential candidate, sued the company for millions in damages for libel. We decided not only to defend the suit against us vigorously but also to sue LaRouche back. LaRouche lost both ways. NBC beat him on the libel suit and won a major judgment against him for his actions against us. It was a delicious victory. Best of all, the Justice Department used much of the evidence from our civil lawsuit to convict LaRouche.

There has been much talk about the role of lawyers in the *60 Minutes* case and much debate about whether lawyers should be making news decisions. In the interest of full disclosure, it should be reported that the author of this article is a law school dropout, having abandoned Harvard Law School after the first year to find more interesting work on a magazine. But good lawyers are essential in cases like this, and CBS had very good lawyers. Their job is to assess the risks and advise what problems exist and what courses of action would be appropriate. But obviously, the responsibility for making hard decisions about whether to go forward and on what basis, rests not with the general counsel but with the head of the news division, and ultimately with the chief executive of the company.

In this instance, CBS was seriously handicapped because of its chief executive's personal and financial entanglements with a major tobacco company. Clearly, too, the pending Westinghouse merger played a not insignificant role, whether overt or subconscious, in how CBS management viewed the issue here, if only in influencing outsiders' perceptions of the reasons behind the decision. But the reality is that nothing can be done about such outside factors as ownership and mergers. News decisions must be made on their own merits, recognizing that those factors inevitably play a role.

What exactly was the role of the lawyers and was there anything inappropriate in what they did? Based on the information reported here, the views of CBS general counsel Ellen Kaden were decisive in the decision to quash the interview. It is apparent that she had reasons to be concerned and that her judgment carried great weight. With regard to the outside counsel, all of them, even the best, the most famous, and the most honorable, inevitably have their perspective influenced by the nature of their charge from the client, their perception of where the client wants to come out. Suppose Ellen Kaden told Cameron DeVore, "Look, this case really bothers me. I'm worried about the people involved. I'm concerned about whether we have all the facts. My instinct and experience, along with the information I have, tell me we are in for trouble. Even the president of the news division and executive producer of the show seem somewhat ambivalent. Please look into this whole matter and let me have your opinion." DeVore would take on the assignment being acutely aware, from the very beginning, of the problems and risks at hand. As an able, independent-minded lawyer, that would not prevent him from concluding after he had researched the issues that in his opinion the risks were minimal. But he would more likely focus on the potential problems than look for ways to go forward with the interview.

On the other hand, suppose the CBS general counsel had said to DeVore, "This is a gangbuster story. It involves serious risks to the health of millions. It comes with problems, I know, but it would be a feather in our cap to pull it off and a great public service as well. If we can do it, it would be a shot in the arm for CBS, for CBS News, and for *60 Minutes*. It could even win us an Emmy. Please look into the issues and let me know if you think they are so insurmountable that we should not run the interview." His conclusions might have been framed rather differently.

The *Times* editorial charged: "The most troubling part of CBS's decision is that it was made not by news executives but by corporate officers, who may have their minds on money rather than public service.... With a $5.4 billion merger deal with the Westinghouse Electric Corporation about to be approved, a multi-billion-dollar lawsuit would hardly have been welcome. Some of the executives who helped kill the *60 Minutes* interview, including the general counsel, stand to gain millions of dollars themselves in stock options and other payments once the deal is approved." Others in the press raised troubling questions about the personal motivation of the lawyers and executives who made the decision.

I have no problem with the press disclosing all the facts that could have influenced the decision, especially facts about who stands to make or lose money, so that readers can come to their own judgment about what is at stake. But I do have problems with the press presuming to read the mind of anyone involved in any story, as the *Times* did in its editorial.

To take a personal example, in 1990 this writer was diagnosed with a rare form of facial skin cancer that required extensive surgery and intensive radiation. Doctors speculated that my cigarette and cigar smoking may have been a cause, but they had no real evidence of it. My wife was sure that my smoking contributed to my cancer, based not on scientific knowledge, but on her own instinct. As a result, I stopped smoking, developed a strong personal interest in issues of tobacco and health, and joined the boards of several nonprofit groups focusing on cancer and heart disease. My interest in the subject may even have been a factor in my decision to write this story. It is useful for readers to know these facts so they can make their own judgments about the reporting and analysis on these pages. But does that mean I cannot do a responsible, professional, fair-minded job of journalism in this case?

What does the *60 Minutes* episode teach us about the newsgathering process, especially if the lawyers are right that the strong First Amendment protections that have been built up for publishing and broadcasting are not matched by comparable First Amendment protection for newsgathering? In 1964, the Supreme Court applied First Amendment principles to defamation law in *New York Times* v. *Sullivan*, making it much more difficult for a public figure to win a libel or defamation judgment for irresponsible publishing or broadcasting. Now the pendulum involving judgments against the media seems to be swinging in the other direction. If that is the case, journalists have to be concerned not only with what they say, publish, or broadcast but also with how they go about gathering their information.

Breaking a law when gathering news, by trespassing, stealing documents, eavesdropping, or even misrepresenting who you really are, are generally unethical and are likely to generate serious legal problems down the road. Interfering with contractual relationships or causing deep emotional stress by using hidden cameras or scare tactics are also more likely today to provoke litigation. Here again, whatever unorthodox procedures

> **Too many questions remained, the general counsel felt, and any further efforts by CBS to find the answers might only serve to solidify the tortious interference case against it**

may have been used, full disclosure is always in order. Once the story broke, *60 Minutes* would have been better served if it had revealed the conditions of the interview, including telling its own correspondents, although that is easier to say in hindsight than to do at the time.

The Wall Street Journal called the veto power that CBS granted the interviewee an "oddity," as indeed it was, but that does not make it wrong or unprecedented. In their book *Strange Justice: The Selling of Clarence Thomas*, two veteran *Journal* reporters, Jane Mayer and Jill Abramson, revealed that Anita Hill insisted on the right to screen their questions in advance and to have her lawyers present at their interview. They also gave her their commitment that "no material from the interview be quoted for attribution until she first cleared it." The reporters decided that getting the Anita Hill interview was worth giving her veto power, and they were right — as long as they revealed the conditions under which they were operating.

In the real world of day-to-day newsgathering, news organizations cannot give away the editorial store to nervous subjects, nor can they afford to go overboard worrying too much about such procedures or they'll end up playing it safe and reporting from press releases rather than aggressively pursuing independent fact gathering. Based on the events in the *60 Minutes* case, Lowell Bergman's efforts to uncover alleged criminal and other malfeasance in the tobacco industry were a model of sound, effective investigative reporting.

The capable investigative reporters I have known (I've never met Bergman) are all of a type. They have a strong sense of right and wrong and a tenacious determination to pursue wrongdoing and wrongdoers. The facts they require almost never drop into their laps unsolicited; the facts need to be uncovered and pursued relentlessly and aggressively. It is usually lonely, painstaking, frustrating work.

Our legal system should do everything possible to protect

2. INFORMATION AND INFLUENCE

responsible investigative reporters and researchers and our trade should honor the best of them. So should their newspaper, magazine, and broadcasting employers. The problem with investigative reporting today is not that there is too much of it, but too little, particularly about serious issues. If one percent of the news resources now being spent on journalistic initiatives in pursuit of the secret lives of TV and movie stars, the private lives of public officials, and the personal peccadillos of sports heroes, were devoted to investigating the bad behavior of big government and big business, the country would be far better served.

Much criticism has poured down on *60 Minutes* for using as its main source in the B&W investigation a former official of that company who had been retained as a consultant on a previous tobacco story. "Checkbook journalism" is almost always deplorable because it tempts sources to tailor their stories to suit the paymaster. But it's an odd criticism to throw around in this case, as if the source could somehow have been seduced into becoming a whistleblower by receiving about $12,000 for ten days' work and out-of-pocket expenses on another project more than a year earlier. Common sense suggests that, regardless of what a plaintiff may try to make of it in the courtroom, there was nothing inherently inappropriate about that process. Why that was held up for criticism by some journalists, even a few inside CBS, is something of a mystery. Perhaps because unlike doctors and cops, some members of the press enjoy nothing more than seizing an opportunity to discomfit one of their own colleagues. If Wigand had the goods, *60 Minutes* was right to move heaven and earth to try to get him on videotape. And once they had him telling his damaging story, understandably scared to death and worried about his family and his future, what is wrong with giving him an assurance that he still had time to think it over, that his interview would not be broadcast without his permission?

In addition, if a source is being used on the air because the producers are convinced he is telling the truth, why not offer to indemnify him against a libel suit, which is the only indemnification CBS originally agreed to? I admit, in my years in television, I never encountered such a written indemnification before. But if an investigative producer had come to me and asked whether it would be all right to commit NBC News to stand behind our source as long as he told the truth, I would have answered, "Of course, go ahead. It's the only honorable thing to do."

In his memo to the troops, CBS News president Eric Ober insisted that the newsgathering process on the tobacco story "was in every respect sound and appropriate" and that "nothing improper was done . . . by anyone involved." Based on everything I've learned so far, Ober is absolutely right about that. Bergman and his colleagues deserve prizes, not pillorying, for their efforts to expose what has evidently been going on in the tobacco industry.

One of the thorniest questions the *60 Minutes* case raises for news executives, and corporate executives whose companies own news divisions, is what obligations do they have to go public with the facts about a decision to kill a story when the threat of litigation is in the air? Can they afford to hide behind the response that journalists hate almost more than any other: "I can't talk about that now, it's in the hands of the lawyers." Goodale argues that "CBS must clear the air. . . . The public is entitled to know what happened." The press, more than any other institution, should be extremely reluctant to withhold information, he says. But the reality is that the journalistic process has always been among the most secretive of all. Journalists rarely allow outside reporters to cover their editorial deliberations. And lawyers can be very convincing that going public can be costly in a courtroom battle.

While the *Times* editorial writers demanded "full disclosure" from *60 Minutes*, that was not what their own newspaper and *The Washington Post* offered last November when the newspaper they both own, the *International Herald Tribune*, agreed to settle libel cases brought against it in Singapore courts for several opinion articles that offended the Singapore government (see "Singapore's Grip," CJR, November/December). The *Herald Tribune* paid damages, published apologies, and agreed to drop an appeal of the Singapore ruling. In response to criticism that the paper had been far too conciliatory, Katherine Graham and Arthur Sulzberger said both of their papers had repeatedly defended the principle of a free press, and added, "To think that we would set a different standard for a newspaper that our companies jointly own is ludicrous." Perhaps, but neither offered any explanation, much less "full disclosure," of why the *Herald Tribune* settled. The result was suspicion that business expediency prevailed over journalistic principles.

The settlement may well have been prompted by a legitimate and praiseworthy need to protect their employees or others in Singapore, in which case their failure to disclose the facts was fully justified. The only answer, in that event, is that a news medium that refuses to answer important questions, even for good reasons, has to know that people will think the worst of it. It comes with the territory. Meanwhile, Goodale points out, "CBS has now cultivated the impression that a company can bring and win an interference suit against the press. This will surely encourage corporations to require secrecy agreements of their employees, encourage judges to consider such suits seriously and encourage the public to believe that the suits are legitimate." Companies have the right to secure nondisclosure agreements from their employees, as allowed by law. But where malfeasance is suspected, the job of the press is to find it out.

One consolation about the press trying to stonewall information about itself: in most cases, the issue becomes moot because the press's stonewall is remarkably porous. Journalists are incurable gossips, a trait that probably attracted them to the business in the first place. Years ago, I suggested to a colleague that the best way to tell the three network news divisions apart was to look at how each one deals with its internal gossip and gripes: At ABC News, theirs ricochet around inside the building. CBS News sprays theirs indiscriminately in public. NBC News leaks theirs anonymously.

THE BOTTOM LINE

Finally, to ask the unfairest question of all: Assuming the facts are essentially as they were described here, what would I have done if I were running CBS News? The question is unfair because hindsight and second-guessing are a thousand times easier to do than making decisions in the midst of the maelstrom.

In real life on the news front, key information comes in dribs and drabs. The atmosphere is filled with distractions: Y's contract needs to be decided upon; X is unhappy with her beat; Z is being wooed by another network; a key program's ratings have begun to plunge; an important senator calls to complain that his party is being stiffed; the White House wants to know why the president got short shrift on last night's news; a big story is breaking someplace where you have no correspondent or producer; the division's budget projections are overdue; you are late for a management meeting. . . . And this one damned story, which everyone is worried about, and which some predict will bankrupt the company, is demanding all of your time and attention. Some argue it is a great scoop. Others insist most of the facts have already come out.

I hope I would have moved heaven and earth to put the tobacco story on the air. Respecting the reservations of counsel, which were reasonable and offered by lawyers for whom I have high regard, I would nonetheless have insisted on getting a second legal opinion. Does that really mean, keep looking for a lawyer until you find one who agrees with you? The answer is yes, within reason. That is what *The New York Times* did in 1971 when its outside law firm, Lord, Day & Lord, advised the paper that the *Times* principals could go to jail and pay enormous fines if the paper continued to defy the federal government and publish the Pentagon Papers. Lord, Day & Lord resigned when the *Times* failed to heed its legal advice. Jim Goodale, the newspaper's general counsel, found other attorneys who had a different opinion. He was convinced that the law would treat the media differently because of the public interest concern and the First Amendment tradition. And he turned out to be right.

Now, the *60 Minutes* interview is hardly in the same league as the Pentagon Papers. For one thing, the Espionage Act is not involved in the tobacco story. Smoking is not a national security issue. So a decision to run the *60 Minutes* interview would not be nearly so momentous. I cannot imagine any court, especially an appeals court, and certainly the Supreme Court, upholding a multibillion-dollar judgment against a news division that is trying to serve the public interest, and ruling in favor of a tobacco company whose practices appear so questionable. A decision against CBS for tortious interference with a contract could be substantial, but is hardly likely to bankrupt a company worth $5.4 billion. The fear of billion-dollar judgments was daunting, but common sense and all precedent suggest it was probably groundless. Corporate executives have a duty to protect the company's stockholders from undue risk. But owning a company with a news division is one of the risks CBS stockholders take. And it does not seem to me at all likely that their stock values or dividends would be hurt in any major way by a decision to run the *60 Minutes* story.

I would have had another argument, too, a self-serving argument in the corporate interest: the very fact that CBS's parent company was in the tobacco business almost demanded that CBS do whatever it reasonably could to put the piece on the air, for its own self-respect and for its reputation. The fact that a merger was pending made the same demand. The worst thing that could happen to CBS would be to have the nation believe that it pulled back from an important news story for self-interested financial reasons, because of the company's impending sale and because of its association with a major tobacco company.

Besides, I have a precedent. In 1980, at PBS, we were faced with the issue whether to broadcast a controversial program, a docudrama called "Death of a Princess," about the execution of a young Saudi princess for adultery. PBS's plan to carry the program prompted powerful objections from the Saudis, the U.S. Secretary of State, most members of Congress, and several of our chief corporate underwriters, the Mobil Oil Co. and Texaco. Mobil launched a major ad campaign urging PBS not to run "Death of a Princess." I decided that on that basis alone, we had no choice but to run the program. PBS could not afford to be seen as knuckling under to pressure from the government or especially from its major corporate underwriters, who, it turned out, continued their support undiminished.

> **One First Amendment lawyer said that if CBS's story was true and in the public interest, any trial would have been a "slam dunk" win**

Suppose the decision to broadcast the tobacco report gets vetoed by someone higher up, the president of the Broadcast Group or the c.e.o., for example. Should people at CBS News resign in protest? Certainly not, as long as the veto (even if mistaken) was prompted by a reasoned and legitimate disagreement with the judgment to run the story. That seems to be what happened in this case. If, on the other hand, there is real and hard evidence that the decision was made solely to protect the special financial interest of the parent company or the personal financial interest of the higher-up, that would be another matter.

The CBS News Division's standards and practices "bible" says, "Investigative reporting, to which CND has a longstanding commitment, often cuts deep and arouses sharp reactions, but must be free, nevertheless, to expose — and indeed we have a responsibility to expose — criminal activity, wrongdoing, and abuses of public confidence and trust." Five states now have sued the major tobacco companies, accusing them of conspiring for decades "to mislead, deceive, and confuse." Other investigations are under way. *60 Minutes* should broadcast its investigative report on an issue that continues to be both timely and big news.

[**Editors note:** On Sunday, February 4, 1996, CBS News' *60 Minutes* presented its interview with Jeffrey Wigand (tobacco industry's whistle-blower). Footage of the old interview, as well as a new interview, were included.]

Defining the Rules

The freedoms of speech and the press are regarded as fundamental American rights, protected under the U.S. Constitution. These freedoms, however, are not without some restrictions; the media are held accountable to legal and regulatory authorities, whose involvement reflects a belief that the public sometimes requires protection from irresponsibility.

Regulatory agencies, such as the Federal Communications Commission (FCC), exert influence over media access and content through their power to revoke or limit licenses to operate. They are primarily, though not exclusively, concerned with electronic media because of spectrum scarcity, the limited number of broadcast bands available in any community. In addition, the courts exert influence over media practice through hearing cases of alleged violation of legal principles, such as protection of privacy or protection from libel. Shield laws, which vary from state to state, grant reporters the right to promise informants confidentiality, although they are regularly challenged.

There is, however, a wide grey zone between an actionable offense and an error in judgment. For example, while legal precedence makes it particularly difficult for "public figures" (those in a position that attracts public attention) to prevail in either libel or invasion-of-privacy cases, it is not necessarily right to print information that might be hurtful to them. Nor is it necessarily wrong to do so. Sometimes being "fair" compromises telling the whole story. Sometimes being "truthful" is insensitive. Sometimes being "interesting" means being exploitive. Media sources are constantly aware that their reporting of an event has the potential of affecting the lives of those involved in it.

The articles in this unit present examples of situations that raise questions of ethical practice. Some media organizations seem to have a greater concern for ethical policy than do others and have attempted to articulate guidelines for practice, such as those that appear in these readings. However, rules rarely can be applied without considering specific aspects of a particular case. Outright fabrication of facts is considered unethical; communicating the essence of what several people said by creating composite quotes falls into a grayer area (see Fawn Germer's report, "Are Quotes Sacred?"). Lying, cheating, and stealing are considered unethical; impersonating a sympathetic lawyer to get inside a criminal operation sometimes wins journalistic commendations.

When Pennsylvania state treasurer R. Budd Dwyer ended a 1987 press conference by putting a gun in his mouth and killing himself, news crews from stations around the state were left with extremely dramatic film footage—and a question of whether or not the probability of offending viewers' sensitivities and causing pain to Dwyer's family was too great to justify its use. When Ted Bundy murdered Caryn Campbell in Colorado in 1975, her family did not realize that they would have to reexperience their pain for almost 14 years, until Bundy's execution in 1989, as broadcasters reminded their viewers of the local angle in almost every story on the Bundy case. Many news stories deal with tragedy. In "How Do You Feel?" Fawn Germer ponders the appropriateness of interviewing a tragedy's victims. What are the appropriate rules regarding sensitivity to subjects and those who love them?

Related issues of sensitivity to a story's subjects have been raised regarding the use of hidden cameras and microphones, as addressed in the essay "Gotcha!" and the practice of "outing" homosexuals, particularly those in prominent positions, in the interest of gay and lesbian rights. When, if ever, is it appropriate for an advocacy agenda to come into play in making decisions about what constitutes news? What responsibility does a news organization have when the subject of a story threatens to kill him- or herself if the story runs? What should news organizations do when the police request that a story not run in order to avoid compromising an ongoing investigation? Writers struggle with the public's right to know, their sense of responsibility in informing readers/viewers, and their culpability if someone is hurt because of a news story.

Is it ethical for journalists to cover stories on issues about which they have strong personal views, or does such practice compromise objectivity? What about their relationship with sources? Is it fair to become a "friend" to win trust? What kind of favors promised are defensible as reasonable reimbursement for information? Is it fair to break through an interviewee's guard with nine innocent questions and go for the jugular with the tenth? If so, what kind of setup is demanded when editing the comments, since surely the tenth response will be central to the story? What standards apply in going public with information from sources who demand anonymity or in deciding whether or not to honor a subject's request, after the fact, that a piece of information not be used or that it appear without attribution? As noted in "Anonymous Sources," this issue was endlessly debated following Watergate and is again the subject of much attention in the wake of the numerous stories based on false information attributed to unnamed sources that were reported during coverage of the O. J. Simpson criminal trial.

UNIT 3

Where some sources wish to remain anonymous, others demand to be paid. Does the exchange of money undermine the credibility of a story and of the press? Can mainstream newspapers compete with the tabloids if they do not pay? If media profit from telling stories, should their profits be shared with the sources of those stories? Louise Mengelkoch's article, "When Checkbook Journalism Does God's Work," argues that when people open themselves to tell "very personal stories . . . that have a real message for the public—it seems only fair that they should be compensated for their willingness to go public."

These are not easy questions, and they do not have pat answers. In "The Media and Truth: Is There a Moral Duty?" Paul Johnson believes that media writers must preside over a moral media "conducted by people with a strong sense of their moral obligation to society. Is that too much to ask? No it is not—and we should not hesitate to ask it." However, as media writer William Henry has observed, "Whether it is staking out [presidential candidate] Gary Hart's bedroom, probing the background of an alleged rape victim, or pondering the number of months that passed between marriage and childbirth for the wives of Ronald Reagan and televangelist Pat Robertson, the press almost always strikes some people as having gone too far." In the final analysis, no code of conduct can prescribe behavior in every possible situation.

Looking Ahead: Challenge Questions

To whom do media practitioners owe allegiance in making ethical judgments? Who, besides the subject of a story, is affected by such judgments?

What is your view on interviewing victims of tragedy? On the use of hidden cameras? On the use of unnamed sources? On paying for interviews? If ratings indicate that the public is attracted to stories resulting from these practices, should the press give—or not give—media consumers what they want?

How would you define the rules of "ethical practice"? To what degree do your rules provide guidance for making decisions in the various cases included in this unit's articles?

THE MEDIA AND TRUTH
IS THERE A MORAL DUTY?

PAUL JOHNSON

Mr. Johnson is a journalist and historian. Adapted from his keynote address at the recent World Media Association meeting in Seoul, Korea:

Not only can the media make a moral contribution to our culture, it must do so. It is, potentially, a great secular church, a system of evangelism for dispersing the darkness of ignorance, expelling error and establishing truth.

I don't know whether any of you have read St. John's Gospel recently. But it could be described as a celebration of the importance of truth—the word is used again and again in all its meanings—and the need to convey it. It is the Gospel of the media, and the Jesus of Nazareth presented in it might almost be called the first journalist—bringing the Good News to mankind. He spoke in the Temple when he was allowed, and in wayside places if need be: anywhere he could collect a crowd. And he aimed his words at the masses, not the elites. Can anyone doubt that the man who once preached to the 5,000 would today use all his resources of the mass-circulation newspaper and, above all, TV? "I am the way, the truth and the life"— those are words of the dedicated reporter; he who brings the news which sets people free.

People would be virtuous and take the right courses so long as they are fully informed of the truth. And the truth reached them essentially through the newspapers. One of the most striking characteristics of the early United States was the rapidity with which newspapers were set up as the frontier expanded. Cincinnati got its first newspaper in 1793 when it had fewer than 500 citizens. In 1808, St. Louis got the first paper west of the Mississippi when less than 1,500 people lived there. Leavenworth, Kan., got its own paper in 1854, when the town consisted of four tents.

ROLE IN A REPUBLIC

Noah Webster, who created the first American dictionary and might be described as the ideologist of freedom of printing in America, as Milton was in England, argued—in the first issue of the newspaper he founded—that the press was essential to the success of republican government because it was the only sure way to correct its abuses. "The best-informed people," he wrote, "are the least subject to passion, intrigue and a corrupt administration." Newspapers, the source of information, should therefore be encouraged by the authorities, just as schools were: "Like schools, they should be considered as the auxiliaries of government and placed upon a respectable footing—they should be the heralds of truth, the protectors of peace and good order."

This was the prevailing view, and government generally helped to finance newspapers by printing contracts and special postage rates. All editors exchange papers—their main source of news in other communities—and these traveled post-free. America got the strongest, the most widely dispersed and the most decentralized press in the world because for most of the 19th century, government subsidized it by these means. Thomas Jefferson himself, third president of the United States and the key man in the growth of its democracy, laid down, in the same year as the Constitution was drawn up: "Were it left to me to decide whether we should have a government without newspapers or newspapers without a government, I should not hesitate a moment to prefer [newspapers]."

Yet it was the same Thomas Jefferson who wrote, 20 years later (1807): "The man who never looks into a newspaper is better informed than he who reads them; inasmuch as he who knows nothing is nearer to truth than he whose mind is filled with falsehoods and errors."

Electronic printing and global satellite communications have transformed media since Jefferson's day, but the dilemma remains: we need the media to make Democracy work at all, but we rightly fear the damage and corruption its frailties inflict on our society. How do we max-

From *Current*, December 1992, pp. 4-7. Originally "Media Morality Function?" by Paul Johnson, from *The Washington Times*, September 7, 1992, pp. E1, E4. © 1992 by News World Communications, Inc. Reprinted by permission.

imize the good, and minimize the evil? The state cannot do it.

Of course the media are subject to the same laws as everyone else—to the monopoly laws, the laws of libel, for instance. But we cannot impose a special legal regimen on it, to compel it to be good. As Milton argued, 350 years ago, such laws would be wrong in themselves, and they would not work anyway. You can impose censorship for a limited purpose and for a limited time—in war, for instance. But in a peace-time society it damages more than it protects, and it always breaks down in the end. The only sure way in which we can have a moral media, serving moral purposes, is by having people work for it who subscribe to moral codes of conduct.

How can this come about? I offer no perfect solution today. Indeed there is none. Instead, I have some hints and guidelines based on over 40 years spent in the media all over the world, in newspapers, magazines, in TV and radio, in lecturing and publishing. And the first necessity is the acceptance by those who work in the media of the power they dispose of. A man or woman sitting in a cubbyhole behind a console, or in a broadcasting studio in front of a mike or camera, may not be conscious of the exercise of power—may never even set eyes on readers, listeners and viewers. But the power is there—often enormous and fearsome power, wielded through print and airwaves. With it go the duties which the exercise of power imposes.

People who work in the media are often insufficiently aware of the obligations of their position—much less so than politicians, for instance. They even see themselves as part of the entertainment industry, operating in the frivolous margins of life. That is false. More so than politics, the media stands right at the center of human activities. There are many aspects of life with which politics does not, and should not, concern itself. We live not in totalitarian societies but in democracies, where government is rightly limited. But there are very few sides of life with which the media do not deal. They are omnivorous, ubiquitous, uncircumscribed and comprehensive. There is no nook or cranny of the world, scarcely a hidden area of the human spirit which they do not seek to penetrate. And most of us want it that way because our own curiosity is infinite. But this means that the journalist, more than the politician, even more than the clergyman, needs to be a moral person, and see with moral as well as professional eyes.

SEVEN DEADLY SINS

Now the journalist, I need hardly say, is not regarded in this light. It is in many ways a disreputable profession or trade; more highly regarded, perhaps, in America than in Britain, more highly in Britain than in France, or Italy, say; but nowhere held in particular esteem. Journalists vary in moral probity more, perhaps, than in any other calling, from the high-minded and idealistic to the ineradicably grubby. But it is important to identify the characteristic weaknesses, which lie behind the general condemnation, if we are to improve or eliminate them. There seem to me to be seven: what I call the Seven Deadly Sins of the Media.

- "Distortion," deliberate or inadvertent. The only safeguard, as that resourceful journalist Dr. Samuel Johnson pointed out, is eternal vigilance, a positive desire to convey the exact truth. Johnson's words ought to be posted in every newsroom and TV studio.
- "Worshiping false images." It applies particularly to TV journalism, where the image captured on tape is allowed to dictate the shape and sense of the news story. Newspapers, too, worship false images when they play down stories that cannot be illustrated by photos, but also when they create stereotype images, the cliches of the news desk. The media must never be more than a sheet of plain glass, through which we see the truth clearly.
- "Theft of privacy." Intrusion into privacy is the most pernicious media sin of our time, and it seems to be growing. Every mortal man and woman has an inalienable right to some degree of privacy. Phone tapping, "staking out," impersonation, telescopic lenses, all can be instruments of theft, as surely as a burglar's bag of tools.
- "Murder of character." The media have always been used for the unconscionable purpose of assassinating the characters of public men and women from a generalized suspicion of authority. In America, the quest for public scandal, in the aftermath of Watergate and the appointment of special prosecutors to investigate government, has become a kind of disease, debilitating the republic and inhibiting good people from serving it.
- "Exploitation of sex," to raise ratings and circulation. Newspapers have employed salacity since the 18th century, but it has never before been so systematically, unscrupulously and shamefully flaunted as a selling-point, up-market as well as down-market.
- "Poisoning the minds of children," by what they see, hear and read.
- "Abuse of the power." In the United States, those who control the editorial policies of the media feel they are the final repository of the nation's honor, and that, if a regularly elected government strays off the rails, they have the ultimate right to get rid of it by a media putsch.

What I would like to see is for all those who hold the levers of power media, publishers and TV bosses, editors, producers, writers and executives alike, to consider and recognize the vast extent of the influence they hold in the world over the day-to-day behavior of countless

3. DEFINING THE RULES

millions of people, as well as the actions of governments—and, in consequence, accept the awesome responsibilities that go with it. The moment they begin to do so, the instant they perceive the magnitude of their ability to mold the future world, they must see that their duties cannot be exercised in a moral vacuum.

TEN COMMANDMENTS

A newspaper or TV station is something more than an objective fact-recording organization that does not make moral choices; indeed if they are not moral human beings they cannot be good professionals either. That means they must have positive moral objectives as well as negative prohibitions.

A moral media, making a contribution to global culture, cannot be legislated into existence, or bullied into existence, either. Having described the negative side of the media—its grievous, habitual sins, let me now look at the positive qualities those who constitute it should possess.

So here are my Ten Commandments—my rules of moral conduct—that apply with particular force to editors and TV producers but are addressed to all those who exercise media power and influence.

The first imperative is the overriding desire to discover and tell the truth. This is much more than a purely negative command not to lie or distort or bend. The truth is often difficult to discern, hidden, evasive, slippery, dangerous, complex and even in the end undiscoverable. What is required is huge energy in search of the truth, objectivity in recognizing it, scrupulosity in telling it and a willingness to make clear to readers and viewers that it is not always simple.

Energetic and positive truth-telling must be balanced by a sense of responsibility. The second commandment is that journalists must always think through the consequences of what they tell. When a riot breaks out in one town, will certain forms of coverage make it certain riots will occur in other towns? What will legitimately inform, and what will needlessly inflame? What will warn—and what will corrupt? Those in charge of the media must always be totting up these moral balances, and while they may not get the answer right every time, the process of evaluating consequences must be both informed and instinctual.

That leads directly to the third commandment: truth-telling is not enough, indeed it can be positively dangerous, without an informed judgment. We all have opinions—too many of them perhaps—so I stress "informed." Journalists should be educated; more important, they should be self-educated too, a lifetime process. They should be reading men and women, taking advantage of the unrivaled opportunities that work in the media brings to broaden and deepen their knowledge of the world and its peoples. Those who own the media must do all in their power to encourage journalists to study and think and sharpen their judgments, and to see and analyze events not merely in their immediate impact but in their long-term implications.

Educated media are essential because its primary function is to educate through information. This is its moral imperative—its principal contribution to the improvement in world culture. So the fourth commandment is that journalists should possess the urge to educate—the missionary spirit. They should not be content to tell the public what it wants—or what they think it wants—to know, but what it ought to know and needs to know. The great American editor Horace Greeley, in creating the New York Tribune in 1841, insisted that his paper would not merely record congressional, domestic and foreign news but also "whatever shall appear calculated to promote morality, maintain social order, extend the blessings of education, or in any way subserve the great cause of human progress in ultimate virtue, liberty and happiness." That is an ambitious aim, and I wonder how many editors today would have the self-confidence and hardihood to endorse it. But they should.

The fifth commandment is in some ways the most difficult one of all to follow, and the most important. Those running the media must distinguish between "public opinion" in its grand, historic sense, that creates and molds a constitutional democracy, and the transitory, volatile phenomenon of "popular opinion." James Madison, the primary author of the American Constitution, argued that in a republic it must be the reasons, not the passions, of the public that sit in judgment.

PUBLIC OPINION

That is why he thought the revision of the Constitution should be possible, but should not be easy. Editors and TV producers in their quest of readers and ratings, find themselves the captive of mass emotions that are no more than moods, rather than genuine, necessary public needs. Northcliffe put up in his office the mystic slogan "It is Ten"—meaning the mental age of Daily Mail readers. H. L. Mencken laid down: "No newspaper ever lost circulation by underestimating the intelligence of its readers." But these are the slippery roads to media delinquency. Moral media conduct a reasoned dialogue with its public, and avoid an emotional one like the plague.

At times, too, the media must show the willingness to lead, the sixth commandment. Power entails responsibility and responsibility means leadership. It is inescapable. A TV network must be prepared to make a moral stand and stick to it in the face of pressures and criticism. A newspaper must not only give its readers news they do not wish to hear but urge them to do things they find unpalatable. The risk of losing readers and viewers must be taken—and can, I believe, be taken with confidence. It is hard to recall any great newspaper that has been permanently damaged by taking an unpopular but principled decision. Leadership that is informed, reasoned and consistent is always respected, and it is usually followed.

COURAGE But to exercise leadership requires courage, and to show courage is the seventh commandment. The older I get, and the more I see of public life and events, the more convinced I become that courage is the greatest of virtues, and the one most lacking in the media. It is required at all levels, from the humblest reporter, who must always evaluate his orders morally, to the richest tycoon risking his fortune to create new media outlets or make existing ones better and more responsible. My old colleague Nicholas Tomalin, killed on journalistic duty on the Golan Heights, was once asked what quality a journalist needed. He replied, "Ratlike cunning." He might have added, "Lionlike courage," which he himself showed.

The eighth commandment, indeed, is also a form of courage—the willingness to admit error. All media organizations inevitably make appalling mistakes of fact and judgment, and are egregiously reluctant to correct them except under the fiercest legal pressure. But where great power is exercised, accuracy is paramount, and judgment and taste must be refined and sensitive to criticism. A willingness to apologize is the mark of a civilized person and a contribution to a dynamic culture always seeking to purge its grossness and imperfections. The handsome and unforced admission of error is the best of all proofs that a newspaper or a TV network has a corporate sense of honour—and possessing such a sense is another way of saying that it has a conscience.

But admitting error is not enough. My ninth commandment enjoins something more positive—a general fairmindedness. If ever there were a moral quality, it is the ability to be habitually fair, because it involves so many others: the imagination to see other points of view, tolerance of them, temperance and restraint in expressing your own, generosity and, above all, a rooted sense of justice. Fairminded newspapers stick out a mile—because they are so rare. All TV networks make a display of their balanced approach, and hardly any display fairness when they wish to make a point. Yet fairness is one of the deepest human yearnings—it is the first moral point a small child recognizes—and lack of it the commonest complaint the public flings at the media. Conversely, nothing is more likely to build confidence in the media than the public's awareness that it prizes fairmindedness.

My last commandment is the most positive of all: respect, value, treasure and honor words. The media, even the image-media, are essentially about words, for words are inseparable from truth, the only way in which it can be conveyed. "In the beginning was the Word"—so St. John's Gospel, which I commended to you earlier, opens. The media have to use words in haste and somtimes in excitement—that is their nature. But they must also and always use them with care, with respect for their precise meaning and nuance, and with reverence for their power. Words can kill, in countless different ways. They can destroy, characters as well as possessions.

But words can also enlighten, comfort, uplift and inspire. They are the basic coinage of all culture, the essential units on which a civilization rests. Respect for words and love of words are two sides of the same coin; and that coin is the currency that will enable the media to make a decisive contribution to world culture in the 21st century. But it must be a moral media, conducted by people with a strong sense of their moral obligations to society. Is that too much to ask? No, it is not—and we should not hesitate to ask it.

"How Do You Feel?"

It's the assignment reporters dread: interviewing the victims of tragedy. Supporters of the practice say it puts a human face on disaster and offers therapy for the grieving. Critics say such reporting is insensitive, exploitative, and unnecessary.

Fawn Germer

Fawn Germer is a reporter for the Rocky Mountain News in Denver.

"We're sorry your son/daughter/husband/wife was killed, but if you've got just a minute, we've got just a few questions."

"How do you feeeeeel?"

Lights on, cameras rolling, mikes in the faces of the grieving. This is the most devastating moment in their lives, just another story to the pack.

Yet while it may appear that journalists pounce on victims and their families and friends without mercy, many are bothered by these stories.

Haunted.

"Who is this? What's going on?"

They didn't know. The FBI hadn't called.

Jonathan Moses wanted to know how they felt, but they didn't even know their son was dead. Three hours earlier, their son had killed himself after holding his coworkers hostage in the Boca Raton bank where he worked.

"I'm sorry," said Moses, then a reporting intern at the Miami Herald. "Please accept my condolences."

Nearly eight years later, after stints at the Washington Post and the Wall Street Journal, Moses hasn't shaken that encounter.

"It's hard just making a call like that when they know," says Moses, who now attends Columbia University Law School. "It is an absolute nightmare to make a call like that when they don't."

Whether it's a dead cop, dead cheerleader, dead bank teller, dead soldier or dead baby, there's a reporter somewhere digging for quotes, hoping for an exclusive, often just wanting to get it over with.

Edna Buchanan knows the burden of this kind of reporting better than anyone. The Pulitzer Prize-winning police reporter, who now works full time writing books, covered more than 5,000 violent deaths in her 18 years at the Miami Herald.

Buchanan had the drill down. When a family member would curse at her or hang up, she'd wait 60 seconds, pick up the phone and call again. By then, the person had changed his or her mind or a more receptive family member would answer the phone.

"This is Edna Buchanan at the Miami Herald," she would say. "We were cut off." She usually got her interview.

While many reporters loathe doing these stories, they say such pieces give meaning to tragedy. If the reader or viewer gets to know the victim as a real person, what happened doesn't get lost in the statistics of murders or plane crashes. Nowhere was that more evident than in Oklahoma City in April, when media from around the world descended to capture the grief after the bombing of the Alfred P. Murrah Federal Building.

Supporters of the practice say talking about the event is sometimes therapeutic for survivors. Talking to the media is one way they can connect with the outside world and share their grief.

But there are those inside and outside the profession who are revolted by such interviews, who see them as unnecessary, insensitive assaults that simply compound the grief of the afflicted. They dismiss the supposedly beneficial aspects of grief reporting as rationalizations for stories whose only purpose is to sell newspapers or drive up ratings.

Many reporters complain that overeager editors and the pressure of competition force them to pounce too soon. Who can afford to give a fam-

> "**People need to know how angry these kinds of senseless acts make you,**" says Mel Kohlberg, whose wife was gunned down in a Colorado restaurant.

17. "How Do You Feel?"

> "You have to remember that these are real people you are reporting about," says Patricia Spradling, whose two-year-old son died after she left him alone in her car.

ily a day or two to get a grip if the competition isn't likely to wait?

So, like Buchanan, everyone has a technique. Some go so far as to send flowers or cards. One reporter shares a slice of personal tragedy she experienced, often prompting the survivor to empathize. Another says she will make the call, and if the survivor declines the interview she will say, "How are you getting along?" She writes her notes in longhand so the sound of a clicking keyboard doesn't alarm the person. When they are finished she says, "I know this interview was hard for you but I think it will tell our readers a little about (insert name). Let me know what you think of the story."

Some reporters hate these stories so much they won't even try to get the interview. They simply tell the editor the family refused to talk.

But Buchanan says these stories are important to the families and the community.

"This is the one moment in time where they have a podium where what they have to say is important and people will listen," she says. "It's really important to give them the chance to reconsider because they might immediately regret hanging up or someone in the room might say, 'You should have talked to the reporter.' If they hang up again, I don't give a third chance. But more than half the time, they'd do it on the second try."

In 1981, as Miami's homicide rate soared, Buchanan insisted on covering every murder and telling the story of every victim. In her view, this is one kind of reporting that tells society what it has become. "It is important for these victims to know that what happened does matter," she says. "It's not only their tragedy, it's a tragedy for all of us."

MINUTES AFTER THE DECEMBER 1993 MASSACRE, reporters wanted to know how Mel Kohlberg felt. His wife Margaret had just been gunned down in a Colorado restaurant along with three teens who worked with her. Photographers and reporters were swarming.

"I thought, 'I am going to see nothing but TV lights and microphones in my face for the next two weeks,'" he says. "But they were absolutely caring and sensitive."

By sharing his grief, he knew his loss would mean something.

"People need to know how angry these kinds of senseless acts make you. If people aren't exposed to those personal feelings, they say 'Oh, great, another shooting.' Just like, 'Oh, great, another cloudy day.' If we are going to hope to have harmony in our lives, we need to share in the emotions of the people who have suffered significant losses."

Some explain this kind of reporting by saying it can prevent tragedy from repeating itself. It might make a drunk think twice before driving. It might teach mothers to watch their children a little more closely.

That was what the reporters told Patricia Spradling.

It was cool the September 1992 morning Spradling forgot her two-year-old son Eric in her van in the parking lot at work in Loveland, Colorado. By the time the boy was discovered, it was a hot day and his temperature was 108 degrees. Everyone in the media wanted to know how she felt about her son's death.

The phone did not stop ringing. The Spradlings would not answer it. Reporters sent letters asking for the story. The Spradlings needed more space than the press would give them, especially while prosecutors were investigating to determine whether charges should be filed against her.

"When you lose somebody, that's the most devastating thing you'll ever have to deal with in your whole life," Patricia Spradling says. "You're not in your normal state of mind. You're not thinking clearly. The press is not your priority. We were so devastated and nothing was making sense to us. It felt like we were just another story."

The calls kept coming.

"There are other stories out there, other things the public needs to know about and can benefit from besides expanding on someone's grief," she says. "I'm not saying the public didn't need to know what happened to Eric. But it was very hard. We heard it on the radio. We saw it on television. It was there in the newspapers. You have to remember that these are real people you are reporting about. You have always got to remember that."

She told her story only after it was announced that no charges would be filed, so other parents might learn from the tragedy.

But others actually seek out the media. That's what happened when Alie Berrelez vanished.

The five-year-old disappeared from the front of her family's Englewood, Colorado, apartment in May 1993. The family sought coverage to find out what happened.

"We wanted to use the media to tell the public that Alie was missing and if anyone saw her they should say something," says the girl's grandmother, Leticia Berrelez. "We had no idea where Alie had been taken or anything that was going on with her. We just wanted everybody to help us look. To do that, we had to have the media's help."

Days later, a bloodhound led police to her body, which had been stuffed in a duffel bag and abandoned in a mountain canyon.

IT'S SOMETHING YOU JUST DON'T SAY TO A MIAMI Herald editor. It just isn't done.

Reporter Tracie Cone's editor wanted to send her to talk to a seven-year-old boy hours after he'd watched his father drown. The boy and his dad had been canoeing when the boat tipped. Both were dumped into the water. The boy could swim, the father couldn't. So the little boy stood there on the shore and watched his father go down.

3. DEFINING THE RULES

"This is a real Tracie Cone," her editor said, assigning her to get an interview with the boy to ask what it was like.

"I can't do that story," Cone replied. She'd never turned down a story in her life.

"What do you mean you can't do that? Why can't you do that?" She burst into tears. "Because it's tooooo saaaaad." And that was how, after four-and-a-half years, Cone ended her career as a police reporter.

"Every day your whole job was to interview people on the absolute worst days of their lives and write about the absolute saddest things that happened to them in their lives," says Cone, who switched to writing news features. She now writes for the San Jose Mercury News' Sunday magazine.

"There had been this incredible frustration and sadness welling up. I think it's one of the reasons reporters often drink so much. They are carrying around the problems of the world.... People think reporters don't care, but how can you listen to all of these stories of tragedy and sadness and not be worried about it?"

Some reporters carry the distaste over these stories for decades.

It was Thanksgiving eve in 1969 when word came down that Mary Mamon had been sentenced to life in a high-profile suburban Philadelphia murder case. The Inquirer city editor approached the area where David J. Umansky sat. He instructed one of the reporters to go ask the woman's parents how they felt, knowing their daughter was going to spend the rest of her life in prison. "I'm off in an hour," the reporter replied. "You going to pay me overtime?"

The city editor then tried Pat McKeown. "I won't do it," she said. Umansky remembers, "The guy was stunned. I don't think anyone in the history of American journalism said no to a city editor before. She said, 'You want me to ask what it feels like for your daughter to get a life sentence on Thanksgiving eve? No.'"

So the editor turned to yet another reporter and told him to talk to the family, then call Umansky. When the reporter checked in, he told Umansky he had gone straight to a bar, and planned to stay there. When the city editor grabbed the phone and asked what was happening, the reporter told him the family wasn't home.

"What struck me was that none of us wanted to do the story. We were sneaking around the issue, and Pat stood up and said she wasn't going to do it," says Umansky, now director of communications for the Smithsonian Institution.

Jacquelyn Mitchard did plenty of these stories, so many that some suggested dialing 1-800-DED-TEEN to reach her. She never saw the humor.

"Before I got there, I always felt like a vulture," the former Milwaukee Journal reporter says of her encounters with victims' families. "When I got there, I felt like a relative. Grief has a mass. You can't be around it without feeling its weight. So when you got there, you ceased being a reporter. You became a witness."

And that was a burden.

"Everything touched me," Mitchard, now a freelance journalist and author, says of her 18 years of reporting. "It never got easier. Every loss and tragedy was brand new. Ultimately, I think that's part of why newspapers are a young person's game. I admire people who do it. It takes the belief that you really do have a reason beyond the salacious to let people speak their grief. What we are trying to do is make sense of the things that none of us can ever make sense of."

At least that's the journalists' line.

Editors Sandra Mims Rowe and Gregory Favre both hated interviewing grieving relatives.

"There's not a reasonable person on the face of the earth who would like doing those stories," says Rowe, editor of the Oregonian. "But people really want to know how others feel about the most significant events in their lives. Part of the reason is we wonder how we would feel."

"It's the only way we can turn victims into real people, to give them personalities, to know more about them," says Favre, executive editor of the Sacramento Bee. "Crime is such an impersonal thing to begin with. When we depersonalize victims, we have an obligation to put some flesh on those folks. And if you don't ask, you're never going to find out."

What is important, both editors say, is how the asking is done.

"There are too many reporters and editors who haven't been there to have the empathy they need," Rowe says. "Perhaps they haven't lost anyone. They need to think it through enough to say, 'If I were in this person's place, how would I feel? What questions would I be able to handle? What would be offensive?'"

Favre thinks reporters should avoid contacting grieving relatives by telephone.

"It ought to be face to face," he says. "You owe it to them. Obviously, there will be times when you may be forced to do it by phone, but that has to be the exception to the rule."

NOT EVERY REPORTER IS BOTHERED BY TALKING TO the bereaved.

"For some people, this is the worst part of reporting," says Lynn Bartels, night police reporter for the Rocky Mountain News. "For me, it's not. I do like it. Part of it is curiosity. We're all just voyeurs at heart."

But there's more to it than that, she adds. Bartels says she gets caught up in the emotions of the tragedy and often cries with the people she interviews. What she loathes about this kind of reporting is the pressure to beat the competition and get the story.

"The pressure here is intense. You have two newspapers that are competing on the same deadline and the TV stations here are good. You have intense pressure to get it first and get it best."

> "BEFORE I got there, I always felt like a vulture," former reporter Jacquelyn Mitchard says of her encounters with victims' families. "When I got there, I felt like a relative."

17. "How Do You Feel?"

> SOME reporters acknowledge the cynicism that exists in the news business. There is a dance that is done to get the story. Today's victim is old news tomorrow.

Most grieving relatives cooperate in such situations, but not necessarily because they want to, says Joe Wheelan, news editor of the Denver bureau of the Associated Press.

"A lot of people aren't thinking clearly to begin with, and some people think they have to do this," he says. "They think they can't say no. When we interview people, we don't give them that option. It's, of course, implied that the person you are interviewing could just hang up and say, 'No comment' or 'I'd rather not talk now.' But when we interview people, I don't think we say, 'You have the option not to answer my questions.'… That's just not done."

Particularly when everybody else is chasing the story.

Joe Avellar dreaded ringing the doorbell of Ronald Goldman's parents, but he had to do it. Nicole Brown Simpson, O.J. Simpson's ex-wife, had just been murdered, and so had Goldman.

"It was awful," said Avellar, then with KCBS in Los Angeles. "You have to go knock on the door of a family who has just lost their son in a terrible tragedy. I felt terrible the whole way up there when we were driving. The photographer and I had a conversation and we understood that neither of us wanted to be there, we were not going to ambush anybody, we were going to respect their loss and would leave if they asked us to."

They knocked. Standard routine. Sorry about your loss. Mind if we ask a few questions?

"A friend of the family said, 'Don't you guys ever go away?' I said, 'We'll go away right now.' And that was that. They were going to see us as vultures regardless. What was important to me is that we could walk away with our own self-respect and dignity intact. If I didn't harass somebody into giving an interview, that's fine. I can live with that."

Some reporters acknowledge the cynicism that exists in the news business. There is a dance that is done to get the story. Today's victim is old news tomorrow. Some will take extraordinary, if not underhanded, measures to get the story.

"I bring flowers," says Todd Bensman, day police reporter for the Dallas Morning News. "I've done that a couple of times. It's completely transparent, but usually, when you get to the door, if they see you've got flowers they can possibly mistake you for being a friend of the family. You can get in the door. Once you're in, you can take it from there."

Bensman recalls doing that when a mother of three left her children with their grandmother. The grandmother set the house on fire killing herself and the children.

"That night I had to interview the mother, who was in shock. I figured it would be a tough one, so I brought the flowers. I managed to get in the door with that, get a few comments before they figured who I was. Then they kicked me out. At least I got something."

This is hardly his favorite part of his job.

"I hate it. Absolutely hate it. I know I am intruding on something that is incredibly private and personal. It's my job to do it, but I hate doing it. I can feel palpably that I am an unwanted intruder. I've had people screaming right in my face, practically splattering me with tears. I've had to hang on to my emotions."

HE APPROACHED WITH THE CAMERA ROLLING. THE Seattle television reporter just knocked on the door, asked if she was the woman's sister and said, "I'm sorry to tell you. She's been shot to death in a police raid."

The woman fell apart right in front of the camera. Great story. The reporter built his entire piece around that woman's grief.

It aired on a Saturday night and Gail Neubert, then the news director of the station, was incensed.

"Sometimes it happens, through no fault of your own, that you end up telling somebody something you thought they knew," she says. "This wasn't the case. He went to the door with the camera rolling. He knew he was going to be informing this woman about her sister and he wanted to capture it on tape."

Another time a reporter said to a photographer, "Let's see if we can find the mom of the crispy critters" while at the scene of a house fire.

Both reporters were disciplined, but that sense of violation and intrusion never left Neubert, who exited the business after 16 years and now works in public relations. Neubert wonders whether grief stories need to be done at all.

"Now that I watch as a viewer, these things really get to me," she says. "Why do you have to talk to the mother of the child who was hit by the car? It seems like an unnecessary intrusion. It's painful. What does it add to the story? People think viewers, listeners and readers all want this stuff. I don't think they do."

STEPHANIE SUND'S STORY BELONGS TO STEPHANIE Sund.

Remember that, she says. It's not yours, it doesn't belong to your readers, your viewers or anybody else. She is not required to talk.

Sund was gunned down by an ex-boyfriend in 1992 as she desperately reached for the front door of the Fort Collins, Colorado, police department. She was shot in the back three times in her futile attempt to get help.

It didn't take long for the media to find her.

She was unconscious in the intensive care unit. "They were pounding on the hospital doors," she says. "Reporters ride on a public misperception of their authority. They wear this 'authority' like a badge on their chest, like it's the authority to intrude on peoples' lives. 'I've got a camera. Let me in.'"

Sund remembers having 15 to 20 photographers following her through the arraignment, trial and sentencing of her assailant.

3. DEFINING THE RULES

"Some of them cared. But others were incredibly unprofessional, callous, uneducated and naive about domestic violence and stalking," says Sund, who is active in the fight to protect abused women. "They acted like they had a right to my story."

She said reporters fixated on the "titillating details" of a sensational finale to an abusive relationship. They didn't ask the hard questions: Why had the police told her she was imagining things when, two days before the shooting, she played the answering machine tape of her ex-boyfriend's vow to kill her? Why didn't the law protect women like her? Instead, they wanted the juice.

"You will always get a neighbor who will say, 'But he was such a nice guy,'" Sund says. "The story always stops there. But if you are going to do these stories, you have to look further. You have to give the victims time to deal with what happened. If you have had tragedy in your own life, don't use that as leverage to get someone to talk. Don't say you understand, because you don't."

But her experience had to stand for something, she is told. Others had to learn from what happened to her.

"I agree," she says. "But with all of the hard questions left unanswered, what did it stand for? Just another tragedy. Just another story."

GOTCHA!

Robert Lissit

Robert Lissit, a former network television producer, teaches journalism at the S.I. Newhouse School at Syracuse University.

"PrimeTime Live" popularized the use of hidden cameras and local stations rely on them for dramatic, high-impact footage. Their prevalence has provoked debate over how and whether they should be used—and lawsuits.

When Attorney Joel Rachmiel sat down to watch television on an August evening in 1993, he was prepared to take his lumps. He knew CBS' "Eye to Eye with Connie Chung" was going to accuse him of wrongdoing in a segment that night on accident insurance fraud.

But Rachmiel says he had no idea he'd not only hear these charges, but see himself on television, in his own office. "I didn't think I was going to be on TV," says Rachmiel, "and when I saw myself I was kind of flabbergasted."

A CBS News correspondent, Roberta Baskin, had covered a series of bus accidents staged by the New Jersey Department of Insurance to catch lawyers and doctors filing fraudulent claims for accident "victims." CBS cameras videotaped one of the incidents in which Baskin was on a bus. Baskin says the only injury she sustained was when a woman stepped on her toe.

The CBS story alleged that a "runner," someone paid to direct accident victims to a particular attorney, sent Baskin to Rachmiel. Baskin and Leslie Hankey, a CBS camerawoman carrying a concealed video camera, visited Rachmiel's office and told him Baskin had been injured. Baskin identified herself as Michelle Wielosynski. Hankey surreptitiously recorded the conversation.

"Eye to Eye" viewers saw Rachmiel say to Baskin, "If you go to Dr. Sherman on a regular basis, you could probably end up in a case like this, you know, $10,000." Baskin said Rachmiel never asked her about her injuries. If Rachmiel was conspiring with a doctor, he would have been violating state rules barring fee-splitting and may have been guilty of insurance fraud. He has not been charged with committing any crime.

Rachmiel has filed a libel suit against CBS News. Among other things, he says CBS News "deceitfully intruded upon a part of professional life... seclude[d] from public gaze, that is, plaintiff's confidential and legally protected professional relationship with his clients."

Baskin declines to comment because of the pending suit. CBS News Vice President Linda Mason says, "CBS News stands by Roberta Baskin's report; we don't feel anything was done improperly. We followed CBS News policy."

That policy requires approval for the use of a hidden camera from a news division vice president and legal counsel. Hidden cameras are used only "in those cases where we would have been denied access," says Mason, "and the element is an important part of the story."

The policy doesn't always hold up, however. Late last year the network was embarrassed by veteran correspondent Mike Wallace's questionable use of a hidden camera. Wallace secretly viedotaped an interview with magazine writer Karon Haller, a source for a "60 Minutes" story who was reluctant to make an on-camera appearance. Wallace later said the hidden camera was used only to convince Haller she'd look good on air. She subsequently agreed to be videotaped, and the hidden camera footage was scrapped. Even so, CBS News reprimanded Wallace and his producer for failing to adhere to network policy, and Wallace apologized during a "60 Minutes" broadcast last December.

Problems with hidden camera stories are not unique to CBS. Over the last six years, the pioneering work of ABC News' "PrimeTime Live," advances in camera technology and the public's apparent interest in "gotcha" journalism have fueled a dramatic increase in the use of hidden cameras on both the national and local level. In turn, growing reliance on hidden cameras has led to embarrassing apologies as well as potentially costly lawsuits (see "The Press and the Law," April 1994).

Some producers and reporters who use hidden cameras say they adhere to strict guidelines and cite numerous stories that couldn't have been done any other way. But unfortu-

3. DEFINING THE RULES

nately the cameras often are used as a substitute for thorough reporting. Moreover, some journalists say hidden cameras shouldn't be used at all. They say they're unethical, and can result in stories that constitute a serious invasion of privacy.

Privacy law has never been as well-defined as libel, and still hasn't been conclusively established by Supreme Court rulings. However, airing audio recorded during a hidden camera investigation is prohibited in some states by laws requiring the consent of both parties to record a conversation. And in California, a judge is threatening to bar ABC News from using hidden cameras in private workplaces in the state. Had that been the law in New Jersey, CBS News wouldn't have been able to record in Joel Rachmiel's office. Some journalists fear cases like the one in California as well as the threat of lawsuits may force reporters to stop using hidden cameras altogether.

The NEWS MEDIA HAVE UTILIZED HIDDEN CAMERAS since 1928, when the New York Daily News sent a photographer to Sing Sing Prison with a small camera strapped to his ankle to secretly photograph an electrocution (see "In the Death Chamber").

Fifty years later, the famous Mirage Bar story pretty much brought an end to newspapers using hidden cameras. The Chicago Sun-Times, in collaboration with a watchdog group, the Better Government Association, set up a saloon monitored by hidden cameras to document licensing inspectors soliciting bribes. The Sun-Times was roundly criticized for the sting and Chicago papers no longer use hidden cameras. In fact, most newspapers no longer consider them appropriate. "Papers can't really show a story through pictures," explains Jeff Kumer, investigations editor at the St. Paul Pioneer Press. "We have to show the story with words."

Television reporters started using concealed cameras in the late 1950s. One noted early example was in 1961, when CBS News producer Jay McMullen staked out a Boston bookie joint, shooting from an apartment building across the street to show the comings and goings of uniformed police. He also slipped a camera, hidden in a lunch box, into the establishment.

Over the years other network and local reporters routinely shot pictures from vans with cameras hidden behind curtained windows. But the impetus for the recent proliferation of hidden camera stories came in 1989, when ABC's "PrimeTime Live," using new miniature cameras, developed an innovative reporting style. Investigative producer Robbie Gordon used hidden cameras to uncover patient abuse in a health care facility in Houston, in Veterans Administration hospitals and in a day care center (see "Out of Sight," December 1994). These were dramatic stories that received favorable attention from the press and attracted large audiences. Without hidden cameras, says Gordon, the stories would have been impossible to do.

Gordon had used hidden cameras years before, but they were bulky and hard to work with. In the early 1980s she snuck a large camera into a hospital emergency room in a suitcase. "It made so much noise when it started up," Gordon remembers, "that we all had to cough to cover up the sound." By 1989, though, Toshiba and Elmo had started producing cameras the size of a lipstick. When carried in a wig, a hat or a stuffed toy, they couldn't be seen or heard. And unlike the previous generation of cameras, microminiatures can deliver an extremely clear picture. They're also relatively inexpensive: A camera and lens cost less than $4,000.

By 1991, the success of "PrimeTime Live," the new cameras' convenience and relatively low cost, and the promise of higher ratings convinced other network shows and local stations to embrace hidden camera technology. That's when major ethical questions started cropping up again.

In 1992, the Society of Professional Journalists (SPJ) and the Poynter Institute for Media Studies took official notice of the growing use of hidden cameras by adopting guidelines drawn up at the institute. A year later SPJ published a handbook, "Doing Ethics in Journalism," which recommended that hidden cameras be used only for stories of profound importance when there's no other way to get the information, and when the information outweighs the potential harm caused by the deception (see "Hidden Camera Guidelines"). SPJ distributed the handbook to thousands of newsrooms.

That same year, Ira Rosen, senior producer for "PrimeTime Live" investigations, attended a Poynter Institute workshop on hidden cameras. He was shocked by what he heard. According to Rosen, some local reporters said their news directors were demanding hidden camera stories. "They'd invested in 'spy cam' technology," says Rosen, "and were compelling reporters to use it without regard to the editorial content."

Rosen reviews undercover stories by reporters applying for jobs at "PrimeTime Live" and says he sees pieces that use hidden cameras unnecessarily. He says he's concerned "their bad work will impact me" by undermining truly legitimate hidden camera investigations.

Some of the "bad work" Rosen worries about includes poorly conceived stories, stories where the final result doesn't justify the inevitable invasion of privacy that goes with the technology, and ones in which stations rely on a quick hit with a hidden camera in lieu of thorough reporting.

▶ In March 1993, KMOV in St. Louis installed hidden cameras and a male prostitute in a downtown hotel room to try to trap a priest into talking about alleged sexual activities of his fellow clergymen. The sting backfired and a local prosecutor launched an investigation to determine if KMOV was guilty of promoting prostitu-

Some producers and reporters who use hidden cameras cite numerous stories that couldn't have been done any other way.

tion. She ultimately determined no laws were broken, but found that the station had shown "bad judgment and poor ethics."

▶ WRGB in Schenectady, New York, gave a hidden camera to a 13-year-old Albany girl in May 1993 to look for examples of discipline problems at her school to dramatize a statewide story. School authorities caught the girl and confiscated the camera. The station apologized to the school superintendent.

▶ Last November, a police officer told a reporter at WLWT in Cincinnati that a man paid a local jewelry store $1,750 for an engagement ring worth only $400. The reporter did not obtain the sales receipt, but used a hidden camera to tape an unsuspecting store clerk who confirmed the value of the ring at $400. After the story aired, the store produced records showing that the customer had paid $400 for the ring. The station aired an apology.

At the time, none of the stations had guidelines, and all three investigations failed to meet SPJ's recommended procedures. All three stations subsequently adopted stringent standards.

Last spring, Minneapolis station WCCO aired a piece that at least one critic says looked like a reporter trying to play police officer. According to University of St. Thomas journalism professor Dave Nimmer, a former Twin Cities print and broadcast reporter, WCCO reporter Tom Gasparoli became "a shill for a detective" trying to solve a crime. The story, on the murder of 3M executive Dennis Stokes, was introduced this way: "WCCO has learned his widow Terri Stokes became a prime suspect within 48 hours of the murder and is still the primary target of the investigation." The report included footage of police interrogating Stokes, filmed through a two-way mirror, and hidden camera footage of a confrontation between Stokes and her mother-in-law, whom Gasparoli wired with a hidden microphone.

Gasparoli says his decision to use a hidden camera is based on his subject's "zone of privacy." He suggests that people have a general right to privacy, but it can be diminished by their actions. If a person is an elected official, for example, that person's zone of privacy is smaller than that of a private citizen. In this case, says Gasparoli, Terri Stokes' "zone of privacy was reduced to the point we felt comfortable putting a wire on the mother and then subsequently airing what was said because she had been named as a suspect in a search warrant." There also were other aspects of the story that led Gasparoli to believe Stokes' zone of privacy was diminished. Stokes has never been charged for the crime.

J. Laurent Scharff, general counsel to the Radio-Television News Directors Association, is uncomfortable with the notion of a zone of privacy. It can be "dangerous for a layman to come up with a test," says Scharff, "however logical it may appear, if it's not sophisticated and accurate enough to reflect all the considerations the law requires."

Scharff says stations should have explicit guidelines and recommends that reporters consult not only with station management but with lawyers as well. In this case, WCCO had no written guidelines, and Gasparoli decided to wire Stokes' mother-in-law the night before her meeting with Stokes without consulting anyone.

Poynter Institute ethics program director Bob Steele, who wrote the SPJ hidden camera guidelines, says the fact that Stokes' widow was taped surreptitiously could foster the perception that she is guilty. Taping someone with a hidden camera implies something is wrong, he says.

IN THE DEATH CHAMBER

The most famous New York Daily News picture may well be a 1928 shot of an electrocution at Sing Sing Prison.

Ruth Snyder was going to the chair because of the love triangle slaying of her husband. The Daily News wanted a picture, but thought prison officials would recognize their regular photographers. So the paper brought in Thomas Howard from the Chicago Tribune.

Howard strapped a tiny camera to his ankle and took the picture. It was splashed across the entire front page of the Daily News. In the caption, the paper said, "The only unofficial photo ever taken within the death chamber, this most remarkable exclusive photo shows closeup of Ruth Snyder in death chair at Sing Sing as lethal current surged through her body."

Not a paper frequently accused of understatement, the Daily News called the scoop "the most talked of feat in the history of journalism."
—R.L.

Therefore, "the very act of obtaining information this way is an ethical question."

ABC News Senior Vice President Dick Wald, who rules on hidden camera requests at the network, acknowledges that hidden camera footage, by its very nature, tends to make anything seem suspicious. "Technology is without ethics," he says. "Our process tries to assure we operate ethically in its use."

SOME LOCAL STATIONS ALSO ARE TRYING TO ENSURE they use hidden cameras responsibly. They subscribe to the SPJ guidelines or they send reporters to Poynter Institute seminars on ethical decision making. There also are reporters who have adopted their own personal guidelines that are more stringent than SPJ's.

Pam Zekman is one reporter who has fashioned her own standards. She's been an investigative reporter at WBBM in Chicago since 1980. Before that, she worked for the Chicago Tribune and the Sun-Times, and was the reporter who did the preliminary work for the Sun-Times Mirage Bar story.

Zekman says it's more difficult to do investigative reporting for television than newspapers because of television's demand for pictures. But more than a decade in TV has shown her that

3. DEFINING THE RULES

> WHEN WBBM's Pam Zekman confronted the repair companies, they accused her of lying. She then simply ran the hidden camera footage for them. "The good thing about the hidden camera," she says, "is it allows no wiggle room."

reporters don't have to resort to a hidden camera. Zekman did an award-winning story on the Chicago police without going undercover. Instead, she did a painstaking records search that revealed the police department had been claiming officers' initial reports were unfounded to make it appear there was less crime.

But Zekman won't hesitate to use a hidden camera when she thinks it's necessary. She says Chicago is a market where "people have demanded undercover reporting as a standard of journalism." In a story that aired last November, Zekman used a hidden camera to document home repair ripoffs. When Zekman confronted the repair companies, they accused her of lying. She then simply ran the hidden camera footage for them. "The good thing about the hidden camera," she says, "is it allows no wiggle room."

Zekman stresses that she is very careful how she uses concealed cameras. She consults with lawyers beforehand and won't use them in private homes. She's never been sued.

Jacquee Petchel at WCCO in Minneapolis is another former newspaper investigative reporter who has managed to avoid lawsuits.

"Hidden cameras should be used primarily in public places where there's no expectation of violations of privacy," she says. In May 1994, Petchel's hidden camera captured city police sleeping, moonlighting at other jobs, and hanging out in strip joints while on duty. Following the reports, two officers were fired, two voluntarily retired and two others were reassigned. The series won a duPont Award in January.

WCCO has no written guidelines on hidden cameras, but Bob Steele of the Poynter Institute has visited the station to counsel news staffers. Petchel herself has a long track record in investigative reporting and was a member of a Pulitzer Prize-winning team at the Miami Herald. She is currently on the board of directors of Investigative Reporters and Editors.

Another station in the Twin Cities market, KSTP, has developed written guidelines based on SPJ standards. The use of hidden cameras requires prior approval by the news director or managing editor, and lawyers.

One of the most notable KSTP investigations in recent years resulted in a series of reports aired in November 1991 on racist department store security guards. The series, by reporter Joel Grover, revealed that guards were targeting black shoppers for no reason other than their race. Grover's hidden camera caught one guard on her hands and knees, peeping into a dressing room as a black shopper tried on clothing. He videotaped another guard saying he follows blacks around the store because "I just don't like them." The series, which won Peabody, duPont and Emmy awards, forced the stores to dismiss some of the guards and to enforce previously ignored regulations regarding equal treatment.

PRUDENT APPROACHES TO HIDDEN CAMERAS DON'T inoculate stations against lawsuits, however.

KSTP, for example, is facing a suit stemming from a series reported by Grover that aired in February 1993. The series, called "The Big Fix," featured hidden camera footage documenting allegedly fraudulent practices of Expertech, a home appliance repair company. KSTP accused the company of charging customers for unnecessary repairs and it went out of business about six weeks after the story ran. The company then filed suit, charging the station "falsely portrayed the business practices of Expertech as dishonest."

KSTP denies any wrongdoing and the case is expected to go to trial later this year. Meanwhile, two other lawsuits against KSTP resulting from other Grover stories, dismissed in lower court, are currently on appeal.

Becky Oliver, a veteran investigative reporter at KDFW in Dallas, has been sued three times over hidden camera stories. Although all three cases were dismissed, she's not as upbeat about the microminiature cameras as she once was: "I'm learning computer-assisted journalism as fast as I can." She says mounting legal challenges are beginning to change TV reporters' attitudes. At the annual IRE convention two years ago she remembers that reporters were enthusiastic about using tiny cameras. At last summer's convention, reporters were talking about lawsuits.

Rosemary Armao, executive director of Investigative Reporters and Editors, says she has received a number of calls over the past year from stations asking about laws governing the use of hidden cameras and microphones. Armao compares the current status of hidden camera reporting to investigative reporting following the Washington Post's Watergate coverage. That story prompted other papers to launch investigative projects, which led to lawsuits. "The same pattern," says Armao, "is taking place with hidden cameras."

In Minnesota, attorney Pat Tierney is representing the plaintiffs in the appeals against KSTP over two Grover stories. Tierney wants to establish the legal concept that hidden cameras constitute an invasion of privacy in his state. In one of his appeals he says, "The Constitution even precludes the government from entering and searching a private residence without compelling cause. To permit the media to engage in this type of outrageous conduct violates privacy rights that are rooted in the Constitution."

Privacy is a relatively new legal concept. Before the late 19th century, the United States, a largely rural nation, had little need for privacy laws. In an apparent response to scurrilous newspaper accounts of the rich and famous, Boston lawyers Samuel Warren and Louis Brandeis wrote an article in 1890 for the Harvard Law Review arguing for laws protecting a person's right to privacy. But such laws have never been formally codified at the federal level and state statutes are inconsistent. As a result, lawyers are jumping in to test the waters.

Perhaps the most important current suit is against ABC's "PrimeTime Live." California Judge Bruce Geernaert has warned he plans to issue an injunction specifically barring ABC News employees from using hidden cameras in private workplaces in his state. In a hearing in January, lawyers argued whether California law already bans hidden cameras. ABC lawyers maintained that "under some circumstances" they are lawful. Geernaert said that is "absolutely wrong."

The injunction would be at the request of attorney Neville Johnson, whose clients already have won a $1 million judgment against ABC for a February 1993 story called "Hello Telepsychic."

For the story, "PrimeTime Live" hired a young woman to go undercover to work for telephone psychics. Using a hidden camera, ABC videotaped the psychics saying things privately that suggested they didn't believe in what they were doing and that they were deceiving callers.

Johnson says one of his clients has suffered constant humiliation since the story aired, and another "relapsed into severe alcoholism…and died." Denouncing hidden camera reporting, he says, "Imagine being scourged and whipped in front of 24 million people. You're tried, convicted, sentenced and buried at sea, with no right of appeal, and you don't know that it is happening to you and have no way to fight back."

Geernaert says the injunction may be necessary because simply awarding damages to the plaintiffs "won't get the attention of ABC." ABC lawyers would appeal the injunction on First Amendment grounds, but they say the jury verdict and the million dollar damage award will stand "as an absolute barrier" to the network's use of hidden cameras in private workplaces in the state.

Some observers say an injunction would represent unconstitutional prior restraint. Others agree it's a bad precedent but nevertheless are concerned about the use of hidden cameras. Poynter's Steele warns, "Even though the access is legal, it may not be ethically justified." Everette E. Dennis, executive director of the Freedom Forum Media Studies Center, believes the injunction would be an intrusion on the First Amendment, but criticizes the use of hidden cameras as a "lazy kind of journalism, driven by ratings and people who don't have a clue about ethics. It's a bulldozer over a lot of things people hold dear."

Both Twin Cities plaintiffs' attorney Tierney and Laura Lee Stapleton, a defense attorney, predict suits involving hidden cameras are going to be a growth industry. "In defamation law," says Tierney, "the future is in attacking television stations which have created news rather than reported it." Says Stapleton, writing in the newsletter Media & the Law, "The First Amendment doesn't seem to immunize the news media from liability when it uses hidden cameras to do investigative reporting."

Some journalists say the legal challenges are only one reason to bar the use of hidden cameras. Former CBS News correspondent Marvin Kalb, now director of the Shorenstein Center on Press, Politics and Public Policy at Harvard University, is opposed to the use of hidden cameras under any circumstances. He believes hidden camera gaffes "may be one reason for the low esteem in which the profession is held."

"Journalists should walk in the front door, not sneak in the back door, even if in doing so they catch a crook with his hand in the cookie jar," says Kalb. "I'd rather introduce myself honestly so people know who they're dealing with."

Steele thinks hidden cameras can serve a valuable purpose, but says that "journalists have misused and overused [them]. They're an important tool to have in the journalistic bag, but we should use them judiciously, conservatively and with the recognition that the stakes are very high, because the consequences for those individuals who are the subject of hidden cameras can be dire and the impact on journalistic credibility is profound."

HIDDEN CAMERA GUIDELINES

In 1992 the Society of Professional Journalists and the Poynter Institute for Media Studies drafted the following guidelines. They say hidden cameras should be used only:

- *when the information obtained is of profound importance. It must be of vital public interest, such as revealing great "system failure" at the top levels, or it must prevent profound harm to individuals.*
- *when all other alternatives for obtaining the same information have been exhausted.*
- *when the individuals involved and their news organization apply excellence, through outstanding craftsmanship as well as the commitment of time and funding needed to pursue the story fully.*
- *when the harm prevented by the information revealed through deception outweighs any harm caused by the act of deception.*
- *when the journalists involved have conducted a meaningful, collaborative, and deliberative decision making process.*

Criteria that cannot be used to justify deception:
- *Winning a prize.*
- *Beating the competition.*
- *Getting the story with less expense of time and resources.*
- *Doing it because "the others already did it."*
- *The subjects of the story are themselves unethical.*

Article 19

ANONYMOUS SOURCES

Alicia C. Shepard

AJR contributing editor Alicia C. Shepard wrote about the Arkansas Democrat-Gazette in our October issue.

Ohio University journalism professor Hugh Culbertson knew he had a hot topic. Editors around the country were agonizing over the use of anonymous sources, fearing they were relying on them too heavily, damaging the press' credibility in the process. Culbertson surveyed more than 200 editors.

The results: Most said competition forced them to use unnamed sources, even though 81 percent considered them inherently less believable. One-third were "unhappy to a substantial degree" with how anonymous sources were handled at their own newspapers, and editors estimated that more than half would go on the record if reporters pushed harder. "They seemed to regard unnamed attribution as a crutch for lazy reporters," Culbertson says.

That was in 1979. It's likely the findings would be similar today. The issue of anonymous sources always makes editors uncomfortable. They debate their use endlessly. But there's no indication nameless officials are going away.

"Certain stories keep bringing this issue to the fore," says Culbertson. "There was Watergate's Deep Throat in 1973, Janet Cooke [who fabricated a story that cited anonymous sources] around 1980... and now O.J. Simpson."

Concern over the use of anonymous or confidential sources is indeed back. Los Angeles County Superior Court Judge Lance Ito angrily threatened to close Simpson's murder trial to television cameras in the wake of one controversial report. In late September, KNBC-TV reporter Tracie Savage told viewers that DNA tests showed a match between blood on a sock found in Simpson's bedroom and his former wife's blood. The link was attributed to a source who refused to be named.

Ito called the report "outrageous" and "irresponsible." KNBC first responded by sticking to its story, but days later admitted the information may not have been completely correct. This was just the latest in a series of high-profile inaccurate stories based on anonymous sources in the Simpson coverage (see "Offside on O.J.").

Pressure to be first on the Simpson case is intense. And with few knowledgeable sources speaking on the record, journalists feel compelled to rely on those willing to talk on a not-for-attribution basis.

"Every time you have a story like O.J. Simpson or Tonya Harding which relies so heavily on sources, we are under increasing pressure to put names in the attribution," says Darrell Christian, the Associated Press' managing editor. "There's a legitimate concern on the part of newspapers that they want their readers to believe what they're writing. The best way to do that is to put names with the facts."

Some would like the Simpson experience to mark the end of the unnamed sources era. "My hope is that the O.J. story will be to anonymous sources what the 'Jimmy's World' story [by Janet Cooke]...was to deception, fictional and composite characters," says Tom Brislin, who teaches journalism at the University of Hawaii and administers the Carol Burnett Fund for Responsible Journalism. If Brislin has his way, in 10 years "we'll look back...on O.J.'s world and anonymous sources as those bad old days in our ethical evolution."

Defenders of confidential sources say they bring to light important stories that otherwise would never surface. If used carefully, they say, unnamed sources are a valuable tool.

"The job of a journalist, particularly someone who's spent time dealing in sensitive areas, is to find out what really happened," says author and Washington Post Assistant Managing Editor Bob Woodward. "When you are reporting on inside the White House, the Supreme Court, the CIA or the Pentagon, you tell me how you're going to get stuff on the record. Look at the good reporting out of any of those institutions—it's not on the record."

But opponents of the practice argue that

A flurry of inaccurate stories about O.J. Simpson based on unnamed sources has rekindled the debate over their use. Detractors say they hurt the media's credibility. Defenders say without them important stories would never be told.

information from unnamed people further undermines journalism's sagging credibility and is simply not worth the price.

"There's not a place for anonymous sources," says Allen H. Neuharth, founder of USA Today and chairman of the Freedom Forum. "I think there are a few major historical developments that happened in journalism—the Pentagon Papers, maybe Watergate—where anonymous sources had a more positive influence than a negative impact. But on balance, the negative impact is so great that we can't overcome the lack of trust until or unless we ban them."

While sensational sagas often bring about a burst of anonymous source stories, there is one place where information from unnamed officials is a journalism staple: Washington, D.C.

"There's just a great deal more tolerance for people going nameless in the newspapers…," says Washington Post Ombudsman Joann Byrd, former editor of the Everett Herald in Washington state. "I think there are more anonymous sources per capita in Washington than there are anywhere else in the world. Nobody has a name in Washington."

Using information from unidentified officials is simply a way of life in the nation's capital, where spokespersons at many agencies routinely speak to journalists "on background."

At the Pentagon every Tuesday and Thursday, an official gives an on-the-record briefing to defense reporters. "After the briefing is over the TV lights go off, AP says thank you and it's over," says David Wood, a Pentagon reporter for Newhouse News Service. "Then people accost the spokesman with the real questions and ask what's really going on. The spokesman can only read from the cards and give the approved line. But after the briefing, he'll talk on background"—with no names attached.

One legendary Washington anonymous source—although he ultimately wasn't all that anonymous—was Henry Kissinger (see "The 'Senior Official,' " November 1992). The former secretary of state was a master at manipulating the media, feeding headline-grabbing tidbits with the proviso that he be identified as a "senior official." During his shuttle diplomacy in the Middle East, Kissinger insisted on anonymity even though the information was reported by the press traveling with him and attributed to the "senior official on the plane." On one of Kissinger's sojourns, humorist Art Buchwald attributed information to a "high U.S. official with wavy hair, horn-rimmed glasses and a German accent."

Periodically, journalists grow weary of the insistence on anonymity and rebel. But generally not for long.

In 1971, then-Washington Post Executive Editor Ben Bradlee ordered that information provided by Kissinger about a pending summit meeting be attributed to him because it was simply too important to be reported anonymously, according to Walter Isaacson's book "Kissinger."

"The Post's action caused a widespread realization that reliance on backgrounders had gone too far," Isaacson wrote. Nevertheless, the White House Correspondents Association soon passed a resolution agreeing to abide by Kissinger's briefing rules.

"Part of the problem is that reporters and sources have become so comfortable with the arrangement here," says Edward Pound, an investigative reporter for U.S. News & World Report who has worked in Washington for 17 years. "If you call somebody at the White House or in an agency, they almost expect to be anonymous and they frequently won't talk unless they are."

Anonymity is not so much of a problem in Congress because many members are willing if not eager to voice on-the-record opinions, says Kevin Merida, who covers the Hill for the Washington Post. At the same time, many Hill aides are under orders not to speak for their bosses and will only talk on an unattributed basis.

At the White House, on-the-record sources are rare.

Karen Hosler of Baltimore's Sun covered the White House for five years, serving a term as president of the White House Correspondents Association. Hosler didn't like White House officials' insistence on briefing reporters without allowing their names to be used, but says she was powerless to change the situation.

"For reporters, it's difficult to unilaterally say you won't take advantage of the information," she adds. "A stand on principle just costs the story…. The White House is the worst and most difficult place to report about. We as a press corps could change things if we as a group did something. But it's much too competitive and cutthroat to do that."

Everyone moans about the excessive use of unnamed sources in Washington copy, but then "they turn around and print [the stories]," says Michael Gartner, former NBC News president and now editor and co-owner of the Daily Tribune in Ames, Iowa, which bans their use. "Sometimes it's a function of laziness. Sometimes it's competitiveness. There's always an excuse…. Both sources and reporters know they can get by with it so they play these little games."

Some think those little games are played at the expense of the credibility of Washington copy.

"When I go to Washington and I see a proliferation of anonymous sources used daily, I don't believe it myself even when I know the authors," says Mary Hargrove, an editor and investigative reporter for the Arkansas Democrat-Gazette. "I think, 'Can't you take that extra step?' It's just cheap shot heaven."

While Washington may be the anonymous source capital, the phenomenon is also widespread on other competitive beats around the country. "It's a disease mostly in Washington,

"MY STORY *wouldn't have been as credible had I used anonymous sources, because the facts were so outlandish and unbelievable,"* says Eileen Welsome, who reported on radiation experiments on humans.

3. DEFINING THE RULES

D.C., and the state capitals," says Steve Weinberg, an investigative reporter who teaches journalism at the University of Missouri. "I don't see it nearly as much outside of political reporting."

Beat reporters spend time developing and protecting contacts. Because of competitive pressure, many print and electronic reporters are quick to grant anonymity, sometimes even before it's requested. When he conducts discussions with journalists about hypothetical ethical dilemmas, says New York Times Assistant General Counsel George Freeman, "reporters are willing to give confidentiality at the drop of a hat."

MANY JOURNALISTS FEEL ABOUT ANONymous sources the way people in troubled relationships feel about their partners: can't live with them, can't live without them.

A few news organizations refuse to quote them at all. Investigative reporters, with plenty of time to devote to projects, tend to use them sparingly. But inexperienced reporters, those covering competitive beats and journalists chasing mega-stories like O.J. and Tonya often rely on them.

Numerous news organizations have wrestled with the anonymous source question and have reluctantly concluded, like Cincinnati Enquirer Editor Lawrence Beaupre: "They're discouraged, but permitted."

Although confidential sources predate Watergate, they were infrequently used before that celebrated story, which produced the most famous unnamed source of all time. Deep Throat, whose identity remains a mystery, helped Washington Post reporters Bob Woodward and Carl Bernstein bring down Richard Nixon in 1974. After that, the use of anonymous sources flourished, with many reporters considering it sexier to have an unnamed source than a named one. Then came Janet Cooke.

In 1980, Washington Post reporter Cooke wrote a disturbing story about "Jimmy," an 8-year-old heroin addict. Cooke convinced her editors, including Woodward, that she could not reveal Jimmy's identity because she had pledged to protect her sources. Post editors didn't find out that Cooke had fabricated the story until after she had won a Pulitzer Prize.

Then the pendulum swung back. Editors began demanding to know source names and became increasingly stingy in allowing reporters to grant confidentiality.

"It was cool to use them in the 1970s because of Woodward and Bernstein," says Theodore Glasser, director of Stanford University's journalism program, who's writing a book about investigative reporters with Northwestern's James Ettema. "But 1981 was a watershed year after the Janet Cooke case. Every journalism publication came out with these long essays saying we can't use anonymous sources anymore.... Everyone beat their breast and said we are going to do

Offside on O.J.

THE O.J. SIMPSON CASE HAS GENERATED SO MANY STORIES BASED on anonymous sources that Los Angeles Daily News writer Ray Richmond has suggested setting up a "Rent-a-Source" service for reporters. It would, he wrote, be an "incredible business opportunity."

"With Rent-a-Source, unsubstantiated information and idle rumor are just a phone call away," he wrote. Sources come in many flavors, he added, including "reliable source: one who has yet to be indicted"; "outside source: a person who has been indicted but has media contacts"; and "unnamed sources: people who don't want their names used because they're just making it up."

Like all good satire, Richmond's is uncomfortably close to the truth. The Simpson case has resulted in numerous erroneous stories based on false information attributed to unnamed sources. Among them were reports that:

▶ A bloody ski mask had been found at the murder site. Prosecutor Marcia Clark later told the court, "There is no ski mask."

▶ The murder weapon was a military digging tool. A deputy medical examiner has testified the murders were carried out with one or more knives.

▶ Simpson acted strangely during his plane flight to Chicago shortly after the murders and kept his hand in a bag during the flight. Several people on the plane said Simpson was not behaving oddly and didn't hide his hand in anything.

▶ At the time of his arrest, Simpson had scratches on his body that made it look as if he had been in a fight. Police witnesses testified Simpson had a small cut and a laceration on one finger.

▶ DNA testing showed that blood on a sock found in Simpson's bedroom matched that of Nicole Brown Simpson. The prosecution, the defense and Judge Lance Ito said the story, reported by KNBC-TV in Los Angeles, was wrong. KNBC initially responded by saying that it had "reported accurately the information our sources have told us." Several days later, the station said part of its report was "in some respect, factually incorrect," although it did not specify what was inaccurate.

—*Jacqueline Sharkey*

better. But I don't think anything's really changed."

Some editors say many good stories would be missed if there were a prohibition on anonymous sources. Whistleblowers would be reluctant to come forward, as would those whose safety or job may be jeopardized by speaking publicly to a reporter.

"I think [anonymous sources] can be a very effective reporting tool," says Beaupre, president of Associated Press Managing Editors. "You simply cannot publish certain stories if you don't give anonymity based on a source's fear of reprisal or a decision that they don't want to be in the spotlight."

One recent example of a significant story based on blind sources concerned former Sen. Brock Adams. The Washington Democrat resigned after the Seattle Times published allegations of sexual misconduct against him in March 1992 (see Free Press, April 1992). Eight women charged Adams with improper behavior ranging from sexual harassment to rape over a 20-year period. None spoke on the record, although they signed affidavits promising to testify if the paper were sued. It wasn't.

The Times was sharply criticized immediately after the story broke, but the criticism faded after it became clear how meticulously the paper had handled the story.

"We feel pretty much about it today the way we did when we published it," says Executive Editor Michael Fancher. "I always go back to the notion that the choice we faced was publishing a story we believed to be true and knew to be important with anonymous sources or publishing nothing at all. Given that choice, I still think we did the right thing."

Eight months after the Adams story, the Washington Post showed that some explosive articles about powerful figures *can* be published with named sources. In November 1992, the Post ran a story in which 10 women accused Sen. Bob Packwood, an Oregon Republican, of sexual misconduct (see Free Press, January/February 1993). Four were named in the original story and six more were identified in follow-ups.

"As you know, the allegations of sexual misconduct were serious and being made for the first time in public...," says Florence George Graves, a freelance writer who developed the story and took it to the Post. "When you are making those kinds of allegations you need to make every effort to get as many on-the-record sources as possible.... I think it's nothing short of a miracle we got as many women as we did to go on the record."

Last year Eileen Welsome reported in the Albuquerque Tribune on government-sponsored radiation experiments on humans in the 1940s (see "Radiation Redux," March). Her articles prompted an investigation by Energy Secretary Hazel O'Leary and a pledge to right the federal government's wrongs. While the broad outline of

---

"On Deep Background"

OFF THE RECORD, ON BACKGROUND, ON DEEP BACKGROUND—DOES everyone know exactly what these terms mean? Does everyone agree? Not entirely.

Off the Record—*Edward Pound*, reporter, U.S. News & World Report: "It means I can't use it unless I can get it elsewhere.... Most sources don't understand it. They tend to think off the record and on background are the same thing."

Steve Weinberg, reporter: "You can listen and you can do something with it but you can't in any way attribute it or even vaguely suggest that it came from a source."

Darrell Christian, managing editor, Associated Press: "You don't use it under any circumstances."

Peter Prichard, editor, USA Today: "It means you can't use it. That's my opinion.... Actually, it means different things to different people."

On Background—*Bob Woodward*, author: "It means that I'm not going to identify the source but I'm going to use it all."

David Hawpe, editor, Louisville Courier-Journal: "Well, that normally means you can use it only for your own information, just so you understand."

Karen Hosler, congressional correspondent, Baltimore's Sun: "On background means you can attribute word for word but you can't use the person's name. At the White House it always has to be a 'senior administration official.'"

Michael Gartner, editor, Daily Tribune, Ames, Iowa: "It means different things to different people. I've never understood it."

Philip Scheffler, senior producer, 60 Minutes: "Hmmmm. Those distinctions are of much greater interest to people who work in Washington."

On Deep Background—*Hosler*: "You can report as 'it was learned.' You can almost state it as fact. Sometimes you have to hedge your words."

So, Are There Differences Between Off the Record and On Background? *George Freeman*, New York Times attorney: "Yes, there are, but I've never quite figured them out. I tell reporters if they really want the source to understand, make it clear. But those words generally cause more confusion than anything else."

3. DEFINING THE RULES

the story had been reported before, Welsome attached names and faces to the victims.

"My story wouldn't have been as credible had I used anonymous sources, because the facts were so outlandish and unbelievable," says Welsome, who has left the paper and is writing a book about the experiments. "By using names, it allowed people to make their own informed judgment about this particular period of history. If I had used 'according to a high-placed Department of Energy official' there would have been more doubts in the public's mind about the nature of the story."

TODAY IN NEWSROOMS ACROSS THE COUNtry there is a consensus that anonymous sources weaken credibility. Yet very few news operations absolutely prohibit their use. Many have policies, written or unwritten, stressing they should be used only as a last resort.

Many editors try to restrict the use of unnamed sources by insisting reporters work harder to get someone on the record, or find a document to corroborate a story. Some insist on having at least two anonymous sources before putting a story in the paper.

Many newsrooms will permit the attribution of facts to unidentified people but not opinions. "We do not allow ambush quotes," says Stuart Wilk, deputy managing editor of the Dallas Morning News. The AP and many other newspapers have similar policies.

If a named source can't be found, according to the Washington Post's guidelines, "reporters should request an on-the-record reason for concealing a source's identity and should include the reason in the story."

Often high-level approval is required for using unnamed sources. For example, Beaupre requires a senior editor to approve their use. At the Dallas Morning News, anonymous sources must be cleared by the executive or managing editor, says Wilk, who can give permission in their absence. At the Albuquerque Tribune, says Welsome, "you need dispensation from the Pope to use an anonymous source in a news story."

News organizations tend to be more reluctant to use anonymous sources than they were 10 or 15 years ago, says William Marimow, a Pulitzer Prize-winning investigative reporter who is now associate managing editor of Baltimore's Sun. He cites a story he wrote while at the Philadelphia Inquirer in 1979 about prospective police commanders getting preferential treatment on promotion exams. Marimow relied on confidential sources in reporting that officers assigned to the chief inspectors—who wrote the tests—had suspiciously high marks on them.

"I think today the editors would have tried their hardest, they might even have demanded, that I get some records somewhere to show where the officers were assigned," Marimow

"In other words, find someone in the personnel department to give me the documents to prove the story."

When an unnamed source is used, some papers and broadcast outlets try to provide readers, viewers or listeners a clue as to where the information is coming from.

New York Times lawyer Freeman says reporters should not simply attribute information to "government sources," but should be more precise—"say what level, what department, something more than that the source is confidential, so you have some understanding where they're coming from."

That's critical to letting a reader understand whether the unnamed source has an agenda and what it might be. "The anonymous source has always been really important to news," says James D. Squires, former editor of the Chicago Tribune. "But you need to identify the source as to its motivations. It gives you a great deal of credibility."

While many associate confidential sources with investigative reporting, those who practice that craft now use them infrequently. They may permit sources to go off the record during preliminary interviews, but by the time they publish or go on the air, they want the facts on the record.

"Of course, you talk to everybody when you begin a story," says Philip Scheffler, a senior producer for CBS' "60 Minutes." "Off the record. On the record. In the record. For background. Not for attribution no matter what. But it's not the raw notes we are talking about. We are talking about what goes on the air." And "60 Minutes" does not use anonymous sources on the air.

Chuck Neubauer, a Pulitzer Prize-winning investigative reporter, rarely uses unidentified sources. In a January 1993 story in the Chicago Sun-Times, Neubauer and colleague Mark Brown revealed a scheme that ultimately became part of the indictment of Rep. Dan Rostenkowski, an Illinois Democrat. They used just one unnamed source.

"I don't very often use anonymous sources...," says Neubauer. "A story based on just anonymous sources would be a hard sell."

Time is a crucial ally for investigative reporters. Stanford's Glasser interviewed about 20 of them and found for the most part, anonymous sources do not play an important role in their work. "They've had four months or more to work on their story," he says. "They are able to get it all on the record. The people who use anonymous sources all the time and abuse it are the ones who are pressured to get stuff into the paper every day."

A notable exception among investigative reporters is Bob Woodward, who relied almost exclusively on anonymous sources for his latest book, "The Agenda," and has used them liberally in other major reporting projects. Woodward notes that just because something is on the record doesn't mean it's true. He says often confidential sources can be more accurate if they aren't worried about losing a job or being reprimanded.

"Look at all the stuff that's been from anonymous sources over the years and very little of it has been wrong," Woodward said at a recent journalism forum sponsored by the Smithsonian Institution and AJR. "In fact, I would argue it's often more correct because the reporter knows his or her rear end is on the line."

People lie just as easily on the record, says Woodward. "You can go up as a White House correspondent and quote the president of the United States in a televised press conference. If it turns out he's lying, as it often has turned out, no one comes back and says to the reporter: 'Why did you print what the president said on the record in public?' The standard has to be: What's the quality of information?"

When Al Neuharth founded USA Today, he instituted a ban on the use of blind sources. He did so, he says, because unattributed information makes it less likely that readers will believe what they read.

During USA Today's second week, White House reporter Ann Devroy phoned in a scoop about President Reagan's plans to appoint his daughter, Maureen, to the Republican National Committee. The only problem was the story was unattributed. "I saw the story and thought it was good," recalls Neuharth. "Obviously it was a plant but we don't run unidentified sources." So he insisted Devroy get Maureen Reagan on the record. Devroy did.

"I think that often happens if you simply have a policy that you don't run anonymous sources," says Neuharth, "I think a majority of sources would go on the record if pushed."

Ten years ago, journalism professor Bob M. Gassaway interviewed 15 people who had been longtime confidential news sources. "A majority of the sources said journalists faced with pressure to identify their sources should 'ask me to reconsider an agreement' of confidentiality," Gassaway wrote in the Newspaper Research Journal.

Neuharth argues that when hiding beneath the cloak of anonymity, sources sometimes tell more than they know, "especially in a political environment like Washington. They often say more than they would if they had to back it up with their name."

Peter Prichard, the current editor of USA Today, says, "We don't exactly have a no anonymous source policy. A better way to put it is we try not to abuse or overuse them."

Veteran newsman Michael Gartner is one of the most outspoken critics of the practice. After the story about O.J. Simpson's DNA match, Gartner wrote, "The lesson is this: Beware anonymous sources. They can lie without accountability. They can fudge without responsibility. They can hide behind anonymity. They can strain readers' credulity and damage journalists' credibility."

Gartner cites a personal experience with confidential sources: After the embarrassing

Using Unnamed Sources

THE CINCINNATI ENQUIRER'S POLICY ON USING ANONYMOUS SOURCES, *written by Editor Lawrence Beaupre:*

▶ The identities of all sources must be verified and confidentially disclosed to the editor and, if requested, to the newspaper's attorney.

▶ Misleading information about the true identity of a source may not be used in a story, even to "throw off" suspicion.

▶ Information supplied by an unnamed source should be verified independently or confirmed by at least one other source. An exception may be made (albeit with risk) for individuals who are the sole possessors of the information or whose integrity is unassailable....

▶ The motive of the anonymous source should be fully examined to prevent our being used unwittingly to grind someone's ax.

▶ We should avoid using anonymous sources on information that calls someone's judgment into question or on statements that are a matter of opinion. For example, it would be wrong to quote an anonymous source saying someone is "dumb." ... If someone wants to take a jab at someone else, he should be compelled to put his name behind it.

▶ Information attributed to an anonymous source must be factual and important to the story. Peripheral information or "just a good quote" aren't good enough reasons for anonymity.

▶ As with on-the-record sources, the Rule of the Best Source should prevail. Reporters and editors should satisfy themselves that the source is appropriate to provide the information sought and that he or she is in a position to know.

▶ When an unnamed source must be used, the story should explain why his or her identity is being withheld, and enough information should be given about the source to establish his or her authority to speak on the subject.

▶ Stories containing unnamed sources may not be published without the approval of the editor or a managing editor. Generally, I want to be consulted.

▶ We should not quote people whose identities we do not know or cannot verify.

3. DEFINING THE RULES

revelation that "Dateline NBC" had rigged an explosion in a crash involving a General Motors truck, Gartner left his job as president of NBC News in March 1993. Associated Press President Louis Boccardi gave a speech around that time urging journalists not to rely on anonymous sources.

"Within an hour [after Boccardi's speech] the AP had moved a story with an anonymous source...," says Gartner. "They had a story that a source told AP that I was fired from NBC. I quit. So I called him up and said, 'What is this bullshit, Lou?'"

Boccardi investigated. A correction ran, recalls Gartner. "It said two sources told AP that I was fired," says Gartner. "Well, Jesus, there were only two people in the room when I quit. Me and [NBC President] Bob Wright."

Investigative reporter Steve Weinberg says he once allowed a source to anonymously criticize someone in a story he was writing about competing news organizations. "It turned out be untrue," says Weinberg.

He no longer uses confidential sources. While researching an unauthorized biography of industrialist Armand Hammer, Weinberg conducted many off-the-record interviews. But he only used information from them that he could document elswhere.

Each time an unnamed source turns out to be wrong or a reporter is caught fabricating anonymous information, journalism's credibility suffers. Even after years of excellent work and more Pulitzers, the Washington Post remains dogged by Janet Cooke and "Jimmy's World."

"I probably have someone bring up Janet Cooke to me every couple of weeks," says Post Ombudsman Joann Byrd, 14 years after the ill-fated story ran. "If they're mad at the Post, they'll say a 'This-is-the-newspaper-that-brought-us-Janet-Cooke' kind of remark. If they're alarmed about something they see in the paper that they're not absolutely sure they believe, then they'll say, 'Promise me this is not another Jimmy's World.'"

While it lends credibility to have a story on the record, some say it's crucial for another reason: to protect against libel charges. Janet Cooke may have cooled the enthusiasm for using unattributed sources, but others feel that massive libel awards in the early 1980s had more to do with changing attitudes about them. "The proliferation of big libel verdicts starting in 1982 and '83 made people more circumspect, more vigilant," says Baltimore's Marimow.

New York Times attorney Freeman says unnamed sources represent one of the most serious libel threats for news organizations. When a paper is sued over a story based on confidential sources, he says, "the plaintiff's lawyer will doubtless complain that either the sources didn't exist or they shouldn't have been relied on. Juries will generally believe that when those people never come into the room."

WHILE GRANTING ANONYMITY MAY induce reluctant or nervous sources to talk, it doesn't guarantee they will say anything worth listening to.

Associated Press Managing Editor Darrell Christian recalls that when he was working in Washington, he called a White House duty officer late one night for comment on a controversial story. The conversation went something like this:

"I'll have to go off the record," the duty officer said.

"Well, all right," Christian replied, "if you have to."

Duty officer: "OK, am I off the record?"

Christian: "Yes."

Duty officer: "Are you sure?"

Christian reassured him. The duty officer was finally comfortable.

"No comment," he said, confident that he'd protected his job and given Christian the quote he needed.

When Checkbook Journalism Does God's Work

Louise Mengelkoch

Louise Mengelkoch teaches journalism at Bemidji State University. She is writing a book entitled Imperfect Justice: A Small-Town Rape and Murder Story.

It seems that at least once a day I read something in the popular press about the shameful nature of the tabloids and, especially, tabloid television. "Checkbook journalism" has become the buzzword for the unsavory practice of paying Michael Jackson's personal servants, or Bill Clinton's bodyguards, or the store clerk who sold O. J. Simpson a knife to tell all, whether it's true or not.

Money taints the truth, we reason. And the stores themselves appeal to the lowest common denominator in terms of subject matter, audience, and focus. Having said that, I'd like to tell about a strange tabloid story in which I became involved.

I've spent the last year immersing myself in reporting on a rape and murder story. During that year, I've changed my thinking drastically about the value of sensationalism and checkbook journalism. Specifically, I now think we, as journalists, and the public would be better served by re-educating ourselves about what the television tabloids are good for, and why.

In August 1993, fourteen-year-old Heather Lory was gang-raped in the wee hours of the morning by three boys, two of them brothers, in a country cemetery near my home in rural northern Minnesota. Later that morning her parents, Richard and Linda Lory, drove to the boys' home to confront them and their family. Richard Lory ended up shooting seventeen-year-old Bruce Bradach Jr., one of the three boys, to death, seriously wounding Bruce Bradach Sr., and accidentally shooting his own wife in the stomach.

I read the account of the incident in our local newspaper, *The Pioneer* of Bemidji, which was based entirely on official sources: the police report, the complaint, the county attorney. It was obviously superficial and incomplete, and that was because of circumstances at the 9,000-circulation daily that I was well aware of; many of my students go on to work there. This is a newspaper that requires its reporters to write an average of seven stories a day (of varying length) and pays reporters little more than minimum wage.

A week later, the *St. Paul Pioneer Press* featured a front-page article on the case, even though we're a long 250 miles northwest of the Twin Cities. This time, the story was based on official sources plus eyewitness accounts by unofficial sources. But more confusion was created by a different kind of resource-allocation problem. The big-city reporter's time was too valuable to spend more than a day or so in the woods of Nowhere, Minnesota. So he interviewed the people who were willing and available: the Bradach family, friends of theirs, a woman who worked with Rich Lory's wife, Linda, and Rich Lory's former employer. Linda Lory was recovering from surgery and was too ill to speak, and the reporter was told by jail administrators that Lory would not grant an interview. What the reporter didn't know was that the county attorney had instructed everyone involved to stay away from the media, and Lory was not even told about the reporter. The Bradachs ignored the instructions and, as a result, were at least able to speak their piece. The Lorys felt they'd been had, especially when the county attorney himself was quoted at length.

Among his off-the-cuff remarks was the assertion that Bruce Bradach Jr., the young man killed, had nothing to do with the rape. (He apparently based that statement solely on the Bradach family's story. Much later, DNA testing strongly suggested otherwise; final DNA testing

3. DEFINING THE RULES

was never done.) After the article appeared, Heather Lory was called a liar, a slut, and a murderer more times than she could count. She was spit upon at football games, received death threats, sometimes on her assignment notebooks. She finally dropped out of school.

For the people in our community, the St. Paul paper's article solidified a few basic "facts" around which everything else now had to fit. When I read it, I was puzzled and intrigued enough to contact the Lorys and ask for an interview. I wanted to hear their side of the story, I said, and perhaps write a commentary for a Twin Cities paper.

They grabbed onto my offer with more hope than I was comfortable with. The Lorys later said they had gone to the Bemidji paper to tell their side, but were rebuffed. The reasons given were the negative effects of pretrial publicity and the need to "protect" Heather's privacy. The Lorys even approached the campus newspaper of the state university at which I teach. The family reasoned, quite rightly I thought, that the story was relevant to our campus because Rich Lory had just graduated summa cum laude that spring with a degree in elementary education, to add to his degree in psychology from some years ago. The *Northern Student* editors didn't know quite how to handle the situation and gave the Lorys mixed messages about their willingness to print their story.

My position was clear — I thought. I would hear their side, interview the Bradach family, and write a short opinion piece decrying twin evils: the timidity of the small-town, corporate-owned press — in this case, the owner was Park Newspapers of Ithaca, New York — in the face of controversy, and the big-city's bumbling parachute journalism. I'd shake hands with all involved and go back to my classroom. It wasn't quite that simple.

The Bradach family had now decided to heed the advice of the county attorney and gave me only one brief, unsatisfying interview. The official sources now mysteriously took the high road and wouldn't discuss either the rape or the killing. The Lory family wanted to talk but were being consumed by several imminent disasters: Linda and the four children were, day by day, fast losing their hold on economic sufficiency. She had lost her job, her car had been repossessed, Rich's phone calls from the jail were costing an average of $150 a month, and the Minnesota fall was fast turning to winter with no money for fuel oil.

Rich Lory was warm and well-fed, but lived in a bleak prison of ignorance about his own case, which, he said, was worse than the actual jail. He had a court-appointed lawyer with whom he'd met only once. The public defender's message was simple — be prepared to spend a long, long time in prison because your case seems pretty open and shut and I'm busy. See you in six months or so. We'll get together about a week before your trial begins. (Lory was also led to believe that pretrial publicity could be damaging to his case and could even cause a change of venue.)

Watching all this go on with my reporter's notebook in hand, I was reminded of photographers documenting acts of violence or horror they could stop if they'd put down the camera. I couldn't stand it. And yet, at the same time, I was beginning to see a larger, long-term story here that I wanted for myself. I worried that if I published part of the story now, I would cut off future sources in opposing camps. When I expressed this concern to my husband, who is also a writer, he agreed, and said he would write a commentary himself.

He entitled it "Is Justice Blind? Or is it Deaf and Dumb in Rural Minnesota?" *The Star Tribune* in Minneapolis wasn't interested, but the *St. Paul Pioneer Press* took notice. They didn't print it, but the editorial page editor called us. We explained the situation, and he passed my husband's piece to the reporter who'd written the original front-page story, who then called us. He said he knew he should have pushed harder to get a wider variety of sources and wondered if we thought the Lorys would agree to be interviewed at this late date. I said it was probably worth a try. He came up.

When Linda Lory asked my advice about granting the interview, I cast aside all pretense of being the disinterested chronicler of events. I warned her that it wouldn't be their story as told through the reporter. It would be his story, and they would undoubtedly be very unhappy with some aspects of it. Furthermore, they would have no way of correcting any new misperceptions the new article caused. The Lorys decided that any publicity that might help find an acceptable lawyer for Rich and clear Heather's name in the community was worth the risk.

The reporter came up and spent several days doing long interviews with the Lorys and re-interviewing the Bradachs and official sources after reading hundreds of pages of transcripts at night in his motel room. He wrote a thoughtful article, focusing on Heather's ordeal, but also mentioning the problems faced by Rich Lory. The Lorys did dislike aspects of the story. But they tried to focus on the long-term good it could do. They were hoping for a break.

It came soon after the story ran in late November. A producer for the *Sally Jessy Raphael* show was visiting her family in St. Paul for Thanksgiving and saw the article. The Twin Cities local television news reporters called. Linda Lory was excited but fearful and uncertain. Rich Lory was impatient and suspicious. Dealing with reporters so intense they wanted to land helicopters on the Lorys' front yard or producers so insensitive they didn't realize the Lorys couldn't afford a long-distance phone call proved to be too much for the family. So my husband and I ended up brokering with the TV producers and reporters for the Lorys.

The *Sally Jessy* show came first, in early December. We negotiated for some extras, beyond all travel expenses, for the Lorys: paid child care for the younger children while Linda and Heather traveled to New York; expenses for the student reporter who had ultimately written the Lorys' story for the campus newspaper; partial expenses for me, and a guarantee that the Bradach family would not appear on the stage with them.

There were some annoying problems. We felt patronized and pressured during the entire experience. Heather was in tears over the inappropriate clothes — too grown-up, too sophisticated — the producers tried to make her wear on stage. Linda Lory was told just to pay her expenses for later reimbursement when she was so broke she couldn't have afforded up-front money to tip the limo driver.

But the show, broadcast in January, was an unqualified success for the Lory family. They had an hour of air time to tell their story to more than six million viewers. Until then they'd assumed that somehow they were responsible for the system's not working, for Heather's harassment, for Rich Lory's frustration. But the professionals who appeared with them on the show and those in the audience reassured them. And the TV appearance gave them a sense of authority in our own community and legitimized their concerns and complaints. Now it was up to the local power structure to respond.

The powers that be were furious. In a front-page story in the local paper, the county attorney vilified the family for their decision to appear on national television and congratulated himself and the Bradach family for taking the high road and refusing to appear. All in all, the town was in an uproar.

After that, things happened fast. *Hard Copy* and *American Journal* wanted the story. We went with *Hard Copy*, the one willing to pay the family $3,000, what the Lorys felt they needed as start-up money to get a lawyer for Rich. That $3,000, and the videotapes of TV appearances, did result — by March, one month before the scheduled murder trial — in a lawyer who agreed to work for expenses only. The lawyer gave the family renewed purpose.

At his trial, Rich Lory was found not guilty of first-degree assault on Bruce Bradach Sr. and not guilty of second-degree murder. He was found guilty of felony murder, a lesser charge in Minnesota. But before sentencing, improprieties in the jury's deliberations were discovered, and a new trial was ordered. The case has been highly scrutinized locally and statewide ever since the national media paid attention.

After the trial, the Lory family, the Bradach family and the defense attorney all appeared together on the Phil Donahue show to tell their stories, the Bradachs by remote hookup from their home, Rich Lory by phone from jail. I was invited to come to offer my observations as well. The entire Donahue organization displayed nothing but the highest degree of professionalism in all our dealings with them. All involved came away feeling they'd had their say. Expenses were paid fully and promptly.

The reporter and producers of *Hard Copy*, as well, were extremely professional in their demeanor and in their editing. They took their time, asked probing and sensitive questions, and followed through on their promises.

The publicity has now died down. One of the Bradach boys, sixteen, and a thirteen-year-old whose mother has since married Bruce Bradach Sr. pleaded guilty to sexual misconduct and were sentenced as youthful offenders to probation and counseling. Rich Lory awaits his new trial, and his wife and children are trying to piece their lives together. But the impact on those lives from their willingness to "sink" to the level of tabloid journalism has been nothing but positive.

Linda Lory has been transformed from a woman too timid to speak to a news reporter to one who was able to put herself on the agenda of a county board meeting and make a public speech about her appearance on national television. Heather Lory has apparently found some healing in public discussion of her case and in support from other women and girls. She has said she hopes that other young women will gain the courage to confront their rapists and trade shame for openness. Rich Lory found a lawyer he probably never would have found otherwise and now faces a maximum of eight to twelve years instead of the forty years the public defender predicted. All three Lorys get phone calls and letters of support. People comment on how grateful they are for the opportunity to try to understand how this happened and prevent it from occurring again.

Another benefit of the tabloid exposure that went beyond the Lory family was the light it shone on local public officials. This normally doesn't happen here. It became apparent as the case progressed that some irregularities had taken place and that such things were considered business as usual. Certain people and offices were so unused to public scrutiny that they trapped themselves over and over by forgetting how things should be done. The Lory trial got gavel-to-gavel coverage from the Minneapolis newspaper and a 2,000-word front-page story when it ended.

There is still the question of that $3,000 payment from *Hard Copy*. I understand all the arguments against checkbook journalism. It's hard not to see the potential abuse and the bizarre extremes to which potential sources will go. But for the powerless in our culture who knowingly open themselves up to very personal stories that should be told — that have a real message for the public — it seems only fair that they should be compensated for their willingness to go public. My only complaint is that the Lorys didn't get more.

This experience has educated me in another way too: I use it in my teaching. I bring into class all the normally private people in our county I can find who've been in the news: the young mother whose ex-husband has been charged with abducting their three-year-old daughter; the woman whose grandson accidentally shot and killed his brother; the student in our class who was shot in her backyard while having a barbecue. We discuss the attention they've gotten, talk about how people like them should handle the media and what they can hope to accomplish from the attention. We talk about how to choose someone to handle the media for you or how to approach a friend who you can see is having trouble handling the media and offer to help. And, yes, we talk about the tabloids and whether negotiating with them would be a wise option in each case.

The tabloids' greatest virtue, I tell my students, is exactly that which makes people sneer at them — they're often foolish and not very selective. As gatekeepers they're lousy, and that's often fortunate for those who need them most. They will listen to your story when nobody else will, if it has the elements and the angles they're looking for. If we truly believe in access, that journalists should be dedicated to comforting the afflicted and afflicting the comfortable, the tabloids must be recognized as sharing that mission.

Article 21

ARE QUOTES SACRED?

Fawn Germer

Fawn Germer, a reporter for the Rocky Mountain News in Denver, wrote about interviewing victims of tragedy in the June issue [of American Journalism Review*].*

THE EDITOR REMOVED THE ELLIPSIS. THE reporter guessed at a word he couldn't quite hear. But it sure made for a great quote. "You got a duty to die and get out of the way," a Denver Post reporter quoted former Colorado Gov. Richard Lamm as saying.

The Associated Press picked up the quote and soon it was everywhere. The New York Daily News ran the story under the headline, "Aged Are Told to Drop Dead. Colo. Gov. Says It's Their Duty." The Boston Globe ran a cartoon of Lamm kicking old people off a cliff. More than a decade later, the quote still resurfaces occasionally (see "The Nexis Nightmare," July/August 1994).

The problem is, that wasn't quite what Lamm said. The actual quote was, "We've got a duty to die and get out of the way with all of our machines and artificial hearts and everything else like that and let the other society, our kids, build a reasonable life."

The Lamm misquote is a classic example of what can go wrong when the printed quote is not a verbatim account of what was said.

Sometimes a misquote stems from human error. But often quotes are altered to make them grammatically correct, or easier to follow, or sexier.

The debate over quotes stretches from the newsroom to the courtroom. While most agree it's no crime to fix a simple grammatical error, there is wide disagreement over the extent to which journalists should alter quotes.

If only sources could say it right the first time. If only they didn't ramble, switch tenses, inject "ummm" or "ah" into sentences and use "gonna" instead of going to. If only their subjects agreed with their verbs. Then there wouldn't be the temptation—or necessity—to ever clean up a quote.

The issue of altered quotes dogged New Yorker writer Janet Malcolm for more than a decade after a libel suit alleged she fabricated five quotes in a profile of a controversial psychoanalyst. Some of the disputed quotes were combined from interviews done many months apart. The most recent jury decison went in her favor, but debate over such tactics lingers.

Some question whether a public official who never uses proper grammar should be the beneficiary of a clean-up job every time his or her remarks appear in print. Others say running poor English might be a deliberate attempt to make someone look bad.

And what about quotes from an ordinary citizen? Should his poor use of language be widely exposed just because he happened to be interviewed once?

21. Are Quotes Sacred?

Some journalists say it's fine to "improve" quotations as long as the meaning isn't changed. Others argue that the practice is dishonest.

It's hard to admit that the purveyors of truth would reconstruct someone's words, then put the doctored version inside a set of quotation marks. Don't quotation marks indicate that what is inside them was actually what was spoken? If a quote needs to be fixed, shouldn't it just be paraphrased instead?

Some say it's not always that simple.

"There is a big difference between changing quotes and cleaning them up," says Sue O'Brien, a media ethics professor and newly named editorial page editor of the Denver Post. "I think cleaning them up is very common. Changing quotes means actually changing the words people use, whether it is for clarity or emphasis. Cleaning them up is leaving out words, substituting a contraction for a bulky phrase. The one place you change a word and call it cleaning it up is changing a tense. But do it with the words they used. It's wrong to change the thrust or context of what someone is saying."

Other professionals say the rules vary.

"I've changed quotes and I've been accused of changing quotes, but I have never been accused of changing a quote I actually changed," says Jon Franklin, a two-time Pulitzer winner who now teaches journalism and creative writing at the University of Oregon. "People don't say what they mean, and they expect you to quote what they mean, not what they say. That is slippery, but it's the reality."

So what should you do when a high-ranking public official says the following: "The indictment certainly came as a shock to all of us. We knew they were requesting a substantial amount of information, and quite frankly, that had us nervous. You've been in this city for a long time, right, and know about me. We are certain that once everything is heard in court, we will be vindicated."

For some this is an easy call. Sentences one, two and four are perfect and fit perfectly together. Sentence three is the sentence from Mars. Just paraphrase it or use an ellipsis. But some would simply delete the third sentence and connect the rest.

While some believe editing quotes is doing the source—and the reader—a favor, others say there's simply no excuse for it.

"You can't. You can't fix quotes. Period," says Susan Feeney, national political reporter for the Dallas Morning News. "If somebody speaks in a way in which quoting them is incomprehensible, you don't use the quote. You use partial quotes. I don't fix them. Ever."

If it's a bad quote, Feeney says, paraphrase. Use ellipses. No cutting, no pasting. For Feeney, there is no debate.

"I'm never going to change my view on this," she says. "I'm one of those people who think quote marks are sacred, and when you are putting quote marks around it, you are telling the reader that this is exactly what the person said."

Contrast Feeney with David Hayes, a Toronto magazine freelancer who has also written three books.

"What I put inside quotation marks is true," he says. "I've compressed and imported quotations most of my career and have only had a subject complain about the content of a quote once or twice. That's because they read their words as they believe they said them—the intent, the meaning is accurate, even though, for example, the five-sentence quote in question is made up of two sentences from a conversation in their car and three from a face-to-face interview in their office."

Yet that is precisely what made history out of New Yorker writer Janet Malcolm's two-part profile of the psychoanalyst who said she cooked up some of the quotes.

Jeffrey Masson sought more than $7 million in damages, accusing Malcolm of falsifying his remarks. Malcolm acknowledged combining statements that were made months apart and changing the setting where remarks were made, but said her work accurately reflected what he was saying. A federal jury found in her favor on libel claims last November. While the jury found two of the five disputed quotations were false, it said Malcolm did not recklessly falsify one of the quotes and the other was not defamatory.

The marathon legal battle ignited debate over the ethics of quotations. Do readers consider the punctuation mark a sacred covenant that signifies every word is reported exactly as it was spoken? That depends on whom you ask.

University of Southern California journalism professor Ed Cray: "Of course. What else are quote marks for?"

University of Oregon journalism professor Jon Franklin: "Some do, some don't, but I don't think it is a big complaint either way. I think journalists think more about it than readers, because we tend to confuse accuracy with truthfulness."

Palm Beach Post Managing Editor Tom O'Hara: "They think that what is between those quote marks is what the person quoted said. But you know and I know and everyone knows that if the county commission chair says, 'I'm gonna vote against this,' it's going to show up in the paper as, 'I'm going to vote against this,' I think that readers have no problem with that and, in fact, expect their newspaper to make that kind of change in a quote."

Says Gene Miller, the Miami Herald's associate editor for reporting and a two-time Pulitzer winner, "If it's garbled and messy, I say, 'Hey, would it sound better like this? And is this what the person said?' And call the person back and get the quote right."

When he has a problem with a quote, Miller says, he goes back to the source. It isn't necessary to put words in their mouths, he says: "If you talk to somebody long enough, they'll say anything."

3. DEFINING THE RULES

Editor Ralph Langer says reporters shouldn't push sources into saying the words that fit best in a story.

But editor Ralph Langer says it's not the reporter's place to push a source into saying the words that fit best in a story. "Our job is to report what people say and think, not to put words in their minds about what they might have said if they were as articulate as we are," says Langer, senior vice president and executive editor of the Dallas Morning News. "We aren't speechwriters for people."

REPORTERS SAY THE DECISION TO CLEAN up a quote is rooted in fairness to the reader and the source. "If reporters relied on transcripts, most of the people they quote would appear blundering and inarticulate," says New York Times reporter Matthew L. Wald. "And the point of quoting someone is generally not to make the person look silly. The solution is generally to put quote marks around the words that the speaker squeezed out in good English."

Often the amount of clean-up depends on the savvy of the source. "Generally, I fix quotes for grammar, especially with average, ordinary people," says Ellyn Ferguson, a regional reporter for Gannett News Service. "I am doing the interview to get information from them, not make them look like idiots."

But it's stickier with public officials, she says. The ones she deals with now are polished and need to be accountable for their words, she says. But it was very different when Ferguson was working in Lakeland, Florida, covering politicians in what was then a rural, undereducated community. Many of the politicians there hadn't graduated from high school and had trouble getting the subject and verb to agree. She would make it work.

"Besides conveying facts, I think our job is to convey coherent information," she says. "Sometimes, when I am standing there doing the interview, it makes all the sense in the world. But when I sit down to write, it makes no sense at all. When that happens, I either paraphrase or I call them back."

Franklin says reporters have to carefully translate spoken English into written English when dealing with regular people. "This is particularly important with someone who is not media wise," he says. "But if I have to change very much, I'll just paraphrase. I think that's probably the solution."

Matt Clark, a freelance writer and former longtime medicine editor for Newsweek, agrees that it's important to consider the source before deciding whether to change a quote.

"A distinguished professor of medicine might utter an ungrammatical phrase and there wouldn't be any harm in cleaning that up," he says. "On the other hand, if you're interviewing an Appalachian miner's wife about tough times, you don't go out of your way to make her sound like a Wellesley graduate, do you? How she talks is part of the story, maybe the most important part. On another level, if the speaker is a pre- sumably distinguished scholar and the issue happens to be his fitness to be head of a university department, you might be expected to leave the ungrammatical parts in, so long as they are quoted accurately."

The Miami Herald's Miller is also a hardliner on changing quotes in certain instances. If the subject is Bill Clinton or George Bush or Richard Nixon "saying something stupid," he says, the quote should run as uttered. If it is voiced in a courtroom or a setting where it is videotaped, the quotes need to be exact, he says.

"But you don't have to use quote marks all the time," he adds. "You paraphrase. You use selected quotes on certain words. You put dots in quite frequently."

In fact, quoting some people verbatim could amount to cruel and unusual punishment.

"If we quoted Mayor Daley correctly every time we dealt with him, he probably wouldn't be embarrassed, but some people would probably be embarrassed for him," says George Langford, the

---

Veteran writing coach Roy Peter Clark offers these tips on handling quotes:

1. Be truthful. Quotes should be faithful to the words and meaning of the speaker.

2. Adding language to quotes is more dangerous than taking stuff out, although both can distort meaning.

3. Because of language prejudice on race and class, be careful with slang and dialect.

4. That said, the American language is a great treasure. If everyone you quote sounds like you, your readers are in trouble.

5. Be polite. Tidy up the quote rather than make someone sound stupid.

6. It's not a good idea to blend quotes from different interviews without a signal to readers.

7. When you quote, imagine that someone has taped the interview, even if you have not.

8. No one takes notes at the speed of light. It's OK to reconstruct a quote using both notes and memory. When you do this, it's always best to read the quote back to the source.

"[I]f you're interviewing an Appalachian miner's wife about tough times, you don't go out of your way to make her sound like a Wellesley graduate, do you?" asks freelance writer Matt Clark.

Chicago Tribune's public editor. "...The way around this is to simply not quote directly. Paraphrase."

Athletes are also in the public eye, and Miami Herald sportswriter Linda Robertson doesn't see anything wrong with giving them a break when it comes to usage. Ballplayers are prone to poor English, particularly after a game, she says.

"You will make the subject and verb agree so Joe Quarterback won't sound like a rube, but you won't change what he is saying," she says. "People appreciate that because most of us aren't public speakers. These aren't people who have taken classes at Toastmasters."

Some say journalists quote exactly only when it is convenient, like when they want to highlight or expose an individual's faux pas to make a point.

Robertson, who has a hard news background, says she is bothered by what she sees as a double standard in reporting quotes. "When we choose to embarrass people, we don't apply *any* of these rules," she says. "When we want to nail somebody, remember how we quote them directly and put sic in there. I'm speaking of the 'we' as the profession as a whole. You'll see an investigative story where clearly they are trying not to paint a flattering picture of someone, and then you'll see this whole tactic of cleaning up quotes go out the window. There are two sets of rules."

Michael Finney, executive editor of the Omaha World-Herald, says double standards can creep in unintentionally. "If we are writing about a bad guy, it is convenient to assume that a guy's bad language will reveal some flaw in his character," he says. "It seems justified to leave embarrassing, destructive quotes in a story. Obviously, there are times and types of stories where those types of things absolutely should run. But that is only when it is powerfully revealing about an important aspect of a story."

When reporters use quotation marks, courts have allowed a degree of latitude. If the remark reflects what the person has said, "the courts have not required precision," says Alice Neff Lucan, a Washington, D.C., newspaper lawyer who runs a libel hotline for the National Newspaper Association and whose clients include AJR. So it is unlikely that a reporter who cleans up dialect or imperfect grammar will be guilty of defamation.

"Remember that for there to be defamation, there has to be falsity," Lucan says. "If the falsity amounts to nothing more than cleaning up the grammar, there's no defamation there. On the other hand, if you put a racist term in someone's mouth when they did not use the racist term, it is very likely that would create liability."

From a legal standpoint, it is all right to delete a clause as long as it doesn't change the meaning. "Courts don't require tape recorder-like precision," Lucan says. But the courts do consider a quotation more sacred than a paraphrase because the reader's expectation is different, she adds.

But even though judges aren't as strict as the purists, Lucan still advises, "Don't screw around with quotes. If you need to interpret something for your readers so they understand it better, take the quote marks off of it."

Sportswriter Robertson wonders why the subject isn't broached more frequently in newsrooms. "There is no set of universal standards," she says. "It would help to have some guidance. It's a really murky area, and it should be taken seriously. What's the most popular complaint of our subjects? That they were misquoted."

One last thing. No quotes were changed for this story. But when the journalists were interviewed about changing quotations, nearly every one of them ended their interviews the same way, the way the Miami Herald's Miller did.

"If I screwed up," Miller said of his own quotes, "fix it."

Newspaper lawyer Alice Neff Lucan offers this advice in the light of recent court decisions:

▸ *If you use a tape recorder, listen to it to verify quotes.*

▸ *Corrections of grammar, syntax, stuttering and filling in explanatory words are all acceptable changes to quotations.*

▸ *It is acceptable to edit out irrelevancies and wandering.*

▸ *It is acceptable to substitute words, without changing the meaning.*

▸ *If you do make changes, consider the whole. Have you conveyed accurately what you think the person meant to say?*

The Power of Images

Time magazine essayist Lance Morrow once observed that taking pictures is a transaction that "snatches instants away from time and imprisons them in rectangles." These imprisoned "instants" leave impressions far more lasting than the words that may accompany them. Our response to pictures is visceral rather than logical. They speak to us more loudly than words.

We tend to accept pictures as the most objective reflection of reality; after all, we reason, a photo does not lie. But, if a picture does not lie, it may not tell all the truth. Most of us can go through boxes of family photographs and find some we like and some we find unflattering, having frozen an expression that was fleeting in reality but seemingly characteristic when captured on film. Seeing the same image over and over again taps into powerful affective responses.

The selection of images seen by mass media consumers is the result of conscious or unconscious gatekeeping decisions on the part of those who create media. When an interview subject is pictured dwarfed behind a huge desk or against an unflattering background, an editorial comment is being made. When heroes are shown composed and calm and enemies shown frowning, agitated, and nervous, editorial comments are being made. When a group becomes a "type" in script after script, perceptions of both in-group and out-group members are influenced. During World War II, conscious decisions affected the selection of media images shared with civilians, censorship intended to maintain civilian morale and shape public attitudes toward the war effort. George Roeder addresses this issue in "Missing on the Home Front." Throughout Hollywood history, less conscious gatekeeping decisions—made more for box office or ratings reasons than in the intent of shaping attitudes—have nonetheless influenced audience perceptions of the press, homosexuality, and racial relations. The essays "Where Have All the Heroes Gone?" "The Final Frontier," and "TV's Black Flight" deal with this subject.

Beyond the power of selection effects, we know that pictures actually can lie, or at least mislead, and we frequently see examples of their doing so. The special-effects blue screen, or chromakey, process allows television weather reporters to stand, on camera, in front of a blank blue screen while their maps are photographed by a second camera. Television cameras translate colors into red, blue, and green chromiance channels for transmission; thus, masking out the blue channel leaves a "hole" behind the announcer that is filled in by the second camera's image when the two shots are superimposed. (If the announcer should be wearing a jacket in the same clear blue that reads exclusively on the blue chromiance channel, her or his body will also disappear.) By watching television monitors hidden at the sides of the blue background, the forecaster can make sweeping gestures in the general area of temperatures or isobars shown on the map. In truth, he or she is not in front of a map at all.

A similar process called rotoscoping, in which computers black out designated parts of photographs and replace them with new images that fit into the "holes," allowed Tom Hanks to appear in newsreel footage with John F. Kennedy and other historical notables in the movie *Forrest Gump*. George Lucas's Industrial Light & Magic, a company founded in 1975 to design the special effects for *Star Wars*, has pioneered a process called digital composing or "morphing" (for metamorphoses) in which film images are reduced to numerical codes that can be manipulated by computer. One image can melt into another, as when the liquid metal villain took on different identities in the movie *Terminator 2*, or when people of different genders and races melted into one another in Michael Jackson's video *Black and White*.

This kind of photo magic is not seen in news reporting; however, digital technology makes more subtle manipulations both easy and tempting (see "Photographs That Lie: The Ethical Dilemma of Digital Retouching"). It is common to remove unattractive backgrounds or unwanted people to make a photo ready to grace the cover of a newsmagazine. A news reporter, broadcasting from in front of a blue screen, can appear to be presenting firsthand accounts of an event superimposed behind her or him. Reenactments of events not actually captured by a photojournalist are labeled as such but often photographed in a grainy, awkwardly composed style similar to what might have been captured by a hidden camera. Audiences may be informed that the images are staged, but their apparent reality carries the same impact and credibility of any other picture. News crews outside the studio with a single camera may concentrate on shooting an interview subject, then later shoot "cut-ins" of the interviewer asking the questions that are edited into the final footage. The possibility exists that differences in inflection, or subtle differences in wording the questions, can alter the way the responses are interpreted. Reporters on television's *60 Minutes* have been accused of intentionally altering the context of a subject's remarks through this process.

Early filmmakers quickly discovered the impact of relational cutting, an editing process that affects audience

UNIT 4

responses and adds implied meanings to a story. Serial images are interpreted in combination rather than separately. When shots of a happy group of children at a birthday party are intercut with shots of a sad and lonely child, the joy of the birthday celebration is interpreted in conjunction with the sadness of the child who is left out. Similarly, news coverage of the president at a posh golf course followed by footage of striking workers or homeless children can—intentionally or unintentionally—communicate symbolic meanings to viewers.

Sometimes photojournalists or news editors take certain liberties in providing images that capture the essence of what was felt in observing an event. As early as the Civil War, Alexander Gardner's battlefield photos were enhanced with additional soldiers' bodies when woodcuts were made for printing. Although he denied restaging the event, it is commonly believed that Joe Rosenthal's Pulitzer Prize–winning photo of U.S. Marines raising the American flag over Iwo Jima was of a reenactment, using an 8-by-4-foot flag to replace the smaller one that was planted first. Obviously, the symbolism of the picture struck a chord—the moment portrayed (large flag and all) was sculpted into a Washington, D.C., monument. Eddie Adams's 1968 footage of the Saigon police chief killing a captive Vietcong officer was aired on American television with a gunshot from a sound-effects record edited in to enhance the effect. Adams has always felt uncomfortable that the drama of the gunshot was used instead of an explanation that would have placed the action in context. The ultimate interpretation of the image was that America was supporting a decadent South Vietnamese regime, not that the act might have been justified. Some critics argue that this was precisely what was intended by liberal journalists with an antiwar agenda.

Earlier in this century, social reformers Jacob Riis and Lewis Hine were instrumental in moving Americans to action through their dramatic photographs of the conditions in immigrant tenements and of children at work in terrible conditions in factories, mines, and mills (a fact widely denied by their employers). Dorothea Lange, Arthur Rothstein, and Walker Evans portrayed the human toll of the Great Depression in photographs that today remain the core impression held in the minds of those who were not then alive. More recently, Alon Reininger's intimate photographs of the devastation wrought by AIDS have helped put a face on the disease, and the future of law enforcement was surely affected by what a video camera recorded of police interaction with Rodney King in Los Angeles (see "What the Jury Saw: Does the Videotape Lie?").

Selection, composition, editing, and technical effects combine to affect the meanings derived from photographic images. Pictures are an essential element of news media's ability to communicate to mass audiences, of advertising media's ability to awaken our desires, and of entertainment media's ability to draw us in. Their messages are often felt more than interpreted, and they must be understood to be an extension of the subjective eye behind the lens.

Looking Ahead: Challenge Questions

If photographs draw their power from emotional more than intellectual interpretation, how can the choice of images seen in news and entertainment media influence the course of history?

Are there different standards of appropriateness for using video in court (such as in California's Rodney King trial for police brutality) and for using segments from the same video in news reports of court proceedings?

What ethical dilemmas are posed by digital retouching of photographs? If your graduation photographs catch you with a bad haircut, would it be appropriate to have them retouched? What about digitally taking off an extra 20 pounds? Or digitally slimming down the president before putting him (or her) on the cover of *Newsweek*? What constitutes ethical use of digital technology?

George H. Roeder, Jr.
Missing on the Home Front

Wartime Censorship and Postwar Ignorance

World War II played a pivotal role in the education of Americans. In the armed services, in addition to receiving basic military training, many Americans learned how to speak a new language or wire a complex electrical apparatus, to cook for hundreds or break codes, to maintain an airplane engine or an operating room. Trainees viewed films such as Frank Capra's Why We Fight series that explained important events in world history, albeit doing little to encourage critical thinking.

Civilians on the home front saw some of these same films, and many learned to identify hundreds of different aircraft or master a new war-generated job. As they followed accounts of the war with keen interest, they learned about the geography of the Soviet Union or the natural resources of Indonesia. Millions of Americans who had never traveled more than a few miles from their birthplace found themselves in distant lands or worked in a war plant far from home. The 1944 Servicemen's Readjustment Act (the "G.I. Bill") extended the impetus to mass education into the postwar period, contributing to a more than doubling of the number of Americans graduating from college between 1940 and 1950.

Wartime policies and circumstances also left a legacy of ignorance. Even as governmental and private organizations provided the public with the massive amounts of information necessary for productive involvement in the war effort, they withheld information deemed detrimental to that effort. This article examines the censorship of visual materials.

Because of the immense popularity of Life magazine, other illustrated publications, and newsreels and films, visual imagery played a major role in educating Americans as to the nature of the war. Military personnel reviewed all pictures taken in American war zones and censored many, most for reasons of operational security, but some because they might raise disturbing questions. Hollywood studios, newspaper editors, and others involved in presenting images of the war occasionally disagreed with official policies (as did some in government), but usually made similar choices as to what the public should and should not see of the war. Thousands of recently declassified photographs in the National Archives reveal that censors suppressed images that blurred the distinction between friend and foe, suggested that the war might bring about disruptive social changes, or undermined confidence in the abil-

22. Missing on the Home Front

ity of Americans to maintain control over their institutions and their individual lives.

The Images We Did Not See

Photographs published during the war created the impression that American bombs, bullets, and artillery shells killed only enemy soldiers. Pictures of young, elderly, and female victims always ended up in the files of censored images. So did photographs of the residents in allied and occupied countries killed in traffic accidents involving military vehicles. Wartime necessities often required weary soldiers to rush these vehicles through unfamiliar terrain. Investigators visually recorded the numerous casualties that resulted. Authorities censored all the documents they produced, such as a poignant photograph showing a little Italian girl killed by an army truck after American troops occupied the southern part of her country.

Atrocities

The enemy committed all visible atrocities. Officials suppressed photographs of G.I.'s taking Japanese body parts as trophies. On rare occasions visual evidence of this practice slipped through holes in the censorship net, such as when *Life* published in its May 22, 1944, issue a photograph of a prim woman from Arizona looking at a Japanese skull that her Navy boyfriend had managed to get smuggled home to her. He and thirteen friends had signed it and added an inscription: "This is a good jap — a dead one picked up on the New Guinea beach." But officials censored all such photographs under their control, such as a 1945 image of a Japanese soldier's decapitated head hung on a tree branch, probably by American soldiers. This was mainly a phenomenon of the Pacific War; in reviewing thousands of censored photographs and tens of thousands of uncensored ones, I never have encountered one documenting that American soldiers took as trophies body parts of European soldiers.

The wish to maintain clear visual distinctions between friends and enemies was one reason for the decision to remove Americans of Japanese ancestry from coastal areas and place them in guarded camps in sparsely inhabited areas of the West. Although political expediency and unfounded fears of espionage were the main reasons for this action, an Office of War Information bulletin sent to the motion picture industry noted that Japanese-Americans were sent to relocation centers partly because they "*look like* our Japanese enemies." The "censorship" of living human beings accomplished by relocation was reinforced by actions that kept out of view photographs that revealed ironies of the process, such as those taken in 1942 by Dorothea Lange during her brief stint with the War Relocation Authority. One showed a Japanese-American, apparently a retired veteran, reporting to the Santa Anita Park assembly center, a first stage in the relocation process, dressed in his military uniform. The uniform markings and ribbons indicated that he had served in the United States Navy for a period of at least twenty years, stretching back to World War I.

Officials also suppressed evidence of disunity within the Allied camp, such as postwar photographs of the bloody interior of the apartment of an English officer whom two Americans had beaten. The government censored all of the numerous photographs, often gory, of victims of G.I. rapes and murders. G.I. criminals as well as G.I. crimes remained largely out of sight, although *Life* and others published photographs that recorded crimes committed in areas not subject to military censorship. Censorship of G.I. crimes helped minimize attention to potential disruptions within American society related to the war effort.

"At a time when home front posters impressed on citizens the need to conserve on behalf of the war effort, officials censored images of waste within the military, such as one showing damaged cans of evaporated milk scattered about in an army warehouse in Australia." From *The Censored War: American Visual Experience During World War Two* by George H. Roeder, Jr. Courtesy of Yale University Press.

4. THE POWER OF IMAGES

Race

Race was the touchiest issue. Wartime imagery urged blacks and whites to work harmoniously together in the common cause, but reassured the white majority that this did not require violations of widely accepted social norms. Propaganda took care of the first task, censorship the second. In 1943, after several newspapers ran pictures of African American G.I.s dancing with English women, the Army hastily ordered censors to stop all photographs showing blacks mixing socially with white women. In the war's final year, black troops' "vigorous protest" of this practice led General Dwight David Eisenhower to call for a slight modification of the restrictive policy. He agreed that publication of such photographs would "unduly flame racial prejudice in the United States," but suggested that army censors allow blacks to mail home the photographs after censors stamped them "For personal use only — not for publication." For part of the war the army also refused to release pictures showing wounded members of the black 92nd Division or burials of soldiers from that unit because of the "tendency on part of negro press to unduly emphasize" its achievements.

Not all censors worked for the government. Local newspapers refused a Maryland post commander's request to run a photograph showing an African American G.I. (Dempsey Travis, now a successful Chicago realtor) who had won a prize for the best-managed PX. Such images threatened a racial status quo based on the assumption of black subordination. The activities of Milton Stark show how intertwined government and private efforts became. Stark, a white who owned several movie theaters with a largely black clientele, also worked as a "racial liaison" for the Office of Emergency Management. During the 1943 Detroit riots he expressed concern because All-American News, a company that made newsreels for theaters with predominantly black clientele, had sent cameramen to Detroit. He hoped the company would not show their footage because that "would serve only to spread further disunity and racial prejudice throughout the entire country." Stark reported that he had talked to the company head, who assured him "that all material in the reels will be *favorable* rather than inflammatory." Stark added, "I feel I can control this to a large degree, since contracts for the newsreel service to theaters which I control personally will represent a large percentage of the total income possibilities of the project." He exaggerated his own economic power, but Stark's position was consistent with that of others in government and business on whose support All-American depended. The company never ran a story on the Detroit riots.

Images of Death

The government initially censored all photographs of Americans who had died in battle, then began releasing such photographs when Allied successes caused officials to be more concerned that the public would take victory for granted than that they would become demoralized. Throughout the war officials censored photographs of the American dead that showed decapitation, dismemberment, and limbs twisted or frozen into unnatural positions. The government censored disturbing images of war's mayhem as it affected Americans for many reasons: out of respect for the feelings of family members, because of a widely shared sense of propriety, and because horrific pictures of the American dead seemed unlikely to help the government's ongoing recruiting efforts. But the army also censored such images because they did not fit seamlessly into a master narrative emphasizing the "we have everything under control" quality of the American war effort. This led the army not only to censor photographs of a field littered with bits of human flesh after the explosion of an ammunition truck, but also photographs of a soldier who fell to his death from a window, and numerous others documenting G.I. suicides.

"Carefully selected images of blacks and whites working together and of black achievements became a more familiar part of the American visual landscape during the war years." From *The Censored War: American Visual Experience During World War Two* by George H. Roeder, Jr. Courtesy of Yale University Press.

22. Missing on the Home Front

Newspapers did run stories that described government mismanagement. However, photographs and film footage from combat areas almost always were presented in a way that reassured readers and viewers that the American war effort was rational not only in its overall goals, but in all of its details, including the mission assigned every soldier. In September of 1943, *Life* accompanied its first photograph of Americans killed in the war — George Strock's powerful, elegantly composed picture of three American soldiers lying dead on Buna Beach in New Guinea — with a full-page editorial. The editors drew on familiar sports imagery to guide viewers' responses: "we are still aware of the relaxed self-confidence with which the leading boy ran into the sudden burst of fire — almost like a halfback carrying the ball down a football field." Such presentations, combined with censorship of photographs showing American corpses piled on top of one another or being tossed onto trucks, placed each American death into a context that made it consistent with a well-ordered life and world.

Maintaining this impression of order required the suppression of photographs that revealed incompetence, irrationality, or loss of control in the United States war effort. Photographs censored at least in part for these reasons ranged from ones that showed Americans and others killed or wounded by allied "friendly fire" or other military blunders to those that showed turkeys intended for soldiers' Thanksgiving meals strewn over the floor of an army warehouse because of careless handling. In addition to suppressing evidence of disorder on the organizational level, the army censored photographs that might raise doubts about how completely individual American soldiers had control of their own behavior. Without such control, how could they consistently resist sliding into undisciplined modes of behavior attributed only to the enemy? Thus censors kept soldiers visibly suffering from severe mental stress out of sight throughout the war and after, despite their large numbers. None of the censored pictures I have encountered in my research illustrate more vividly the human inability to keep complete control over war's chaos than those of "shell shocked" soldiers screaming and flailing out at their fellow soldiers and at the horror of their situation.

Throughout the war officials censored photographs of the American dead that showed decapitation, dismemberment, and limbs twisted or frozen into unnatural positions.

The Consequences of Ignorance

I agree with decisions that kept out of view those photographs of soldiers in the midst of mental breakdowns in cases where publication would have violated the privacy of individuals. However, censors suppressed many pictures not to protect individuals, but to conceal unpalatable truths. The images which Americans encountered during World War II sustained a less complex understanding of the nature and meaning of that war than Americans might have achieved had they also seen the censored images. Visual expurgation of black achievements, unpalatable to many because they undermined belief in white supremacy, hindered postwar struggles against racial bigotry. Visual denial that American soldiers sometimes lost control of themselves left citizens ill-prepared to evaluate their country's policies in Vietnam, or understand the experiences of the young men who fought there.

These shortcomings in the education of the American public took on special significance when the United States emerged from World War II with more economic, technological, and military power than any country had ever possessed. Visual acknowledgment during the war of the uncertainties, injustices, and potential miseries attendant upon the exercise of such power, even on behalf of good causes, might have encouraged more circumspect use of it in the following decades, whether for interventions abroad, or for environmentally and socially consequential projects at home.

Censorship decisions made fifty years ago continue to have consequences. The Smithsonian Institution, under intense pressure from Congress and veterans' organizations, recently canceled plans to include photographs of the victims of the atomic bombing of Hiroshima in its exhibition of the plane that dropped the bomb, the *Enola Gay*. This is consistent with wartime censorship policies and with official practices since then. The site of the exhibition, the Smithsonian's National Air and Space Museum, never has displayed pictures of the victims of Allied bombing. Although debates over the decision to drop the bomb will continue throughout the lifetime of all readers of this article, there can be no doubt that it caused great suffering. Documenting this suffering in an exhibition on the bombing does not imply criticism of the decision to use the bomb, but commitment to historical truth. This truth includes commitment to the proposition that actions have consequences and ac-

4. THE POWER OF IMAGES

knowledgment that in actual historical situations, good and evil are seldom delineated as clearly as they are in most of the war movies made between 1941 and 1945.

Such acknowledgment would help visitors comprehend two clashing ideas about World War II. The first is that American involvement in that war helped bring about the defeat of repugnant and dangerous authoritarian regimes. Allied victory greatly improved the prospect of a dignified life for hundreds of millions of people in the postwar world. Those who contributed to this victory deserve the respect and gratitude of future generations. The second idea is that the nature of this most costly of all wars ensured that one consequence of American involvement would be infliction of terrible pain on people of all ages in many different countries. The suffering that occurred under the mushroom clouds in Hiroshima and Nagasaki in August of 1945 was unique in some ways, in that it included radiation sickness and other new horrors, but it also was representative of what war had become by that date, when all countries involved abandoned distinctions between military and civilian targets. Whatever the obstacles, American educational institutions such as the Smithsonian Institution must do everything they can to encourage this simultaneous comprehension of difficult-to-mesh realities. As the destructive power at humanity's disposal increases, so does the cost of ignorance.

George H. Roeder, Jr. is the chair of the Undergraduate Division in the School of the Art Institute of Chicago and a lecturer in history at Northwestern University. His recent publications include "The Visual Arts" in Stanley Kutler, ed., *Encyclopedia of the United States in the Twentieth Century* (MacMillan, 1995) and *The Censored War: American Visual Experience During World War II* (Yale University Press, 1993; paperback edition, 1995).

Where Have All the Heroes Gone?

CHRISTOPHER HANSON

Christopher Hanson is Washington correspondent for the Seattle Post-Intelligencer *and a contributing editor of* CJR.

When the film *All the President's Men* opened to great acclaim in 1976, the country embraced Hollywood's depiction of reporters as heroes, portrayed by superstars Dustin Hoffman and Robert Redford, embodying the best of American values. What a difference twenty years makes. When Oliver Stone's *Nixon* was released a couple of months ago, the role of Bob Woodward and Carl Bernstein in exposing Watergate had been reduced to about thirty seconds of offhand dialogue in a three-hour, seventeen-minute film. Stone said sneeringly in a *Newsweek* interview that *All The President's Men*, produced by Redford, had "glamorized" an undeserving press.

Hollywood is less concerned with the accuracy of a characterization than with its fidelity to the mood of the times and its box-office potential. And Stone—who once celebrated the courageous truth-seeking reporter in *Salvador* (1986) but more recently portrayed a journalist as the lowest form of life in *Natural Born Killers* (1994)—doesn't appear to think much of the reporter-as-hero archetype anymore.

He's not alone. Consider *Quiz Show* (1994), about the TV game-show scandal of 1958. In reality, newspaper investigators played a big role in uncovering how contestants on the program *Twenty-One* were secretly given the answers in advance. On screen, there are no newspaper investigators. The case is cracked by a lone Senate aide. It is noteworthy that this film was produced and directed by erstwhile press "glamorizer" Redford.

Or consider *Just Cause* (1995), based on a novel of the same title by John Katzenbach. In the book, the main character is a journalist who wins a Pulitzer Prize for disclosing evidence that frees a death-row inmate and who then discovers he is guilty and tries to bring him back to justice. But in the movie, the journalist disappears from the plot entirely, replaced by Sean Connery as an idealistic law professor.

All of which demonstrates a striking change in the journalist's place in American pop culture. A cinematic staple in past decades was the journalist as idealist—gruff and hard-bitten yet unwilling to yield to cynicism, intolerant of bullies and crooks and always ready to fight for the right: think of Joel McCrea in *Foreign Correspondent* (1940), whose all-American values help him expose a Nazi plot: Humphrey Bogart in *Deadline USA*, putting his life at risk as an editor taking on the mob; Jane Fonda in *The China Syndrome* (1979), defying big business to expose a nuclear nightmare.

Today, with the odd exception (Denzel Washington as an ace reporter in 1993's *The Pelican Brief*), such characters have faded away, while the journalist as boob or bounder is becoming more marketable. In *Bob Roberts* (1992), for instance, the TV reporters covering a charlatan Senate candidate are so cretinous that you expect to see drool trickling from their lips; only one obscure reporter for an alternative newspaper catches the candidate's dark side. *Hero* (1992) portrays witless TV checkbook journalists who try to squeeze ratings out of an airline crash story and end up losing $1 million to a con man who poses as the missing crash scene samaritan.

Other contemporary films cast those in the news business as outright villains. In *Newsies* (1992), Joseph Pulitzer (Robert Duvall) is shown as a cold, ruthless cad who cuts the income of his impoverished street-urchin newsboys to boost his profits. And he is a nice guy compared to aspiring TV news star (Nicole Kidman) in 1995's dark comedy *To Die For*. She is one of the most amoral, calculating film villainesses in recent memory, stopping at nothing, including murder, to catapult herself

4. THE POWER OF IMAGES

Deadline USA, 1952

Natural Born Killers, 1994

from cable weather girl to the next Diane Sawyer. Stone's even more disturbing *Natural Born Killers* features a swaggering TV crime reporter (Robert Downey, Jr.) who pretends to be appalled by acts of violence he actually loves. He ends up gunning down some innocent folk just to experience the "purity" of the act. A mass murderer who takes him hostage tells him: "You're a hate.... You're not even a hate, you're a media person. Media is like the weather only it's man-made.... You're scum.... Killing you and what you represent is a statement...."

all philosophy metastasized through our news organs, weakening their standards and enfeebling their public spirit. Hollywood comes to reflect shifts in American culture and its institutions, but slowly. There is a lag between when an institution develops the symptoms of an illness and when the movies respond, by which point the disease is often far advanced. When it comes to journalism, the Robert Downey, Jr., and Nicole Kidman characters are like bad news on a lung biopsy.

As Katzenbach (an ex-*Miami Herald* journalist who has had two novels made

than a journalist to establish in quick strokes as a person of integrity.

It's no surprise, then, that the few films that depict journalists as relatively benign generally evoke an earlier period, from the thirties to the fifties, when the journalist was still in good enough standing to be projected as Everyman. It was a time when, in the old films (often scripted by ex-journalists idealizing the gritty authenticity of their pre-Hollywood days) reporters were men of the people in trench coats and rumpled suits, with press cards in their hats, who skewered hypocritical

For every celluloid press villain like Charles Foster Kane, Hollywood once gave us a half-dozen crusading white hats

The movies have always featured press villains or anti-heroes (some fully realized and three-dimensional, like the narcissistic, truth-twisting publisher in *Citizen Kane*, 1941). But for every celluloid journalist who embodies the worst in human nature (the corrupt Big Boss publishers in Frank Capra films, the character-assassin Winchellesque columnist in 1957's *Sweet Smell of Success*, the super-manipulative reporter who delays a rescue of a man who fell down a mine shaft to build suspense and circulation in 1951's *The Big Carnival*), Hollywood once gave us a half-dozen crusading white hats.

No longer. And this points up the antipathy to the news media that has been building for well over a decade, as sensationalism and a profits-above-

into films) pointed out in an interview, "Because of the explosion of tabloid TV, tabloid journalism, and the mob approach to reporting, the journalist is seen as a ghoul.... Hollywood always reflects, sooner or later, the public feelings — all of those polls showing that newspaper reporters rank down there with dentists and serial killers."

He also points out that Hollywood prefers to paint its characters with lots of white or black and relatively little gray and to sketch them quickly, tapping the preconceptions of the audience. Although he did not write the screenplay for *Just Cause*, he suspects his novel's main character was transmuted from journalist to scholar on screen because a professor is today far easier

politicians and other pretentious types, chased fires and crime stories and shouted "Stop the presses!"

Three recent films echo such old movies, though not very effectively. In *The Paper* (1994), Michael Keaton is the city editor of a down-at-heel tabloid who rejects a job at the snooty *New York Times*esque *Sentinel*, chases down a crime story and then takes glee in yelling "Stop the presses!" for the first time in his career. (Alas, Keaton's hard-boiled idealism is a shadow of his cinematic forebears': he helps prevent his managing editor from knowingly printing a false story so the paper can carry on in its sub-mediocrity without additional taint.)

In *I Love Trouble* (1994), Nick Nolte and Julia Roberts are trench-coated police reporters who fall for each other while competing, no holds barred, on a crime story. Although it is set in the present like *The Paper*, this film struggles lamely to draw upon such charming flagpole-clutching Man vs. The Elements bout when a huge storm hit Florida last October) to the celebrity trials that TV has made the new center of national debate.

In *Network*, which seemed like wild caricature when it opened in 1976, an entertainment programmer seizes control of a nightly news show with lagging ratings. She starts broadcasting sensational footage of actual crimes committed by terrorists and letting ordinary people vent frustrations on the news (in a nightly segment called "Vox Populi")—shades of today's reality-based crime and prime-time call-in shows. She also showcases aging anchor Howard "Mad as Hell" Beale (Peter

Malice conveys a sense of outrage at the way things can really work in the news business, but by the time we get to *Broadcast News* (1987), a more complaisant or cynical tone is becoming evident. The film deals with the encroaching shallowness in TV journalism but uses it as a backdrop for romantic interplay between news producer Holly Hunter and William Hurt, the inexperienced reporter-anchor hired for his looks. We are evidently supposed to see Hunter as a symbol of old-line journalistic integrity: she bridles at the show-biz gimmicks and news division budget cuts imposed by management, hates fakery so much that she breaks up with Hurt after learning that he pretended to cry on the air to dra-

In recent productions, the myth of the Truth-Seeking Reporter, who will stop at nothing to keep the public informed, has met its demise.

rogue press films of yore as *His Girl Friday* (1940). The underwhelming *Public Eye* (1992), in which Joe Pesci plays a rumpled, eccentric, intense, super-aggressive free-lance photographer, is set in New York in 1942. He's about as far removed from today's standard college-educated yuppie journalist as you can get.

Slouching toward extinction along with the hero films have been those that once lampooned the press with the hope — naively idealistic, it turns out — that this institution might be rehabilitated. Back in 1971, for instance, when Cronkite was still going strong but trivialization of the network news was becoming a worry, Woody Allen opened his film *Bananas* with a TV sports reporter — Howard Cosell, playing Howard Cosell — going live for the assassination of a Latin American president ("He's . . . DOWN! It's over! It's all over for El Presidente!") Today, of course, reality has caught up and it's almost a cliché to point out that news divisions actually do reduce life to a spectator sport, from wars (served up live with special video logos and stirring martial theme music) to natural disasters (recall "Hurricane" Rather's

Finch) because he has gone crazy and can be counted on to build ratings by saying bizarre things as the "mad prophet of the airwaves." Today there are many such prophets on the real airwaves, not only on talk radio but on the news "discussion" shows of major networks, fulminating and yelling predictions to grab attention.

After *Network*, the technique of exaggerating dangerous trends in journalism was used sparingly, perhaps because filmmakers were becoming more jaded and realized that press excesses had become so flagrant there was no longer any need to exaggerate. *Absence of Malice* (1981), for instance, is not a lampoon but a somber account of how an over-ambitious newswoman (Sally Field) is manipulated into falsely reporting that a local businessman is a murder suspect. Journalism's cynical arrogance is encapsulated by her paper's house lawyer: "As a matter of law, the truth of your story is irrelevant. We have no knowledge the story is false, therefore we are absent malice. We've been both reasonable and prudent. . . . We may say whatever we like . . . and he is powerless to do us harm. Democracy is served."

matize an interview with a rape victim. Strangely, however, the plot has her benefiting from staff cuts by the bottom-line boys she detests, becoming a bureau chief and later pole-vaulting to the managing editor slot when pretty boy Hurt is elevated to anchordom. The unintended, subliminal message of her success is hardly idealistic: you can moralize a little but in the end you go along to get along, even if that includes becoming a tool of airhead journalism.

Even more jaded, in their own way, were the seemingly harder-hitting *Natural Born Killers* and *To Die For*, whose journalistic characters are so incorrigible that they can be rehabilitated only with a bullet to the head and are accordingly done in.

What we are seeing in recent productions is the demise of a myth that has been a mainstay of American film — the Truth-Seeking Reporter who will stop at nothing to keep the public informed and who, to quote sociologist Michael Schudson, tells us "what we may have been once, what we might again become . . . ." This myth has given rise to its share of Hollywood hokum, to be sure, but it has also been a beacon in the fog for aspiring journal-

4. THE POWER OF IMAGES

ists and even some veterans of the trade.

In many of the older press films, there comes a point when a journalist-hero gives voice to the myth directly, as when Jason Robards as Ben Bradlee tells his two Watergate reporters: "You guys are probably pretty tired. . . . Go on home, get a nice hot bath, rest up — fifteen minutes — then get your asses back in gear. . . . Nothing's riding on this except the First Amendment to the Constitution, freedom of the press, and maybe the future of the country."

One of the myth's corniest distillations is in the Jack Webb day-in-the life-of-a-newsroom film *–30–* (1959; available on video; best watched with press colleagues while imbibing heavily). In one scene, a harried copy boy played by David Nelson, of *Ozzie and Harriet* fame, tells a co-worker he's quitting the paper. His friend commiserates, saying: "What is it? A newspaper, that's all. It's not like we joined the priesthood." Overhearing this, the gruff, hard-bitten city editor (William Conrad, later the fat gumshoe in TV's *Cannon*) tears into them and reveals that he, like so many gruff, hard-bitten cinematic city editors before him, is an idealist at heart: "That's right, Aristotle. . . . Do you know what people use these for? They roll them up and they swat their puppies for wetting on the rug, they spread them on the floor when they're painting the walls, they wrap fish in them . . . BUT *[pause as he cups the paper reverently, with two open hands, like a Bible, as stirring background music begins]* this also happens to be a couple of more things. It's got print on it that tells stories that hundreds of good men all over the world have broken their backs to get. . . . It gives a lot of information to a lot of people who wouldn't have known about these things if we hadn't taken the trouble to tell them. It's the sum total of the work of a lot of guys who don't quit. . . . It only costs ten cents, that's all. If you read only the comics section and the want ads, it's still the best buy for your money in the world." Needless to say, young David Nelson stays on the job.

Like everything else produced, directed and acted in by Jack Webb, *–30–* is so bad it's almost good, so square it's almost hip. But for me — to my mild chagrin — the city editor's soliloquy had more than just the camp appeal of an old *Dragnet* episode. It actually evoked a twinge or two of genuine feeling. Webb was a straight arrow's straight arrow, an anti-elitist who was in the business of affirming the best of mainstream America as he saw it. And in 1959 that America included the news business. A kid could see a film about reporters and come away thinking, "I bet it would be really great to be one."

Those were the days.

The Final Frontier

Two new movies pose the question, Can't Hollywood treat gays like normal people?

RICHARD CORLISS

As the nightclub crowd waits impatiently downstairs, Starina, the headliner, sits at her dressing table. She powders away the age lines. She applies mascara to the eyes that have bewitched a thousand sailors. She runs an electric shaver over her chin stubble. It's hard work being a drag queen, as Starina (Nathan Lane), diva deluxe of *The Birdcage*, can testify.

And as any moviegoer can tell you, it's even harder to find much evidence of homosexuals on the Hollywood screen. *The Birdcage*, opening this week, is the rare exception. This gently supportive comedy about gays, a sweet parable of family values, has Robin Williams and Gene Hackman for star quality, writer Elaine May and director Mike Nichols to provide 80 years of comedy know-how, and a famous property for box-office insurance—the hit French play and film *La Cage aux Folles*. In short, this new version is no more threatening to mainstream American sensibilities than the pro-Indian *Pocahontas*.

Maybe once a year, a big studio trots out a big picture with similarly sympathetic gay characters in leading roles: *To Wong Foo Thanks for Everything Julie Newmar* last year, *Philadelphia* before that. Is this enough to constitute enlightenment?

Hardly, as a spiffy new documentary, *The Celluloid Closet*, amply demonstrates. For nearly a century, Hollywood has done a shoddy, often slanderous job of showing what it is like to be homosexual. Adroitly assembled by Rob Epstein and Jeffrey Friedman, with narration written by Armistead Maupin (*Tales of the City*) and read by Lily Tomlin, *Celluloid Closet* is by turns funny and poignant. It interlaces old clips (for instance, a peignoired Cary Grant declaring, in *Bringing Up Baby*, "I just went gay all of a sudden!") with cogent commentary by Gore Vidal, Harvey Fierstein and others. It should be getting raves at Oscar time—except that, like *Crumb* and *Hoop Dreams* last year, *Celluloid Closet* was denied a nomination by the Academy's documentary committee.

In this film (and in another enticing compilation, David Johnson's *The Lavender Lens: 100 Years of Celluloid Queers*, available in some video stores), we see gay characters haunting the corners of the film frame. From the early days of silent films (when Charlie Chaplin, in a barbershop, gives a cruel hairdo to an effeminate man) to the '90s (when gay or bisexual murderers lend lurid pizazz to *The Silence of the Lambs* and *Basic Instinct*), American films—like America itself—have typically treated gays as a joke or a curse.

Homosexuality was described as a disease, a mental illness, the most mortal of sins. Its carriers were monsters or, the luckier ones, martyrs. With few exceptions they have been members of the movies' creepiest underclass: the men more feminine than the heroine, foils to make the hero look more masculine; the women as big as truck drivers and miles meaner. And that was on the rare occasions when they were there at all. Mostly, homosexuals have had nonperson status in movies. What a destiny, in movies or in life: to be either reviled or invisible.

Briefly, in the early '30s, gays were familiar screen types: "pansies" (often played by Franklin Pangborn) for comic relief and, more heroically, bisexual heroines (incarnated by Garbo and Dietrich) who looked thrillingly glamorous in their tuxedos and bachelor togs. That was old Hollywood's highest compliment to a woman—that she acted and thought like a man—just as new Hollywood accepts films with transvestites, men who act and think like women. In the '50s, gayness could be viewed as a social disease (in *Tea and Sympathy*) or with oblique rapture (in the torrid gaze of Stephen Boyd's Messala at Charlton Heston's Ben-Hur).

When gays were not figures of suave or silly decadence, they were figures of fear, preying on normal people and meriting Hollywood's sternest judgment. They were murdered—and a good thing too—in *Caged* and *Suddenly, Last Summer*. The nicer ones were left to their own misery, suicide being the only solution for characters who either had a homosexual fling (Don Murray in *Advise and Consent*) or were accused of one (Shirley MacLaine in *The Children's Hour*). Moral: the only good gay was a dead gay. It took the 1970 film of Mart Crowley's hit play *The Boys in the Band* to find good news amid the woe. As one character noted, "Not all faggots bump themselves off at the end of the story."

The movies, as commentators of every political stripe have noted, are a glamorous mirror of society. Growing up, we all find ourselves, in part, by finding aspects of ourselves onscreen. Gays didn't. "You feel like a ghost," essayist Susie Bright (author of *Sexwise*) says in *The Celluloid Closet*, "a ghost that nobody believes in." So gays went looking for kinship in any movie character who was artistic, flamboyant, wounded. They still do, and some of the subtextual readings in *The Celluloid Closet* result in eyestrain. "We know the Sal Mineo character in *Rebel Without a Cause* is gay," asserts British film historian Richard Dyer, "partly because he has a picture of Alan Ladd in his locker." Well, maybe Mineo was just ... *sensitive*. But even if these interpretations are wrong, they are telling: they indicate how desperate some gays have been to find their reflection onscreen—even in code or in could-be, should-be wish fulfillment.

The Celluloid Closet tells us things are

4. THE POWER OF IMAGES

better now. But that is mainly on the independent scene, where nobody's betting real money. In the films most people see, gays are still crippled in some way. Tom Hanks can be the good, dying gay man in *Philadelphia*—but no passionate kiss for your boyfriend, please. In the thriller *Copycat*, the gay character is not the serial killer, he is the heroine's best friend—but he still gets murdered. And gay baiting is still acceptable; "faggot" remains the epithet du jour of movie machismo. In Mel Gibson's *Braveheart*, early line favorite for the top Oscars, the English prince who will become Edward II dares to have a male lover at court. The King's response: he throws the lover out a high castle window, then contemptuously swats his whining son aside.

Maybe *The Birdcage*—with its *Romeo and Juliet* plot about two young lovers and their opposing families, one gay, one straight—will challenge a few prejudices. For a start, it's funny, with two of the world's most gifted comics, Lane and Williams, as the drag queen and his slightly more butch companion. Lane is wildly endearing: a tempestuous wife, a doting mother and every inch the great lady. The film gets less comic mileage, but more political kick, from the right-wing politician (Hackman) who is the butt of the film's genial jokes.

A Gay Gaze

A new documentary, *The Celluloid Closet*, recounts how gays were first ignored in movies, then portrayed derisively, then as heroic victims—but rarely as ordinary people with stories worth telling. A brief history:

MOROCCO (1930) Dietrich was sexy when she boldly kissed a woman—but, Kenneth Tynan once asked, *which* sex?

BEN-HUR (1959) Writer Gore Vidal got Stephen Boyd to suggest, sub rosa, a hot, homoerotic tryst with Heston

THE CHILDREN'S HOUR (1962) Slander about lesbian love drives MacLaine to suicide and Audrey Hepburn to despair

THE BOYS IN THE BAND (1970) Campy, melodramatic, yes; but the boys were honestly gay—and nobody had to die

He might be Pat Robertson or Pat Buchanan on a bad day. In the mistaken-identity dinner party that serves as the film's third act, it is his function to be enlightened—not to forgive the gay couple for any crime against nature but to realize that charm and devotion have their place in every family, every life-style.

The Birdcage is about reconciliation: of two families, of opposing social and sexual points of view, but also of the two meanings of gay; the word can suggest happiness as a part of homosexuality. The film is bold enough to propose the integration of gays—and by extension of anyone "different"—into an America that at the moment seems ready to take up arms and shoot holes in the melting pot. Indeed, that may be a part of Hollywood's continuing reluctance to confront the issue. As exotics—drag queens or dying swans—gays are fine fodder for movies. But Hollywood sees little need to show that the vast majority of gays are ordinary, reasonably complicated people. They are the folks who work next to you at the steel press or in the sales office.

Or in the film studio. For the final irony is that Hollywood, with its dozens of gay stars, its hundreds of gays in positions of creative and executive power, is afraid to depict homosexual life—the world it knows and could persuasively dramatize. The whole town, timid as ever, prefers to reside in one huge, beautifully appointed celluloid closet. Or a gilded birdcage with a cover over it. The world looks safe and cozy from inside. Why would anyone want to come out?

TV's Black Flight

The fall schedules are out, and shows with predominantly minority casts have landed in the low-rent neighborhoods.

CHRISTOPHER JOHN FARLEY

THERE'S A STANDARD EXPLANATION that white-run companies employ when they are taken to task for having homogeneous work forces. "Hey," upper-level management types will say, "we looked for qualified folks. There just were no black candidates." It's the old "N.B.C." answer, and in the face of a historic turnabout, the National Broadcasting Co. happens to be using said answer to defend its just-announced fall season. NBC, the network that broadcast the pioneering *Cosby Show* in the '80s, the network that carried the *Nat King Cole Show* in the 1950s when virtually no advertisers were willing to sponsor a variety show hosted by a black man, will not have a single minority-themed series in its fall lineup. A fluke? Don Ohlmeyer, president of NBC West Coast, says the simple fact is none of the ethnic shows they had in development were good enough to air. "To look deeper," he adds, "is an attempt to attribute false cause and effect."

Indeed, failed pilots are hardly news. But is there a more complicated explanation than NBC's N.B.C. answer? Perhaps. TV seems to be undergoing a racial restructuring, a kind of ethnic *perestroika*. The four biggest networks, ABC, CBS, NBC and Fox, which finished announcing their prime-time fall lineups last week, appear to be turning away from minority programming. CBS will have only one black-themed show next fall, a new Bill Cosby sitcom. ABC will have only the aging sitcom *Family Matters* and the new sitcom *Common Law*, with Latino stand-up Greg Giraldo. Fox, once a bastion of black comedy, is down to *Martin, Living Single* and the multiracial drama *New York Undercover*. All told, that's six minority-themed shows on the Big Four networks. Three years ago, there were 12.

Today the networks are scheduling either all-white shows (the sitcoms *Friends, Seinfeld, Ellen* and *Mad About You* are set in urban centers, but the only thing black on them is the coffee) or, increasingly, shows with multiethnic ensemble casts, like the NBC dramas *ER* and *Homicide* or Fox's new sitcom *Lush Life*, which stars two female friends, one white and one black, as does ABC's new *Clueless*. A significant number of minorities still appear on TV, but they are only intermittently at the center of the action.

However, the two newer, smaller networks, the upstart United Paramount Network and the Warner Bros. channel, are embracing minority-themed programming as a way of differentiating themselves from the bigger, established players in the TV game. In a classic case of counterprogramming, the two mininetworks will between them air 11 ethnic-themed shows in the fall—nearly twice the big-network total.

Top 10 Television Shows
Show / NETWORK (Ranking for other group)

FOR WHITE VIEWERS
1. ER / NBC (20)
2. Seinfeld / NBC (89)
3† Friends / NBC (111)
3† Caroline in the City / NBC (106)
5. The Single Guy / NBC (125)
6. Home Improvement / ABC (53)
7. Monday Night Football / ABC (9)
8. Coach / ABC (60)
9. NYPD Blue / ABC (23)
10. 60 Minutes / CBS (22)

FOR BLACK VIEWERS
1. New York Undercover / FOX (122)
2. Living Single / FOX (124†)
3. The Crew* / FOX (124†)
4. In the House / NBC (79)
5. The Fresh Prince of Bel Air* / NBC (76)
6. Martin (Sun.) / FOX (117)
7. Family Matters / ABC (61)
8. Martin (Sat.) / FOX (127)
9. Monday Night Football / ABC (7)
10. The Preston Episodes* / FOX (128)

*Canceled †Tie
Source: BBDO Special Markets, Black Television Viewing based on Nielsen ratings, Sept.-Dec. 1995

4. THE POWER OF IMAGES

Some of them star familiar names like Sherman Hemsley, Malcolm-Jamal Warner and Robin Givens. One, UPN's *Homeboys in Outer Space*, is a must-see for the high-concept title alone. Some are refugees from the Big Four: *Moesha*, an urban sitcom starring teen singer Brandy Norwood, was developed for CBS, but after the network passed, UPN put it on the air in January and saw it blossom into a moderate hit.

The newer, scrappier networks say their programming is a natural result of their efforts to establish themselves. Building a distribution system is a key challenge for start-up networks, and it begins by serving stations in the top 50 cities, which, as urban centers, are characteristically more ethnic than the rest of the country. Minority shows can also appeal to demographically desirable younger audiences. According to this year's *Special Report: Black Television Viewing*, an annual production of the BBDO ad agency, younger viewers are more willing to cross racial boundaries. Of the 20 most popular shows for black households and for white ones last fall, only two appeared on both lists—*Monday Night Football* and *ER*. But blacks and whites ages 18 to 24 have six shows in common on their respective Top 20 lists. The smaller networks hope ethnic shows will hook young blacks and whites—and eventually their families too. Says Garth Ancier, programming chief for the WB: "The networks have largely abandoned the family audience at 8 p.m. Our formula is to reach families who watch TV together."

Yet another factor in the rise of black shows on the WB and UPN is the competition for on-camera talent. "If I'm looking for a white leading man from 30 to 35 years old, I'm fifth in the food chain," says Michael Sullivan, UPN's president of entertainment, referring to his network competition. "But there is an underutilized pool of younger black actors."

The big networks argue that it is their very size that prevents them from catering to niche audiences. Says Janice Gretemeyer, vice president of media relations for ABC: "We can't afford to program for one segment, whether age-based or race-based. As a broadcast network, we must develop programs that appeal to the largest segment of viewers in the country. We want to bring in viewers from every age, gender, religious and ethnic group." But critics charge that networks are shying away from minority shows not because of economics but in spite of it. Says Lisa Navarrete, spokeswoman for the National Council of La Raza: "Minorities, particularly Hispanics, watch more TV than other people do, and Latinos are a $200 billion annual market and growing. There is money to be made by being responsive to this community."

So why would network suits turn down good money if in fact there is money to be made in ethnic programming? One answer: success is relative. Says NBC's Ohlmeyer: "*Moesha* might be a big hit for UPN, but we can't live on a five share." Another possible answer: network-TV programmers, who are mostly white, are out of touch with minority communities. "It's not a conspiracy of exclusion," says Brett King, director of current programming for Twentieth Century Fox Television and an African American. "But nobody wants to bring up the issue of race, which is still an incredible tinderbox. We suffer from the politics of disinterest and denial." TV shows that do deal with race are often self-conscious and clumsy. One of the first jokes on the interracial sitcom *Buddies*, a short-lived ABC show, involved a white mother-in-law mistaking a black man for a prowler; when *Grace Under Fire* added a black couple to the cast recently, one of the first jokes was—yes—a white mother-in-law mistaking one of the new neighbors for a prowler.

And while UPN and the WB are showing an interest in ethnic programming now, some wonder whether the interest will last much longer than a commercial break. "Just as Fox was edgy when it started, these smaller networks are creating a name brand for themselves," says King. "It's a way to build a network. Unfortunately, once that reputation has been built and the network has been established, it is a safe bet that edgy black shows will give way to more mainstream programming."

—*Reported by Sylvester Monroe and Jacqueline Savaiano/Los Angeles and William Tynan/New York*

What the Jury Saw Does the Videotape Lie?

MICHAEL B. ROSEN

Michael B. Rosen is Associate General Counsel at Boston University.

With the videotape as evidence what more was needed? The beating of Rodney King was seemingly fortuitously captured by an amateur's use of his video camera. The videotape (or portions) were shown repeatedly on national television. After a lengthy trial of the police officers, the jury's verdict: acquittal. The national response to the verdicts: condemnation, outrage, and anger. Even President Bush decried the verdicts: "What you saw and I saw on the TV video was revolting. I felt anger. I felt pain." In Los Angeles, the anger fueled riots.

ABC-News reporter Dave Maresh tried to raise a question about the video itself:

"What George Holliday's video camera saw seemed as clear-cut as black and white: Rodney King suffering a merciless beating at the hands of Los Angeles police officers.... Video looks so real, so capable of bringing all of the sorrow and destruction of a riot scene right into your living room. But is it real? The most basic question of all and the hardest for viewers to answer."

The question that defied answer for many was how a verdict of acquittal could have been reached if the jury had seen the videotape. Was the jury racist? Was the prosecution inept? But the leading nature of the question is the assumption or premise that the videotape was clear and convincing evidence, beyond a reasonable doubt, of a beating rather than of police using reasonable force to subdue a potentially dangerous individual. Put another way, perhaps the most important question is whether television, through the medium of videotape, is—or should be—taken at face value in court.

In the Rodney King case, the videotape was shown over

4. THE POWER OF IMAGES

and over again, including slow motion and stop-frame, and was used by defense counsel as well as by the prosecution as evidence in support of the positions being advocated.

The fact that the Rodney King beating was captured on videotape may have been unusual. But the planned or serendipitous videotaping of "live" events as evidence to both public opinion or a jury in a court of law will become increasingly commonplace. A noted litigator on issues involving the press, Floyd Abrams, states:

"The whole notion of how our society is changing because of these new cameras and the proliferation of the cameras is really a stunning one. For the first time in our history, we have people who don't work for the press, who don't work for the police, being the ones first on the scene."

As a medium for communicating emotional and evocative images, photography has a power that human, "live" testimony often lacks. As more accidents, crimes, arrests, or political demonstrations are captured by amateur or professional videocamera operators, will this improve the accuracy of court verdicts?

The basic story of the Rodney King case is familiar: A motorist — often minority — engages in some traffic infraction, major or minor. When asked to pull over by police, he fails to do so and a chase ensues. Other police officers join the case. The motorist is finally stopped and arrested. Between the time he is stopped and the time he is brought before a magistrate and charged with a crime, he has suffered serious bodily injury. The motorist charges that he has been beaten by the police after he was stopped. The police ascribe any injuries of the motorist to reasonable force used to subdue a potentially dangerous and violent person.

From the police viewpoint, a driver who has refused to stop when ordered to do so by police and has then endangered himself and others by driving away, often at high speed, represents a risk to the public's safety until the individual is in police custody. Having already shown a willingness to place others at risk by engaging in an attempt to drive away from the police, the motorist is an unknown risk to the police. Does he have a gun? Will he attempt to use violence to avoid being arrested? The use of *reasonable force* to place the individual in restraint and insure that he has no weapon is proper police procedure. If attacked or threatened by the motorist, the police may under appropriate circumstances even use *deadly force* to protect their lives or the lives of others.

But to many people, the issue is whether police have used excessive force to administer a "punishment" to the driver who was foolish enough to try to drive away. Frequently the above scenario is played out before no witnesses other than the immediate participants.

But in Rodney King's case there was an unexpected witness: the videocamera. Unknown to any of the participants, George Holliday used his videocamera to photograph and record some of the incident after the chase had stopped. The 81-second videotape segment was shown on nationwide television and what might have been a depressingly familiar story — motorist who led police of high speed chase alleges he was beaten by police — became a national outrage of documented police brutality.

The video segment shown on television — or the portions of the segment that found air time — appeared to show police officers raining blows with their batons on a helpless Rodney King who was either kneeling or lying on his face. Did the video lie? Regardless of one's opinion about the outcomes in the Rodney King case, the acceptance of video as virtual reality must be examined.

THE MIRROR WITH A MEMORY

In its infancy, photography was limited to still lifes. In the 1830s, in order to make a living while attempting to promote commercially his invention of the telegraph, Samuel F.B. Morse opened a portrait studio in New York, utilizing the latest methods of the master, Daguerre. But the rigors of the subjects having to sit from ten to twenty minutes, out of doors, on the roof of a building, in the full sunlight or indoors using mirrors to reflect the sunlight usually resulted in portraits with the eyes shut (or tears streaming down the cheeks). The photographic venture was unsuccessful for Morse and he was forced to close his studio (fortunately, the telegraph proved more successful). It was not until the year 1840 that John William Draper, a professor in New York, succeeded in taking the first known photographic portrait in which the subject's eyes were *open* — an amazing achievement for the time.

As photography became quicker and more portable, the ability of photographs to capture eloquently and movingly the drama of actual events was demonstrated by the photographic record of war. From Roger Fenton's "Valley of the Shadow of Death" in the Crimea in the 1850s to the photographs of Union and Confederate dead at Fredericksburg, Antietam, and Gettysburg by Mathew Brady, Alexander Gardner, and Timothy O'Sullivan, photography became evidence: a record of apparent objectivity.

Perhaps the power of the photograph lies in the fact that it is presented as an objective image of life but at the same time is known to be a partial and limited view, a snapshot, a frozen portion of time. The bodies lie before our eyes on the road to Antietam. That they are dead is assumed. We do not know how they died, but the fact of their death is the inescapable truth, more powerful than the verbal account of an eyewitness could ever be.

Still photographs are accepted routinely as evidence in ordinary life and in the courtroom. The ease with which they are accepted may stem from the fact that once they are authenticated by the photographer or witness who vouches for the accuracy of the representation contained in the photograph, they are *actual evidence*. But because they are limited in time, they are not self-explanatory. As in Alexander Gardner's famous photo of the dead at Antietam, we know only that they are dead, not how they died.

The transition from still photographs to videotape or other moving pictures does not always convince. Simply because the videocamera or motion picture camera can capture many still photos in succession does not mean that in viewing the multiple sequenced photos that make up a film we are convinced that we have seen all that there is to see. With the still photograph we know there is more beyond the lens.

Indeed, the carnage of the American Civil War had an unintended research by-product that led to the development of motion pictures: with amputation the usual surgery for wounds to limbs, the need for artificial legs that would actually enable a person to walk led a prominent Boston physician, Dr. Oliver Wendell Holmes (the father of the jurist) to put together in sequence photographs of people walking in order to capture with precision how human limbs move and bend when humans walk. Writing in the *The Atlantic Monthly* in 1863, Holmes said of his discovery that by using the "instantaneous photograph" in sequence, the actual motion of "human locomotion" could be studied. What Dr. Holmes called "the mirror with a memory" would soon be pushed to new uses.

E.J. Muybridge used multiple cameras to record a horse's gait. His photographs astounded conventional wisdom and showed that a horse's actual gait was totally different from that normally assumed and shown in paintings. The *Scientific American* in 1878 printed eighteen drawings taken from Muybridge's photographs and instructed its readers that if the illustrations were pasted on a strip and mounted on a topless drum known as a *zoetrope*, by rotating the drum, "the actual motions" of the horse could be seen. In 1880, Muybridge used a similar device to project the "motion pictures" onto a screen.

By 1893, the inventions by George Eastman of continuous film and Thomas A. Edison's patented camera for "taking a large number of photographs of a moving object in such a manner that any two successive pictures are almost identical in appearance" (U.S. Patent No. 403, 534) and his "apparatus for exhibiting photographs of moving objects" (U.S. Patent No. 493, 426) formed the basis for motion pictures.

Edison's own description in the 1893 patent of the projector made clear that he understood that it is the illusion of motion that is recorded and played back: "a single composite picture is seen by the eye, said picture giving the impression that the object photographed is in actual and natural motion."

Videotaped evidence is fine as far as it goes. If we want to see a witness testify so that we can judge his facial expressions and mannerisms as he speaks and he cannot be in court, a videotape of his statement can provide the missing factors. But when the events in question are in dispute, the videotape record is not unambiguous. It may be objective in that it records what it was focussed upon. But without information as to the events beyond the lens, the record on the videotape is not self-explanatory.

THE MARION BARRY CASE

"They had the mayor using cocaine on video but it showed the theory of entrapment that the defense wanted to show." ABBE LOWELL, *former special assistant to the Attorney General and currently a Washington, D.C., attorney.*

U.S. District Judge Thomas Penfield Jackson, who presided over the trial in 1990, of Washington, D.C., Mayor Marion Barry, told a law school symposium that he had been disappointed that the jury did not convict "Barry of the more serious charges because he had "never seen a stronger government case." Key to the evidence as to one of the charges on which Barry was acquitted was an 80-minute videotape, made by secret camera installed in the Vista Hotel. The camera was installed by and operated by the FBI. The videotape showed Barry meeting with a woman in a room at the hotel. The fact that Barry smoked cocaine is shown clearly and unambiguously on the videotape. Laboratory reports and other trial testimony established beyond doubt that the substance being smoked was cocaine.

The jury's verdict of acquittal on this count demonstrated the jury's acceptance of the defense of entrapment: when the government goes to the time and expense to prepare for the commission of a crime, including renting the hotel room, providing the crack to be smoked, and having prepositioned camera crews there to film the scene, the defense may or may not establish entrapment as a matter of *law*. In the judgement of the jury the video was evidence of entrapment. Unless Barry could be lured to the set where the lights, camera, film crew and other accessories were ready to record the crime for posterity, and unless, once there, he could be convinced to do that which he may have done repeatedly elsewhere, there would be no movie to show to the jury — and to the nation as snippets on the national news shows.

In the Barry case, the jury listened to the evidence not merely as to what was on the film but to find out what the film showed. The circumstances surrounding the filming and the testimony of the participants all contributed to presenting the visual image in a fuller setting. The jury must have shared Thomas Edison's understanding that the film merely gives the "impression that the object photographed is in actual and natural motion." Having been lured to the hotel room and invited to smoke the crack cocaine, for the jury Barry was not seen in "actual and natural motion." We may all believe that the Mayor of Washington, D.C., should not use con-

4. THE POWER OF IMAGES

trolled substances. But are we prepared to say that the jury made the wrong decision as to the criminal charge on this particular count?

TRUTH OR PROPAGANDA
"One picture is worth a thousand words"

If one picture is worth a thousand words, what is the value of sixteen frames per second? To say that film is propaganda is not to say that what is seen is false. Some of the earliest and greatest propaganda films were those made by and for the Third Reich. The mass rallies showing thousands of Hitler Youth (*Hitlerjungend*), armed with shovels, pledging a frenzied fealty to the Führer, were not imaginary. They actually took place. The young people were not paid actors but fervent devotees of the Nazi cause. The fact that the cameras were rolling and the film taken shows a nation of young and old dedicated to the Führer, and this film could be distributed worldwide, were no accidents — it was often part of the reason for the rallies to be held in the first place.

We have neither time nor space here to explore the range of issues of film and propaganda. Some are discussed elsewhere in this issue in Professor Murray-Brown's article, "Desperate Deception." But in the context of videotape in court, the value of film as propaganda is clear.

The natural affinity of film and trials is immediately obvious to any attorney. If we think of a trial as an attempt by both sides to present a picture of reality, the value of film is apparent. Each side attempts to present to the "trier of facts" (jury, or sometimes a judge) evidence that will convince the trier of facts that one side's picture of the events in question is more believable than the other side's. While we can use euphemisms that the search is for truth, attorneys know that it is persuasion, not truth, that is the job of the attorney. (This is not a statement about the ethics of an attorney. Attorneys are — or are supposed to be — bound by ethical principles that impose obligations about presenting truth and not presenting known falsehoods to the court.) To bring a case to trial is, for the attorney, the effort to present a picture and to attempt to convince the trier of facts to adopt the client's position as the truth instead of the picture that the advocate on the other side will attempt to create. (The burden of and amount of persuasion may vary on a issue. For example, in a criminal case, the prosecution must establish its case "beyond a reasonable doubt." But it is still pictures of reality that must be presented to the jury.)

Increasingly, some savvy trial attorneys prefer the evocative effect of video over "live" testimony from a client to generate sympathy for or understanding of the client's position. In addition to the power that a video may have in showing pain, suffering, and other aspects of a client's life "after the accident," the risk that live testimony may falter can be eliminated. Interviewed on CNN, Washington trial attorney John Coale put it succinctly:

"I'll take a video tape over a live witness any day. Sometimes we videotape on purpose and use that instead of a live witness, because studies have shown and my experience shows that . . . you capture the attention of a jury for a much longer time. It's just better. People are used to watching television. They're not used to evaluating testimony, but they are used to seeing the tube."

A whole jurisprudence has developed over the use of "Day-in-the-Life" videos. Used extensively in personal injury litigation to demonstrate the pain, suffering, and life impairments suffered by the alleged victim, these made-for-court videotapes of the injured person going about, or attempting to go about the tasks of living are often major factors in the jury's award of damages. As Milwaukee attorney J. Ric Gass has written:

"The reason that these videos are prepared is relatively straightforward: they effectively convey selected portions of an individual's life to a jury in a very powerful, extremely memorable and highly credible manner. The use of the graphic video and its typical presentation on a television set makes for a potent combination."

RODNEY KING: THE TRIAL AND THE VIDEOTAPE

My biases should be made known: I do *not* believe that justice was done in Simi Valley and I believe that after the chase, Rodney King became victim, unlawfully punished by the police.

Most who have formed their opinion about the beating of Rodney King have done so based on the brief portions of the George Holliday videotape they may have seen on television as well as other press coverage. Most people have had neither the opportunity nor reason to examine the videotape with care or to review the trial testimony. It is easy to overlook the fact that much of the evidence at the Simi Valley trial came from sources other than the videotape. Fifty-six witnesses testified over the course of the seven-week trial, including observers (some of whom were police officers) as well as expert witnesses. The videotape (which in fact lasts more than nine-minutes) was shown both at full speed, slow motion, and frame-by-frame to illustrate the actions of the defendants and Rodney King.

It may overstate the obvious, but is has been decidedly unfashionable for any commentator to point out, as did Eric W. Rose and Steven S. Lucas in a nationally syndicated column published the day after the Simi Valley acquittals were announced, that, "for the jury, the videotape was one of many pieces of evidence to evaluate in a complex case. For the public, the videotape was the sole piece of evidence."

The discrepancies between what people thought they saw at

26. What the Jury Saw

home and the evidence in court has been ably summarized in a controversial article by Roger Parloff in the June 1992 issue of the *American Lawyer*, titled "Maybe The Jury Was Right." Noting that "I can't remember a time when I have ever felt so hesitant to say what I believe," Parloff effectively compares the actual content of the video to the trial testimony to conclude that the Simi Valley jury had a basis for its acquittals.

To understand that video presents ambiguities rather than right and wrong is to remember the function of the jury, a function video cannot replace. We may disagree with the verdict of the jury, but, as Parloff argues meticulously with reference to the actual testimony introduced at trial and its relationship to what the video did and did not show, it is possible to understand the argument that the video supported the defense that the police acted to subdue King, not to punish him.

Those who have seen only the video would not know that it was not disputed that after his car was stopped, King refused to be searched for weapons or be handcuffed, that he danced around and, when two officers attempted to put handcuffs on him, he shook them off and stood up. That is not on the video; as Parloff makes clear, it was essentially uncontradicted testimony.

Those who have seen only the video would not know that Sergeant Koon then ordered King to get on the ground or he would fire a taser dart. He then fired the first dart. He repeated his instructions and warning and, when King did not get down, fired the second dart. That too is not on the video, but as Parloff tells us, is part of the uncontradicted testimony the jury heard.

The video starts after the second dart has hit; instead of being rendered immobile by the darts, King gets fully to his feet and rushes either at or toward Officer Powell. Powell swings his baton and hits King — possibly in the head, possibly in the neck or on the shoulder. The video is not clear. King falls to the ground. With the video out of focus and a car partially blocking the view, the video shows Powell raining blows onto King while King apparently continues to try to raise himself. As Parloff's article points out to an incredulous readership, the *prosecution's expert* on use of force did not find this to be unreasonable force.

King lies on the ground. When he moves or attempts to raise himself, he is hit with blows from the baton, pushed to the ground by an officer's foot, and kicked. It is not clear from the video that any of the baton blows from this point on hit King in the head.

The famous shot of Officer Briseno putting out his hand to stop Officer Powell is seen clearly on the video. Officers Powell and Wind are seen on the video poised over King with their batons, striking him when he attempts to get up, arguably in a least one case, continuing to do so after he is on the ground.

Regardless of how you define the offense, the issue the jury "decided" in Simi Valley was whether these officers should be *convicted of a crime* for using excessive force (and whether the commanding officer, Sergeant Koon, committed a crime by failing to prevent his subordinates from using excessive force). Again, as Parloff points out, what the video can never show and only testimony can present is the mindset of the officers. On many points their testimony was supported both by the video and by other testimony: King had shown a reckless disregard for life by forcing the high-speed chase. King had shown both extraordinary strength and unwillingness to submit peacefully to arrest. King had not been searched and could have been concealing a weapon (in addition to his own physical strength).

It is against that backdrop that the officers' defense went

PERSUASIVE IMAGES

Students of propaganda should not neglect the poster. In "Persuasive Images: Posters of War and Revolution" (Princeton University Press), authors Peter Paret, Beth Irwin Lewis, and Paul Paret demonstrate the flexibility and power of the medium in wartime. The posters reproduced here all come from the collection of the Hoover Institution of Stanford University. The uses to which the poster was put in wartime were many: to encourage men to enlist, to persuade women on the home front to save materials for the war effort, to inflame the general public toward even more hatred against the wicked foe, to stiffen the resolve of a side facing imminent defeat. There are images based on racism and some silences: the atrocities of the Nazis against the Jews found no expression on posters. There are a few lapses in the text of the book: for a few of the Russian posters, the translation is incomplete or, in one case, wrong (in #145, the Russian does not mean "Take your rifle and hand to the Polish front" but simply "Take your rifle to the Polish front"). Contexts provided for each poster underscore the role propaganda played in its creation and reception. The study of such posters may help to immunize some readers against the power of propaganda. One must be grateful to the compilers and to Princeton University Press for a collaboration that has produced a first-rate example of book-making.

4. THE POWER OF IMAGES

beyond the lens to put a perspective on the video: in showing that King in fact did repeatedly either get to his feet or attempt to get to his feet; in the case of Officer Wind, to show that he never hit King in the head with his baton. The ability of the defense to present a context for the police officers' actions, a context of perceived threat and danger, was sufficient to convince the jury that there was reasonable doubt as to the prosecution's case.

The video did not lie; nor did it present the full story. The jury evidently accepted the argument made by Sargent Koon's attorney that Rodney King was at all times "in control" of the situation: he could have avoided or ended the beating simply by ceasing to resist the arrest.

The argument begs the question. If a police officer shoots a fleeing defendant because he did not stop after the officer has shouted, "Stop or I'll shoot," it may be true that the fleeing defendant was "in control" of the situation and could have avoided being shot if he stopped fleeing. But that does not answer the question as to whether the force used was excessive. The legal right of a police officer to use reasonable force or deadly force is not defined by whether an order has been disobeyed. Rather, the definition goes to the need to use force in the first place. An officer can command the fleeing purse snatcher to stop; he may use reasonable force to apprehend him. But, under principles of American law, he can't shoot and kill the purse thief on the ground that if he didn't the thief would get away. Yet at all times, the purse thief was "in control."

The argument that the person being arrested controls his fate was rejected by the Supreme Court as a justification for the use of deadly force on a nondangerous suspect. It is the police officer who is responsible for the amount of force used, not the suspect. Under the Constitution, according to the Supreme Court, "It is not better that all felony suspects die than that they escape . . . A police officer may not seize an unarmed, nondangerous suspect by shooting him dead." Writing for the majority in a 1985 case, Justice White stated "The use of deadly force is a self-defeating way of apprehending a suspect and so setting the criminal justice mechanism in motion. If successful, it guarantees that the mechanism will not be set in motion." *Tennessee v. Garner*, 471 U.S. 1 (1985).

But the fact that the "in control" argument proves too much is a legal distinction. Whether it was the composition of the jury, the quality of the advocacy, or simply the weight of the evidence, the jury in Simi Valley looked not only at the video but at the larger picture painted by the testimony and other evidence. The jury concluded that under the circumstances the defendant police officers found themselves in that evening, they would not or could not, from the vantage point of hindsight, find the officers guilty of a crime.

The Parloff article does a service by taking the time to show how the jury could have acquitted the defendants. And it is clear that the jury did not ignore the videotape, but relied on it, to confirm a view presented by the defense that the officers, acting out of fear of the unknown, did not use unreasonable force intended to cause "great bodily harm." The jury's hung verdict on the lesser count against Officer Powell *left open* the question as to whether he had unreasonably continued to beat King when it was not "necessary" to do so in order to subdue him.

The issue the American public judged through an inadequate viewing of the video was whether it was necessary to beat and continue to beat Rodney King. The jury in Simi Valley had a bigger picture presented through the seven-week trial and answered a different question. The videotape may be instrumental in "proving" that Rodney King was "in control" in that had he not resisted (or moved from pain and agony from the taser dart and prior blows), he would not have continued to have been beaten. The video shows this clearly. For the jury, that was consistent with the view that the use of force was not criminal.

But for society, the video left unanswered the question of whether police should beat a man who is on the ground every time he tries to get up until he is beaten into submission. Police officials across the country condemned the scenes shown on the video because modern police methods answer that question in the negative.

The media's repetitive showing of snippets of the video contributed to a mass judgement that was to a large extent uninformed by the full content of the video and, as the trial went on, the other evidence at trial. For many, the judgement was made once a portion of the video was seen, and repetition merely reinforced the judgement to the point of certainty. In these circumstances, the jury's verdict defied rational explanation because our collective judgement had already been formed.

When video is used in court, there are controls to prevent misuse, including control of the trial by the presiding judge as well as the natural checks and balances of the adversary system so that misleading use of a video can and will be pointed out by the advocates on the other side. On television we have no such controls and by sheer repetition alone an image is accepted as reality, as appearing to represent the impression that the object photographed is in actual and natural motion.

Videotape as a part of court proceedings is here to stay. We will always have to be vigilant to ensure that we do not mistake this illusion of "actual and natural motion" for the full story of what what lay beyond the lens. And for those concerned with the impact on police work of the proliferation of amateur video cameras, the best and last word belongs to my colleague Dean Edwin Delattre, who works with police across the nation:

"Since the savage beating of Rodney King . . . when working on ethics with police, I am now often asked, 'What should we do about video cameras out there?' The answer is not complex: . . . Do your job the right way, the way you have been trained — use only minimum necessary force and respect the people you serve — and you don't have to worry about cameras."

Photographs That Lie

The Ethical Dilemma Of Digital Retouching

J. D. Lasica

J. D. Lasica is a features editor and columnist at the Sacramento Bee.

A few years ago I wandered into a seminar touting the wonders that technology would bring to the photographs of tomorrow. Up on the screen, a surreal slide show was in progress. One slide showed Joan Collins sitting provocatively on President Reagan's lap. *Click.* Joan was now perching, elfishly, on the president's shoulder. *Click.* Reagan had grown a third eye. *Click.* Now he was bald. *Click.* And so on.

A representative from the Scitex Corporation, a Bedford, Massachusetts, company that manufactures digital retouching equipment, said that computers could now alter the content of photographs in virtually any manner. The slides had all been produced electronically—with no trace of tampering.

The audience, clearly dazzled, tossed off a dozen or so questions about whether the machines could do this or that. Finally a hand shot up. "Nobody's said a word about the potential for abuse here. What about the ethics of all this?"

"That's up to you," said the representative.

Welcome to journalism's latest ethical nightmare: photographs that lie.

In the past few years, this razzle-dazzle digital artistry has begun to turn up at the nation's largest newspapers, magazines and book publishing houses. The trend has a lot of people worried.

Consider what has taken place already:

• Through electronic retouching *National Geographic* slightly moved one of the Great Pyramids at Gîza to fit the vertical shape of its cover in 1982.

• An editor at the *Asbury Park Press*, the third-largest newspaper in New Jersey, removed a man from the middle of a news photo and filled in the space by "cloning" part of an adjoining wall. The incident prompted the paper to issue a policy prohibiting electronic tampering with news photos.

• The *Orange County Register*, which won a Pulitzer Prize for its photo coverage of the 1984 Summer Olympics, changed the color of the sky in every one of its outdoor Olympics photos to a smog-free shade of blue.

• The editors of the book *A Day in the Life of America* could not choose a cover photo from the thousands of pictures taken by the world's leading photojournalists. They solved the problem electronically by taking a photo of a cowboy on horseback, moving him up a hillside and, for good measure, enlarging the crescent moon. "I don't know if it's right or wrong," says co-director David Cohen. "All I know is it sells the book better."

• For one of its covers, *Popular Science* used a computer to place an airplane from one photo onto the background of another aerial photo. And a number of magazines have combined images of people photographed at different times, creating composites that give the false appearance of a single cover shot.

• The *St. Louis Post-Dispatch* used a Scitex computer to remove a can of Diet Coke from a photo taken of Ron Olshwanger, winner of the 1989 Pulitzer Prize for photography.

Faster than you can say "visual credibility gap," the 1980s may be the last decade in which photos could be considered evidence of anything.

"The photograph as we know it, as a record of fact, may no longer in fact be that in three or five years," warns George Wedding, director of photography for the *Sacramento Bee*.

4. THE POWER OF IMAGES

Jack Corn, director of photography for the *Chicago Tribune*, one of the first papers to buy a Scitex system, says the stakes are enormous. "People used to be able to look at photographs as depictions of reality," he says. "Now, that's being lost. I think what's happening is just morally, ethically wrong."

Digital technology's impact will be no less dramatic in other areas.

Within a decade, consumers will be able to buy a hand-held digital camera that uses a microchip instead of film, allowing the owner to "edit" photos. Soon you'll be able to remove your mother-in-law from that otherwise perfect vacation snapshot.

In the cinema, some experts are predicting the day when long-dead movie stars will be re-animated and cast in new films. "In 10 years we will be able to bring Clark Gable back and put him in a new show," John D. Goodell, a computer graphics consultant, told the *New York Times*.

Beyond such fanciful applications of digital technology, Goodell raises a dark scenario: Consider what might happen if the KGB or a terrorist group used such technology to broadcast a fabricated news bulletin about a natural disaster or an impending nuclear attack—delivered by a synthetic Dan Rather.

More likely than an assault by the Islamic Jihad on our airwaves will be an assault on our trust in visual images. Will photos be admissible evidence in a courtroom if tampering cannot be detected? Can newspapers rely on the truthfulness of any photo whose authenticity cannot be verified? As the price of these machines comes down, what will happen when the grocery-store tabloids start using—or abusing—them?

In television, too, the potential for abuse is great. Don E. Tomlinson, assistant professor of journalism at Texas A&M University, foresees the day when news producers try to re-create news events that they failed to capture on camera using exotic technology whose use was once confined to cinematic special effects. Airing such a simulation on a nightly newscast could confuse viewers about whether they're watching the real thing.

Tomlinson goes so far as to suggest that an unscrupulous TV reporter might use digital technology to fabricate an entire story because of ratings pressure, for career advancement or simply to jazz up the news on a slow day. A shark lurking near a populated beach, for example, could be manufactured using file footage and a digital computer.

While digital machinations on television may pose the greatest threat to the credibility of visual images in the long run, today the war is being waged in print.

Ironically, publishers are snapping up these systems not for their photo-altering capabilities but for economic reasons. Newspapers and magazines are using digital computers to achieve huge savings in labor and materials, enhance the quality of color photo reproduction, push back editorial deadlines (because of the time saved) and transmit color separations to remote printing plants via satellite.

Among the publications already employing the technology are *Time*, *Newsweek*, *U.S. News & World Report*, *USA Today*, *Newsday*, the *Atlanta Journal* and *Constitution*, the *Providence Journal-Bulletin* and, most recently, the *New York Times*. (Incidentally, while Scitex is the industry leader in producing these machines, it is not alone in the field. Crosfield Electronics of East Rutherford, New Jersey, and Hell Graphics Systems of Port Washington, New York, also manufacture digital retouching systems.)

"People have no idea how much alteration is going on," says Michael Morse of the National Press Photographers Association. "When you're looking at that *Redbook* or *Mademoiselle* or *Sports Illustrated* tomorrow, there's a good chance somebody has done something to that picture."

Of course, some of this photo modification is familiar terrain. Pictures have been faked since the earliest days of photography in the 1850s. Retouching photos by hand was once common practice in many newsrooms, and photographers can change the composition of a black-and-white print in the darkroom. But over the years, ethical standards have tightened. Today retouching a news photo is forbidden at most publications, and faking a photo can be grounds for dismissal.

As the tools of the trade change, however, the rules of the game evolve as well. Altering a photo has never been so fast and seamless. Digital systems allow an editor or art director to capture, display, alter, transmit and publish a picture without it ever seeing photographic paper.

A photographer in the field is now able to capture an image on a light-sensitive semiconductor chip and send it to the newsroom via telephone line, microwave or even satellite. The image—a collection of hundreds of thousands of pixels, similar to the makeup of a TV screen—is then reassembled on the video monitor of a picture editing station, or "electronic darkroom," where an editor can size it, crop it, enhance the contrast and tone and correct minor flaws. From there the image is sent to a color laser plotter, which converts the pixels into signals of zeros and ones (representing the densities of magenta, cyan, yellow and black printing inks) and produces a color separation. While conventional processing reads a transparency or photo by exposing it to light, electronic scanning creates an instant digital representation of an image. *Voilà!* A process that would normally take hours is accomplished in minutes. With a plaything this seductive, it's easy to understand the temptation to "improve" a news photo at the stroke of a few keys.

Rolling Stone magazine used a digital computer to erase a pistol and holster slung over the arm of "Miami Vice" star Don Johnson after he posed for a 1985 cover shot. Editor Jann Wenner, an ardent foe of handguns, ordered the change; using a computer saved the time and expense of having the cover re-shot.

Unquestionably, this high-tech process is here to stay. The question thus becomes: Where do you draw the line?

"If someone wants to remove a tree from a photo or move two people closer together, that's crossing the line," says Dennis Copeland, director of photography for the *Miami Herald*. "The media's image has been hurt because of those few people who've abused the technology."

While a spot survey of editors, art directors and picture editors at major newspapers nationwide found no one who supported the notion of using digital technology to tamper with the integrity of a documentary news photograph, there was far greater acceptance of using it to create conceptual or illustrative photos.

The distinction is far from academic. Documentary photographs aim to portray real events in true-to-life settings. Conceptual photos are meant to symbolize an idea or evoke a mood. Because a studio shot of, say, a truffle is more akin to a still life than to the hard-edge realism of photojournalism—indeed, because the shot is staged in the first place—art directors and page designers are given wide latitude in altering its content.

What is happening, many photographers and picture editors fear, is that the distinction between the two styles is blurring, partly due to the new technology. Scott Henry, chief photographer for the *Marin County* (California) *Independent-Journal*, detects in photojournalism "a quiet shift toward pictures as ornamentation or entertainment rather than reportage."

And George Wedding of the *Bee* says of tampered photographs, "Fabricated images that look authentic on first glance sometimes taint the believability of the pictures around them."

Wedding sees a trend toward increased reliance on conceptual photos, caused in part by the recent influx into newsrooms of art directors and designers who take their visual cues from art schools and the advertising field, where manipulation is the name of the game. "These people have not been taught the traditional, classic values and goals of documentary photojournalism," he says.

Joseph Scopin, assistant managing editor for graphics at the *Washington Times* (which uses the Scitex system), thinks those fears are overblown. "If you run a photo of someone holding a 4-foot-tall, 300-pound

152

strawberry, it's pretty obvious to the reader we're playing with the images," he says.

Sometimes, however, the distinction can be lost on the reader.

The *Asbury Park Press* ran into that difficulty in 1987 when it ran a cover story in its "Health and Fitness" section on a new kind of beef with lower cholesterol. Says Nancy Tobin, the paper's design director, "We had a head-on shot of a cow munching hay and a studio shot of a beautiful salad, and [we] combined the two images on Scitex. People came up to us afterward and said, 'How'd you get that cow to eat that salad?' We labeled it *composite photo illustration*, but some people were left scratching their heads."

Readers may grow more accustomed to digital photography's use as it spreads from the feature sections to the rest of the paper. Last summer the *Hartford Courant* ran a Page One color photo that showed how the city's skyline will look after several new skyscrapers go up; the feat was accomplished with *Newsday*'s Scitex equipment. Experts say it won't be long before newspapers' real estate pages display computer-created photos, rather than rough "artist's conceptions," of planned developments.

But some observers worry that increased use of digital retouching will make readers skeptical about the integrity of even undoctored images.

"People believe in news photographs. They have more inherent trust in what they see than what they read," says Kenneth Kobre, head of photojournalism studies at San Francisco State University. "Digital manipulation throws all pictures into a questionable light. It's a gradual process of creating doubts in the viewer's mind."

It was precisely that concern that led *National Geographic*, the magazine that moved a pyramid, to rethink its position. Jan Adkins, former associate art director, explains: "At the beginning of our access to Scitex, I think we were seduced by the dictum, 'If it can be done, it must be done.' If there was a soda can next to a bench in a contemplative park scene, we'd have the can removed digitally.

"But there's a danger there. When a photograph becomes synthesis, fantasy rather than reportage, then the whole purpose of the photograph dies. A photographer is a reporter—a photon thief, if you will. He goes and takes, with a delicate instrument, an extremely thin slice of life. When we changed that slice of life, no matter in what small way, we diluted our credibility. If images are altered to suit the editorial purposes of anyone, if soda cans or clutter or blacks or people of ethnic backgrounds are taken out, suddenly you've got a world that's not only unreal but surreal."

Adkins promises that, at *National Geographic* anyway, "the Scitex will never be used again to shift any one of the Seven Wonders of the World, or to delete anything that's unpleasant or add anything that's left out."

But even if other publications begin to show similar self-restraint, critics warn, digital technology is making additional inroads that threaten the credibility of visual images.

Already, there are a half dozen software programs on the market, such as "PhotoMac" or "Digital Darkroom" for the Macintosh, that allow the user to edit photographs digitally. The programs retail for about $700.

And then there is the digital camera, a sort of hand-held freeze-frame video camera that should be in stores within a decade, at a price within reach of the average buyer. What disturbs many people about this device is that the original image exists in an electronic limbo that can be almost endlessly manipulated. The camera differs from Scitex digital retouching equipment, which works with an original photo or negative.

"The term *photographic proof* may already be an archaic term," says the *Bee*'s Wedding. "You used to be able to hold up a negative and see that the image is real. With the advent of digital technology, you're going to hold up a floppy disk and you're not going to see anything."

Adds Tobin of the *Asbury Park Press*: "This is scaring everyone, because there's no original print, no hard copy. From the moment the shutter is snapped, it exists only as a digitized electronic impulse. Talk about the ability to rewrite history! It literally will be possible to purge information, to alter a historic event that occurred five years ago because no original exists. There's enormous potential for great wrong and great misuse."

Scitex spokesperson Ned Boudreau says the digital industry addressed such concerns long ago. "To hear the critics tell it," he says, "it's like we've unleashed Joe McCarthy all over again. We haven't."

He says safeguards, such as an archiving system that stores originals where no one can get at them, can be built into the digital equipment. At present, however, manufacturers do not provide such options unless requested.

John Derry, director of graphic services for Chromaset, a San Francisco creative-effects studio that has used digital retouching for dozens of corporations' advertising campaigns, thinks Americans will learn to accept the technology as it becomes pervasive. "Maybe it's generational," he says. "My mother could never tell the difference between videotape and movies, between the hard, sharp edge of Johnny Carson and the soft look of motion picture film.

"As we move into this new technology, perhaps there will be people who won't be able to discern electronically manipulated images from undoctored images. But I think most of us are already pretty savvy about this stuff. If you show someone a picture of Reagan punching Gorbachev, most people won't think it's real. They'll think, Oh, look at this doctored photo. How'd they do that?"

None of this assuages the critics of digital technology, but even its detractors concede this much: It's not the technology itself that's the culprit. Machines aren't ethical or unethical; people are.

"You've got to rely on people's ethics," says Brian Steffans, a top graphics photography editor at the *Los Angeles Times*. "That's not much different from relying on the reporter's words. You don't cheat just because the technology is available."

Wedding of the *Bee* is less sanguine about the future of news photography: "I hope that 10 years from now readers will be able to pick up a newspaper and magazine and believe what they read and see. Whether we are embarking on a course which will make that impossible, I don't know. I'm afraid we have."

A Word from Our Sponsor

Advertising is the major source of profit for newspapers, magazines, radio, and television, and advertising tie-ins are a common element in motion picture deals. While media writers may have the potential of reflecting their own agendas and social/political viewpoints as they produce media messages, they depend largely upon financial backing from advertisers, who have their own interests to protect. Advertisers use media as a means of presenting goods and services in a positive light. They are willing to pay generously for the opportunity to reach mass audiences: In 1993 Procter and Gamble spent $624 million to advertise on network television programs; General Motors spent $454 million, Philip Morris $374 million, and PepsiCo $310 million. However, advertisers are unwilling to support media that do not deliver the right kind of audience for their advertisements or that do not provide an appropriate "frame" within which to view them. And advertisements themselves sometimes introduce icons of popular culture that seep beyond the confines of 30-second spots. They may annoy consumers, entertain them, move them, or create considerable controversy. The readings in this unit explore the relationships among advertising, media content, and popular culture.

Mass advertising developed along with mass media; in fact, commercial media have been described by some as a system existing primarily for the purpose of delivering audiences to advertisers. While this may be an overly simplistic indictment, it reflects the marketplace orientation of the American media system, which depends on advertising revenue to offset enormous production costs and turn a profit. In 1994 the average cost of a 30-second spot on television's *Home Improvement* was $305,000, on *Roseanne* $261,000, on *60 Minutes* $188,700, and on the *Late Show with David Letterman* $30,700. A 30-second spot during the 1994 NCAA finals cost $214,600; a similar advertisement during the 1995 Academy Awards ran $685,000 and cost $1,000,000 during the 1995 Super Bowl broadcast. Advertising revenues provide approximately two-thirds of the income of a daily newspaper, which, in turn, devotes 50 to 75 percent of its space to advertisements. *Ms.* magazine began publishing without advertisements in June of 1990, a move that required raising subscription rates to $40 for 6 issues from $16 for 10 issues of the old *Ms.* with advertisements.

The dependent relationship between those who make decisions regarding media content and those who underwrite the production and distribution of that content has been an issue of some concern among media critics. Protecting advertising accounts can contribute to editorial decisions. Some advertising account executives admit, and others deny, that they consider a publication's overall trend in supporting their product category and that they also look at whether or not their brands or companies are featured favorably when they are mentioned in news or editorial copy. In "Sex, Lies, and Advertising," Gloria Steinem provides examples of "insertion orders" that both stipulate placement of advertisements and dictate topics considered unacceptable for discussion anywhere within magazines in which particular companies will buy advertising space. Editors at *Good Housekeeping*, which does not accept tobacco advertising, report facing similar pressure against printing articles on the dangers of smoking because they stand to lose revenue from nontobacco subsidiaries of the tobacco companies. Newspaper publishers report pressure to print favorable reviews of restaurants that buy advertising space and to downplay mention of brand names in news articles associated with an advertiser's product; thus, bank robbers are reported as having escaped in "a small car" rather than a Volkswagen.

Sometimes "news" or feature stories are developed specifically to attract or placate advertisers. As editor of *Vanity Fair*, Tina Brown reversed a 1984 advertising slump by running a series of feature stories about fashion designers Bill Blass, Giorgio Armani, Ralph Lauren, Calvin Klein, and Yves Saint Laurent, who subsequently became loyal advertisers. Sometimes product pitches creep into entertainment media, often striking below the level of consumer awareness. The 1995 television movie *Derby*, sponsored by Wendy's and cowritten by the fast-food chain's executive vice president for marketing, cast Wendy's founder, Dave Thomas, in a small role in its climactic scene. Asked for a comment on the ethics of this casting, ABC spokesperson Judd Parkin noted, "The guy is paying for the movie, he can do what he wants." Nine 30-second Wendy's spots aired during the broadcast. In "Hollywood the Ad," Mark Crispin Miller examines the influence of advertisers in cutting product placement deals with moviemakers, a practice that Miller believes has transferred some of the creative authority "out of the hands of filmmaking professionals and into the purely quantitative universe of the CEOs." In "Your Show of Shills," Leslie Savan discusses incidents of similar practices in television.

Advertisers are sensitive to controversy and are prone to avoid supporting controversial media content. When consumer groups threatened to boycott companies advertising on television's *Married ... with Children* because they objected to the show's content, the companies looked carefully at whether or not it was in their best

UNIT 5

interest to remain associated with the program. Several advertisers withdrew; others refused to commit to further advertising unless they could screen and approve individual episodes. As a result, Fox asked the producers to tone down the scripts. For the same reason, NBC had a difficult time finding sponsors for its 1989 television movie *Roe v. Wade*, which involved the controversy over abortion rights, and ABC canceled reruns of episodes from *thirtysomething* (showing two gay men in bed discussing friends who had died from AIDS) and *Roseanne* (focusing on teenage drinking) because advertisers' boycotts of the first showings cost the network over $1.5 million in lost revenue.

Finally, advertisers' interest in not only how many but also what kind of consumers select the media within which they advertise exerts influence on media content. Circulation data (for print media) and ratings data such as that provided by the A. C. Nielsen and Arbitron organizations (for television and radio) are instrumental in determining rate scales for advertising sales. Advertisers are becoming increasingly attentive to the demographic data included in such reports, since age, gender, ethnic background, and income are factors that determine how a given consumer might respond to a product pitch. Target marketing puts a premium on reaching certain advertiser-desirable groups by sponsoring media most likely to reach those groups. In television, programmers are able to assess a "premium program surcharge" for commercials aired during shows that attract the upscale viewers (especially women) whom advertisers most want to reach; thus, programming for that kind of audience becomes particularly attractive. Conversely, *Gunsmoke*, which was still receiving very high ratings after 21 seasons, was canceled in 1975 because advertisers felt that its viewers were becoming too old and too rural to attract sponsorship (see "Why Won't Television Grow Up?"). According to Kathryn Montgomery in "Children in the Digital Age," target marketing has also brought product pitches into school environments and educational media, and is creeping into the Internet.

There is no question that mass media availability is directly related to its inclusion of advertising. Without the support of corporate sponsorship, both information and entertainment media would be restricted only to those able to pay much higher costs of access. Some critics contend that advertising has moved beyond its acceptable boundaries and left no segment of mass media content untouched by its influence; that advertising has created a climate in which even critically acclaimed media face uncertain futures if they do not appeal to enough consumers, or to the right consumers. Countercritics give media consumers credit for being savvy interpreters of commercial messages, citing research that shows that even very young children are quick to recognize an advertisement once they have been taught to do so. They further suggest that the marketplace orientation of media businesses has had the desirable outcome of making the public the ultimate media gatekeeper, since advertisers will support only what audiences desire.

Looking Ahead: Challenge Questions

How do responses to advertiser attempts to influence editorial copy affect a newspaper or a magazine's credibility? What short-term and long-term considerations are salient in deciding where to draw the line between business realities and editorial integrity?

Why did *Ms.* magazine decide to drop advertising? Why did it have problems attracting enough advertising revenue to break even? Gloria Steinem is highly critical of advertisers' relationships with *Ms.* and with women's magazines in general. What is defensible, from a business standpoint, in advertising policies as Steinem describes them?

What is subliminal advertising? What subliminal effect do product placement plugs within films have on viewers? How have product placement trends affected the creative process and art of filmmaking?

What is the difference between television programming that will appeal to older versus younger audiences? What evidence do you see of age bias in network television programming?

If given the option of either paying access fees for information on the Internet or receiving that information free of cost along with commercial messages, which would be your choice? Why? What are the arguments for and against a ban on advertising in all children's media?

Sex, Lies & Advertising

GLORIA STEINEM

Gloria Steinem was a founding editor of "Ms." in 1972 and is now its consulting editor. She is also at work on "The Bedside Book of Self-Esteem" for Little, Brown.

About three years ago, as *glasnost* was beginning and *Ms.* seemed to be ending, I was invited to a press lunch for a Soviet official. He entertained us with anecdotes about new problems of democracy in his country. Local Communist leaders were being criticized in their media for the first time, he explained, and they were angry.

"So I'll have to ask my American friends," he finished pointedly, "how more *subtly* to control the press." In the silence that followed, I said, "Advertising."

The reporters laughed, but later, one of them took me aside: How *dare* I suggest that freedom of the press was limited? How dare I imply that his newsweekly could be influenced by ads?

I explained that I was thinking of advertising's media-wide influence on most of what we read. Even newsmagazines use "soft" cover stories to sell ads, confuse readers with "advertorials," and occasionally self-censor on subjects known to be a problem with big advertisers.

But, I also explained, I was thinking especially of women's magazines. There, it isn't just a little content that's devoted to attracting ads, it's almost all of it. That's why advertisers—not readers—have always been the problem for *Ms.* As the only women's magazine that didn't supply what the ad world euphemistically describes as "supportive editorial atmosphere" or "complementary copy" (for instance, articles that praise food/fashion/beauty subjects to "support" and "comple-

■ Suppose archaeologists of the future dug up women's magazines and used them to judge American women. What would they think of us—and what can we do about it?

ment" food/fashion/beauty ads), *Ms.* could never attract enough advertising to break even.

"Oh, *women's* magazines," the journalist said with contempt. "Everybody knows they're catalogs—but who cares? They have nothing to do with journalism."

I can't tell you how many times I've had this argument in 25 years of working for many kinds of publications. Except as moneymaking machines—"cash cows" as they are so elegantly called in the trade—women's magazines are rarely taken seriously. Though changes being made by women have been called more far-reaching than the industrial revolution—and though many editors try hard to reflect some of them in the few pages left to them after all the ad-related subjects have been covered—the magazines serving the female half of this country are still far below the journalistic and ethical standards of news and general interest publications. Most depressing of all, this doesn't even rate an exposé.

If *Time* and *Newsweek* had to lavish praise on cars in general and credit General Motors in particular to get GM ads, there would be a scandal—maybe a criminal investigation. When women's magazines from *Seventeen* to *Lear's* praise beauty products in general and credit Revlon in particular to get ads, it's just business as usual.

I.

When *Ms.* began, we didn't consider *not* taking ads. The most important reason was keeping the price of a feminist magazine low enough for most women to afford. But the second and almost equal reason was providing a forum where women and advertisers could talk to each other and improve advertising itself. After all, it was (and still is) as potent a source of information in this country as news or TV and movie dramas.

We decided to proceed in two stages. First, we would convince makers of "people products" used by both men and women but advertised mostly to men—cars, credit cards, insurance, sound equipment, financial services, and the like—that their ads should be placed in a women's magazine. Since they were accustomed to the division between editorial and advertising in news and general interest magazines, this would allow our editorial content to be free and diverse. Second, we would add the best ads for whatever traditional "women's products" (clothes, shampoo, fragrance, food, and so on) that surveys showed *Ms.* readers used. But we would ask them to come in *without* the usual quid pro quo of "complementary copy."

We knew the second step might be harder. Food advertisers have always demanded that women's magazines publish recipes and articles on entertaining (preferably ones that name their products) in return for their ads; clothing advertisers expect to be surrounded by fashion spreads (especially ones that credit their designers); and shampoo, fragrance, and beauty products in general usually insist on positive editorial coverage of beauty subjects, plus photo credits besides. That's why women's magazines look the way they do. But if we could break this link between ads and editorial content, then we wanted good ads for "women's products," too.

By playing their part in this unprecedented mix of *all* the things our readers need and use, advertisers also would be rewarded: ads for products like cars and mutual funds would find a new growth market; the best ads for women's products would no longer be lost in oceans of ads for the same category; and both would have access to a laboratory of smart and caring readers whose response would help create effective ads for other media as well.

I thought then that our main problem would be the imagery in ads themselves. Carmakers were still draping blondes in evening gowns over the hoods like ornaments. Authority figures were almost always male, even in ads for products that only women used. Sadistic, he-man campaigns even won industry praise. (For instance, *Advertising Age* had hailed the infamous Silva Thin cigarette theme, "How to Get a Woman's Attention: Ignore Her," as "brilliant.") Even in medical journals, tranquilizer ads showed depressed housewives standing beside piles of dirty dishes and promised to get them back to work.

Obviously, *Ms.* would have to avoid such ads and seek out the best ones—but this didn't seem impossible. *The New Yorker* had been selecting ads for aesthetic reasons for years, a practice that only seemed to make advertisers more eager to be in its pages. *Ebony* and *Essence* were asking for ads with positive black images, and though their struggle was hard, they weren't being called unreasonable.

Clearly, what *Ms.* needed was a very special publisher and ad sales staff. I could think of only one woman with experience on the business side of magazines—Patricia Carbine, who recently had become a vice president of *McCall's* as well as its editor in chief—and the reason I knew her name was a good omen. She had been managing editor at *Look* (really *the* editor, but its owner refused to put a female name at the top of his masthead) when I was writing a column there. After I did an early interview with Cesar Chavez, then just emerging as a leader of migrant labor, and the publisher turned it down because he was worried about ads from Sunkist, Pat was the one who intervened. As I learned later, she had told the publisher she would resign if the interview wasn't published. Mainly because *Look* couldn't afford to lose Pat, it *was* published (and the ads from Sunkist never arrived).

Though I barely knew this woman, she had done two things I always remembered: put her job on the line in a way that editors often talk about but rarely do, and been so loyal to her colleagues that she never told me or anyone outside *Look* that she had done so.

Fortunately, Pat did agree to leave *McCall's* and take a huge cut in salary to become publisher of *Ms.* She became responsible for training and inspiring generations of young women who joined the *Ms.* ad sales force, many of whom went on to become "firsts" at the top of publishing. When *Ms.* first started, however, there were so few women with experience selling space that Pat and I made the rounds of ad agencies ourselves. Later, the fact that *Ms.* was asking companies to do business in a different way meant our saleswomen had to make many times the usual number of calls—first to convince agencies and then client companies besides—and to present endless amounts of research. I was often asked to do a final ad presentation, or see some higher decision-maker, or speak to women employees so executives could see the interest of women they worked with. That's why I spent more time persuading advertisers than editing or writing for *Ms.* and why I ended up with an unsentimental education in the seamy underside of publishing that few writers see (and even fewer magazines can publish).

Let me take you with us through some experiences, just as they happened:
■ Cheered on by early support from Volkswagen and one or two other car companies, we scrape together time and money to put on a major reception in Detroit. We know U.S. carmakers firmly believe that women choose the

5. A WORD FROM OUR SPONSOR

upholstery, not the car, but we are armed with statistics and reader mail to prove the contrary: a car is an important purchase for women, one that symbolizes mobility and freedom.

But almost nobody comes. We are left with many pounds of shrimp on the table, and quite a lot of egg on our face. We blame ourselves for not guessing that there would be a baseball pennant play-off on the same day, but executives go out of their way to explain they wouldn't have come anyway. Thus begins ten years of knocking on hostile doors, presenting endless documentation, and hiring a full-time saleswoman in Detroit; all necessary before *Ms.* gets any real results.

This long saga has a semihappy ending: foreign and, later, domestic carmakers eventually provided *Ms.* with enough advertising to make cars one of our top sources of ad revenue. Slowly, Detroit began to take the women's market seriously enough to put car ads in other women's magazines, too, thus freeing a few pages from the hothouse of fashion-beauty-food ads.

But long after figures showed a third, even a half, of many car models being bought by women, U.S. makers continued to be uncomfortable addressing women. Unlike foreign carmakers, Detroit never quite learned the secret of creating intelligent ads that exclude no one, and then placing them in women's magazines to overcome past exclusion. (*Ms.* readers were so grateful for a routine Honda ad featuring rack and pinion steering, for instance, that they sent fan mail.) Even now, Detroit continues to ask, "Should we make special ads for women?" Perhaps that's why some foreign cars still have a disproportionate share of the U.S. women's market.

■ In the *Ms.* Gazette, we do a brief report on a congressional hearing into chemicals used in hair dyes that are absorbed through the skin and may be carcinogenic. Newspapers report this too, but Clairol, a Bristol-Myers subsidiary that makes dozens of products—a few of which have just begun to advertise in *Ms.*—is outraged. Not at newspapers or newsmagazines, just at us. It's bad enough that *Ms.* is the only women's magazine refusing to provide the usual "complementary" articles and beauty photos, but to criticize one of their categories—*that* is going too far.

We offer to publish a letter from Clairol telling its side of the story. In an excess of solicitousness, we even put this letter in the Gazette, not in Letters to the Editors where it belongs. Nonetheless—and in spite of surveys that show *Ms.* readers are active women who use more of almost everything Clairol makes than do the readers of any other women's magazine—*Ms.* gets almost none of these ads for the rest of its natural life.

Meanwhile, Clairol changes its hair coloring formula, apparently in response to the hearings we reported.

■ Our saleswomen set out early to attract ads for consumer electronics: sound equipment, calculators, computers, VCRs, and the like. We know that our readers are determined to be included in the technological revolution. We know from reader surveys that *Ms.* readers are buying this stuff in numbers as high as those of magazines like *Playboy;* or "men 18 to 34," the prime targets of the consumer electronics industry. Moreover, unlike traditional women's products that our readers buy but don't need to read articles about, these are subjects they want covered in our pages. There actually *is* a supportive editorial atmosphere.

"But women don't understand technology," say executives at the end of ad presentations. "Maybe not," we respond, "but neither do men—and we all buy it."

"If women *do* buy it," say the decision-makers, "they're asking their husbands and boyfriends what to buy first." We produce letters from *Ms.* readers saying how turned off they are when salesmen say things like "Let me know when your husband can come in."

After several years of this, we get a few ads for compact sound systems. Some of them come from JVC, whose vice president, Harry Elias, is trying to convince his Japanese bosses that there is something called a women's market. At his invitation, I find myself speaking at huge trade shows in Chicago and Las Vegas, trying to persuade JVC dealers that showrooms don't have to be locker rooms where women are made to feel unwelcome. But as it turns out, the shows themselves are part of the problem. In Las Vegas, the only women around the technology displays are seminude models serving champagne. In Chicago, the big attraction is Marilyn Chambers, who followed Linda Lovelace of *Deep Throat* fame as Chuck Traynor's captive and/or employee. VCRs are being demonstrated with her porn videos.

In the end, we get ads for a car stereo now and then, but no VCRs; some IBM personal computers, but no Apple or Japanese ones. We notice that office magazines like *Working Woman* and *Savvy* don't benefit as much as they should from office equipment ads either. In the electronics world, women and technology seem mutually exclusive. It remains a decade behind even Detroit.

■ Because we get letters from little girls who love toy trains, and who ask our help in changing ads and box-top photos that feature little boys only, we try to get toy-train ads from Lionel. It turns out that Lionel executives *have* been concerned about little girls. They made a pink train, and were surprised when it didn't sell.

Lionel bows to consumer pressure with a photograph of a boy *and* a girl—but only on some of their boxes. They fear that, if trains are associated with girls, they will be devalued in the minds of boys. Needless to say, *Ms.* gets no train ads, and little girls remain a mostly unexplored market. By 1986, Lionel is put up for sale.

But for different reasons, we haven't had much luck with other kinds of toys either. In spite of many articles on child-rearing; an annual listing of nonsexist, multi-racial toys by Letty Cottin Pogrebin; Stories for Free Children, a regular feature also edited by Letty; and other prizewinning features for or about children, we get virtually no toy ads. Generations of *Ms.* saleswomen explain to toy

28. Sex, Lies, and Advertising

You may be surprised to learn, as I was, that in the ratio of advertising to editorial pages in women's magazines, the ads average only about 5 percent more than in "Time," "Newsweek," and "U.S. News." That nothing-to-read feeling comes from editorial pages devoted to "complementary copy"; to text or photos that praise advertised categories, instruct in their use, or generally act as extensions of ads.

To find out what we're getting when we actually pay money for these catalogs, I picked random issues, counted the number of pages (even including letters to the editors, horoscopes, and so forth) that are not ads and/or copy complementary to ads, and then compared that number to the total pages. For instance:

Glamour, April 1990
339 pages total;
65 non-ad or ad-related

Vogue, May 1990
319 pages total;
38 non-ad or ad-related

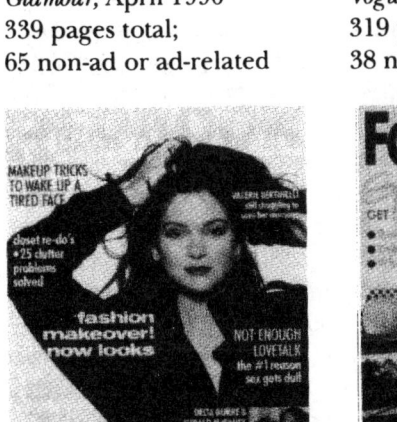

Redbook, April 1990
173 pages total;
44 non-ad or ad-related

Family Circle, March 13, 1990
180 pages total;
33 non-ad or ad-related

manufacturers that a larger proportion of *Ms.* readers have preschool children than do the readers of other women's magazines, but this industry can't believe feminists have or care about children.

■ When *Ms.* begins, the staff decides not to accept ads for feminine hygiene sprays or cigarettes: they are damaging and carry no appropriate health warnings. Though we don't think we should tell our readers what to do, we do think we should provide facts so they can decide for themselves. Since the antismoking lobby has been pressing for health warnings on cigarette ads, we decide to take them only as they comply.

Philip Morris is among the first to do so. One of its brands, Virginia Slims, is also sponsoring women's tennis and the first national polls of women's opinions. On the other hand, the Virginia Slims theme, "You've come a long way, baby," has more than a "baby" problem. It makes smoking a symbol of progress for women.

We explain to Philip Morris that this slogan won't do well in our pages, but they are convinced its success with some women means it will work with *all* women. Finally, we agree to publish an ad for a Virginia Slims calendar as a test. The letters from readers are critical—and smart. For instance: Would you show a black man picking cotton, the same man in a Cardin suit, and symbolize the antislavery and civil rights movements by smoking? Of course not. But instead of honoring the test results, the Philip Morris people seem angry to be proven wrong. They take away ads for *all* their many brands.

This costs *Ms.* about $250,000 the first year. After five years, we can no longer keep track. Occasionally, a new set of executives listens to *Ms.* saleswomen, but because we won't take Virginia Slims, not one Philip Morris product returns to our pages for the next 16 years.

Gradually, we also realize our naiveté in thinking we *could* decide against taking cigarette ads. They became a disproportionate support of magazines the moment they were banned on television, and few magazines could compete and survive without them; certainly not *Ms.*, which lacks so many other categories. By the time statistics in the 1980s showed that women's rate of lung cancer was approaching men's, the necessity of taking cigarette ads has become a kind of prison.

■ General Mills, Pillsbury, Carnation, DelMonte, Dole, Kraft, Stouffer, Hormel, Nabisco: you name the food giant, we try it. But no matter how desirable the *Ms.* readership, our lack of recipes is lethal.

We explain to them that placing food ads *only* next to recipes associates food with work. For many women, it is a negative that works *against* the ads. Why not place food ads in diverse media without recipes (thus reaching more men, who are now a third of the shoppers in supermarkets anyway), and leave the recipes to specialty magazines like *Gourmet* (a third of whose readers are also men)?

These arguments elicit interest, but except for an occasional ad for a convenience food, instant coffee, diet drinks, yogurt, or such extras as avocados and almonds,

5. A WORD FROM OUR SPONSOR

this mainstay of the publishing industry stays closed to us. Period.

■ Traditionally, wines and liquors didn't advertise to women: men were thought to make the brand decisions, even if women did the buying. But after endless presentations, we begin to make a dent in this category. Thanks to the unconventional Michel Roux of Carillon Importers (distributors of Grand Marnier, Absolut Vodka, and others), who assumes that food and drink have no gender, some ads are leaving their men's club.

Beermakers are still selling masculinity. It takes *Ms.* fully eight years to get its first beer ad (Michelob). In general, however, liquor ads are less stereotyped in their imagery—and far less controlling of the editorial content around them—than are women's products. But given the underrepresentation of other categories, these very facts tend to create a disproportionate number of alcohol ads in the pages of *Ms.* This in turn dismays readers worried about women and alcoholism.

■ We hear in 1980 that women in the Soviet Union have been producing feminist *samizdat* (underground, self-published books) and circulating them throughout the country. As punishment, four of the leaders have been exiled. Though we are operating on our usual shoestring, we solicit individual contributions to send Robin Morgan to interview these women in Vienna.

The result is an exclusive cover story that includes the first news of a populist peace movement against the Afghanistan occupation, a prediction of *glasnost* to come, and a grass-roots, intimate view of Soviet women's lives. From the popular press to women's studies courses, the response is great. The story wins a Front Page award.

Nonetheless, this journalistic coup undoes years of efforts to get an ad schedule from Revlon. Why? Because the Soviet women on our cover *are not wearing makeup.*

■ Four years of research and presentations go into convincing airlines that women now make travel choices and business trips. United, the first airline to advertise in *Ms.*, is so impressed with the response from our readers that one of its executives appears in a film for our ad presentations. As usual, good ads get great results.

But we have problems unrelated to such results. For instance: because American Airlines flight attendants include among their labor demands the stipulation that they could choose to have their last names preceded by "Ms." on their name tags—in a long-delayed revolt against the standard, "I am your pilot, Captain Rothgart, and this is your flight attendant, Cindy Sue"—American officials seem to hold the magazine responsible. We get no ads.

There is still a different problem at Eastern. A vice president cancels subscriptions for thousands of copies on Eastern flights. Why? Because he is offended by ads for lesbian poetry journals in the *Ms.* Classified. A "family airline," as he explains to me coldly on the phone, has to "draw the line somewhere."

It's obvious that *Ms.* can't exclude lesbians and serve women. We've been trying to make that point ever since our first issue included an article by and about lesbians, and both Suzanne Levine, our managing editor, and I were lectured by such heavy hitters as Ed Kosner, then editor of *Newsweek* (and now of *New York Magazine*), who insisted that *Ms.* should "position" itself *against* lesbians. But our advertisers have paid to reach a guaranteed number of readers, and soliciting new subscriptions to compensate for Eastern would cost $150,000, plus rebating money in the meantime.

Like almost everything ad-related, this presents an elaborate organizing problem. After days of searching for sympathetic members of the Eastern board, Frank Thomas, president of the Ford Foundation, kindly offers to call Roswell Gilpatrick, a director of Eastern. I talk with Mr. Gilpatrick, who calls Frank Borman, then the president of Eastern. Frank Borman calls me to say that his airline is not in the business of censoring magazines: *Ms.* will be returned to Eastern flights.

■ Women's access to insurance and credit is vital, but with the exception of Equitable and a few other ad pioneers, such financial services address men. For almost a decade after the Equal Credit Opportunity Act passes in 1974, we try to convince American Express that women are a growth market—but nothing works.

Finally, a former professor of Russian named Jerry Welsh becomes head of marketing. He assumes that women should be cardholders, and persuades his colleagues to feature women in a campaign. Thanks to this 1980s series, the growth rate for female cardholders surpasses that for men.

For this article, I asked Jerry Welsh if he would explain why American Express waited so long. "Sure," he said, "they were afraid of having a 'pink' card."

■ Women of color read *Ms.* in disproportionate numbers. This is a source of pride to *Ms.* staffers, who are also more racially representative than the editors of other women's magazines. But this reality is obscured by ads filled with enough white women to make a reader snowblind.

Pat Carbine remembers mostly "astonishment" when she requested African American, Hispanic, Asian, and other diverse images. Marcia Ann Gillespie, a *Ms.* editor who was previously the editor in chief of *Essence*, witnesses ad bias a second time: having tried for *Essence* to get white advertisers to use black images (Revlon did so eventually, but L'Oréal, Lauder, Chanel, and other companies never did), she sees similar problems getting integrated ads for an integrated magazine. Indeed, the ad world often creates black and Hispanic ads only for black and Hispanic media. In an exact parallel of the fear that marketing a product to women will endanger its appeal to men, the response is usually, "But your [white] readers won't identify."

In fact, those we are able to get—for instance, a Max Factor ad made for *Essence* that Linda Wachner gives us after she becomes president—are praised by white readers, too. But there are pathetically few such images.

■ By the end of 1986, production and mailing costs have risen astronomically, ad income is flat, and competition for ads is stiffer than ever. The 60/40 preponderance of edit over ads that we promised to readers becomes 50/50; children's stories, most poetry, and some fiction are casualties of less space; in order to get variety into limited pages, the length (and sometimes the depth) of articles suffers; and, though we do refuse most of the ads that would look like a parody in our pages, we get so worn down that some slip through. . . . Still, readers perform miracles. Though we haven't been able to afford a subscription mailing in two years, they maintain our guaranteed circulation of 450,000.

Nonetheless, media reports on *Ms.* often insist that our unprofitability must be due to reader disinterest. The myth that advertisers simply follow readers is very strong. Not one reporter notes that other comparable magazines our size (say, *Vanity Fair* or *The Atlantic*) have been losing more money in one year than *Ms.* has lost in 16 years. No matter how much never-to-be-recovered cash is poured into starting a magazine or keeping one going, appearances seem to be all that matter. (Which is why we haven't been able to explain our fragile state in public. Nothing causes ad-flight like the smell of nonsuccess.)

My healthy response is anger. My not-so-healthy response is constant worry. Also an obsession with finding one more rescue. There is hardly a night when I don't wake up with sweaty palms and pounding heart, scared that we won't be able to pay the printer or the post office; scared most of all that closing our doors will hurt the women's movement.

Out of chutzpah and desperation, I arrange a lunch with Leonard Lauder, president of Estée Lauder. With the exception of Clinique (the brainchild of Carol Phillips), none of Lauder's hundreds of products has been advertised in *Ms.* A year's schedule of ads for just three or four of them could save us. Indeed, as the scion of a family-owned company whose ad practices are followed by the beauty industry, he is one of the few men who could liberate many pages in all women's magazines just by changing his mind about "complementary copy."

Over a lunch that costs more than we can pay for some articles, I explain the need for his leadership. I also lay out the record of *Ms.*: more literary and journalistic prizes won, more new issues introduced into the mainstream, new writers discovered, and impact on society than any other magazine; more articles that became books, stories that became movies, ideas that became television series, and newly advertised products that became profitable; and, most important for him, a place for his ads to reach women who aren't reachable through any other women's magazine. Indeed, if there is one constant characteristic of the ever-changing *Ms.* readership, it is their impact as leaders. Whether it's waiting until later to have first babies, or pioneering PABA as sun protection in cosmetics, *whatever* they are doing today, a third to a half of American women will be doing three to five years from now. It's never failed.

But, he says, *Ms.* readers are not *our* women. They're not interested in things like fragrance and blush-on. If they were, *Ms.* would write articles about them.

On the contrary, I explain, surveys show they are more likely to buy such things than the readers of, say, *Cosmopolitan* or *Vogue*. They're good customers because they're out in the world enough to need several sets of everything: home, work, purse, travel, gym, and so on. They just don't need to read articles about these things. Would he ask a men's magazine to publish monthly columns on how to shave before he advertised Aramis products (his line for men)?

He concedes that beauty features are often concocted more for advertisers than readers. But *Ms.* isn't appropriate for his ads anyway, he explains. Why? Because Estée Lauder is selling "a kept-woman mentality."

I can't quite believe this. Sixty percent of the users of his products are salaried, and generally resemble *Ms.* readers. Besides, his company has the appeal of having been started by a creative and hardworking woman, his mother, Estée Lauder.

That doesn't matter, he says. He knows his customers, and they would *like* to be kept women. That's why he will never advertise in *Ms.*

In November 1987, by vote of the Ms. Foundation for Education and Communication (*Ms.*'s owner and publisher, the media subsidiary of the Ms. Foundation for Women), *Ms.* was sold to a company whose officers, Australian feminists Sandra Yates and Anne Summers, raised the investment money in their country that *Ms.* couldn't find in its own. They also started *Sassy* for teenage women.

In their two-year tenure, circulation was raised to 550,000 by investment in circulation mailings, and, to the dismay of some readers, editorial features on clothes and new products made a more traditional bid for ads. Nonetheless, ad pages fell below previous levels. In addition, *Sassy*, whose fresh voice and sexual frankness were an unprecedented success with young readers, was targeted by two mothers from Indiana who began, as one of them put it, "calling every Christian organization I could think of." In response to this controversy, several crucial advertisers pulled out.

Such links between ads and editorial content was a problem in Australia, too, but to a lesser degree. "Our readers pay two times more for their magazines," Anne explained, "so advertisers have less power to threaten a magazine's viability."

"I was shocked," said Sandra Yates with characteristic directness. "In Australia, we think you have freedom of the press—but you don't."

Since Anne and Sandra had not met their budget's projections for ad revenue, their investors forced a sale. In October 1989, *Ms.* and *Sassy* were bought by Dale Lang,

5. A WORD FROM OUR SPONSOR

owner of *Working Mother, Working Woman,* and one of the few independent publishing companies left among the conglomerates. In response to a request from the original *Ms.* staff—as well as to reader letters urging that *Ms.* continue, plus his own belief that *Ms.* would benefit his other magazines by blazing a trail—he agreed to try the ad-free, reader-supported *Ms.* you hold now and to give us complete editorial control.

II.

Do you think, as I once did, that advertisers make decisions based on solid research? Well, think again. "Broadly speaking," says Joseph Smith of Oxtoby-Smith, Inc., a consumer research firm, "there is no persuasive evidence that the editorial context of an ad matters."

Advertisers who demand such "complementary copy," even in the absence of respectable studies, clearly are operating under a double standard. The same food companies place ads in *People* with no recipes. Cosmetics companies support *The New Yorker* with no regular beauty columns. So where does this habit of controlling the content of women's magazines come from?

Tradition. Ever since *Ladies Magazine* debuted in Boston in 1828, editorial copy directed to women has been informed by something other than its readers' wishes. There were no ads then, but in an age when married women were legal minors with no right to their own money, there was another revenue source to be kept in mind: husbands. "Husbands may rest assured," wrote editor Sarah Josepha Hale, "that nothing found in these pages shall cause her [his wife] to be less assiduous in preparing for his reception or encourage her to 'usurp station' or encroach upon prerogatives of men."

Hale went on to become the editor of *Godey's Lady's Book,* a magazine featuring "fashion plates": engravings of dresses for readers to take to their seamstresses or copy themselves. Hale added "how to" articles, which set the tone for women's service magazines for years to come: how to write politely, avoid sunburn, and—in no fewer than 1,200 words—how to maintain a goose quill pen. She advocated education for women but avoided controversy. Just as most women's magazines now avoid politics, poll their readers on issues like abortion but rarely take a stand, and praise socially approved lifestyles, Hale saw to it that *Godey's* avoided the hot topics of its day: slavery, abolition, and women's suffrage.

What definitively turned women's magazines into catalogs, however, were two events: Ellen Butterick's invention of the clothing pattern in 1863 and the mass manufacture of patent medicines containing everything from colored water to cocaine. For the first time, readers could purchase what magazines encouraged them to want. As such magazines became more profitable, they also began to attract men as editors. (Most women's magazines continued to have men as top editors until the feminist 1970s.) Edward Bok, who became editor of *The Ladies' Home Journal* in 1889, discovered the power of

Elle, May 1990
326 pages total;
39 non-ad or ad-related

Lear's, November 1989
173 pages total;
65 non-ad or ad-related

advertisers when he rejected ads for patent medicines and found that other advertisers canceled in retribution. In the early 20th century, *Good Housekeeping* started its Institute to "test and approve" products. Its Seal of Approval became the grandfather of current "value added" programs that offer advertisers such bonuses as product sampling and department store promotions.

By the time suffragists finally won the vote in 1920, women's magazines had become too entrenched as catalogs to help women learn how to use it. The main function was to create a desire for products, teach how to use products, and make products a crucial part of gaining social approval, pleasing a husband, and performing as a homemaker. Some unrelated articles and short stories were included to persuade women to pay for these catalogs. But articles were neither consumerist nor rebellious. Even fiction was usually subject to formula: if a woman had any sexual life outside marriage, she was supposed to come to a bad end.

In 1965, Helen Gurley Brown began to change part of that formula by bringing "the sexual revolution" to women's magazines—but in an ad-oriented way. Attracting multiple men required even more consumerism, as the Cosmo Girl made clear, than finding one husband.

In response to the workplace revolution of the 1970s, traditional women's magazines—that is, "trade books" for women working at home—were joined by *Savvy, Working Woman,* and other trade books for women working in offices. But by keeping the fashion/beauty/entertaining articles necessary to get traditional ads and then adding career articles besides, they inadvertently produced the antifeminist stereotype of Super Woman. The male-imitative, dress-for-success woman carrying a briefcase became the media image of a woman worker, even though a blue-collar woman's salary was often higher than her glorified secretarial sister's, and though women at a real briefcase level are statistically rare. Needless to say, these dress-for-success women were also thin, white, and beautiful.

In recent years, advertisers' control over the editorial content of women's magazines has become so institutionalized that it is written into "insertion orders" or dictated to ad salespeople as official policy. The following are recent typical orders to women's magazines:

- Dow's Cleaning Products stipulates that ads for its Vivid and Spray 'n Wash products should be adjacent to "children or fashion editorial"; ads for Bathroom Cleaner should be next to "home furnishing/family" features; and so on for other brands. "If a magazine fails for 1/2 the brands or more," the Dow order warns, "it will be omitted from further consideration."
- Bristol-Myers, the parent of Clairol, Windex, Drano, Bufferin, and much more, stipulates that ads be placed next to "a full page of compatible editorial."
- S.C. Johnson & Son, makers of Johnson Wax, lawn and laundry products, insect sprays, hair sprays, and so on, orders that its ads "*should not be opposite extremely controversial features or material antithetical to the nature/copy of the advertised product.*" (Italics theirs.)
- Maidenform, manufacturer of bras and other apparel, leaves a blank for the particular product and states: "The creative concept of the ____ campaign, and the very nature of the product itself appeal to the positive emotions of the reader/consumer. Therefore, it is imperative that all editorial adjacencies reflect that same positive tone. The editorial must not be negative in content or lend itself contrary to the ____ product imagery/message (e.g. *editorial relating to illness, disillusionment, large size fashion, etc.*)." (Italics mine.)
- The De Beers diamond company, a big seller of engagement rings, prohibits magazines from placing its ads with "adjacencies to hard news or anti/love-romance themed editorial."
- Procter & Gamble, one of this country's most powerful and diversified advertisers, stands out in the memory of Anne Summers and Sandra Yates (no mean feat in this context): its products were not to be placed in *any* issue that included *any* material on gun control, abortion, the occult, cults, or the disparagement of religion. Caution was also demanded in any issue covering sex or drugs, even for educational purposes.

Those are the most obvious chains around women's magazines. There are also rules so clear they needn't be written down: for instance, an overall "look" compatible with beauty and fashion ads. Even "real" nonmodel women photographed for a woman's magazine are usually made up, dressed in credited clothes, and retouched out of all reality. When editors do include articles on less-than-cheerful subjects (for instance, domestic violence), they tend to keep them short and unillustrated. The point is to be "upbeat." Just as women in the street are asked, "Why don't you smile, honey?" women's magazines acquire an institutional smile.

Within the text itself, praise for advertisers' products has become so ritualized that fields like "beauty writing" have been invented. One of its frequent practitioners explained seriously that "It's a difficult art. How many new adjectives can you find? How much greater can you make a lipstick sound? The FDA restricts what companies can say on labels, but we create illusion. And ad agencies are on the phone all the time pushing you to get their product in. A lot of them keep the business based on how many editorial clippings they produce every month. The worst are products," like Lauder's as the writer confirmed, "with their own name involved. It's all ego."

Often, editorial becomes one giant ad. Last November, for instance, *Lear's* featured an elegant woman executive on the cover. On the contents page, we learned she was wearing Guerlain makeup and Samsara, a new fragrance by Guerlain. Inside were full-page ads for Samsara and Guerlain antiwrinkle cream. In the cover profile, we learned that this executive was responsible for launching Samsara and is Guerlain's director of public relations. When the *Columbia Journalism Review* did one of the few articles to include women's magazines in coverage of the influence of ads, editor Frances Lear was quoted as defending her magazine because "this kind of thing is done all the time."

Often, advertisers also plunge odd-shaped ads into the text, no matter what the cost to the readers. At *Woman's Day*, a magazine originally founded by a supermarket chain, editor in chief Ellen Levine said, "The day the copy had to rag around a chicken leg was not a happy one."

Advertisers are also adamant about where in a magazine their ads appear. When Revlon was not placed as the first beauty ad in one Hearst magazine, for instance, Revlon pulled its ads from *all* Hearst magazines. Ruth Whitney, editor in chief of *Glamour,* attributes some of these demands to "ad agencies wanting to prove to a client that they've squeezed the last drop of blood out of a magazine." She also is, she says, "sick and tired of hearing that women's magazines are controlled by cigarette ads." Relatively speaking, she's right. To be as censoring as are many advertisers for women's products, tobacco companies would have to demand articles in praise of smoking and expect glamorous photos of beautiful women smoking their brands.

I don't mean to imply that the editors I quote here share my objections to ads: most assume that women's magazines have to be the way they are. But it's also true that only former editors can be completely honest. "Most of the pressure came in the form of direct product mentions," explains Sey Chassler, who was editor in chief of *Redbook* from the sixties to the eighties. "We got threats from the big guys, the Revlons, blackmail threats. They wouldn't run ads unless we credited them.

"But it's not fair to single out the beauty advertisers because these pressures came from everybody. Advertisers want to know two things: What are you going to charge me? What *else* are you going to do for me? It's a holdup. For instance, management felt that fiction took up too much space. They couldn't put any advertising in that. For the last ten years, the number of fiction entries into the National Magazine Awards has declined.

"And pressures are getting worse. More magazines are

5. A WORD FROM OUR SPONSOR

more bottom-line oriented because they have been taken over by companies with no interest in publishing.

"I also think advertisers do this to women's magazines especially," he concluded, "because of the general disrespect they have for women."

Even media experts who don't give a damn about women's magazines are alarmed by the spread of this ad-edit linkage. In a climate *The Wall Street Journal* describes as an unacknowledged Depression for media, women's products are increasingly able to take their low standards wherever they go. For instance: newsweeklies publish uncritical stories on fashion and fitness. *The New York Times Magazine* recently ran an article on "firming creams," complete with mentions of advertisers. *Vanity Fair* published a profile of one major advertiser, Ralph Lauren, illustrated by the same photographer who does his ads, and turned the lifestyle of another, Calvin Klein, into a cover story. Even the outrageous *Spy* has toned down since it began to go after fashion ads.

And just to make us really worry, films and books, the last media that go directly to the public without having to attract ads first, are in danger, too. Producers are beginning to depend on payments for displaying products in movies, and books are now being commissioned by companies like Federal Express.

But the truth is that women's products—like women's magazines—have never been the subjects of much serious reporting anyway. News and general interest publications, including the "style" or "living" sections of newspapers, write about food and clothing as cooking and fashion, and almost never evaluate such products by brand name. Though chemical additives, pesticides, and animal fats are major health risks in the United States, and clothes, shoddy or not, absorb more consumer dollars than cars, this lack of information is serious. So is ignoring the contents of beauty products that are absorbed into our bodies through our skins, and that have profit margins so big they would make a loan shark blush.

III.

What could women's magazines be like if they were as free as books? as realistic as newspapers? as creative as films? as diverse as women's lives? We don't know.

But we'll only find out if we take women's magazines seriously. If readers were to act in a concerted way to change traditional practices of *all* women's magazines and the marketing of *all* women's products, we could do it. After all, they are operating on our consumer dollars; money that we now control. You and I could:

- write to editors and publishers (with copies to advertisers) that we're willing to pay *more* for magazines with editorial independence, but will *not* continue to pay for those that are just editorial extensions of ads;
- write to advertisers (with copies to editors and publishers) that we want fiction, political reporting, consumer reporting—whatever is, or is not, supported by their ads;
- put as much energy into breaking advertising's control over content as into changing the images in ads, or protesting ads for harmful products like cigarettes;
- support only those women's magazines and products that take *us* seriously as readers and consumers.

Those of us in the magazine world can also use the carrot-and-stick technique. For instance: pointing out that, if magazines were a regulated medium like television, the demands of advertisers would be against FCC rules. Payola and extortion could be punished. As it is, there are probably illegalities. A magazine's postal rates are determined by the ratio of ad to edit pages, and the former costs more than the latter. So much for the stick.

The carrot means appealing to enlightened self-interest. For instance: there are many studies showing that the greatest factor in determining an ad's effectiveness is the credibility of its surroundings. The "higher the rating of editorial believability," concluded a 1987 survey by the *Journal of Advertising Research,* "the higher the rating of the advertising." Thus, an impenetrable wall between edit and ads would also be in the best interest of advertisers.

Unfortunately, few agencies or clients hear such arguments. Editors often maintain the false purity of refusing to talk to them at all. Instead, they see ad salespeople who know little about editorial, are trained in business as usual, and are usually paid by commission. Editors might also band together to take on controversy. That happened once when all the major women's magazines did articles in the same month on the Equal Rights Amendment. It could happen again.

It's almost three years away from life between the grindstones of advertising pressures and readers' needs. I'm just beginning to realize how edges got smoothed down—in spite of all our resistance.

I remember feeling put upon when I changed "Porsche" to "car" in a piece about Nazi imagery in German pornography by Andrea Dworkin—feeling sure Andrea would understand that Volkswagen, the distributor of Porsche and one of our few supportive advertisers, asked only to be far away from Nazi subjects. It's taken me all this time to realize that Andrea was the one with a right to feel put upon.

Even as I write this, I get a call from a writer for *Elle*, who is doing a whole article on where women part their hair. Why, she wants to know, do I part mine in the middle?

It's all so familiar. A writer trying to make something of a nothing assignment; an editor laboring to think of new ways to attract ads; readers assuming that other women must want this ridiculous stuff; more women suffering for lack of information, insight, creativity, and laughter that could be on these same pages.

I ask you: Can't we do better than this?

Hollywood the Ad

Mark Crispin Miller

A prolific media critic, Miller often focuses on issues raised by the commercialism of the television, recording, and film industries. He is author of Boxed In: The Culture of TV *(1988), and* Seeing through Movies *(1990).*

"This approach to human beings strikes me as utterly cynical, and directly contrary to the democratic ideal." Such was the sharp response of Dr. Lewis Webster Jones, the head of the National Conference of Christians and Jews. Other clergymen agreed: this new technique could mean the twilight of democracy. It was not only God's ministers who sensed a threat. This technique, Aldous Huxley declared, made "nonsense of the whole democratic procedure, which is based on conscious choice on rational ground." The public protest was immense. The National Association of Radio and Television Broadcasters felt obliged to ban the use of the technique by any of its members, and the three major television networks also publicly rejected it. The New York State Senate unanimously passed a bill outlawing the technique. When KTLA, an independent TV station in Los Angeles, announced that it would soon start using the invention to discourage littering and unsafe driving, the station "received such a torrent of adverse mail," *Life* magazine reported, "that it cancelled the campaign."

Meanwhile, there were some who were not emitting "yelps of alarm," according to the *Wall Street Journal*. Indeed, certain forward-looking managers were rather taken with the idea, despite its dangers, or perhaps because of them. "Chuckles one TV executive with a conscious eye on the future," *Time* magazine reported in its coverage of the controversy, "'It smacks of brainwashing, but of course it would be tempting.'"

The invention that sparked the national panic, and that was also quietly thrilling certain corporate salesmen, was "subliminal advertising"—a phrase coined by the first of its practitioners, James M. Vicary, "a young motivational researcher and amateur psychologist," as the *Journal* called him. On September 12, 1957, Vicary, the vice-president of the Subliminal Projection Company, held a press conference to tout the results of an experiment that he had just concluded at a neighborhood movie theater in Fort Lee, New Jersey. For six weeks, using special equipment, he had flashed imperceptible allurements onto the screen during the theater's showings of *Picnic,* a Columbia release. Projected every five seconds for one three-thousandth of a second, those unnoticed coaxings, Vicary said, had dramatically boosted concession-stand sales of the items subliminally hyped on the big screen. Vicary had projected two terse bits of copy: "Hungry? Eat popcorn" and "Drink Coca-Cola."

BLATANT IMPOSITIONS

Today what matters most about Vicary's experiment is not his "findings"—which Vicary fabricated. His invention turned out to have had no effect at all on how much Coke or popcorn people swallowed, but was a mere sales gimmick to promote the Subliminal Projection Company itself. Although his "results" were valueless, the outrage stirred by his announcement is important. Back then the rumor that one movie had been temporarily polluted with an advertising pitch—"Drink Coca-Cola"—was enough to elicit a great wave of angry protest. That was in 1957. Let us now look at two clips from movies of the 1980s—movies that nobody protested.

In *Murphy's Romance*, released by Columbia in 1985, Sally Field is a youngish divorcée, poor but plucky, who has just moved with her sweet pre-adolescent son to a friendly little Texas town. At the start of the film she wanders into an old-fashioned drugstore, owned, we soon discover, by James Garner, a very benevolent curmudgeon ("Murphy"). On her way in, Field passes, and so

---

Extracted from the introduction, "The Big Picture," pp. 5-13, from *Seeing through Movies* by Mark Crispin Miller. © 1990 by Mark Crispin Miller. Reprinted by permission of Pantheon Books, a division of Random House, Inc.

5. A WORD FROM OUR SPONSOR

we see (she's moving slowly so that we'll see), not one but *three* bright Coca-Cola signs (the merry red, the bold white script)—one on each front window, one on the front door. And then, as Field plunks herself down cutely at the soda counter, and as the seemingly brusque but really very kindly Garner comes to serve her, there is the following exchange:

Field: I'll have a banana split. No, I won't. I'll have a Coke.
Garner: A Coke?
Field: A lemon Coke.

Much is later made of Garner's cherished 1927 Studebaker, which sits out front; Garner refuses to put it elsewhere, despite a daily parking ticket. Although this business does say something obvious about Garner's character ("That Murphy! Stubborn as a mule!"), the car's visual function is to say "Drink Coca-Cola," because it shares the frame with, and is the same deep merry red as, those three prominent Coca-Cola signs. (The movie, incidentally, has a happy ending.)

Toward the beginning of *Who's Harry Crumb?*, a 1989 Columbia release, John Candy sits next to Jim Belushi on a bus. A fantastically inept detective, Candy is on his way to meet his employers in a big kidnapping case. Here, in all its comic brilliance, is the entire scene with Belushi:

Candy (eating cherries, offers one): Cherry?
Belushi (reading): No fruit, thank you.

Candy pulls a can of Diet Coke (silvery cylinder, red block letters) out of his bag.

Candy: Coke?
Belushi: No, thank you.
Candy: Mix 'em together, ya got a cherry Coke. Ah ha ha ha ha ha! A cherry Coke, ha ha ha ha!

Later, dining with his wealthy clients, Candy pours a can of Diet Coke into a brandy snifter full of ice cream, holding the (silvery) can up high so that its (red) name is not just legible but unavoidable.

What is the difference between James Vicary's ploy and these later cinematic tricks to make an audience "Drink Coca-Cola"? In 1957 Vicary tried to boost his business by implanting a commercial message in a Columbia release (and then by making false claims for the failed experiment). In 1982 Coca-Cola bought 49 percent of Columbia Pictures and began at once to plug (its own) products in (its own) movies—trying, just like Vicary, to profit by turning movies into advertising.

(The company kept it up until it sold Columbia Pictures to Sony, in 1989.) Certainly there is a difference in degree. Whereas Vicary's method was a furtive imposition on the movie, used in only one theater, and only temporarily, the come-ons embedded in Coke's movies are there forever, in whatever prints or tapes you choose to see, because those messages are worked—overtly— right into the movies' scripts and mise-en-scène.

In this overtness, one might argue, these later exhortations to drink Coca-Cola differ crucially from Vicary's gimmick, because his appeal was "subliminal," whereas the later cans and signs beckon us openly, like illuminated billboards. Such a distinction, however, rests on too crude an understanding of subliminal effects—which result not from invisible implants but from words or images that are, in fact, explicitly presented yet at best only half perceived. These latter-day plugs for Coca-Cola, for example, work as subliminal inducements because their context is ostensibly a movie, not an ad, so that each of them comes sidling toward us dressed up as non-advertising, just as other kinds of ads now routinely come at us disguised as "magalogues" and "advertorials"; rock videos; "educational" broadcasts, newsletters, filmstrips, and posters; concerts, art exhibits, sporting events, magazines, newspapers, books, and TV shows; and a good deal of our daily mail—in short, as anything and everything but advertising.

The subliminal impact of the Coke plugs arises not only from their cinematic camouflage but also from the pleasant welter of associations that in each movie efficiently glamorize every Coca-Cola can or logo; Garner's personal warmth and fine old car, John Candy's would-be riotous antics (and, in each case, the very fact of stardom itself), are attractions serving as oblique (that is, subliminal) enhancements to the all-important product. Precisely because of this benefit Coca-Cola has understandably been very careful in its choice of cinematic vehicles—and has also used them to stigmatize the competition.

In *Murphy's Romance*, Field's nice son goes looking for a job; and while "Coca-Cola" sheds its deep red warmth throughout Murphy's homey store, in a big supermarket where the kid is told abruptly that he isn't needed, two (blue) Pepsi signs loom coldly on the wall like a couple of swastikas. In fact, the company used such tactics before it bought Columbia. In Costa-Gavras's *Missing*, a Universal picture made just before the purchase, Jack Lemmon plays a very decent father searching Chile for his son, who has been kidnapped by Pinochet's soldiers. In one scene this haggard, loyal dad, while talking things out, takes rare (and noticeable) solace in a bottle of Coke— whereas inside the nightmare stadium where the army does its torturing and murdering there stands a mammoth Pepsi machine, towering in this underworld like its dark idol.

Although Pepsico owns no movie studio (yet), its officers began fighting back at once. A special manager tackled the job of keeping Pepsi on the silver screen, and from that moment the spheric Pepsi logo (white/blue/red) became a film presence almost as prevalent as big handguns. In the movies Pepsi is the choice of a new generation—that is, of every generation. The suburban kids are drinking Pepsi in *Ferris Bueller's Day Off*, like the poor kids in *Stand and Deliver* and *Lean on Me*, and like the old folks in *Cocoon: The Return*. Jennifer Beals is drinking Diet Pepsi in *Flashdance*, Kathy Baker is buying Pepsi in *Clean and Sober*, in *Always* a brightly lit Pepsi logo lengthily upstages Holly Hunter, and in *Legal Eagles* Debra Winger keeps her Pepsi cold and blatant in a refrigerator otherwise full of blank containers. Pepsi glides through the Texas of the fifties in *Everybody's All-American*, pops into the cute Manhattan of *Crossing Delancey*, and drops in on Norman Bates's milieu in *Psycho II* and *Psycho III*. And Pepsico, too, has tried to move against its major rival, declining to place a Pepsi ad on the cassette of *Dirty Dancing* unless Vestron, the video company, cut every scene that showed a Coca-Cola sign. Vestron passed. (All these movies have happy endings.)

PRODUCT PLACEMENT

Such subliminal tactics are certainly not peculiar to the mighty cola rivals. They are also used today—aggressively—by every other major advertiser. Indeed, cinematic product placement became so common in the eighties that it now sustains a veritable industry. Formerly plugging was a marginal (if common) practice in the movie industry, the result of direct bartering between studio and advertiser. In the eighties the plugging process became "rationalized," as dozens of companies formed to broker deals between advertisers and film producers. Usually the advertisers—and sometimes the studios themselves—keep the brokers on retainer with an annual fee; the advertisers are then charged extra for specific "placements." In return for the plug the advertiser will help defray the ever-rising costs of filmmaking, not only by providing props or costumes but often—and more important—by mounting a tie-in promotional campaign that will sell the movie in many ads, in thousands of bright aisles, on millions of clean boxes.

The arrangement seems to work wonders for the budgets of all concerned. The advertisers love it: "More and more companies now recognize that movies are an alternative advertising and promotional medium," a plugster exults. And this offer is one that financially pressed filmmakers can't refuse. "Obsessed with the bottom line, studios no longer snub promotion tie-ins—much to the delight of marketers eager to reach the last captive media audience," *Incentive* magazine reports. An executive at Walt Disney Pictures and Television says, "Add the magic of movies to a promotion, and you can rise above the clutter to get people's attention."

Always in search of the perfectly closed-off setting, advertisers have for decades been eyeing cinema, whose viewers can't flip the page or turn their chairs away. It is this interest in a captive audience that has the marketers delighting in the movies—which, now crammed with plugs, offer about as much magic as you would find at K-Mart, or at Lord & Taylor. Watching them, there is no way that you "can rise above the clutter," because they *are* "the clutter."

Consider one of Sylvester Stallone's big hits, *Rocky III*, which showcases in passing Coca-Cola, Sanyo, Nike, Wheaties, TWA, Marantz, and Wurlitzer, and—in actual ads within the film (with Rocky, now a big celebrity, as endorser)—Nikon, Harley-Davidson, Budweiser, Maserati, Gatorade, and American Express. Or consider *Over the Top*, a box-office disaster in which Stallone plays a humble trucker who, estranged from his son, must win the lad back by taking first prize in a major arm-wrestling tournament. Even before the opening credits are over, the movie has highlighted Budweiser, Colgate shaving cream, and Michelin tires; and daubed across the side of Stallone's giant rig is a huge full-color ad for Brut cologne, which shows up grandly in the film's big landscape shots. (Brut and the film's producers had a tie-in deal.) Moreover, each of the many arm wrestlers who roar and shudder at the Big Event bears the imprint of some corporate sponsor, so that the movie displays not only Hilton Hotels, TWA, Alpine car stereos, Leaseway Transportation, Nintendo—and Pepsi—but also Volvo *and* Toyota, Nike *and* Adidas, and Valvoline, Duracell, Soloflex, and AlkaSeltzer. (Both films have happy endings.)

These are two examples of Hollywood's new commercialism at its most grotesque, and there are many others—for example, the . . . 007 entry, *License to Kill*, in which James Bond ostentatiously smokes Larks, a plug for which Philip Morris paid $350,000; or *Back to the Future II*, a very loud and manic "romp" that lovingly showcases the futuristic wares of at least a dozen corporate advertisers; or *The Wizard*, a children's movie that is essentially a long commercial for Nintendo; or, in what may be (you never know) the most glaring case of rampant plugging yet, the children's movie *MAC & Me*, a shameless *E.T.* knock-off in which a handicapped child befriends an alien, MAC, who lives on Coca-Cola. (In just over a month this movie grossed $34 million.)

5. A WORD FROM OUR SPONSOR

The practice of plugging is just as obvious in movies that do not resemble comic books. Take *Bull Durham,* which begins with the cute rookie pitcher Nuke LaLoosh (Tim Robbins) on the mound, the Pepsi logo plain as day on the outfield wall behind him, its colors reproduced exactly on his uniform. As the film proceeds, it also plugs—repeatedly—Budweiser, Miller, Jim Beam, Oscar Mayer, and a host of Alberto-Culver products. (*Bull Durham* has a happy ending.) Or take *Mr. Mom,* a feeble "issue" comedy about the travails of a green house-husband, which showcases McDonald's, Domino's pizza, Terminix exterminators, Folgers coffee, Lite beer, Jack Daniels, Van Camp's chili, Ban deodorant, Windex, Tide, Spray 'n Wash, Borax, Clorox 2, and Downy fabric softener. (*Mr. Mom* has a happy ending.) Or, finally, take *Murphy's Romance,* which showcases (aside from Coke) Purina, Heinz 57 Steak Sauce, Wesson Oil, Nike, Huggies, Vanish toilet-bowl cleaner, Fuji film, and Miller beer. There are also *two* bottles of Ivory Liquid at Sally Field's kitchen sink, and at one point she asks James Garner, "Could I have two Extra-Strength Tylenol and a glass of water, please?" At another point she shouts enticingly, "Campbell's tomato soup!"

Such bald intrusions into dialogue are no longer rare. Usually the spoken plug comes in the form of a casual request: "Want a Coke?" Eliot asks E.T. "Gimme a Pepsi Free," Michael J. Fox tells the soda jerk in *Back to the Future*—and since they didn't have that choice back in 1955, the jerk's snide retort is really funny. To the advertisers, such a soft gag is ideal, especially if it quotes an established piece of copy. For instance, in *Vice Versa,* one of the late 1980s' several comedies about adults and children swapping bodies, the apparent child, in line at the school cafeteria, betrays his inner maturity in this way: "I don't suppose you have any Grey Poupon?" (All these movies have happy endings.)

TV programs, routinely interrupted by pure ads, need not themselves display the labels quite so often, or so dramatically (although they do display them). American movies nonetheless have a televisual counterpart: Brazilian soap operas, a daily spectacle in which the products play so large a role that some multinationals, among them Coca-Cola, sign annual contracts with Brazil's largest television network, TV Globo, to keep their products constantly written into the shows' ongoing "stories." Down there in Rio the practice, which the Brazilians call by the English word "merchandising," is defended just as Hollywood defends the practice here—by attesting to its powerful naturalism. "Most soap operas are about daily life in which people go shopping and drive cars and drink beer," TV Globo's head of product placement says. "That's why it is so natural."

Likewise, a Hollywood plugster argues that since films "are pushing more toward reality," plugging is imperative: "A can that says 'Beer' isn't going to make it anymore."

In a few . . . movies—the eerie satire *Heathers,* the exquisite *Drugstore Cowboy*—the subtle use of products does make the fictive milieu more believable than generic items would. Usually, however, product placement does not seem natural at all but is deliberately *anti*-realistic: its sole purpose is to enhance the product by meticulously placing it within the sort of idealized display that occurs nowhere in real life but everywhere in advertising—which is itself just such display. In the world as advertised, the label or logo always shines forth like the full moon, whereas in our world, where "people go shopping and drive cars and drink beer," the crucial symbols reach us (if at all) with none of that sudden startling clarity—for the very ubiquity of advertising has paradoxically also worked to hide it from us. To live the daily life in which people go shopping is to be bombarded into numbness; and it is this stupefaction that movie plugs, like advertising proper, have been devised to penetrate.

As such plugs are anti-realistic, so also are they anti-narrative, for the same movie-glow that exalts each product high above the clutter of the everyday also lifts it out of, and thereby makes it work against, the movie's story. Even when half turned toward us, coquettishly, or placed in some marginal position, the crucial can or box or bottle tends (as it were) to make a scene. An expert rhetorical missile in the first place, and with its force enhanced a thousandfold by advertising, the product cannot even sneak by without distracting us at least a little, its vivid, pleasant features calling, "*Hey! It's me!*"

And when shoved right into the spotlight, the product doesn't just upstage the actors but actually stops the narrative. In *Uncle Buck,* John Candy appears sitting on a sofa, holding a big box of Kellogg's Frosted Flakes at his side, as prominent and boldly hued as an armorial shield—and on that sight the camera lingers. At such a moment the loud package wipes out its co-stars and surroundings, becoming the only thing we notice. (*Uncle Buck* has a happy ending.)

The rise of product placement has, however, damaged movie narrative not only through the shattering effect of individual plugs but also—more profoundly—through the partial transfer of creative authority out of the hands of filmmaking professionals and into the purely quantitative universe of the CEOs. All the scenes, shots, and lines mentioned above represent the usurpation by advertising of those authorial prerogatives once held by directors and screenwriters, art directors and set designers—and by studio heads, who generally cared about how their films were made, whereas the managers now in charge are thinking only of their annual reports. "Hollywood has changed," says Ed Meyer, of the ad agency Saatchi & Saatchi DFS Compton. "Unlike the old days, the bankers and M.B.A.s are calling the shots."

Thus the basic decisions of filmmaking are now often made, indirectly, by the advertisers, who are focused only on a movie's usefulness for pushing products. Take the case of costume designers, who have often in the eighties been displaced by "promo-costuming"—an arrangement that, according to *Premiere* magazine, either showcases the wares of name designers (Oscar de la Renta did *Bright Lights, Big City;* Giorgio Armani did *The Untouchables*) or, more frequently, "involves manufacturers of such branded staples as jeans and sneakers, which have visible logos that make them much easier to promote." In 1987, for example, Adidas shod and clad many of the characters in some sixty movies.

The plugging process is as thorough and exacting as the work of those professionals whose skill it has long since superseded. The pre-production effort is exhaustive: "Friendly producers," the *Wall Street Journal* reports, "send scripts to [Associated Film Promotions] weeks and even months before filming starts, and the company analyzes them scene by scene to see if it can place a product—or advertising material, a billboard perhaps—on, under, or behind the stars." While the advertisers may not be as idealistic about movies as, say, David O. Selznick, they are just as dictatorial: "We choose projects where we have maximum control," says one plugster. "We break a film down and tell the producers exactly where we want to see our clients' brands."

Such subordination of the movie is essential to plugging, which is based on the assumption that the movie will in no way contradict—will, indeed, do nothing but enhance—the product's costly, all-important aura. The plug, in other words, must not just "foreground" the crucial name or image but also flatter it—that is, brightly reaffirm the product's advertising. When its brokers argue that plugging enhances realism, they are implying that reality is only where the products mean just what their advertising says they mean: "power" or "safety" or "old-fashioned goodness."

Now and then in the eighties an American movie has invoked products critically, or at least in a way that is poetically telling and not just promotional. In Garry Marshall's *Nothing in Common,* a surprisingly grim and moving (if uneven) comedy about a successful young adman (Tom Hanks) and his dying scoundrel of a father (Jackie Gleason), the same product appears in two shots—not to sell it but as a chilling metaphysical implication and a visual hint that father and son, despite their mutual loathing and antithetical lifestyles, are fundamentally alike. Placed casually in each man's kitchen—the one tidy and state-of-the-art, the other bare and slovenly—is a box of the same cereal: Life. (*Nothing in Common* does not have a happy ending.)

Such dark suggestiveness is precisely what advertisers do not want, and so they, or their brokers, will back away from any movie that might somehow cast a shadow on their advertising. For advertisers are obsessed not just with selling their own specific images but also with universalizing the whole hermetic ambience for selling itself—the pseudo-festive, mildly jolting, ultimately tranquilizing atmosphere of TV and its bright epiphenomena, the theme park and the shopping mall.

CROSSOVERS

Even if, armed with some marvelous zapping gizmo, you could sit and blast away every obvious product as it passed through the frame or glowed in close-up, today's Hollywood movie would still seem like an ad. This is in part because movies now tend to look and sound a lot like TV commercials, as if the major film schools were teaching not, say, the best movies out of Warner Brothers but the latest campaign by the Saatchi brothers. Like ads, movies now tend to have a perfectly coordinated total look, as if they'd been designed rather than directed—a tendency so marked, in some cases, that the movie and some well-known ad can hardly be distinguished. Thus *The Color Purple,* with its lush score, hazy golden images, and long climactic round of teary hugs, leaves you thinking not that you should read the novel but that you really ought to call your mother ("Reach out—"), while the parodic *Raising Arizona* uses precisely the same wide-angle distortion and hyped-up, deadpan acting that Joe Sedelmaier used in his famous ads for Federal Express ("When it abso*lute*ly, posi*tively*—"), while *Top Gun,* the blockbuster salute to navy fliers, is in its action sequences identical to those spectacular commercials that allured the young with "It's Not Just a Job: It's an Adventure!" or (yes!) "Be All You Can Be!"—expert recruitment propaganda that was probably well known to the film's director, Tony Scott, who came to the movie business as a famed director of TV ads, most notably for Diet Pepsi. (These three movies leave you feeling good.)

Such crossovers are the usual thing in today's media industry, many of whose filmmakers learned their craft (and continue to work) in TV advertising. Ten years ago a stellar group of such professionals migrated from the ad shops of London to the studios of Hollywood, where they helped to alter modern cinema. Like his brother Tony (who, the year after *Top Gun,* directed the repetitious *Beverly Hills Cop 2*), Ridley Scott is a

5. A WORD FROM OUR SPONSOR

prolific ad-maker, most notably for Chanel, W. R. Grace, and Apple Computer. He is also the auteur of the inspired and nauseating *Alien;* the brilliant *Blade Runner;* a thriller designed, as if by computer, to stroke lonely women, *Someone to Watch over Me;* and finally the unforgivable *Black Rain.* The ad-maker Hugh Hudson has turned out such gorgeous, empty films as *Chariots of Fire* and *Greystoke: The Legend of Tarzan, Lord of the Apes.* Having made hundreds of short ads, Adrian Lyne came to Hollywood and made such ad-like films as *Flashdance, 9-1/2 Weeks,* and also the gynophobic crowd-pleaser *Fatal Attraction.* Alan Parker, whose films include *Midnight Express, Fame,* and *Mississippi Burning,* is easily the most successful of the British émigrés, because the most adept at stirring our worst impulses. Many American ad-makers have also become filmmakers, including Stan Dragoti, the director of the "I Love New York" ads and the plug-ridden *Mr. Mom;* Howard Zieff, the director of Alka-Seltzer's "Spicy Meatball" ad and the incoherent *Private Benjamin;* and Joe Pytka, the director of numerous Pepsi ads and the deadly racetrack comedy *Let It Ride.*

Meanwhile, as more and more admen direct films, more and more filmmakers are directing television ads—simply in order to keep working, now that the huge costs of moviemaking have made it nearly impossible to get a project going. Directors can no longer afford to scorn the sixty-second pitch: "There *was* a stigma in the past," Jerry Bernstein, the head of the Association of Independent Commercial Producers, observed in 1988. "The feeling was [that the ad] was not a great art form." That feeling is passé, if not extinct, now that Robert Altman, Martin Scorsese (Armani), Federico Fellini, Jean-Luc Godard, Francis Ford Coppola (Fuji), John Frankenheimer, John Badham, Tony Bill (Bud Light), John Schlesinger, David Lynch, Penny Marshall (Revlon), David Steinberg, Stephen Frears, and Errol Morris (7-Eleven), among others, are making ads. Cinematographers, too, have turned to advertising: Sven Nykvist, Nestor Almendros, Gordon Willis, Eric Saarinen, and Vilmos Zsigmond, among others. And filmmakers have even been doing celebrity turns in ads: Richard Donner for Amaretto di Saronno, George Lucas for Panasonic (in Japan), Bernardo Bertolucci for Pioneer, Spike Lee for the Gap, and for Nike (which he plugs throughout his movies) in a commercial that he also directed.

If movies look like ads, then, the transformation may owe something to this exchange of personnel—which delights the powers of advertising, who want their ads to look like movies (so that the restless TV viewer won't zap them). "Advertisers and agencies want their commercials designed with the look of the hottest features," one ad producer says. Crossovers have helped erase the old distinctions between movies and commercials: "The two disciplines—feature films and commercial films—have blended together to the point now where it's just filmmaking," says a senior vice-president at the ad agency DDB Needham, in Chicago. It might seem that through this convergence each "discipline" would somehow benefit the other—but in the era of the VCR it is advertising that has affected cinema, and not the other way around. Now that most movies are produced with an eye toward their eventual re-release on videocassette for the home audience, and now that TV, moreover, has induced a universal taste for TV's pace and tone, the new "filmmaking" takes its lead primarily from those who create the small screen's most hypnotic images. "There's not a good filmmaker alive who doesn't look to us for inspiration," Bob Giraldi, the director of ad spots for GE, Sperry Rand, McDonald's, Miller Lite, and many other corporations, claimed in 1984.

GRABBERS

Just as the product plug halts or weakens the movie narrative, so has this general drift toward ad technique drastically reduced the movies' narrative potential, for cinematic narrative works through a range of visual conventions or devices, and the recent rise of ad technique has all but wiped out that earlier diversity, coarsening a various and nuanced form into a poundingly hypnotic instrument—a mere *stimulus,* and an ugly one at that.

There is, first, the all-important difference in scale. "This is just like doing a small feature," Ridley Scott assured his crew on the set of a Pepsi ad in 1984. "I see commercials as short films," Adrian Lyne told *Advertising Age* in 1985. But to suggest that commercials are just like movies, only smaller (in both space and time), is to negate the crucial ground of cinematic art: an expansive visual field, broad enough to imply a world beyond, behind, more varied than, the glamorous item in midframe. TV is, to say the least, different. Watching *The Last Emperor* on your set is like trying to survey the Sistine Chapel ceiling by peeping at it through a toilet-paper roll. TV, however, has reduced the movies not just by putting blinders on the viewers of wide-screen epics but also by establishing a compositional norm of close-ups, two-shots, and other setups whereby the action is (just as in advertising) repetitiously *foregrounded.*

Such is now the norm of cinema. Today there are few scenes shot in deep focus (as in Renoir and Welles, *Vertigo* and *The Godfather Part II,* or, for that matter, *The Night of the Living Dead*). Likewise, we rarely see the kind of panoramic composition that once allowed a generous impression of quasi-global simultaneity, as (most elaborately) in the movies of Robert Altman and Jacques Tati, and that also, more subtly, enriches the frame in most great movies, whose makers have offered *pictures,* composed of pleasurable "touches" and legible detail. These moving tableaux often, as André Bazin argued, gave their viewers some choice, and required some (often minimal) interpretive attention. Only now and then, and in films that don't come out of Hollywood—Terry Gilliam's *Brazil,* Stanley Kubrick's *Full Metal Jacket*—do we perceive such exhilarating fullness. In contrast, today's American movies work without, or against, the potential depth and latitude of cinema, in favor of that systematic overemphasis deployed in advertising and all other propaganda. Each shot presents a content closed and unified, like a fist, and makes the point right in your face: big gun, big car, nice ass, full moon, a chase (great shoes!), big crash (blood, glass), a lobby (doorman), sarcasm, drinks, a tonguey, pugilistic kiss (nice sheets!), and so on.

Thus today's movie not only foregrounds but also serializes, for just as TV's narrowness has superannuated deep focus and the movies' (sometime) lateral complexity, so has the speedy pace of TV's ads superannuated most of cinema's earlier transitional devices. As John Frankenheimer (*The Manchurian Candidate,* Fiat, AT&T) told *Advertising Age* in 1988, "No longer do films use the fade to black and the slow dissolve the way they used to." This laconic, and correct, observation hints at a grievous cinematic loss, because the fade and the dissolve are no quaint old movie mannerisms. Rather, the dissolve is a succinct and often beautiful means of conveying the passage of time or the onset of a memory; although it has no exact linguistic counterpart, to drop it from the movies would be somewhat like dropping the past tense from verbal language. The fade to black works like a curtain to cover some event too painful or intimate for exhibition, or as a means of conveying loss of consciousness, or as a somber sort of visual cadence, a way of saying, "It's over: now consider what you've seen." In today's ad-saturated "filmmaking" these devices not only seem too slow but are, in different ways, too suggestive of mortality for the movies' bright mall atmosphere, and so they have been dumped in favor of that most basic of connectives, the simple cut, the overuse of which has helped transform the movies into ad-like serial displays.

Such displays show us nothing—not only because each image in the series is as unambiguous as a brand-new belt but also because the serial rush itself is mesmerizing, and so it blinds us to the flashing items that compose it. Large, stark, and fast, the mere contrast stuns us pleasantly—a response that is, as it were, subvisual, as the ad-makers know very well. Thus both marketing and advertising always aim directly at the lowest levels of the mass (that is, your) brain, seeking a reaction that is not just "positive" but unconscious and immediate. Although the pillars of the ad world still use the word "persuasion" to (mis)represent their business, the whole selling project now depends on moves that are less rhetorical than neurological. "Color goes immediately to the psyche and can be a direct sales stimulus," one typical package designer says. Such blithe and simplistic Pavlovianism is wholly characteristic of the admakers and marketers, who like it when we respond without even knowing it, much less knowing why. Thus Philip Dusenberry, of the ad agency BBDO, in New York, claims to have learned (from making Pepsi ads) "that it wasn't important that the viewer read every scene—just that they get the impact of the message."

That last remark could as easily apply to the movies, which now, like advertising, rely heavily if not exclusively on techniques that work directly on the nervous system. Of course, the movies have always used gratuitous tricks to keep viewers riveted: pointless close-ups of a baby's smile to get the women cooing, martial music to tense up the men, sad violins to get the whole house sniffling. Indeed, some of cinema's basic rhetorical devices, it could be argued, are inherently non-narrative, subvisual: crosscutting for suspense, say, or the weepy reaction shot (which moves the viewers to weep). The point, however, is not that such tricks are new but that they are now all-important—for their power has been fantastically augmented by computer science, Dolby sound, great strides forward in the art of mock mayhem, and other technological advances.

Music, for example, has long been overused by Hollywood, as James Agee noted in 1945. Watching John Huston's war documentary *San Pietro,* which he admired immensely, Agee found it "as infuriating to have to fight off the emotional sales pressure of the Mormon Choir as it would be if all the honored watches and nasal aphrodisiacs insisted on marketing themselves against a Toscanini broadcast." At its pushiest, movie music "weakens the emotional imagination both of maker and onlooker, and makes it virtually impossible to communicate or receive ideas. It sells too cheaply and far too sensually all the things it is the business of the screen itself to present."

Watching the movies that Agee found overscored, most people now would probably agree with him, since the aesthetic errors of the past are easy to laugh at decades later. What may be less obvious today is the persistent relevance of Agee's argument, for the movies have, as visual events, been largely devastated by their "music"—a vast and irresistible barrage of synthesized sound, a hyper-rhythmic full-body stimulus far more effective, and a whole lot louder, than the old choral

5. A WORD FROM OUR SPONSOR

yawpings or symphonic sweeps that now seem so corny. Starting somewhere out there and back to the left, the "music" thrums and zooms and jumps and jangles right on through you, clearing out your head with such efficiency that not only is it impossible to receive ideas but the whole movie, once over, seems to have gone in one ear and out the other—except that it's not just your head that has functioned as a throughway but every vital organ.

It is the Dolby system, sometimes enhanced by George Lucas's more recent THX Sound System, that gives the music such prostrating force. Even on cassette, however, the music works an antivisual effect (just as it does throughout TV's shows and ads), imposing an upbeat mood on images that are, per se, so mundane that they would bore or even depress you if the music weren't there telling you to dance. In *St. Elmo's Fire,* Emilio Estevez drives off in a car, and the music makes it sound as if he's just won gold at the Olympics. At the end of *Private Benjamin,* Goldie Hawn walks down a lonely road, and the score exults as if she were attending her own coronation. (Both those movies have happy endings.)

More and more, the movies' very images are also—paradoxically—nonvisual, because, like the music, they try to force our interest or reaction through a visceral jolt that stuns the mind and shuts the eyes. Some of the movies' latest grabbers are very old, like the gooey close-up of some wondering baby ("Awwww!"), a device no less sickening in *Ghostbusters II* (1989) than it was in *Bachelor Daddy* (1941). Generally, however, the latest grabbers are more technologically sophisticated and (a lot) more violent than those sentimental moments—and far more commonplace, now that movie narrative has been supplanted by such blinding jabs.

As special effects have since *Star Wars* become more mind-blowing and yet more believable, they have also grown more important to the spectacle—and have changed in tone. In many instances the effects now *are* the movie, whether it's *Indiana Jones and the Last Crusade* or *A Nightmare on Elm Street 3,* films you can sleep through for twenty minutes without then having to ask, "What did I miss?" And as the effects have become the whole show, they have ceased to represent some ambiguous looming force, uncanny or apocalyptic—as they did in the first *King Kong, The Day the Earth Stood Still,* and *2001: A Space Odyssey*—and have instead become the tools for a light show that both stimulates and reassures, like fireworks on the Fourth.

In other words, whereas the effects were once used by and large to fake some scary threat to all humanity, they now routinely fake, in one way or another, someone's annihilation—and it is *good.*

The wipe-out might be violent, as at the end of *Raiders of the Lost Ark,* when the Nazis are melted down or shriveled up by the wrathful ark light, or as in the horror movies, where, say, Jason burns, zaps, and mangles several teens, until some teen burns or zaps or mangles Jason. Whether the killing force is righteous or demonic, the spectacle of its, his, or her destructiveness or destruction invites your rapt gaze of wondering assent, just like those movies that present the wipeout as a sweet translation into outer space (that is, heaven): *E.T., Close Encounters of the Third Kind, Cocoon, Cocoon: The Return*—films whose (grateful) characters finally disappear into the all-important light show, just like the films themselves.

For all their visual sophistication, these effects are meant to move us beyond, or back from, visual experience, by either having us nearly *feel* those razors rake that throat or having us *feel* as if we, too, were dissolving in a celestial bath of light. The same kind of experience—antivisual, non-narrative—is commonplace even in films that have no supernatural or "alien" component. In the eighties the car chase, for instance, became the movies' main story substitute, offering the illusion of dreamlike forward speed and the gratifying sight, sound, and feeling of machinery bucking, squealing, blowing up—elements that have become so frequent that to catalogue them here would fill a page, since they compose whole sections not only of the cop films (*The Presidio, Cobra,* and two *Lethal Weapons,* the two *Beverly Hills Cops, Red Heat*) but also of many comedies, even ones that didn't need such filler (*Midnight Run, The Blues Brothers, Throw Momma from the Train*). The pleasure here is not visual but physically empathic—the centrifugal tug, that pleasing *crash!*: mock thrills that have only gotten punchier and more elaborate as the car stuff has become routine. Likewise, screen violence in general, a relentless story substitute, has become both commonplace and often horribly sadistic. (The movies named in the above two paragraphs all have happy endings.)

THE IMPERATIVE OF VIOLENCE

The empathic function of today's screen violence has changed the character of movie heroics. In *Bullitt* (1968) and *The French Connection* (1971), in *The Searchers* (1956), and in the movies of Sam Peckinpah, the violence, however graphic, was muted by a deep ambivalence that shadowed even the most righteous-seeming acts of vengeance, and that therefore suppressed the viewer's urge to join in kicking. In contrast, screen violence now is used primarily to invite the viewer to enjoy the *feel* of killing, beating, mutilating. This is most obvious in the slasher films, in which the camera takes the stalking murderer's point of view, but the same empathic project goes on throughout the genres. There is no point to Rambo's long climactic rage, or Cobra's, or Chuck Norris's, other than its open invitation to *become him* at that moment—to ape that sneer of hate, to feel the way it feels to stand there tensed up with the Uzi. The hero's inner kinship with the villain used to seem uncanny, as in Hitchcock's and Fritz Lang's movies, and in Clint Eastwood's excellent *Tightrope*—whereas Stallone's Cobra gets a charge out of being *exactly* like the psychopaths he chases, just as we are meant to feel *exactly* like him.

Moreover, it is not just the overt paeans to machismo that thus incite us but also films that seem politically unlike, say, *Rambo III*—and like *Mississippi Burning*. Hailed for having a plot based on a key event in the history of the civil rights movement, it actually has no plot, nor is it even slightly faithful to that history. The movie is, in fact, nothing more than one long grabber. After an hour of watching white trash inflict atrocities on helpless blacks (and a nice white woman), we watch the kick-ass Gene Hackman argue hotly with his FBI superior, the tight-assed Willem Dafoe, who has from the outset rebutted Hackman's vigilantist urgings with the boring creed of rules and regulations. They fight at length (shouts, punches; a gun is even pulled)—and then, suddenly, Dafoe just up and *changes*: "New rules. We nail 'em any way we can. Even your way." This absolute reversal, although absurd in terms of character, makes sense rhetorically, since it's now time to have the three of us (audience, Dafoe, Hackman) all fold into Hackman, who is thereby freed to punish all those ugly rednecks in the ugliest of ways—crushing their testicles, threatening them with castration, maiming them with straight razors, and otherwise permitting "us" to act, through him, just like the Klansmen we presumably detest, while the blacks remain helpless throughout. (*Mississippi Burning* has a happy ending.)

Over and over, conventional narrative requirements are broken down by the imperative of violence—which need not be inflicted by "us," through the movie's hero, but is just as often used *against* us, by the movie's anti-hero, for what matters above all, it seems, is that we feel the stimulus. Thus we are victimized by the "sight" of the vampires in *The Lost Boys* biting off bright red gobbets of their victims' heads ("Ow!"), and by the sight and sound of the good guy having his fingers broken (*Blade Runner, Blue Thunder*) or receiving a ballistic kick between the legs (*Shoot the Moon, Black Moon Rising*). Likewise, the movies now more than ever shock us with the old nonvisual trick of going "Boo!"—a crude startler once used mainly in horror films but now recurring in thriller after thriller (and often heightened by the deep "*lub*-dub-*lub*-dub" that stimulates your fearful heartbeat).

The primacy of stimulation has, in short, made the movies increasingly cartoonlike. In the cartoon world nothing stands between the wish to look at violence and the enactment of that violence: no demands of plot or character, no physical limitations (space, gravity), no mortality. Ingeniously, and with cruel wit, the cartoon presents a universe wherein the predatory are punished again and again for their appetite by the very hills and trees, the doors and crockery. Full of rage and purpose, those victim-predators get nowhere, and yet never die, pushing on forever, despite the anvils falling on their heads, the steamrollers flattening their bodies out like giant pancakes, the cannonballs caroming down their throats—torments at once severe and harmless, and which occur exclusively because we want to see them happen.

It is not just *Batman* and *Who Framed Roger Rabbit* that invoke the cartoon but all those movies that present a universe wherein the stimulus is gross, never-ending, and immediate, the human "characters" appearing just as easily tormentable, and yet (usually) as indestructible, as Wile E. Coyote or Yosemite Sam. Thus *Lethal Weapon II*, which begins with the old Looney Tunes theme playing over the familiar Warner Brothers logo, includes several scenes in which Mel Gibson casually brutalizes Joe Pesci—squeezing his badly injured nose, for instance. And thus in *Dragnet*, as a car runs over Dan Ackroyd's feet there is a sound as of the crushing of a bag of walnuts, and Ackroyd pales and winces. And thus Jason, although dead, keeps coming back to life, like Freddy Kreuger, like Michael Myers, and, for that matter, like the dead ballplayers in *Field of Dreams*, like the vanished old folks in *Cocoon: The Return*, like the dead E.T.—all of them coming back forever and ever, because the cartoon always has a happy ending.

SURPLUS WISH FULFILLMENT

The convergence of the movies with both ads and cartoons makes sense, because the ad and the cartoon each present a fantasy of perfect wish fulfillment: that is, wish fulfillment that seems both immediate and absolute, arising, on the one hand, from a purchase (which will make life perfect *now*) or, on the other hand, from the animated spectacle itself (in which the universe appears responsive to one's wishes). This effect has been compounded in the movies, which now purvey a wish-fulfillment fantasy as extreme as, and far more compelling than, any Coke spot or Tom and Jerry free-for-all.

Your Show of Shills

Think there are too many ads on TV? The networks don't, so they're sticking them in programs too.

LESLIE SAVAN

What were those hokey dancing taco-and-bell doing on the premiere of Dana Carvey's new comedy show two weeks ago—was this a plug or a parody of lead sponsor Taco Bell? It was hard to tell as the fast-food duo sang, "We're paying him a fortune to use our name, 'cause he's a shameless whore!"

In fact, this was an odd TV moment when parody and plug became one. *The Taco Bell Dana Carvey Show* was intended to be an ironic resurrection of 1950s-style brand-name TV shows like *The Lux Video Theatre* or *The U.S. Steel Hour*. The deal originally struck between ABC and Pepsico, Taco Bell's parent company, was that each week a different member of the Pepsi family would serve as "both title and target" for Carvey's wry satire, positioning the sponsor as quite the cool dude for rope-a-doping a few edgy punches.

But maybe it sounded better on paper. Taco Bell pulled out of future Carvey shows the day after the premiere, though the company wouldn't say whether it objected to the ribald skits (which included a prosthetically enhanced President Clinton breast-feeding animals) or the darts aimed at the ad business. ABC quickly promised to tame the show, and Pepsico decided to limit sponsorship to its less familiar, more attitude-seeking brands, and thus was born last week's somewhat safer episode, *The Mug Root Beer Dana Carvey Show*.

Whatever its fate (or name), the Carvey show illustrates the increasingly blurred line between programming and ads on network television. Of course, the ad-driven medium has never been a pristine art form, its practitioners not generally averse to bending over backward to please sponsors. But lately, advertising's osmotic bleed into entertainment has turned into an arterial gush. *Murphy Brown* wrote John F. Kennedy Jr. into a script so he could promote his magazine, *George*; Diet Coke hired the writers and producers of *Friends* to create a mini episode-cum-ad starring the entire cast; and, most famously, Elizabeth Taylor spritzed her way through four CBS sitcoms in a single night last month—including *Murphy Brown*, again—to push her new fragrance, Black Pearls.

No network has indulged more aggressively in this kind of stunt than Fox. As part of a complex $1 million package deal last fall that included a viewer contest, Fox had a character on its *Party of Five* ask, "Got milk?"—the tag line for the multimillion-dollar America's Dairy Farmers' ad campaign. In a similar marketing scheme, Dr. Dre spouted AT&T's "Know the code" on *New York Undercover*. The upcoming Mother's Day episode of *Living Single* will top that for MCI when a character calls mom by dialing 1-800-COLLECT. "Whatever we do, we try to look for a natural integration with a show," says Fox senior vice president Doug Binzak. "Our main concern is to make sure viewers don't feel everything is over commercialized."

Viewers, however, may no longer know what it means to be overly commercial. Polaroid has gone so far as to buy ads within ads, sponsoring the networks' own promotional trailers. Recent spots for upcoming shows—from Fox's *Melrose Place* to this Thursday's entire NBC lineup—begin and end with the new Polaroid slogan, "See what develops," and the company's logo. Meanwhile, some of the world's largest advertisers are simply starting up their own sitcoms. In a partnership with Paramount TV, Procter & Gamble is now airing *Home Court* on NBC and, on CBS, *Almost Perfect* and *Good Company*. The latter show is set at an ad agency where copywriters spent most of one episode ridiculing a "toilet paper with baking soda"—a product actually sold by P&G rival Scott Paper. While P&G also owns several long-running daytime soap operas, the baking soda gibe is the sort of "product message" (a.k.a. advertisement) that gains mileage and legitimacy when slipped sub rosa into a prime-time showcase. (P&G swears that all creative decisions are Paramount's.)

The phenomenon of sponsor-owned shows in the 1950s began to fade when advertisers realized they could better reach a target market by spreading their ad budget across many shows rather than by socking it into one. But that's not so easy in a world of 500 channels and ever more "new media" outlets. "There's more competition in the marketplace," says Cheryl Kroyer, director of media services at Polaroid's ad agency, Goodby, Silverstein & Partners. So advertisers who can afford it are going back to sheer, unavoidable visibility—and there are few things more visible than the Church Lady dancing with a life-size taco. Kroyer notes that the networks have powerful economic reasons for getting ever cozier with advertisers. "With more networks and TV channels chasing the same dollars, [TV executives] are willing to give more than just basic air time for 30–sec. ads."

Do the writers, actors and producers who must do their sponsors' bidding feel used? Not necessarily. Carvey says the parody-as-plug idea was his. "It was just kind of boring to call it *The Dana Carvey Show*, he says. "The idea came off of sports shows like the Doritos Cotton Bowl." Actually, it was the Mobil Cotton Bowl, so maybe in-show product placement isn't as effective as advertisers hope. At any rate, Carvey isn't quite the "whore" his show alleges. Though Pepsico pays ABC extra for the special treatment, "if they were paying me more, I wouldn't do it," Carvey says, adding that he okayed the deal only after Pepsico "agreed to have no input into the show."

After winning its Tuesday-night time slot on its first outing, Carvey's show slipped to third place last week—though he still scored No. 1 with the coveted market of men ages 18 to 49. Many of them are in that key demographic group that likes to think of itself as ad resistant. But for these cynics with disposable income, advertisers have been devising below-the-radar approaches for years, come-ons that are harder to detect and resist than dancing tacos or Liz galumphing through *The Nanny*. These are all the rebel ads and anti-ad ads of recent vintage, from former "underground" beat poet/heroin addict William Burroughs flacking for Nike to Sprite's "Image Is Nothing" campaign that attacks advertising as a bunch of lies; from the spot that insists buying an Audi is "a declaration which screams out 'I will not wallow in conformity' " to the bad-boy "Do the Dew" ads for Mountain Dew. These ads are aimed squarely at Carvey's "counter-cultural" audience, as he's called it—not coincidentally, Mountain Dew is his next title sponsor. Rather than spoof an advertising form that really doesn't exist anymore, Carvey might find more stinging satiric subject matter in ads that shamelessly flatter his audience, telling them they're too hip to be sold to.

Wouldn't that be special?

Why Won't Television Grow Up?

> **SUMMARY**
>
> The big broadcast networks are controlled by a conspiracy, say the authors. While their executives scramble to reach shrinking youth markets, they ignore a growing number of experienced, affluent, older consumers. The execs are blinded by outdated thinking, skewed statistics, and their own youth. Selling to maturity will require big changes in the networks, but it has to happen—and here's how to do it.

Vicki Thomas and David B. Wolfe

Vicki Thomas is president of Thomas & Partners in Westport, Connecticut, a promotional agency specializing in mid-life markets. David B. Wolfe heads the Wolfe Resources Group of Reston, Virginia, and is a frequent contributor to American Demographics.

America's aging population fills the hearts of business leaders with optimism and fear. Marketers and CEOs are challenged by the opportunities that arise from this huge shift in U.S. consumer markets, and they fear that appealing to older consumers will make their products less attractive to younger consumers.

The anxiety surrounding this trend may be most acute in network television. To put it bluntly, many network executives don't like the fact that their audiences are growing older by the day. Neither do their advertisers. As a result, programs and advertisements that appeal to a huge audience of mature viewers are often viewed as unimportant. ABC, for example, has had tremendous success with television magazine shows like "Primetime Live" and "20/20." But one ABC executive believes that these shows have a weakness because they are so popular with people over age 50. "We've got to figure out how to make this format more appealing to younger viewers," he says.

Americans aged 45 and older are the largest television audience. They have and spend more money than all other adults combined. The demographic tides are flowing in their direction, and the result will be decades of growth. Yet the networks are obsessed with pleasing young adults, for two reasons. First, advertisers are still willing to pay a premium to reach this less affluent and shrinking group. The second reason is attitudinal: when network executives look at aging audiences, they see nothing but problems.

Why are networks and their advertisers so reluctant to come to terms with an aging U.S. population? Some say the youth of copywriters, commercial directors, and media buyers is at the heart of the matter. Others fault ad-agency clients who still insist on youthful images for their commercials and the shows they support. But whatever the reasons, the results are the same. Networks and their advertisers have a huge blind spot whenever they look toward the future.

A CONSPIRACY AGAINST AGE

We recently interviewed executives with 20 of the top 100 television advertisers, along with a number of their agencies, to find out their attitudes toward advertising and an aging population. We found that

31. Why Won't Television Grow Up?

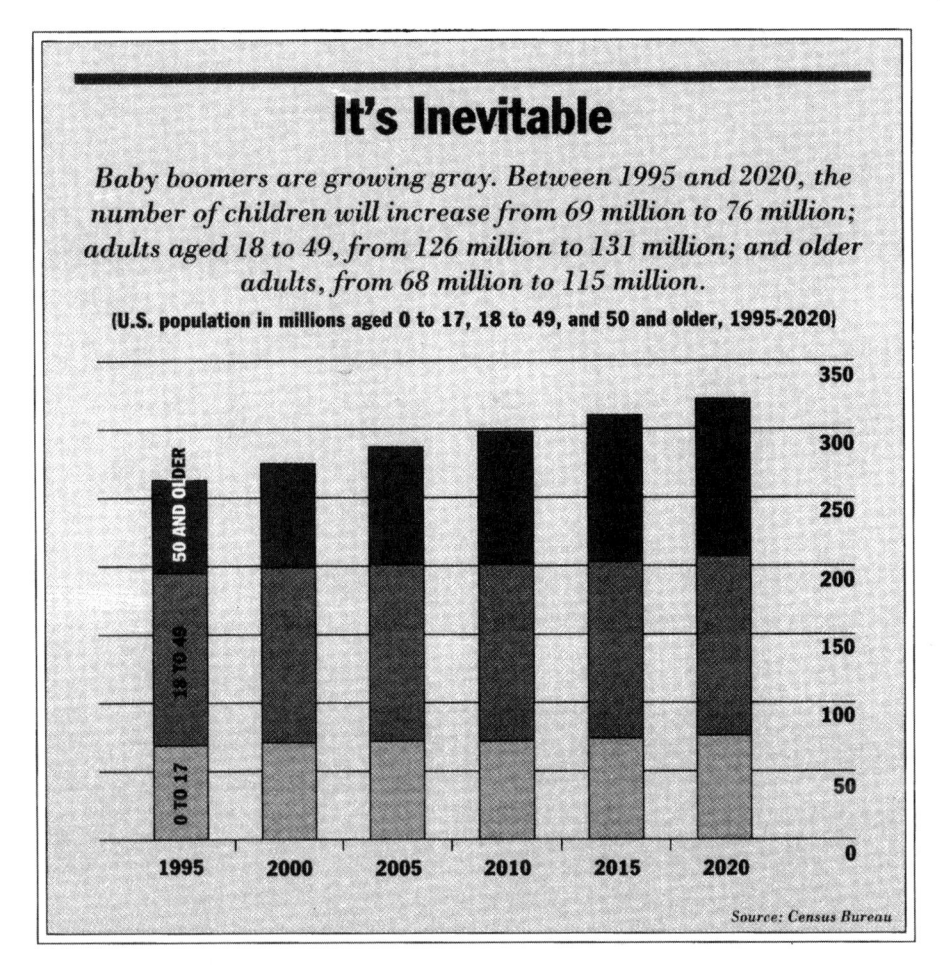

It's Inevitable

Baby boomers are growing gray. Between 1995 and 2020, the number of children will increase from 69 million to 76 million; adults aged 18 to 49, from 126 million to 131 million; and older adults, from 68 million to 115 million.

(U.S. population in millions aged 0 to 17, 18 to 49, and 50 and older, 1995-2020)

Source: Census Bureau

both groups share the responsibility for TV's anti-age bias. Slightly more than half of our interview subjects said that target audiences are primarily determined by advertisers. A significant minority said that the targeting decisions are joint efforts between advertisers and ad agencies.

We also found evidence that relatively few media or advertising executives have had any first-hand experience with aging. In our survey, the average age of advertisers' representatives was 31, and the average age of agency representatives was 28. Their youth sends subtle but powerful messages to older people. A 57-year-old marketer at ABC recently attended a meeting with 30 people from a major ad agency. By his reckoning, all but two of them were in their 20s. He remembers thinking, "How many of these people know anything about my age group and can relate to me in any meaningful way? To them, I am ancient. They think I'm not important as a consumer."

Another problem is that few of these young decision-makers are knowledgeable about demographic trends. When we asked our sample of major advertisers and agency people to name the median age of U.S. adults, one-fifth said 35 and half of them said 39. Only two respondents had the right answer.

The median age of U.S. adults (18 and older) is 41.3, and it will be 49 in about 25 years. Moreover, the 18-to-49 age group will not experience significant growth in the next 25 years. Yet the 50-plus group is projected to increase more than 60 percent by 2020.

The broadcast industry's ignorance about aging may stem from the way it chooses to receive its information. To find out about their markets, television advertisers and agencies must rely on Nielsen ratings, which are the only comprehensive source of information about television audiences. But in markets where older adults are a potent and growing force, the standard Nielsen numbers do not adequately describe viewers or their buying habits.

Nielsen data typically describe television audiences by their age. Roger Morrison, director of media at Eastman-Kodak, would rather have them described by their stages of life. Morrison believes that an empty-nest householder will spend differently than will a parent with a teenager, and that the age of each householder is less important than the householder's stage of life. A few years ago, he asked Nielsen to produce audience estimates based on life stage. The company responded by doing a series of special tabulations, but Morrison was dissatisfied because he could not use the data in his everyday decision-making.

The current ratings system "is like being back in the horse and buggy days," says Morrison. "With all of today's technology, we should be doing a lot better." Several network-sponsored efforts to improve the ratings system have been attempted, but these have always fizzled out.

SKEWED STATISTICS

Households headed by someone aged 45 to 54 have the highest per-household spending of any age group, according to the Bureau of Labor Statistics' Consumer Expenditure Survey (CE). Those aged 55 to 64 have the highest per-capita spending. And householders aged 65 to 74 have a high percentage of total income that is discretionary. In other words, the most lucrative markets of the 1990s consist of people aged 45 and older. But if you want to learn about older Americans' television viewing habits, the standard Nielsen reports won't help you. They only report aggregate viewing of all persons aged 50 and older.

The networks are under great pressure from advertisers to boost their young-adult audience ratings and play down their older audiences. The result is skewed statistics and a long-term erosion in the usefulness of Nielsen data.

Last year, NBC executives happily reported that the show "seaQuest DSV" was succeeding because it ranked highly in a measure based on "viewers per

5. A WORD FROM OUR SPONSOR

viewing household." As a result, NBC was able to charge premium rates for a show that was experiencing a decline in total audience ratings. Nielsen statistics showed that "seaQuest" ranked 60th in total audience. In contrast, a show with a loyal but older following, "Murder, She Wrote," ranked 7th. But buying a 30-second ad on "seaQuest" cost $101,000. Thirty seconds on "Murder, She Wrote" —which appeared in the same time slot—cost $75,000.

"Viewers per viewing household" refers to the number of viewers in specific age groups in a show's total audience. "SeaQuest" cost more than "Murder, She Wrote" because it performed better in the 18-to-49 age group. For every 100 households tuned to "seaQuest," 106 people aged 18 to 49 were watching. For every 100 households tuned to "Murder, She Wrote," only 42 young adults were watching.

The logic of this system is straightforward. "There is more competition among advertisers for younger viewers, so that runs up the air-time charges for shows that are popular with them," according to one advertiser. "Because older people watch more television, we can have them any time."

True, younger viewers are harder to reach with television. But should advertisers pay a premium to get their attention? In the 1990s, the most desirable audiences don't watch shows like "seaQuest." Media buyers could serve their clients better by estimating the total sales they could register by advertising on a particular TV program. Using this measure, "Murder, She Wrote" would clearly beat "seaQuest" in virtually all product categories, with the possible exceptions of motorcycles and beer.

The current situation in network advertising brings to mind the story of the emperor whose nakedness went unchallenged until someone was brave enough to point it out. The vast majority of industry executives we interviewed said that once a product is targeted at a particular demographic segment, that segment will generally remain its target for the life of the product. Some respondents added that consumers change so slowly that there is no point in frequently re-examining target markets. And while many respondents agreed that the Nielsen ratings need an overhaul, most believe the industry has no alternative to using what Neilsen gives them.

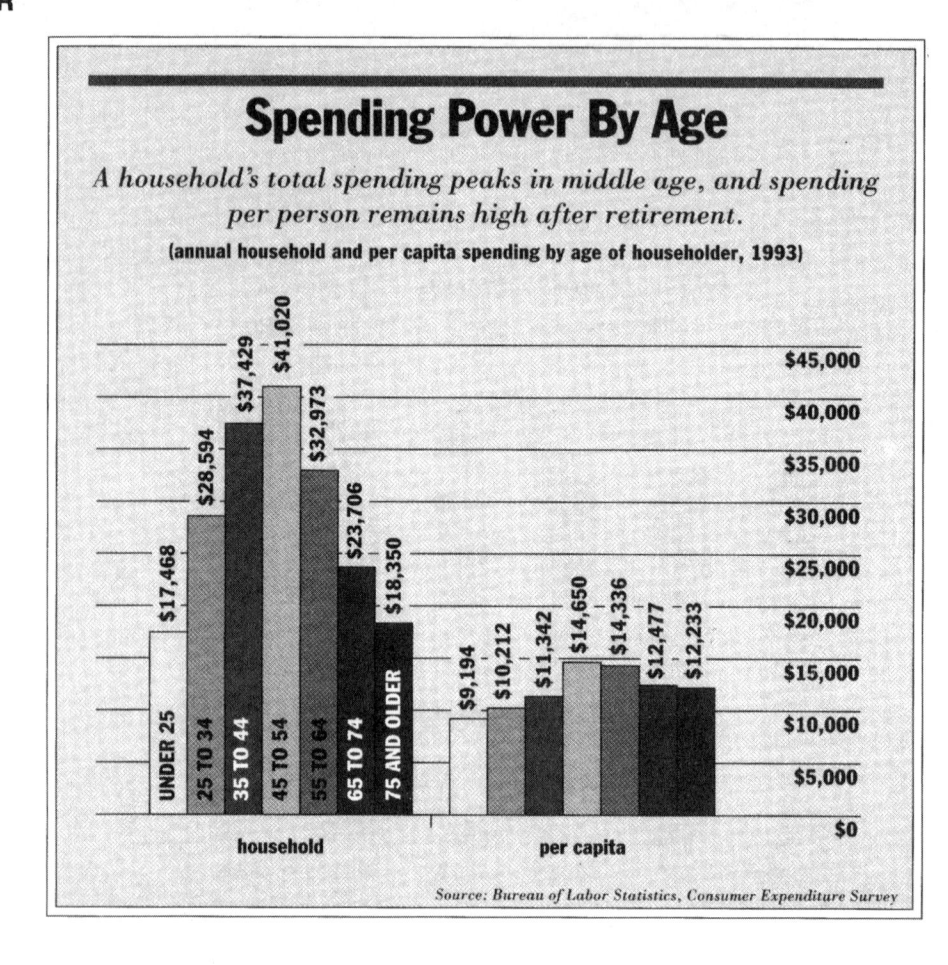

These attitudes are cop-outs. An aging population is changing consumers in fundamental ways, making it necessary to re-evaluate one's target markets regularly. Moreover, any data provider, including Nielsen, will collect and sell data in the manner demanded by its subscribers. In fact, the life-cycle segmentation Nielsen created for Kodak is still available to anyone who wants to buy it, along with a wide variety of demographic and lifestyle segmentations. But according to Clay Herrick, eastern regional manager for Nielsen Media Research in New York City, few clients are interested in the life-cycle product.

Spending Power By Age

A household's total spending peaks in middle age, and spending per person remains high after retirement.

(annual household and per capita spending by age of householder, 1993)

household
- UNDER 25: $17,468
- 25 TO 34: $28,594
- 35 TO 44: $37,429
- 45 TO 54: $41,020
- 55 TO 64: $32,973
- 65 TO 74: $23,706
- 75 AND OLDER: $18,350

per capita
- UNDER 25: $9,194
- 25 TO 34: $10,212
- 35 TO 44: $11,342
- 45 TO 54: $14,650
- 55 TO 64: $14,336
- 65 TO 74: $12,477
- 75 AND OLDER: $12,233

Source: Bureau of Labor Statistics, Consumer Expenditure Survey

EXPERIENCED CONSUMERS

Advertisers are fond of repeating the adage that half of their budget is wasted, but they don't know which half. Perhaps they should find out. It's time for advertisers to stop targeting shrinking markets and start following the growth markets. It's time for them to stop using meaningless age distinctions and switch to more meaningful life-cycle distinctions.

Networks often set their advertising rates based on how well their shows attract men and women aged 18 to 34, 18 to 49, 25 to 54, and 55 and older. But relatively few ads that appeal to an 18-year-old will also motivate a 49-year-old, and advertising targeted at a 50-year-old worker will be ineffective on a 75-year-old retiree. Even if you're selling a product that is bought by people of all ages, a four-person household headed by two 35-year-olds often will represent less sales potential for a given product than a more affluent two-person household headed by people in their 50s. Yet millions of dollars are spent by advertisers who never seem to think about such matters.

Some of our respondents said that their media buying decisions are based on the cost of reaching 1,000 viewers with their message (CPM). But this tactic ignores qualitative measures of audience value, which are often more important in predicting sales. When younger markets stop expanding, advertising decisions based on CPM will not deliver as much bang for the buck.

Younger consumers are more inexperienced consumers. It's often easier to persuade them to buy something than it is to persuade a more experienced older consumer. When the ratio of novice consumers to experienced consumers goes down, the result is a lower net response to a mass-marketing ad campaign. People who market to older consumers know that as a person's age rises, so too does the cost of marketing needed to make the first sale. It takes more money, time, and effort to persuade older consumers to switch brands or try something new. Yet older people will switch, and advertisers who try to persuade them are often rewarded.

In fact, there may be no age-related differences between younger and older consumers in willingness to try new products or switch brands. Older consumers are generally willing to buy a new product or change brands, according to research by George Moschis, head of the Center for Mature Consumer Studies at Georgia State University. Yet older consumers switch for more practical reasons, he says. They are less likely than younger consumers to try a new product simply to enhance their social appearance or status.

SELLING TO MATURITY

Perhaps it is the networks and their advertisers who are unwilling to try something new. Most advertisers are comfortable with youth-based marketing, and they simply don't want to learn how to market to older consumers. The mature mind is far more complicated than its youthful counterpart.

In middle age, a person's spending habits typically become more discretionary. People in their middle years may spend more, but they are usually required to buy less. As a result, persuading them to buy requires greater skill and more exquisite means of seduction. Many marketers don't want to take on that challenge, so they stay focused on a shrinking market of young adults. As the population continues to age, this strategy of denial will become more and more costly.

What should broadcasters and advertisers do to switch their efforts to an aging marketplace? First, move away from the notion that consumers are best segmented by age. Consumers' needs originate more from levels of personal growth and from levels of social development achieved in family, job, and other social circles. Age is primarily a coincidental factor, not a determining factor. When you divide a market by age, you're going against the grain of life's realities.

Developmental psychologists tell us that the values of narcissism, hedonism, and materialism begin to ebb at the onset of middle age. This does not mean that people begin to spend less. They may spend more, but they do it more selectively and thoughtfully. And they will be turned off by advertising that appeals blatantly to narcissism, hedonism, and materialism.

Second, target consumers by using emotional cues appropriate to their life stages. Research shows that as people grow older, they are less motivated by emotionally neutral information such as commercials that focus on product attributes and benefits. Commercials that tell mini-stories with gentle humor or human interest are often more effective with older viewers, even if they make no mention of what a product can do.

One of the most successful commercials ever aimed at the mature market was a spot for McDonald's called "New Kid." The commercial showed a white-haired, grandfatherly man preparing for his first day at a new job. His wife checks his appearance. He squares his shoulders and walks down a small-town sidewalk to meet his new colleagues—a group of fresh-faced teenagers at the local Golden Arches. The commercial makes older people feel good about visiting McDonald's without telling them anything about a Big Mac.

Third, sponsor shows that appeal to the values of older audiences. In mid-life and beyond, viewer interest tends to move away from farcical, fierce, or sardonic programs. Older viewers prefer programming that is ironic, gentle, or factual. Hard-hitting, fact-based programs like "Sixty Minutes" have been top-rated shows among older audiences for years. Gentle mystery programs like "Murder, She Wrote" and "Matlock" consistently top the charts among older audiences. But truly mature viewers will shy away from sitcoms based on put-down humor or crude sexual innuendo. With maturity comes the knowledge that insults are unkind and unacceptable acts.

Older adults generally like adventure, but they are not interested in graphic violence. They love romance, but not graphic sex. And like children, they want to see good vanquish evil in the end. We believe that advertisers and their agencies will not alienate the young by creating programs and commercials that reflect these mature values. Rather, we see an aging U.S. population leading society to the realization that a person's age does not determine values, attitudes, or behavior. And as society becomes ageless, television needs to follow its lead.

TAKING IT FURTHER

For more information about Nielsen Media Research, contact Clay Herrick at (212) 708-7631. The Center for Mature Consumer Studies at Georgia State University conducts surveys and publishes reports and a newsletter; contact George Moschis at (404) 651-4177. David Wolfe's book *Serving the Ageless Market* was published by McGraw-Hill in 1990. Also, see "Targeting the Mature Mind," *American Demographics*, March 1994.

CHILDREN IN THE DIGITAL AGE

KATHRYN C. MONTGOMERY

Kathryn C. Montgomery is co-founder and president of the Center for Media Education.

After 50 years of controversy over the impact of television on children, a new world of online media is emerging that may have even greater impact on them. Almost one million children in the United States are now using the World Wide Web, according to a research and consulting firm specializing in interactive technology, and 3.8 million have Web access—figure that will grow rapidly in coming years. Like adults, children will increasingly be connected to a vast digital universe that transcends the family, the local community, and even the nation. Education will expand beyond the classroom and other traditional settings, as more interactive "edutainment" becomes available. New personal and portable technologies will enable children to inhabit their own separate electronic worlds.

The dazzling graphics and engaging interactivity of the new multimedia technologies will make them potent forces in the lives of children. If harnessed properly, the new media could enhance their drive to learn, provide them with access to a rich diversity of information and ideas, and enable them to reach across community and national borders. But there is also peril: Video game channels, virtual shopping malls, and manipulative forms of advertising targeted at children could further compound the problems in the existing media that have troubled parents, educators, and child advocates for decades.

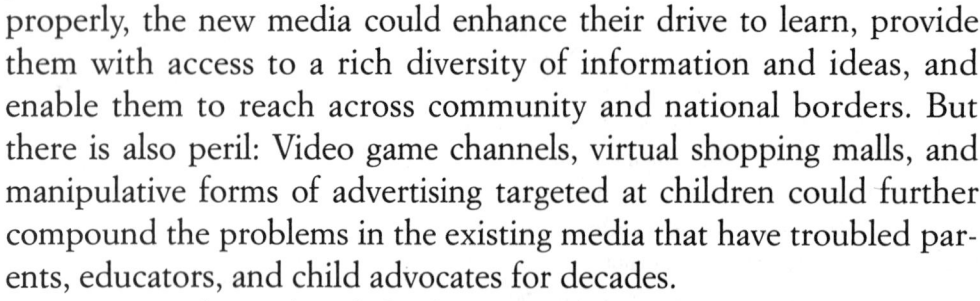

We are in the midst of the formative stage of this new digital age. Government policies are being debated and enacted, marketing and programming strategies are being developed, and services for children are being designed. If we are to believe some hyperbolic visions of cyberspace, the information superhighway will be a great equalizing force that will bring unprecedented opportunity for all. Improvements in education and other benefits for children are often

32. Children in the Digital Age

have already poured vast amounts of money into lobbying to shape the 1996 Telecommunications Act. From the beginning, corporations were able to frame the debate. While some political leaders, such as Al Gore as a senator, compared the new information superhighway to the interstate highway system, the Clinton administration's vision quickly became a privately built and operated national information infrastructure (NII). The Telecommunications Act is designed to encourage competition by deregulating the telecommunications market. Public interest advocates, though pitifully underfinanced, were able to win only a few positive provisions for consumers. The interests of children were not central to the legislative debate, and the little attention paid to children was misdirected at indecent content on the Internet. As a result, the law ignores or inadequately addresses critical issues that will have a significant long-term effect. In the wake of the legislation, we need a new strategic understanding of what needs to be done to make the best of the new media—and to avoid the worst.

at the center of these visions. But history offers us cautionary lessons. In this century enthusiasts have hailed every new medium—from radio to FM to television to cable to satellites—with claims that it would reinvigorate our culture, expand educational opportunities, and enhance the democratic process. None has lived up to these claims. In each case, powerful commercial forces have used civic values to gain support for the new medium—and then squelched the very policies necessary to serve the public good.

In this recent phase, powerful media companies

ELECTRONIC INCLUSION

While traditional media are sometimes viewed as unnecessary diversions, digital media will soon become an integral part of daily life. Those without access to the communications system are likely to fall behind in education and be unable to compete in a highly selective job market. Yet just as access is becoming imperative, the number of children living in poverty, with little or no access to technology, is growing at an alarming rate. According to a 1994 survey, 11 percent of families with incomes of less than $20,000 have a computer, compared to 56 percent of families with incomes above $50,000.

181

5. A WORD FROM OUR SPONSOR

One out of ten children under the age of six lives in a home without a telephone.

To its credit, the Clinton administration has raised the issue of disparities between the information rich and information poor. In its 1993 Agenda for Action, the White House called for all schools, libraries, and hospitals to be connected to the national information infrastructure by the year 2000. The idea was to provide equitable access through these institutions, even if it couldn't be assured for all homes. At present, there are a handful of government programs intended to encourage innovation and pay for pilot projects, but the administration has mostly relied on private, voluntary efforts to meet this goal.

Some promising projects have emerged, such as California's NetDay, a one-day effort in March 1996, spearheaded by Sun Microsystems, in which volunteers across the state strung miles of wire to connect elementary and secondary schools to the Internet. Relying heavily on such voluntary efforts, however, will likely leave many communities and schools unconnected. The vast majority of public schools, particularly for minority and low-income children, lack the basic technology and training to provide students access to computer networks.

Even if more children are able to use the new media through schools and libraries, they will still be at a disadvantage relative to children with access at home. An hour or two of computer laboratory time in school is not enough to acquire the technological competence that colleges and many jobs will require. Some argue that the costs of the equipment will go down dramatically in the next few years, making computer communications as affordable as televisions and VCRs. But monthly service charges are another barrier, and communications services that are now free or very inexpensive may become unaffordable. While some form of over-the-air television is likely to remain free, most other video services will require payment. For families in poverty, either the upfront cost of equipment or service charges may be insurmountable barriers.

The Telecommunications Act could have created comprehensive policies for ensuring equitable access to the national information infrastructure. But because of the conservative political climate, the federal deficit, and unprecedented lobbying expenditures and campaign contributions by the telecommunications industries, the legislation dealt very narrowly with the issue. The education and library communities were able to win a provision that requires telecommunications companies to offer less expensive connection and service charges to schools and libraries than to homes and businesses. But the Federal Communications Commission (FCC) must define what "affordable" means. In consultation with the states, the FCC is now supposed to develop a universal service policy for the new digital era that includes the provisions for schools and libraries.

A NEW MEDIA ENVIRONMENT

Access isn't the only challenge; the quality of the new media culture for children also raises concern. Unlike TV, online media are dynamic and two-way. This participatory quality makes them particularly compelling to children. Such technological breakthroughs as real-time audio, real-time video, and virtual reality modeling language (which allows programmers to turn Web sites into three-dimensional environments) are transforming online media. Eventually, this interactive online world could supplant traditional television as the most powerful and influential medium in children's lives.

Many online services are now available that seek to challenge children by exposing them to places, people, and ideas far outside their everyday experiences. For example, Plugged In, a Web site created by a community computing center in Palo Alto, California, allows poor children to explore the Internet, produce their own art, and display it to other children around the world. Another Web site, Cyberkids, enables children to write and share their own stories in an online magazine. Special networks have been established to foster online communities for children. With help from a federal grant from the National Telecommunications and Information Agency, the National Youth Center Network is addressing such problems as violent crime and unemployment by elec-

> Access isn't the only challenge; the quality of the new media culture for children also raises concern.

tronically linking youth centers in low-income neighborhoods.

These educational and civic services, however, are in danger of being overshadowed by a powerful interactive commercial culture with an unprecedented ability to capture children's attention. Marketing to children has become a multibillion dollar business. The direct spending power of children, almost all of it discretionary, has risen rapidly in recent years. In 1995, according to *Interactive Marketing News* and *Youth Markets Alert*, children under 12 spent $14 billion, teenagers another $67 billion, and together they influenced $160 billion of their parents' annual spending. As an executive for Turner Home Entertainment recently explained: "Probably for the first time in the consumer business, kids are now being recognized as a truly gigantic part of the consumer purchasing block." In the last decade, these trends triggered a proliferation of new TV networks aimed at capturing a segment of the hot children's market, including the controversial classroom news service Channel One, the highly profitable Nickelodeon cable channel, CNN's Cartoon Channel, and the Fox Children's Network.

With the FCC's deregulation of children's television in the mid-1980s, toy manufacturers began the wholesale creation of "kidvid" series that served as half-hour commercials for a line of licensed products—from He-Man to the Care Bears to the Transformers. Character licensing has become the driving force not only in children's television, but also in much of the rest of children's culture. Cross-promotion of licensed products through TV, movies, magazines, discount stores, and fast food restaurants has produced a proliferation of licensed characters that permeate every facet of a child's life.

The new online services for children are being developed in the context of this highly commercialized children's media culture. Children are a disproportionately important market for the new interactive media because they are early adopters of high-tech products. Marketers who view children as the "lucrative cyber-tot category" see the emerging media as a fertile new frontier for targeting children. As an executive from Saatchi and Saatchi, a leader in the online kids' marketing field, recently proclaimed, "There is nothing else that exists like it for advertisers to build relationships with kids."

Advertisers are already aggressively moving into cyberspace. A new Coalition for Advertising Supported Information and Entertainment (CASIE), led jointly by the American Association of Advertising Agencies and the Association of National Advertisers, is spearheading lobbying efforts to ensure that advertising becomes the dominant mode for funding online content and to ward off government restrictions. The coalition claims that advertiser support for online services is the only way to make information services affordable to all.

> Federal regulations limit TV advertising to children, but no such rules exist in cyberspace.

But the consequences of making advertising the key to universal access for children are troubling. Advertisers are not just supporting online content; they are shaping much of the virtual landscape for children. At Saatchi and Saatchi, psychologists and cultural anthropologists have perfected a variety of techniques—including play groups, art, and games—to probe children's feelings and behavior when they go online. They are also studying the nature of "kids' culture" as a separate set of experiences and values from that of adults. Knowing that children often use computers alone, marketers are carefully cultivating this separateness in the design of online services that circumvent parental authority. One online children's service recently published results from a survey that asked children whom they trusted more—their parents or their computers. The majority of respondents said they put more trust in their computers.

According to advertising researchers, going online quickly puts children into a "flow state," that "highly pleasurable experience of total absorption in a challenging activity." This is an optimal condition for advertisers to reach children. Traditional commercials will not work online. "Anything that is perceived as an interruption of the flow state," explained a Saatchi and Saatchi executive, "whether it's artwork being downloaded

5. A WORD FROM OUR SPONSOR

or an ad that is obtrusively splattered on a screen, is going to get a negative reaction." So the solution is the seamless integration of content and advertising in "branded environments." The goal of these environments is to "get kids involved with brands"—including "brand characters, brand logos, brand jingles, and brand video."

Major children's advertisers have Web sites where children are encouraged to come and play for extended periods of time with such product "spokescharacters" as Ronald McDonald, Kellogg's Snap, Crackle, and Pop, and Chester Cheetah. The aim is to encourage children to develop ongoing relationships with the characters—and the products. Within days of visiting the Kellogg's Web site recently, for example, one child received unsolicited e-mail from Snap, Crackle, and Pop, urging her to return for more fun.

The new interactive media are being designed to compile personal profiles on each child to help in developing individually tailored advertising known as "microtargeting" or "one-to-one marketing." The sites get children to volunteer such personal data as e-mail address, street address, the identity of other family members, and purchasing behavior and preferences. Sophisticated computer software can track every move a child makes online and give marketers "clickstream data" or, in the vernacular of the business, "mouse droppings."

Federal regulations limit TV advertising to children, but no such rules exist in cyberspace. Marketers can pursue children with few restraints. Nothing prevents them from collecting personal information from children and selling it to third parties. The lines among advertising, entertainment, and information—already dangerously blurred in television and other media—are likely to disappear entirely in the new online environment. "What is really happening [on the Web]," explains one industry expert, "is what will ultimately happen on interactive television: the infomercialization of all programming." Adds another: "The blending of entertainment with advertising will work if packaged correctly: just look at how the toy industry has taken over production of Saturday morning cartoons."

Even traditionally noncommercial services are likely to be shaped by the norms of this new unregulated media environment. While PBS is prohibited from most forms of advertising on television, there are no restrictions on its use of advertising online. Children's Television Workshop, producer of such highly acclaimed noncommercial programs as *Sesame Street* and *Ghostwriter*, has recently begun developing advertiser-supported cable and online services for children.

AN AGENDA FOR REFORM

Although the 1996 Telecommunications Act established a broad framework for federal policy, there are still opportunities to influence the shape of the new electronic media. Three key goals should guide public and private voluntary efforts.

Ensuring universal access. Every child, regardless of income, should have access to the advanced communications technologies and services necessary for their education and full participation in society. Providing access to telecommunications can in no way be a technological quick fix for more complex social and political problems. But those problems will only intensify unless we adopt policies—and invest significant resources—to ensure access for all segments of society.

Political participation needs to be expanded beyond those groups that have traditionally been involved in telecommunications policy. Child advocacy, parent, health, and other constituencies need to understand what may seem to be a highly technical subject. Targeted strategic interventions at the state level could have a positive influence on local communications services. In such states as Ohio, coalitions of education, consumer, and low-income advocates have succeeded in obtaining substantial resources for community computing centers, educational technology, and training. Public interest groups need to monitor the plans of telecommunications companies to prevent "electronic redlining"—omitting low-income neighborhood from new initiatives. Public hearings can help raise the level of the debate and create a forum for articulating a public vision for how the new telecommunications can serve children. Such organizing efforts could lay the groundwork for a national movement on behalf of children's interests in the national information infrastructure.

Developing safeguards. Preventing the commercialization of online media for children may be impossible, but there is an important opportunity to influence the design of new interactive services. A report issued in late March by the Center for Media Education, the organization of which I am president, documented the emerging patterns of online advertising and marketing to children. In response, a few companies have stopped some of the most egregious practices, and industry trade associations have promised to adopt guidelines to regulate their own conduct. As past experience has shown, however, self-regulation is likely to have little impact unless there is effective government oversight and enforcement. New screening software programs, such as Net Nanny, Cyber Patrol, and SafeSurf, may enable parents to screen out certain content areas or restrict the information that children can give out, but these tools are unlikely to be sufficient. Because children are a particularly vulnerable audience, effective legal safeguards will be necessary to prevent manipulation by advertisers and to protect children and their families from invasions of privacy.

The Center for Media Education and Consumer Federation of America have jointly urged the Federal Trade Commission to develop guidelines for advertising to children in cyberspace. These rules would restrict the collection of personally identifiable information from children and require disclosures of data collection practices on all Web sites and online content areas directed at children. In addition, we are calling on the FTC to require clear separation between content and advertising in online services targeted at children. These rules should also apply to the interactive television services under development. Although the U.S. district court decision on June 12 restricts government regulation of indecent content on the Internet, it does not prohibit either regulation of commercial speech or government safeguards to protect online privacy.

The global nature of the Internet also calls for international efforts to develop standards for new media programs and services targeted at children. Since many countries already have stricter policies for protecting children than we do, international guidelines could raise the standards for children's interactive media in the United States.

Creating a noncommercial children's civic sector. The emerging media environment should serve children not only as consumers, but also as citizens. While a number of exciting services for children are available on the Internet, they may disappear or be overshadowed by an all-pervasive commercial culture that will capture and dominate children's attention. If, as current trends suggest, the dominant method of financing the new media is likely to be advertising, we need to assure the availability of noncommercial educational and informational services for children. Just as we have public spaces, playgrounds, and parks in our natural environment, so we should have public spaces in the electronic environment, where children will be able to play and learn without being subject to advertising, manipulation, or exploitation.

New models for producing and distributing noncommercial services need to be explored. For example, an alliance of nonprofits, artists, film makers, and educators might create a new children's service that combined the traditions of public television with the innovative potential of the Internet. Public and private funds might help launch a children's version of C-SPAN—"Kidspan." A consortium of government and private program suppliers from various countries might create an international children's programming service.

To ensure long-term survival, noncommercial programs and services need a dependable source of funds. One untapped revenue source could be the sale of broadcast spectrum, valued at as much as $70 billion. Other possibilities include the creation of a trust fund exclusively for children's services, using a combination of public and private money.

There is also a need for more civic-minded research to think through these issues. The telecommunications industries have enormous resources for sophisticated economic analysis, but the public interest community has been ill-equipped to compete. New models for financing universal access and achieving other reform objectives need to be explored.

This is the ideal time for efforts to insure this new media system serves the needs of children. Once the new media institutions are firmly entrenched, it will be almost impossible to change them. The system is still fluid enough for those who care about the character of our culture and our children to create a rich electronic legacy for future generations.

The State of the Nation

America's political system is based on the choices of its people. A candidate's success in being elected to public office depends on his or her ability to communicate to mass audiences; thus, mass media have always been central to the political process.

Section 315 of the Communications Act of 1934 provides that all legally qualified candidates for office be afforded equal opportunity to use broadcast media to communicate their messages to the public. It further states that broadcast licensees shall not censor the content of material broadcast under this provision. (Broadcasters were initially concerned about their responsibility for libelous comments made in these uncensored messages; however, their exemption from being sued for libel under such conditions has been upheld by the Supreme Court.) When candidates appear on bona fide newscasts or news interview programs, the necessity to provide equal time is not applied, though most broadcast operations attempt to even out coverage of candidates even in exempt categories.

Besides equal access to broadcast time, Section 315 specifies that all candidates be given the opportunity to buy advertising time at the same rate. During the 45 days before a primary and the 60 days before a general election, advertising must be made available to all candidates at the station's "lowest unit charge" (in other words, the cheapest rate available to any advertiser in a given time period). Paid political advertising provides an opportunity for candidates to make points that might have been ignored or downplayed in "free" news coverage of the campaign. Such advertising has become a controversial element of campaigns for several reasons, including its tendency to go for knee-jerk emotional responses and its negative tone. In 1996 local and national candidates spent over $1 billion on their campaigns, about half on television advertising with the remaining investment split among radio, cable television, newspapers, direct mail, and new media such as on-line services (see "The Boys on the 'Net").

There is little question that television has changed politics. Although it is true that images have always been important to some degree—getting on the cover of a newsmagazine, for example, has traditionally required that a striking vertical-composition shot be provided for the photographers covering a story—television has made visual images particularly powerful.

Professor Martha Cooper (Northern Illinois University) explains that television combines sound and picture to present an aesthetic rather than a logical experience, using a narrative rather than a discursive approach. Discursive presentations, such as those in print and aural media, are sequential and linear. With print media, we read each sentence from beginning to end before going on to the next. With aural material, such as radio, we perceive only one piece of information at a time. People tend to be analytical about discursive material, to look for what assertions are being made and how they are supported. By contrast, narrative material is processed out of sequence. A photograph, a painting, or a television picture requires the viewer to shift focus to analyze

UNIT 6

the foreground, the background, the different elements of the image. People's reaction to narrative material emphasizes the aesthetic or affective response rather than the informative value.

In today's narrative media environment, candidates for public office often find themselves evaluated more in terms of appearance than on the substance of their words; media commentary devoted to how Bill Clinton looks in running shorts equals commentary devoted to his positions on foreign policy. Campaign strategists focus as much on providing good backgrounds for news photographers as they do on drafting the candidates' speeches. Political advertisements are created using the same visual metaphors that are used to sell Pepsi. The ability to speak in sound bites—snippets likely to be picked up on the evening news—is cultivated. (In 1968 the average sound bite for presidential candidates on network news was 42 seconds; in 1996 it was less than 8 seconds.) Campaign staffs engage regularly in "spin patrol," a process of trying to influence the slant that reporters will take in interpreting both campaign news and noncampaign news, such as the state of the economy, that might affect voter attitudes. Once in office, news spin continues to affect public perceptions of how political leaders are doing, and both their supporters and detractors continue in attempts to influence its direction.

Politicians are not supposed to admit that they like or know how to use television, but ever since Dwight Eisenhower's administration in the 1950s, media consultants have been routinely engaged to assist with political campaigns. Campaign managers are acutely aware of "packaging" the candidate, much like any other product. Their response to criticism is that they are simply doing what is necessary to get today's candidate elected. They did not, they argue, invent the game; they just know its rules and help their candidates play to win. In "Hoodwinked!" James McCartney traces a history of strategic successes in influencing media agendas during presidential campaigns from 1960 through 1992.

Today's political leader governs in a climate of expanded media options and new forms of media scrutiny. In "Reshaping the World of Politics," Lee Edwards contends that electronic town meetings, electronic referenda, and "real time participation" in public affairs present new opportunities for both involving and manipulating the electorate. Howard Fineman notes that fast-growing television and radio talk-show formats generate "tidal waves of switchboard-clogging calls and letters-to-your-congressman" that influence government agendas in his essay, "The Power of Talk." In "Over the Line?" Sherry Ricchiardi describes the impact of advocacy reporting that hits hard in covering national policy and presidential decisions.

The media have a fascination with politicians as personalities. The implicit agreement between politicians and the press that kept the adulteries of presidents Warren Harding, Franklin Roosevelt, Dwight Eisenhower, John Kennedy, and Lyndon Johnson out of the public eye no longer holds. It is arguable that disclosures such as these give voters valuable insight into the character of the candidates under consideration, and that is often a point made by reporters who bring such stories forward. It is also arguable that the interest generated by such stories overrides the public's focus on what is important: where candidates stand on issues. News media tend to be highly conscious of this criticism and very committed to providing a forum for candidates to discuss issues, but they are also sensitive to competitive pressures.

The media are not without blame in either sensationalizing or trivializing politics, but they are also not entirely responsible for these trends. As *Time* magazine's Richard Zoglin has pointed out, catchy campaign slogans and the practice of oversimplifying issues were not invented by television people. Successful leaders have always had to adapt to the medium of their time. They must be able to forge an emotional bond with the people. Perhaps, to a certain degree, it is appropriate that politicians, who will need to use media to communicate themes and dreams while in office, "audition" for that role as a part of running for office. But it is also appropriate that voters learn the difference between style and substance in mediated politics.

Looking Ahead: Challenge Questions

How can news spin influence a political leader's success both during the campaign for office and while serving in office? Has the press been fair in its coverage of current Washington leadership?

Politicians are often portrayed as victims of the press; however, according to James McCartney, they can also be sophisticated manipulators of news coverage. Which side do you believe is more at fault in creating public cynicism about the American political process? Why?

Public interest in government and politics has declined over recent years. To what degree do you believe media have contributed to voter apathy? What changes in campaign and campaign coverage practices would you recommend as likely to change this trend?

Is knowledge of a political candidate's personal conduct relevant to your voting decision? Why should or should not this information be available to the public? How should it be treated by mainstream news media?

Do call-in talk shows enhance or compromise democratic ideals?

RESHAPING THE WORLD OF POLITICS

Television has contracted political time and changed the way elected officials communicate with the people.

LEE EDWARDS

Lee Edwards is senior editor for the Current Issues section of THE WORLD & I and teaches politics and mass media at Catholic University of America.

The leader of every nation, north and south, rich and poor, democratic and authoritarian, acknowledges the awesome power of the electronic media to shape the politics of his nation.

When Polish leader Lech Walesa was asked what effect Radio Free Europe had on Solidarity's activities in communist Poland, he responded, "Would there be Earth without the Sun?" A spokesman for the "No" opposition that upset Chilean dictator Augusto Pinochet in a plebiscite remarked, "In 15 minutes' television time, we destroyed 15 years of government publicity for the dictatorship."

Chinese Communist Party General Secretary Jiang Zemin stated that Tiananmen Square illustrated the "chaos" that will result "if the tools of public opinion are not tightly controlled in the hands of true Marxists." In his Harvard commencement address, Alexander Solzhenitsyn declared that "the press has become the greatest power within the Western countries, more powerful than the legislature, the executive, and the judiciary."

In particular, the electronic media continue to change the politics of the oldest democracy in the world—the United States. Political candidates used to be picked behind closed doors by party bosses. Because of the media's demands, political parties now rely on primaries to decide their nominees for offices from the statehouse to the White House. All but the richest politicians once depended on their party for money and workers. Today, through the power of television, even those with the most modest of means can raise their own money and create their own organization.

The communications systems of the political parties have become thin shadows of their once-substantial selves. The electronic media now serve as the bulletin boards of political information. Parties have become so weakened that split-ticket voting—voting for candidates of different parties—is common.

The media's impact has been greatest on the office of the presidency. While John F. Kennedy was the first TV president in 1960, Ross Perot was the first talk-show presidential candidate in 1992. Both used television to talk directly to the voters without being filtered—that is, mediated—through the critical judgment of traditional journalists and politicians.

The media revolution is occurring so rapidly that increasingly a distinction is made between "new" and "old" media.

33. Reshaping the World of Politics

Going to the people: **Candidate Bill Clinton scores a point during election debate with President George Bush and independent Ross Perot.**

The new media range from cable TV and satellites to computers and fiber optics. The old media include broadcast TV, newspapers, and telephones. The new media explode previous limits on the volume of information, making it possible to exchange information without regard for time and space.

Author George Gilder argues that "the force of microelectronics will blow apart all the monopolies, pyramids, and power grids of established industrial society." He predicts that all hierarchies will become what he calls "heterarchies," systems in which "each individual rules his own domain."

OLD AND NEW

Sometimes the difference between the new and the old media is not that great. Walter Wriston, the former chairman of Citicorp, has described personal computers as electronic throwbacks to the Committees of Correspondence during the American Revolution that kept patriots advised of the latest developments in the war with England. Today, private PC users communicate through thousands of electronic bulletin boards that carry news about everything from personal experiences to political messages.

"Old" media like the *New York Times* and the broadcast networks like ABC and CBS will continue to have an impact on American politics for years to come, but, with satellites, candidates can hold rallies in different parts of the country at the same time. Campaign strategists in separate cities and states can meet in teleconferences. Direct mail is being supplemented by videocassettes—a tactic already used by Pat Robertson in the 1988 Republican primaries.

In the area of governing (as opposed to campaigning), nothing is more controversial than Perot's suggestion of a nationwide electronic town meeting—a sort of continental impulse of the moment that would delight Jean-Jacques Rousseau and dismay James Madison. As envisioned by Perot, after the presi-

6. THE STATE OF THE NATION

dent and members of Congress and various experts presented the proposed legislation or policy on national television, voters would register their "yes" or "no" opinion through a button on their TV set or by telephone.

As Perot told his favorite talk-show host, CNN's Larry King, "It's either up or down or sideways," prompting the response: Was he referring to the fate of the legislative proposal or the U.S. Congress? Futurist John Naisbitt declares that we have already "outlived" the usefulness of representative democracy.

Most political analysts would strongly disagree, arguing that precisely because electronic town meetings and similar feedback mechanisms can be easily manipulated, American politics needs more deliberation and discussion to prevent American democracy from becoming a crudely majoritarian system. A demagogue could misuse TV to create an electronic mob; historical antecedents that immediately come to mind are Huey Long and Father Coughlin in Depression-era America and Hitler in Nazi Germany.

Electronic referenda would further weaken political parties, increase voter volatility, and expand single-issue politics. Although some scholars continue to be intrigued by the possibilities of "real-time participation" in public affairs, Perot himself has had second thoughts, saying that what he really meant was using interactive TV to allow millions of Americans to participate, symbolically, in the legislative process.

Ted Koppel, anchor and managing editor of ABC's highly praised *Nightline*, has condemned the notion of "an ongoing electronic plebiscite," stating that it would paralyze our government. The last thing lawmakers need, he says, is "a permanent electrocardiogram, hooked up to the body politic."

Watchdog or Attack Dog?

The founders of the Republic were agreed that the media (or the press, as they knew it) had a dual role to play: (1) as *middleman* between the government and the people, providing necessary information about affairs of state and politics; and (2) as *watchdog*, investigating public officials and exposing scandals. They did not anticipate that the media would turn into an attack dog and engage in what political scientist Larry Sabato calls a feeding frenzy—where a critical mass of journalists pursue the same story intensely, excessively, and sometimes uncontrollably. They did not foresee that journalists would seize center stage in the political process, creating, not reporting, the news and altering the shape of politics and the contours of government.

Nor did Washington, Jefferson, Madison, and the other founders consider the possibility that one particular means of communication would dominate the mass media. The average American adult spends more than four hours a day watching TV, compared to less than an hour reading a newspaper. Time spent with the mass media has jumped 40 percent since the advent of television, mostly at the expense of other leisure activities. The public's heavy dependence on television is certain to increase with the widespread use of satellite TV with its hundreds of channels.

The CNN Phenomenon

CNN (the Cable News Network) deserves a special place in any discussion of the electronic media. What a computer does within an office, CNN does around the world, giving millions of viewers on different continents the same information at the same moment. It has become the common frame of reference for the world's power elite—from Boris Yeltsin and Deng Xiaoping to Bill Clinton and Saddam Hussein.

Don Hewitt, founding producer of CBS' award-winning *60 Minutes*, concedes that CNN has become *the* source of knowledge in a crisis, particularly an international crisis. It has come closer than any other network so far to creating the global village that media guru Marshall McLuhan spoke of, because now, says Hewitt, "the minute that anything happens [we] all run to CNN and think, 'The whole *world* is sharing this experience with me.'"

CNN has also changed America's politics. It has, for example, contracted political time. No longer do politicians have a week or even a day to draft a response to a crisis. Their deadline is one hour away, when CNN presents its next edition of *Headline News*, monitored by every other major broadcast and print media organization in the nation.

It has reshaped political rhetoric. Rather than the carefully crafted, inspiring speeches of FDR and Churchill, we have the staccato sound bites of Bush and Clinton ("Read my lips—no new taxes" takes just four seconds to say).

It has changed the way that public officials communicate. In the Clinton White House, as author Tom Rosenstiel has pointed out, CNN has become a means to communicate to the press corps and the public without having to hold briefings or face reporters. The White House press secretary talks to CNN's White House correspondent, who immediately goes on the air and gives what he has been told to everyone.

How responsible?

Given their enormous influence, it must be asked: How responsibly are the electronic media wielding their power? Even on its best days, American television seems obsessed with the tawdry and the trivial—with O.J. Simpson, Tonya Harding, the Bobbitts, and the Menendez brothers rather than health care, welfare reform, the civil war in Bosnia, and the elections in Germany, our most important European ally.

The media almost seem to have made a Faustian bargain, trading respect and integrity for higher ratings and increased circulation. Their profits may be going up, but they are creating a distorted image of America that is damaging democracy. And their stress on scandal and bad news is also affecting public attitudes about them.

In 1973, according to a University of Michigan survey, 23 percent of the public had a great deal of confidence in the press, while only 15 percent had hardly any. Twenty years later, only 11 percent of the respondents had a great deal of confidence, while 39 percent had hardly any confidence in the press. Among 13 major institutions in America, only Congress lost more public confidence than the press between 1973 and 1993.

Journalists continue to resist reform, especially from outside the profession, invoking the First Amendment, which states that Congress shall make no law abridging the freedom of the press. Media scholar Doris Graber argues that communications policy making by the government is best kept to the barest minimum, recalling Chief Justice John Marshall's warning nearly two centuries ago that the power to regulate is the power to destroy.

Still, more and more journalists concede they must improve their performance and raise their standards.

That process must begin with an evaluation of how journalists make their decisions about what to broadcast and print. Some follow a libertarian philosophy, insisting that the public has a right to know everything about everything. They are practitioners of a "new journalism" that emphasizes confrontation, advocacy, and cynicism.

Other journalists, usually younger, adhere to a social responsibility philosophy that claims a higher standard (civil rights at home, human rights abroad) but also follows the popular will (Jesse Jackson as president, Mikhail Gorbachev as "Man of the Decade"). This kind of social responsibility, relentlessly utilitarian, often degenerates into social correctness.

The media's obligation to be responsible comes from their privileged position in American society. The First Amendment guarantees the media freedom and power like no other institution or business in America. But the founders assumed that the media would use their liberty and their power prudently and in the cause of a constitutional republic.

The First Amendment is not a license to make money, win Pulitzer prizes, or form a fourth branch of government. The First Amendment is intended to protect the media from government censorship. It is there to ensure that the people will receive the information they need to make intelligent, informed decisions about their government and their politics.

American journalists need to exercise a true sense of responsibility—moral and political. Moral responsibility stress-

6. THE STATE OF THE NATION

es the cardinal virtues of wisdom, courage, justice, and, above all, prudence. The purpose of moral responsibility is to appeal to reason rather than emotion in decision making.

Political responsibility is founded on the concept of limited constitutional government. It stresses duties as well as rights, order as well as liberty. The purpose of political responsibility is to uphold the constitutional framework that protects the rights of all citizens, including journalists.

In both the moral and political areas, journalists have a responsibility to act not only for their own self-interest but for the good of the free society in which they live and prosper.

Their critical importance

Abraham Lincoln understood how critical the media are to politics, commenting, "With public sentiment, nothing can fail; without it nothing can succeed. Consequently he who moulds public sentiment goes deeper than he who enacts statutes or pronounces decisions."

Journalists must accept the responsibility of power and believe in the power of responsibility. They must steer a middle course between the Scylla of libertarianism and the Charybdis of social responsibility. Their guiding principle should be the golden mean, rooted in wisdom, courage, justice, and prudence.

For the journalist, the middle way would lie between lying to get a story and depending on a government handout. For a politician, it would fall between covering up a break-in of the opposition's headquarters and never trying to find out what the opposition was up to. For a voter, it would be between not voting and voting the straight party ticket.

Where there is adequate political and intellectual freedom, most people have little difficulty in making the right decisions. They are the natural outflow of courage, common sense, self-control, and fair-mindedness—the qualities important to any culture that wishes to survive.

A global turning point

Over the last several decades, gulags and political genocide along with economic failure and corruption have brought down rightist authoritarians and leftist totalitarians. Democratization has been greatly advanced by mass communications. The computer, fax machine, and satellite TV have erased national borders and broken governmental monopolies over communications while inspiring widespread desires for freedom.

Historian Francis Fukuyama argues that monarchy, fascism, and communism all failed because they were imperfect vehicles for freedom, while liberal democracy triumphed because it allowed the greatest possible freedom. But liberal democracies, he says, are not self-sufficient: "The community life on which they depend must ultimately come from a source different from liberalism itself."

The founders of the American Republic would agree. They understood that they were not simply rational individuals motivated by self-interest but members of a group of states bound by a common moral and religious code.

Liberal democracy in any century requires societal consensus as to what constitutes good politics, fair economics—and responsible media. It requires a people who demand a politics founded on these words of John Adams:

"Public virtue is the only foundation of republics. There must be a positive passion for the public good, the public interest, honor, power and glory, established in the minds of the people, or there can be no republican government, *nor any real liberty.*"

HOODWINKED!

The media have failed to pierce campaign myths in election after election. Will the 1996 run for the White House be different?

JAMES McCARTNEY

IN EVERY PRESIDENTIAL ELECTION SINCE Richard Nixon faced John F. Kennedy in 1960, the American press has fumbled the ball in some significant, often memorable way. Candidates have gotten away with outright lies, deliberate misrepresentations, phony assertions and, on occasion, ridiculous, unachievable proposals. In each instance the public and democracy have been poorly served.

Yet it is by no means certain that the media have learned obvious lessons. It is as though the press, collectively, has no institutional memory, plunging from one campaign to the next while ignoring the history of its own failures.

With the 1996 campaign under way, a reasonable question might well be: How will the media be hoodwinked this time? Will it fall for some last-minute "surprise"? Will someone find a new Willie Horton? Will a new and untried national savior appear on the scene to ignite media mania?

Consider the record:

■ In 1960 John F. Kennedy asserted there was a "missile gap" between the United States and the Soviet Union, to the Soviet advantage. It was not true.

■ In 1964 Lyndon Johnson campaigned as a peace candidate in Vietnam. He was secretly planning an escalation of the war.

■ In 1972 Richard Nixon permitted his national security advisor, Henry Kissinger, to announce that "peace is at hand" in Vietnam. It was not.

■ In 1980 Ronald Reagan promised to cut income taxes, substantially increase defense spending and balance the federal budget—all at the same time. It sounded impossible, and it was.

■ In 1988 George Bush managed to make convicted murderer Willie Horton a household name in an effort to depict Michael Dukakis as soft on crime. It was a phony issue.

These cases are part of a roll call of failure on the part of the media. Time after time, presidential candidates have managed to mislead the American people, and get away with it.

These days the press is often accused of being overly negative and too aggressive, of damaging if not destroying the public's faith in government with its cynical, confrontational approach.

But when it comes to presidential campaigns, history suggests that is not the problem. It suggests instead that the press often does not probe hard enough, does not dig deep enough. It suggests that the press tends to accept all too readily the spoken word and the patently self-serving political declaration without critical examination. That principle has been illustrated many times over the last 36 years.

1960 JOHN F. KENNEDY'S MYTHICAL "missile gap" was a case of calculated political manipulation of an easily wooed, transfixed press.

Kennedy was searching for a political weapon to offset the superior background in national security affairs of his opponent, Nixon.

It was a bogus issue, which Kennedy knew as early as September from private briefings by the outgoing administration. The media probably could have figured this out if they had made a serious effort.

Kennedy was inaugurated on January 20. Less than three weeks later, his defense secretary, Robert McNamara, admitted to reporters that the Pentagon had tentatively concluded that there was no missile gap.

During the campaign the media essentially accepted Kennedy's assertions without challenge. He said it. They reported it. Even the sainted Walter Lippmann, the most influential columnist of the time, appeared to accept the missile gap without question. "The military power of the United States is falling behind that of the Soviet Union: We are on the wrong side of a missile gap," Lippmann wrote.

Even after the election, when the truth began to emerge, Theodore White, famed chronicler of presidential campaigns, failed to perceive the significance of the issue, even though

6. THE STATE OF THE NATION

Washington Post political writer and columnist **DAVID BRODER** *says it is very difficult for the media to uncover deliberate deception by a candidate.*

The St. Petersburg Times' **PHIL GAILEY** *says the press should have looked more closely at the gubernatorial records of Jimmy Carter and Bill Clinton.*

it had been a central part of Kennedy's campaign. White didn't even bother to list the missile gap in the index of his book, "The Making of the President, 1960."

It is difficult to believe that the press could not have done better. It is true that the Eisenhower administration's obsession with secrecy on nuclear issues was an obstacle, but top Pentagon officials knew Kennedy was off base. And an effort to obtain information from Republicans on the Senate Armed Services Committee should have made it possible to present a more accurate picture.

1964 THE MEDIA WERE EQUALLY INEFFECtive in the face of Lyndon Johnson's deception about Vietnam in 1964, revealed in all its cynicism in the Pentagon Papers. Johnson was plotting an escalation of the war while campaigning as a man of peace.

Johnson apparently was considering a more aggressive war effort as early as Christmas of 1963. In Stanley Karnow's book, "Vietnam: A History," he is quoted telling the Joint Chiefs of Staff at a White House reception on Christmas Eve, "Just let me get elected, and then you can have your war."

But Johnson, running against Republican hawk Barry Goldwater, repeatedly declared during the 1964 campaign that he opposed sending "American boys" to Vietnam. Two weeks before the election he said, "We are not about to send American boys nine or 10 thousand miles away from home to do what Asian boys ought to be doing for themselves."

The Pentagon Papers reveal, however, that a consensus to bomb North Vietnam was reached at a White House strategy meeting in early September of 1964, two months before the election. On September 9 Johnson secretly authorized U.S. retaliation against North Vietnam in the event of any "special" attacks against American units.

But the most dramatic example of Johnson's duplicity came on Election Day itself, November 3, 1964. A committee headed by William Bundy, assistant secretary of state for the Far East, formally recommended bombing the north. The peace candidate's bombing campaign began in February, and two months later Johnson authorized American ground troops.

"While the press corps in those years diligently reported what the government said about Vietnam...too few sought out opposing viewpoints and expertise until too late...," political writer Jules Witcover explained in a 1970 analysis of the behavior of the press. "There is strong evidence the reason is too many reporters sought the answers...from the same basic source—the government."

The fact is that the press was completely captivated by Johnson. It accepted at face value his disingenuous promises to keep "American boys" out of the war. But there was a solid basis for tough questions that never got asked.

In April 1964, Senate Minority Leader Everett Dirksen publicly accused the president of hiding the fact that U.S. military forces were engaged in combat operations in Southeast Asia. In July, South Vietnamese Air Marshal Nguyen Cao Ky openly boasted of flying combat missions against the North. In August Goldwater, who had close ties to the military, was publicly demanding a "full, frank" disclosure of American policy in Vietnam. And the administration's high-pressure request for the famed Gulf of Tonkin resolution in August, authorizing whatever military action might be necessary in Vietnam, should have been a dead giveaway.

Furthermore, high administration officials who declined to be identified were discussing the possibilities of a wider war with at least some reporters. But none of these hints that something was going on were followed up aggressively.

James Reston of the New York Times, certainly one of the most respected journalists of the era, was deeply puzzled. On October 2 he wrote that "it is difficult to understand why prominent officials, a few weeks before a national election, should be talking so openly about expanding the war...almost lobbying for such a course of action...talking casually about how easy it could be to 'provoke an incident' in the Gulf of Tonkin."

It is obvious in retrospect that the press should have been reporting in hard news stories on page one what these unidentified high officials were saying in contrast to what the president was saying on the campaign trail.

But the major mistake of the press during the 1964 campaign was its failure to examine Lyndon Johnson's character. There was much in his personal history, available on the public record, to suggest that the president was capable of blatant deception. The record of his disputed election to the Senate in 1948, documenting how the election had been stolen, was available at the Supreme Court building, across the street from the Capitol, for any reporter who wanted to read it.

1968 THE WORLD KNOWS WELL TODAY that in 1968 there was no "New Nixon." The Watergate tapes tell it all. He was the same cynical, insecure, embittered man who sneered at the press in 1962 after losing a race for the California governorship, "You won't have Nixon to kick around anymore."

What was new in 1968 was Harry Treleaven, a New York advertising guru, and Frank Shakespeare, an 18-year-veteran of CBS.

Nixon's victory was a triumph of advertising-age merchandising, told best by Joe McGinniss in his classic, "The Selling of the President 1968." Treleaven and Shakespeare systematically repackaged the Nixon of 1962 and sold him, like so much soap, to the public and the press.

34. Hoodwinked!

The key was total control. They kept Nixon away from the traveling press, presenting him instead in regionally televised "citizen panels" in which he was quizzed by Republican stalwarts firing carefully scripted questions. The stalwarts were instructed when to clap and when to laugh.

The traveling press was not permitted in the studios and was forced to watch on monitors from adjacent studios. As one of Nixon's men explained, "It is a TV show, and the press has no business on the set."

Image-making, of course, has long been an integral part of politics. But in 1968 Nixon set a new standard, and his approach was widely copied in subsequent years.

The press did not make a serious effort to penetrate the shield. It accepted the staged shows as part of the game, with print reporters docilely recording what they saw on the monitors. Little was written about the adaptation of Madison Avenue advertising techniques to presidential politics, which turned out to be *the* story of the campaign.

Essentially, the press bought into the notion that there was indeed a "New Nixon." The full story of the master media manipulation by Treleaven and Shakespeare didn't emerge until McGinniss' book was published, well after Nixon was ensconced in the White House.

1972 On October 27, just before Election Day 1972, National Security Advisor Henry Kissinger declared that peace was "at hand" in Vietnam.

It wasn't. The heaviest bombing of the war was soon to follow with the infamous "Christmas bombing" of North Vietnam.

(It has been reported that Nixon was enraged by Kissinger's statement, although he never rebuked him. Kissinger himself has said he believed the carnage was about to stop and was simply wrong.)

According to Walter Isaacson's biography of Kissinger, on October 25 the national security advisor called Max Frankel, then Washington bureau chief of the New York Times, and invited him to lunch at the fashionable Sans Souci near the White House. Frankel's front page story the following day quoted "American officials" as saying that a cease-fire could come very soon "barring a supreme act of folly in Saigon or Hanoi."

That night, as Frankel's story was being printed, Hanoi was publicly broadcasting details of the agreement—and how Saigon had scuttled it, Isaacson later wrote. The deal had already gone sour.

This development did not restrain Kissinger from declaring in a televised news conference in the majestic East Room of the White House that peace was imminent. Kissinger apparently had hoped that the announcement itself would force Saigon's hand. It didn't.

The stock market soared. "It has been a long time," James Reston wrote in the New York Times, "since Washington has heard such a candid and even brilliant explanation of an intricate political problem." Newsweek's cover featured an American GI with "Goodbye Vietnam" splashed across his helmet, and the magazine published an article on "How Kissinger Did It."

The following week Nixon trounced his hapless Democratic opponent, Sen. George McGovern.

What could the press have done? It certainly couldn't ignore the secretary of state's bombshell. But it might have pointed out that last-minute political surprises often turn out to be false. More significantly, it might have stressed more prominently that neither the North nor South Vietnamese would confirm Kissinger's announcement.

Instead, the media—and the voters—were had.

1976 Success in politics often stems from the manufacturing of myths. Jimmy Carter understood that principle well.

The media accepted John F. Kennedy's assertion that there was a "missile gap" in which the United States trailed the Soviet Union. There was no gap.

6. THE STATE OF THE NATION

Columnist **JAMES RESTON** *wrote of the "brilliance" with which Henry Kissinger explained that peace was imminent in Vietnam. It wasn't.*

His reigning genius was Atlanta advertising executive Gerald Rafshoon. In early 1976, with Gerald Ford in the White House following Nixon's resignation, Carter and Rafshoon perceived that the basic question on the minds of millions of troubled Americans was simple: Could they trust their government?

Carter's campaign featured two themes: "I'm an ordinary, decent American, a peanut farmer from Georgia who wants to do good," and "I will never lie to you."

During the Democratic primaries Rafshoon produced a memorable television spot showing Carter in denim work clothes and boots, walking slowly across a neatly plowed field, sifting the soil through his fingers. A common man. A man of the earth.

Rafshoon recounted later that he had had little contact with Carter. The two had one meeting in November 1975, he told authors Edwin Diamond and Stephen Bates, in which they went over a list of possible topics for commercials. Then, Rafshoon said, he worked on his own for the next six months. Carter had told him, "I don't have to look. You make sure they're good."

But those carefully crafted TV images did not reflect the real Jimmy Carter, according to Phil Gailey, who covered Carter for the Atlanta Constitution when he was governor of Georgia.

Gailey, now editorial page editor of the St. Petersburg Times, was astonished that the public and the national media were buying the Rafshoon image. Carter had demonstrated again and again as governor that he was rigid, self-righteous and moralistic, Gailey told colleagues in the Knight-Ridder Washington bureau, where he worked at the time. As it became clear that Carter would be the Democratic presidential nominee, Gailey made a prediction. "When the public sees the real Jimmy Carter after he's been in office for a while," Gailey said, "they'll turn against him." His prediction proved prescient. By the time Carter ran for reelection in 1980, his charm had long since worn thin, and he became an easy target for Ronald Reagan.

A fitting description of the press coverage of Carter's 1976 campaign came from CBS' Lesley Stahl at a post-election review with top network brass. "I think the truth is that the candidates have learned to manipulate us almost 99-and-a-half percent," she said.

Martin Schram, author of "The Great American Video Game: Presidential Politics in the Television Age," obtained a transcript of the meeting in which there was a consensus that Stahl was essentially right. Schram wrote, "In 1976, the CBS summiteers discussed whether they had been had by the candidates and their strategists, whether they had paid too much attention to visuals and cosmetics, too little attention to issues and substance. There were grand resolves pronounced, but the campaign coverage of 1980 saw only modest changes made."

What could the press have done differently? For starters, it could have looked far more closely at Carter's record as Georgia's governor. And it could have spotlighted the paucity of substance in his campaign.

1980-84

IT WAS CLEARLY THE impossible dream. But the press and the public bought it not once, but twice, from Ronald Reagan. It was Reagan's contention that he could simultaneously cut income taxes, drastically increase defense spending *and* balance the federal budget.

The chimera, as we now know so well, laid the groundwork for today's debt crisis. In retrospect, the failure of the press to focus on the gathering storm seems remarkable. Reagan talked fiscal responsibility while spending wildly, yet the mounting deficit never became a major national issue.

When Reagan took office in 1981 the budget deficit was $78.9 billion. When he was reelected it was $185.4 billion. But that staggering growth never stopped him from touting his dedication to fiscal restraint. In his 1985 inaugural address he declared that "an almost unbroken 50 years of deficit spending has finally brought us to a time of reckoning. We've come to a turning point...."

In an exhaustive post-election examination in the National Journal of the media's performance in 1980, Dom Bonafede, a journalism professor at American University, found that the media often trivialized fundamental questions.

He cited a Washington Post story on November 3, 1980, the eve of the election, which said, "On most points of domestic policy, Carter and Reagan are already more alike than different." In fact, Bonafede said, "there were distinct differences between them on virtually every domestic issue, including welfare, abortion, school busing, school prayers, the Equal Rights Amendment, aid to education, national health insurance and defense spending."

But the press never laid a glove on Reagan; the legend still lives. Reagan proved as much as anyone in modern politics that image can overwhelm intellect, that the public and the press, when manipulated with style and brilliance, are perfectly willing, sometimes even eager, to suspend rational judgment.

During the campaign Reagan's rivals challenged the notion that he could pull off his unlikely trifecta. As early as January 5, 1980, in a debate in Iowa, the candidates were asked how Reagan's plan could possibly be achieved. Independent candidate John Anderson responded, "You do it with mirrors, because it can't be done." Reagan's chief Republican rival at the time, George Bush, also saw the impossibility, coining the phrase "voodoo economics."

Political writer **PAUL TAYLOR** *left the Washington Post in part because he felt the press was contributing to disenchantment with the nation's political system.*

196

34. Hoodwinked!

We now know that both were right, but the message was never presented loudly or clearly by the media. Imagery triumphed.

Bonafede says that the media failed to focus on the fundamental questions: Did Reagan's approach make sense? Could it work? I asked Bonafede recently, "Were the central elements of Reagan's program a nonissue in the press?" He replied: "I think that's true."

1988 IN THEIR BOOK "WHOSE BROAD Stripes and Bright Stars?" political writers Jack Germond and Jules Witcover described the 1988 race between George Bush and Michael Dukakis as "a campaign of distortion, character assassination and division." What came to symbolize that campaign was a convicted murderer named Willie Horton.

When Michael Dukakis was governor of Massachusetts, Willie Horton was granted a weekend furlough from which he did not return. A year later he resurfaced in Maryland where he kidnapped a family, raped the wife and stabbed the husband. The law establishing the furlough program was enacted under a Republican governor, Frank Sargent. Dukakis, under pressure from a newspaper campaign, had repealed it.

But when the late Lee Atwater, Bush's national campaign manager, learned about the Horton case, he and Bush's media consultant, Roger Ailes, decided to use it to label Dukakis as soft on crime. They tested their theory in a focus group in Paramus, New Jersey, and found that it resonated with potential voters. "If I can make Willie Horton a household name," Atwater is reported to have said after the session, "we'll win the election."

Bush began talking of the Horton case on the campaign trail. Ailes also produced a now-legendary television commercial showing prisoners, most of them black, leaving jail. A narrator intoned that Dukakis' "revolving door prison policy gave weekend furloughs to first-degree murderers not eligible for parole." It was a blatant and unfair appeal to fear, with heavy racist overtones.

The Willie Horton gambit, however, was only part of the strategy orchestrated by Atwater and Ailes. They portrayed a Dukakis veto of a bill to require the Pledge of Allegiance in classrooms as an unpatriotic act. They set up a Bush appearance in a flag factory. They produced a TV commercial depicting scum and dead fish in Boston Harbor, using footage taken elsewhere.

After the election, Jack Corrigan, a Dukakis adviser, observed, "We were surprised that they paid no penalty for running this kind of campaign." On the contrary, Bush's negatives declined while disapproval of Dukakis rose.

The media magnified the deliberate Republican distortion. Rather than exposing the GOP chicanery, the press granted it free air time. Kathleen Hall Jamieson, a media expert at the University of Pennsylvania, has pointed out that Willie Horton's face got more exposure on network news programs than it did in the political ads.

In his book "See How They Run," former Washington Post political writer Paul Taylor reported that Horton became the "most powerful symbol" of the entire campaign. At a post-election seminar at Harvard University, Dukakis campaign manager Susan Estrich pointed out that Bush mentioned Horton's name regularly in his speeches. "Each time he

Richard Nixon (left) convinced voters in 1968 that there was a "New Nixon." There wasn't.

American GIs reading a news account of Henry Kissinger's declaration that peace was "at hand" in Vietnam.

6. THE STATE OF THE NATION

The Brookings Institution's **STEPHEN HESS** *believes that the press has performed admirably in covering presidential campaigns.*

The 1988 Bush campaign made furloughed murderer **WILLIE HORTON** *a household name in its effort to label Michael Dukakis soft on crime.*

did," she said, "or at least often when he did, it would lead to a network story. We would have a little network recap and a bunch of newspaper stories that would show a picture of Willie Horton."

Once again, the media fell for a phony issue. The Bush managers understood well the weaknesses of the media, their unblinking willingness to search for interesting angles, however bogus. Bush and his cohorts were playing the race card, and the media tagged right along.

It is true that Michael Dukakis failed to mount a vigorous response to the Horton onslaught. But that is no excuse for the media to permit themselves to be suckered. The media had a responsibility to expose the facts and the cynicism of the Bush campaign. They should have presented an intense critical examination of the Horton ads and explained the unsavory strategy. Instead, they acted as a megaphone.

1992 AS THE 1992 ELECTION APproached, there was a pervasive sense among journalists that something had gone terribly wrong in their coverage of the previous presidential campaign. It was widely agreed that George Bush had run a deceptive campaign and that the media had done little to expose it.

The mainstream press collectively, if uncertainly, made an effort to change its approach. And it made some progress.

Nevertheless, it failed in what most journalists would agree should be its central objective—the presentation of an intelligent, meaningful and understandable picture of the personalities and basic issues in the campaign.

One widely shared conviction was that the press over the years had allowed campaign managers, advertising wizards and consultants to dominate discussion of the national agenda through phony events staged largely for the TV evening news programs. Election campaigns had been reduced to battles for sound bites.

The most ambitious effort to change came from ABC. Shortly after Labor Day Peter Jennings announced a radical new approach. "We'll give you the day's headlines," he said, "but we'll only devote more time to a candidate's daily routine if it is more than routine. There will be less attention to staged appearances and sound bites designed exclusively for television."

Within days CBS announced a policy of expanding its political sound bites from 7.3 seconds to 30 seconds, though it soon retreated to 20 seconds, and sometimes a little less. NBC more or less stood pat.

In an examination of ABC's performance in his book "Strange Bedfellows," Tom Rosenstiel, at the time a Los Angeles Times media writer, concluded that "for a year, the American press had taken responsibility for its coverage, even if it did so grudgingly. It had conceded that what it published and broadcast had consequences, that the act of observation altered the event—a step toward intellectual honesty."

One lesson from the Willie Horton debacle did stick: Something had to be done to tell voters about deceptive ads. The networks and major newspapers began running "ad watches" to point out what was true, and what wasn't, in political advertising. That alone was a major improvement.

Perhaps the media's greatest single shortcoming in 1992 was their failure to pin down Bill Clinton on his plans for dealing with the economy. Clinton made the economy the centerpiece of his drive, blaming Bush for its lackluster performance. But Clinton never produced a detailed economic plan of his own, a point almost totally overlooked by the press.

"I think the failure to push Clinton on his budget stuff was a much greater failure than anything we did about Bush," says the Washington Post's David Broder, arguably the nation's premier political writer. Reporters became enamored of Clinton, he says, and thought Clinton would be more interesting than Bush. "There was," he adds, "a suspension of critical judgment about the economic plan."

O F COURSE, NOT EVERYONE AGREES THAT PRESIdential campaign coverage consistently falls short of the mark. Stephen Hess, a longtime student of the media at Washington's Brookings Institution, believes that on the whole, the press has performed admirably in presidential campaigns over the last 36 years. "I think the press could do a lot better," he says, "but I am sympathetic with what they have to put up with.... There are some awfully good reporters out there."

Many in the media who had key roles in covering the 1992 campaign seem satisfied with their performance. According to a survey of more than 250 members of the press by the Times Mirror Center for the People & the Press (now the Pew Research Center for the People & the Press), "eight in 10 journalists rated press coverage of Campaign '92 as excellent or good. Fewer than one out of five (18 percent) judged press performance as only fair or poor. The survey also found the press thinking it did a good job on most of the major elements of the campaign coverage"—including coverage of the economy.

Some respected reporters and students of the press, however, are troubled, even though they differ widely on the degree of concern.

It's very difficult to penetrate deliberate deception, "when a candidate says one thing, when in fact he intends to do something else," Broder says. "In a broad sense, the only way you can deal with that is to try to look at character, and that is a very tricky area for us. What we're trying to do is to have a very talented reporter look at the pattern of a person's life."

Broder recalls historian Doris Kearns Goodwin telling a conference before the 1988 cam-

198

34. Hoodwinked!

paign of how she developed serious doubts about Lyndon Johnson's integrity. In researching a book on Johnson she found he had repeatedly said his grandfather had died in the battle of the Alamo, but she could find no record of that. She confronted Johnson, who conceded that his grandfather had in fact died in the battle for Texas independence at San Jacinto—but since people outside Texas wouldn't know about the battle of San Jacinto, he'd embroidered a little. Later she found out that Johnson's grandfather had died in bed.

"She pointed out that no matter how trivial the incident may seem, when you find somebody who lies about their personal history, it may be someone who can fake a Gulf of Tonkin," Broder says. "I remember chills running down my spine."

Marvin Kalb, director of Harvard University's Shorenstein Center on the Press, Politics and Public Policy and a former CBS mainstay, says that television networks must accept far more responsibility for presenting candidates to the public.

"Number one, there must be longer interviews with the candidates, and more substantive interviews," he says. "Number two, these interviews have to be built into the television schedule on a regular basis."

The Center has advocated what it has called a "Nine Sundays" program, in which in-depth, hour-and-a-half interviews would be conducted during prime time on the nine Sundays before the election, on alternating networks.

"The issue of length is as important as the issue of predictability—that the American people would know that there will be those long, serious interviews," Kalb says.

Paul Taylor, the former Washington Post political writer, agrees with Kalb that the road to better campaigns must lie with television but has a different solution in mind. He would like the networks to provide five minutes of prime time for Republican and Democratic candidates every day of the week during the four or five weeks before the election.

Taylor wants to expose the politically disenchanted, the dropouts who have become disgusted with politics, to serious discussion of issues in bites small enough for them to tolerate. Taylor quit the Post in part because he feels the press is contributing to widespread disenchantment with the political system. "Our conventions," he says, "lead us to write the half-empty version rather than the half-full."

American University's Dom Bonafede doubts that much is going to change. The answer, he says, lies with television, because television so completely dominates modern American life and modern campaigns.

"If they took an issue and devoted an hour to it—welfare, or the budget, or Bosnia, any issue—yes, that would help," he says. "But by the nature of television they are not going to do it, they are not going to do anything, because they are controlled by the ratings."

Compounding the problem, he adds, is that newspapers "now tend to follow television," although the best papers do a fine job in covering issues—often devoting a full page to exploring a particular topic.

Bonafede fears the 1996 campaign may be just as tawdry as 1988, possibly even worse, given the growing tabloidization of the media. "The print press is going along with this," he

The media failed to make clear that it would be very difficult, if not impossible, for Ronald Reagan (left) to simultaneously cut income taxes, increase defense spending and balance the budget.

Many critics asserted that George Bush ran a deceptive campaign in 1988 and that the media did little to expose it.

6. THE STATE OF THE NATION

> **THE PRESS has not learned how to handle deliberate manipulation. It failed with Kennedy's missile gap, Johnson's duplicity on Vietnam, the "New Nixon" and Willie Horton.**

predicts. "Hillary Clinton is going to be the Willie Horton of 1996."

So is there any underlying, unlearned lesson, any grand principle to be gleaned from these performances over the last 36 years? Perhaps the most obvious is that the press has not learned how to handle deliberate manipulation. It failed with Kennedy's missile gap, Johnson's duplicity on Vietnam, the "New Nixon" and Willie Horton.

The press continues to have great difficulty in examining substantive issues, particularly the meaning and the implications of campaign promises. Television simply ignores most issues that don't produce pictures.

As recently as the 1994 congressional elections the media failed to examine the implications of Newt Gingrich's "Contract With America." In general, they portrayed the contract as a cheap PR stunt. Neither the Washington Post nor the New York Times made a serious effort to examine its implications. To the networks it was a sound bite.

And in 1995 Colin Powell became a national icon, the media's candidate for president, without ever suggesting what he would do about the economy or how he would handle Medicare.

History does have its lessons. And they are there to be drawn from the last 36 years if we are wise enough to apply them.

One: Legitimate presidential candidates must be provided substantial free, or at least reasonably priced, air time on television to present their views in depth.

But it is not enough to just let them talk. They must be subjected to intense questioning before a national audience by seasoned reporters or informed political observers. This is essentially what Marvin Kalb has concluded, and he is right.

Two: The press must do a far better job in examining the character of candidates. It is tough, as David Broder has suggested, but it is not impossible.

The major failures of the last 36 years involved Lyndon Johnson in 1964 and Richard Nixon in 1968 and 1972. Evidence of their character weaknesses was abundant. It was there in Lyndon Johnson's 1948 campaign for Senate. It was there in Nixon's campaigns in California. What is needed is detailed reportorial research of candidates' families, friends and enemies over their lifetimes. As Doris Kearns Goodwin noted, tiny lies tell their own story.

Three: The press must pay far more attention to the public record of candidates—what they have actually done in office. Phil Gailey is right that Jimmy Carter's record as governor of Georgia was there for all to see. It was not examined closely enough by the national press.

Moreover, Gailey adds, the press corps "did the same goddamned thing for Bill Clinton in 1992 that they had done for Jimmy Carter in 1976. All this temporizing, the compromising. All these traits were obvious in Arkansas when he was governor.... Instead of lifting the sheets to look for a Gennifer Flowers, the press should have been examining his record."

Broder agrees: "There is nothing Clinton has done since he became president that wasn't foreshadowed by the way he acted as governor."

If the nation's media learn these lessons from the last 36 years, the 1996 campaign could be deeper, richer and more rewarding. The public and the cause of democracy would be better served.

James McCartney, a Washington journalist since 1959, is a columnist for Knight-Ridder newspapers and teaches a course in politics and the media at Georgetown University. He has written about coverage of Newt Gingrich and the myths about the Cuban missile crisis for AJR.

OVER THE LINE?

Powerful reporting by Christiane Amanpour and others focused the world's attention on Serb atrocities in Bosnia. But did these journalists go too far when they became both reporters and advocates?

SHERRY RICCHIARDI

Sherry Ricchiardi, an AJR contributing writer, teaches journalism at Indiana University and directs an International Media Fund project in Croatia. She has written numerous pieces on coverage of the Balkan conflict for AJR.

NATO JETS SWOOPED OVERHEAD AS A shield of blackness settled over Sarajevo. A curfew forced stragglers to take shelter from the firestorm that sent shivers of terror through the city. But CNN had a 2 a.m. broadcast.

The seasoned crew, accustomed to front line duty, methodically set up in the ghost-like streets where a dog's bark echoed for blocks and children went to bed hungry. All around, Serb gunners lurked in the hills, their fingers on triggers that in a heartbeat could turn apartment buildings into tombs.

The glow of TV lights was tempting fare for sharpshooters. But during this CNN broadcast viewers would witness another kind of volley—a collision via satellite on the information superhighway, as a TV critic later described it.

There was a chill in the air that night and Christiane Amanpour recalls that she wasn't feeling well as she took her place before the camera to confront the president of the United States live from Sarajevo on CNN's "Global Forum," an interactive public meeting with journalists around the world.

Moments later, the famous war correspondent locked glances with President Clinton, and with millions watching, accused him of wavering on his Balkan policy. "As leader of the free world, as leader of the only superpower, why has it taken you, the United States, so long to articulate a policy on Bosnia? Why, in the absence of a policy, have you allowed the U.S. and the West to be held hostage to those who do have a clear policy, the Bosnian Serbs?

"And do you not think that the constant flip-flop of your administration on the issue of Bosnia sets a very dangerous precedent and would lead people such as [the late North Korean leader] Kim Il Sung or other strong people to take you less seriously than you would like to be taken?"

The president shot back a hostile glare. "No, but speeches like that may make them take me less seriously than I'd like to be taken," Clinton responded coldly. "There have been no constant flip-flops, madam."

Amanpour stared back. The confrontation, which many considered a bold, if not improper, move, made headlines in May 1994 and placed the London-born superstar in the eye of a controversy.

Amanpour's unabashed style epitomizes an evolving advocacy approach to journalism that some say is the only proper way to cover some events, such as the brutal war in the Balkans. For Amanpour, her commitment in Bosnia is simple: "In certain situations, the classic definition of objectivity can mean neutrality, and neutrality can mean you are an accomplice to all sorts of evil. In this case, genocide and crimes against humanity."

Some question whether journalists like Amanpour are crossing a fine line between reporting and crusading, and are trying to influence foreign policy rather than simply report facts. In an article for London's Independent, award-winning journalist Nik Gowing noted that United Nations officials often complained that reporting from Bosnia omitted crucial facts that would supply context and balance. Gowing, former diplomatic editor for London's Channel 4, wrote: "As many sources confirmed, America can only cope with 'one black hat'—one cowboy bad

6. THE STATE OF THE NATION

guy—in any given crisis. Stories that were critical of the Bosnians were often spiked or diluted."

But Bob Steele of the Poynter Institute for Media Studies believes that good, tough investigative reporting can sometimes be mistaken for advocacy journalism. And when reporting atrocities, such as those that occurred during the Bosnian war, he says, presenting the other side in the interest of neutral reporting is "simple-minded."

AMANPOUR'S QUESTIONS TO CLINTON, part scolding, part lecture, were a clear challenge to the apparent reluctance of the world's superpower to stand up to a band of bullies who use murder, rape and torture as weapons of war. The next day, a Dallas Morning News headline read: "When it Rains, It Amanpours." A Washington Times headline read, "Clinton Flares at 'Flip-Flop' Suggestion." Media pundits nationwide questioned the propriety of Amanpour's challenge.

"I am not a pit bull or an attack dog type of person," Amanpour told AJR. "The question wasn't designed to be rude to the president. Clearly, it was motivated by my gut and from my experience here. And I think I was right."

But did Amanpour's passion for the story, driven by the human misery she had witnessed, overwhelm her journalistic sensibilities?

Getting too close to a story is always a danger, says Jackson Diehl, the Washington Post's assistant managing editor for foreign news. Particularly for journalists who witness horrific events, he says, "being as objective as possible, being an observer and not taking sides is something they all struggle with." But Diehl doesn't believe his reporters crossed the line in the stories they filed from Bosnia, even though their reporting was informed by their reactions to the war.

In 1991, Post reporter Blaine Harden was among the first journalists to document "barbaric violations" of the Geneva Convention on War Crimes, "including widespread mutilation of Croat corpses, deliberate destruction of churches, hospitals, [and] organized looting of personal property."

In a highly personal Washington Post Magazine piece, reporter Mary Battiata, who covered the war in its early stages, provided a glimpse of the passion that drives those who bear witness in Bosnia. She wrote: "In the place you have just left, ordinary people sitting in ordinary living rooms much like yours are still being blown into red mist by Serb guns. The smells, sounds and sights of the carnage are a visceral video that plays in your head.

"But in official Washington, the war is an 'issue,' and issues exist to be worked—bloodlessly, professionally, placidly. Like a cow chewing her cud."

The debate over whether journalists had become partisans against the Serbs is a "sideshow," says Battiata. "I feel more strongly about this than anything in my entire journalism career. We did nothing different [in Bosnia] than we as reporters do anywhere else. This was not a Muslim story or a Serb story. There was only one story—a war of aggression against a largely defenseless, multi-ethnic population. It was very simple."

In his book, "Love Thy Neighbor, a Story of War," Peter Maass of the Washington Post describes experiencing "journalistic impotency" and tells of efforts to resist what in Bosnia is described as "horror porn." "You were on the lookout for these stories [of murder, rape and torture] not because anybody back home was going to do anything about it, but because it was good copy. The agony of Bosnia was being turned into a snuff film," he wrote.

That kind of intimate relationship with the human condition in its most vulnerable form may be a driving force behind what some view as advocacy or partisan reporting in the Balkans. According to Amanpour, it was exactly that kind of closeness that motivated her. "What I admire most, and what kept me going during the war, was the incredible resistance among ordinary people to the indignities they were undergoing. Bosnia really was a war against civilians and against their dignity," she says.

These debates along lines of conscience trigger hot buttons for some media professionals. On one side are proponents of neutral, dispassionate reporting that keeps the media as close as possible to impartiality and a balanced representation of all parties. For instance, if a shell explodes in a Sarajevo marketplace killing 68, as it did in February 1994, these journalists would remind the audience that a crater analysis by the U.N. was unable to pinpoint which side—the Serbs or the Muslims—fired the shot. They might also report Serbian allegations that Muslims shelled the marketplace themselves to gain sympathy and spark international intervention.

On the flip side, some say there is a danger in drawing a "moral equivalence" between victim and aggressor, espousing the belief that neutrality can inadvertently lead to siding with wrongdoers.

In reporting the marketplace story, "I put [the shelling] in context," says Amanpour. "What I said was that over the years, our [U.N.] briefers had explained to us and shown us, numerically and by their own measure and statistics, that the overwhelming number of mortar shells and sniper fire and fire into the city was from the Serb side. Therefore, statistically, the likelihood is that it came from the Serb side. And furthermore, there's never been any forensic evidence to suggest that the Bosnians were shooting at themselves," a notion she calls "disgusting."

Journalists in this camp would define objectivity as giving all sides a fair hearing, but would cringe at the notion of treating all sides equally.

"With this war, it was not possible for a human being to be neutral," says Amanpour, the only broadcast journalist to win a News and Documentary Emmy, a George Polk Award and

> **GETTING TOO close to a story is always a danger, particularly for journalists who witness horrific events and "being as objective as possible, being an observer and not taking sides is something they all struggle with," says Jackson Diehl, a Washington Post editor.**

a George Foster Peabody Award. "Life obviously is full of gray areas most of the time. But sometimes in life, there are clear examples of black and white.... I think during the three-and-a-half-year war in Bosnia, there was a clear aggressor and clear victim."

But mention the debate over "moral equivalency" to veteran foreign correspondent David Binder of the New York Times and he snaps, "That's bullshit, complete bullshit. It's a garbage argument out of garbage minds. Our job is to report from all sides, not to play favorites."

Binder, who has covered Eastern and Central Europe since the 1960s, begs off targeting individuals for their "propaganda-style" reporting out of Bosnia, but he cautions against journalists "playing God."

"These arrogant Joe Blow reporters go into a country without a shred of knowledge of the area, no language, no knowledge of the literature. Who gave them the right to decree morality?" he asks.

But Amanpour would take exception with Binder. "An element of morality has to be woven into these kinds of stories," she says. "I don't think it has anything to do with an agenda. Simply it has everything to do with what is going on in front of your eyes.

"Governments, particularly in the West, were telling their versions of the truth about Bosnia. If we had blindly repeated that in the name of so-called objectivity, and not said, 'But hang on. In fact, this is what we know is going on,' then we would be giving eternal life to the lies."

Bill Kovach, curator of Harvard University's Nieman Foundation, is skeptical of what some consider advocacy journalism. "The value of objective journalism is that it is the sole source of information to which the public has access," he told AJR. "As human beings, it is often impossible for journalists not to feel strongly about stories of death, disease or destruction, and to hope something will be done to alleviate the pain and suffering." This, he says, can cause journalists to "lose their unique and irreplaceable standing."

The journalist's role, Kovach believes, is to provide as much detailed information from as many valid sources as possible. "That does not mean all sides in conflict are presented in a context of moral equivalency," he says. "But it does mean that all sides do have standing in the stories and that standing rises and falls of its own weight. Advocacy journalism lets reporters off the hook by allowing them to fill gaps in knowledge with emotional opinion."

OBJECTIVITY VERSUS SUBJECTIVITY IS an issue that's not new to the profession. In his 1977 book, "Existential Journalism," media scholar John C. Merrill maintains that there are two basic journalistic instincts: The first is a tendency toward involvement and the second is a tendency toward aloofness. The first, he says, is more "sense oriented"—or subjective—and the second is more "fact oriented"—or objective.

Merrill says that subjective journalists want to bring themselves, their intelligence, their sensitivities and their judgments to bear on the news of the day. They are not satisfied to be mere bystanders. The aloof journalist, on the other hand, maintains that journalism is primarily a disinterested activity in which the audience should not be encumbered by journalists' biases, prejudices, judgments, feelings or opinions. Merrill says that most journalists tend to be objectivists who give short shrift to personal judgments and advocacy journalism.

Merrill warns that journalists who fit snugly into the objectivist camp might fall prey to "robopathy," a term coined by author Lewis Yablonsky in his book, "Robopath: People as Machines." For these journalists, lack of passion is what defines their natural journalistic state, writes Merrill.

Drawing from writings by Jean-Paul Sartre, who argued that to be truly human one has to be engaged and rebel against the idea of "standing at a distance," Merrill defines existential journalism as "not isolating oneself, trying to be some kind of recluse; rather it is plunging into dangerous waters and being willing to take chances."

This sort of reporting was perhaps best exemplified during the Vietnam War. It was in Vietnam that journalists first broke close ties with the military that existed during World War II and the Korean War and began exposing the lies and distortions delivered during briefings dubbed the "Five o'clock Follies." Vast differences existed between official versions of events on the battlefield and what journalists were witnessing.

Marvin Stone, a former editor of U.S. News & World Report who covered the Korean and Vietnam wars, says reporting on Bosnia is different. "Most of the guys assigned to Korea either had fought in World War II or covered it. When the military handed out the daily communiqué, they believed it," recalls Stone. "In Vietnam, press briefings were a matter of hilarity. Nobody believed the military."

But in Bosnia, American reporters are covering a third-party war in which the United States, for the most part, has been a bystander. There is little risk of being labeled "unpatriotic" for reporting that is out of sync with official policy.

"Just the pure act of reporting the immorality you witness on the ground in Bosnia makes you an advocate. You don't always get two sides to the story, particularly in wartime," says Stone, who is on a Knight International Press Fellowship in Croatia.

Frank McCulloch, who covered the Vietnam War for Time magazine, says he also has seen a transition in war coverage over the years. "In World War II there was no doubt what the reporters' role was, especially from the U.S. point of view. They had full censorship, accepted it and saw the need for it," says McCulloch, a former executive editor of McClatchy Newspapers.

6. THE STATE OF THE NATION

"Korea essentially still was a pro-war mission for the media. But in Vietnam we shifted, not toward a Communist point of view, but in doubting and challenging the U.S. mission, both in terms of how adequately it was fulfilled and whether it was a worthy mission to begin with. That's the first time we questioned what the U.S. was doing and if they were doing it well.

"It's obvious," he adds, "the Serbs are getting clobbered [in media coverage], and I think probably they deserve it. I have an uneasy feeling that there must have been significant Muslim and Croatian atrocities that got little coverage. To that extent coverage might be a little lopsided. But the Serbs thoroughly earned that kind of coverage. Overall I think it's pretty damn good reporting.... It is thorough and reasonably measured, by which I mean fair."

During a four-month study at Harvard's Kennedy School of Government, British journalist Nik Gowing set out to test the "conventional wisdom" as he calls it, that TV images drive public policy (see "The CNN Effect," May). Gowing interviewed more than 100 diplomatic and military insiders in Europe and the U.S. who were involved in the Balkan war and documented a growing discontent with the quality and fairness of media coverage of events in Bosnia. U.N. officials criticized the media for having a "blood lust" and an anti-Serb bias. Many said that, at critical moments, the accuracy of real time television coverage, and the ensuing impact, were skewed by the "absence of critical facts in the reporting."

In his report Gowing wrote that "bitter U.N. officials describe some journalists and their reporting as 'glamour without the responsibility.' " At the height of the war, as Bosnian Serb forces tightened their grip on Sarajevo, Gowing quotes one "leading correspondent" asking a colleague over breakfast, "What is it going to take us to get the U.S. and their allies to intervene here?" as evidence of partisanship.

But Steele, director of the Poynter Institute's ethics program, says sometimes issues of neutrality are not black and white. He believes that high-quality reporting that places complex issues in context may be misinterpreted as advocacy journalism.

"In many cases, we might label as 'advocacy' stories that present a deeper meaning because the reporter has done a better job of digging and asking probing questions that carry information beyond the basic five Ws," he says. "When a journalist presents layers in a story that builds evidence to prove a point, some may interpret this as advocacy when, really, it is good, solid reporting."

Steele thinks reporters can step over the line, however, when they take an ideological stance and argue a point of view based on personal beliefs. Here, he says, is where it's up to editors to provide checks and balances.

James O'Shea, deputy managing editor of news for the Chicago Tribune, says that striving to cover all sides doesn't mean printing information that the reporter knows to be untrue. "If a guy from the Serbian Information Ministry tells you a bunch of baloney, you have absolutely no obligation to report it unless you're going to characterize it for what it is," says O'Shea, who has visited Belgrade and the Bosnian battlefields. If the weight of the facts and evidence reporters collect suggests that one side has a relative advantage in terms of truth, journalists have the responsibility to reflect that, O'Shea adds.

Amanpour believes the Serbs did themselves an "incredible disservice" by denying CNN and other Western media better access to the territory they controlled. When journalists did receive permission to travel behind Serb lines they were closely monitored. "Every time we wanted to go to the Serb side it was like the old communist mentality—they didn't want us to do this, that or the other," says Amanpour. "But no wonder. There were some very unsavory things going on."

THE DEBATE OVER OBJECTIVITY ALSO begs the question of whether reporting influences government policies or spurs the international community into action. (See "When Pictures Drive Foreign Policy," December 1993.)

There is little doubt that tenacious reporting by Newsday's Roy Gutman forced the Red Cross and other human rights groups to react to charges of genocide committed against Muslims and Croatians back in 1992. Sylvana Foa, a U.N. spokeswoman, credits Gutman with saving thousands of lives with his documentation of human slaughter in Serb-run "death camps."

And perhaps NATO would not have reacted as strongly in the fall of 1995 if David Rhode of the Christian Science Monitor hadn't slipped into Serb-held territory to document reports of massacres around the "safe haven" of Srebrenica. Rhode's case was further dramatized when he was held prisoner by the Serbs.

Rhode, Gutman and John Burns of the New York Times all have won Pulitzer Prizes for their reports from the Balkans. Was it their reporting, coupled with powerful images from CNN, the BBC and other major networks, that eventually led the Clinton administration to a call for action at the Dayton, Ohio, summit last year?

Many journalists assigned to the Balkans were disappointed that, despite the mountains of evidence, the brutality went unchecked. After Newsday's Gutman won the Pulitzer in 1993, he told AJR: "This would be recorded as the first genocide in history where journalists were reporting it as it was actually happening and governments didn't stop it. It's outrageous and hypocritical." The award was bittersweet, Gutman said, because, "we [the media] did our job, but didn't make any difference."

But caution lights flash in the minds of some media experts when reporters begin dwelling on "making a difference." In his study, Gowing concluded that the "emotive" television coverage

PUTTING *aggressor and victim on the same footing, Amanpour maintains, is drawing "moral equivalence." From there, it is a short step toward neutrality, and "an even shorter step to becoming an accessory to all manner of evil."*

and "alarmist" newspaper accounts formed a barrage of pressure for Western military intervention and may have led to NATO air strikes. Gowing says he found a strong consensus among U.N. officials that the media often omitted crucial facts that would have supplied balance to the war coverage.

In "Dateline Yugoslavia: The Partisan Press," an article in the December 1993 issue of Foreign Policy, Peter Brock charged that the media had become "a movement, co-belligerents no longer disguised as noncombatant and nonpartisan. News was outfitted in its full battle dress of bold headlines, multipage spreads of gory photographs and gruesome footage.

"The clear purpose was to force governments to intervene militarily," Brock wrote. A special projects and politics editor for the El Paso Herald-Post, Brock documented what he portrayed as the death of objective and fair reporting in the Yugoslav war.

Brock, whose name appears on a Serbian Unity Congress membership list, attempted to show the superficiality of coverage and singled out journalists for their sensational reporting, specifically about Serb death camps and systematic rape by Serbs. Brock alleges that crimes committed by Croats and Muslims were not given equal play.

During research for an upcoming book, Balkan analyst Obrad Kesic interviewed some 60 Western European and American journalists who covered the Balkan war. He calls the preliminary conclusions "troubling."

Kesic identified a common thread, particularly among younger reporters, that to be neutral was to abandon "some grand moral code." "These journalists saw themselves as crusaders. They believed they not only should decide what information we receive, but how we should digest and process it," he says. He wonders, for instance, why more reporters didn't write about Serbian children who were targeted by snipers or about Serbian refugees forced into exile.

Johanna Neuman, author of "Lights, Camera, War," and foreign editor for USA Today, does not believe impassioned newspaper reports and graphic TV images sway policy. Neuman, who compiled research on the subject while on a fellowship at Columbia University, argues that it is political leadership, or the lack of it, that determines the impact of the media.

Neuman cites Bosnia as proof that the media often have little influence on diplomacy, despite four years of a steady drumbeat from Bosnia, backed by images of children blown to bits, marketplace massacres and gripping TV interviews of women recounting rape.

"If images were driving policy, the U.S. Marines would have marched into Bosnia a long time ago," says Neuman, who lectures at George Washington University's Elliott School of International Affairs.

The Post's Jackson Diehl also doubts the ultimate impact of reporting on U.S. policy and the international community. "Bosnia clearly was a more complicated, risky operation. Policy makers are less likely to be swayed by the media in a situation like that," says Diehl, who maintains that other political and military factors more likely motivated U.S. action.

The New York Times' David Binder believes journalists tend to take their lead from governments in setting reporting agendas. In Bosnia, he says, that led to an anti-Serb bias. "When the American government, very early in the 1990s, singled out the Serbs for everything wrong in the former Yugoslavia, that set a pattern that exists even to this day."

For her part, Amanpour staunchly defends her reporting. "We're not perfect, and there are probably many, many flaws, but in the face of a relentless desire to keep this [the atrocities] secret, to stop intervention and not do anything about the worst atrocities that have happened in Europe since World War II, we journalists fought that," she says. "…They were forced out in the open by journalists. We have done our jobs; we have everything to be proud of."

ON MARCH 9, 1995, A PAGE ONE STORY by Roger Cohen of the New York Times told of a CIA report that faulted the Serbs in 90 percent of the atrocities in the Balkans. And that, Cohen noted, made "nonsense" of the view that the Bosnia conflict is a civil war for which guilt should be equally shared by Serbs, Croats and Muslims.

For journalists like Amanpour, who believe—and reported—along those lines, the Cohen story offered a form of vindication. She says the reaction by the U.N. and others was often contradictory. "I strongly believe there was an attempt by the international community to make the war in Bosnia sound like a quote 'civil war' with all sides equally guilty, built on centuries of ethnic hatred," she says. "None of that is accurate." In fact, she says, it was the international community that found the Serbs guilty. "It's not me who put sanctions against Serbia," she says. "It's not me who created safe areas to protect Muslims from besieging Serbs. It was the international community, which shows there was an acceptance of the overwhelming burden of guilt on one side."

But she was the one who decided to confront President Clinton back in May 1994, and in the end, after his icy response, Clinton ultimately bowed to Amanpour. Later in the program, referring back to her, Clinton said, "That poor woman has seen the horrors of this war, and she has had to report on them. She's been fabulous. She's done a great service to the whole world on that. I do not blame her for being mad at me. But I'm doing the best I can on this problem."

Amanpour stared back, silent.

The Power of TALK

Call-in democracy ignited the presidential race. Now it's shaking up government, rattling Clinton—and driving Washington's agenda.

HOWARD FINEMAN

Let's talk about the power of talk, of calling in to your favorite show:

■ A Florida man goes on CNN's "Larry King Live." He says his wife died of cancer because she used a cellular phone. There is no scientific study on the question. The cellular industry scoffs and declines to put a spokesman on the show. Big mistake. The lines light up. By last Friday—eight days after "King"—a share of stock in Motorola, Inc., the biggest maker of cellular phones, has dropped 20 percent. The federal government, at the industry's urging, gears up to study the issue.

■ It's two days before Bill Clinton's Inauguration. On public radio in Washington, host Diane Rehm goes to the "open phones." Much of her audience is, literally, inside the Beltway, people who might be sympathetic to Zoë Baird's child-care problems. The lines light up. Opinion makers and politicos are listening. The verdict: Zoë's got to go. "If that's the feeling here," Rehm muses, "what's happening in Sioux City?" Washington begins to get the message. Three days later Baird withdraws.

■ On Tuesday the Joint Chiefs of Staff meet with Secretary of Defense Les Aspin in the "Tank," their Pentagon conference room. The topic: whether to allow avowed homosexuals in the military. The Chiefs are against it on military grounds. But they have other arguments. Top brass are not known for the common touch, but they tell the president: look at the polls, listen to the radio. Three days later Clinton moves far more cautiously than he had wanted, merely ordering the services to quit asking new recruits if they are gay.

Talk-show democracy changed politics in the presidential race last year, bringing candidates phone to phone with voters. With his vision of teledemocracy and his surprisingly strong showing in November, Ross Perot woke up the establishment to the voters' anger. Now comes the next step: call-in government. Having tasted power, voter-callers want more; having risen through talk, Clinton is being rattled by it. "People want two-way talk," says King. "They say, 'We want to talk to our government!'" Americans can do it through the burgeoning phenomenon of call-in shows, led by King, Rush Limbaugh and Brian Lamb on C-Span, and mirrored locally by dozens of tart-tongued, influential hosts. These shows, in turn, generate tidal waves of switchboard-clogging calls and letters-to-your-congressman. Call-in government is a needed jolt to sclerotic Washington. But it also raises the specter of government by feverish plebiscite—an entertaining, manipulable and trivializing process that could eat away at the essence of representative democracy.

It's hot: It's probably inevitable. Call-in shows are a fast-growing format, accounting for nearly 1,000 of the nation's 10,000 radio stations. "Larry King Live" is the highest-rated show on CNN. This week he switches his 15-year-old late-night radio call-in show to afternoon "drive time" on more than 300 stations, quadrupling his radio audience. Television networks, which experimented with call-in formats during the campaign, are studying ways to use them again. "You're going to see a lot more call-in on the networks," predicts King. "It's hot and they know it."

Technology and demographics are the agents of change. Cheap satellite time allows local hosts like Mike Siegel of Seattle to go national with ease. Many mobile-phone services now have special deals with call-in shows, enabling motorists to punch a single button to dial in. King's new show will be carried live on United Airlines planes, most of them equipped with phones. Two decades ago baby boomers turned on, tuned in and dropped out of politics. Now, says Atlanta radio consultant Jon Sinton, they are tuning in again, abandoning rock for talk. Flying to the coast, or idling on a clogged freeway, they can get in touch using the same cellular technology King's guest told them to worry about. "Now you can call Larry and get cancer at the same time," jokes Sinton.

Politicians are getting with the program, literally. New York Gov. Mario Cuomo is a pioneer; he's hosted a regular call-in show for years. Other local politicians are dong the same. At the Democratic National Committee, new chairman David Wilhelm is laying plans for Clinton and other administration officials to make themselves available for call-ins. If he needs any advice, he can ask Susan Estrich. A former Harvard law professor, she ran Michael Dukakis's famously out-of-touch campaign in 1988. She left Cambridge, Mass., for Los Angeles, where she now teaches law—and hosts a call-in show. "Anybody who ever spent five minutes in radio," she

---

NEWSWEEK POLL

Do you have a favorable opinion of Hillary Clinton?
60% Favorable
20% Unfavorable

Do you approve of Bill Clinton naming his wife to lead administration efforts to reform the country's health-care system?
61% Approve
32% Disapprove

Will Hillary Clinton do a good job coming up with a health-care plan?
62% Yes   21% No

NEWSWEEK Poll, Jan. 28-29, 1993

says, "could have told you that gays in the military would strike a chord."

You could have learned the same lesson by watching C-Span. Though it is available in 58 million homes, its audience is rarely more than 2 million. But a new survey shows that an astounding 98 percent of its viewers voted in 1992, and the network provides instant feedback from them. During breaks in the Baird hearings, C-Span's Lamb fielded viewer calls in his deadpan manner. The voices grew angrier with each break—and they were being heard by the same Capitol insiders who were watching the hearings. "In the old days people would have had to wait for details on Baird," says lamb. "Now it's in real time."

The next layer of the call-in system is CNN. Increasingly the network is including viewer call-in segments in its news shows to complement King's prime-time appearances. The network's ratings rose sharply during the election year and stayed there. CNN's newest star is White House communications director George Stephanopoulos, whose boyishly evasive briefings garner high daytime ratings. "He's getting some of our highest numbers," says a CNN official. CNN is likely to continue carrying Stephanopoulos—and wrap call-ins around him.

NEWSWEEK POLL

Should homosexuals be able to serve in the armed forces?
CURRENT
53% Yes   42% No
11/92
48% Yes   44% No

Should the military temporarily stop asking about inductees' sexual orientation while the new administration consults about changing policy on gays in the military?
44% Yes   48% No

NEWSWEEK Poll, Jan. 28-29, 1993

Until recently, and with the important exception of Ralph Nader, Democrats and their allies largely ignored the power of talk broadcasting. Conservatives have always understood and relied on it. While Franklin Roosevelt sold his New Deal in radio "fireside chats," Father Coughlin and Gerald L. K. Smith developed their own vast audiences of naysayers. Long before he became president, Ronald Reagan sharpened his antigovernment message on the radio. Pat Buchanan honed his combative style as a call-in host in Washington. "The fact is that liberals feel empowered and conservatives don't," says Limbaugh.

If conservatives feel any sense of "empowerment" these days, it's due in large part to Limbaugh. His show is the most listened-to in talk radio (15 million tune in each week on 560 stations). His best-selling book, "The Way Things Ought to Be," has sold 2 million copies in hardback; his TV call-in show is fast approaching Letterman-Leno ratings, and a new newsletter has 170,000 subscribers. Only nominally a call-in affair, Limbaugh's show offers group therapy for mostly white males who feel politically challenged and who would rather hear Rush's voice than their own. But they react. In Sacramento, Calif., last week, a Democratic lawmaker banned Limbaugh's show from the internal broadcasting system in the California capitol. Limbaugh, who began his broadcasting in Sacramento, put the issue to his listeners. Within minutes, calls poured in. His show was back on the system that same day.

As famous as King, Limbaugh and Lamb have become, the roots and power of call-in

---

Look Who's Talking

Ross Perot didn't invent rule by phone, he merely tapped into a network that's been giving millions of Americans someone to talk to for years. Last week the phone lines crackled with discussion about Bill Clinton, Zoë Baird and gay soldiers. But a survey of some leading chat shows reveals that there was still plenty of room for local news, gossip—and ego.

MICHAEL JACKSON, Los Angeles
Hot Topic: Gang violence
Audience: 1,150,000
Political Slant: Liberal
Pet Peeve: Proposed license fee for L.A. hiking trails

MIKE SIEGEL, Seattle
Hot Topic: Gays in the military
Audience: 800,000
Political Slant: "Pragmatist"
Pet Peeves: Seattle's "politically correct" police chief, crack houses

IMHOTEC GARY BYRD, New York
Hot Topic: Haiti
Audience: 1 million
Political Slant: Liberal, Afrocentric
Pet Peeve: Double Standards

JERRY WILLIAMS, Boston
Hot Topic: Local water rates
Audience: 250,000
Political Slant: "Pragmatic"
Pet Peeves: Big government, high taxes

LARRY KING, Washington
Hot Topics: Foreign-policy hot spots, gas taxes
Audience: 8,520,000
Political Slant: Nonpartisan
Pet Peeve: Long-winded callers

RUSH LIMBAUGH, New York
Hot Topic: Clinton's promises
Audience: 15 million
Political Slant: Conservative
Pet Peeves: Liberals, "Feminazis," tree-hugging environmentalists

BRIAN LAMB, Washington
Hot Topic: White House press access
Audience: (Not available)
Political Slant: "Completely neutral"
Pet Peeve: People who call more than once a month

DIANE REHM, Washington
Hot Topic: Zoë Baird
Audience: 100,000
Political Slant: Liberal
Pet Peeves: Callers who disregard women's rights

ROE CONN, Chicago
Hot Topics: Mike Ditka, the Chicago Bears, the "Home Alone" family
Audience: 500,000
Political Slant: Liberal
Pet Peeve: The recession

DAVID GOLD, Dallas
Hot Topics: Zoë Baird and gay soldiers
Audience: 138,000
Political Slant: Conservative
Pet Peeves: Liberal media and big government

Special Features
New York celebs **Don Imus**, **Howard Stern** and **Bob Grant** have mass appeal, attracting a million listeners a week each. **Malin Salu**, whose New York call-in show is in Spanish, and Washington African-American conservative **Armstrong Williams** wield influence in their communities. Veteran hosts **Bob Hardy** (St. Louis) and **Brad Davis** (Hartford) draw big audiences interested in consumer and community affairs.

6. THE STATE OF THE NATION

democracy are local. Call-in shows first turned political in New York and Boston, cities in which arguing in public about politics—or anything else—is a way of life. The recent history of call-in clout begins with 35-year veteran Jerry Williams in Boston, who in 1989 teamed up with Ralph Nader and others to protest a congressional pay raise. They succeeded in delaying it six months. Williams, Siegel and others founded the National Association of Radio Talk Show hosts—a kind of Continental Congress of call-in government.

Talk-show hosts can get results—and have been doing so for years before Rush Limbaugh arrived. In Seattle, Siegel took his microphone to a crack house and got it shut down. In Boston, Williams helped derail the state's seat-belt law, the proposed location of a state prison and numerous legislative pay increases. In 1986, he got 2,000 people to show up on Beacon Hill in a snowstorm to decry a Dukakis tax increase. "It's nothing new," Williams says of the Limbaughs of the world. "It is they who have been asleep."

With Nader in the lead, others outside the conservative movement are exploring the power of talk radio. National Public Radio has launched a successful call-in show, "Talk of the Nation." It's now heard on more than 70 stations, most in major markets. Jim Hightower, a feisty Democrat and former agriculture commissioner in Texas, is launching a national show he says will attack an establishment the right rarely touches: Wall Street and big corporations. He's resisting pleas to turn the program into a call-in ("I don't want to be chained to a studio"), but if he is going to be true to his populist roots, he may have no choice.

Secular religion: This may all be great broadcasting, but is it good government? Perot, who's busy wiring his "town halls," obviously thinks so. So do many of the 19 million Americans who voted for him. Conservatives think it's grand—a more accurate reflection of grass-roots opinion than the evening news. Radio consultant Sinton agrees—even though he is advising Hightower and calls Limbaugh "Hitler Light." "The grass roots are basically conservative," says Sinton. "And our medium, radio, is much more representative of America than others." Free expression is America's secular religion. Tuning in—and calling in—is just a high-tech way of honoring it.

But it can be honored too much. What King calls the "hum" of talk radio can be misleading. Only the most devoted and outraged of listeners call—rarely more than 2 or 3 percent of an audience. Politicians who react slavishly can be deceived. "It's a potential early-warning sign, like radar in Greenland," says Democratic polltaker Harrison Hickman. "You don't launch a strike based on that evidence alone." And its effects can be oversold. "Talk shows didn't get rid of Zoë Baird," says Limbaugh. "She got rid of herself."

The more troubling question is whether America needs a government of its angriest voices. "Only the people who feel most strongly call us," says Rehm. "But they aren't the only ones who vote." Dial-in democracy is attracting the same forces of manipulation that prey on other levers of power; interest groups on the right and left have the technology and determination to patch themselves into the national conversation. The intensity, speed and entertainment value of talk radio has a downside in a society already plagued by long-lasting problems and a short attention span. Ratings count and boredom is the enemy. There's enormous pressure to keep the "board lit" by moving to the next hot topic.

But it's obvious how this controversy will come out. On CNN last week, "Crossfire" debated the pros and cons of dial-in democracy. The weekend shows discussed it. Rehm has scheduled a call-in show about . . . call-in shows. So all you need to do now is pick up the phone and give your opinion.

With DONNA FOOTE *in Los Angeles,*
PATRICIA KING *in San Francisco,* MARK STARR
in Boston and GINNY CARROLL *in Houston*

THE BOYS ON THE 'NET

The campaign beat now includes home pages on the World Wide Web.

WENDELL COCHRAN

MARK 1996 AS THE YEAR politics discovered the computer as a communications tool. The Internet, the World Wide Web and e-mail have all become resources of choice for politicians and journalists who cover them.

"A political reporter who's not online is behind the curve a little bit," says Jeffrey Weiss, a Dallas Morning News reporter. And by all accounts, journalists can only look forward to seeing more and more campaign-related activities move to the Internet and other online sites. David L. Haase, Washington correspondent for the Indianapolis Star & News, says he checks political sites on the 'Net much like "doing office rounds if you're covering a [congressional] delegation."

Much of this move to get online has come about because politicians have recognized that the Internet and other electronic communications media give them powerful new ways to get their messages out, to citizens as well as journalists.

To see what might be a prototype for how political issues are framed and communicated in the electronic world, drop in on the World Wide Web's Flat Tax Home Page (http://www.house.gov/armey.flattax/), courtesy of House Majority Leader Dick Armey of Texas and Sen. Richard Shelby, an Alabama Republican, cosponsors of one of many flat tax proposals. You can get "flat-tax-related press releases." You can connect to the Internal Revenue Service's home page. (Don't, however, expect a discussion of the flat tax on the IRS site.)

One document on Armey's page invites you to "click here for excerpts from a representative sample of thousands of letters Mr. Armey has received." Typical: "Hurray for a flat tax!"—Kathleen, Mt. Pleasant, South Carolina. But viewers looking for a quote like "This flat tax is awful" will search in vain.

The page also has the obligatory summaries of the Armey-Shelby proposal and, for the truly wonked-out, the full text of their bill, which as of yet has gone nowhere in Congress. Seven months after it was introduced, the bill had a single cosponsor in the House and two in the Senate.

The Armey-Shelby page is one of many sites where you can get flat tax information. There are flat tax discussions on the "Forbes for President" page and other Web pages related to taxes. And there are numerous chat groups,

6. THE STATE OF THE NATION

mailing lists, newsgroups and bulletin boards where "ordinary people" log on to express their flat tax views.

The flat tax is just one example of how issues are being voiced on the Internet. Every serious presidential candidate has a home page on the World Wide Web (and some who aren't so serious, like Pat Paulsen). These sites offer press releases, biographies, reports of favorable polls, rosters of campaign staff, addresses of campaign offices, position papers, schedules and other information about the campaign. Sen. Bob Dole's home page solicits campaign contributions; donors sending more than $25 will be given an official "Bob Dole for President" mousepad.

Many major publications have also developed Web sites that primarily provide access to political and government information. And many reporters are finding that it's getting so they can't cover aspects of politics and government without first hooking up to the online world. They are also discovering that cyberspace needs to be covered as an increasingly important part of the campaigns themselves.

RECOGNIZING THIS TREND, several newspapers have assigned journalists to write about the electronic campaigns.

Brock Meeks is covering the 1996 campaigns in his new capacity as chief Washington correspondent for Wired magazine and Hotwired, its electronic counterpart, and is up against a 6 p.m. daily deadline. He uses the home pages of the presidential candidates frequently. "I can often find their press releases faster in the home page than on PR Newswire or the fax machine," he says. When Meeks was searching for information on the flat tax, he used the PoliticsUSA site, offered by a partnership between National Journal and the American Political Network, to find references to past stories, which he passed along to a researcher. "This all happens within 15 minutes," Meeks says. "It would take hours to track down and at much greater expense" using conventional means.

PoliticsUSA is one of the most popular Internet sites among political journalists. Doug Bailey, a former Republican political consultant and cofounder of the American Political Network, says the aim is to make the Internet site "a first-stop shopping" location for journalists and others interested in politics. The site offers extensive coverage of the 1996 presidential candidates, but its most useful features for journalists are the archives of The Hotline, a daily roundup of political news from sources around the nation published by Bailey's company, and a fully searchable edition of the Almanac of American Politics, considered by many to be the political bible.

Several other major organizations have also entered the market: Congressional Quarterly offers American Voter '96; the Washington Post, Newsweek and ABC News are collaborating on a venture called Electionline; Time and CNN have joined forces to operate a site called AllPolitics; and C-SPAN is operating a site called "Campaign '96." Dozens of local and regional newspapers also are devoting extensive coverage of the campaign through their electronic editions. Most of these sites are not aimed directly at journalists, but many have proved useful to reporters.

It's not surprising that Meeks uses the Internet to supplement his reporting. He is a pioneer in the use of electronic communications systems by journalists, and his publication is devoted to coverage of the online world. But scores of other reporters and publications are also discovering the value of having an Internet connection when it comes to covering politics.

"I'm just starting to explore, but I anticipate it's going to be an increasingly useful tool," says Kathy Kiely, Washington bureau chief of the Arkansas Democrat-Gazette. Kiely says she expects Internet connections to be "really helpful on the road. That's where you need it." For example, she envisions being able to connect to the Little Rock paper's home library while she's traveling with President Bill Clinton during the 1996 campaign.

Kiely, who took a computer-assisted journalism seminar in 1993, might have moved to using electronic tools sooner, but until recently her bureau, like many others around the country, didn't have the computer horsepower it takes for a full-scale Internet hookup. Editors and managers are discovering the need to upgrade their equipment now that the use of the computer has become more integral to journalism. Many journalists, like Indianapolis' Haase, find their office computers are less suited to Internet-based reporting than their home machines. "I do a lot of trolling the 'Net there," says Haase, who writes a weekly column about the Internet and politics. It appears in the newspaper's electronic version, StarNews Online, but not in the printed editions.

Haase isn't covering the presidential campaign daily, though he used the 'Net to keep track of the ill-fated presidential campaign of Indiana Republican Sen. Richard Lugar day to day. Among other things, he subscribed to a University of New Hampshire-based electronic mail service that tracks the candidates for the Republican nomination. Haase thinks he could get a story off the Internet every other day.

Electronic reporting doesn't often produce information that reporters couldn't find through some other means. But it makes it possible to access large amounts of data more quickly and more easily.

"It's a matter of rearranging my time," says Rick Dunham, national political correspondent for Business Week. He checks America Online and other sources to keep up with breaking stories. And he drops in on presidential candidate Internet sites and other locations daily. For example, he says, it's been possible this year to track schedules "without having to call nine different people."

Haase finds easy access one of the Internet's most important advantages. "If I need to compare positions I can call three campaigns, play a little phone tag with press secretaries and then get a canned statement. Or I can go to Project Vote Smart," an independent political organization based in Oregon that encourages participation in the political process by collecting and disseminating candidate information online. That kind of access is really important to many regional reporters in Washington, as well as to those who aren't based there. "If you're not the Washington Post or the New York Times or one of the networks, it's hard to get one of these campaigns to respond to you in a timely manner," Haase says.

Journalists also are finding that electronic mail can give them quick and direct access to sources, and can also serve as a fast way to receive press releases and other material. Dunham has begun to make extensive use of electronic mail. When the Democratic Senatorial Campaign Committee began to issue a weekly update, Dunham asked for it electronically and the committee obliged. "I look at a press release that comes electronically," he says. And a message in his e-mail account "catches my attention more than some of the fax stuff."

Eventually, many observers expect electronic mail to become a primary means of political communication. Mail lists let candidates communicate directly with a targeted audience of commit-

37. Boys on the 'Net

ted supporters. For now it appears that many politicians, especially members of Congress, are wary of e-mail, which could, in time, overwhelm their ability to answer constituent correspondence.

But Doug Bailey predicts e-mail will become the most common method of political fundraising. Pat Buchanan's campaign, which many journalists think runs one of the best candidate home pages, also has one of the most active mail lists.

Some campaigns and political organizations are starting to use e-mail for direct mail. Ross Perot's United We Stand America Party relies on e-mail to keep the movement's adherents in touch with one another. Jeffrey Weiss of the Dallas Morning News recently began using e-mail to help his newspaper keep track of the often fractious disputes that have characterized the Perot camp since the 1992 campaign. Getting access to some of this e-mail might become a problem, especially when the campaigns become more sophisticated about its use and learn ways to shut out those they don't want eavesdropping.

Weiss and other journalists find the online world to be a good way of keeping track of what ordinary citizens are saying about the candidates and political issues. Every online service has areas devoted to political discussions. The Internet newsgroups, known collectively as Usenet, also can be busy sites for lively talk.

The chat groups are "the cyberspace equivalent to hanging out in New Hampshire in a coffee house," Meeks says. Haase says he checks in with the newsgroups to "see what the crazies are talking about. It hasn't produced a lot of copy, but it has kept me informed."

But the journalists who use these groups to keep in touch with political feelings are wary of them as sources. Few reporters would feel safe quoting from an electronic poster who had not been contacted directly to confirm the information and the identity of the writer.

Chuck Raasch, who's covering the campaign for Gannett News Service,

T*HE DALLAS Morning News' Jeffrey Weiss says the most important reason to monitor the electronic aspects of modern campaigns is to determine whether "online actually is affecting the non-online universe."*

says it's possible "this is going to be the new avenue of underground attack stuff." Raasch says that already a school board race in Great Falls, Montana, was affected by negative material that was spread by way of bulletin boards and other electronic means. Tracking such attacks could be made more difficult in the electronic realm, given that users who know what they are doing can post material anonymously. Michael Tackett, national political writer at the Chicago Tribune, agrees. He says the electronic communications systems offer ways to "attack someone in a spurious, sinister way." He wouldn't be surprised to see ads similar to the infamous Willie Horton spot from the 1988 campaign appear on the Internet.

Weiss says the most important reason to monitor the electronic aspects of modern campaigns is to determine whether "online actually is affecting the non-online universe." He says that for electronic campaigning to "have any real meaning it has to affect the outside world."

M*OST OBSERVERS DON'T* think that the Internet and other online politicking have made that leap yet. Says David Fink, politics and government editor at the Hartford Courant, "I have no illusions. I don't believe a huge number of people are going to get their news from the Internet this year." The numbers of hits on the presidential candidate home pages remains relatively small. Still, Fink has decided to devote about half of one reporter's time to tracking computerized campaigning.

There's also one other sign of the importance of this new medium to politics: Political humor has moved to the Internet. Several satirical political sites have popped up to make fun at the expense of presidential candidates. On one you can watch Bob Dole's head explode. The Forbes campaign is lampooned on another. Unwary visitors have to be careful: The addresses for these pages are very similar to the addresses for the real deal. And the official Buchanan pages contain what appears to be a poke at the press: In some Web browsers, the background graphic for the Buchanan press page is a stone wall.

With campaigns getting more computer-savvy by the day, the way of the future for political journalists is clear: Get connected and stay connected. "The people who are using it now are pioneers," says Haase. "In another four years it will be standard. By 2004, it will be assumed that reporters will get most of their information off the Internet."

Wendell Cochran teaches journalism in the School of Communication at American University.

Politics Online

NEWS ORGANIZATIONS

Washington Post / Newsweek / ABC News Electionline
http://www.electionline.com

American Political Network / National Journal PoliticsUSA
http://politicsUSA.com

Time / CNN AllPolitics
http://allpolitics.com

Congressional Quarterly's American Voter '96
http://voter96.cqalert.com

C-SPAN Campaign '96
http://www.c-span.org/campaign/campfram.htm

PRESIDENTIAL CAMPAIGNS

President Bill Clinton
http://www.whitehouse.gov

Buchanan for President
http://www.buchanan.org

Dole for President
http://www.dole96.com

Forbes for President
http://www.forbes96.com

Keyes for President
http://www.keyes.gocin.com

INDEPENDENT GROUPS

Project Vote Smart
http://www.vote-smart.org

League of Women Voters
http://www.electriciti.com/~lwvus/

The Shape of Things to Come

In 1926, U.S. inventor Lee De Forest, the "father of the radio," noted, "While theoretically and technically television may be feasible, commercially and financially I consider it an impossibility, a development of which we need waste little time daydreaming." In 1946, Darryl Zanuck, head of the 20th Century-Fox motion picture studio, predicted that "[Television] won't be able to hold onto any market it captures after the first six months. People will soon get tired of staring at a plywood box every night." De Forest and Zanuck have been proven wrong. Contrary to their predictions, television established itself as a mass medium with unexpected speed. It took 80 years from the time the telephone was invented until it was available in 80 percent of American homes, 25 years for radio to enter 80 percent of homes, and only 10 years for television to reach 80 percent of the population. Nielsen Media Research tells us that 98 percent of American households now have televisions. People have not tired of staring at a plywood box every night; however, television is surely not the final word in media technology.

The articles in this section provide their own predictions of changes to come. In "The Age of Convergence," Philip Moeller speculates on the future of news media in an interactive media environment that integrates computers, fiber optics, and cable systems into a delivery system for multimedia content. Writing in early 1994, Moeller noted that "the most dramatic signs of convergence have been the far-reaching mergers announced or proposed by many of the biggest players—telephone companies, cable systems, and video powerhouses." By the end of 1995, news of media megamergers between Rupert Murdoch's News Corporation and long-distance telephone company MCI, Disney and Capital Cities/ABC, Westinghouse Electric and CBS, Gannett News and Multimedia, Inc., and the Turner Broadcasting System and Time Warner rocked the media industry in quick succession. The Disney–Capital Cities/ABC merger created a company with combined revenues of $16.5 billion and ownership of the ABC Television Network, 10 large-market local television stations, 21 radio stations, the Disney Channel (as well as 80 percent ownership of ESPN, 50 percent ownership of Lifetime, and 38 percent ownership of A&E), Walt Disney Pictures, Touchstone Pictures, Hollywood Pictures, Miramax, Buena Vista Home Video International, Hollywood Records, Hyperion Books, Fairchild Publications, 7 daily and 75 weekly newspapers, 56 shopping guides and real estate magazines, 55 diversified niche publications, 8 financial service and medical journals, Walt Disney Records, Walt Disney Publishing, the Anaheim Mighty Ducks hockey team, and several theme park and resort properties. Critics of the deal have questioned whether there is anything with meaningful entertainment value that Disney does *not* own, or will not soon absorb.

Not surprisingly, the current trend toward media mergers and maverick spinoffs, such as HotWired, has been viewed from varied perspectives. Some fear the impact of consolidated corporate structures on independent news reporting and the loss of multiple independent voices reflecting diversity of opinion. Some predict merely a coming of more avenues competing for audiences via similar content produced in similar bad taste. Others foresee an exciting evolution that turns today's passive media forms into a two-way, interactive information highway offering endless variety, convenience, and flexibility—where the tools currently used in video and computer games immerse entertainment as well as information seekers in a three-dimensional world of illusion controlled by the consumer (see "The Amazing Video Game Boom" and "Cyberspace Journalism").

Most media futurists admit that one important unknown factor in the portrait of media to come is the direction of government regulatory policy. Merger mania among media industries has been fueled by an extended run of deregulatory sentiment in Washington. Restrictions enacted in 1970 to restrain the three major television networks from monopolizing the production and distribution of programming expired in November 1995. Regulations pertaining to the reach and saturation of any one media owner's holdings are being systematically relaxed. Ann Okerson in "Who Owns Digital Works?" explains legal battles yet to be fought, such as the interpretation of copyright law as applied to material created for and/or "published" over the Internet. Issues of free speech and equal access have become hot topics in anticipating the

UNIT 7

nation's transition to media interactivity. According to Jeff Baumann, executive vice president and general counsel of the National Association of Broadcasters, "Things are happening so quickly in the marketplace, regulatory-wise and technologically, that it's difficult to get a grip on it. I don't think the public is aware and I don't think the Congress and the FCC have taken time to reflect on what these innovations really mean."

A second unknown factor addressed in these articles is media consumers' ultimate acceptance of new media technology, for just as a marketplace orientation has shaped present-day media, it will influence media of the future. In "Immaculate Reception," Marshall Jon Fisher describes the development and promises of digital television technology, but then asks two critical questions: Does the public want high-definition television enough to pay for it? And why should broadcasters spend $10 billion or so to convert their stations to digital simply to show their viewers the same old programs? Michael Krantz questions in his report, "The Biggest Thing Since Color?" whether newly minted NetTVs, designed with both cable and Internet connection ports, will find the average couch potato interested in waiting for a Web page to download when *NYPD Blue* provides far more action. "Media of the Future" test projects, such as GTE's Main Street interactive shopping and information service in Cerritos, California, have failed to attract the expected subscribers. Michael Noll, dean of the Annenberg School of Communications at the University of Southern California, suggests that "the level of satisfaction with current technology is likely to keep most consumers from making sizable investments in new electronics" and predicts that "rather than damning or enlightening humanity, a turbocharged home entertainment and information center most likely will be put to the same everyday uses as were its ancestor appliances—in short, to make life a little more diverting, inspiring, productive and convenient." The results of a recent Harris poll indicate that at least two-thirds of Americans currently do not know what the information highway is, much less what they think of it or whether they want to travel it.

Media futurists, however, estimate that between 5 million and 30 million households will be using new media by the year 2010. By tracking the preferences and reactions of these change leaders, media providers will come to understand the kinds of innovations that will ultimately be accepted by the mainstream. And even if new media forms are not ultimately widely embraced, their impact will be felt as current media evolve to compete with the attraction of their variety, novelty, and interactivity.

Looking Ahead: Challenge Questions

What projections of new media technology are the most attractive to you? Do you predict that new media forms will be more attractive for information or entertainment uses? Why?

Why do you think pilot tests of new media have failed to attract the expected interest among subscribers? What attributes do new media forms need to win mainstream adoption?

It has been argued that spectrum scarcity, the driving force behind FCC regulation of electronic media, is no longer an issue. Is there still a need for regulation of spectrum access? Of media content? Why or why not?

The age of convergence

Phone companies, cable systems and entertainment producers are rushing headlong into the new interactive electronic world while the print media try to figure out how they fit in.

Philip Moeller

In the pleasantly upscale Cascades housing development in Northern Virginia, Bell Atlantic has created a deceptively low-key "Intelligent Home" at 20648 Bellwood Court. Each room displays interactive services and tools that address family members' daily needs. The kids' bedroom features education, the kitchen is equipped for shopping, while the living room is for entertainment.

The technology pales in comparison with the new virtual-reality rides at major theme parks—until you realize there's nothing virtual about the reality in Bell Atlantic's home. Most of its services are here or close to being here, including the massive upgrading of cables, curbside wiring and computer systems needed to make it all happen.

The Intelligent Home then becomes an exciting distillation of the opportunities and technologies that seem destined for American households. But it is also a sobering vision for newspapers, and that was even the case before Bell Atlantic startled the communications world last fall by announcing it planned to buy the huge cable and programming company, Tele-Communications Inc. of Denver.

Newspapers have already begun to develop electronic ways to deliver news and information (see "The Future Is Now," October 1993). But most have not done much beyond annointing an electronic news editor and throwing together some audiotex and fax offerings. And still fewer have responded to Bell Atlantic and the host of equally imposing powerhouses that are laying the groundwork for multimedia empires. But across the country the tempo has picked up and it's clear this is a game newspapers very much want to play.

Omaha, Orlando and Castro Valley, California, are just a few of the unglamorous settings for one of the most glamorous events of not one but two millennia—the coming of the Age of Convergence of computers, fiber optics and cable. These cities will host some of the highest profile, best-funded research and development efforts to determine if consumers want—and can afford—this new "interactive multimedia."

In the more plebian settings of online services, equally significant content and packaging shifts are underway that are of more immediate significance to print journalism. The personal computer clearly will be a major delivery vehicle for multimedia content, as well as a more friendly environment for the newspaper industry's efforts to develop interactive products.

The Appeal of News

With a limitless library of movies and games soon to be only a keypad away, news and information services don't rate too highly in many surveys of likely demand for multimedia products. That's not surprising, however, because respondents probably have a clear idea of the movies and games they'd order, but little familiarity with interactive news products.

People do love to talk, and online conversations have proven big winners with the large online companies as well as smaller computer bulletin boards. Responsiveness, timeliness and some sense of individual control are key. And plain old text does just fine in this medium.

Dataquest Inc., a large Silicon Valley research firm, polled 200 families last summer about their attitudes toward multimedia. Bruce Ryon, the firm's principal analyst for multimedia research, notes that survey participants had to have $30,000 or more in annual household income and own either a computer or video game system. The resulting group was hardly representative of the general population; 90 percent of the households surveyed included married couples, with an average of two children around 12 years of age.

The research firm was interested in getting opinions from people who were already users of new technologies and, presumably, would be heavily represented among early users of multimedia products. What it also got was a group that highly values news and information services, and hard-core newspaper readers. In fact, 88 percent of the respondents were newspaper subscribers, and 36 percent received two or more dailies.

"My initial hunch was that they would be more interested in entertainment than in information," Ryon says, "but they were actually more interested in information, and news ranked fairly highly in the information category."

Asked to rate various types of interactive content, the respondents ranked news highest, with a rating of 52 percent. Educational information was next (45 percent), trailed by interactive game shows (38 percent) and directories, including program listings and restaurant menus (30 percent). Bringing up the rear were entertainment (29 percent), financial information (26 percent) and games (22 percent). These were responses from parents; presumably, teenagers and young adults would vote somewhat differently.

Beyond the interest in news, Ryon says, consumers also expressed a strong desire to gain some control over the flow of information that is inun-

38. Age of Convergence

dating them. That control is one of the most attractive features of interactive media, permitting users to retrieve what they want when they want it. "People want to be able to view TV news the same way they read a newspaper," Ryon says.

Corporate Convergence

The most dramatic signs of convergence have been the far-reaching mergers announced or proposed by many of the biggest players—telephone companies, cable systems and video powerhouses.

Bell Atlantic's planned merger with Tele-Communications Inc. was the biggest of the deals, perhaps even big enough to send members of Congress and Justice Department officials scurrying for antitrust statutes that were placed in storage during the Reagan-Bush years. But the battle between the QVC Network and Viacom International for control of Paramount Communications focused even more attention on the growing popularity of marrying huge storehouses of content—mostly movies, game shows and syndicated and cable series—with powerful new platforms for on-demand delivery to consumers. Almost lost in the shuffle: American Telephone & Telegraph's $13 billion deal for McCaw Cellular Communications, and at least two other big-bucks efforts to develop a national network for wireless cellular communications. These networks will carry a new generation of personal information products that can bypass traditional phone service.

At first glance, the wave of multimedia alliances seems to be a good deal for newspapers and magazines. Although print often has been forgotten in the glow of multimedia developments, it has been rediscovered as a provider of content to the new digital dynamos. Newspaper stocks, in the dumps for most of the stock market's march to record highs last year, were sharply higher last October after Wall Street analysts recognized that someone has to bring food to the party.

The search for the digital Holy Grail is taking these growing giants into several high visibility test sites, although with as much as $100 billion already wagered on interactive media, there's clearly no turning back. In the 1970s, Knight-Ridder and Times Mirror were ahead of the curve with videotex systems, and walked away from those experiences with some minor wounds and institutional savvy. Today, however, companies ahead of the curve will more likely try to redefine the curve instead of walking away.

Choice and Control

Three major trials of viewer-controlled programming delivered to TV sets are scheduled for launch this year, and there are numerous, smaller-scale efforts. They all will be using high-capacity, glass-fiber and coaxial cable to provide digitized information—text, audio and visuals—that can be ordered on demand.

A lot of attention will be focused on ease of use. In fact, the early stars of multimedia are less likely to be the content than the television set-top units that viewers will use to communicate with the service, and the hand-held remotes they will use to help them navigate.

Clearly, for a society that can't program VCRs, wading through lots of new offerings will be tough. Behind the scenes, the experimenters will also gauge the delivery capabilities of the participating telephone systems, which have been beefed up with fiber optics and computerized switching systems.

The "multi" in these early applications will be dominated by visual material. People don't plop down in front of their TVs to read the dictionary or to punch in checkbook balances for an electronic bill-paying service. And text is difficult to read on TV screens, which lack the resolution of computer monitors. Moreover, while kids' noses seem to break the plane of the TV screen regularly, most older people prefer to sit 10 to 15 feet away.

Therefore, the potential of delivering newspaper-like content on television is not clear, says Bob Meyers, Viacom's vice president of corporate development for interactive television. "We really haven't come to grips with how you transition something that's a printed, portable medium with what's an entertainment, visual medium." Meyers believes computer screens may be the more appropriate delivery vehicle for information products that have heavy text and graphics elements. In Viacom's test with AT&T in Castro Valley, California, the emphasis will be on visual entertainment.

Meyers stresses that Viacom, which owns MTV, Nickelodeon and Showtime, "sees itself as a programming company," so it needs to adjust as much as newspapers and other content providers do. "As the technology changes," says Meyers, "we, too, have to figure out how we are going to be distributed." Castro Valley, he says, is "a playground and gigantic focus group."

Lexicon

Audiotex: Automated telephone information, such as stock prices, sports scores and personals.

Bandwidth: The width of an electrical transmission path or circuit, or a measure of the volume of communications traffic that a channel can carry. The large bandwidths of optical fibers and, to a lesser extent, coaxial cable, make possible the home delivery of large amounts of information and visual material.

Coaxial Cable: The most common wiring used by cable TV operators.

Digital/Digitized: Any type of information that can be output, transmitted and interpreted as discrete bits of binary information, using electrical or electromagnetic signals that can be modulated to convey their specific content.

Digital Compression: Many multimedia products would not be feasible today if it were not for software advancements that greatly condense the digital information needed to replicate images on a recipient's viewing screen.

Fiber Optics: Glass strands that use light waves to transmit vast amounts of digital information.

Information Superhighway: The shorthand description for the growing network of computer-based, digital communication pathways.

Interactive: Information services that permit users to respond to the information provider. Electronic mail, home shopping on TV and pay-per-view TV are all examples of interactive content.

Modem (modular-demodulator): The device that links personal computers to a telephone line, allowing them to send or receive digital information.

Multimedia: Information products that include text, audio and visual content.

Online Services: Subscription-based providers of information and entertainment that can be accessed using a personal computer and a modem.

Source: "The New Telecommunications," by Frederick Williams (Free Press, New York)

7. THE SHAPE OF THINGS TO COME

In Cerritos, California, not many cable customers have subscribed to Main Street, even though its sponsor, GTE, has spent four years and millions of dollars to develop it. Main Street provides about 60 sources of special content and is interactive. But it hasn't caught on and is viewed in some circles as a cautionary tale that consumers are not ready for or interested in a mass market product that delivers interactive entertainment, information and transactions.

Other detractors say Main Street has not been a fair test of consumer attitudes because it's a technological clunker victimized by the limited transmission capabilities of coaxial cable and copper wire. The content and visual presentation might be fine if users were expecting a low-resolution online service, but not for a television product. GTE officials did not respond to repeated requests for an interview.

Time Warner Cable, which is putting together in Orlando what is billed as the most extensive test of interactive media, envisions a more direct role for the kind of content newspapers might provide. "We believe there is a substantial benefit... to form local alliances with newspapers, to provide a variety of on-demand information," says company spokesman Michael Luftman. Besides parent Time Warner, other investors include Toshiba and U S West, one of the seven regional phone companies.

The major informational resources of Time will be used to create multimedia news offerings, putting consumers in control of tailoring the content, duration and delivery time of the news. This product, while relying heavily on video, will be accompanied by text that can be output over new Hewlett-Packard printers that are being developed and tested especially for the Orlando project.

The Orlando Full Service Network (FSN), as the project is called, expects to offer some content by April to an audience of some 4,000 customers of the local Time Warner cable system. The Orlando Sentinel will likely provide some local content for the test, but details of the relationship are still being worked out. The Sentinel is also developing an online product that users will access from America Online, similar to what its sister paper, the Chicago Tribune, has done.

"No one's going to be making any money out of this for a long, long time," Sentinel Editor John Haile says. "But I think we're going to be learning an awful lot.

"As a core structure, you need to have the newspaper online, and we will do that," he says. "But that's not the most important thing.... We're looking at national services, things about Florida that people around the country would be interested in."

Because digital products can move around the world as easily as across the street, a broader market for certain newspaper content makes sense. Larger markets can also justify capital investments that wouldn't otherwise be prudent for local or regional papers. And while current R&D efforts don't have to pay for themselves, commercial ventures do.

In addition, Haile says, his newspaper will have to adjust to the real-time demands of electronic publishing, providing constantly updated information. And adding value to information will be more clearly seen as a requirement of a successful product. Here, Haile says, newspapers have strengths that can't easily be matched by others because editors and reporters are trained to distill the most important information from a story.

"The core job of the newsroom is the same," Haile says. "When you have 500 choices for information, the role of the editor becomes all that more important. That's one of the reasons I'm so optimistic about the future of newspapers."

Modem Mania

Today the computer screen is a more sensible place than TV for newspapers. It is much easier to read text on high-resolution monitors and, even with big gains in the amount of information that can be piped over telephone lines, it will be some time before large amounts of visual content can be handled the same way. Newspapers are becoming increasingly adept at generating and storing color graphics and photographs in digital form, and this fits in nicely with the technology curve on which online services now sit. And don't assume that computer screens will be limited for long by low-capacity phone lines for outside communications. Cable TV companies are working on providing access to computers in the home over their commodious broadband systems, and online services are now testing cable modems hooked up to personal computers.

Further, the prospect of 500-channel cable systems is hardly intimidating to veteran online "surfers." CompuServe, the H&R Block subsidiary that is the largest commercial online service, already offers 1,700 databases and forums. With more and more content being added almost daily, commercial online services are gathering valuable knowledge about how to present information.

With such a bewildering array of content, brand-name sources of information can become strong magnets. For example, people are much more likely to access critiques by Siskel and Ebert than "generic" movie reviews. And newspapers are seen as very good providers of trusted information, especially in their local markets.

America Online, the newest and most aggressive of the major online services, provides access to the most publications, including the Atlantic Monthly, Consumer Reports, National Geographic, the New Republic and Time. It's also the only service so far to provide access to electronic subscription products from daily newspapers, first with Chicago Online from the Chicago Tribune and later with Mercury Center from the San Jose Mercury News.

CompuServe and Prodigy, the

"No one's going to be making any money out of this for a long, long time. But I think we're going to be learning an awful lot."

—Orlando Sentinel Editor John Haile

Sears-IBM partnership, have since joined in, with the most noteworthy alliances being those made with Prodigy by Times Mirror and Cox Newspapers. Cox also is working with BellSouth on interactive advertising products and, along with the Tribune Co., has been particularly active in pushing information products onto new platforms.

Prodigy views newspapers as essential to its development. "They have local content, promotional capabilities and contacts that we, as a company located in White Plains, New York, do not have," says Gerry Mueller, vice president of new business ventures.

Mueller says Cox's Atlanta Journal and Constitution, and probably Times Mirror's Los Angeles Times and Newsday, will offer subscriptions on Prodigy that can be purchased and used by customers without accessing or paying for other Prodigy services. Chicago Online and Mercury Center, by contrast, are accessed through America Online.

"We're talking to many newspaper groups," Mueller says, stressing that each relationship is different, depending on the paper and how it would fit into Prodigy's offerings. The negotiations involve pricing, content, costs, advertising and revenue splits, and what papers will do to promote the service.

At CompuServe, interactivity is paramount, says Kevin Knott, director of product marketing. Partly for this reason, Knott is lukewarm about newspapers whose electronic products consist of simply putting each day's paper online. "There's not much added value" in that for a CompuServe subscriber, he says. Knott is very interested in time-sensitive schedules and similar service information and reviews—movies, plays, restaurants—that showcase newspaper skills and can reside on the system for reference.

CompuServe has the reputation of being the most serious of the major online services, which to some detractors means it's the most difficult to use. It relies heavily on providing specialized information and forums, which are premium services that carry hourly charges, unlike 48 basic CompuServe services covered by the minimum monthly $9 charge.

Roughly half of CompuServe's use is related to the forums, Knott says, and that model is appropriate for newspaper partners. It's also a less expensive proposition for the newspaper than creating the staffing structure for a full-fledged electronic product, which is what Knight-Ridder has done with its Mercury Center project in San Jose.

Knott says CompuServe looked at Mercury Center and decided it wasn't an appropriate model. "There's still not enough of a market to make it worth a major investment on their part" in developing an electronic product, he says, but "every paper we've talked to is interested in developing" one.

Knott has heard all the stories about how newspapers leave 90 percent or more of the available news out of each day's paper, and that this material can flow online as an added benefit. But additional newspaper staffing is needed to turn this "content" into publishable material, and newspapers can't afford to hire new staff for the meager returns now available from online services.

A Multimedia Primer

For journalists, a quick course in Multimedia 101 begins with the rush toward a world where all pictures, sound and words can be "digitized"—expressed in the binary language of computers as a series of "0s" and "1s."

Inside the computer, this language is associated with either the presence or absence of electrical energy. The two possibilities, energy or no energy, correspond to the zeros and ones. Each zero or one is a "bit" of information, and while individual bits can't "say" much, they can be assembled into larger groups that can convey complex information that is organized and interpreted by the computer.

These larger groups of bits are known as "bytes," and advances in computers have allowed them to process ever-increasing sizes of bytes.

Outside the computer, digitizing information means that every dot of color in a photograph can be given a digital home, or address, and its precise shade defined by a number that can be translated on any computer screen as the same hue. The same is true for text and sound. They then can be blended together with relative ease.

Once expressed digitally, information can be shipped at the speed of light and, when using optical fibers, converted into light pulses and reconverted into digital form at its destination. When that information is received, it can be converted into precise images, sounds and text.

Each new generation of computer chips has greatly increased the speed and storage capabilities of computers, making it economically feasible to manipulate, move and store large amounts of digitized information. Even so, the fanciest personal computer would have a hard time downloading and displaying even Walt Disney's 1928 cartoon, "Steamboat Willie," were it not for equally impressive advances in digital "compression"—software that compresses the information needed to convey accurate images.

While better compression programs have been shrinking video transmission files, faster transmission speeds have been introduced to ship these files on their way. The telephone modem, which produces that eardrum-splitting noise you hear when you accidentally pick up a fax or computer line, only a handful of years ago was boasting speeds of 300 bits per second. The newest devices now offer speeds of 28,800 bps, with afterburners that can boost transmission to more than 230,000 bps.

But even such digital hot rods would be of limited value if the information highway were not made wider to accommodate more traffic. In this world, where transmission bandwidth is crucial, fiber optics and other transmission media have created a phenomenon that has been called the "Bandwidth Bonanza." Even plain old copper phone wires are being souped up.

Tele-Communications Inc., the cable TV giant, is rushing to upgrade its systems and bring on the age of 500 cable channels. But even this vast programming environment would be topped by the marriages of cable and telephone technologies now being celebrated, if not yet consummated.

The telephone industry has a marvelous switching system, which is moving quickly to become completely digitized. It allows you to pick up your phone whenever you want and dial just about any other telephone in the world. Now, imagine if those other telephones weren't Aunt Ruthie but individual programming choices such as movies, home shopping and interactive video games, all available on demand, delivered over coaxial cable or glass fiber. The idea of 500 channels suddenly becomes a moot concept, replaced by a world that can produce any one channel—the one you want—on demand. —*P.M.*

7. THE SHAPE OF THINGS TO COME

Making It Work

The Washington Post looked at the relationships between newspapers and online services and decided they weren't appropriate or lucrative enough, says Donald K. Brazeal, editor and publisher of the company's new electronic information unit, Digital Ink. "We believe newspapers should continue to be [the primary] publishers" in an electronic world, he explains, which for the Post means controlling the advertising and news content and supplying its electronic information directly to its subscribers.

As last year drew to a close, Post managers were still considering the types of hardware and software they need for a new online product, and hoping to be able to offer customers by mid-1994 more satisfying graphics, pictures and sound than current online services do. Brazeal isn't sure the Post will opt for working with an online provider, though. He says current newspaper-online relationships don't create a strong enough connection between the user and the newspaper. "In the Washington area," he says, "we want to have the 'Washington Post window on the world' rather than the 'America Online window on the world' or the 'Prodigy window on the world.'"

Whether the Post offers its product through an online service or not, it plans to include access to Internet, the sprawling collection of publicly accessible networks created by the government. The paper also is considering national electronic products integrating news and advertising.

Moving advertising into an electronic environment may be the most difficult challenge newspapers face. "We have a sense that [online] advertising is far more interactive [and] more akin to classified than display," says Brazeal, referring to classified advertising's emphasis on text and timeliness.

At the San Jose Mercury News, content, not advertising, is the focus, and Executive Editor Bob Ingle makes no apologies. Newspapers "haven't got financial resources compared to our emerging [electronic] competitors, we don't have the entertainment, and we don't have the technology," he says. "So, if we ain't got the content, we're sunk."

Ingle, Mercury Center director Bill Mitchell and others involved in the news side of online delivery experiments all stress that it's too early in the digital era to focus too much on revenue. The revenue will be there eventually, they say, but newspapers might not be in a position to cash in on commercial efforts unless they learn their lessons now.

"Where we are right now is at a very early, crude stage," Ingle says. "What we basically still have is text on a screen." Today's online services, he says, "are the Model Ts, the horseless carriages of the information future."

Beyond adapting to new technology, newsroom attitudes must change. "We need to be figuring out ways of using our newspapers to lead people into these new directions, and that's a fundamental premise of Mercury Center...," Ingle says. "The better younger journalists, and there's an age thing here, begin to see that the power is not on the printed page—the power is in the information."

Mitchell, who oversees a staff of 15, says the service has about 5,100 paying customers. Users subscribe to Mercury Center in addition to the newspaper, and one of the service's goals is to link the print and electronic products. "People tell us they use the printed paper very much as a guide to Merc Center," he says.

Besides the online service, Mercury Center customers also have access, for a fee, to the paper's audiotex and fax service, News Call. All services are promoted in the pages of the Mercury News.

"There's kind of a hidden dimension of all of this," Ingle says. "It heightens the need to have a very clearly defined strategy of how you're going to get from here to there, and how you're going to get there along the way." Over the years, he says, newspapers have allowed a lot of competitors to if not "eat our lunch, at least to nibble at it a lot. We have not been very creative at looking at changing economic conditions and market conditions and reader interests.... If we don't get fast-moving, lean organizations to compete in this new world, we ain't going to make it."

Digitize or Die?

In fact, newspapers are already getting used to lean, but job cuts and freezes also have been the order of the day at the Baby Bells. The key difference is that most newspaper staff reductions have been reactive, whereas the

> Today's online services "are the Model Ts, the horseless carriages of the information future."
>
> —San Jose Mercury News Executive Editor Bob Ingle

telecommunications industry is slimming down to gird for new market conditions and the kind of fast-moving environment that is clearly the norm for computer-driven communication. So while newspapers may not be looking at large revenues from interactive products anytime soon, virtually no one thinks they can afford to stay out of this new business.

"They better adapt to new ways of doing things," cautions Kenneth T. Berents, a media analyst and head of research at Wheat First Securities in Richmond, Virginia. Berents, a former newspaper reporter, sees continued staff downsizings at newspapers as a fact of life, but thinks the industry is well-positioned to provide electronic content on several platforms. "I think [newspapers] are terrific, but only if they adapt to the conduits out there. Otherwise, they're dead meat."

"They have to get involved," agrees Alan Brigish, head of 10 information newsletters published by SIMBA Information/Communication Trends Inc. in Connecticut. Brigish points out that online services make money from subscriptions, advertising and transactions, and says that papers

38. Age of Convergence

Previewing the Future

Companies are working together across the country to test interactive multimedia services. Below is a sampling of what may be coming soon to your neighborhood.

Castro Valley

This summer Viacom International and AT&T will test new interactive services over Viacom's cable system, which is located 20 miles southeast of San Francisco and serves about 13,000 customers.

By the end of September the partners plan to have at least 1,000 homes receiving interactive content, including video-on-demand, a home-shopping service and an on-screen program guide. Viacom also will test some interactive versions of programming from its current networks, including MTV, Nickelodeon and Showtime.

Cerritos

For four years, GTE has tested interactive TV using what have been the standard distribution conduits—coaxial cable and copper-wire telephone lines. Working with Apollo Cablevision, the 60 information services of GTE's Main Street have been provided to 350 cable customers in Cerritos, 25 miles south of Los Angeles.

In the past year, Main Street also has been offered by two other cable systems to 35,000 Continental Cablevision customers in six towns west of Boston and 50,000 subscribers of Daniels Cablevision in the San Diego area. Thus far, GTE says 700 customers in Massachusetts and another 2,000 have signed on in San Diego.

Main Street content in the Boston area includes educational references, home shopping, travel services, financial services and entertainment. Main Street's news and sports information is provided by UPI and Accu-Weather.

Omaha

Early this year U S West will begin testing video services as part of its announced plans to install a high capacity network using fiber optics throughout its 14-state territory. The company says its projected 100,000 customers in the Omaha test will have access to video on demand as well as interactive games, educational programs and home shopping by the end of this year.

U S West will work with several technology partners, including DSC Communications Corp., AT&T Network Systems and Scientific-Atlanta Inc., which will provide video equipment for the network.

Orlando

Beginning in April, 4,000 households will test Time Warner's Full Service Network, an interactive information and entertainment system to be delivered over Time Warner's local cable system. CUC International has signed on to provide access to its electronic shopping service, which sells 250,000 products.

FSN subscribers also will be able to output images from their TV. Time Warner Cable has entered into a venture with Hewlett-Packard that will allow FSN customers to print on a high-resolution color printer any image, such as coupons, retail ads and promotions, maps, invoices and articles, from their TV screens. —*P.M.*

---

have to start thinking about the latter, which can be lucrative.

Chicago Online's Ticketmaster service is cited as an early example of a blend of transactions with information similar to that provided by newspapers. Users can order tickets as well as scan schedules of events and even download seating plans of Chicago theaters.

At Reuters America, which serves newspapers and also will be a competitor of sorts in electronic information, top editor Andrew Nibley sees an accelerated pace of change in news organizations, including his own. Parent Reuters has a major television news arm and is expanding those efforts as well as its links with electronic distributors. For example, it will be feeding news updates to customers of Motorola's wireless communications system, called EMBARC.

"The great majority of the industry took a wait-and-see attitude," Nibley says. "But I think there's been a big shift in the industry's thinking over the last couple of years and now they're struggling with how they're going to fit in. Everyone thinks they have to do something; the question is, what?

"In some ways it should be very encouraging for journalists in that there will be new outlets for what they do. I think what the whole multimedia craze has done is show that...all of the things we write about are very important. It's just that the customer wants to see it in a different form."

Philip Moeller, a former business editor and electronic news editor at the Sun in Baltimore, is a communications consultant and writer based in West Hartford, Connecticut.

Article 39

CYBERSPACE JOURNALISM

There's no doubt that electronic newspapers and magazines are the flavor du jour. But are they more flash than substance? And will they ever make money?

Carol Pogash

Carol Pogash (pogash@hooked.net), a former reporter and columnist for the San Francisco Examiner, is writing online satire (http://www.sjmercury.com/lastbest/) to accompany a serial about Silicon Valley in the San Jose Mercury News and Mercury Center. She has written about Times Mirror Chairman Mark H. Willes and the evolving Los Angeles Times for AJR.

They said HotWired looked like a newsroom. Not like any newsroom I've ever seen. Ringed with cloudy windows, the former sewing factory has been transformed into a cavernous space. As HotWired grew, seamstresses fled; walls were crushed and open space now is brimming with young, enthusiastic cyber-editors and producers pioneering their way onto the World Wide Web.

Hot pink and black wires snake across the ceiling. Evian and Crystal Geyser waters are the beverages of choice. Maria, a yellow lab belonging to the design director, moseys by, wearing a blue ribbon to protest censorship on the Net and a tasteful set of pearls. She's the most dressed up member of HotWired. Women don't wear makeup. With a few exceptions, men don't wear ties.

The chief operating officer, the marketing director and the legal counsel share space with the newsroom staff. Nobody has an office. A surreal six-foot flower-like lamp looks like vegetation from Neptune. On the sign-in sheet, one person gave as a reason for visiting: "spiritual enlightenment"; another wrote "kicks and giggles."

"I'm working more hours, making less money, but I'm happier," says HotWired's copy chief, Pete Danko, a recent emigré from the San Francisco Examiner. "I feel better about my future. I have a feeling it's going somewhere."

The switch meant a departure from tradition, a new way of thinking, of editing, including the incorporation of audio and video into stories. It meant tossing out the AP Stylebook in favor of rules established by Wired magazine, the ad rich, beautiful print cousin of HotWired. Wired's Ten Commandments, which sit by Danko's elbow, include "Don't Sanitize" and the "We're not in newspapers anymore" directive: "Invent New Words."

So much happens so fast on the Net that HotWired, which has been in existence since October 1994, is considered old and established. To Danko, Web years are like dog years. Flourishing for a few fortnights is a feat. Stagnate and you die.

HotWired is constantly evolving, not into a newspaper, not into an entertainment magazine, but into something interactive and different. But is journalism being committed here? Or are these people simply larding up cyberspace with splashy graphics, news of the Net and fun factoids? Is this the future of news? Or is it some fantastic but short-lived journey?

The stampede to put information on the Net may have begun with individual self-expression. Now it's clearly market driven. Stand-alone news and feature services have popped up online while the number of daily newspapers in cyberspace has tripled in a year, with some 175 now on the World Wide Web. Millions upon millions of dollars are being spent, even though no one yet knows how to turn a profit, or what effect newspapers online will have on circulation figures at their print parents.

Despite the costs, nearly all the news on the Net is being served up free to everyone (although that's beginning to change, so enjoy these halcyon days). Each site is trying to make itself so clever, colorful and appealing that it becomes a daily habit. Each is competing not only against other forms of media, but also against thousands of other sites. So much experimentation is going on so fast that you can observe the changes daily. In the two months since AJR's last Internet-related feature ("The New Journalist," April), the Wall Street Journal (full text) and the Los Angeles Times have been launched online. And other sites have changed dramatically.

"This is not a land grab," says David Simons, president of Digital Video Corp., an online business development firm. "This is jockeying for position in sand dunes. Nobody is making money that I know of. Certainly not on the content side."

Observes Paul Sagan, president and editor of new media for Time Inc., "It's the chicken or the egg. Which comes first, the content or the audience with the money?" Pathfinder, Time Warner's megasite, offers a Coney Island of publications, including People (updated daily), a daily Time, Asiaweek, Money Magazine, Fortune, Sports Illustrated, Sports Illustrated for Kids, Entertainment Weekly, dozens of others—enough detours to get lost for days.

Most of the newspapers on the Net are producing "shovelware," print stories reproduced on Web pages, with few changes other than key words painted hypertext blue that offer readers links to stories with greater depth.

For the most part, HotWired's features tend to be about the Web. Swathed in natural fibers, young people are scrunched over HotWired's computers, trolling for sites and stories on the Net that they can write about for their site. A basic difference between this setting and a traditional newsroom is that these people don't go out to cover stories. They largely cover what's on the Internet, which is what many sites do. It's as if most of those working on the Web are standing in a circle holding up mirrors to one another. HotWired just does it better than most.

"We make plenty of mistakes every day," says Chip Bayers, one of HotWired's executive producers, "and we're proud of it. We're still learning the form. It's like the early days of radio when people read newspapers on the radio."

And HotWired has begun branching out, producing stories from around the world beyond the Net. Newspaper journalism with attitude.

Under the direction of David Weir, a onetime editor at Mother Jones and Rolling Stone, and cofounder of the Center for Investigative Reporting, HotWired runs some of the best political coverage anywhere. It's politics among consenting adults.

The Netizen, HotWired's political section, provides "Daily Braindumps from the Campaign Front," spicy, incisive accounts of the candidates' activities. A piece by staffer John Heilemann, formerly of the Economist and now HotWired's "boy on the bus," described Sen. Robert Dole, the presumptive Republican presidential nominee, as "muttering, mumbling, spitting out staccato bursts of simplistic assertions that have been the hallmark of his campaign this year."

Authored by such writers as iconoclastic media critic Jon Katz and Netraker Brock N. Meeks, HotWired's political pieces may be laced with the kind of street lingo that would cause mass cancellations if they ran in daily newspapers. Stories tend to be heavy on opinion and angle, zippier, looser in language yet tighter in length than in a newspaper or magazine.

After the Republican primaries wound down, the Netizen seemed to falter. But by late April, it was breaking ground again with Heilemann shadowing Clinton in Japan. One piece contrasted a Clinton speech praising Japan's receptiveness toward more American imports, specifically cell phones, with a visit to Japanese electronic stores, where Heilemann had a tough time finding a Motorola.

"We have to prove there is an audience," Weir says. If enough people visit the Netizen (you can track the number of "hits" or visits to a site per day) there could be more news-driven stories to follow.

"I think what you're looking at," Weir says, "is honestly the birth of a new mass media. It's happening right before our eyes…it's global…and it's headquartered in San Francisco."

ONLY A FEW MILES FROM SILICON VALLEY AND A jog away from San Francisco's dailies, the Examiner and the Chronicle, many Internet-related businesses have taken root in what is dubbed Multimedia Gulch. Their location makes it easier for local journalists to emigrate to cyberspace.

Steven Chin was working as the Examiner's City Hall reporter when he developed an idea for covering Asian American news and entertainment online. "The next day, during my lunch break, I went into the offices of some of these companies and started talking to people about my ideas," he says. Then he began looking for investors. Chin, who is on sabbatical from the Examiner, anticipates closing a deal with a commercial online service soon.

More than any other paper in the nation, the Examiner has been strip-mined by cyberspace, losing its publisher, editor, travel editor, arts and features editor, associate editor, chief editor of the day copy desk, movie critic, book critic, TV reviewer, and national and foreign editor to the Internet.

The exodus was ignited by the bitter San Francisco newspaper strike of 1994 and its aftermath. During the strike, the Newspaper Guild launched a Web site to compete with management's anemic online effort. The Guild site, which published every important columnist from both newspapers and broke local stories, received national attention.

The success of the union's online newspaper was not lost on Examiner employees. Three months after the strike ended, former Associate Editor Bruce Koon left to become managing editor of Mercury Center, the San Jose Mercury News' online site. The Examiner's publisher, William Randolph Hearst III, left soon afterwards. He's now CEO of the futuristic @Home, an interactive, multimedia, TV, print, entertainment and news service be-

> "We make plenty of mistakes every day," says HotWired's Chip Bayers, "and we're proud of it. We're still learning the form. It's like the early days of radio when people read newspapers on the radio."

7. THE SHAPE OF THINGS TO COME

ing developed in conjunction with Tele-Communications Inc. (TCI), the cable giant.

The Examiner's former arts and features editor, David Talbot, defected to the online world to start a pioneering cultural magazine (see "The New Journalist," April). "I was getting increasingly frustrated at the Examiner because of the downsizing and the management style of kick butt," he says. Talbot's never ending schemes to launch a magazine were almost a newsroom joke. He considered starting a magazine about the Pacific Rim or the 21st century.

A print magazine might cost $10 million to $20 million to launch. A Web magazine would be far cheaper. Joined by David Zweig, a Harvard MBA with a background in newspapers, magazines and software, Talbot, a supreme salesman of haute culture, convinced Adobe Systems and Apple Computer to invest.

Swiping the Examiner's theater critic/digital columnist Scott Rosenberg, crack TV reviewer Joyce Millman, foreign and national editor Andrew Ross, cerebral book editor Gary Kamiya and even the paper's former cartoonist, the biting "Tom Tomorrow" (Dan Perkins), Talbot began Salon, a classy cyberspace magazine.

Discouraged by what he calls the lack of "quality" writing on the Net, Talbot views his competition as National Public Radio, The New Yorker, Atlantic Monthly and Harper's. Much of what he's doing is what he'd done for the Examiner, but the highbrow tone seems better suited to the Net than to a family newspaper. "We wanted to do journalism as intelligent as we are," he says, "and not write down to our readers."

Unlike print magazines, Talbot can alter his product dramatically in a nanosecond. And he has. "We were too deep and not timely enough," Talbot says of his launch five months before. "People don't want to stay on one site for too long. They skitter through it."

Shorn of tradition, everyone plays multiple roles at Salon. "It's better than getting slotted into one thing which you do over and over again for years," says Rosenberg, Salon's senior editor/technology. "It's healthier. It's also a lot more chaotic."

Salon's staffers, who tend to be older than their counterparts at other sites, aren't making as much as they once did in newspapers. Cyber-salaries tend to be lower than at newspapers because the sites aren't making money and because the industry is filled with young people in their first and second jobs.

Salon eschews what Talbot calls "traditional features," its articles scrolling a fast 800 words. As with many other sites, readers can react instantly, conversing with the author or among themselves.

And like every other site with news and information, it's trying to find the road map to profitability. While living off its start-up money, Salon has picked up some ads, such as narrow billboards for Saturn, or reminders that if you want to purchase the book discussed in a piece,

In place of newspaper cynicism and gallows humor, Don George has found "spirited, enthusiastic people bursting with creative excitement" at his online job.

click on Border Books, a major sponsor of the site. To survive, Salon is syndicating its articles to content-starved sites.

Salon's lineup includes uncensored stories by such writers as Camille Paglia, John Le Carre and Jamaica Kincaid. But with the kaleidoscopic competition from over 100,000 sites on the Web, Zweig has found "it's increasingly difficult to make people aware of you."

NET WRITERS DON'T HAVE TO WRITE DOWN TO THEIR readers, but they must accommodate the medium. Don George, cyber-columnist at Global Network Navigator (GNN), a lively Internet service and content provider, has found that "long, reasoned sentences do not do as well as punchier, livelier, snap, snap, snap sentences." Pieces can't run more than 1,500 words, he's found, or readers will bail out, which they may do anyway with all the lure of hypertext.

Last year George left his post as Examiner travel editor, crossing the Bay to Berkeley, where he's planted his red backpack on the floor of his just built office. George marvels at the newness of the medium. At 42, he's the old man in the office. In place of newspaper cynicism and gallows humor, he's found "spirited, enthusiastic people bursting with creative excitement." Oddly, perhaps, for a newspaperman, he seems to like the optimism.

"The subtext of meetings is, 'What are we doing here and how are we going to do it?'" George says. "In newspapers, that was decided a long time ago."

In Seattle, Michael Kinsley is also feeling his way around the new medium. He begins,

---

Global Network Navigator
http://gnn.com

HotWired
http://www.hotwired.com

Los Angeles Times
http://www.timeslink.com

Mercury Center
http://www.sjmercury.com

New York Times
http://www.nytimes.com

Pathfinder
http://www.pathfinder.com

Salon
http://www.salon1999.com

Songline Studios
http://www.songline.com

Wall Street Journal
http://www.wsj.com

Washington Post
http://www.washingtonpost.com

he says, "with the assumption that we may have to make compromises on length but not on quality." A former New Republic editor, newspaper columnist and "Crossfire" mainstay, Kinsley is creating Slate, a weekly online magazine of opinion, politics and the arts for Bill Gates' Microsoft.

Kinsley's analysis of what works on the Net (print-style writing, weekly rather than daily publication) differs from that of many cyberspace pioneers. "The idea that you have to write in a different form of prose for cyberspace is something I'm going to assume is wrong," he says, adding, "I may be proven wrong myself."

While much of the writing will be farmed out to freelancers, Kinsley recently hired three big hitters: Jodie Allen, who had been editor of Outlook, the Washington Post's weekly commentary section; former New York magazine columnist and editor Judith Shulevitz; and Jack Shafer, longtime editor of Washington City Paper and most recently editor of San Francisco Weekly.

Virtually every major paper is establishing itself on the Web. At the beginning of the year the New York Times launched its free online service. The site looks pretty much like, well, the New York Times, with a few CyberTimes stories written for the Web, some of which are informative, others of which have more cool than content. The Times seems among the least willing to bend to the interactivity or the immediacy of the medium. The newborn Los Angeles Times site is more user friendly and, with Associated Press updates, more timely.

In Arlington, Virginia, not too far from the Washington Post newsroom, the Post is preparing to go onto the Net this summer with washingtonpost.com. It will phase out its initial online venture, Digital Ink, which was never on the Web. Stories from the Post will appear on the Net with deep hypertext. Readers who click on, say, "Egypt," will be able to see stories about Egypt that appeared in the Post in the last 60 days or were transmitted by the Associated Press over the past two weeks, as well as information from the CIA World Fact Book and State Department background notes.

Editor Jason Seiken works with 20 producers and content developers—"not really reporters per se." Everyone who works in editorial is a journalist, he adds, "just not in the traditional sense. There's no real demarcation between reporter, editor and copy editor."

Seiken says the Post's primary mission will be "to serve the local area" with data about crime, schools, anything that's important to a community. While the Net is global, many news outlets are anxious to win over local readers and local classified ads. The competition will be fierce, with America Online, Microsoft and smaller companies offering flashy city sites of local entertainment and arts news to lure local readers.

B UT IT TAKES MORE THAN CLASSIFIEDS TO TURN a profit. And major advertisers are not clamoring for space on the Net. So where's the payoff?

"We're seeing the beginnings of interesting stuff," says Time Warner's Sagan. "But if all this disappeared tomorrow, a lot of people might be bored but their lives wouldn't come to a crashing halt. It's not habit forming, except for surfing the Net. It's not like if you took away their TVs. If you did that, there'd be riots. I think it will get there because of the interactive component. It has that potential. But it also could just collapse under the weight of its own load."

Time Warner has spend many millions more on its popular site than the $2 million it pulled in from advertising last year, although the company says it's doing better this year.

The current free-for-all cannot last forever. A handful of sites receive more than half of the Net's ad revenue.

Experimenting online can fast turn into a sinkhole for funds. AT&T spent more than $50 million on its Inter-change Online Network in 1994, just about the time the world discovered the Web.

But in three years, people may look back on the Web "as a hilarious, speculative bubble," says Salon's Scott Rosenberg. "People may say, 'That was a bizarre episode.' I don't believe that will happen, but I think there will be a shakeout and some handful of these institutions will survive."

"There are real exciting things you can do online," says Dale Dougherty, the creator and president of Songline Studios, which produces Web news, Web reviews and the hit cyberspace soap opera, "Ferndale." The key question, he adds, is "how can we create a business and make a living at it? It's not clear yet."

"Over the next year," he says, "I think we'll begin seeing publishers like ourselves either begin moving toward limited distribution for qualified users or toward a user pay model." He adds, "I just can't see how you can survive without user support." (The Wall Street Journal is planning to charge $49 a year for its interactive edition, and others are studying the possibility of charging for online content.) Dougherty syndicates his Web material on AOL and GNN.

One of Dougherty's mainstays is Stephen Pizzo, who says working for a start-up online publication is like working for a small town paper: He writes a column and knocks out quick hit stories, all the while digging for investigative jewels. Pizzo, a former newspaper reporter, seems to understand the Web's journalistic potential more than most. The author of the bestselling book, "Inside Job: The Looting of America's Savings and Loans," he wrote online about the Ethel and Julius Rosenberg case, linking his story to recently released decoded cables from the KGB.

7. THE SHAPE OF THINGS TO COME

For now, though, Songline Studios and HotWired are exceptions. More typical is the Los Angeles Times site, which employs 27 people with titles such as electronic editor and technical coordinator. No one is listed as a writer or reporter.

At Pathfinder, Sagan has found that original writing works. His most popular sites are those such as Time Daily that provide more frequent and original news than a reader can find in print. But, he points out, "costs go up when you do it."

"Get past the technological whizzy whiz," says San Jose Mercury Center Managing Editor Bruce Koon, "and content still matters." Considered the granddaddy of news on the Net, Mercury Center is developing some original content: stories from Silicon Valley, breaking stories that appear on Merc Center hours before the next edition of the newspaper is printed. At some point, Koon says, "everyone will have to deal with original content." Because anyone can put up news. More and more sites are expected to feature Reuters and AP.

Knight-Ridder executives say they expect Merc Center to become profitable this year. It relies on five revenue streams: ads, Newshound (which offers customized news), the news library, its site on America Online and subscriptions for the latest news.

What is the key for newspapers to flourish in cyberspace? "They should play their historical role online," says HotWired business columnist David Kline. He thinks newspapers should become the civic resource and the community glue.

If they are to succeed, Kline says, news sites should become "less cool and more useful." He says online newspapers should help customers find a washing machine repairman, reserve theater tickets, reach city services, e-mail their city council members, renew their driver's licenses, check the test scores for neighborhood schools.

No one can predict whether the Salons, the Songlines and other creative online sites will be bigfooted by the New York Times, CNN, Pathfinder and USA Today. Since no one has yet figured out how to make money off news on the Net, the sites that survive will be those with deep pockets and creative solutions. Some contend that the cyberspace news sites that are up first and are the best will win the loyalty of consumers. Others argue that it doesn't matter what you do now, because the established players with brand names will win when the market is ready and the average American goes online.

"It's a full employment act for writers," says John Markoff, who covers high technology and the computer industry in Silicon Valley for the New York Times, of the burgeoning Web. So many start-up ventures are being created he says, all of them "hungry for people who write." An unabashed optimist, he believes "original content is coming." And while much of the focus is on computer-related subjects, he says that too will change as technology improves, cyberspace becomes easier to navigate, and more and more people start to surf.

Markoff characterizes these days as equivalent to the time "before the Model T." He adds, "The problem most people have is imagining journalism in a decade. Their imagination is based on the technology being used today."

"Give this another five years," Markoff advises, "before you make a judgment."

The Amazing Video Game Boom

Kid stuff has become serious business as Hollywood and Silicon Valley race to attract a new generation to the information highway

Philip Elmer-Dewitt

The kids get it right away. Nobody has to explain to a 10-year-old boy what's so great about video games. Just sit him down in front of a Sega Genesis or Super Nintendo machine, shove a cartridge into a slot and he's gone—body, mind and soul—into a make-believe world that's better than sleep, better than supper and a heck of a lot better than school.

Grownups, as a rule, don't get it. Which may be why the video-game craze has been seen by most adults—including the captains of the entertainment industry—as a dead end. For 20 years they have watched the advent of Pong and Pac-man, the rise and fall of Atari, the arrival of the Japanese, and have dismissed videogaming as a temporary detour far removed from the mainstream of modern American culture—which is to say, movies and prime-time television.

Until now. What once seemed like a passing fad for preteen boys has grown into a global moneymaking machine that is gobbling up some of the most creative talents in Hollywood and tapping the coffers of media and communications conglomerates eager to get in on the action. Video games rake in $5.3 billion a year in the U.S. alone, about $400 million more than Americans spend going to the movies. Globally, game revenues exceed $10 billion each year, and the worldwide sales of a single hit can top $500 million. Last week players from Times Square to Paris to Tokyo queued up in stores to buy Mortal Kombat, one of the hottest (and most violent) games ever made. In the next few weeks, Disney/MGM will release the game version of *Aladdin*; Propaganda Films will debut Voyeur, a new kind of adult-oriented interactive movie; and a start-up company named 3DO will launch the riskiest merger of games and multimedia yet, with a $699 superpowered machine designed to blast the market into new levels of graphic reality and financial risk.

The video-game industry is being propelled forward by a technological imperative that is reshaping most forms of entertainment. America's telemedia giants—from AT&T and Time Warner to Tele-Communications Inc. and the proposed Paramount-Viacom combo—are spending billions to turn today's passive television broadcast system into a two-way, interactive information highway capable of delivering not just movies, sitcoms and news on demand, but the world's greatest video games as well.

Suddenly a new medium—and a new market opportunity—has opened up in the place where Hollywood, Silicon Valley and the information highway intersect. Games are part of a rapidly evolving world of interactive amusements so new that nobody knows what to call them: Multimedia? Interactive motion pictures? The New Hollywood? And like the proverbial blind men feeling their way around the elephant, everybody involved in it has a different idea of what this lucrative beast is, depending on what part of it touches them. Hollywood executives tend to see the emerging market as a way to distribute movies and TV shows. Computer types see it as a way to get their machines into every home. Cable TV companies see it as a Pied Piper that will lure a generation of young viewers onto the

7. THE SHAPE OF THINGS TO COME

data superhighway-and get their parents to pay for pricey service connections and set-top cable boxes that might otherwise seem intimidating.

But right now, it's the video-game designers who have the electronic ball. The rapid advance of technology in the past decade has given them a set of tools with almost unimaginable power: high-speed computer-graphics chips that can create millions of bright colors and flash them on a screen in a fraction of a second; digital compression schemes that can squeeze the equivalent of a complete set of an encyclopedia onto a single silver disc; fiber-optic cable that can beam limitless quantities of data around the world at nearly the speed of light; simulation techniques that can immerse players in a three-dimensional world of illusion.

Like children with a new box of crayons, video-game makers are taking up these tools and using them to transform the cartoonlike earlier hit games—Super Mario Brothers, Sonic the Hedgehog, Street Fighter II—into something with lifelike action and plots. Meanwhile, the programmers have been joined by a new generation of Hollywood executives who, having tasted the power of computerized special effects, are eager to create a whole new form of entertainment that can be beamed over a cable line, bought in a cartridge or played from a compact disc. Both sides talk excitedly about making interactive movies with synthetic actors, of allowing players to take full control of the character's action and even, with the proper equipment, to enter a virtual reality in which they *are* the character.

Over the past 18 months, two groups, one representing Silicon Valley, the other Hollywood, have been meeting at trade shows, visiting labs and quietly cross-fertilizing. Several prominent executives have jumped ship—most notably Strauss Zelnick, who quit his job as president of 20th Century Fox Film Corp. this summer to head a video-game company called Crystal Dynamics. This fall dozens of these ventures are at last starting to roll out real products. Among the attractions coming soon to a living-room screen near you:

- Mortal Kombat, whose release last week in a $10 million Hollywood-style media blitz set off a nationwide debate about the escalating violence in video games *(see box)*. The brutal kick-and-punch game is expected to bring in more than $150 million by Christmas—roughly equivalent to ticket sales of a hit movie like *The Fugitive*.
- Aladdin, which may be the most beautiful video game ever made, features the first game characters hand-drawn by Disney's studio artists. Aladdin's release will be closely tied to that of the home-video version of the movie, which Disney predicts will be the best-selling videotape in history.
- Voyeur, a kinky murder mystery created by the Hollywood production company that made Madonna's *Truth or Dare*, stars Hollywood veterans Robert Culp (from the old *I Spy* series) and Grace Zabriskie (from *Twin Peaks*). A true hybrid, it shows real motion pictures on the screen while players control which of hundreds of twists and turns the plot will take.

The most closely watched video-game event of the season is not a game at all, but the arrival of a new game player. Next week Panasonic will introduce a VCR-size black box called REAL Multiplayer, designed by the hot Silicon Valley start-up company 3DO. With a 32-bit processor, packing twice the punch of the 16-bit Super Nintendo and Sega Genesis systems, and two special-purpose graphics chips, the Multiplayer is the most powerful video-game system ever marketed to the home. That in itself is no guarantee of anything. Other companies have tried and failed to use sheer power to steal the hearts and minds of the Nintendo generation, and this machine carries the added disadvantage of a price tag seven times as large as that of a Sega or Nintendo. But the industry—and Wall Street—is taking 3DO seriously, in large part because the company is backed by some of the biggest players in the information-highway business and headed by one of America's most charismatic entrepreneurs.

Trip Hawkins, founder and chairman of 3DO, was one of the first to see that Hollywood and the video-game industry were headed toward a happy collision. With his salesman patter and show-biz smile, he has for years been telling anyone who would listen that video arcades were more popular than movie houses—and he would rattle off the numbers to prove it. As chairman of Electronic Arts, maker of video games (and the first to treat its programmers like rock stars), he also railed against the electronics industry for failing to agree on a single game standard—a failure that kept the industry locked in the Beta-versus VCR stage. When nobody appeared interested in building the machine of his dreams, he set out to build it himself. He kept thinking, he says, of an old *New Yorker* cartoon showing two vultures sitting glumly on a limb. "I'm sick and tired of waiting," one says to the other. "Let's go kill something."

Hawkins set out to combine the visual Hollywood power of a Hollywood movie with the interactivity of a video game. His solution, whether it succeeds in the marketplace or not, points in the direction that all interactive media are likely to go.

Hawkins will sell his games on compact discs—the same silver platters that have taken over the music business and been adapted as storage devices for machines built by Sega, Philips, Commodore and all the major computer manufacturers. But unlike most of his competitors. Hawkins sees CDs as a temporary solution. Ultimately, he says, interactive motion pictures will be delivered to home game machines not on a disc but through the fiber-optic networks being built by cable and telephone companies. This summer he announced plans to sell a new version of the Multiplayer that plugs directly into a coaxial cable, where it can serve both as a cable TV and VCR controller and as a gateway to the information highway.

It was in part the clarity of Hawkins vision of that highway, and how video games fit on it, that made him so attractive to investors—and to more than 350 of the cleverest video-game designers in the business. His early backers include AT&T, Time Warner and Matsushita (which owns Panasonic and Universal, one of the biggest Hollywood studios).

Unfortunately for Hawkins and his partners, he is not the only one with his eye on the information-highway prize. Atari has announced a $200 game system called Jaguar that could steal some of 3DO's sparkle this fall. Both Sega and Nintendo are rumored to have 3DO-class machines in development. And last month Nintendo announced plans to leapfrog ahead with a game machine built around a 64-bit chip, which has twice the power of 3DO's.

Sega, meanwhile, has made a couple of deals that could prove prescient. In one, Time Warner and Tele-Communications Inc. have agreed to create a special Sega channel on their cable-TV systems that would give subscribers access to 50 games each month. In another important pact, Sega has allied itself with AT&T to create a special cartridge called the Edge 16 that would enable Sega Genesis owners to compete with similarly equipped players anywhere in the world over ordinary telephone lines.

John and Shelly Bain already have a pretty good idea of what that's like. Almost every night after dinner, instead of clicking on their TV set and waiting to be entertained, they sit down at their computers and entertain themselves. Dialing a local access number from their San Francisco living room, they enter the virtual amusement park of the ImagiNation Network, a combination Las Vegas, Nintendo and Sunday-afternoon social club, where they can compete against fellow computer users in everything from bridge and blackjack to medieval role-playing fantasies.

The Bains are video-game addicts by almost any definition of the word. Shelly, 40, pays $129.95 a month to spend unlimited time on the network, while John, 43, a police officer, pays $79.95 for a 90-hour-a-month package. The two of them spend hour after hour perched in front of their computer screens playing games and exchanging E-mail messages with old friends, newfound acquaintances and even, sometimes, each other.

The Bains may not know it, but their nocturnal habits are of intense interest to the entertainment industry. What Hollywood needs to know is whether the Bains are a curious exception or the wave of the future. If videogaming is going to be one of the popular attractions in the mix of entertainment offerings on tomorrow's interactive TV systems—and many are gambling that it will—the people who create and market those games will have to know what makes people like the Bains tick. What do they want to play? Why? And, most important, how much are they willing to pay?

Until now the core audience for video games has been boys ages 8 to 14. It is with this group that the power of interactivity can be seen in its purest form. Unlike young girls, who seem to be able to take video games or leave them, boys tend to be drawn into the games at a deep, primal level. Many simply can't tear themselves away, to the detriment of their schoolwork, their eating habits and their health.

What is going on? According to psychologist Sherry Turkle, author of *The Second Self*, the key lies in the rates of development of young boys and girls, which to their mutual pain and embarrassment are usually out of synch. Girls in their preteen years tend to mature faster than boys—socially and sexually. Normal day-to-day interactions with these girls can be stressful and troubling for the boys, who tend to withdraw to a safe place—sports, scouting, computer gaming—where they can hang out until they are ready to hold their own with the girls, a process that can take years. Most home video games, unfortunately, are derived from coin-operated arcade models that were designed not to build up a lad's fragile ego but to defeat him and take away his quarters.

Over the past decade, video-game companies have struggled to extend the market beyond that audience of preteen boys. Games built around characters such as Barbie and the Little Mermaid are clearly pitched to girls. On the other end of the spectrum are sports games like John Madden Football (an early Trip Hawkins hit) designed to give older boys and men an excuse to extend their game-playing habits well into adulthood.

But nobody has yet found a way to make video games broadly attractive to that part of the market that consumes the biggest share of books, movies and television drama: adult women. That's where Hollywood comes in. The idea is that nobody knows better than moviemakers how to put stories on a screen and bring them to life. "My own belief," says Voyeur's Zabriskie, "is that the sooner the better actors and the better directors get involved, the sooner this will be a medium that everybody will want to get into."

The Hollywood–Silicon Valley connection goes back to the early 1980s, when movie companies and video-game makers found it mutually convenient to license cartoon and film characters (usually for a modest 5% to 10% of net sales) for use in video games. At one point Atari had deals lined up to make video games out of Peanuts, Mickey Mouse and the Muppets. Then in 1982 Atari licensed *E.T.* for $23 million and proceeded to turn it into one of the worst video games ever made. The resulting disaster, known in the industry as "the crash of 1984," brought Atari into bankruptcy court and nearly dragged down its corporate parent, Warner Communications, as well. Some of those unsold E.T. cartridges can still be found on the dusty back shelves of retail stores.

The licensing game never died, however. Now Hollywood is making movies and TV shows out of video-game characters (witness this summer's *Super Mario Brothers* feature and the two Sonic the Hedgehog cartoon shows coming this fall), and kids assume that any film or series with any action in it will come out in a game cartridge within six months. Besides Aladdin, vidkids this Christmas will be able to choose from games based on *Cliffhanger, Last Action Hero, Ren and Stimpy, Bram Stoker's Dracula, Home Improvement, Jurassic Park* and a whole sub-genre of Bart Simpson adventures, including The Simpsons: Escape from Camp Deadly, Bartman Meets Radioactive Man, Bart vs. the Space Mutants, Bart vs. the Juggernauts and Bart vs. the World.

As the video-game business exploded over the past few years, people in Hollywood couldn't help noticing that their 10% cut was becoming bigger and bigger. "They started getting these huge royalty checks that were doubling every year," says Gilman Louie, chairman of Spectrum Holobyte, publisher of the popular game Tetris. "Finally someone said, 'Why aren't *we* in that business? Why are we leaving the rest of that money on the table?'"

Thus began a massive consolidation in which every major Hollywood studio either bought a video-game company, started its own in-house interactive department, or did both. "People used to ask, What's the risk of getting in this business?" says

7. THE SHAPE OF THINGS TO COME

Too Violent For Kids?

Johnny Cage kills his victims with a bloody, decapitating uppercut. Rayden favors electrocution. Kano will punch through his opponent's chest and rip out a still-beating heart. Sub-Zero likes to tear his foe's head off and hold it up in victory, spinal cord twitching as it dangles from the neck.

Renegades from the Late Late Movie? No, these are characters from Mortal Kombat, America's top-grossing arcade game last year and the focus of a growing debate about whether violence in video games has finally gone too far. The issue came home for millions of parents and kids last week when Acclaim brought out four new versions of Mortal Kombat designed to play on the Sega and Nintendo systems found in some 50 million U.S. households.

To head off complaints, Nintendo chose to delete the digitized blood in its versions and replace the so-called finishing moves with less realistic endings, although the final product is still pretty brutal. Sega decided to use a warning label alerting parents that the game is not suitable for children under 13, but few expect that to have the desired effect. Peggy Charren, founder of Action for Children's Television, believes that the labels will actually make the game more attractive to kids: "It's a warning to the children that tells them, 'This is what I want.'"

Mortal Kombat is not the first violent video game—or even the worst. In Night Trap, a controversial compact-disc game that plays on the Sega system, five scantily clad women are stalked down by bloodthirsty vampires who like to drill holes in their victims' necks and hang them on meat hooks. In both Night Trap and Mortal Kombat, live-action video technology makes the violence that much more realistic.

Are games like these bad for kids? There are no definitive scientific studies, in part because it is difficult to sort out the effects of the violent acts in video games from those of the mayhem seen in movies, TV shows and city streets. According to Parker V. Page, president of the Children's Television Resource and Education Center in San Francisco, preliminary research suggests that such games make children "more aggressive or more tolerant of aggression." That jibes with the experience of parents who will drag their kids away from a kick-boxing video game only to watch them start kick-boxing with each other in the backyard.

University of Southern California professor Marsha Kinder, who is a member of several video-game review panels, believes that the games are different from other media because they actively engage children in violent acts: "It's worse than TV or a movie. It communicates the message that the only way to be empowered is through violence." Enthusiasts counter that the games serve as a harmless way to let off steam. As one video-store manager put it, "You had a bad day, so you can go in there and rip a couple of heads off and feel better."

Of course, there are better ways to let off steam. As it is, American kids who have video-game machines already play, on average, nearly 1.5 hours a day. For many parents, the problem is not what their children are doing on their Nintendo systems, but what they are *not* doing while locked in Mortal Kombat—reading books, playing outdoors, making friends. When the information highway comes to town, bringing with it a thousand new reasons to spend time in front of a video screen, that may be a growing problem not just for the kids, but for all of us.

—*By Philip Elmer-DeWitt. Reported by John F. Dickerson/New York*

Steve Eskenazi, an analyst at the investment firm Alex. Brown & Sons. "This year the question is, What's the risk of *not* getting into the business?"

Now when a movie studio agrees to license a video game, it gets involved in the game's design from the start. When Steven Spielberg realized that a plot he was considering for a movie would work better as a game, he took it to his friend George Lucas, whose own video-game operation turned the idea into a spelunking adventure called The Dig. At Sony Interactive, every movie script that Columbia buys is screened by the video-game department for its game potential. If it looks promising, says Olaf Olafsson, president of Sony Electronic Publishing, a separate scriptwriting team develops the game version. In some cases the movie script is actually changed to add what Sony's creative team calls IPMs—interactions per minute—to make for a better game.

When film crews go out to the set, the video-game people are right behind. Sony used footage from *Cliffhanger* and *Dracula* to create the backdrops of the CD versions of those games. Spectrum Holobyte is doing the same for a version of *Star Trek: The Next Generation* it is creating for 3DO. In some cases, extra footage is shot on location to provide additional material for the games.

To make the characters in video games more realistic, actors are being recruited to serve as models. Acclaim, the video-game company that made Mortal Kombat, has created a special "motion capture studio" for this purpose. A martial-arts expert with as many as 100 electronic sensors taped to his body sends precise readings to a camera as he goes through his moves—running, jumping, kicking, punching. The action is captured, digitized and synthesized into a "naked" wire-frame model stored in a computer. Those models can then be "dressed" with clothing, facial expressions and other characteristics by means of a computer technique called texture mapping.

To make Voyeur, Propaganda Films shot live actors in an empty room and then combined their digitized images with computer-generated sets—beds, desks, windows. To make Switch, an interactive motion picture to be released next year, director Mary Lambert rented Sound Stage 5 at the Hollywood Center Studios. Watching a scene in which actress Deborah Harry, dressed in a skintight dress with a plunging neckline, strides into a chamber decorated with ancient Egyptian props is like stepping back into the studios of the 1930s.

"Wow," someone says, as giant columns begin to crumble around her. "The whole place is a gigantic vault."

"And cut!" shouts Lambert. "Thank you everybody. That was nice."

Intriguing as such productions are, there is no guarantee that any of this will produce a game that is fun to play. The very best designers—and there are only eight or 10 with track records for making video-game hits—are as rare as Spielbergs and Scorseses are in Hollywood. They have to know how to design puzzles that are hard but not too hard. They have to pace the dangers and rewards and have an intuitive feel for the nature of the medium. "Hollywood knows nothing about interactivity," says Brian Moriarty, who designed some of the best-selling Zork games and is working on Spielberg's The Dig. "If they are looking for a quick killing, they are in for a disappointment. There are no quick killings here."

It remains to be seen which needs the other's talents more: Hollywood, with all it has to learn about computers, or Silicon Valley, with all it needs to discover about telling a story. But the tale of their meeting and their subsequent romance has all the makings of a terrific movie. And if someone can figure out how to make it interactive and put it on the info highway, it might even make a good game.

—*Reported by John F. Dickerson/New York and David S. Jackson/San Francisco*

IMMACULATE RECEPTION

Will digital TV and the newly passed communications act give birth to a monster or to a screen saviour?

MARSHALL JON FISHER

MARSHALL JON FISHER has written for THE ATLANTIC MONTHLY, the LOS ANGELES TIMES MAGAZINE and other publications. He is a coauthor of TUBE: THE INVENTION OF TELEVISION, which is published by Counterpoint.

On a chilly January morning in 1928 the citizens of Berlin were greeted with a curious sight. Leafing through the *Berliner illustrierte Zeitung* (Berlin Illustrated newspaper) while riding the Strassenbahn, they came upon a full-page drawing: a man was shown lying in bed, steering an apparatus on his lap while watching a mountain panorama on a projection screen. "Marvels that we might still experience: viewing the world from bed through television," read the caption. "The viewer operates, by remote control, an airplane that carries the filming apparatus."

The Berlin artist must have been inspired by the Scotsman John Logie Baird, whose "televisor" had lately been enjoying abundant publicity. The televisor used a large spinning disk drilled with holes in a spiral pattern to scan an image and turn it into an electrical signal. At the receiving end, another disk turned the signal back into a picture.

Baird's system was doomed to fail: disks could never spin fast enough to render a fluent moving picture. But in the 1990s the idea that viewers might one day tell their televisions exactly what to broadcast no longer seems so futuristic. The concept is now called "interactive programming," and digital television will soon make it a reality.

The televisions in people's living rooms today work much as did the ones designed by Philo T. Farnsworth and Vladimir K. Zworykin in the 1930s. (Zworykin, the chief scientist at the Radio Corporation of America—RCA—garnered most of the credit for inventing electronic television. Farnsworth, a college dropout with private financing, deserved at least half the credit, but he died a penniless, bitter man, virtually unknown.) True, televisions have offered color since the 1950s, but programs are transmitted and received in the same basic way: scan an image with a beam of electrons to create an electrical signal; then, at the receiving end, turn that signal back into an electron beam and bombard a fluorescent screen with it, thereby recreating the image.

Digital televisions will be machines more worthy of the information age. Images will still have to be scanned, but the resultant analogue signals will be converted to binary ones. The signals will assign bits of code to each pixel, or picture element, on a television screen, defining the color and brightness of the pixel and recreating the original image.

As straightforward as it may sound, that technology is rewriting the rules of broadcasting. In the wake of congressional passage of the Telecommunications Act of 1995, debates over digital standards and broadcasting frequencies will soon come to a head. No matter how the act shapes up, digital televisions will do more than show the same old programs. They will send and receive electronic mail (or video mail) and gain access to the Internet. They may offer a choice of camera angles from which to watch tennis at the U.S. Open. They may even enable viewers to steer remote aircraft through breathtaking mountainscapes. The one thing they may not offer is what the public most expects: high-definition television, or HDTV.

The past two decades have not been good to the American television industry. Beginning in the 1970s Japanese manufacturers took over the television, videocassette recorder and stereo businesses in quick succession. Then, in January 1987, the Japanese launched their version of Sputnik. At a meeting in Washington, D.C., representatives from the Japanese public-television network demonstrated a new system, known as MUSE. Although in most ways it was a conventional analogue system, MUSE generated pictures of stunning quality by doubling the number of horizontal scan lines in the picture. Stung into action at last, the United States launched some acronyms of its own. In September 1988 the Federal Communications Commission (FCC) created the Advisory Committee on Advanced Television Service (ACATS). ACATS declared an open competition to create an American version of HDTV and promptly received twenty-three proposals. All the proposed systems were analogue: conventional wisdom held that digital television would not be ready until the twenty-first century.

But then, as often happens, conventional wisdom was confounded. In June 1990 the world's first all-digital system was proposed in San Diego. Its creator, appropriately enough, was named VideoCipher.

DIGITAL TELEVISION WAS AN IRONIC CHANGE of pace for VideoCipher. A division of the General Instrument Corporation in Chicago, VideoCipher had for years specialized in blocking telecasts—not transmitting them. Its electronic scramblers prevented freeloaders from tapping in to cable programs meant for paid subscribers. The advent of HDTV, however, threatened to make the standard scrambling system obsolete.

VideoCipher's engineers went to work. First they figured out how to compress digitized HDTV broadcasts into twelve-megahertz satellite channels. Then they began to wonder if they could compress the signal into the six-megahertz channels that regular antennas pick up. Most engineers considered those channels too narrow to carry HDTV. With the ACATS proposal deadline approaching, Woo Paik took a week off to see if he could prove them wrong.

Paik has been called the engineering world's "premier HDTV celebrity." Korean born, with a Ph.D. from the Massachusetts Institute of Technology, he was put in charge of VideoCipher's digital-HDTV project in 1989. Now, less than a year later, Paik had to say whether or not he could deliver.

"We had the compression simulated," Paik told me, "but the system requires transmission and other things, which I just had to develop right there in my mind. I had to extrapolate based on what was known, and say we could make it work."

All of which went against Paik's grain. Paik is "a hands-on guy, more empirical than theoretical," says Robert M. Rast, vice-president of the communications division of General Instrument. "He doesn't want to sit and analyze things forever, he wants to go and do it." Nevertheless, after only a week Paik declared the project feasible. VideoCipher's proposal to ACATS, submitted at the last possible moment, bumped up the digital-television timetable by a decade.

TO BRING DIGITAL HDTV INTO PEOPLE'S homes, Paik and his colleagues had to squeeze HDTV transmissions into about 1 percent of their original space. How did they do it? The solution lies in what Rast calls "compression tricks." A standard, analogue television system transmits a complete picture frame thirty times a second. Because most of the picture does not change from one frame to the next, a lot of redundant information is transmitted. Paik's digital system does away with that redundancy by transmitting a complete picture at intervals, and transmitting only changes to the picture between times. When a newscaster is on the air, for instance, almost nothing in the picture changes except the newscaster's mouth. By not retransmitting images of the desk and the backdrop, one can save millions of bits a second. Even when objects do move, they often do not change appearance. Instead of redescribing a moving car in each of 1,000 frames, the VideoCipher system describes the car once and then assigns it a motion vector.

There are many other compression tricks. "But the fundamental rule is: Only transmit what changes," says Andrew Lippman, director of the Television of Tomorrow research program at the MIT Media Laboratory. "Never, never send a frame if you can avoid it."

A few months after VideoCipher's announcement, both the Zenith Electronics Corporation and the David Sarnoff Research Center (a division of SRI International), in Princeton, New Jersey, announced their own digital systems. "It was more a coming out of the closet than a crash effort," says David H. Staelin, a professor of electrical engineering at MIT. "The technical people had been working on it in the back room for a long time; they just hid it." The following year, 1991, VideoCipher (now called DigiCipher) built its first prototype, the DigiCipher I. "And the thing worked," says Rast. "It did. To the amazement of many people."

The race was on: HDTV would provide a new proving ground for American industry, a second chance to thrive in the promised land of television. It soon became clear, however, that digital television was too big a territory for one pioneer to stake out. Over the next two years, opposing alliances took shape, and the digital-television industry began to look like Europe in 1914, with treaties binding entities that had long been fierce competitors. Then, in May 1993, the alliances merged, forming a coalition of all the major players: the AT&T Corporation, General Instrument, MIT, Philips Consumer Electronics, Sarnoff, Thomson Consumer Electronics and Zenith. The coalition chose a name for itself worthy of Kaiser Wilhelm: the Grand Alliance.

Free to combine the best features from a number of systems, and unfettered by court actions between rival corporations, the alliance moved quickly. Within a year it had settled on an audio system and other technical details. In the summer of 1994 the alliance members held field tests in Charlotte, North Carolina. The following April they began to demonstrate their system to members of the FCC and to anyone else who might influence the agency. The age of digital television, the alliance insisted, had arrived.

LAST FALL, AT THE ANNUAL MEETING OF THE Association for Maximum Service Television (MSTV) in Washington, D.C., it was hard to argue with the alliance's claims. On HDTV sets in viewing rooms, a golfer hit his ball out of a sand trap, and individual grains fell from his club with perfect clarity. A kingfisher diving for prey in a snowy lake raised no pulses from a distance; but the closer I got, the more eerily lifelike the picture became. Even looking at it point-blank, I could make out no lines, and the snowflakes remained distinct and sharp; I felt I was just seeing farther and farther into the picture. I was ready to sell my wife's car for cash as soon as those things came on the market.

Then I talked with experts outside the industry and came

7. THE SHAPE OF THINGS TO COME

back down to earth. "The Grand Alliance is just a bunch of entrepreneurs trying to peddle a modulation system," said

HDTV IS DEAD, SAY MOST EXPERTS. Instead, broadcasters will squeeze six standard-definition programs and services into a single channel.

Richard J. Solomon, associate director of MIT's Research Program on Communications Policy. Rigid standards are unnecessary, Solomon went on. Digital televisions will be able to "handshake" just as computers with modems do now, adapting to the greatest common denominator for scanning rate, aspect ratio and other variables.

"The Grand Alliance system has lots of limitations and problems," agreed the MIT physicist William F. Schreiber. "Many people are going to be surprised when they have to put up a $100 antenna. You can forget about rabbit ears; they won't do the trick." The first Grand Alliance televisions will cost several thousand dollars—as much, in today's terms, as the first television sets cost in the 1940s and the first color sets cost in the 1950s. The difference is that many consumers already own high-definition, digital monitors: the ones that came with their computers. Why not let people use them for digital television instead of forcing them to buy expensive new units? "So we get to HDTV," Lippman says. "But we get to it by creeping up on it, the same way we got hi-fi."

BENEATH ALL THE DICKERING OVER DIGITAL systems lies a much deeper question: Does the public want HDTV at all? According to the MIT contingent, most consumers are relatively undemanding where television images are concerned. "Our studies showed that if people liked a program, then they would put up with terrible picture quality," Schreiber says, "as long as the sound was okay and the picture was reasonable."

According to Donald West, editor of *Broadcasting & Cable* magazine, fewer than half of today's broadcasters are interested in transmitting high-definition programs. Why should they spend $10 billion or so to convert their stations to digital, simply to show their viewers the same old programs? As Jonathan Blake, general counsel to MSTV, puts it, "There will be no net gain in the eyeballs which they can sell to advertisers." Solomon is even blunter: "I don't think there's any prospect for HDTV in our lifetime."

Even as they turn their backs on HDTV, however, broadcasters are embracing digital television. Thanks to the new compression technology, a six-megahertz channel can carry five or six standard-definition digital programs. "Multicasting" several programs, with that much more advertising, promises to be much more profitable than broadcasting one HDTV program. What's more, because digital televisions are computers in their own right, broadcasters could offer electronic mail, two-way paging and Internet access. HDTV is dead, say most experts. The future belongs to ATV (advanced television).

And yet some prominent broadcasting figures still profess faith in HDTV. According to Richard E. Wiley, chair of ACATS and a former FCC chair, research shows that experts and lay viewers strongly prefer HDTV to regular television. "HDTV is a whole new video platform, a quantum leap forward in the state of the art," he proclaimed at the MSTV meeting. At the same meeting representatives from ABC and NBC reaffirmed their commitment to HDTV.

Not many people seem to believe them. As Lippman explains, "The goal with HDTV was to seize the revenue from broadcasters and shift it to the consumer-electronics industry. It was a bankrupt goal, and now it's basically a nonevent. The broadcasters don't want HDTV, and if they tell you they do, they're being disingenuous." The motive for such chicanery seems apparent to some. One FCC official told me, "There's only one reason they're asking for an HDTV mandate: to justify getting the new spectrum."

In the 1940s the FCC parceled out chunks of the electromagnetic spectrum to television broadcasters free of charge. Ever since then, six-megahertz television channels have been separated by six-megahertz chunks of empty spectrum to prevent interference. Now, thanks to the new digital technology, stations can occupy adjacent spaces in the spectrum without interfering with one another. The FCC plans to assign the "taboo" channels to digital television for a transition period of fifteen years or so. Then the old analogue spectrum will be given back to the FCC for auctioning.

Many people, including Larry Pressler (R., South Dakota), chair of the Senate Commerce Committee, would like to see broadcasters bid for the new frequencies, which are worth between $10 billion and $40 billion on the free market. If broadcasters can squeeze six programs into one channel, why not ask them to pay for their new space? In the past year the government has raised more than $9 billion by auctioning other parts of the radio spectrum. Putting television frequencies on the market, proponents say, might help balance the federal budget.

Broadcasters, naturally, disagree. They cannot afford to compete with cash-wealthy cable and satellite companies, they say, and still provide television for free. A recent editorial in *The New York Times* called the plea of insufficient wealth "bogus," but the broadcasters have stuck to their story. Free television is a mainstay of American broadcasting. The FCC wants to keep it that way, and the broadcasters know it. The question is, Will they really use the new frequency to simulcast their programs in HDTV? Or will they use it to broadcast several standard-definition programs, as well as other, more profitable services?

THE *TIMES* WOULD HAVE LOVED ONE SCENE AT the MSTV meeting. "You'll be happy to know," Don West told the broadcast executives in a panel he was moderating, "there is great suspicion in Washington that you'll never give the spectrum back." There was an awkward pause while the panelists grinned nervously at one another. Then John Rohrbeck, president of NBC Television Stations, leaned toward his microphone: "Well, I think, if the law says we have to . . . now, I can't speak for Ed [Edward Reilly, president of McGraw-Hill Broadcasting]. . . ."

The 200 broadcasters in the auditorium broke into laughter as Rohrbeck added: "Are you giving us a choice?"

"The public owns these coveted airwaves," says Andrew Blau, director of the Communications Policy Project at the Benton Foundation in Washington, D.C. "For the government to give them away with no additional public-interest safeguards and no compensation to the American taxpayer is scandalous." The majority of the media and a host of public-service organizations, both liberal and conservative, agree with him, but to no avail. "Broadcasters out there shot us down, to put it mildly," Senator Pressler said of an early effort last year to pass a bill requiring auctions. As Solomon puts it, "If you're a congressman, you're not going to get re-elected if your local TV station doesn't like you."

In addition to money and political clout, the broadcasters hold one trump card: the Communications Act of 1934 prohibits the FCC from auctioning the television spectrum. There is a bill before Congress asking the FCC to consider auctions. But the FCC official I spoke with doubted it would pass. "Congress doesn't have the spine to auction," he said. "They fear the wrath of the broadcasters."

Regardless of whether the new spectrum is given away or auctioned off, television will probably go digital in the next fifteen years. Flat, active-matrix monitors, many feet wide and high but only a few inches thick, will hang like paintings on walls and will serve as computer screens as well as televisions. Nicholas Negroponte, the founder of MIT's Media Lab and author of *Being Digital,* predicts that someday "smart televisions" will scan through thousands of hours of daily programming, picking out clips of particular interest to their owners.

BY THAT TIME THE INTERNET ITSELF MAY WELL be a broadcasting venue, with videos as well as text and photographs. Instead of home pages, users will have their own virtual television stations on the Net. "Any rational social commentator would have to say that television is going to become more like the Internet, and vice versa," Lippman says.

Just who would watch all those personal sitcoms is another question. And of course digital technology, no matter how much it improves television pictures, will do nothing to improve network television programs. "I wonder if perhaps we are aiming our video quality standards too high," Ian Childs, engineering policy adviser for the BBC, recently said. "Perhaps we should save money on compression and spend more on program quality."

And that will be the day *Masterpiece Theatre* tops the Nielsen ratings.

Who Owns Digital Works?

Computer networks challenge copyright law, but some proposed cures may be as bad as the disease

Ann Okerson

Millions of readers since 1926 have found A. A. Milne's stories of Pooh and Piglet and their friends Eeyore and Tigger delightfully simple and yet profound. So it is not surprising that James Milne (no relation) of Iowa State University thought that it would be a wonderful idea to put *Winnie-the-Pooh* on the World Wide Web. A computer attached to the Internet could take a few files containing linked text and pictures from the books and make them available to children of all ages around the world. In April 1995, shortly after he created the Web site, Milne received a *very* polite letter (as have other Pooh fans) from E. P. Dutton, the company that holds the rights to the text and classic Pooh illustrations, telling him in the nicest way imaginable to cease and desist. His other choice was to sequester a substantial part of his life's savings for the coming legal bills.

About the same time, a scandalous new book about the private life of former French president François Mitterand was banned from distribution in print in France. It turned up anonymously on the Internet days later. There was little anyone could do to prevent its rapid digital dissemination.

Some network enthusiasts assert that "information wants to be free," but an equally vociferous band of digital pioneers contend that the real future of the global Internet lies in metering every drop of knowledge and charging for every sip. How will society's legal and cultural institutions react? Will tomorrow's readers be able to browse electronic works as easily as they have been able to peruse books at their favorite bookstore? Will they be able to borrow from virtual libraries? Authors, publishers, librarians and top-level government officials are debating these questions.

No More Yawns

Even five years ago few people would have thought of electronic copyright as an issue for heated national controversy. But today there are vast sums to be gained—or lost—as a result of the inevitable legal decisions to be made regarding ownership of "intellectual property" transmitted via electronic media. By the early 1990s the core copyright industries of the U.S. (which include publishing, film and music) accounted for more than $200 billion in business annually, or about 3.6 percent of the gross domestic product. In 1993, when QVC and Viacom battled for control of Paramount and its archive of classic films, it became clear that both companies believe the future lies in ownership of "content." Since 1981 the National Writers Union has sued large publishing organizations, including the New York Times Company and Mead Data Central, for allegedly selling unauthorized digital copies of its members' works. Even universities now think about how to maximize the return on the intellectual property they produce, rather than simply assigning full rights to publishers.

For the most part, the copyright industries create mass-market products such as trade books, films and related items. (The novel *Jurassic Park*, for example, spawned a major movie, videotapes, audiotapes, T-shirts, toy dinosaurs and other derivatives, all protected by various rights.) Scholarly and literary publishing—the scientific, critical and artistic record of human knowledge, culture and experience—accounts for only about half a percent of the total, or $1 billion a year. (Publicly funded government information, freely distributed, plays no important part in that market.)

Most scientists and scholars are far more interested in the widest possible distribution of their work to their professional colleagues than in capturing every possible royalty dollar. The Internet can deliver information more quickly and cheaply than traditional print formats can, which makes it an appealing vehicle for publishing. An electronic copy of a document or program will also usually be identical to the original and exactly as functional.

Yet such authors are merely passengers on a mass-media ocean liner, required to abide by the same copyright laws as the makers of action-figure toys based on Saturday-morning cartoons. And publishers' exhilaration about new products and markets is offset by fear that a single sale to a library or an individual could result in the endless reproduction of a document over the global Internet, eliminating hopes of further revenue.

Questions about how to apply current copyright law to new formats and media abound: To what extent are works on the newer—let alone not yet created—electronic media protected by law? Is cyberspace a virtual Wild West, where anyone can lay claim to anyone else's creations by scanning and uploading them or simply copying a few files? Many works are being created through extensive electronic communities or collaborations—who owns and benefits from these? How can we track who owns what, assuming that ownership makes sense at all? How do we efficiently compensate information owners when their works can be sold by the word, phrase or even musical note? What are the liabilities of Internet access providers, who may be unaware of copyright violation over their facilities? Should we dispense with copyright as we have known it entirely and seek new paradigms, as the Office of Technology Assessment advocated in 1986?

Where the Law Stands

The roots of copyright are old, and the lines along which it has grown are complex. One of the earliest copyright disputes, from sixth-century Ireland, sets the tone: St. Columba had copied out for himself a manuscript of the Latin Psalter, and the owner of the original, Finnian of Druim Finn, objected. The king ruled: "As the calf belongs to the cow, so the copy belongs to its book." A war ensued; the "copyright violator" prevailed and held on to the book. (The manuscript has had a long history as a good luck charm for the Columba clan's military adventures and survives to this day in the library of the Royal Irish Academy in Dublin.)

The Statute of Anne, enacted in England in 1710, was the first national copyright law. It gave authors rights to their work and limited the duration of those rights; it served as a model for the first statute governing copyrights in the New World, enacted in 1790. On both sides of the Atlantic, copyright in its nascent stages balanced neatly the interests of private property and public use. Indeed, the constitutional authority for U.S. copyright is based on its potential to "promote the progress of science and useful arts."

In successive revisions, Congress has extended the period of copyright, expanded the types of works that are protected, and joined in global copyright agreements, such as the Berne Convention. Berne signers agree to give copyrighted works from other countries the same protection they would have if they had been produced in the home nation.

American publishers have not always been so scrupulous in observing foreign copyrights. Pirate editions were common during the 19th and early 20th centuries (when, according to an argument made by Paul Goldstein of Stanford University and others, the U.S. was a net importer of intellectual property). British artists then, from Gilbert and Sullivan to J.R.R. Tolkien, were acutely aware of such trespasses. Today, however, Americans look at such lax-copyright countries such as China as disapprovingly as Britain looked westward 100 years ago.

Some observers have argued that cyberspace is a similarly underdeveloped territory with respect to intellectual property—many words and images from other media find their way there, but relatively few cyberworks have crossed in the opposite direction. That asymmetry is changing rapidly, though: the land rush of media companies to the Internet in the mid-1990s may already have put an end to the frontier era. And, of course, because cyberspace has no physical territory, its citizens are subject to the laws of whatever jurisdiction they live in.

A Tilted Playing Field

The most recent revision of the U.S. copyright law, made in 1978, is far more thorough than its predecessors. It protects creative works in general, including literature, music, drama, pantomime, choreography, pictorial, graphical and sculptural works, motion pictures and other audiovisual creations, sound recordings and architecture. (Patents and trademarks are governed by their own laws, as are trade secrets.) Copyright explicitly grants the owners of the expression of an idea the right to prevent anyone from making copies of it, preparing derivative works, distributing the work, performing it or displaying it without permission.

At the same time, the law limits the exclusive rights of owners in various ways. The most important of these exceptions is fair use, which allows copies to be made without either payment or permission under certain conditions. Fair use includes copying for purposes of research, teaching, journalism, criticism, parody and library activities.

Much of the current debate about electronic copyright stems from questions about the future of fair use raised by the Lehman Commission, known more officially as the National Information Infrastructure Task Force's Working Group on Intellectual Property Rights, chaired by Bruce A. Lehman, the U.S. commissioner of patents and trademarks. In mid-1994 the 25-member group released a first draft of its report for comment. Hearings were held in Washington, D.C., Chicago and Los Angeles, and the group took comments by post, fax and e-mail. Individual readers and copyright market participants offered well over 1,000 pages of opinion. In September 1995 the group released its final draft—a white paper—containing a legislative package intended to update the current Copyright Act.

In general, the information-producing industries have greeted the white paper's recommendations with relief and acclaim. It forestalls publishers' and authors' worst-case scenario, which could have reduced income to the point where there would be no incentives to produce new works and market them on-line. The tighter controls over digital reproduction proposed in the white paper appear to secure the industry's financial well-being in the on-line environment.

In contrast, library and education groups, on-line services and private citizens have been mostly negative—and very voluble—in their responses to the Lehman proposals. Their nightmare future is one in which nothing can be looked at, read, used or copied without permission or payment. Many libraries are already feeling pinched as costs for information, particularly scientific books and journals, increase by 10 percent or more annually.

Fees charged for electronic information licenses (which give libraries or schools permission to use material that they do not own) are generally even higher than prices for the equivalent books or periodicals. Thus, the working group's suggestion that the use of licensing should be greatly expanded has an ominous ring for librarians in most American institutions. Under the typical license, such terms as price, permission for users to download sections of a database, liability and long-term ownership favor the information provider in significant ways. If li-

7. THE SHAPE OF THINGS TO COME

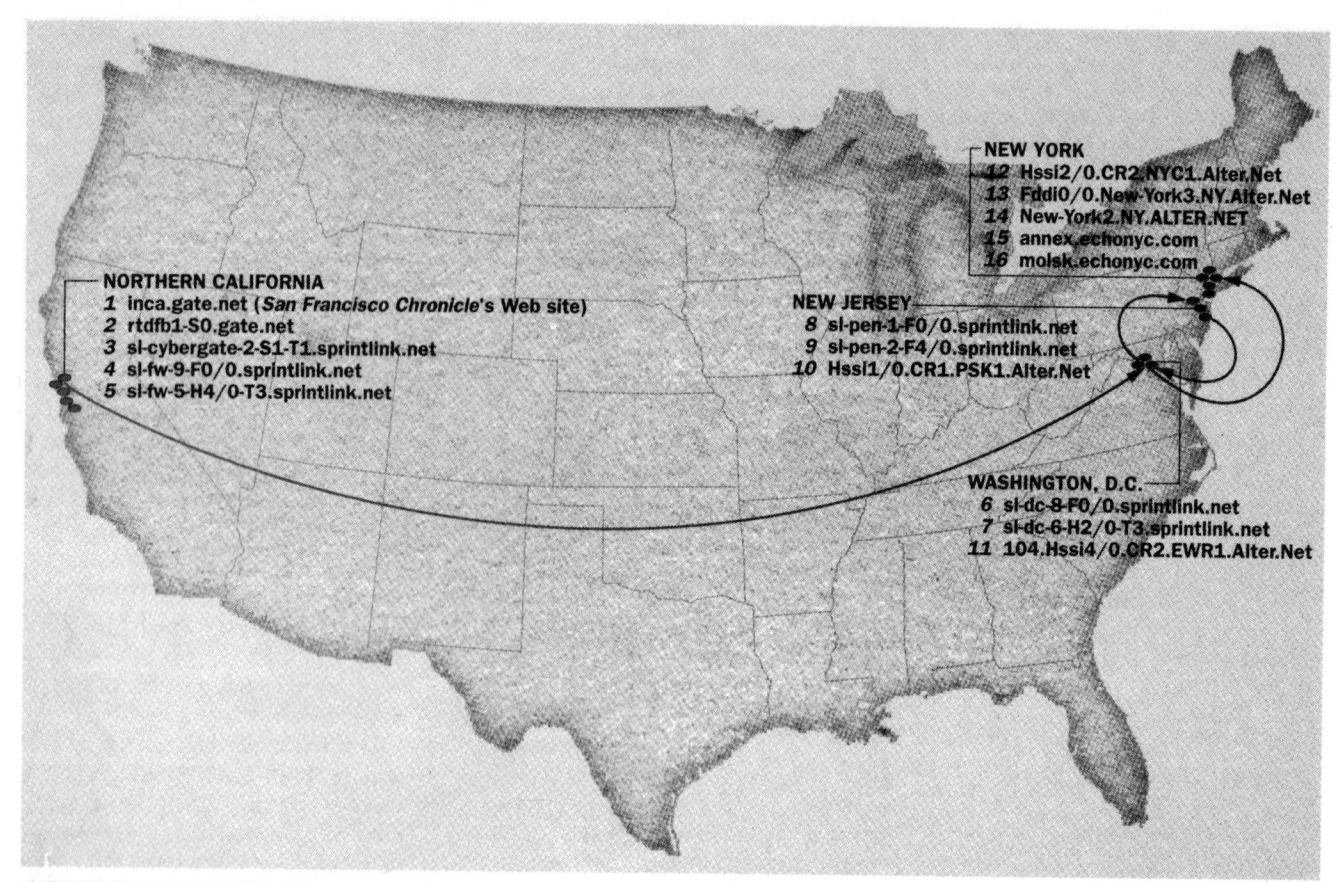

NORTHERN CALIFORNIA
1. inca.gate.net (*San Francisco Chronicle*'s Web site)
2. rtdfb1-S0.gate.net
3. sl-cybergate-2-S1-T1.sprintlink.net
4. sl-fw-9-F0/0.sprintlink.net
5. sl-fw-5-H4/0-T3.sprintlink.net

NEW JERSEY
8. sl-pen-1-F0/0.sprintlink.net
9. sl-pen-2-F4/0.sprintlink.net
10. Hssi1/0.CR1.PSK1.Alter.Net

NEW YORK
12. Hssi2/0.CR2.NYC1.Alter.Net
13. Fddi0/0.New-York3.NY.Alter.Net
14. New-York2.NY.ALTER.NET
15. annex.echonyc.com
16. molsk.echonyc.com

WASHINGTON, D.C.
6. sl-dc-8-F0/0.sprintlink.net
7. sl-dc-6-H2/0-T3.sprintlink.net
11. 104.Hssi4/0.CR2.EWR1.Alter.Net

MULTIPLE COPIES OF A DIGITAL TEXT may be made as it travels across the Internet from source to destination. In the example above, information passes through 14 different computers (*shown by name and approximate location*) on its way from the *San Francisco Chronicle*'s World Wide Web site to a browser in New York City. Some copyright experts assert that each of these copies must be sanctioned by the copyright owner. As the proposed law now stands, the owners of all the intermediate machines might be found liable if it is determined that infringement has occurred.

cense terms continue to make electronic information more expensive than its print counterparts, and the digital domain continues to grow, libraries will eventually be unable to afford access. At that point, of course, this imbalance will have to change, because there can be no marketplace without a ready supply of customers to buy new products.

Furthermore, in the eyes of many citizens and legal scholars, the Lehman commission's suggested changes upset the balance that the current law maintains between the rights of copyright owners and those of users. For example, the commission affirms that any information alighting in a computer's memory for any length of time—however fleeting—is "fixed" for purposes of copyright. The Copyright Act governs only ideas "fixed in a tangible medium of expression, when its embodiment... is sufficiently permanent or stable to permit it to be perceived, reproduced, or otherwise communicated for a period of more than transitory duration."

This distinction is crucial. The white paper implies that anyone who for any reason transfers a sequence of bits representing copyrighted information between computers without permission of the copyright owner breaks the law. Indeed, the working group recommends that the Copyright Act be amended expressly to recognize that transmissions fall within the exclusive right of the copyright owner. Even the act of viewing a Web page, which involves transmitting it from a server to a user's computer, could be interpreted as illegal without specific prior authorization.

In addition, the group refuses to extend to electronic copies the so-called doctrine of first sale. Someone who buys a book or magazine can sell or give away that copy without paying additional royalties, but this would not be true in cyberspace. This apparently illogical recommendation follows the argument that during an electronic transfer, a work is "fixed" in at least two computers, even if only for a few milliseconds—and hence is duplicated rather than being trans-

ferred the way that a book might be. Legitimate ways for a lawful owner of a copy of an electronic work to sell the copy or to give it to a friend, an act that is perfectly legal in the world of print-on-paper, are left unexplored. As a result, in the electronic information omniverse, the ability even to glance at materials, an act we take for granted in libraries and bookstores, could vanish. Browsing works on-line without permission could be considered a violation of the law.

Universities and other organizations that supply access to the Internet are particularly concerned by the commission's assertion that they should be liable for any copyright violations committed by their users. Such a situation would force them into the role of unpaid digital police, checking on every piece of data that students, staff or subscribers read or published.

Although the white paper proposes a future inconsistent with the grand tradition of public access, one way around these controversies might be disarming-

42. Who Owns Digital Works?

Who Owns the Pieces?

Multimedia creation involves taking text, pictures and sound from many different sources. Each item (*as shown below*) may belong to a different entity. The resulting issues of ownership and compensation are complex and can hamper the creative process.

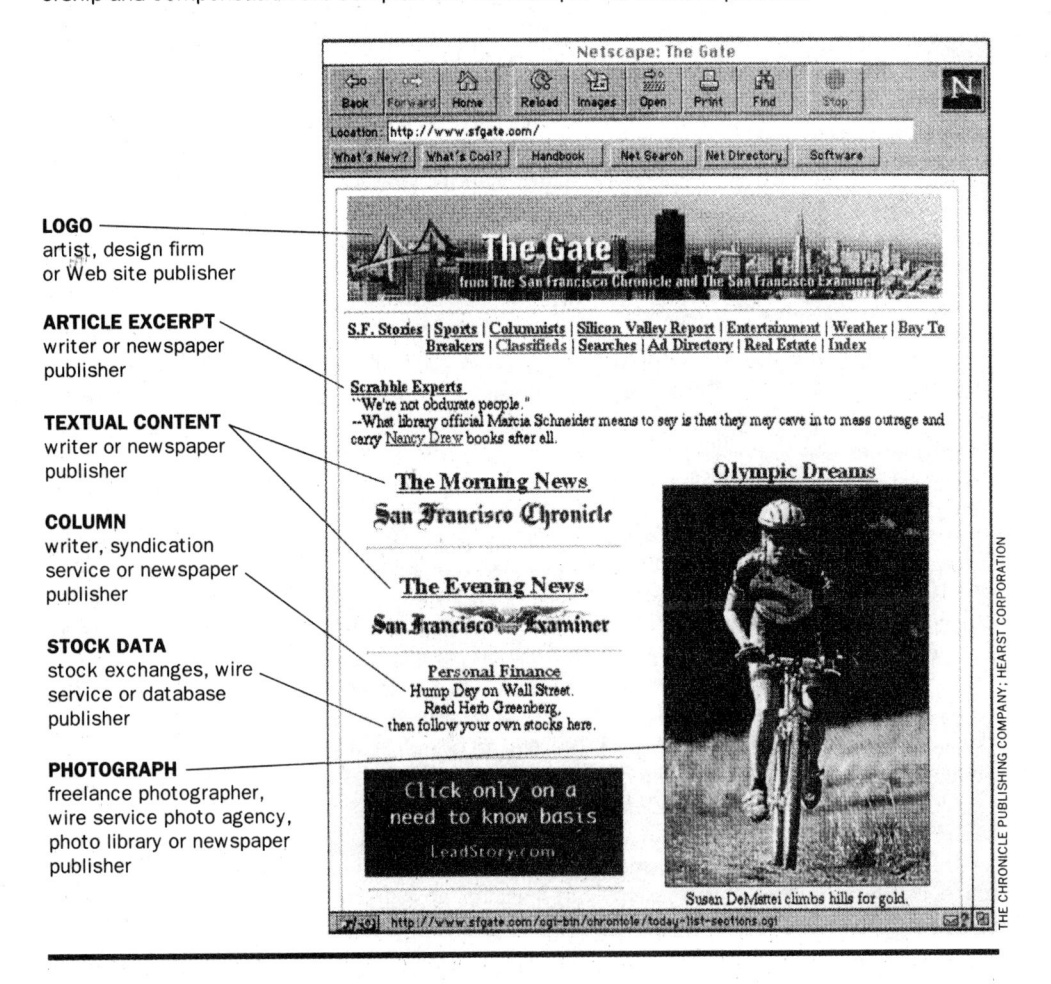

LOGO
artist, design firm or Web site publisher

ARTICLE EXCERPT
writer or newspaper publisher

TEXTUAL CONTENT
writer or newspaper publisher

COLUMN
writer, syndication service or newspaper publisher

STOCK DATA
stock exchanges, wire service or database publisher

PHOTOGRAPH
freelance photographer, wire service photo agency, photo library or newspaper publisher

---

ly simple. The commission emphasizes technological aspects of "transmission" and "fixation," but many critics have found those discussions imperfect precisely on technological grounds. A more thorough analysis of the range of technological possibilities for transferring files—including cryptographic methods that effectively limit the number of permanent copies produced—might make the Lehman approach more useful than it now seems likely to be.

Fair Use—The Balancing Act

If access to electronic materials without payment for every use is to be recognized, then fair use is the area in which the bridges can be built between the rights of copyright owners and those of information users. At least that is where they have been built in the medium of the printed word.

Just what fair use means in the electronic environment is unclear. Other than stating that fair use should continue in the electronic realm and that the need for it will diminish as licenses and other automatic accounting techniques become more widespread, the white paper says little about it. Advocates of readers' and users' rights find this imprecision particularly troubling. Although the Lehman commission made a clear statement in favor of owners' rights, it balked at the chance to clarify users' rights similarly.

Lehman's office has, however, continued to foster an unofficial series of meetings, at which between 50 and 70 users, authors, librarians, lawyers and publishers' representatives meet every month in Washington, D.C., in an attempt to evolve guidelines for electronic fair use. This Conference on Fair Use is affectionately called CONFU, a reference to the CONTU (Commission on New Technological Uses) group that drafted the guidelines that have helped to clarify the 1978 copyright revisions. From the start of CONFU, it quickly became clear that little agreement would be reached by the time the white paper was due or copyright legislation would be introduced and debated on Capitol Hill.

What policymakers may not appreciate is that the inability of the CONFU participants to agree is by no means bad. On the one hand are fears that without a set of electronic fair use guidelines, confusion about the law and the likelihood of litigation will increase—particularly damaging for elementary schools

237

7. THE SHAPE OF THINGS TO COME

and others who can least afford the risk. Yet on the other hand are the advantages of proceeding slowly with legislation. Because there are not a lot of rules about the new media, publishers, librarians and scholars are free to conduct electronic experiments—many of them governed by written agreements between commercial publishers and educational or library organizations.

Progress in the creation and distribution of electronic information is being made nicely, though not rapidly. Commercial copyright owners seem a long way from suing libraries or elementary schools. The individual scientist or teacher preparing a Web page may be in technical violation of one or another owner's rights but seems similarly immune, at least for now, from legal action. (If this truce breaks down, of course, the consequences for electronic distribution of information could be grim.)

In the view of many participants, the disagreements at CONFU meetings deserve to be cherished. Many believe the technology is not mature enough for agreement about fair use guidelines. They shy away from making legal commitments before they really understand the implications of what they agree to, and at this writing it appears that the process of reaching adequate voluntary electronic fair use agreements will take a long time.

Coming to Terms with the Future

For all the criticism that some aspects of the Lehman commission's report have generated, there is substantial consensus on many others. Many recommendations have generated dissension not so much about their general appropriateness as about the degree to which they should be codified in law. For example, few take issue with the notion that malicious tampering with encryption methods intended to secure copyright should be illegal. Questions arise only about how draconian the punishment for such an offense should be and whether investigators should be able to presume guilt.

Similarly, everyone, except for the small minority who believe copyright protection has no future on the Internet, agrees that there is an urgent need to educate citizens about copyright. Now that everyone with a computer and modem is a publisher, rules that once applied to only a few companies bind millions of people.

How society ultimately changes the Copyright Act will largely determine the nation's information future. The power of new technologies already transforms the way creators work and how authors and publishers deliver information. Is it too much to hope that widely and cheaply accessible public and academic information will coexist with information sold by publishers at prices that earn profits and foster the copyright industries? We do have the potential, if we act wisely and well, to arrange matters so that most participants in the new technologies will be winners.

Further Reading

THE NATURE OF COPYRIGHT: A LAW OF USERS' RIGHTS. L. Ray Patterson and Stanley W. Lindberg. University of Georgia Press, 1991.
COPYRIGHT'S HIGHWAY: FROM GUTENBERG TO THE CELESTIAL JUKEBOX. Paul Goldstein. Hill and Wang, 1994.
COPYRIGHT, PUBLIC POLICY, AND THE SCHOLARLY COMMUNITY. Association of Research Libraries, Washington, D.C., July 1995.
COPYRIGHT LAW OF THE UNITED STATES OF AMERICA. Contained in Title 17 of the United States Code. Obtain copies from U.S. Government Printing Office or the Copyright Office at the Library of Congress.
For access to the World Wide Web site maintained by the creator of the Pooh FAQ: http://www.clark.net/pub/rinzel/muppooh/
For current information on copyright law: http://www.library.yale.edu/~okerson/copyproj.html

---

ANN OKERSON is associate university librarian at Yale University, where her work includes making digital materials available to the library's users. Before going to Yale in September 1995, she was director of the Office of Scientific and Academic Publishing for the Association of Research Libraries in Washington, D.C. Okerson received her M.L.S. in library and information science from the University of California, Berkeley, in 1967. Since January 1993 she has been co-moderator of NewJour, an electronic mailing list that announces new electronic journal, magazine and newsletter start-ups. The list's World Wide Web site (http://gort.ucsd.edu/newjour/) has links to the journals described in the announcements and handles about 1,000 searches a day.

THE BIGGEST THING SINCE COLOR?

Ready or not, computer and television makers are racing to bring the Internet to the boob tube

MICHAEL KRANTZ

HE WAS AMERICA'S QUINTESSENTIAL media consumer: a hardworking breadwinner who settles down after dinner with his feet up and his thumb on the remote. So Tim Bajarin, an analyst at the research firm Creative Strategies, was curious about how the man would react to a focus-group presentation of Silicon Valley's latest hot idea: using a TV receiver to cruise the Internet. As Bajarin watched, the subject waited patiently a full 30 seconds for a sports-related Web page to fill the screen. He studied it for a minute, then looked up and asked, "When do the movies start?"

That may be the question of the year. The man represents the Internet industry's most coveted market: the estimated 85% to 90% of American homes that aren't yet connected. For this Passive Majority, most of whom don't even own a computer, let alone a modem, "Net TV" would seem to make perfect sense. After all, nearly everybody in America has a TV and a telephone, and many are presumably curious to learn what the World Wide Web is all about. If they could use their existing sets to access the Infobahn from the comfort of their La-Z-Boys, the Web might finally become the mass medium its promoters have been promising all along.

To that end, some half a dozen companies plan to begin selling a Net TV of one sort or another between the end of summer and the beginning of next year. Rich Doherty, a director of the Envisioneering Group, estimates that 1 million Net TV devices will be sold in the first year, and that a third of American homes will have one by 2002.

These devices, in their simplest form, consist of a television with two ports in the back: one for cable, the other for an Internet connection (usually a phone line). Once their link to the Net is established, viewers will, in theory, be able to navigate Websites with their trusty remotes as easily as they now surf TV channels.

There are, however, as many variations on this latest get-rich-on-the-Internet scheme as there are firms that want to cash in on it. Companies like Zenith and Curtis Mathes are building new TVs that come out of the packing crate Net ready; others like ViewCall America, are designing set-top boxes that plug into ordinary TVs and make them Web capable. Sony and Philips, for example, are licensing set-top technology from WebTV Networks, a company partly financed by Microsoft co-founder Paul Allen. Sega and Nintendo, meanwhile, are adding Internet capability to their video-game machines, and this fall Apple is expected to market its long-delayed Pippin computer as a $600 Web-browsing set-top box that also plays Macintosh CD-ROMs.

The TV-PC hybrid idea is attractive to computer makers, although most would prefer to add TV reception to their PC lines than get into the TV business. Direct-mail giant Gateway 2000 is already selling Destination, a $3,500-to-$4,500 hybrid TV-PC. NetTV, Inc. introduced its competing World-Vision in March, and Compaq and RCA are expected to follow suit early next year.

Whatever approach they favor, Net TV makers share one belief: that the era of stand-alone desktop computers, if not quite over, is on the wane. "The lock that PCs have had will be broken," says Joe Gillach, chief operating officer of Silicon Valley start-up Diba, which is providing Web-browsing technology for Zenith's NetVision TV as well as Internet circuitry for a variety of VCRs, set-top boxes and cable converters; a deal to make Internet appliances with NEC will be announced this

---

SURFING THE WEB
The new players in the Net-TV game:

Zenith
NetVision TV debuts this fall for $1,000

Sony | Philips
Both will offer WebTV's $200-$400 set-tops in October

Thomson/Compaq
Their high-end, $2,000-$4,000 TV-PC is due in early 1997

Apple
Its Pippin computer, due this fall, is a TV plug-in Net browser and CD-ROM player

Gateway 2000
Their Destination is a $3,500-plus wide-screen TV-PC

Other Players
NetTV, Inc.
ViewCall America
Curtis Mathes

TIME Chart by Bryan Christie

7. THE SHAPE OF THINGS TO COME

week. "The Internet TV," Gillach says, "is the Trojan horse for bringing technology in a non-PC form into the home."

Even if the PC revolution can be decoupled from PCs, however, it is by no means certain that the boob tube is the device to do it. Television's very familiarity is a double-edged sword. Yes, TV may help seduce the Passive Majority into trying the Net, but if today's Net fails to meet their entertainment expectations, they may just change the channel. The Web is info-rich, but it's still a poor entertainment medium. It takes agonizingly long for even a fast modem to download the average Web page, and that page, by and large, offers mostly still pictures, graphics and plain text—hardly fare to set a couch potato's heart aflutter. "People aren't going to sit there waiting for something to develop on the screen," says Peter Krasilovsky, a new-media analyst at Arlen Communications. "We don't believe in TV as a reading vehicle."

Even if he's mistaken—even if there are millions of folks who think TV's problem is that it isn't enough like a magazine—Net TV users may find that the Web's most exciting pages don't work right on their machines. Netscape and Microsoft, whose Web-browsing software dominates the market, are currently engaged in a life-or-death struggle to be the first to introduce the newest and whizziest Internet embellishments. Net TV's programmers may be hard pressed to keep up with the big boys. "Nobody is targeting [browser] improvement at set-top boxes," says Josh Bernoff, a senior analyst at Forrester Research. "The gulf between the two will only get wider and wider."

Then there is the eye-straining challenge of reading screenfuls of text from eight to 12 feet away—the distance most people sit from their TV sets. Net TV designers have tried to solve the problem by redesigning Web pages for larger type, but that limits the number of words that can fit on a screen. "It's going to take a dozen scrolls to see one [traditional] Web page," complains Bernoff. "These devices are not going to be able to deliver a complete Web experience."

Net TV makers say they never intended to do that. To judge Net TV by current Web standards, its boosters say, is to miss the point. "This is a brand-new architecture," argues WebTV Networks CEO Steve Perlman, whose company won licensing deals with Sony and Philips in part by delivering the best-looking Web pages seen on any TV screen. "We view Web TV as a complement to the TV experience," he says. Perlman is trying to get TV producers to jazz up their standard prime-time fare with Web content that can be displayed with the press of a button. Soap operas, for instance, could conduct mid-episode viewer polls; baseball fans could get statistics updated with every pitch.

If this sounds familiar, it may be because equally dreamy scenarios were spun only a few years ago by telephone and cable-TV companies—including Time Warner—convinced that the interactive TV of the future would be carried over privately owned fiber-optic and cable-TV lines. Billions were spent designing proprietary technology that would enable TV viewers to shop at virtual 3-D malls and order movies on demand. The rise of the Internet has eclipsed those efforts, at least for now, as those same phone and cable-TV companies race start-ups like @Home to deliver ever-faster access to the Web.

Whether it will ever be fast enough to satisfy that quintessential couch potato remains to be seen. "My general view," says Adam Schoenfeld, senior analyst with Jupiter Communications, "is that these people are crawling all over each other to provide a service that has no proven demand." If the Net TV makers are wrong, they could find themselves offering pallid, expensive hybrids of services millions of PC owners and TV junkies already enjoy. If they're right, however, and they manage to attract tens of millions of new viewers to the Web, a lot of Internet business plans that were looking pretty iffy will suddenly start making a lot more sense. —*Reported by Daniel Eisenberg/ New York*

Index

ABC, 198; influence of mergers on, 60, 61, 62–63, 64; lack of black programs on, 143; medical reporting on, 77–78, 79
Absence of Malice, 139
addiction, television as, 6–11
advertisers, in magazines, and control over editorial content, 17–18, 156–164
advertising, 29, 165–173; to children on Internet, 183–184; lack of reproductive issues in magazines and, 17–18; in magazines, 156–164; pathologizing of human body by, 29–30; sexuality in, 18; stereotypes of women in, 28; subliminal, 165–173; within programs on TV, 174–175
advocacy approach, to journalism in Bosnia, 201–205
African Americans. *See* blacks
Against Our Wills: Men, Women, and Rape (Brownmiller), 31, 32
"Age of Convergence," 214–219
aggression, against women and media stereotypes, 23–32
alienation, of public, 50–53
All the President's Men, 137
Amanpour, Christiane, 201, 202–203, 204
America Online, 216, 218
American Civil War, development of motion pictures and, 147
American Medical Association (AMA), 80
Annals of Internal Medicine, 80
anonymous sources: issues surrounding, 116–122; guidelines for use of, 121
anxiety, of young children and television watching, 34
Arnot, Bob, 77–78, 79, 81
Atwater, Lee, 197

Bailey, Doug, 210
Barbie "Math class is tough" doll, 25
Barry, Marion, 147–148
Battiata, Mary, 202
Bazell, Robert, 78–79, 80
beauty, cosmetic surgery and, 30
beauty products, advertisement of, in magazines, 156–164
Beavis and Butt-Head, 19–22
bereavement, tragedy and reportage and, 106–110
Berne Convention, 235
Binder, David, 203, 205
Birdcage, The, 141, 142
blacks: censorship of accomplishments of, in World War II, 134; lack of programming for, on TV, 143–144; sex in mass media and, 16, 17, 20
Bok, Edward, 162
Bonafede, Dom, 199–200
Bosnia, advocacy approach to journalism in, 201–205
Bradlee, Ben, 96, 117
Brady, Matthew, 146
Brazil, violence on TV and, 46
Britain, violence on TV and, 46
Broadcast News, 139
Brock, Peter, 205
Brown, Helen Gurley, 162
Brownmiller, Susan, 31, 32
Bush, George, 193, 196, 197–198

Canada, television violence in, 46
Capital Cities/ABC. *See* ABC
Carter, Jimmy, 195–196
CBS, 198; influence of mergers on, 60, 63, 64; lack of black programs on, 143; medical reporting on, 77–78; 79, 80
Celluloid Closet, The, 141–142
censorship, in World War II, 132–136
Centerwall, Brandon, 36–37
checkbook journalism, 98, 123–125
children: media influences on aggression in, 33–40; universal access to Internet and, 180–185
Civil War, development of motion pictures and American, 147
Clinton, Bill, 45, 181, 182, 198
CNN (Cable News Network), 190–191, 206–208; medical reporting on, 78, 79–81; use of VNRs on, 65, 67
Collings, Tim, 45–46
CompuServe, 217–218
computers. *See* Internet
Conference on Fair Use (CONFU), 236–237, 238
consumerism, television advertising and, 176–179
Contract with America, 50, 51, 52
convergence, of media formats, 214–219
Cooke, Janet, 116, 118–119, 122
copyright law, Internet and, 234–238
corporate convergence, 215–216
Crossfire, 208
"cultivation hypothesis," 19
cultural issues, division of, 52
culture, influence of television on, 102–105
CyberKids, 182

Daguerre, 146
Dana Carvey Show, 174
deep background, 119
Deep Throat, as anonymous source, 116, 118
Diehl, Jackson, 205
digital compression, 215
digital technology, impact of photography and, 151–153, 154
distortion, in journalism, 103
doctrine of first sale, 237
Dole, Bob, 45
Don't Touch That Dial: Impact of Media on Children and the Family (Hattemer), 33
Dougherty, Dale, 223
Draper, John William, photographic portraits of, 146
Dukakis, Michael, 197, 198

Eastman, George, 147
Edison, Thomas A., patented camera of, 147
"edutainment," sexuality in mass media and, 20
electronic copyrights, 234–238
electronic magazines, on Internet, 220–224
electronic referenda, 190
entrapment, of Marion Barry, 147–148
Erikson, Wendy, 58–59
Europe, television viewing in, 46

"fake news," 65–70
Faludi, Susan, 26

FCC (Federal Communications Commission), 40, 46, 182
fiber optics, 214–219
First Amendment, 95–96, 97, 115, 191
flat tax, promotion of, on Internet, 209–210
forced sex, male attitudes toward, 30–31
Fox, black programs on, 143, 144
"framing," 19
Frankel, Max, 195
f/X, 60, 61

Gailey, Phil, 196, 200
gender, influence of media on views of, 23–32, 165–173
"Gendered Media," 23–32; normalization of violence against women and, 30–32; sterotyped portrayals of men and, 24–25; stereotyped portrayals of relationships between men and women and, 25–26; stereotyped portrayals of women and, 24–25; underrepresentation of women and, 23–24
General Electric (GE), 61, 62–63
George, Don, 222
Germany, television viewing in, 46
Gillach, Joe, 239–240
Glamour, 17
global village, 214–219; teenager consumer preferences and, 12–15
Godey's Lady's Book, 162
Goodwin, Doris Kearns, 198–199
Gospel of St. John, contemporary media and, 102–105
Gowing, Nik, 201–202, 204–205
Greeley, Horace, 104
grief reporting, 106–110
Gutman, Roy, 204

Hasse, David L., 209, 210, 211
Hattemer, Barbara, 33–40
Hearst, William Randolph, 76
"heterarchies," 189
hidden cameras, use of, 111–115
Hill, Anita, 97
Holmes, Oliver Wendell, M.D., instantaneous photography and, 147
homicide, television watching and, 36–39
homosexuality, treatment of, in movie industry, 141–142
Horton, Willie, 197
HotWired, 220, 221, 224
human body, pathologizing of, by media, 29–30
Huxley, Aldous, 165

I Love Trouble, 139
Implant Circus, The, 30
Intelligent Home, The, 214, 215
interactive television, 239–240
Internet: electronic copyrights and, 234–238; electronic pubishers on, 220–224; political campaigns and, 209–211; on TV, 239–240; universal access for children on, 180–185

Japan, violence and television and, 46
Jefferson, Thomas, 102
Johnson, Lyndon, 193, 194, 199
Johnson, Timothy, 77–78, 79

Journal of the American Medical Association (JAMA), 80
journalism: advocacy approach to, in reporting on Bosnia, 201–205; anonymous sources and, 116–122; decreasing violence in local news shows and, 54–59; network medical reporting and, 77–81; political, 188–192, 206–208; portrayal of, by movie industry, 137–140; public, 71–76; tabloid, 125
Judge, Michael, 41, 42–43, 44
Just Cause, 137, 138

Kalb, Marvin, 72, 75, 115, 199, 200
Karstens, Bob, 56, 57, 59
Kassirer, Jerome, 80
Katzenbach, John, 137, 138
Kennedy, John F., 193–194
Kiely, Kathy, 210
King, Brett, 144
King, Larry, 206–208
King, Rodney, 145, 146; use of videotape in trial of, 149–150
Kinsley, Michael, 222–223
Kissinger, Henry, 117, 193, 195
Kneeland, Carole, 56, 57, 58–59
Koppel, Ted, 190
Kurtz, Howard, 84
KVUE-TV, decreasing of violence in local news on, 54–59

labels, ineffectiveness of parental advisory, 40
Ladies Home Journal, The, 162
Ladies Magazine, The, 162
language, 105
Lehman Commission, 235, 236–238
Lieberman, Joseph, 45
Lincoln, Abraham, 192
Lippmann, Walter, 193

magazines: advertiser's control of content in, 17, 156–164; gender stereotypes and, 28–29, 156–164; sex and reproductive issues in, 17; teen, 18
Maggio, Judy, 57
Maier, Daniel, 80
"mainstreaming," 19
mature audiences, target marketing of, 176–179
McCulloch, Frank, 203–204
McFeatters, Cathy, 55–56, 57, 59
Media Circus (Kurtz), 84
Medialink, 65
medical reporting, on TV news programs, 77–81
Meeks, Brock, 210, 221
men, portrayal of, in media, 23–32, 165–173
Mencken, H. L., 104
menopause, negative marketing of, 29
merger, influence of, on networks, 60–64
Merrill, John C., 203
Merrit, Dave "Buzz," Jr., public journalism and, 71–76
minority programming, lack of, on TV, 143–144
"mirror with a memory, the," 146–147
"missle gap," 193–194
modems, news services and, 216–218
moral media, 104–105
Morse, Samuel F. B., 146
Motion Picture Production Code, 38, 40

motion pictures, development of, and American Civil War, 147. *See also* movie industry
movie industry: commercialism of, 165–173; portrayal of journalists in, 134–140; treatment of homosexuality in, 141–142. *See also* motion pictures
Ms., 17, 28, 156–164
MTV, 24, 28, 42–44; globalism and, 13, 14, pornography and, 30; sex in music videos and, 17; sexual violence on, 28–30; women as sex objects on, 28
multimedia formats, 214–219
"murder of character," media and, 103
Murrah Federal Building, bombing of, 106
music, violence in, 39–40
Muybridge, E. J., 147

National Information Infrastructure Task Force's Working Group on Intellectual Property Rights, 235, 236–238
National Television Violence Study, 47
Natural Born Killers, 137, 138, 139
NBC: influence of mergers on, 61, 62–63; lack of black programs on, 143; medical reporting on, 77–78, 79, 80
"Net TV," 239–240
NetDay, 182
Netizen, 221
Network, 139
Neuharth, Allen H., 117
New England Journal of Medicine, 80
New York Post, 60, 61
New York Times, 223
newspapers: decline in circulation for, 83; ombudsmen for, 84–85, 87, 117; on-line, 223
Nielsen ratings, 177
"Nine Sundays" program, 199
Nixon, Richard M., 83, 193, 194–195
nurturing, responses to violence and, 40

objectivity, vs. subjectivity in journalism, and Bosnia, 201–205
older people, media and, 24, 176–179
Oklahoma City, Oklahoma, bombing in, 106
ombudsmen, 84–85, 87, 117
on-line services, 214–219

Packwood, Bob, 119
Paper, The, 138–139
Paramount Pictures, 41
parental advisories, ineffectiveness of, 40
Pentagon Papers, 98, 117
People Project: Solving It Ourselves, 73
Persuasive Images: Posters of War and Revolution, 148
photographic proof, as archaic term, 153
photography: digital retouching and, 151–153; history of, 146–147; use of, as evidence, 145–150; "visual credibility gap" and, 151–153, 154
"Photomac," digital photoediting software, 153
Plugged In, 182
PMS (Premenstrual Syndrome), media hype and, 29
political campaigns, 188–192, 193–196; Internet and, 209–211
Politics USA, 210
pornography, 30, 35; MTV and, 30; violence against women and, 30; youth and, 35
presidential ad campaigns, 85, 193–196
Prime Time Live, hidden cameras and, 111–115

privacy, journalistic mandate and, 8
privacy law, 86, 112–115. *See also* First Amendment
Procter & Gamble (P&G), 174–175
Project on Public Life and the Press (New York Unversity), 73
propaganda, 148
pubic journalism, 71–76; cautions concerning, 75–76
public service announcements (PSAs), sexuality in mass media and, 20

quotations, 127–129; editing of, 127; ethical guidelines for, 128, 129; legal use of, 129; use of partial, 127

radio, sex in, 17
Rafshoon, Gerald, 196
rap music, 40
rape: legitimization of, by media, 30–32; myths concerning, 31; rising incidence in reporting of, 30; as school problem, 35; as violent crime, 30–31
Reagan, Ronald, 193, 196–197
responsibility, in journalism, 102–105
Reston, James, 194, 195
Roosevelt, Franklin D., "fireside chats" of, 207
Rosen, Jay, 71–76
Rowland, Rhonda, 81
Rutz, Dan, 78, 79–81

Saatchi and Saatchi, 183
Sagan, Paul, 221, 223, 224
Salon, 222
San Francisco Examiner, 221–222
Sassy, 18
Scitex Corp., digital photograph editing and, 151, 153
Serbs, advocacy approach to journalism toward, 201–205
sex role, portrayal of, in media, 23–32, 165–173
sexual violence, normalization of, by media, 30
sexuality, in mass media, 16–22
Shakespeare, Frank, 194, 195
Simon, Paul, 45
Simpson, O. J., 53, 116, 118
60 Minutes, tobacco industry reportage by, 88–99
soap operas, sex and, 16
socioeconomic sectors, as factor in media consumption, 50–53
soft-cure pornography, high school populations and, 35
Songline Studios, 223
spy cam technology, 111–115
St. John's Gospel, 102–105
Stait, George, 77–78, 81
Statue of Anne, 235
Steele, Bob, 202, 204
Steinem, Gloria, 28, 156–164
Stephanopoulous, George, 207
stereotypes, gender, 23–32, 165–173
Stone, Oliver, 137, 138
subliminal advertising, 165–173
subjectivity, vs. objectivity in journalism, and Bosnia, 201–205
Suffragists, 162
suicide, as response to rape trauma, 31
Sulzberger, Arthur Hays, 98

tabloids, 125

Talbot, David, 222
talk shows, sex and, 16
Taylor, Elizabeth, 174
Taylor, Paul, 199
teen magazines, sexuality in, 18
teenagers, culture of consumption and, 12–15
Telecommunications Act of 1996, 181, 182, 184
television, 6–11, 33–40, 41–44, 190; advertisements within programming on, 174–1785; decreasing amount of violence in local news shows on, 54–59; effect of, violence on children, 45–47; influence of mergers on, 60–64; Internet on, 239–240; lack of black programming on, 143–144; medical reporting on, 77–81; sexual issues and, 16–17; as shared environment, 6–11, 190
"theft of privacy," 103
-30-, 140
Tie Me Up, Tie Me Down, 26
Time Warner, 61–62, 216, 221, 223
To Die For, 137–138, 139
tobacco industry, reporting on, 88–99

tragedy, instant reporting on, 106–110
Treleaven, Harry, 194, 195
truth imperative, 102–105
TV Guide, attack on VNRs and, 68, 69

United Paramount Network, black programs on, 143–144

V Chip, effect of television violence on children and, 45–47
video news releases. *See* VNRs
videos, sex and, 16–17
violence: decreasing amount of, in local news shows, 54–59; early influence of TV and, 33–34; effect of, on development of children, 23, 33–40, 45–47; normalization of, against women by media, 28, 30–32, 35; research studies on television, 36–39; youth and, 33–40
virtual reality, 145–150
VNRs (video news releases), 65–70; definition of, 65; media ethics and, 69–70; medical reporting and, 80

Walesa, Lech, 188

Wallace, Mike, 88–99, 111
Walt Disney Co, 60, 62
Warner Bros. (WB) network, black programs on, 143–144
Washington Post, 223
Webster, Noah, 102
Westinghouse, 60, 63, 64
white paper, 235, 236–238
White, Theodore, 193–194
Whitewater affair, 52
Wigand, Jeffrey, 88–99
Wolfe, Sidney, 77, 78
women: portrayal of, in media, 23–32, 165–173; normalization of violence against, 30–32; underrepresentation of, 23–24
Woodward, Bob, 120–121
words, as cornerstone of journalism, 105
World War II, censorship during, 132–136
World Wide Web. *See* Internet

youth crime, 33–40

zoetrope, 147
zone of privacy, 113

Credits/Acknowledgments

Cover design by Charles Vitelli

1. Living with Media
Facing overview—Dushkin Publishing Group illustration by Mike Eagle.

2. Information and Influence
Facing overview—Sygma photo by A. Tannenbaum.

3. Defining the Rules
Facing overview—EPA Documerica photo.

4. The Power of Images
Facing overview—United Nations photo by Y. Nagata.
133–134—National Archives photo. 138—Photos from Photofest.

5. A Word from Our Sponsor
Facing overview—Photo by Rebecca Holland.

6. The State of the Nation
Facing overview—AP/Wide World photo by Wilfredo Lee.

7. The Shape of Things to Come
Facing overview—Apple Computer photo. 82—*Scientific American* map by Laurie Grace.

PHOTOCOPY THIS PAGE!!!*

ANNUAL EDITIONS ARTICLE REVIEW FORM

■ NAME: _____ DATE: _____

■ TITLE AND NUMBER OF ARTICLE: _____

■ BRIEFLY STATE THE MAIN IDEA OF THIS ARTICLE: _____

_____

■ LIST THREE IMPORTANT FACTS THAT THE AUTHOR USES TO SUPPORT THE MAIN IDEA:

_____
_____
_____
_____

■ WHAT INFORMATION OR IDEAS DISCUSSED IN THIS ARTICLE ARE ALSO DISCUSSED IN YOUR TEXTBOOK OR OTHER READINGS THAT YOU HAVE DONE? LIST THE TEXTBOOK CHAPTERS AND PAGE NUMBERS:

_____
_____
_____
_____

■ LIST ANY EXAMPLES OF BIAS OR FAULTY REASONING THAT YOU FOUND IN THE ARTICLE:

_____
_____
_____
_____

■ LIST ANY NEW TERMS/CONCEPTS THAT WERE DISCUSSED IN THE ARTICLE, AND WRITE A SHORT DEFINITION:

_____
_____
_____
_____

*Your instructor may require you to use this ANNUAL EDITIONS Article Review Form in any number of ways: for articles that are assigned, for extra credit, as a tool to assist in developing assigned papers, or simply for your own reference. Even if it is not required, we encourage you to photocopy and use this page; you will find that reflecting on the articles will greatly enhance the information from your text.

We Want Your Advice

ANNUAL EDITIONS revisions depend on two major opinion sources: one is our Advisory Board, listed in the front of this volume, which works with us in scanning the thousands of articles published in the public press each year; the other is you—the person actually using the book. Please help us and the users of the next edition by completing the prepaid article rating form on this page and returning it to us. Thank you for your help!

ANNUAL EDITIONS: MASS MEDIA 97/98
Article Rating Form

Here is an opportunity for you to have direct input into the next revision of this volume. We would like you to rate each of the 43 articles listed below, using the following scale:

1. Excellent: should definitely be retained
2. Above average: should probably be retained
3. Below average: should probably be deleted
4. Poor: should definitely be deleted

Your ratings will play a vital part in the next revision. So please mail this prepaid form to us just as soon as you complete it.
Thanks for your help!

Rating	Article	Rating	Article
	1. TV without Guilt: Group Portrait with Television		23. Where Have All the Heroes Gone?
	2. Can TV Save the Planet?		24. The Final Frontier
	3. Sexuality and the Mass Media: An Overview		25. TV's Black Flight
	4. Gendered Media: The Influence of Media on Views of Gender		26. What the Jury Saw: Does the Videotape Lie?
	5. Cause and Violent Effect: Media and Our Youth		27. Photographs That Lie: The Ethical Dilemma of Digital Retouching
	6. Battle for Your Brain		28. Sex, Lies, and Advertising
	7. Chips Ahoy		29. Hollywood the Ad
	8. Tuning Out the News		30. Your Show of Shills
	9. Should the Coverage Fit the Crime?		31. Why Won't Television Grow Up?
	10. All in the Family		32. Children in the Digital Age
	11. VNRs: News or Advertising?		33. Reshaping the World of Politics
	12. The Gospel of Public Journalism		34. Hoodwinked!
	13. A Medical Breakthrough		35. Over the Line?
	14. Under Siege		36. The Power of Talk
	15. CBS, *60 Minutes*, and the Unseen Interview		37. The Boys on the 'Net
	16. The Media and Truth: Is There a Moral Duty?		38. The Age of Convergence
	17. "How Do You Feel?"		39. Cyberspace Journalism
	18. Gotcha!		40. The Amazing Video Game Boom
	19. Anonymous Sources		41. Immaculate Reception
	20. When Checkbook Journalism Does God's Work		42. Who Owns Digital Works?
	21. Are Quotes Sacred?		43. The Biggest Thing Since Color?
	22. Missing on the Home Front		

(Continued on next page)

ABOUT YOU

Name _____ Date _____

Are you a teacher? ☐ Or a student? ☐

Your school name _____

Department _____

Address _____

City _____ State _____ Zip _____

School telephone # _____

YOUR COMMENTS ARE IMPORTANT TO US!

Please fill in the following information:

For which course did you use this book? _____

Did you use a text with this *ANNUAL EDITION*? ☐ yes ☐ no

What was the title of the text? _____

What are your general reactions to the *Annual Editions* concept?

Have you read any particular articles recently that you think should be included in the next edition?

Are there any articles you feel should be replaced in the next edition? Why?

Are there other areas of study that you feel would utilize an *ANNUAL EDITION*?

May we contact you for editorial input?

May we quote your comments?

ANNUAL EDITIONS: MASS MEDIA 97/98

BUSINESS REPLY MAIL		
First Class	Permit No. 84	Guilford, CT

Postage will be paid by addressee

Dushkin/McGraw·Hill
Sluice Dock
Guilford, Connecticut 06437

No Postage
Necessary
if Mailed
in the
United States